THE DEMOCRATIC MOVEMENT
IN GERMANY,
1789–1914

D0503336

THE
JAMES SPRUNT STUDIES
IN HISTORY
AND POLITICAL SCIENCE

Published under the Direction of
the Departments of History and Political Science
of The University of North Carolina at Chapel Hill

VOLUME 55

_____

Editors

J. CARLYLE SITTERSON, *Chairman*
FEDERICO G. GILL
JOHN D. MARTZ
GEORGE V. TAYLOR
GEORGE B. TINDALL

THE DEMOCRATIC MOVEMENT IN GERMANY, 1789–1914

by
John L. Snell

edited and completed by
Hans A. Schmitt

THE UNIVERSITY OF NORTH CAROLINA PRESS
CHAPEL HILL

Copyright © 1976 by
The University of North Carolina Press
All rights reserved
Manufactured in the United States of America
ISBN 0-8078-1283-8
Library of Congress Catalog Card Number 76-10254

Library of Congress Cataloging in Publication Data

Snell, John L, 1924-72
    The democratic movement in Germany, 1789-1914.

    (The James Sprunt studies in history and political
science; v. 55)
        Bibliography: p.
        Includes index.
        1. Germany—Politics and government—1789-1900.
    2. Germany—Politics and government—1888-1918.
    3. Democracy—History. I. Schmitt, Hans A., joint
    author. II. Title. III. Series.
    DD203.S63   320.9'43   76-10254
    ISBN 0-8078-1283-8

CONTENTS

PREFACE

In the summer of 1958, while I held a visiting appointment at Tulane University, John Snell showed me the first chapter of a book that he was then planning to be titled "Germany Enters the Democratic Era." It was bulky as such chapters go and reviewed the history of German representative institutions, together with the efforts to expand their range and power, since 1870. Correspondence about the work with publishers and colleagues indicates that the work was making rapid progress at the time I first learned of its existence, and in 1959, when Snell published his *The Nazi Revolution: Germany's Guilt or Germany's Fate?* in D. C. Heath's Problems in European Civilization, he announced on page 94 that *Germany Enters the Democratic Era* "should appear" before the year was out.

Eight years later the book remained far from complete and the earlier announcement, as Professor Snell wrote a friend on 31 March 1967, "was one of my worst predictions." The delay was, however, not the result of idleness. In addition to the Heath booklet, he published in 1959 his *Wartime Origins of the East-West Dilemma over Germany*, and he was already working on his study of the diplomacy of World War II, *Illusion and Necessity*, which was to appear in 1963 under the imprint of Houghton, Mifflin Company.

The study of the genesis of German democracy, meanwhile, had not been neglected, but by 1961 John Snell was no longer certain that he could do justice to the subject in one volume. While he still anticipated putting the years 1789 to 1918 between two hard covers, he also expressed the expectation of writing a number of sequels covering the Weimar, Nazi, and post–World War II years. Before such designs could take shape, however, and while *Illusion and Necessity* was going to press, John Snell became dean of the Graduate School of Tulane University. Administration proved to be a far from happy detour for the scholar, but more importantly it put German democracy back on the shelf.

The interruption turned out to be particularly inopportune because it came at a time when the literature of modern German history was beginning to increase at break-neck speed. The late 1950's had witnessed the beginning of Ernst Rudolf Huber's monumental modern German constitutional history (four volumes to date), accompanied by the publication of equally indispensable parallel volumes of documents. The papers of Friedrich von Holstein were appearing at a rapid clip, as were numerous other sources on whom John Snell would be drawing heavily in years to come, such as the Kautsky and Spitzemberg memoirs, the letters of Moses Hess, and Peter Rassow's and Karl Born's *Akten zur staatlichen Sozialpolitik.*

This torrent grew during the three years of John Snell's deanship. In the sector of documentation the harvest of primary sources on socialism became especially plentiful. The production of seminal secondary works grew at an even more overwhelming rate. These were the years during which Helmut Böhme finished *Deutschlands Weg zur Grossmacht*, during which Fritz Fischer became if nothing else a *cause célèbre*, while Rolf Dahrendorf published the first version of *Society and Democracy in Germany*, and Otto Pflanze delivered the first volume of his most sensible Bismarck biography. Michael Balfour gave us what remains the best biography of William II (*The Kaiser and his Times*), and Jacques Droz added another penetrating segment to an unexcelled *oeuvre* on German history and culture in his *Romantisme allemand et l'état*. We welcomed Klaus Epstein's first, and alas only, volume on the *Genesis of German Conservatism*, Adalbert Hess's study of the Prussian parliament "which resisted Bismarck," the Jürgen Bertram monograph on the German elections of 1912, and a brace of pioneering studies on the German labor movement by Dieter Fricke, Wolfgang Schieder, and Hedwig Wachenheim. When John Snell retired from his administrative chores, he had fallen behind badly, and his industrious colleagues on both sides of the Atlantic saw to it that he would not soon catch up with them. The flow of Socialist documentation continued, while writing the history of political parties and pressure groups under the empire seemed to have become a particularly fashionable pursuit among the younger generation of German scholars. Within the space of less than a year, for instance (1966–67), the conscientious student of modern Germany found his library enriched by Jürgen Puhle's revelations about agrarian pressure groups, Hans Jaeger's treatment of the German entrepreneur in politics, and Hartmut Kaelble's revised dissertation on the *Centralverband Deutscher Industrieller*. Even if we were to continue this report and confine it to major works of substantive importance, it would expand this introduction beyond reasonable length. Suffice it to add, therefore, that the bibliography at the end of this volume would shrink significantly if the titles published after 1963 were stricken from its pages.

With knowledge expanding at such an unmanageable rate, John Snell's subject came to rest on an increasingly unwieldy body of information. It could no longer be contained within its original confines. By 1967 John had decided that Germany must enter the democratic era by way of two volumes. One of these would carry the story from 1789 to the beginning of World War I, while the second would provide a far more detailed record of German political developments during the war and would conclude with the establishment of the Weimar Republic. Neither prospective publishers nor colleagues asked to read various parts of the manuscript encouraged this expansion. But the author persisted. "The movement for democracy in Germany did not fail before 1914 because it was nonexistent or weak, but because it was opposed by powerfully entrenched political and social groups and institutions," he explained in 1967 to one such sceptic. "At least, that is my thesis. If it is a sound one, the opposition must be treated fairly carefully if the book is to be of value to senior and graduate students as well [as] to (or more than to) fellow specialists in German history." And in the summer of 1969 he justified his plan once more in these words:

> I am determined that this shall be a two-volume work. The story Volume I tells is not well known, even among Germans; and the present version tells it clearly and in readable English. I know of no comparable volume in English or in German. . . . Like Pflanze's first volume [on Bismarck], mine is based upon little archival material but upon thorough coverage of other types of sources. It synthesizes a mass of monographic literature, including the most recent. It is carefully footnoted, and the footnotes should be

of use to many students interested in researching some of the many aspects of my larger study.

At that point the first ten chapters of Volume I, about 376 manuscript pages, had been completed. The problem of keeping abreast of the "mass of monographic literature" was not diminishing and it had been complicated by two moves. In 1966 the author had left Tulane to accept an appointment at the University of Pennsylvania. Two years later he returned to his alma mater, the University of North Carolina, as University Distinguished Professor.

In the autumn of 1969, then, John Snell seemed to be settling down, revising once more what he had completed so far and looking forward to completing his most important project at the university where, some twenty years earlier, he had learned his history and taken the first precocious steps as a scholar. But when death struck him down at the age of forty-eight, less than three years later, the first volume remained a fragment. He had received a research grant for 1972–73 to begin archival research on the second but did not live to exploit this opportunity.

Only days were left to him when Professor Snell asked me to finish what I am sending to the printers with this introduction. I agreed, and between June of 1972 and January of 1974, I carefully reviewed what had been done and filled in the gaps. These were few in number at the beginning, and the first half of this volume required little editorial polish. After that divide the work to be done increased rapidly and much of the last four chapters can be said to be a fusion of John Snell's research and my writing.

Throughout, and regardless of my own physical involvement, I have sought to formulate John Snell's approaches and views, not mine. Since he did not leave any conclusions, I finally decided against adding any. Anything I could have added beyond a perfunctory summary of contents would have injected my interpretations into another man's work. Rather than risk the dissonance to which such a merger might have given rise, I put down my pen at the end of Chapter 13.

Clearly I did not and could not complete the work John Snell began almost twenty years ago. I finished what he left, and the result remains a fragment. The year 1914 presents no great divide in the history of German democracy, but unfinished as it is, the extant portion of this work tells us indeed much that is not well known, and it tells it clearly. It draws together a monumental mass of information, both substantive and bibliographic, which students at all levels will not be able to locate between two covers anywhere else for many years to come.

To the extent that it succeeds, then, *The Democratic Movement in Germany, 1789–1914* accentuates the impression of incompleteness and failure. How much more we could have learned if John had lived to complete the companion volume. But no executor of his intentions can make up for that loss. The editor and coauthor's residence at the Center for Advanced Studies of the University of Virginia from 1971 to 1973 provided time for research and writing without which this volume could not have been completed on schedule. Miss Frances Lackey typed the entire manuscript. Her prodigious energy and profound respect for the English language contributed significantly to the final product.

Hans A. Schmitt
Charlottesville, Va.
February 1976.

THE DEMOCRATIC MOVEMENT
IN GERMANY,
1789–1914

I.

THE BEGINNINGS,
1789–1815

"To bow down to the ground in the presence of princes is only an external honor. . . . God wishes that they be honored also in the internal recesses of every heart . . . by valuing and loving them; by wishing them long life, a happy government, and all other blessings; and by obeying all of their commands."

The exhortation was delivered in 1789 by the German Catholic bishop of Speyer to his flock. In any earlier year the words would have seemed in no way unusual to his fellow Germans, for in all of Europe there was no democratic nation and, indeed, no significant agitation for democracy. If so liberal a German of the years before 1789 as Friedrich Schiller described the idea of majority rule as "nonsense," the liberal Frenchman Voltaire was even more vehement, commenting that average human beings "are cattle and what is wanted for them is a yoke, a goad, and fodder."

For Germans as for the French themselves, the outbreak of the French Revolution in 1789 aroused hopes of making democracy something more than an abstract theory.[1]

Much attention has been focused on the supposed "national character" of the Germans in attempts to explain why they lagged behind in the development of democracy.[2] Whatever judgments social psychologists might finally reach, it is not necessary to attribute unchanging national characteristics to the Germans to understand why they were not democratic in institutions or in spirit in 1789. Geography and a complex history suggest well enough why the concept of popular sovereignty had few supporters among Germans on the eve of the French Revolution, and they help to explain why the principle so slowly won converts among them in the decades that followed.

A central and exposed location in Europe and a lack of natural frontiers had denied the German people the geographical protection that greater isolation afforded Great Britain, the United States, Switzerland, and even France. Much of Germany's authoritarian political behavior before and after 1789 can be explained in terms of accentuated insecurity. Beset for centuries by fear of attacks from east and west, and particularly vulnerable to them, Germans had been willing to accept rule from above and feudal class structure in return for military protection, however inadequate.[3]

The military vulnerability of the Germans was perpetuated by their political fragmentation. In the eighteenth century striking differences existed between the myth of a great Germanic community and the political reality of central Europe. For hundreds of years the small German states had been linked together in the Holy Roman Empire. But the emperor was only as powerful as his own dynastic state within the empire allowed him to be, and the empire was a loose diplomatic and dynastic association of some three hundred kingdoms and principalities, ecclesiastical states, and city-states. Austria— whose Habsburg ruler was also emperor of the Holy Roman Empire—and Prussia were the most powerful of these states.

Failure to make a timely transition from a feudal patchwork of small states to national unity was one of the greatest sources of frustration for the German people. Their more highly unified neighbors kept them weak and insecure by encouraging their hostilities against one another, playing the ancient game of "divide and rule." Richelieu had played the game in the Thirty Years' War, and its rules had been written into the Peace of Westphalia in 1648. They were also to be written into Napoleon's diplomacy of war and peace.[4]

Division into small states bred a virulent localism, a sense of "states rights" stronger than that known to John C. Calhoun's South Carolina. Since about 1829 the Germans have called this "particularism" (*Partikularismus*), but the feeling existed long before it was named. For centuries it made them obstruct advances toward national unity. Their particularistic loyalties caused the Germans occasionally to fight among themselves without any foreign inspiration. Their internecine rivalries intensified their sense of insecurity, their dependence upon state power, and, as a consequence, their respect for authority. Insecurity developed mental blockages that were difficult even for democrats to overcome; whatever "really injures the state," one of them remarked in 1788, "must be forbidden."[5]

Because they lived in small states under authoritarian rulers, Germans did not learn the freedom that distance from authority can bring. Long after French government was centered near Paris and the British knew but one monarch, Germans were never far from one of some three hundred rulers. "In this very multiplication of authority," Friedrich Meinecke wrote, "we see the chief means by which the mentality of the authoritarian state penetrated so deeply into the pores of German life."[6]

Religious authority reinforced that of the secular rulers. German Catholicism as well as Lutheranism in the sixteenth century had established the principle that the religion of the prince should be the religion of his subjects, and Catholics experienced at least as much hierarchy in their religious observances as was confronted in the churches of Luther and Calvin. Even in the twentieth century, Catholics who wanted to rebel against Hitler could find in their doctrine no basis for revolt. Indeed, it was easier to find such a basis in Luther's example and in his doctrine of justification by faith alone. The radical nineteenth-century political writer Heinrich Heine admired Luther's defense of freedom of conscience, calling him "the greatest German." But the majority of German Protestants in the eighteenth century remembered the other Luther, the Luther who taught that there were "no better works than to obey and serve all those who are set over us as superiors." The philosophical principle of freedom powerfully attracted Protestant intellectuals in Germany; the practice of political freedom did not. Johann Wolfgang von Goethe (1749–1832) reflected the true accents of Luther when he wrote that politics should be left to "the great, the powerful, and those versed in the affairs of state."[7]

The greatest significance of the Protestant Revolt for the history of democracy in Germany may not lie in the ambiguous impact of Luther's teachings, but in the effects of the religious struggle upon the German mentality. Because of the intimate relationship of church and state in sixteenth-century Europe, the Reformation was a political struggle as well as a religious upheaval. It was for Germany the supreme revolutionary experience of modern times, demanding personal sacrifices as few revolutions have demanded of any people, and lasting intermittently from 1517 until 1648. The Protestant Revolt burned out the revolutionary spirit of the German people for a long time to come. By 1648 they had lost both the energy and the naiveté that upheavals require. In the years that followed, the teachings of Catholic priests and Protestant pastors alike trained Germans to show respect for those destiny had placed above them in the social hierarchy—for all authorities (*die Obrigkeiten*) and, most of all, for their rulers.[8]

In the seventeenth and eighteenth centuries economic development in Germany did no more to foster a democratic spirit than did political geography, history, and religion. Most Germans were engaged in farming, which encouraged neither individualism nor equality. The migration of farmers to the eastern frontier had occurred in the late Middle Ages and under conditions that preserved and strengthened authority and class awareness. Unlike the rural Americans of the eighteenth century, Germans of that period had no frontier of forest or plains in which to taste a large measure of equality and to develop self-reliance; in which to find freedom from both political and ecclesiastical authorities; in which, in short, to cultivate the psychology of democracy. Most of their arable land had been turned to crops by the time America was opened to European settlement. While democratic attitudes slowly grew in the virgin lands of the New World, Germans were bound more tightly into socially stratified obedience by economic pressures; many peasants became serfs only during the seventeenth century, and serfdom still held sway in 1800 in most of Germany.

Economic development had, by 1789, created neither a power-hungry "bourgeoisie" in the Marxist sense (a capitalist class) nor a "proletariat" (industrial working class) that believed itself to be exploited by capitalists. The proletariat was nonexistent. There was a German "middle class," but few capitalists were included in it. Besides the small number of great merchants, it consisted chiefly of civil servants, professional people, pastors, intellectuals, small shopkeepers, and owners of tiny factories that had only rudimentary machinery. The German middle class was not large. The shift of trade routes in the sixteenth century and the Thirty Years' War in the next had caused an absolute as well as a relative decline in the size, wealth, and importance of Germany's "free cities." The towns of Germany had languished. They harbored an old middle class, rich in memories and preserving its traditional cultural and political influence; but it was a middle class that tended to be relatively timorous in the late eighteenth century and prideful of its hierarchical privileges. Middle-class Germans were inclined to seek additional privileges and enhanced social status for themselves under the established governments, but not the right to run those governments.[9]

Intellectual forces did more in the eighteenth century than did economic conditions to promote desires for change in Germany. The Enlightenment in Britain and France found its counterpart in the German states, though the German *Aufklärung* started earlier and was largely independent. The arbitrariness of monarchical and bureaucratic government, the lack of freedom in economic life, the censorship of publications, the privileges of the feudal aristocracy, serfdom, and the unimaginative education of children—all these were of concern; but the German Enlightenment was, above all, religious in origins and in aims. From such centers as the new Pietist University of Halle innovators like August Hermann Francke modified traditional theology and called for greater religious toleration. The movement was in no sense "democratic," but it added to the foundation of ideas upon which the liberalism of later years could stand.

In a few of the German states the rulers themselves and their more forward-looking civil servants embraced the critical spirit of the Enlightenment in attempts to make government more efficient and their states more powerful. The "enlightened despots" thus effected a number of needed reforms. A somewhat greater degree of religious toleration was introduced, bureaucracy was made more efficient, the lot of the serfs was improved, roads were built, swampy lands were drained and brought under cultivation, and some industry was stimulated. Enlightened despots like Karl Friedrich, the ruler of Baden, and Frederick the Great of Prussia led the way. But the changes they introduced stopped short of fundamental social political alterations. Frederick the Great tentatively decreed the abolition of serfdom in

1763, but backed down in the face of stiff arguments from the nobility that freedom would make the peasants harder to handle. And Karl Friedrich of Baden, who eventually did liberate the serfs of his state in 1793, strongly defended the aristocracy as the most superior of "races among men."

The enlightened despots rejected all proposals to limit their own royal powers. The tradition that the dynasty was an end in itself was not diminished in Hohenzollern Prussia when Frederick the Great self-effacingly called himself the "first servant" of the state. On the contrary, the Junkers—noble owners of Prussia's large estates—as well as lesser folk were subordinated to the royal will as never before when Frederick died in 1786. Two years earlier, already ailing, the aging monarch had concisely revealed the unflattering view he held of representative government; his blood, he wrote to his brother Henry, was "as badly disordered as the British Parliament." Far from weakening royal authority, enlightened despotism resulted in exactly the reverse; by accomplishing needed reforms, the enlightened rulers increased respect for monarchical government among their subjects.[10]

Like the other German states, Prussia before 1789 was governed rigidly, and it became more highly regulated under enlightened despotism. In the very act of protecting the rights of the individual against the customary authority exercised by his family and other social groups, the state arrogated greater power to itself. Thus, while striving to increase individual independence, the reformed legal code of Prussia specified in 1794 that every healthy mother was "obligated to nurse her own infants." More than any other German principality, Prussia was a service state. Its bureaucracy, giving its discipline and obedience to the monarch, expected obedience and respect from mere citizens. The tradition of authoritarianism that the bureaucrats helped to foster was also nourished by the military. The army in Prussia, built as elsewhere as a means to an end, was so important by about 1740 that it was beginning to shape the political, economic, and social life of the state. Frederick the Great, his own personality remolded by it, used the army to double the size of his dominions and to discipline his subjects.[11]

Before the development of absolutism and its strong armies and bureaucracies, the powers of the rulers within the German states had been checked by feudal assemblies or "diets," which were controlled by the upper classes. Nobles, the clergy, and the patrician officials of the towns were recognized as separate status groups or "estates" (the German plural was *Stände*) and had the right to representation in the diets, which had begun to meet in the fifteenth century. In some states the landowning peasantry also held representation in these diets. The right to elect representatives was denied the propertyless. The powers of the diets were limited by the inherited rights of individual noble or dynastic families. The assemblies could state grievances and in some cases refuse to authorize taxation until their complaints were acknowledged, but they did not pass legislation. They were not true parliaments.

Nonetheless, the diets had provided checks against the princes' efforts to centralize government control and to create standing armies. As a consequence, the enlightened despots sought to weaken the diets or to eliminate them altogether. In several states they simply were not called into session; where they continued to exist they were diminished in importance during the late seventeenth and eighteenth centuries. But they did not disappear everywhere. In the southwestern German state of Württemberg the diet's rights were reaffirmed in 1770 after a period of challenge by the ruler, and members of the recognized status groups (*Stände*) prided themselves on the large measure of control over taxation that they enjoyed. These corporative assemblies left a tradition of limits on monarchy, though they did not foster the development of democracy.[12]

Where diets existed, they approximately reflected the structure of German society. Shaped by centuries of slow developments, that society was highly stratified. Each man's place was largely determined by the *Stand* into which he was born, though some upward mobility was possible. Each man knew his place and showed respect for those whom birth or acquired status had placed above him, while looking down on those below him. Johann Georg Schlosser, a leading official of Baden and brother-in-law of Goethe, accurately reflected the *Stände*-consciousness of German society when he wrote in 1785: "The . . . nobility is rather arrogant. It regards the lesser court servants [middle-class officials like Schlosser himself] with hearty contempt; they in turn have as much contempt for the businessmen; the business-men and office holders have not much regard for the craftsman, and the craftsman is just as arrogant towards the peasant." The peasants could feel superior only to those inhabitants who were treated by law as well as by social practice as the inferiors of all other Germans, regardless of wealth or class status—the Jews. A movement for legal emancipation and religious tolerance was underway by the 1770's—one of the more attractive aspects of the German Enlightenment—but many years would pass before its aims were achieved.[13]

Even this brief sketch should leave no doubt that by the 1780's geography and history had created serious mental and material obstacles to democracy in Germany. Insecurity which resulted from wars among the great powers on German soil and from strife among the German states, exhaustion from religious strug-gle, obedience taught by priests and pastors, the relative lack of social mobility that faster economic development might have brought, and the patronizing favors and exactions of hundreds of enlightened and unenlightened princes and nobles—all these had made the social and political structure and the "national character" of Germany what it was in 1789, and the people were not democratic in principle, liberal in practice, or revolutionary in spirit. But the news of political developments in England and America had begun to quicken the imagination of a few Ger-mans, and the outbreak of revolution in France in 1789 stirred others.

The Puritan and Glorious revolutions of seventeenth-century England had passed with little notice in Germany, but interest in British government was increased after 1714, when the ruler of the German state of Hanover assumed the British crown as George I. Voltaire's *Letters Concerning the English Nation* (1733) and Montesquieu's *Spirit of the Laws* (1748) also stimulated Ger-man interest in British political liberty. By the 1770's some Ger-mans who had traveled in Great Britain were pointing to the excellence of its constitution, especially to its combination of monarchy with an elected assembly—the House of Commons. Then in 1776 the American War of Independence called forth an unaccustomed consideration of revolution and of democratic constitutional principles.[14]

A good many Germans had settled in America by 1776, and a few German travel books and histories of the colonies had been published; but it is scarcely an exaggeration to say that the Declaration of Independence marked the "discovery of America" by Germany. German soldiers fought on both sides in the struggle. Articles in journals and newspapers brought news of conditions in America to German readers. At least three hundred items published in Germany in the years 1776–83 were partly or wholly concerned with the American colonies, and no fewer than 180 appeared during the three-year period from 1787 to 1789 when the United States Constitution was being drafted and ratified. The views of Edmund Burke were read, and in 1786 Thomas Paine's more radical justification of the American rebellion, *Common Sense*, was published in a German edition. By 1800 the first important German student of American affairs, Christoph Daniel Ebeling, had published five volumes of his seven-volume work on the geography and history of America.

Many Germans viewed the American Revolution at first as simply a struggle for national independence. Its revolutionary implications for Germany were so muted that Frederick the Great—seeing that it would keep Britain busy outside Europe—commented favorably on it. Those who saw a more radical meaning in the revolt across the Atlantic did not welcome it unanimously. In Hanover, whose ruler was the king of England, the Göttingen professor, August Ludwig von Schlözer, was moved by the American Revolution to denounce democratic government in general, contending that "no freedom, no human happiness of a higher kind" was possible in a democracy. On the other hand, the poet Friedrich Gottlieb Klopstock in 1781 described the revolution as "the dawning of a great day coming." A much lesser-known writer, Johann Christoph Schmohl, was even more radical in interpreting its meaning in a book that he anonymously published at Königsberg in 1782 (*Ueber Nordamerika und Demokratie*). "Europe," he predicted, "shall receive its salvation from America." But in the 1780's it was easier to seek salvation in America than to wait for America's salvation of Europe, and Schmohl was one who migrated. Georg Forster, the German explorer, scientist, and political pamphleteer who accompanied Captain James Cook around the world, complained to his wife in 1793: "I still cherish hope that public happiness will come also to our continent; but nobody can foretell how long we shall have to fight, because compared with the cold-blooded Americans we are mad-caps and our principles are rotten to the core."[15]

Germans who thought of applying the principles of the American Revolution at home were exotic and lacked influence before 1789. Then an astonished Germany learned that the common folk of Paris were storming the Bastille, that peasants in the French countryside were rising against aristocrats, and that both middle-class Frenchmen and liberal-minded nobles were limiting the power of King Louis XVI.

The uprising in Paris in 1789 was at first applauded in all classes of German society. Even Prussian officials celebrated the upheaval as a French victory for enlightened monarchy, reason, justice, and the principles of government that Frederick the Great had followed. (They also congratulated themselves that no such upheaval was needed in Prussia.) Isolated revolts broke out among the peasants of Saxony in 1790 and among peasants and craftsmen in Silesia in 1792 and 1793. The rebels sometimes invoked French revolutionary principles in support of their risings, and they were put down only by troops. Here and there a few middle-class Germans would suggest the need for revolution in the years that followed.

Yet there was scarcely a chance that Germans might actually instigate a revolution of their own in the years 1789–92. There was not yet a sufficient "revolution of the mind"—to use R. R. Palmer's expression; and sociopolitical conditions in the German states had not prepared the people for a national uprising. Paris radicalized the French Revolution, and orders from Paris carried it to all parts of France; but there was no Paris in Germany—no large concentration of middle-class citizens and artisans to revolt, no established economic and political center to influence the country as a whole. Furthermore, many Germans who initially welcomed the French Revolution began to lose sympathy when mob violence prevailed in Paris. By 1790 tracts began to appear in condemnation of conditions in France and in defense of German political institutions, and their arguments were strengthened in 1793 by the execution of King Louis XVI.[16]

The outbreak of war in 1792 between revolutionary France and the two largest of the Germanic states, Prussia and Austria, introduced additional complications. At war and hard pressed by powerful enemies, the French government tried to inspire rebellion against the German governments. The French *Guerre aux châteaux, paix aux chaumières* soon was echoed in German: *Friede den Hütten!–Krieg den Palästen!* When French armies moved into the Rhineland in the fall of 1792, urging the "oppressed Germans" to collaborate with them, they found some hearty responses. Georg Forster, the admirer of America, welcomed the French occupation of the electorate of Mainz, whose archbishop-ruler he had served; in November 1792 he celebrated the transformation of "silent serfs of a priest into upright, vocal, free citizens, into daring friends of liberty and equality." But the French found little spontaneous support. In Mainz they rigged it artificially. Elections were influenced to obtain popular assemblies that would favor annexation to France. "All the deputies named so far are our friends," wrote one French official from Mainz in 1793, "for I took the precaution of proposing them myself or of having them proposed."

In the Rhineland the leaders of the pro-French faction were professors, students, doctors, and lawyers, though only a small minority of these occupational groups. Most of the pro-French Rhinelanders at first hoped to create under French sponsorship a constitutional monarchy or a republic of their own. Some wanted a German republican state stretching from Alsace to Holland; the revolutionary journalist A. G. F. Rebmann saw this as a first step toward making "Germany a republic and the Germans a nation." But thousands—under both persuasion and pressure—signed petitions asking for annexation to the French Republic. Georg Forster was one of those who went to Paris to promote the proposal. While varying portions of the Rhineland belonged to France between 1800 and 1814, Rebmann and others were glad to accept official positions under the French regime. Meanwhile, little pro-French or prorepublican sentiment was evident east of the Rhine.[17]

But if the French Revolution called forth no comparable revolt in Germany, it did—directly or indirectly—bring important changes, and in this sense Napoleon Bonaparte, as Georges

Lefèbvre succinctly put it, "prolonged the Revolution." One of the casualties of change was the Holy Roman Empire. By 1801 both Prussian and Austrian armies had felt defeat at the hands of Napoleon. Instead of banding more closely together against the first consul, the leading princes of Germany cooperated in his reorganization of the empire to their separate territorial advantages. The more powerful of the southern German dynasties established their sovereignty over "free cities," small noble states that had been autonomous within the Holy Roman Empire, and church-states that had been governed in the past by bishops. Bavaria, Württemberg, and Baden made the largest gains, winning greater strength vis à vis Austria. When the Habsburg House of Austria in 1805 again made war against Napoleon, Baden, Bavaria, and Württemberg aided the French ruler rather than their "own" emperor. As a result, Austria was defeated and Vienna occupied. In 1806, after several German states had seceded from the empire, the last Holy Roman emperor laid down the ancient crown. The Holy Roman Empire ceased to exist, though the Austrian Empire, newly proclaimed, would be preserved under Habsburg rule until 1918. For the next several years after 1806, Napoleon provided what little unity there was among the German states, several of which were brought together in the Confederation of the Rhine, but for the most part they went their separate ways. Out of the breakup of the Holy Roman Empire, particularism was broadened, transformed, and strengthened.

One by one the German states carried out modernizing reforms in the French pattern. In Baden, Württemberg, and other states the rulers themselves inaugurated reforms from above, here in compliance with French demands, there to strengthen the defensive ardor of their subjects against the French, and often simply to knit together the diverse parts of their enlarged territories. The reforms of these years did not introduce democracy, but they established some essential prerequisites for its development later. In 1789 serfdom was still entrenched in the German states. Now it was eliminated, though feudal dues lingered on. The reforms also introduced the principle of equality before the law. Beginning steps were taken, under French pressure, toward constitutional government.

The constitution of 1807 for Westphalia, for example, was made in Paris (though several Germans helped to draft it), sent to Germany by Napoleon, and applied under the rule of his own brother, Jerome Bonaparte—made king of Westphalia at twenty-three. A kind of parliament was allowed to function in Westphalia from 1808 until 1810. Substantial reforms were accomplished there, in the annexed Rhineland, and in the southwestern state of Baden, and somewhat more tenuous ones in Württemberg and Bavaria.[18]

Prussia, beaten by the French in 1795 but occupied only after another defeat in 1806, was a special case. Even before 1806, King Frederick William III had shown interest in improving the lot of the peasants, and by 1805 all serfs on royal estates were freed. The nobles, however, clung to their own serfs, and the Prussian government did not want to take the risk of leading a free people with acknowledged political rights. As late as 1803 a government decree asserted: "The children of the working classes are to read the catechism, Bible and Hymn Book; to fear and love God and act accordingly; to honour authority. Whoever attempts to stuff them with more than this, sets himself a useless and thankless task."[19]

The defeat of Prussia by Napoleon's armies in 1806 opened the way to more substantial changes. The Treaty of Tilsit temporarily reduced by half the size of a humiliated Prussia, placed it under French occupation, and levied a tribute that the treasury could pay only with difficulty. A Prussian army officer who had gone to Canada in 1782 as a young man, Count Neithardt von Gneisenau, was among the first to draw the necessary conclusions from the failure on Prussia's old regime: Prussian officials and aristocrats, in cooperation with the monarch, must voluntarily initiate progressive domestic changes. Such a "revolution from above" (*Revolution von oben*) would head off revolution from below and revitalize the Prussian state in the midst of its adversity.[20]

Baron Karl vom Stein was the grand designer of the Prussian *Revolution von oben* of 1807–13. Though no democrat, this scion of a family of imperial knights from Nassau concluded that a larger measure of freedom must be introduced into Prussia if the kingdom was to be reinvigorated to overthrow French domination. "If the nation is to be ennobled," he wrote in 1807, "the oppressed sections of the population must be endowed with freedom, independence, and property." On October 9, 1807—more than half a century before slavery was abolished in the United States—Stein's first great reform as the king's chief minister provided that serfdom must end in 1810. The few former serfs who could produce the purchase price could now buy and own land. Four years later peasants were allowed to gain clear title to land by surrendering their claim to a third of the acreage they previously had used as serfs. The major result of this was to increase the landholdings of the nobles, but by this method or by making monetary payments, 240,000 peasants would become proprietors in Prussia by 1846.[21]

Since free men must constitute the basis for the realization of democratic ideals, the decree of 1807 was a precondition for the eventual development of political democracy in Germany. But democratic results were not to be apparent for a long time. For many decades the majority of rural Prussians would continue to be landless and dependent upon a local noble and consequently poor material for representative government. Stein realized this. Men "must be gradually accustomed to act on their own initiative before they are convened in large assemblies and entrusted with great issues to discuss," he noted in 1807.

A year later, through the reorganization of city government, another move was made to develop initiative. The right of Prussian cities to regulate their own affairs autonomously had been limited sharply by the growth of absolute monarchy in the eighteenth century. In November 1808 a large measure of local control was restored. Each city was provided with an elected assembly, which in turn chose members of the city council and the mayor. This did not make city government democratic because only inhabitants who owned property could vote for the city assemblymen; furthermore, municipal law enforcement remained under the control of the state. But municipal government henceforth was representative. The city assembly controlled taxes and the city budget.

Through his reforms, Stein had antagonized powerful Prussian nobles who had the ear of King Frederick William III, and his German nationalism antagonized the French. While preparing other reforms, Stein was dismissed at the end of 1808 amidst domestic intrigue and French pressure, but a number of his associates continued to pursue his goals. A liberal-minded and patriotic nobleman, Wilhelm von Humboldt, was placed in charge of Prussian education just before Stein's dismissal. Before being sent to Vienna as Prussian ambassador in June 1810, Humboldt founded the University of Berlin and charted a system of teachers' colleges to improve public schools and train his fellow Germans for responsible freedom. In the years that followed, he worked to create a Prussian constitution and called for equality for Prussia with Austria in the leadership of a more united Germany. In his draft constitution of December 1813, he proposed to organize Germany as a union of federal states.

Humboldt's hope for a German constitution was doomed to failure, but one of its chief assumptions was taken up by others. Humboldt was convinced that "only a nation externally strong can preserve within itself the spirit from which all internal blessings flow." That faith was shared by a number of military leaders who set out to reform the Prussian army. Urged on by Generals Gneisenau, Gerhard von Scharnhorst, and Hermann von Boyen, the king in 1808 almost totally eliminated corporal punishment. The reformers also eased the way for middle-class Prussians to become officers; and finally, in 1813, they introduced universal conscription. These and other changes made the army more effective, though they did not nourish a democratic spirit; the Prussian army continued to inculcate recognition of authority and strict obedience rather than democratic values.[22]

Gneisenau, like Stein and Humboldt, wanted the king to grant Prussia a constitution. After Stein was dropped this aim was pushed by Baron Karl August von Hardenberg, a member of the nobility of Hanover who had collaborated in the Prussian reforms but had assisted in the dismissal of Stein. For Hardenberg, even more than for Stein, domestic change was not primarily an end in itself but a means to strengthen the state. With this in mind, Jews living in the old provinces of Prussia were granted equality before the law in 1812. More broadly, Hardenberg sought for a decade after becoming chief minister in 1810 to persuade the king to introduce a constitution. In this he faced the same arguments that Stein had met—arguments that would be repeated almost word for word by Prussian conservatives a full century later: elected representatives would seek only their private advantage; no good could come of the representation of the stupidity which they associated with common folk; monarchical government could maintain itself only through "an intermediary class"—the aristocracy—whose function was to restrain the masses.[23]

Faced with this opposition and feuding with other reform leaders, Hardenberg eventually abandoned his own attempts to obtain a constitution and representative government. Five times his monarch, Frederick William III, would promise to grant the people of Prussia a constitution, but he never made good his promises. Hardenberg's proposal of an Assembly of Notables—representing all of Prussia but only advisory in its capacity—ran into the particularist arguments that would be stated and restated against parliamentary government in Germany during the next century: the nobles cried out that a national assembly would create a centralized Prussian state and thus violate the autonomy of the provinces. The idea of a statewide assembly of notables was allowed to die after one assembly met briefly as the first such consultative body ever to be convened in Prussia. What finally emerged from Hardenberg's efforts for constitutional government was not a Prussian legislature, but only diets for each of the eight Prussian provinces, heavily weighted in favor of the nobility. These were created in 1823, a year after his death. By then it had been obvious for several years that Frederick William III was not going to continue the *Revolution von oben*. As early as 1815 the king who had patronized Stein after the defeat at Jena was bestowing a medal upon a pamphleteer who had attacked "the hatching of constitutions" as a "characteristically French vice." For in 1815 the crisis that had given rise to reforms had passed.[24] As Napoleon's humiliation of Prussia in 1806 had frightened Frederick William III into granting reforms, so the defeat of the emperor in 1814–15 had encouraged the Prussian king and other German rulers to turn their backs on innovation.

On June 25, 1812, Napoleon had made the mistake of invading Russia. The king of Prussia, cowed by the power of Napoleonic France, lent support to the venture, but by the end of the year the czar's armies, harrying the French out of Russia, were on the

Prussian frontier. On February 28, 1813, a Prussian-Russian treaty was signed. It invited the assistance of other German princes to help reestablish German independence from France. The German "War of Liberation" was underway, and Baron vom Stein, now an adviser to Czar Alexander, worked furiously to arouse a national uprising against Napoleon and enthusiasm for German unity. For the first time, a virile and widespread nationalism found expression among the Germans.

German responses to the early incursions of French armies into the territory of the Holy Roman Empire had been either parochial or cosmopolitan; there was no German "nationalism" at that time. A few writers, most notably Johann Gottfried von Herder, had begun to create an awareness of cultural nationality among intellectuals, but in the early 1790's it was a rare German who felt any need or desire to create a German nation. Then Napoleon had progressively extended his influence over Germany. In several areas French influence had given way to French control, and French control had meant humiliation and exploitation of the Germans. Simultaneously, literary Romanticism had provided an intellectual stimulus to national aspirations by offering an idealized and mystical view of the German past.

"Out of the myths of the past and out of the dreams of the future," as Hans Kohn has written, German authors "created an ideal fatherland long before an actual fatherland . . . became a reality." Neither parochialism nor cosmopolitanism would die quickly. But by 1806, when Prussia was forced to kneel before "the Conqueror of Europe," nationalistic proclamations in prose and poetry were beginning to be heard from literati such as Ernst Moritz Arndt and Friedrich Schlegel, the theologian Friedrich Schleiermacher, and the philosopher Johann Gottlieb Fichte. German nationalism could not become a mass contagion within seven years, but by 1813 there could be no doubt that a nationalistic movement had developed. It fed upon resentment against Napoleonic France, was given intellectual respectability by a dozen or so major writers, and was used during the War of Liberation to create still more resentment against the French. "I hate all Frenchmen without distinction in the name of God and of my people," Arndt proclaimed in 1813.[25]

The advent of German nationalism enormously complicated

the task of achieving representative government among the Germans. Those who wanted both popular sovereignty and a genuine national community would find it much more difficult to accomplish both objectives than only the first, for to unite the Germans into a nation would call for changes at least as profound as those the democratization of the separate German states required. Those who favored both objectives would, after 1813, repeatedly find it necessary to decide which to put ahead of the other, and the achievement of national unity generally would take priority over democratization. Some nationalists would concede that greater political equality was essential to strengthen the national spirit of the masses. Many others, however, would argue that attempts to attain democracy jeopardized the national movement by creating divisions among the German people. Democracy's enemies also could capitalize on the resentment against the French that was so pronounced a part of the new nationalism, denouncing the principles of liberty, equality, and popular sovereignty as French inventions and labeling the men who supported these principles as pro-French.

The immediate goal in the spring of 1813 was to defeat Napoleon. To do this the Prussians and Russians needed the help of the Habsburg lands, but Prince Clemens von Metternich, the Austrian chief minister, was reluctant to join them. Rather, he sought the restoration of a balance of power in which Austria's leadership over the separate German states would be reasserted. At first Metternich tried to achieve his objectives by urging the warring powers to make peace. By August, however, it was clear that Napoleon's price for peace was too high; thus Metternich joined in the struggle against Bonaparte. Together, Austria, Prussia, and Russia won a celebrated victory over Napoleon around Leipzig in October 1813; he was then beaten in France in March 1814, was forced into exile, reappeared at the head of French troops, and was decisively defeated at last at Waterloo on June 18, 1815, by British and Prussian contingents.[26]

For the rulers of Germany the successes of 1813–15 seemed more than a victory over Napoleon; they marked a belated and partial triumph over the revolution that had produced him. In the years that followed, the specter of revolution at home would continue to prompt some German princes to make additional concessions to constitutionalism, but it would cause others to respond with scorn and repression.

Contradictory results thus emerged from the impact of the French Revolution and the Napoleonic Empire on Germany. Reforms were accomplished that would never be taken away. Some German serfs had been freed, the principle of equality before the law had been recognized in several states, and constitutions had been granted in a few. Democratic institutions had been established nowhere in Germany, and there was very little democratic spirit, but the period 1789–1815 marks the beginning of aspirations for democracy and even for a democratic republic among a tiny minority of Germans. At the same time, the urge to create a unified nation had arisen amidst resentment against French domination during the Napoleonic years. Henceforth, Germans who wanted democratic or republican government would find it difficult to live down the fact that the French had been the first to test their ideas on streets and battlefields. They would find it equally difficult to overcome the habits of mind and body, of the bowed head and the bent knee, that centuries of subservience to authority had instilled in the German people. The struggle for democracy had begun, but no early success for it could be imagined in 1815.

II.

REPRESSION AND NEW IMPULSES

"I hope with the help of God to strike down the German revolution, as I have defeated the Conqueror of Europe." With this somewhat exaggerated appraisal of his past accomplishment, Prince Clemens von Metternich acknowledged the ambitious aim that guided him through the years 1815–48. In his attempts to hold back the rise of liberalism and democracy, Austria's chief minister had much help from the princes of the several German states. They were especially anxious to check agitation for national unity, for all of them knew that they stood to lose their particularistic sovereignties if their states should ever be merged to form a united German nation. All the while, however, new impulses in German society sustained the movement for political change and ensured its slow growth amidst repression.[1]

Throughout the Metternich era the people of Germany continued to live under authoritarian governments in particularistic states. Napoleon had remade the map of Germany, and the Congress of Vienna only cautiously disrupted the new status quo. Prussia was much enlarged—having regained some of the Polish provinces, won two-fifths of Saxony, and annexed new Rhineland territories as a buffer against France. Instead of trying to restore the dozens of tiny states that had existed before 1789, Metternich chose to support the existing thirty-nine and to keep them separate and sovereign. With its many non-German subjects, the Habsburg monarchy had neither the will nor the ability to become part of a genuine German nation. On the other hand, unity without German Austria would banish Habsburg influence over north-central Europe and sharply diminish the great-power status of the monarchy. Thus Metternich wanted only a loose union of the German states, one in which Habsburg influence would prevail.

The resulting German Confederation was simpler than the old Holy Roman Empire, and it provided a somewhat more unified policy for its component parts. As Metternich had wished, Austria played the leading role in its affairs. The Confederation's Diet, presided over by the Austrian representative, consisted of delegates appointed by the separate sovereigns. It regularly met in Frankfurt, the coronation site of the Holy Roman Empire. There it planned common diplomatic actions and coordinated the struggle of the state governments against the agitation of democrats and liberals.

The reality of 1815–16 was terribly disappointing to those who, during the national rising of 1813, had hoped for the unity of a free Germany. Faculty members and students in the universities felt the disappointment with special keenness. Beginning in 1815 at Jena, the students—many of whom were veterans of the War of Liberation—formed new organizations (Burschenschaften) in several of the universities. Diverse motives inspired the members (Burschenschafter). Some were so highly nationalistic and so intolerant in their Christianity that they barred Jews from membership; some, while talking of liberty, did not hesitate to burn the books of antinationalist writers. In 1818 the character and aims of the liberals among them were sensitively summarized by Heinrich von Gagern, a nineteen-year-old student who had served at Waterloo. Emphasizing that "love of the Fatherland" was the leading Burschenschaft credo, young Gagern added: "We want a constitution for the nation that conforms to the spirit of the age, to the Enlightenment, not one that each prince gives his people to suit his fancy and serve his private interests." For more than thirty years Gagern was to speak for the liberals of Germany. In 1818, Karl Follen spoke even more radically. Another veteran of the War of Liberation, Follen became a lecturer in civil law and a leader of the Burschenschaft at the Hessian University of Giessen. His "Great Song" of 1818 captured both the principles and the passion of his fellow liberal democrats:

> Only the equality of man, the will of the people, is
> Sovereign by the grace of God.
> Up, up, my people, God created you free,

> Call yourself from slavery's wasteland
> To the haven of freedom.

August von Kotzebue was a scornful critic of the whole Burschenschaft movement. Trained as a lawyer, Kotzebue had become a prolific dramatist and a conservative man of the world who had been in and out of the Russian state service since 1781. In 1817 he had become an agent and publicist in Germany for the Russian government. Denouncing both the nationalism and the liberalism of the Burschenschafter, Kotzebue epitomized all they hated. On March 23, 1819, young Karl Sand, an ardent follower of Karl Follen, stabbed the Russian agent to death in Mannheim.

Metternich already had taken alarm at the Burschenschaft movement. The "evil" in the universities had to be restrained, he cautioned, before "a whole generation of revolutionaries" was trained. For him, both liberalism and democracy—like nationalism—were cancers in the body politic of Europe, and conceiving himself to be a kind of "social physician," he thought only in terms of cutting out the disease. The assassination of Kotzebue made it certain that he could count on the help—even the initiative—of the German rulers. He met with their representatives at Carlsbad in Bohemia in August 1819, and the resulting resolutions, adopted by the Diet of the German Confederation in Frankfurt on September 20, 1819, came to be called the Carlsbad Decrees. They provided for censorship of newspapers, pamphlets, and other publications and required the dissolution of the Burschenschaften. To make certain that the "evil" in the universities was eliminated, they created a system of police supervision and inspection. The Carlsbad Decrees were not perfectly enforced in all the states, but for almost three decades these and similar measures handicapped advocates of political change.[2]

Metternich equated the granting of even a conservative constitution with victory for "revolution" and "democracy," and he did not hesitate to poison the mind of the Prussian monarch against Hardenberg and Wilhelm von Humboldt. Events in Prussia after the dismissal of Humboldt in 1819 should have set even Metternich's mind at rest. Frederick William III ruled as Prussian kings had ruled before 1789, with the advice of his nobles, the support of his army and—he said—by the grace of God. Bureaucratic rule reached an all-time high, and more nobles than before filled administrative positions. Middle-class Germans who rose as officials were absorbed into the nobility, which also dominated local administration. In the state as a whole in 1820, 72 percent of the royal administrators in the counties (*Landräte*) were nobles; in 1845, 73 percent were nobles. Notwithstanding a promise in 1808 to eliminate preference according to social class in selecting officers, the Prussian army still belonged to the nobility as well as to the king: 7,264 of its 9,434 officers in 1842 were nobles (77 percent). Thus a contemporary poet–critic, in lines that became immortal, hinted that the Prussian nobles not only served but controlled the Prussian king: Adalbert von Chamisso suggested that their King was absolute, so long as he did their bidding. On the most fundamental issues, however, there was no great difference between the will of the nobles and the royal will in the period 1815–48; monarchy and aristocracy worked together in opposition to liberal and democratic demands.[3]

Between 1815 and 1848, in Prussia as in the other states of Germany, the churches—staunch supporters of kings and nobles —exerted a powerful influence upon public opinion. After the settlements of 1814–15, one-third of Prussia's population remained Catholic, but the bishops and priests taught obedience to the Protestant monarchy that destiny had placed at their head. When they challenged the Prussian king it was for religious rather than political reasons, and even then the power of the state sharply limited their public opposition. The only serious contest came in 1837 over the religious education of children born to marriages between Catholics and Protestants, and this dispute was resolved in 1840.

Trouble between the Prussian monarch and the Protestant churches had come earlier. In 1817 the Calvinist King Frederick William III, had celebrated the anniversary of Luther's revolt against the Catholic church by calling for a union of Lutherans and Calvinists. The Evangelical Christian church was the result. Similar Protestant unions were formed with congregational ap-

proval in Baden, Nassau, Hesse-Darmstadt, and in the new
provinces of Bavaria by 1821. In Prussia, however, the king, not
content to settle for administrative unity, insisted upon a unified
statement of belief. The noted theologian Friedrich Schleiermacher protested that the change would secularize Protestantism, and there was considerable opposition from the six
thousand Protestant clergymen of Prussia; but those who complained wanted to protect traditional religious rights, not to
attain political rights for the citizens of the state.

With rare exceptions, Catholic priests and Protestant ministers
treated those who demanded political democracy before the
1840's as though they bore the scriptural Mark of the Beast.
Political radicals responded with equal zeal, denouncing the
churches and religion generally as foes of human progress.
"The world would be happier if it had never heard of God,"
proclaimed Karl Gutzkow, a well-known radical litterateur, in
1835.[4]

As Gutzkow's outburst suggests, forces were developing to
foster irreverence for traditional authority, even in the age of
reaction. The degree of irreverence varied among those who
called for political change, and they lacked clear-cut programs,
well-defined political organizations, and standard terminology
to describe themselves. Most of the prominent reformers before
1848 thought of themselves somewhat vaguely as "liberals," if
they thought of a label at all. The established authorities, on the
other hand, often categorized all reformers as "democrats" in an
attempt to conjure up visions of mob rule and to stir responsible
opinion against them. The resulting semantic problems have
continued to trouble historians. The imprecision and lack of
standardization of the historical vocabularly have reflected the
real linguistic conditions of the reform movement before 1848.
In a history of the struggle for democracy in Germany, however,
it is important to identify as clearly as possible those reformers
who, in fact, can legitimately be described as "democrats," and
to indicate the criteria by which they are judged to have been
"democrats" rather than simply "liberals."

What gave liberalism as such its special identity before 1848
was its call for freedom—freedom for the German nation
through unification and freedom for the individual in political,

religious, and economic affairs. In this volume, therefore, the term "liberal" is used to describe men who demanded these freedoms but who did not favor the full political equality that genuine democracy implies. They believed with Wilhelm von Humboldt that "only harmful consequences" could flow from the "chimerical ideas of equality"; that democracy would breed demagoguery and be incompatible with freedom. The one measure of equality demanded by such liberals was designed to achieve freedom: they insisted that all men should be treated as equals by the police and the law courts of Germany. For most Germans who considered themselves liberals in the period 1815 –48, egalitarianism stopped with legal equality. They opposed equal voting rights, and they abhorred the idea of social equality. Many justified their claim to liberty as a product of historical development within the state; for others, it was an abstractly rationalized "natural right" of mankind to be won and defended against historically inherited governments.

Those liberals who were also genuinely democratic are denoted in this volume as "liberal democrats." They tended to draw more inspiration from natural law concepts and from the cosmopolitan rationalism of the Enlightenment than did other liberals. They favored all the classical liberal freedoms, but were not content to stop with them. They stood for a large measure of political equality as well as for legal equality. Beyond this, the democrats themselves in time divided. By the 1840's, some would favor various forms of social and economic equality as well as political equality, but these "social democrats" would remain poorly organized and small in numbers until late in the century. Until then, the movement for democracy in Germany would be led by liberal democrats. A minority of these believed that democratic aims could be realized only in a republic. Others were content to seek reforms within a monarchical framework of government, as were virtually all liberals who were not democrats.

The major differences and similarities between the liberals and the democrats slowly began to harden in discussion of specific political issues during the three decades after 1815. Several differences pivoted around one central practical question: How representative should government be? Genuine democrats insisted upon the creation of parliaments that would set and control state policies. Most liberals, as loyal supporters of monarchical government, were content to have the parliaments merely influence policy. Democrats demanded that the parliaments represent all the people equally. Thus they favored elections based on *universal* and *equal* suffrage for adult males, and they increasingly insisted that the suffrage should be *direct* and *secret* as well. All four characteristics were indispensable if the suffrage was to be made fully democratic. Those who are identified in this volume as liberals, on the other hand, favored a more restrictive suffrage, one that would enable the middle class to gain political power, but without allowing it to slip into the hands of the masses.

What separated liberals and liberal democrats in the Metternich era was of fundamental importance, but there were issues on which they agreed. The desire for a united German nation was shared by many liberals and democrats. Both sought relief from the repressive measures of the existing German governments. Both favored government in accordance with a written constitution. Both desired government by representatives of the people, organized in parliaments, although they disagreed over who should vote, how they should vote, and how much power the parliaments should have. Both strove for the abolition of secret judicial proceedings and for trial by jury to secure equality under the law. And both insisted upon much greater individual liberty, freedom of the press, and right of assembly than Germans enjoyed before 1848. Thus liberalism served in these years to clear the way for the rise of democracy, though most of the leading liberals did not intend it to do so.[5]

By 1820 the efforts of both liberals and liberal democrats were beginning to be facilitated by nascent parliamentary bodies in several German states. In attempting to mobilize popular backing for the War of Liberation, several princes in 1814–15 had promised to grant their states more or less aristocratic constitutions and parliaments in which the "better" elements of society would find representation. Article XIII of the 1815 statutes of the German Confederation had promised that constitutions could "exist in all German states." Metternich had hoped to frustrate its implementation, but before he could organize princely opposition to further reform, several German rulers had granted their states constitutions (or, in the Austrian minister's own words, "committed the unpardonable error of giving their States institutions copied from those of France"). Thirteen states of the German Confederation, most of them small, adopted constitutions by 1820. Prussia, sprawling across all of northern Germany, notably did not. Bavaria, Baden, and Wurttemberg, all southern states, became the most important proponents of government by blueprint.[6]

Most German state constitutions of 1814–20 were patterned fairly closely after the French Constitutional Charter of 1814. The lower houses of the parliaments created in the era of restoration (except Baden's) were made up of delegates elected separately by the traditional corporate status groups (*Stände*)—the churches, the universities, the nobles, the towns, and the landowning peasantry. They represented only parts of the population. Baden—greatly enlarged during the Napoleonic era and the state most in need of integration to survive—was the only one in Germany to bring the people as a whole into the electoral process, and its parliament (Landtag) in Karlsruhe became a kind of "mother of parliaments" for the Germans. Here as elsewhere, the proclamation of constitutions left many traditional institutions unchanged, and from their first meetings the men who sat in the new parliaments raised demands for additional concessions. In many speeches and letters, Metternich would warn against the "party" of reform in the several German parliaments, exaggeratedly asserting that it was "inimical to every kind of authority."[7]

If the reform agitation of parliamentarians worried Metternich, the existing limitations on parliamentary activity were galling to many representatives in the early legislatures. In each Landtag the upper house was a stronghold of aristocratic privilege, and the deliberations of the lower houses were only partly public. Word-for-word publication of speeches was forbidden, and reports of Landtag actions commonly were censored. The parliamentary agenda normally was determined by the ruler and his minsters. Cabinet ministers were responsible to the ruler, not to the representatives of the people. Most important, the essential right of real parliaments, the power to control finances, was restricted. Still, in southwestern Germany, the creation of state parliaments by 1820 had laid the basis for a slow evolution toward more fully representative government and majority rule.[8]

In the years that followed, other forces fostered political reform. Developments in philosophy, science and education; the rise of popular journalism; the coming of the Industrial Revolution; and the examples of liberalism and democracy in other countries—all were important if slow subverters of the status quo in German politics.

The case for the importance of ideas in history can be put concisely and simply: "action follows from belief"; or, in the newer language of psychiatry, "it is on the perception of individual human beings that everything depends."[9] The beliefs of educated Germans for many years after 1815, and the ways they perceived, were determined by Kant and Hegel as well as by the traditional church teachings. Their emphasis on Reason became a weapon against the status quo.

Liberal and even democratic aspirations had been stimulated by the writings of Immanuel Kant (1724–1804), notwithstanding the contradictions in his message. Kant talked of a "republican constitution," but actually had in mind a limited monarchy. Influenced by Rousseau, he preached contract theory and the ideal primacy of "the general will" in politics; but he rejected the democratic practice of popular sovereignty. While he viewed the French Revolution as a moral act, he was reluctant to condone revolution as a means of achieving reform. Yet he undoubtedly gave intellectual force to the liberal movement. Kant explicitly opposed hereditary aristocracy; wrote that every man should develop himself through his own efforts and Reason; insisted upon the right of all citizens to criticize all existing laws and to propose new ones; and declared that unrepresentative government was "an irrational thing" (*eine Unform*). Kant demanded that monarchs govern according to the interests of their subjects: "What a people may not decree for itself can even less be decreed . . . by a monarch."

G. W. F. Hegel (1770–1831) generously borrowed from Kant in further developing his own philosophy of Idealism. Hegel was the most influential philosopher in Germany in the first half of the nineteenth century. The elements of liberalism in his thought have been obscured by his glorification of the Prussian state and by the tendency of some of his followers to subordinate their longing for freedom to the goal of national unity. But in three important ways he gave strength to the political reform forces. First, by elevating historical change into a metaphysical dogma he encouraged contemporaries to believe in the impermanence of their present, and this faith nurtured political reformers. Second, by emphasizing the need for political consciousness among thinking people in any state worthy of the name, he prodded German academicians into their most vigorous period of political concern in the country's history. Third, in describing constitutional monarchy as "the typical achievement of the modern world" he justified a reform demanded by contemporary German liberals.

Hegel glorified the state, but only an ideal one. The state of his *Philosophy of Right* was "absolutely rational," one in which freedom "attains its highest right." A strong glimmer of liberalism shines through the turgid Hegelian philosophical formula, often quoted in the nineteenth century: "the idea of the will is in general the free will which wills the free will." And the push Hegel gave to liberalism was even more apparent in his forthright statement that "world history is nothing else but the development of the concept of freedom."

Reason, celebrated by Kant and Hegel, would have called forth a number of German liberals even if French muskets had never crossed the Rhine after 1789. The revolutionary poet Georg Herwegh defined liberalism as "rational knowledge applied to our existing conditions," and declared that "freedom and reason are the same." The liberal Heinrich von Gagern could tell the parliament of Hesse-Darmstadt in 1833 that "every rational being strives for freedom," as if he were only stating the obvious. The Hegelian political radical, Arnold Ruge, declared that humanity could reform itself by applying abstract rules of reason to the exigencies of everyday life.[10]

Everyday life could be improved not only by applying Reason, some German scientists were saying, but by applying what could be learned through empirical investigations. The very need for freedom of inquiry predisposed scientists and their admirers against both religious and political curbs on the human mind, and the experimental approach that was winning out in the natural sciences suggested the possibilities of bettering society through political and economic experimentation.

By about 1830 progress in medicine was showing that men could improve their lot on earth by turning empirical science against the threats to human health. It is hardly surprising, therefore, that a good many German doctors were active as political reformers and even as revolutionaries. In 1833 a young physician, Gustav Bunsen, was one of the three leaders of an abortive revolt in Frankfurt. A more scholarly physician, Johann Lukas Schönlein, made Würzburg a noted medical center through his pioneering laboratory experiments and clinical demonstrations, only to fall into disfavor with the Bavarian authorities because of his liberal political views. Schönlein sought refuge at Zürich in 1833, but he was called to the University of Berlin in 1840. One of his Würzburg medical students, Friedrich Adolph Wislizenus, had participated in the Frankfurt revolt in 1833, and when it failed, followed him to Zürich.

Another of Schönlein's students at Berlin, Rudolf Virchow, was later to win fame as a pioneer in cellular pathology. Twenty-seven-year-old Virchow wrote in 1848 to his father: "As a natural scientist I can be but a republican." His democratic view of the future political order was in harmony with his knowledge of cells: "No longer shall the king have his will; no longer shall there be privileged classes. . . . .Everybody shall have the same rights. This is corresponding to nature." Carl D'Ester was yet another physician who self-consciously linked his discipline to his political radicalism. Born in 1813, he practiced among the poor in the 1840's and became a social democrat and an individualist. As a member of Prussia's revolutionary Constituent Assembly in 1848, his approach to the *Staatsorganismus* would reflect his scientific training. He told his fellow delegates on August 10, 1848: "I know from my medical experience that one must remove the cause of sickness if one wants to achieve a good recovery."[11]

The tendency of science to promote desires for political change in Germany before 1848 is further suggested by the experience of the Büchner family of Hesse. Ernst Karl Büchner was for a time a regimental surgeon in Napoleon's armies before settling down as a medical official in the Grand Duchy of Hesse. His first son, Georg, was born on October 17, 1813. Georg Büchner is most often remembered as the precocious author of plays that foreshadowed the expressionist drama of the twentieth century, *Danton's Death* (1835) and *Woyzeck* (1837); but by the time these were published he had flared like a young comet amidst the conservative gloom of the Metternich era.

Young Büchner studied medicine at Strasbourg from 1831 to 1833, then continued his medical studies in the small Hessian university town of Giessen, where Karl Follen had put a democratic stamp on the Burschenschaft fifteen years earlier. There, already a dedicated democrat and republican, he became increasingly impatient with the status quo. At the beginning of 1834 he joined other radical students and a few artisans to form and lead a conspiratorial "Society for the Rights of Man" (Gesellschaft der Menschenrechte). Büchner had become one of Germany's early socialists, castigating the relationship between rich and poor as "the only revolutionary element in the world." Blending scientific materialism with idealism before Karl Marx, he took an unusually tough view, for reformers of his generation, of what was needed to shape the future. "If in our time anything will help, it is power," he concluded, and he turned to the lower classes to try to mobilize power that could break the status quo.

In July 1834, Büchner wrote a radical appeal to the peasants of Hesse. It was set into type by an Offenbach printer, and members of the Gesellschaft der Menschenrechte stuck it into the doors and windows of peasant cottages at night. In this leaflet Büchner resurrected the subversive propaganda slogan that Cambon had given the revolutionary armies of France in 1792: "War against the palaces! Peace with the cottages!" He did not speak in abstract terms, but in language the peasants could understand, calling them to class struggle: "The life of the rich is one long Sunday, . . . The life of the peasant is one long workday, . . . his sweat is the salt on the rich man's dinner table." Although the peasants did not rise, the leaflet moved the authorities into action. With friends already under arrest, Büchner fled Giessen. In 1835 he engaged in scientific research in Strasbourg. The next year, aided by a liberal-nationalist physician who had left Germany in 1832, Lorenz Oken, Büchner was awarded a doctorate and appointed to the faculty of the University of Zürich to teach comparative anatomy. Here he was befriended by Johann Lukas Schönlein. But before he was long in Zürich he was struck down by typhus in 1837—not quite twenty-four years of age.

Georg Büchner's brother Ludwig, eleven years younger, earned his medical degree in 1848, just before the outbreak of the revolution. After postdoctoral study with Virchow in 1850, he became a professor at Tübingen, only to be dismissed after publishing in 1855 a controversial book of materialistic philosophy (*Kraft und Stoff*). Resuming private medical practice in Darmstadt, Ludwig Büchner won leadership among local workers as a pronounced advocate of liberal democracy. For six years he served in the Hessian state parliament. Luise, the sister of Georg and Ludwig, became a novelist and a passionate early protagonist for Germany's new mid-century feminists. One of her several books, *Die Frauen und ihr Beruf*, was in its fifth edition by 1884, a few years after her death. Her brother Alexander (born in 1827) also won recognition as a novelist and as a literary historian after becoming by twenty, in his own words, a "horrendous democrat." He wrote for a republican newspaper in the Revolution of 1848. Another brother, Wilhelm (born in 1816), studied briefly at Giessen with Justus von Liebig, founder of organic chemistry. As the creator and owner of one of Gerany's early chemical factories, in 1840 Wilhelm Büchner was elected to the state parliament of Hesse as a democrat and served five consecutive terms. After the unification of Germany, his fellow citizens at Darmstadt sent him to the Reichstag (national parliament), where he sat with the Progressives of Eugen Richter, Bismarck's tenacious opponent.[12]

The Büchners of the nineteenth century do not loom large in German history. Indeed, many histories of the century fail to mention even Georg Büchner, the most spectacular of the brothers. But their story hints at the corrosive if very slow growth of democratic impulses beneath the hard crust of conservatism, a growth in which before 1848 science played a significant part.

Scientists were joined by other products of the German system of education in the liberal and democratic agitation of the Metternich era. The early nineteenth century was a period of rapid expansion of educational opportunities for the people of Germany. Elementary schools grew rapidly in numbers; by 1840 there were about thirty thousand in Prussia. Attendance reached 93 percent in the Prussian province of Saxony. Though illiteracy was not eliminated, the great majority of Prussians could read and write by the 1840's. Elementary school education was far from democratic, but the pedagogical ideas of the Swiss educator Johann Heinrich Pestalozzi encouraged many teachers to develop the individualism of their pupils, and acquisition of literacy enabled many humble Germans to continue to read on their own after leaving school. Some of them thus acquired political and social ideals that school authorities had no desire to encourage.

A small percentage of the pupils were able to continue their education in the Gymnasia, ten-year schools that placed heavy emphasis upon Greek and classical studies. It was unusual for children of the poor to enter one of these high schools, and the education they received was less likely to encourage independent political thought than Wilhelm von Humboldt had hoped it might. Graduates of the Gymnasia with lasting liberal political convictions were a minority of all those who attended, but they caused the conservative state authorities much concern after 1815. Some complained that the study of Greek and Latin was making republicans out of German youths. In actuality, classical studies in the universities as well as in the Gymnasia served as too good an entrée to positions in state service to turn many students toward political radicalism. The scarcity of positions in relation to the increasing numbers of graduates stimulated some discontent, but it probably did much more to encourage conformist behavior.[13]

Nevertheless, in a few universities the Burschenschaften continued to work secretly, winning a few hundred members among the thirteen to sixteen thousand students enrolled (1830–33). And the Carlsbad Decrees only partly purged the faculties of liberals. Throughout the period 1815–48 a few dozen "political professors" played a significant part in the civic education of their fellow Germans.

One of the most influential academic liberal democrats was Karl von Rotteck. Son of the head of the medical faculty at Freiburg im Breisgau, Rotteck taught history there from 1798 until 1818, and then jurisprudence. He learned French from his mother, a native of Alsace-Lorraine, and throughout his life Rousseau and Rousseau's best-known German interpreter, Kant, remained his favorite authors. In the upper house of the Baden parliament from 1819 until 1824 he called repeatedly for reforms to make inherited institutions conform to natural law, and in his nine-volume history of the world—a "best-seller" while being published, 1812–26—he saw the past through the eyes of a liberal democrat. For Rotteck's readers the French Revolution became an inspiring historical fact, and America emerged as the hope of the world. Even dismissal from his academic post did not diminish Rotteck's political impact. Forced out of his professorship in 1832, he continued until 1840 to hold a seat in the lower house of the Baden parliament, to which he had been elected in 1831.

With his liberal Freiburg colleague, Karl Theodor Welcker, Rotteck began in 1834 to bring out an immediately famous encyclopedia of political science that was completed in fifteen volumes in 1843. He frankly announced in its first volume that his purpose was to provide "a political confession of faith . . . around which all dispassionate, moderate, sensible liberals might rally." Rotteck and Welcker themselves wrote 270 of the 870 articles, and they found willing academic contributors in several other German states, north and south. Rotteck died in 1840, but the *Staats-Lexikon* was so successful that his collaborator brought out a second edition between 1845 and 1848.

Soon after the first edition of the *Staats-Lexikon* began appearing, seven other distinguished scholars took a different stand for the moderate liberalism in which they believed, protesting in 1837 against the unconstitutional actions of a new ruler in Hanover. The "Göttingen Seven" were dismissed by the king with the contemptuous remark that "professors, whores, and ballet dancers can be had anywhere for money," to which Friedrich Christoph Dahlmann, one of the seven, gave an enduring reply: "As a man of honor I would rather give up teaching altogether than sell to my audience as truth that which is a lie and deceit." Six of the dismissed professors, including the brothers Jacob and Wilhelm Grimm—compilers of the well-known fairy tales—soon found other posts; and the widely publicized incident did more for the cause of liberalism than it did for autocracy.[14]

For this the academic liberals could thank the political journalism of 1815–48. While the schools were rapidly increasing the population of reading citizens, the journals and newspapers of Germany slowly expanded in number and circulation, giving currency to liberal, liberal-democratic, and nationalistic principles.

A political press had scarcely existed in Germany before 1813, but the War of Liberation had produced an outburst of protests against Napoleonic France in the newspapers of the day. Several of the journalists who then helped to inflame the spirit of nationalism called also for representative government. The most noted of these was a Rhineland Catholic, Joseph Görres, born in the year of the American Declaration of Independence. For more than a year after his *Rheinische Merkur* was founded in 1814, the Prussian government welcomed its demands that all the territory of the Rhine be made German—and profited from the propaganda by annexing much of it in 1814–15. But when the author continued to call for individual freedom and representative government within the Prussian state after 1815, he encountered the wrath of the authorities.

Görres hoped to realize liberal principles through evolutionary and monarchical means. Indeed, in his pamphlet on "Germany and the Revolution" (1819), he prophetically warned that a German republic would breed a conquering military despot like Napoleon ("another and more fortunate Wallenstein") who would "overthrow, even to the confines of Asia, the fragile system of the European state edifice." To prevent such a cataclysm, Görres proposed that the ruling princes sponsor reforms from above, accomplishing a marriage between "the monarchical and democratic principle." Elective provincial assemblies should be set up to assist in the framing of laws, and general assemblies should be created "to co-operate with the ministry in the regulation of the concerns of the whole nation."

After twelve thousand copies of Görres's pamphlet had been distributed, the Prussian government retaliated. The proposal of restricted suffrage and parliamentary bodies that would influence but not control government policies made it clear that the writer was a liberal rather than a democrat, notwithstanding his talk of "democracy," but even his state-conserving demands were considered dangerous by the Prussian authorities. He was forced to flee the country to escape arrest, and the same fate befell several other political journalists. "The greatest and consequently the most urgent evil now is the press," Metternich wrote in 1819. But because the censorship established by the Carlsbad Decrees of that year was not fully enforced in the German states, liberal journalists made many subsequent contributions to the movement for reform.

One of these was Baron Johann Friedrich von Cotta, owner of the distinguished press that had published the works of Schiller, Goethe, and other leading writers. Cotta had lobbied for freedom of the press at the Congress of Vienna and later in the Diet at Frankfurt. His newspaper, the Augsburg *Allgemeine Zeitung*— widely read by liberals—took a critical position on issues of the day, as did he himself and his son in the Württemberg state parliament.

By 1832 more radical journalists were openly demanding that Germany be transformed into a democratic republic. One of these was Bavaria-born Johann Georg August Wirth, who published his *Deutsche Tribüne* at Homburg in the Bavarian Palatinate. After Wirth demanded the unification of Germany as a constitutional monarchy under Prussian leadership in mid-1831, censorship and confiscation frequently interrupted the regular appearance of the *Deutsche Tribüne*. In retaliation the publisher became increasingly outspoken. In the issue of January 30, 1832, he denounced moderation, asserting that it would not achieve "desired goals." This issue even sounded a call for revolution: "When an oppressed people has no lawful and impartial agency to regain those inalienable rights which have been violated and withheld, then it has the authority, yes, even the duty to help itself in justifiable self defense."

On the day before this issue was published, Wirth, speaking at a political banquet in Zweibrücken, proposed the creation of a German-wide society for the promotion, financial support, and defense of a free press. The result was the Deutsche Press-

und Vaterlandsverein, which within six weeks won financial contributions from more than eighteen hundred persons in various parts of Germany. A catalogue of each area from which more than a dozen supporters sent contributions provides a crude index of the distribution of democratic and nationalist sentiment in Germany early in 1832: Palatinate, 684 contributors; other parts of Bavaria, 73; Frankfurt am Main, 411; Baden, 242; Hesse-Darmstadt, 157; Saxe-Coburg-Saalfeld, 53. From the outset, the German Press and Fatherland Association meant to be more than a press organization; it sought to give general direction to the movement for a democratic republic. It may be regarded, therefore, as a primitive prototype of the organized political parties that came later in Germany. In its first public program this organization described a "free press" as the only means for the spiritual "reunification of Germany." The Bavarian authorities ordered its dissolution after only two months of existence, but it continued for some time to function surreptitiously.

If the press was never completely free in this period, it was seldom completely prevented from publishing critical political comment. When Baden in 1831 permitted full freedom of the press, other states of the German Confederation forced a retraction; but in the same year the Bavarian king was pressed by his parliament into dismissing a minister of the interior who had tried to impose total political censorship. Meanwhile, scores of journalists went on telling the people of Germany that those who tried to extinguish the fires of liberty would themselves go up in flames. Then in 1832 the more strident newspapers were banned, a restriction that lasted a decade.

Those newspapers that continued to appear at all remained small, but technology facilitated publishing in these years. Shortly after 1820, presses driven by steam engines were introduced in Leipzig, Augsburg, Stuttgart, and a few other towns. By 1847 the liberal *Kölnische Zeitung* was being published in editions of 9,500 copies, the *Allgemeine Zeitung* of Augsburg in 10,400, and Berlin's *Vossische Zeitung* in 20,000. As printing by movable type had abetted Luther's revolt in 1517, the steam-driven press did the same for the liberal movement in the 1830's and 1840's. Even under restrictions, liberal journalists helped to prepare middle-class Germans to demand political reform.[15]

Meanwhile, technology was at work in other ways. By the 1840's steamboating on the rivers of Germany and the beginnings of a railroad network had promoted the circulation of newspapers and expanded personal as well as business contacts among Germans. The first short railroad line was constructed between Nuremberg and Fürth in 1835. Progress was slow, only four thousand miles of railway being completed by 1850; but a line from Switzerland through Heidelberg to Frankfurt was opened in 1847, and this occasionally brought in democratic propaganda. Better postal service came with the railroads, facilitating communication and early attempts to coordinate activity among German reformers. But the more nebulous effects of the early trains—their impact on the minds of contemporaries—were probably of more importance to political reform than was any immediate tangible result. The very sight of the "fiery dragons," spewing sparks and smoke and noisily pulling a long line of carriages, was shocking to the senses of Germans in the 1830's. The vivid symbol of technological progress seemed to some Hegelian intellectuals to give proof to their philosophical assumptions about the inevitability of change; and it made even those who had little or no knowledge of Hegel aware that they lived in an era of flux. The effusive comment of the time on the early trains reflected an awareness that technological innovation would bring with it fundamental changes in values, social relations, and political life.

As the civil servants and merchants of the German states began to sense the potentialities of steamboats and railroads for the growth of trade, a powerful incentive was added to efforts already underway, through tariff agreements, to create larger free trade areas. In this movement Prussia was as progressive as she was backward in her domestic politics. Beginning in 1819, Prussia had worked out customs agreements with several small states in the north. Between 1828 and 1834 a German Customs Union (Deutscher Zollverein) came into existence under Prussian leadership. By promoting trade, the Customs Union stimulated industry. It also multiplied contacts among middle-class Germans of the various states and fostered the hope among some nationalists that Prussia might lead Germany to political unity.[16]

Meanwhile, the early growth of mechanized industry was

underway. As early as the 1780's a few steam engines had been constructed in Prussia, and in the 1820's Friedrich Harkort, a political liberal, began to supply engines to drive machinery in textile, sugar, paper, and other factories. But mechanization in Germany developed at a snail's pace before 1848, lagging behind that of the other countries of western Europe. In the 1840's Belgium alone produced more iron than all the German states combined. In 1848 only about 4 percent of all the cotton looms in Prussia were driven by power. Most factories were small. By 1848, Saxony had a few plants that employed hundreds of workers each, but they were exceptions. Krupp of Essen in 1848 employed only 140 workers; the Borsig steam engine factory in Berlin, new and exceptionally big, gave work to 1,200. The 516 factories in Baden employed an average of 32 workers each. The German industrial working class—a "proletariat"—emerged only slowly. Baden had 16,600 factory workers in a population of 1,300,000 in 1848; Bavaria, 155,000 in a population of 4,500,000. Only about 4 percent of the people of Germany as a whole worked in factories in 1848, and it was a rare worker who was attracted to socialism, though many already hated capitalism.

The slow development of trade and industry first contributed to the rise of the reform movement by gradually creating a new group of middle-class entrepreneurs with their own economic, social, and political grievances. Many of this group felt that the German states inadequately supported economic progress.

The German governments aided the economy by building roads and canals, sponsoring the introduction of new technology, and developing the Zollverein, but their fiscal and credit policies did not adequately serve the needs of ambitious private industry and trade. For example, the owners of large landed estates and influential bureaucrats—predominantly from agrarian backgrounds—for several years discouraged the use of state funds to promote construction of railroads in Prussia by private enterprise, and they generally sought to inhibit the transfer of capital from agricultural and governmental investments to industrial development. The Zollverein brought with it no uniform currency, and the state governments only hesitantly approved and then closely restricted the circulation of the paper money needed for an expanding commerce. The states were slow to set up state banks, refused requests for subsidies to infant industries, and were extremely cautious in the regulation of credit; thus, many German merchants and manufacturers found it necessary to create their own banks to help finance expanding operations. State policy in Prussia and other German principalities also angered enterprising merchants and manufacturers by requiring unnecessarily large amounts of capital for the formation of corporations. All of these economic policies caused a number of German merchants and industrialists to add their voices to demands for political reform. What many of them wanted was not a policy of laissez-faire but government support.[17]

Meanwhile, emerging capitalists and many other middle-class Germans reacted to the constant irritant of persisting social and political privileges for the nobility. In a report to the Prussian Ministry of the Interior in February 1844, the royal governor of the Rhine Province would caution that the well-to-do led political opposition in the province. Middle-class spokesmen knew they had reason to be discontented when they noted that the one hundred thousand inhabitants of Cologne and Aachen sent three delegates to the Provincial Landtag (diet), while only seven thousand nobles sent twenty-five. They were prompted to political action by the knowledge that conditions like these were changing in favor of the middle classes in countries to the west.[18]

For any generation of mankind, political aspiration is only one part of its complex spiritual and material experience. The desire for representative government in Germany just after 1815, though felt by only a small minority, was rooted in the totality of German life. Ideas, technology, and economic needs converged to transform this desire into an indigenous and vital force, though one that was vigilantly repressed. While it transcended class lines, it was fundamentally a movement of the broad middle class, in which the "bourgeoisie" of the Marxists—capitalists as a class—formed only a small part, both in numbers and in monetary promotion. State and local officials, professors, lawyers, journalists, artisans, and small merchants formed more of the movement than did large merchants, industrialists, and bankers. Data available on contributors to the Deutsche Press- und Vaterlandsverein in 1832 sharpen the meaning of this generalization. Of 749 contributors who indicated their occupations, 477 were artisans or merchants; 104 students; 63 lawyers, civil servants, or officials; 34 publishers, journalists, or writers; 17 estate owners; 17 laborers; 16 physicians or pharmacists; 8 teachers; 7 peasants; and 6 pastors or priests. While it did not lack economic motivation, the movement for reform before 1848 could not have been created or sustained without the moral and intellectual convictions that more vitally motivated it.[19]

By the 1830's the new parliaments in several states, Reason, science, education, the press, improved transportation, growing trade, and the beginnings of mechanized industry were moving a minority of Germans to demand political modernization. Change was in the air, no matter how strongly tradition might resist it, no matter how much conservatives might deplore it. As one diarist noted in 1842, "Each day life becomes more turbulent, more noisy, more broken up; the Customs Union and the railroad but also the newer ways of thought in general contribute to that. . . . My feelings toward the world have become entirely different in only 10 years."[20]

The new developments gave liberals and democrats what was most needed by a minority that worked for change in the midst of repressive efforts to preserve the status quo: an unswerving confidence that it represented *Zivilisation*, progress, the forces of "movement"—in short, the swelling and irreversible tide of history that sooner or later would sweep its opponents away. The faith of Germany's few liberals and democrats that the future was on their side was being confirmed, meanwhile, by developments west of the Rhine. These became particularly persuasive in the period 1830–48.

III.

FOREIGN MODELS AND DOMESTIC AGITATION, 1830—1847

The hatred felt in 1813 for Napoleon's France never completely disappeared in the third of a century that followed, but neither did the admiration of German reformers for the principles of the French Revolution. France, Cotta's *Allgemeine Zeitung* commented in May 1832, "has become the focus of constitutional life in Europe, notwithstanding all mistakes and shortcomings."[1] Britain and the United States also inspired German liberals and democrats. Thus, while conditions within Germany were giving rise to indigenous demands for political change, foreign examples encouraged and helped shape agitation for liberalism and democracy throughout the Metternich era. Propaganda from German political refugees abroad served the same function. The status quo, shaken in 1830, would be vulnerable to general revolution in 1848.

The restoration of 1814–15 in France, like the Metternich system in Germany, aroused widespread criticism, and in July 1830, Paris unseated the last Bourbon king. The July Revolution in France stimulated the most abrupt political changes that the German states experienced between 1819 and 1848.

In Braunschwieg friction had been increasing between Duke Karl II and his subjects for several years. The news from Paris turned discontent into rebellion. On September 7, 1830, a crowd surged into the ducal palace and set it afire. Duke Karl fled—the first modern German ruler to be overthrown by his own people. Moderate nobles and middle-class leaders got Karl's brother named head of the state, but they circumscribed his powers with a constitution and a single-chamber parliament. In Hesse-Cassel, too, rioting made it possible for liberals to bring in constitutional government. In Saxony riots broke out in September 1830 in Leipzig and Dresden, spreading to Chemnitz and Freiberg. A new element was introduced in the Saxon disturbances: while leaders of the liberal opposition were content to demand representative government, workers briefly directed their protests against factory owners. New outbreaks in Dresden in April of the following year forced promulgation of a constitution that created a two-house parliament. In Hanover, unrest after the July Revolution in France was followed by outright rebellion in January 1831, in which university students played a major role. After the student revolt in Göttingen was crushed by the army, Hanover's liberals continued to demand more representative government, and in 1833 the king agreed to a new constitution. The new parliament preserved the power of the upper classes, but it also gave greater representation to the peasants and townsmen.[2]

In 1831–32, meanwhile, the French Revolution of 1830 had radical effects in other parts of Germany. The radical student clubs, the Burschenschaften, reappeared. Growing rapidly in size, they were emboldened as never before. "The path of revolution is the only one that should be pursued for the present," Burschenschaft leaders resolved at a Stuttgart meeting in 1832. That year marked the first national demonstration for a unified democratic republic in Germany, the so-called "Hambach Festival" of May 27–30, 1832.

The holding of banquets and festivals was the answer of the age to the prohibition of political parties. Festivals of a liberal or radical character were held in various parts of Germany in 1832, but the one at Hambach attracted the greatest attention. Staged near the southwest German town of Speyer, the fest was organized by the short-lived Deutsche Press-und Vaterlandsverein. Plans to hold it were publicized by the press well in advance of May 27. Then, amidst the black-red-gold banners of the Burschenschaften, which became the symbol of a democratically united Germany, some twenty thousand persons assembled at Hambach. Meeting ostensibly to celebrate the granting of Bavaria's constitution more than a decade before, instead a variety of orators advocated the overthrow of princes and the creation of the "United Free States of Germany" as a first step toward a "Confederated Republic of Europe." The participants—

democrats and nationalists—came not only from the surrounding Palatinate countryside, but from other parts of Bavaria, Alsace, Baden, Württemberg, Hesse-Darmstadt, Nassau, Frankfurt, the Rhine province of Prussia, Electoral Hesse, Hanover, and Saxony. Most were small farmers and students, but journalists, lawyers, doctors, and even one or two state legislators and pastors were among them; many would later be leaders in the German Revolution of 1848.

Even before the participants assembled, the *Allgemeine Zeitung* predicted that the Hambach Festival "coperhaps receive in the future a place in history." The great demonstration conceivably might have sparked a general revolt throughout Germany in 1832 except for the countermeasures taken by the state governments. To Metternich the "scandalous scenes" did not as yet constitute a revolution, but he regarded them as "its immediate precursors"; clearly alarmed, he urged new repressive measures upon the states of Germany. When the Bavarian authorities recovered their wits and their nerve, they arrested Wirth and other Hambach republicans or sent them scurrying into exile in France or Switzerland. A special commissioner was appointed for the Palatinate on June 22, with half the Bavarian army at his disposal. Leaders who were caught were brought to trial in 1833 (in the first German court proceedings to be recorded stenographically).[3]

The German repercussions of the French Revolution of 1830 stand as evidence of a rising assertiveness among liberals and democrats, but they brought about no significant social changes. Social ranks were reflected as before in the prescribed forms of address one inhabitant was expected to use in speaking to another. For example, the official *Adressbuch* for Rhineland-Westphalia in 1833 prescribed that state officials of high rank were to be titled *Exzellenz*; that all noblemen were to be addressed as *Hochwohlgeborener* (literally, "High Well Born"), a salutation also to be accorded commoners who were state officials or army officers; that any person of some status but not enough to be called *Hochwohlgeborener* was to be addressed as *Wohlgeborener*—a title, for example, for nonnobles who were mayors, judges, professors, merchants, owners of estates, or artists. Lesser commoners had to be content with *Geehrter Herr*

("Honored Sir") or simply *Herr* ("Sir"). Social inequalities were reinforced daily by usage of these and many other titles. As irritants they helped to make some persons politically radical.[4]

Most decisive about the revolutionary activity of 1830–32 is that neither of the German great powers was much affected by it, except to become more reactionary. Still unhampered by constitutions, the governments of Prussia and Austria were able to use their influence to stifle the insurgent political forces in other German states.

Since the July Revolution of 1830 in France, the governments of Austria and Prussia had been trying to win the support of other states in the German Confederation for more restrictive legislation. After the Hambach Festival, the "Six Acts" proposed by the two governments were unanimously adopted by the Frankfurt Diet on June 28, 1832. These obligated the princes of all the separate states to uphold the monarchical principle more firmly vis á vis the state parliaments, whose powers and whose freedom of debate were to be restricted; provided for creation of a supervisory commission to report on infringements upon the law of the Confederation that might occur within any federal state; and called for new restrictions of the press.

The Six Acts and the other repressive measures adopted from 1832 to 1834 were not uniformly implemented in the various states of Germany; but in the general reaction that followed the Hambach Festival, many newspapers were suppressed and censorship was tightened over those that were allowed to continue publication. Political associations, political meetings, and political speeches were all prohibited by the laws of the Confederation. The Burschenschaften were almost completely suppressed at last; death penalties and many years of imprisonment were handed out by the courts against persons found guilty of mere membership in them. Troops were used when necessary: the plot by Gustav Bunsen and some fifty other young radicals to touch off a general democratic revolution in April 1833 by seizing the police guardhouses and then the Diet of the German Confederation in Frankfurt ended with thirty-one rebels, soldiers, and police dead or wounded.

By 1834 authority had been fully restored in all of the German states, but nobles were still discussing with alarm "the daily attacks of the democratic movement." Close surveillance by a central investigating office of the German Confederation helped repress radicalism from 1833 to 1842. But by compiling two lists of 2,140 persons who were politically suspect, this office also recorded its inability to eliminate democratic and nationalistic aspirations in the Metternich era.[5]

Men who were forced to take flight in the 1830's helped significantly to prepare Germany for revolution. France offered many of them both a place of safety and more direct contact with her revolutionary tradition. The "July Monarchy" hardly exemplified democratic principles in action, but the memory of 1789 was alive in Paris, and French political and social theorists—especially Saint-Simon and other Utopian Socialists—exercised a radicalizing influence upon a number of German intellectuals. Furthermore, even the France of Louis Philippe permitted greater freedom of the press than did the German states; Paris thus became a base from which refugees could send trickles of revolutionary propaganda into Germany.

The political émigrés increased the ranks of some thirty thousand or more Germans in Paris in the decade after 1830; some estimates run as high as eighty-five to one hundred thousand. At least half were journeyman artisans who were in France as part of the custom of "wandering" to find work and to gain a varied experience before settling down in a German town to practice their trade. In 1834 the political radicals in Paris began organizing small clubs that included journeymen. Among the most radical were the League of Outlaws (*Bund der Geächteten*) and, a few years later, the League of the Just (*Bund der Gerechten*). They never involved more than a few hundred members in any one year; but there was considerable turnover as members returned to Germany and other potential recruits came to Paris, and the wandering artisans helped to transmit the basic ideas of both political and social democracy to the German states. By 1840 various German radical groups in Paris had formed a loose association, the Confederation of the Germans (*Bund der Deutschen*). The Frankfurt Diet's investigators of subversion collected the names of some 390 persons who belonged to the affiliated groups, intellectuals as well as craft journeymen.[6]

The best known of the émigrés in France and the one most

widely read in Germany during the period 1830–48 was the poet Heinrich Heine. Born in 1797 of Jewish parents and educated as a lawyer, Heine had embraced Christianity in 1825 and the next year forsook the law for full-time literary work. Traveling in western Europe, he came to conceive of himself as a "soldier in the war for the liberation of mankind." While living in Paris after 1830, Heine became neither a consistent republican nor a consistent Saint-Simonian, but he remained an apostle of liberty and humanism and a constant critic of conditions in Germany. His views were made known in the German states through articles that he wrote as the Paris correspondent for Cotta's *Allgemeine Zeitung*, four volumes of his travel diaries published between 1827 and 1833 in Hamburg, and other books of lyrical poetry and prose. In all of these he satirically contrasted oppression in Germany with the more liberal conditions in France, and he did so well before the French government began in 1835 to pay him a secret pension. Heine was a bitter critic of aristocratic privileges and of monarchy. "A curse upon our king, the king of the rich," he wrote in 1844. Through his verse, many Germans sustained their faith in a democratic future:

> Ein neues Lied, ein besseres Lied,
> O Freunde, will ich euch dichten:
> Wir wollen hier auf Erden schon
> Das Himmelrich errichten.

Another member of the German colony in Paris, Ludwig Börne, had been born in the ghetto of Frankfurt in 1786 and became a radical in defense of the right of Jews to full citizenship. Like Heine, Börne accepted baptism, but remained a radical. In Paris after the French Revolution of 1830, he attracted widespread attention through literary letters (published as *Briefe aus Paris* in 1832) reflecting his hope for a German republic. Unlike Heine, he refused even temporarily to accept the gospel of Saint-Simon, but his admiration for France and his sense of indebtedness to her were fervently set forth in an essay he published in 1837, the year of his death: "It was France which so shook the German feudal state structure that all the props that

fear and caution can devise will not protect it from collapse. . . .
Thus, whoever hates France or slanders it . . . is a traitor to his
own Fatherland, whatever his Fatherland may be; is an enemy
of God, of humanity, of justice, of liberty, and of love."[7]

The admiration for France felt by Heine and Börne amalga-
mated their longing for a free Germany of the future and their
sense of rejection by the Germany of their own time. The same
amalgam brought Arnold Ruge to Paris. Arrested in 1824 for
membership in the Burschenschaft, he was sentenced to prison,
released in 1830, soon became a radical Hegelian, and grew
even more outspoken after failing to obtain a professorship. In
1840, influenced by Börne's writings, he began to pay turgid
Hegelian compliments to France. France had rejuvenated Spain,
Portugal, and England, Ruge wrote, and generated a constitutional climate in Germany, at least outside of Prussia. By 1840
the intellectual magazine Ruge edited had become a forum for
the writings of other "young Hegelians." Among its contributors were the best-known critics of theology and the churches
during this period, David Friedrich Strauss, Bruno Bauer, and
Ludwig Feuerbach. When the magazine was banned in Prussia
and then in Saxony, Ruge went to Paris at the end of 1843. There
he and Karl Marx briefly edited another magazine before parting
company. While Marx took up the class struggle, his collaborator
in 1845 moved on to Zürich in his restless search for effective
ways to strengthen the humanistic spirit—materialistic, democratic, and individualistic—among the Germans.

Convinced that they were participants in a universal movement, Heine, Börne, and Ruge lived in exile because they were
denied the right to publicize their views in the German Confederation. (Metternich, alarmed by the ideas and influence of
Heine in particular, had arranged in 1835 for the Diet to ban
dissemination of the writings of "the literary school known as
Young Germany," with which these exiles were loosely identified.) Though they loved Germany, they brought a cosmopolitan impulse to the movement for reform. All could say, as did
Ruge: "A free Frenchman is dearer to me than a German reactionary, because he belongs to my party and pursues the same
idea toward which I strive." For these men France was more

than a nation; it symbolized a political program for German reform.[8]

Other countries also offered political principles and places of refuge for Germany's malcontents. Both Switzerland and Belgium were readily accessible and usually hospitable havens for those who had to flee the German Confederation.

The exodus of German radicals to the Swiss cantons had begun after the Carlsbad Decrees were proclaimed in 1819. Here in the 1820's Karl Follen and other Burschenschafter had paused briefly before moving on to England and America; others remained. Liberal monarchists as well as republicans followed after the Six Acts were decreed in 1832. Karl Mathy was one of the former. A young tax official in Baden in 1832, Mathy used his spare time to edit a journal which disseminated progress as he understood it. Forced to choose between his career as a Baden bureaucrat and his liberal political convictions, he chose the latter. In May 1835, Mathy applied to the authorities in Switzerland for sanctuary with his family.

Switzerland after 1832 also harbored a number of German democrats. Julius Fröbel fled there after the Hambach Festival, working for a united Germany that would offer equal voting rights to all men. Through marriage to the daughter of a Swiss silk manufacturer, this son of a Thüringian pastor acquired the fortune that enabled him to publish the writings of many German leftists. Calling his ideal a "republic," Fröbel published the early ideas of Karl Marx, but refused to become a Marxist. He also printed for the first time the song by the radical scholar-poet August Heinrich Hoffmann von Fallersleben, that became the battle hymn of the liberal and democratic movement for German unity (and, in 1922, Germany's national anthem)— *Deutschland über Alles*. Fröbel romantically hoped that Switzerland might become part of a united Germany and that ·Germany would find its place in a united *Mitteleuropa*— a democratic central European union to which Poles, Hungarians, Rumanians, and Southern Slavs would also belong.

In Switzerland exiled German radicals organized a branch of Giuseppe Mazzini's "Young Europe" movement. The leaders of "Young Germany" hoped to indoctrinate German workers in Switzerland with republican and nationalist ambitions. In 1835 this group claimed some two hundred members in fourteen branch clubs which were in touch with other wandering craftsmen from Germany; some ten thousand or more of these were in Switzerland during the 1830's, and the constant goings and comings helped transmit democratic ideas into the German states.

Many German refugees joined in the civil war that erupted in Switzerland in November 1847. The more conservative Catholic cantons, which had opposed attempts by Swiss liberals and democrats to increase the authority of the federal government, were defeated within three weeks. The victory of the liberal and democratic Swiss lifted the spirits of Germans who subscribed to similar objectives while creating consternation among the rulers of the German Confederation. The short war also gave many German participants their first battle experience.[9]

Like Switzerland, Belgium after 1830 offered both a haven for political refugees and inspiration for reformers who remained in the states of the German Confederation. In 1830, Belgian liberals declared the country independent of the Dutch. The interest of Germany in the Belgian experiment was stimulated by the selection of Prince Leopold of Saxe-Coburg as the first king and by the desire of Rhenish merchants for close commercial relations with the new state. The Belgian Constitution of 1831 was immediately celebrated as a model by Germany's moderate liberals, who admired its parliamentary system based upon a restricted suffrage. The economic prosperity of Belgium impressed German merchants, bankers, and manufacturers. Its rapid economic development after 1835 helped convince the emerging German bourgeoisie that liberal political reforms at home would bring them similar advantages.[10]

The economic development of Great Britain exercised much the same effect upon Germany's merchant and industrial liberals. English economic power became apparent to Germans with every passing decade after the first British steamship puffed its way past the still unfinished steeples of Cologne's cathedral in 1816. Though the radical poet Georg Herwegh was moved by envy to favor construction of a German fleet (to "drive a nail in the coffin of Albion"), other reformers hoped to gain the strength England displayed by achieving more representative government. Some of the emerging industrialists hoped, through constitutional reforms, to install governments that would promote their interests by granting them state subsidies and credits or by building railroads. Others expected constitutional reform to free the new economic forces from existing regulations and restrictions that hampered growth. For these, English economic theory provided an important stimulus to demands for liberal reform in Germany. Adam Smith's *The Wealth of Nations*, published in 1776, had been quickly translated into German and printed in two volumes in Leipzig in 1776 and 1778. *Smithianismus*—"Manchesterian liberalism" and its implementation in Britain in the 1830's and 1840's—encouraged German liberals in their efforts to reduce barriers to trade and to eliminate the privileges of the guilds during these decades.

Even in the Rhineland province of Prussia, where liberalism first had been awakened by the example of France, English practices were inspiring imitation by the 1840's. There, Ludolf Camphausen and David Hansemann were among the most important spokesmen for the political and economic reform of Prussia on the British model. Camphausen, son of a merchant, became a banker in Cologne and pioneered in the promotion of steam shipping and railroad building. At thirty-six he was president of the Cologne Chamber of Commerce, a position he held from 1839 to 1847. A man of cool calculation, active in politics throughout the 1840's, Camphausen would be well prepared to assume a leading position as a liberal in the Revolution of 1848. Like many other liberals, he desired free trade as well as freer constitutional life.

An Aachen merchant who, like Camphausen, promoted railroad building, David Hansemann chafed under the failure of the Junkers and bureaucrats of Prussia to give it support. Politically Hansemann was no more a democrat than was his fellow liberal. In 1828 he wanted to limit the right to vote to persons who paid substantial taxes; by 1843 he was willing to broaden the suffrage, but would add multiple voting for property owners. His aim in both cases was a suffrage that would give political power to the upper middle class. In this as in his desire for constitutional and parliamentary government, Hansemann was a true liberal of the *Vormärz* (the two decades before the

March 1848 revolutions). As early as 1830 he had written to the Prussian king urging the need for liberal reform. Only a free Prussia, he cautioned, could resist if there should be a future French invasion of Germany in the name of "liberty, equality and fraternity."

England was no military threat to Germany, as many believed France to be in the 1840's, and British institutions had long been admired by Germans who favored cautious rather than radical political reform; as early as 1815, Friedrich Christoph Dahlmann had portrayed them as models for his country to follow. Britain became an even more attractive foreign model for some German liberals when the Whigs gained power there and showed, through the Reform Bill of 1832, how constitutional development could be accomplished without revolution and within a monarchical structure. In the parliament of Hesse-Darmstadt, for example, Heinrich von Gagern consistently and repeatedly through the 1830's and 1840's held up the example of Britain's parliamentary and jury systems as patterns for the transformation of his own state. What inspired admiration in Gagern elicited condemnation from Metternich; in April 1833 he blamed German unrest quite as much on the Reform Act of the previous year as on the revolutions in France and Belgium.

Yet many Germans were slow to grasp the full significance of the British Reform Bill of 1832. University students continued to study translations of William Blackstone's *Commentaries on the Laws of England* and Montesquieu's *Spirit of the Laws*. Both of these classics portrayed the government of Britain as one in which the crown, the House of Lords, and the House of Commons checked and balanced one another. Thus the German view of the British constitution saw the power of the crown as greater than it was. Consequently, while the German liberals as a whole admired Britain's jury system and freedom of the press, they were divided in their attitudes toward what they believed to be Britain's governmental structure. The more conservative liberals such as Dahlmann and Theodor Welcker saw and liked strong aristocratic and monarchical elements in the government of Britain. More radical liberals such as Friedrich Murhard and Welcker's fellow reformer in Baden, Karl von Rotteck, formed much the same outdated view of Britain and were critical.

In Württemberg and generally among German academic liberals, the more empirical and up-to-date writings of Robert von Mohl favorably portrayed British government. Mohl began to attract attention by his early publications on government affairs in the 1820's. He later described his political attitudes of that decade as those of "an English Whig, a French member of the left-center, and an American Federalist." In 1829, preparing an argument for more liberal administration, he wrote to his brother: "I would like to see if I cannot become the Adam Smith of the Police." He became a leading spokesman for reform in Germany; the journal he founded in 1844, the *Zeitschrift für die gesamte Staatswissenschaft*, was a major organ of academic liberalism.

Camphausen, Hansemann, Dahlmann, Gagern, Welcker, and Mohl were to exercise significant leadership among liberals in the German Revolution of 1848. It should come as no surprise that these and other German admirers of Britain's limited monarchy would then counsel moderation amidst the clamor for radical change. Migratory German artisans, on the other hand, living in England in the 1840's, transmitted more radical ideas back to Germany—democratic and socialistic conceptions that owed little to existing British government, but instead reflected less visible undercurrents of discontent among English workers. An estimated twenty thousand German workers lived in England in the period 1830–48. [11]

While Germany's liberals saw examples to follow in the government of Great Britain, Germany's democratic republicans were even more enthusiastic about the democracy across the Atlantic. The American experiment with republican and democratic government, largely eclipsed by the French Revolution, aroused new interest during the Metternich era.

Germans were informed about the United States by diverse sources. The major newspapers carried frequent reports on North America, and books published by travelers began to increase awareness of America; by 1850 more than fifty had appeared in print. An additional and more romantic image of the United States was created by German editions of works by American authors, especially those of Washington Irving and James Fenimore Cooper.

Germans who migrated to America greatly influenced the
image of the New World among friends and relatives who remained at home. Upon leaving Europe in 1825, Karl Follen
poetically called for followers to the free Fatherland of all mankind:

> Lass uns wandern, lass uns ziehn
> Mit der Sonne nach Westen hin.
> Dort an des Meeres andrem Strand,
> Dort ist die Freiheit, dort des Menschen Vaterland

From his post at Harvard, the former Burschenschaft leader
informed other liberal democrats in Germany about American
social and political affairs. In 1827 he was joined in Boston by
another émigré reformer, Francis Lieber, who soon started the
Encyclopaedia Americana and in time gained recognition as a political philosopher in the United States. From 1827 to 1837 Lieber
served as a correspondent for the Cotta press.

Economic hardship in Germany motivated most of the 180,000
small farmers, craftsmen, and shopkeepers who came to the
United States in the 1830's; they could not fail to note the greater
degree of religious and political freedom in their new country.
Letters to relatives and friends back home were passed from
hand to hand and discussed in hundreds of village taverns and
family gatherings. Occasionally a permanent or temporary re-
turnee brought first-hand news of America. Johann Ludwig
Tellkampf spent five years in the United States, then took up a
professorship of political science at Breslau in 1846 and advised
reforms along American lines. (He was to be elected to the
National Assembly in 1848.) Gustav Dresel, the son of a liberal
member of the Nassau parliament, returned in 1841 to the family
home, where Hoffman von Fallersleben and other prominent
liberal visitors were enthralled by his tales of struggle in Texas
and the chance for fulfillment on the frontier.[12]

A number of patriotic Germans saw the loss of so much
population to America as proof of the need for political and
economic reform at home. Cotta's *Allgemeine Zeitung* spoke for
many of its readers when it commented that "Germany could

undoubtedly support its entire population if it pleased the governments to govern less, to abolish guilds and feudal dues, and to allow free movement for all." That was in 1847. But the theme was constant: as early as 1816 the newspaper had contended that the best way "to counter the passion to emigrate would doubtless be to treat men so that they would wish to stay."[13]

Germans who wanted to remain at home and reform their states rather than migrate could find plenty of discussions in German of the American constitutional system. Not all painted a pretty picture. Friedrich Schmidt drew a sharp contrast between the theory of government in America and its reality, concluding that the United States was only "the dead hull of nominal freedom." But the Cotta press, which had presented Schmidt's account in 1822, two years later published a more favorable book by the young Robert von Mohl, who thought the United States Constitution excellent for American conditions. Cotta also published in 1827 a strongly favorable account of American political, religious, and social conditions by the novelist Charles Sealsfield, whose Anglo-Saxon pseudonym successfully concealed the identity of Karl Anton Postl from Poppitz in Moravia.

A more analytical and significant report became available when the first volume of Alexis de Tocqueville's *Democracy in America*, published in French in 1835, appeared in two German translations in 1836. Tocqueville favorably portrayed American government. "Democratic liberty," he wrote, "rarely completes its projects with the skill of an adroit despotism. But in the end it produces more than any absolutism . . . . .Under its sway the grandeur is not in what the government does, but in what is done without it or outside it." The message in Tocqueville's preface must have seemed particularly congenial to Germany's democrats as they felt the repression of the Metternich era: "The gradual trend toward equality of conditions is a work of Providence. . . . It is universal, it is enduring, it constantly eludes human powers of control. . . . Would it be wise to believe that a social movement of such remote origins will let itself be stopped by the effort of one generation?"

Tocqueville's study opened up a considerable scholarly discussion in Germany that went beyond his American subject to include the merits and demerits of such principles as popular sovereignty, majority rule, and federal union. German views varied. Robert von Mohl was prompted by *Democracy in America* to renew his professions of liberalism and his objections to democracy as a form of government for Germany. More democratic liberals, rejoicing over Tocqueville's portrayal of democracy, were inspired by the America he described. In Baden, Karl von Rotteck described the United States as "the noblest, most splendidly flourishing community...in the world." Knowing that Germany could not be made into a republic, he hoped for the building of a constitutional monarchy that would be filled with "republican spirit." Rotteck's Baden colleague, Karl Theodor Welcker, was more conservative, but even Welcker thought federal governments the most appropriate for large nations and of all federal constitutions he regarded the American as the best.

Like Tocqueville, the Berlin historian Friedrich von Raumer was convinced that one must look "not only in Europe" to learn "the probable future of humanity." The product of his first-hand observations in America in the early 1840's was a two-volume historical, sociological, and political analysis, published in Leipzig in 1845. Perceptively and with a high degree of objectivity, Raumer reported on many aspects of American life. Like other German writers, he gave much attention to slavery, presenting the American arguments pro and con on the issue and leaving no doubt of his conviction that gradual steps must be taken to end it. But his praise of America greatly outweighed his concern. "In no country in the world," he wrote, "is there so little rule from above and so much left to the people to determine . . . as in the United States."[14]

While moderate German liberals like Welcker and Raumer were attracted by the federal system of the United States, considering it a structure suitable for unifying Germany, Karl Heinzen saw something more. Heinzen first attracted attention among Germany's reformers—and the police—by publishing in 1845 a slashing criticism of the Prussian bureaucracy, a pamphlet that clearly said that his ideal state was a republic. With an order out for his arrest, he fled to Holland, then to Brussels, and soon to Zürich, where he collaborated with Arnold Ruge to produce revolutionary propaganda aimed at Germany. In December 1847 he visited the United States. From New York Heinzen advised his fellow Germans: "You must all recognize that your salvation can be achieved just as little through liberalizing twaddle as through phrase-turning majesties . . . just as little through constitutional lies as through an absolutist decree. . . . .Revolution is the beginning and a rational . . . republic is the conclusion. Without revolution no republic, and without the republic no salvation!"

In one way or another the gospel of democratic republicanism—reinforced by the American example—was reaching the German people by the winter of 1847–48. When peasant revolts occurred in southwest Germany in March 1848, a leaflet proclaimed: "We want a state whose business is conducted by a parliament elected by us and by its president; we want a *republic like that in America.*" The leaflet continued: "To those who say that in a republic all laws and all order cease to exist, we will say: Just stretch your nose in the direction of America; there a republic has existed for almost 100 years with no disorder. . . . *We want a republic and nothing else!*"

It is understandable that well before 1848 the United States had come to be regarded by conservative Germans as a dangerous example. The Prussian Ministry of Interior in 1836 directed officials to watch out for letters from America that might, by overly enthusiastic descriptions of conditions there, create unrest; and Metternich was only the most powerful of those who worried about America's revolutionary effect upon Germany.[15]

While the institutions of the West were admired by Germany's liberals and liberal democrats, the ideas of Robert Owen in England and of several French writers contributed to the emergence of socialism among several German intellectuals in the late 1830's. In Paris and Belgium the Westphalian Karl Grün condemning "the verbal swindle of liberalism," saw the future as one of proletarian socialism, and he found publishers in Germany despite the censorship. So did Moses Hess, who embraced dialectical materialism through the study of Hegel and the writings of the French Utopian Socialists. A one-time Magdeburg tailor's apprentice, Wilhelm Weitling, also slowly transformed Utopian Socialism into a harsher doctrine. By 1839, Weitling was the moving force in the small *Bund der Gerechten* in Paris. There, and after 1841 in Switzerland, Weitling led in organizing various socialist groups among migratory artisans and intellectuals. In 1847 a number of these groups were collaborating in the Communist League, which was to be made famous by the subsequent careers of two of its members, Karl Marx and Friedrich Engels.

Marx, born in the ancient city of Trier in 1818, was the grandson of a rabbi and the son of a lawyer who joined the Lutheran church the year before the boy's birth. In 1835—the year Marx began his studies in jurisprudence, history, and philsosphy at Bonn—David Friedrich Strauss published his critical study of the life of Jesus. The next year young Marx enrolled in the University of Berlin, where he became a full-blown atheist under the influence of the radically Hegelian Bruno Bauer. By 1842 he was turning his primary concern from philosophical questions to political and social problems. Vaguely democratic, he now was republican as well. He spent much of 1842 and the early months of 1843 as a writer and editor of a new newspaper in Cologne, the *Rheinische Zeitung*, founded by middle-class liberals (Ludolf Camphausen was a principal stockholder), in an environment in which socialist ideas were being widely discussed. Marx's own ideas were in flux, and censorship made it risky to set forth a clear, positive program for change; but he was critical of the religious and political policies of the Prussian monarch and sensitive to the problems of Germany's poor. When the paper was suppressed in the spring of 1843, Marx and his bride, Jenny von Westphalen, chose exile in Paris. By now he considered himself a socialist—well before he undertook any serious study of economics.

The ideas Marx wanted to publish in 1844 were set forth in the only issue of a radical magazine he and Arnold Ruge brought out that year with money from Ruge's wife. The emancipation of the German people, the twenty-six-year-old Marx wrote, would lead to the emancipation of mankind. To achieve revolution in Germany, the proletariat must be radicalized by the intellectuals. To succeed, the industrial working class must identify itself as the "general representative" of society as a whole; only in that way could it "justify its claim to universal power." Furthermore, it must brand another class—the bourgeoisie—as the "undisguised enslaving class," the enemy of society as a whole. In a writing style and a conceptualization still ponderously Hegelian, Marx described the proletariat as a class "which cannot emancipate itself without liberating itself from all classes of society and thereby freeing all other classes of society; a class which in one word represents the total loss of humanity, and thus can gain control over its own destiny only through the total reconquest of humanity." An article sent from England by Friedrich Engels—who had met Marx casually in Cologne in 1842—was couched in more specific economic terms. Increasing concentration of wealth was an "imminent law" in the development of the "industrial revolution," Engels wrote; the tendency to divide all people into "millionaires and paupers" would prepare the way for social revolution, which alone could forestall pauperization and open the way to the creation of a socialistic economy.

Like Marx, Engels had become an atheist under the influence of the Young Hegelians. By 1842 he found his way to socialism through the writings of Wilhelm Weitling and personal contact with Moses Hess. His father, an exemplary member of the bourgeoisie, owned textile mills in the Rhineland and in England. This enabled young Engels to observe at first hand the results of the Industrial Revolution in the country where it was most advanced. His first book described *The Condition of the Working Class in England*. Largely prepared in 1844, it was published in May 1845 in Leipzig. In it Engels predicted the ultimate overthrow of capitalism by the oppressed workers.

In 1846 and 1847, Marx and Engels developed their commitment to a firmly materialistic and revolutionary line. While scathingly criticizing more idealistic socialist writers, they preached the necessity of a bourgeois-democratic revolution as a precondition for a proletarian-socialist revolution. Engels became a tireless advertiser of Marx, and both fostered international collaboration among radical democratic groups in Paris, Brussels, London, and Germany. When the branch of the League of the Just in London called a conference there of all its member clubs in 1847, one of Marx's associates was sent to represent the Brussels organization, and Engels—then in Paris —got himself elected as the representative of the branches in the French capital. Meeting in June 1847, the congress in London renamed the League of the Just the Communist League. Marx attended a second congress in London in December 1847, and here he and Engels were authorized to prepare a manifesto for the League. The document was published in German in London in February 1848. This *Communist Manifesto* proclaimed that Germany stood "on the eve of a bourgeois liberal revolution" and that this would be "the prelude to an immediately following proletarian revolution." Decades later this document would become the best known of all Marxist writings, but it would be a mistake to attribute much significance to it in the onset of the German Revolution of 1848.

The emergence of socialism had ambiguous effects on the movement to democratize Germany. By identifying political democracy with the social demands of the slowly increasing numbers of factory workers, the socialists helped to establish a mass base for the democratic movement. At the same time, however, the fear that democracy would lead to socialism probably dampened enthusiasm for democratic reform among many peasants and artisans as well as among middle-class Germans. Socialism in the 1840's aroused both fear and hope in Germany. The widespread talk about it during that decade was symptomatic not so much of its actual appeal as of increasing concern about existing economic unrest.[16]

Though there were few industrial workers in Germany in the 1840's, the term "proletariat" was heard on all sides. Loosely, the term meant persons who were employed, socially dangerous, or simply poverty-stricken. Some of these happened to be employed in factories, where women and children as well as men worked from five or five-thirty in the morning to about seven in the evening. The term was also applied to farm workers, to peasants who were accustomed to crafting articles in their tiny huts to maintain subsistence, and to apprentices and journeymen of the guild trades. The artisans, whose labor could not keep pace with machine production, were among the most discontented of Germans in the 1840's. Occasionally they submitted petitions that won no benefits for them. At times they smashed the machines of nearby factories to vent their frustration. In June 1844 some five thousand hand weavers attacked the homes and mills of manufacturers in southeastern Prussia before the Prussian army crushed their rebellion. The revolt of these Silesian weavers—which became a classic episode in the early history of the Industrial Revolution—made many Germans for the first time acutely aware of the social problems being created by industrialization.

For both the rural and urban poor in Prussia and other German states, conditions grew worse rather than better after 1844. Three years of crop failures beginning in 1845, especially potato famines, aggravated unrest in Germany as in all of western Europe. The price of food rose rapidly, if it could be obtained at all. Summer and winter alike in 1846 and 1847, bands of hungry beggars made their piteous way through the villages and towns in search of handouts. Dysentery reached epidemic proportions in parts of Germany in the summer of 1847, and it was followed by typhus; together, these diseases and starvation took some fifty thousand lives and left about ten thousand orphaned children in Upper Silesia alone by early 1848. Poverty became equally chronic in western Germany. In January 1847, Heinrich von Gagern wrote his father that misery was increasing around his estate in Rhenish Hesse: "We . . . have food prepared twice a week for about 20 persons, 9 families: soup and a piece of meat. . . . .But how much better our conditions are in comparison with those in France, Ireland!"

Such comparisons did nothing to mollify those Germans whose children went to bed with empty stomachs only to face another day with little or no food. It took the royal Prussian cavalry four days to suppress hundreds of hungry Berliners who tried in April 1847 to take in the city's markets what they could get in no other way. Blood was spilled in Leipzig that same month in similar rioting. In May there were demonstrations in Ulm and in Stuttgart, where one of the rioters was killed and many wounded by the royal troops; the king of Württemberg simply blamed the disturbances on the "revolutionary rabble" in Switzerland.[17]

Not knowing how to cope with the economic hardships of the lower classes, the governments of the German states in the

1840's were unwilling to concede to the demands of middle-class reformers. Their armies protected them against revolution; their ministries and bureaucracies formed barriers against demands for reform; the censors continued to restrict the press; troublesome professors were reprimanded or dismissed.

These circumstances largely determined the immediate demands of the liberal and liberal-democratic reformers, who wanted to require the armies to take oaths to support the constitutions of the German states instead of the customary personal oaths to support the rulers. There was a growing call for legalized arming of the citizenry—for the creation of local militias or national guards as liberal counterweights against the authoritarian influence of the traditional military forces. To these demands were joined insistence upon freedom of the press, freedom to form associations, freedom of assembly, trial by jury, and public rather than secret court proceedings. Where parliaments existed, some argued that ministries should be made responsible to them rather than to the ruler. Many liberals as well as democrats wanted suffrage to be made more nearly universal. Growing numbers wanted to make of the Germans a united nation—especially after 1840 when France, through its aggressive policy in the Middle East, defied the other great powers. Many Germans feared that the Rhineland was again in danger. If the French Revolution continued to inspire German liberals and democrats to demand internal reforms, recollections of Napoleonic imperialism spurred demands among them for German unity.

While the liberals and democrats could agree on some goals, they could hope to achieve them only through better organization, which was difficult because political parties were illegal. Meetings had to be held in secret or "front organizations" exploited. Among the latter were Germany's new national organizations of scholars and professional men. The first of these annual gatherings was that of the natural scientists and physicians, called into existence in 1822 by Lorenz Oken. The philologists began meeting annually in 1838. University teachers of history, law, and the German language organized in 1846. In all of these annual gatherings of intellectuals, there was considerable talk in formal sessions of the need for German unification;

and the participants found much free time to carry on more radical discussions informally and behind the scenes.

The professors of history, law, and the German language were particularly political-minded. The men who called the first meeting included such staunch liberals as Dahlmann, Georg Gottfried Gervinus, the Grimm brothers, Ludwig Uhland, and Karl Mittermaier. This very first Congress established a committee to report on the pros and cons of trial by jury, under the chairmanship of Mittermaier because he had declared that law in Germany stood disregarded and often defied the postulates of the common good. It came as no surprise when the committee's report in 1847 endorsed trial by jury—one of the most frequent liberal demands for reform. Mittermaier held up England as an example to follow in reforming German law.

If scholarly concerns helped liberals organize when political organizations were forbidden, so did common economic interests. As early as 1833 a few liberals had met in an attempt to develop a common attitude toward the *Zollverein*. This small conference brought together Heinrich von Gagern and his senior colleague in the liberal movement in Hesse-Darmstadt, Karl Jaup; Rotteck and Welcker from Baden; Paul Pfizer and Friedrich Römer, leaders of the liberal movement in Württemberg; and a few other opposition leaders from the same three states. These men would work together closely in the Revolution of 1848; several met for the first time at the conclave in 1833. Thereafter, they exchanged letters about their activities.

The circle was enlarged in the 1840's, chiefly on the initiative of Adam von Itzstein. A civil servant before being dismissed as a critic of the government in Baden's parliament, Itzstein was a leader of the liberal opposition in the 1830's. He had sought to bring liberals, democrats, and republicans into a common front through meetings at his estate at Hallgarten in the Rheingau. In 1843 the sixty-eight-year-old Itzstein hosted a meeting of fellow reform leaders from as far away as Hanover, Altenburg, and Saxony. Another meeting was arranged for Leipzig in the spring of 1845 and yet another at Hallgarten in 1846. Through these conferences the reform leaders coordinated demands in the various states on behalf of freedom of the press, public court proceedings, trial by jury, ministerial responsibility, restrictions on the military forces, and German unity.

Itzstein's efforts to bring liberals and democrats under a single roof were not very successful, but in 1847 the liberals found a new outlet for their opinions and strengthened their relationships across state lines. Early in that year Karl Mathy of Baden, Heinrich von Gagern, and Georg Gottfried Gervinus organized an immediately influential newspaper, the *Deutsche Zeitung*. The editor in 1847–48 was Gervinus, who for a decade had argued the need to educate the German people for political action. Until 1847 his efforts had been confined largely to his historical writings and the limited audiences he reached through his lectures at Göttingen and Heidelberg. His basic political principles were those of liberal democracy, which he had first encountered upon entering Giessen a few years after Follen's dismissal. Now they were expressed in the pages of the *Deutsche Zeitung*, which encouraged a new sense of unity among Germany's liberals. The goal of the newspaper, as defined by Gervinus in January 1847, was "to achieve the advantages of a political revision without violent movements." The revision favored by the men who founded the newspaper was "constitutional monarchy...in all its consequences and for all parts of the fatherland."

On October 10, 1847, moderate liberal leaders from Rhenish Prussia, Nassau, Hesse-Darmstadt, and the southern states met in the town of Heppenheim, between Darmstadt and Mannheim, to coordinate strategy. The roster of this conference reads like a *Who's Who* of the liberal leadership in the Revolution of 1848. These were men of means and education: David Hansemann from Prussia (who had called the meeting), Heinrich von Gagern from Hesse-Darmstadt, Friedrich Römer from Württemberg, the Baden merchant Friedrich Bassermann, Adam von Itzstein, and others. The conferees resolved to reinvigorate their efforts for the unification of Germany, and they agreed to press common reform goals within their separate states.

More radical reformers in Baden, meanwhile, had met separately on September 12 at Offenburg, halfway between Karlsruhe and Freiburg, under the leadership of two of Itzstein's democratic acquaintances, Gustav von Struve and Friedrich Hecker. Several points in their program (freedom of the press, freedom of religion, trial by jury, and a parliament for all of Germany) would have harmonized in a purely liberal setting.

But the Offenburg democrats enthusiastically added some principles that set them apart from the liberals: the right of citizens to bear arms, income taxation, protection of labor, and improvements in relations between labor and the owners of industry. The Offenburg demands reflected a rising insistence upon the need for social reform. Struve proclaimed in his newspaper that the masses yearned not so much for constitutional freedom as for succor from poverty. His fellow lawyer and Mannheim political associate, Friedrich Hecker, advocated a rudimentary social democracy. Struve and Hecker had been the most prominent democrats in Baden in the 1840's, and by 1847 they commanded a considerable following.[18]

The effects of Reason, science, and social and political unrest had shaken the churches of Germany, and by 1845 religious dissent was providing front organizations for Hecker, Struve, and other reformers. The "Protestant Friends" and the "German-Catholics" were similar in motivation and ideas. Both bore considerable resemblance to the Unitarian churches of the United States. While their first concern was to reconcile science and Hegelian Reason with the ethical teachings of Christ, both movements included men who demanded social welfare and political democracy.

In June 1841 several Protestant clergymen in the Magdeburg area (Prussian Saxony), disturbed by official criticism of a pastor who rejected a literal interpretation of the scriptures, agreed to band together to aid one another "in word and deed." They had come together at the suggestion of forty-two-year-old Leberecht Uhlich, who had prepared for the ministry at Halle and had been a pastor in the Evangelical church since 1824. Under Uhlich's energetic leadership their circle quickly broadened. In September some fifty clergymen and laymen from various parts of Prussia, Saxony, and other states met in Halle to create a more formal organization. The resulting Society of Protestant Friends pledged its members to test religious beliefs by Reason; and they promised, as far as possible, "to work for the Kingdom of Jesus around us." Critics were soon derisively calling the Protestant Friends Lichtfreunde or Illuminati (Friends of Light). But local branches grew in number and membership, as did attendance at their conventions at Köthen, in the Duchy of

Anhalt about ninety miles southwest of Berlin and an accessible railroad junction. In September 1843 some four hundred persons attended the convention; even more were on hand in the spring of 1844. At that time Pastor Gustav Adolf Wislizenus outraged the church hierarchy by proclaiming "the living spirit within ourselves" to be a higher authority for contemporary Christians than the Bible.

Suspension of Wislizenus by the provincial consistory of the Evangelical church in Prussian Saxony in the spring of 1845 provoked protests from all sides. The Whitsuntide meeting at Köthen in 1845 drew two to three thousand persons who gathered for outdoor services. The authorities took alarm; that summer the governments of Bavaria and Saxony forbade any activity by the Lichtfreunde within their territories, and in August the Prussian government denied them the right to hold mass meetings or to form "closed societies." The removal of one of their ministers, Julius Rupp, from his pastorate in Königsberg finally provoked the Protestant Friends to secede from the state church. Rupp and laymen who supported him agreed to form a church of their own, and this became the first of the Protestant Free Congregations (Freie Gemeinden). Similar congregations quickly were organized in Halle, Magdeburg, Halberstadt, Nordhausen, Breslau, and other places in central and eastern Germany. By late 1846 there were about one hundred Free Congregations with possibly as many as twenty-five thousand members, chiefly in Prussia.

Several leaders of the Free Congregations were moving speakers and prolific writers. Wislizenus was their most radical spokesman. As a *Burschenschafter* at Halle he had been imprisoned during the 1820's. In 1846, removed from his pastorate in Halle, he became the leader of the Free Congregation there. He believed Christianity should be founded on the spirit of truth and love for humanity rather than on literal interpretations of the scriptures. In political life as well as in religion, he demanded full freedom for the individual. He won a little support, but also much opposition, within the Free Congregations in his advocacy of a form of Christian socialism to improve the lot of the poor. Leberecht Uhlich was less radical but an effective publicist and a capable organizer. The only son of a tailor, his rational theology, like that of Wislizenus, dated back to his student days at Halle. Dismissed from his church in 1847, he served henceforth as pastor of Magdeburg's Free Congregations.

The persistent growth of the Free Congregations was reluctantly acknowledged by the Prussian government in the spring of 1847; a royal decree then recognized the right of the dissidents to separate from the established church. But the persecution from the state they had experienced left a firmer impression on many members of the Free Congregations than did the belated and partial grant of toleration. Though at first not much interested in politics, a number of their leaders participated in the Revolution of 1848. Julius Rupp became a leader of the revolution in Königsberg; Wislizenus a member of the Vorparlament; Uhlich was elected to Prussia's revolutionary Constituent Assembly and to the National Assembly at Frankfurt; Eduard Baltzer, another leader of the Protestant Friends, won a seat in the Frankfurt Parliament, as did Max Duncker and Rudolf Haym, prominent lay intellectuals in the movement.

During the years the Lichtfreunde had organized to oppose the Protestant hierarchy in Prussia, similar religious dissent had resulted in the creation of the separatist German-Catholic movement. Its leading figure was Johannes Ronge. The son of a Silesian peasant, Ronge had become interested in the political ideas of Karl von Rotteck while studying at Breslau in 1836–37. After his ordination he was disciplined for criticizing church officials. He became a public figure in 1844. In that year the church hierarchy provoked widespread protests among Catholics by encouraging a massive pilgrimage to Trier to view the alleged robe of Christ. In an open letter to the bishop of Trier, on October 1, Ronge denounced the whole affair as a "most unChristian exhibition." He was swiftly excommunicated.

Ronge responded to excommunication by deliberately setting out to create a separate church, "free from Rome." In February 1845, under his leadership, a thousand supporters founded the first significant German-Catholic congregation. In the same month Robert Blum organized a German-Catholic congregation in Leipzig, and Franz Wigard emerged as the leader of one in Dresden. Blum was a self-made radical journalist. Wigard learned shorthand from its inventor, Franz Xaver Gabelsberger, then taught stenography in Dresden and recorded the minutes of Saxony's parliament; he was elected to preside when representatives of fourteen congregations met in Leipzig in March 1845 to create a united German-Catholic church. Their proposals included the provisions that local congregations were to be fully independent, electing their own ministers and elders. The mass was to be conducted in German. Priests were not required to observe celibacy.

Between April and December 1845, Ronge toured much of Germany to win support for the new movement. He met a great deal of political and religious enthusiasm in Württemberg and Baden. At Ulm fifteen thousand persons packed into the old Münster, its towering spire not yet completed, to hear him proclaim that the new church must not be exclusively concerned with spiritual affairs; that it must strive to relieve poverty and to reduce the differences that separated rich and poor. At Offenbach in Hesse twenty thousand persons attended his open-air service. In Stuttgart he met Friedrich Römer and Paul Pfizer, the leaders of the liberal movement in Württemberg. Gervinus and Welcker were his hosts at Heidelberg. In Mannheim another of the chief Baden liberals, the merchant Friedrich Bassermann, opened the garden of his villa for the crowd to hear Ronge, and other Baden liberals and democrats—Mathy, Itzstein, and Hecker—received him with enthusiasm.

Officialdom reacted differently. Austria, Bavaria, and Hanover repressed the German-Catholic movement with special ruthlessness. Public worship in Saxony was forbidden in the autumn of 1845, but was legalized in June 1846; prohibitions by the governments of Baden and Hesse-Cassel were maintained until 1848. In Prussia, Ronge was arrested several times, and meetings were allowed only in private homes until a somewhat greater degree of toleration was granted in March 1847. In spite of the restrictive measures everywhere, by the beginning of 1848 some fifty thousand members were organized in about two hundred German-Catholic congregations.

The German-Catholics tended to be more openly and vigorously interested in political and social questions than were the Protestant Free Congregations. While generally demanding changes, they disagreed among themselves about particulars. In

Württemberg, Heinrich Loose helped to organize the German-Catholic groups in Stuttgart and Esslingen and edited a socialist newspaper, *Die neue Zeit* (*The New Age*). The Baden democrats Gustav Struve and Friedrich Hecker became German-Catholics, as did Gervinus and many other liberals. In 1848, Blum, Wigard, and at least three other German-Catholics were elected to the National Assembly in Frankfurt. Ronge, finding that body too conservative, helped organize a democratic movement outside it. Christian Gottfried Nees von Esenbeck, a German-Catholic professor at Breslau, was a democrat in the Prussian Constituent Assembly and active in attempts to organize associations of workers.

Religion remained a powerful force among the people of Germany in the 1840's. Consequently, the Free Congregations and the German-Catholic movements were especially significant purveyors of political discontent. One critical observer noted in 1847 that "this supposedly religious movement of the present is really not a religious but a political movement." This underestimated the profound religious concern of both the Free Congregations and the German-Catholics, but the year 1848 was to prove that both groups—and the efforts to suppress them—had readied many Germans to participate in revolution. Their churches were especially important in providing organizational contacts in an era that allowed no strictly political organizations.[19]

The same decade had witnessed the growth of political awareness among German Jews, some 350,000 to 400,000 of whom lived within the German Confederation. For the Jews, the reaction after 1815 had held special meaning. Napoleon's policy of Jewish emancipation had ceased after the Congress of Vienna. In Prussia, the decree of 1812 that had granted equality before the law in the older provinces was not extended to include the new territories until 1847, and even then Jews were expressly denied access to administrative positions in the civil service and to certain other professions. Though a number were elected to municipal assemblies in Prussia and other states, they were almost never appointed to public offices. Four or five Jewish converts to Christianity won seats in state parliaments, but practicing Jews held none before 1848.

Notwithstanding the discrimination they experienced, most

Orthodox Jewish spiritual and lay leaders admonished their followers to respect their rulers; thus, for example, the *Treue Zionswächter* reminded its readers in 1845 that Orthodox Jewry recognized state authority "as a holy instrument of the divine will." But rejection of the Judaic religion by increasing numbers of Jews and the rise of Reform Judaism brought forth many demands for social and political change. Those who found their own religion antiquated and who either abandoned it or moved to modernize it could also find much to criticize in state and society—as was made clear by the examples of Heine, Börne, Hess, and Marx. During the first half of the nineteenth century, liberalism was especially attractive to Jews because it held the promise of full civic rights for all and solidly called for religious toleration. Some rallied to the liberal standard for purely selfish reasons, but many of these in time fully endorsed liberalism's broad vision of human rights.

Gabriel Riesser emerged in the 1830's as the outstanding liberal spokesman for German Jewry. After earning a doctorate in jurisprudence, Riesser first sought an academic position. Such appointments almost never went to Jews, however, so Riesser became a lawyer in Hamburg. There he began his crusade for Jewish emancipation with two pamphlets in 1831 and with a short-lived journal (*Der Jude: Periodische Blätter für Religion-und Gewissensfreiheit*) that he edited in 1832–33. He quickly concluded that the cause of Jewish rights could best be served by winning legal equality and political rights for all citizens within a united Germany. "If I were offered on the one hand [Jewish] emancipation," he wrote, "and on the other the fulfillment of the beautiful dreams of the political unity of Germany in political freedom, I would choose the latter without a moment's thought; for I am of the firm, deepest conviction that the latter will bring the former."

Riesser's magazine gave hope, courage, and liberal conviction to Jews in many parts of Germany. In faraway East Prussia a twenty-five-year-old physician, Johann Jacoby, was prompted by an early issue to write Riesser declaring his appreciation and support. This merchant's son had been enabled by Prussia's Jewish emancipation of 1812 to obtain a good education. Completing his medical doctorate in 1827 at the local university, he

studied for a time at Heidelberg in the southwest before returning to Könisberg in 1830 to practice. Though brought up
under relatively favorable circumstances, he had suffered discrimination as a Jewish youngster and was left with an abiding
resentment. It confirmed Jacoby's sense of Jewish identity, for
he saw much to change in the traditional Mosaic faith as a leader
of Reform Judaism in Königsberg in the 1830's. His resentment
of discrimination led him to liberalism by 1832.

Jacoby absorbed all of Riesser's message, and by 1837 he was
no longer thinking in purely Jewish terms. "Just as I am a Jew
and a German at the same time," he then wrote, "so the Jew in
me cannot be free without the German, and the German not
without the Jew." Acting on this conviction, in 1841 he published a bold call for a Prussian constitution. In this pamphlet—
Vier Fragen, beantwortet von einem Ostpreussen—Jacoby demanded
a consitution "as a proven right" rather than "as a favor."
Charged with lèse-majesté, after drawn-out legal proceedings,
he was sentenced in 1843 to a term of thirty months in prison.
Subsequently he was acquitted by the court of appeals, but the
pamphlet and the publicity concerning the trial made liberals
more insistent than ever on the need for constitutional rule in
Prussia, and they publicized Jacoby throughout Germany as a
vigorous proponent of democracy.

Other Jewish-born Germans took up active roles in the movement for political modernization in the 1840's. Another Königs-
berger, August Lewald, was a convert to Christianity who had
begun in the 1830's to publish a liberal magazine, *Europa*. Karl
Weil published another in Stuttgart in the 1840's. In Breslau a
Christianized Jew, Heinrich Simon, won recognition as a liberal
leader after resigning his judgeship in 1844 in protest against
royal interference with the judiciary. During these same years
Aaron Bernstein, co-founder of the Reform Jewish congregation
in Berlin, began to attract attention as a liberal-democratic journalist.[20]

Until 1848 the growing agitation for reform only increased the
Prussian government's resistance to liberals and democrats.
Prussia in the 1840's remained virtually an absolute monarchy.
In the eight provincial diets—representing the nobility, middle-
class townsmen, and peasantry—the nobility dominated. In the

provincial diet of Rhineland Prussia, for example, the few nobles and princes elected a total of 30 representatives, the peasantry 25, and the designated towns 25. In the towns, only persons who paid substantial taxes could vote; for example, in the town of Solingen, 6 percent of the inhabitants, in Düsseldorf only 1 percent. Attempts in the mid-1840's to broaden the suffrage were vetoed by the Prussian king.

In 1840 the death of Frederick William III had led to the succession of the deeply religious Frederick William IV, forty-five years of age when he became king. Hoping for a happy reign, he had begun it by conciliating the Roman Catholic hierarchy, calling a few liberals to professorships, and somewhat relaxing the censorship. On the other hand, he was pedantic, lacked judgment, and felt a crushing responsibility before God to preserve the authority of the Hohenzollern dynasty. Thus, although impulses to try the new were evident in the early years of his reign, they were at war in his breast and mind with impulses to preserve the old. The result of this ambivalence and of contradictory advice was a marked tendency to avoid firm decisions. Bismarck's appraisal decades later was accurate: "His rich phantasy lacked wings as soon as it ventured on the domain of practical resolve." Frederick William IV was "deficient in resolution and consistency."

Practical suggestions for the alleviation of public unrest were brought to the attention of the king from several quarters. Josef von Radowitz, a conservative general, held out before him the possibilities of carrying through a "revolution from above" in the tradition of Frederick the Great and Stein: the masses would be pacified by a royal program of social welfare and prolabor policies; the middle classes would gain recognition in a national parliament made up of representatives of Prussia's corporate groups (*Stände*). In 1847 it appeared for a time that the king had accepted the Radowitz proposal, at least in part. Needing to increase the state debt in order to build a railroad from East Prussia to Berlin, he called members of the Prussian provincial diets to Berlin for a joint meeting.

This United Diet was the first semiparliamentary body for all of Prussia. When it met on April 11, 1847, hopes soared that the king would meet the demands for a constitution and a statewide parliament in order to win the financial support of the liberals. These hopes crashed when the new ruler told the United Diet: "Never will I permit a written sheet of paper to come between God in heaven and this land." He refused to agree to periodic meetings of the United Diet, as David Hansemann and other liberals requested. In turn, the members refused (360–179) to approve the proposed financing of the railroad from Königsberg to Berlin. The United Diet adjourned on June 26, 1847.

While still following the impulse to break with tradition, the monarch had permitted newspapers to publish verbatim reports on the debates of the United Diet. This marked a temporary but highly significant departure from the tight censorship that previously had handicapped discussion of political affairs. The meetings of the United Diet thus had given rise to avid public consideration of political issues and high expectations of progress toward a constitution. In Saxony, Hesse-Darmstadt, and other states, they had aroused the hopes of some liberal nationalists that a reformed Prussia might lead Germany to unity. The barren outcome deepened dissatisfaction. In several features, therefore, the whole affair was like a restaging in railroad-era Prussia of Louis XVI's ill-fated Assembly of Notables of 1787.[21]

Before 1848 democrats who dared lift their voices had done so in vain. The liberals had been only slightly more successful; they, too, felt deep and many-sided frustration, particularly in Austria and Prussia, and they were much more numerous than the democrats. In Königsberg, for example, it is estimated that in 1848 only about fifty of the fourteen hundred active liberals stood on the extreme left.[22] Probably the balance of forces was not very different in Germany as a whole. When the year 1848 began, the rulers of Germany had passed up many chances to accomplish political change through evolution within their separate states. They also had refused to give serious consideration to the problems underlying unification of the German people. The more radical democrats were increasingly confident that political modernization was possible, if only through revolution; countries west of the Rhine had shown them the way. Neither the democrats nor the liberals formed a cohesive revolutionary movement, but they were groping toward organization. They remembered Ferdinand Freiligrath's poetic advice of 1841 to "stand upon a higher watch-tower than the battlements of a party," but Georg Herwegh had penned what growing numbers accepted as a suitable rejoinder: the party, Herwegh had written, was "the mother of all victories."[23] Meanwhile the economic hardships of the 1840's had prepared craftsmen and peasants for radical action. When news came in February 1848 of yet another revolution in France, both the Metternich system of repression and the German democrats were put to the test of the first genuine political revolution to reach into all corners of Germany.

IV.

1848: LIBERALS AND
DEMOCRATS REVOLT

In 1848 as in 1789 and 1830, Paris transformed unrest into revolution. The revolt that began on February 22 quickly unseated King Louis Philippe. With France once again a republic, monarchs all over Europe trembled and democrats impetuously sought to realize their long-frustrated ambitions. The revolutions in Germany were part of this general European phenomenon.[1]

Blood and violence were not characteristic of the German revolutions. Most were accomplished by street demonstrations, public assemblies, and petitions to the rulers. But the armed clashes that did occur were of decisive importance. In the central German Thuringian states and in southwestern Germany—in the Black Forest, the Odenwald, Franconia, and Nassau—peasants armed with scythes and axes destroyed records of property and tax obligations. Sometimes, for good measure, they put the torch to homes of nobles and to state office buildings. In Mannheim, Mainz, and a few other places, artisans attacked factories and smashed machines. In Vienna and Berlin bloody street fighting raged briefly. As a result, governments felt threatened everywhere, causing rulers to make quick concessions to the liberals in hopes of winning their support against the more radical demands of the democrats. The strategy of the princes divided their enemies, and it worked, for the violence that tore at German flesh and property in the spring of 1848 greatly accentuated the differences between liberals and democrats.[2]

These generalizations suggest the broad character and tendencies of the German Revolution of 1848–49. To understand its early successes and its failures it must be more closely examined where it actually took place—in the diverse states that made up the fragmented political landscape of the German Confederation.

Disturbances broke out in Bavaria almost a month before the French Revolution began. Bavarians, like other Germans, had felt the pinch of famine in 1847. Industry had been slowly developing—only one Bavarian out of twenty-nine was a factory worker in 1848—but its rise disquieted handicraftsmen in town and country. Munich, having almost doubled in size since 1813, was a city of one-hundred thousand inhabitants. King Ludwig had fostered cultural creativity and beautified his capital; but he also had sharply limited the powers of parliament and tightened the censorship since the mid-1830's, and these restrictions provoked political dissatisfaction. The immediate cause of Ludwig's downfall was, however, considerably more exotic. In the autumn of 1846 a twenty-six-year-old fancy dancer of international background had come to Munich seeking employment at the court theater. Rejected, Lola Montez managed to see the king himself. She enchanted the sixty-one-year-old ruler. He said he liked the way she read Calderón and Cervantes to him, but the Catholic hierarchy and the solid citizens of Munich spoke openly of scandal. They and students at the university were outraged by the monarch's attachment to Lola. After the customary "Grüss Gott," Ludwig and Lola figured prominently in the daily talk of peasants and townsmen from the Alpine meadows around Berchtesgaden to the marketplace at Aschaffenburg.

The chief minister, Karl von Abel, resigned, warning his king of revolution, but Ludwig refused to part with his mistress. He conferred Bavarian citizenship on her, endowed her with the title of a Countess Landsfeld, and built her an expensive villa in Munich. Lola made matters worse by interfering in political affairs and identifying herself with anticlericalism. By the beginning of 1848, Bavarians of all classes were determined that she must go. On January 29 demonstrations began in Munich. On February 11 the king finally agreed that she should leave the city, and with a crowd in tumult around her villa the fallen favorite had no choice but to resume her travels. She eventually made her way to Switzerland, the United States, and other ports of call.

News of the revolution of February 22 in Paris set off new

demonstrations in Munich. Bavarian moderates, hoping to avert a more radical upheaval, called upon the monarch to grant a number of liberal reforms. Instead, Ludwig began bringing troops from outlying areas to the city. Against this danger, citizens armed themselves; on March 4 a crowd stormed the arsenal in Munich, seizing weapons and demanding the abdication of the king. Two days later, Ludwig attempted to save his crown by promising liberal reforms. But neither promises nor the decision a week later to create a new ministry could calm the agitation. On March 20 he abdicated. That same day his son and successor, Maximilian II, took an oath to the constitution.

Under a new ministry, reform laws were drafted to give Bavaria a more genuinely representative government. The lower house of parliament was to be elected by the equal votes of all taxpayers. The ministry was made responsible for the acts of the king. Freedom of the press was guaranteed by law. Peasants were relieved of the remnants of feudal obligations. Trial by jury was introduced. Court proceedings were to be made public. Moderate liberals managed the revolutionary government in Munich,[3] but Ludwig's abdication and his successor's concessions to liberalism allowed the Wittelsbach dynasty to continue to reign.

In neighboring Württemberg revolt assumed less militant forms. The reform forces in the capital city of Stuttgart, both liberal and democratic, demanded greater civic freedom and change in the structure of the German Confederation. King William I at first counted on military assistance from Prussia and from his Russian brother-in-law. But when local demonstrations threatened to turn into revolution, he agreed on March 2 to the major demands of the liberals, whose two chief spokesmen—Friedrich Römer and Paul Pfizer—were shortly brought into a new ministry.

Thus, under the shadow of revolution more than under its impact, Württemberg experienced a number of moderate reforms in March 1848. The state parliament in Stuttgart passed laws that authorized the bearing of arms by the citizens, guaranteed freedom of the press and of assembly, and abolished remaining feudal obligations. The king agreed on March 18 that the army should take an oath to uphold the constitution. A week later he called for the election of a new lower house. With these measures, the Württemberg liberals tended to become satisfied allies of the monarch; the liberal ministry acted swiftly in April to suppress republican agitation. The king, on the other hand, regarded collaboration with the moderate liberals as a distasteful compromise, which he hoped to end as soon as possible. When democrats as well as liberals were elected in May to the new parliament, William delayed its meeting until September 20, and there were no significant new reform measures in Württemberg in 1848. The ruling dynasty had not even been subjected to the indignity of an abdication.[4]

Meanwhile, more violent revolutions had occurred elsewhere, notably in the largest capitals of the German Confederation. Before the French Revolution of 1848, Metternich or the king of Prussia would have sent troops to aid the rulers of Bavaria and Württemberg, but in the moments of need in March 1848, neither of the two most powerful German governments was able to defend the status quo. Each had to contend with its own revolution.

News of the February Revolution in Paris touched off disturbances in Vienna; on March 13 these developed into a full-scale civil conflict when troops fired on demonstrating students, workers, and middle-class citizens. The mob burned factories, plundered stores, and demanded the dismissal of Metternich. A conference of state ministers and members of the royal family decided to make concessions. They raised no protest when the state chancellor offered to step down. That night the man who for forty years had been the leading conservative in central Europe resigned while the revolutionaries went about establishing their mastery over Vienna.

Seeking to save what could still be preserved, the royal court on March 15 decided to appeal to the liberals against the radicals by promising a constitution. Time being short, Emperor Ferdinand on April 25 simply decreed a constitution based on the Belgian model of 1831. Vienna's democrats liked neither the method nor the constitutional terms. On May 15 a second Viennese revolution broke out. The emperor left the city for Innsbruck, where he sought to organize resistance against the radicals. Meanwhile, revolution had temporarily broken the power of the Habsburgs in Hungary and Italy and sharply limited it in Bohemia. In the spring of 1848, therefore, the dynasty was in no position to obstruct revolution in the states of the German Confederation, and it appeared that Austria could no longer stand in the way of German unity.[5]

Earlier, Prussia had joined with Austria to form the vanguard of opposition to reform, but in March 1848 the Hohenzollern kingdom in the north was no more able than was the Habsburg empire in the south to hold back change. Prussia itself was shaken by revolution, and the capital city was the epicenter of the earthquake.

Since 1814, Berlin's population had increased from one hundred eighty thousand to more than four hundred thousand, making it slightly larger than Vienna. The Berlin of 1815 had been an overgrown court and garrison town. The Berlin of 1848 was a sprawling mixture of settled and raw urban districts. It was a city of outdoor privies and deep gutters that carried waste from the few houses with water closets into the sluggish Spree River—if it did not seep along the way into hundreds of public fountains and the thousands of wells from which Berliners drew their drinking water. Typhus, typhoid fever, and cholera took a heavy toll in infant mortality, especially in the poorer districts. In the city's new northern sections factories employed thousands of artisans and industrial workers, many of whom lived in squalor. Early in March the Borsig steam engine factory laid off four hundred workers—about a third of its total labor force—and other manufacturers also cut back production. Hundreds of Berlin workers were thus free to roam the streets and join in demonstrations. Unemployment in other Prussian cities likewise facilitated the mobilizing of crowds.

Middle-class leaders realized both the opportunity and the danger as soon as they heard of the revolution in France. First from Cologne and other Rhineland cities and then from central and eastern Prussia, petitions were sent to the government in Berlin from chambers of commerce, asking for the reforms being demanded by the liberals in the south German states. In Berlin itself, news from France aroused both hope and consternation. An observer in the Prussian capital on February 28 noted the "amazement, the terror, the confusion" provoked there by the "latest reports from Paris crowding on each other almost hourly."

As early as March 7 public gatherings were calling for liberal and democratic reforms. On March 13 revolutionary demands were heard in a large Tiergarten demonstration. Sporadic clashes between soldiers and the crowd became widespread the next day when the troops tried to clear demonstrators from Berlin's streets and squares. The crowds reacted by erecting barricades out of barrels, timber, stones, and other materials and defending themselves. Again during the night of March 15 there were street battles. The following day Berliners heard the news of Metternich's fall from power; once more street fights broke out, leaving several dead and wounded.

The king's inclination to make concessions was strengthened by the news from Vienna. On March 17 he decided to lift the censorship, and the following morning he received delegates bearing demands for reforms. Frederick William IV informed his visitors that he was calling a United Diet to meet on April 2 to plan the drafting of a constitution for Prussia; further, that he would propose the creation of a unified Germany with a German parliament. When this news reached crowds preparing to march to the royal palace to press their demands, they came instead to thank the monarch, who appeared on the balcony and was greeted with an ovation. But the citizenry felt only hatred for the army that had been shooting into its ranks for several days, and there were demands that the troops be removed entirely from the city.

The festive mood at the palace on March 18 quickly turned into tragedy. Shouts for removal of the army increased. The king, fearful of the mob, was unwilling to move his army out of Berlin and ordered troops to clear the courtyard. With drawn swords, the soldiers managed to expel most of the demonstrators without injuries, but then two shots were fired and pandemonium broke loose. Driven out of the palace grounds, students, intellectuals, other middle-class citizens, and large numbers of workers threw up hundreds of barricades. For eight hours into the frenzied night, liberals and radicals fought elbow to elbow against the Prussian army. Some 255 revolutionaries and probably as many soldiers were left dead. A few industrial workers and a much larger number of artisans accounted for a majority of the dead revolutionaries.

With fifteen thousand troops in or around the city, resolute continuation of the fighting probably would have ended the Berlin revolt in short order. But such an end might have provoked a broader revolution throughout Prussia. No one will ever know because the indecisive ruler again determined to appease the crowd. He issued a conciliatory appeal to his "dear Berliners" and ordered practically all troop units off the streets in the morning of March 19. At about noon the royal couple—the king showing the black-red-gold colors that the liberals had taken over from the Burschenschaften—paid respect to the dead rebels, whose corpses were borne to the palace by their apparently victorious comrades. ("We all crawled on our bellies," Frederick William later recalled.) Having agreed to the creation of a militia, the king withdrew the last units of the regular army from the city on March 20 and 21. On the latter day he rode through the streets of Berlin again wearing a black-red-gold arm band. That night he issued another proclamation to his subjects "and to the German *Volk*," pledging himself to work for German unity. The creation of a German national state seemed assured.

On March 22, Frederick William repeated his promise of a constitution for Prussia and added assurances of freedom of association and assembly, a responsible ministry, introduction of trial by jury, and other reforms. The victory of the revolution seemed as complete as middle-class liberals wanted it to be when the king on March 29 created a new ministry led by the Cologne merchant-banker Ludolf Camphausen, with David Hansemann the new minister of finance. But for many liberals the revolution had already gone too far. Fear of the workers began to replace concern about the king and the conservative nobles. As early as March 24 young Rudolf Virchow noted that middle-class Berliners were "already considering how to distribute the political rights unequally among the various members of the nation."

When the United Diet promised by the king met on April 2 to arrange for election of a Constituent Assembly for Prussia, even more conservative voices were once again heard in public. Otto von Bismarck, a thirty-three-year-old Junker and a loyal monarchist, refused to join in an expression of thanks to the new ministry; he could not "rejoice" and be "thankful," he said, for what he considered "to have been a mistaken course." But the majority of the United Diet was sufficiently concerned about the sensitivities of the lower classes to provide for equal and secret suffrage for all adult males not receiving poor relief. At the same time, wanting to spare the Constituent Assembly the full democratic effects of universal suffrage, the Diet also provided for indirect election of the delegates. Thus, even in the midst of revolution, the future Prussian constitution was to be the work of an elite, though this group would be more open than the hitherto dominant aristocracy.

The Constituent Assembly elected on May 1 was nevertheless generally representative of the Prussian people. It included craftsmen, peasants, salaried employees, intellectuals, merchants, lawyers, doctors, clergymen, and a good many nobles. Reflecting government opinion, the British minister to Prussia incorrectly reported to London that the Kingdom's first parliamentary gathering contained an excess of members from the lower orders. When the assembly met for the first time on May 22 its majority of liberals was challenged by a large group of democrats. Prussia's future appeared to hang in the balance between these divided heirs of the revolution.[6]

Prussia, the toughest ally of Metternich's Austria in obstructing reform before 1848, had itself experienced the most violent revolution of all the north German states. With neither of the two great powers able to impede its course, upheaval shook most of the remaining state capitals of Germany in March 1848.

In Saxony, Alexander Braun, lawyer and president of the lower house of parliament, and Heinrich Brockhaus, a Leipzig publisher, led the liberal opposition against the conservative ministry in Dresden. Democrats, lacking parliamentary power, gathered support from the factory workers and the lower middle class, especially in Leipzig. The court city of Dresden escaped the first agitation of March 1848, but it too experienced general unrest when King Friedrich August rejected demands presented from more radical Leipzig. Under mounting pressure, the king by March 13 raised the censorship, created a more genuinely liberal ministry under Braun's leadership, and called the parlia-

ment to meet on March 20. In the months that followed, legislation was passed to provide freedom of assembly, trial by jury,
and even a democratic suffrage. Saxony's democratic leaders
held no positions in the government, and neither the king nor
his ministry showed real enthusiasm for German unity; but in
the spring of 1848 the consolidation of liberalism in Saxony
seemed an assured result of the revolution, which had been
marked by little violence.[7]

Demonstrations and petitions in Hanover had convinced King
Ernst August that his conservative principles must give way if
he wanted to keep his throne. "Our King . . . has made unheard
of concessions," the noted chemist Friedrich Wöhler wrote in
March to his distinguished collaborator Justus von Liebig in
Giessen. In March and April the king decreed freedom of the
press; created a new ministry including Carl Bertram Stüve, the
leader of the liberal opposition and a former *Burschenschafter*;
consented to the creation of a militia; and agreed to restore the
constitution of 1833. The liberals were satisfied, although the
right to vote was not gained by all Hanoverians.

Neighboring Braunschweig's ruler, after a little hesitation,
agreed to the March 3 demands for freedom of the press, the
right of citizens to bear arms, trial by jury, public court proceedings, and endorsement of a national assembly for Germany.
During the spring and summer new suffrage legislation gave all
adult males in Braunschweig the right to vote, though not in full
equality. Meanwhile, nearby Oldenburg also experienced the
revolution. When a large crowd demonstrated outside his palace
on March 10, the grand duke granted a constitution for his
previously absolutist state, and he further agreed on March 18
that the ministry should be made responsible to the future
parliament. In feudal Mecklenburg, the grand duke and the
estates had ruled before 1848 without benefit of popular representation; but unrest in Schwerin and Rostock persuaded the
monarch on March 23 to promise "that Mecklenburg would join
the ranks of constitutional states."[8]

The luck of the reformers-turned-revolutionaries was mixed
in the republics of Hamburg, Bremen, and Lübeck. Each of
these three important port cities was controlled before 1848 by a
handful of wealthy merchant families; in each, most inhabitants

were denied the right to vote. In April 1848 the city fathers of
Lübeck quickly accepted a new constitution that had been under
consideration for two years. After outbreaks occurred in the fall
of 1848, universal and equal manhood suffrage was introduced.
In Bremen, meanwhile, the ruling Senate had bowed on March
8 before the movement for reform. A constitutional assembly,
elected by equal and universal manhood suffrage, worked slowly
from April 19 on into the next year.

Hamburg before 1848 recognized as full citizens only those
inhabitants who had inherited homes of their own. These—a
small minority of the total population—were entitled to attend
town meetings (*Bürgerkonvente*) somewhat like those in the Swiss
cantons. In normal times few bothered, leaving the patrician
Senate to run the city-state. But on March 3, 1848, liberals and
democrats demanded reforms. At first they accomplished only
the lifting of censorship. The arrest of democratic leaders in
August provoked greater popular support for the left. The arrested men had to be released, and in September the Senate
gave in to the joint demands of liberals and democrats for the
election through equal suffrage of a constitutional assembly.
Friction between liberals and democrats within this body and
disagreements between it and the conservative Senate persisted
through the winter and even beyond 1849. (In fact, the new
constitution of Hamburg was not enacted until 1861.)

In the west German states of Hesse-Darmstadt and Hesse-
Cassel, democrats were active in March 1848, but they were
quickly put down by coalitions of princes and liberals.

In Hesse-Darmstadt, concessions made early in March by
Grand Duke Ludwig II—brought to power after the disturbances
of 1830—were made in vain. Ludwig was forced to abdicate in
all but title. A reform ministry then undertook to enact the
classic liberal reforms. It was headed at first by Heinrich von
Gagern, who had led vigorous parliamentary criticism of government policy during 1847 and early 1848. Under Gagern the liberal
ministry acted with shrewdness and force against the uprising
of peasants and town workers in the Odenwald, Upper Hesse,
Mainz, and Worms. Though democrats in Hesse-Darmstadt were
far from satisfied and peasant unrest in the Odenwald was not

pacified, the liberal ministry's control of army and police was decisive.

In Hesse-Cassel the March revolution boiled up from the factory town of Hanau in the southern part of the state. Elector Frederick William, who had just begun his reign in 1847, approved the characteristic liberal demands, including election of a national German parliament. The liberal ministry he created soon implemented freedom of religion, press, and assembly; trials in public and by jury; and subordination of the army to parliamentary control. It also restored order. Democrats were not satisfied, but the liberals and moderate conservatives controlled the state.[9]

Thus the revolution in March and early April 1848 had scored triumphs for liberalism in all parts of Germany: from the Russian frontier to France, from Lübeck on the Baltic to the Main River and on down to the tollgates of Switzerland one could travel through contiguous but separate German states, all governed in April by ministries in which liberals worked side by side with conservative bureaucrats—bureaucrats who had thwarted them before the princes discovered in conservatism's Ides of March that the liberals were not such bad fellows after all.

The new coalition of liberals and moderate conservatives took on a national dimension in April 1848. The German Confederation had served from 1815 as an alliance of princes to repress liberalism and democracy in all the states of Germany. Soon after liberal successes were achieved in the state revolutions in March, a loose alliance of the liberalized governments of the various states began to develop an unwritten compact, the purpose of which was to make certain that liberalism and limited monarchy would prevail everywhere against both reaction and democracy. The first place in which the democrats in a single state were set back by the intervention of liberal-conservative governments in other states was Baden. For it was here that the democrats and republicans were strongest, most uncompromising, and in the spring of 1848 most willing to use force.

The Baden of 1848 had a few mills in its small towns, but for the most part it was a picturesque country of hills, trees, and little streams that rushed white past one turn to lie in crystalline tranquillity around the next. The two largest towns, Mannheim and Karlsruhe, had populations of only twenty thousand each; Freiburg, the third largest, had only 15,300. From sparkling Lake Constance in the south to the cloud-shrouded firs of the Black Forest slopes in the west, the outward eye saw the land and its people much as they had been for centuries. But the complaints of the hill people had been intensified by hunger in 1847, and the ideas that circulated were more modern than the countryside appeared. Baden was at the confluence of radical ideas and radical men, crossing its borders from France in the west and from republican Switzerland to the south, or coming down the Rhine—especially after steamboating enabled Mannheim to become an inland port in the 1840's—from Belgium, England, and even America. Badeners had long been receptive to liberal doctrines and interested in reports of democracy from across the ocean. Spokesmen for political reform were stronger than ever before in the state parliament elected in 1846. They lost no time in 1848 in pressing their demands upon Grand Duke Leopold, and they found impatient supporters outside the Landtag.

On February 27 democrats and liberals met together in Mannheim, where the Neckar flows into the Rhine. There they agreed on a set of common demands: the right to bear arms, freedom of the press, trial by jury, and creation of a national parliament for Germany. On March 1 armed demonstrators from all parts of the country swarmed into Karlsruhe—impressive in the geometrical rationality of its planning as an eighteenth-century palace town—to present their demands to the state parliament. Friedrich Hecker—lawyer, German-Catholic, and democrat— was their spokesman, and he added other requests to those that had been drafted in Mannheim. The old insistence that the army be sworn to support the constitution instead of being bound by only a personal oath to the ruler was heard again, as was the call to make ministers responsible to the parliament rather than to the grand duke. The lower house of the state parliament quickly adopted all these demands.

Grand Duke Leopold was shrewd enough to cultivate the liberals in an attempt to ward off the more radical reformers led by Hecker and Gustav von Struve. On March 9 he created a

coalition ministry under the leadership of Karl Georg Hoffmann, since 1831 a liberal member of the Landtag.

Karl Mathy—once a Burschenschafter of Heidelberg, a participant in the Hambach Festival of 1832, and an émigré in
Switzerland, but now a lawyer—became an undersecretary in
the ministry and a leader of those who wanted to block Baden's radical revolutionaries. Karl Theodor Welcker, liberal
professor and veteran member of the state parliament, was
designated as Baden's new representative in the Diet of the
German Confederation—a step that seemed to endorse the movement to create a national parliament for a unified Germany.

The prospects of stopping the revolution with liberal successes
in no way satisfied Hecker and Struve. They and several hundreds of their supporters met on March 19 in the town of
Offenburg, about halfway between Karlsruhe and the Swiss
border, to plan their next moves. Inspired by the knowledge
that autocracy had been humbled in a dozen other states, including Austria, the crowd at Offenburg endorsed Hecker's and
Struve's demands for democratization of Baden's parliament,
separation of church and state, the replacement of all existing
taxes by a progressive income tax, merger of the regular army
into the citizen's militia that had been created earlier in March,
and confisication of the royal domains as state property. Beyond
this, Hecker and Struve hoped to replace the monarchy with a
republic, and the two extremists set about constructing a tightly
organized political party toward this goal. Winning a good many
of the government's troops to their movement, they organized
other armed bands of their own.

All this was alarming to Grand Duke Leopold and to Baden's
liberals as well. On April 8 the Hoffmann ministry began to curb
revolutionary tendencies by arresting a radical editor and leader
of the democrats in Constance. If Hecker was going to create a
republic, he had to act without delay, and he did. Sticking cocks'
feathers into a colorful hat and wrapping belt pistols around a
bright blue blouse, he quickly marched sixty followers out of
Mannheim to mobilize his revolution. He crossed the Rhine,
made his way inside the frontier of newly republicanized France
down to Switzerland, and reentered Baden at Lake Constance.
In the town of Constance he proclaimed the republic on April 12,

asking all the people of Baden to support his provisional government. All able-bodied men were urged to assemble with their
weapons in the town of Donaueschingen. The lines were thus
definitively drawn between liberals and democratic republicans.

Almost a third of Baden's people were peasants on the large
estates of the aristocracy, with social grievances aplenty, and
rural revolutionaries were available in considerable numbers.
On the other hand, it was impossible to concentrate all the
armed rebels in one place. A force of eight hundred men gathered in Donaueschingen under Hecker; near Lake Constance a
former Baden army officer, Franz Sigel, organized another band
of three thousand men; several hundred more were led by an
innkeeper, Josef Weisshaar, on the Upper Rhine. In Switzerland
a German Legion of exiles assembled and armed near Basel for
an invasion of Baden under the leadership of a socialist republican, Johann Philipp Becker. Becker had been one of the speakers
at the Hambach Festival; living in Switzerland since 1838, he
had participated in the Swiss civil war in 1847. The poet Georg
Herwegh, meanwhile, gathered German émigrés in France at
Strasbourg, just across the Rhine from Baden. Altogether, the
rebels mobilized some six thousand armed men in their various
camps, and Hecker fully expected many soldiers of Baden's
army to desert to his side as soon as the battle was joined.

The liberal-conservative ministry was unwilling to depend
exclusively upon its own army to crush the republican uprising.
Before the end of March the grand duke asked for support from
the German Confederation, and the Confederation now came to
his assistance. On April 15 the leaders of the Confederation in
Frankfurt ordered into Baden a contingent of troops from Hesse-
Darmstadt and Nassau. The liberalized ministries of Hesse and
Nassau knew that their own future as well as that of liberalism in Baden was at stake. While Heinrich von Gagern served as
the new minister-president of Hesse-Darmstadt, his brother
Friedrich went south in Baden in command of the intervening
armies. The liberal-conservative ministry in Stuttgart was also
alarmed, and a division of the Württemberg army participated in
this first intervention of the liberalized state governments in the
affairs of a member state of the Confederation.

The opposing forces met on April 20 not far from the Swiss

frontier. Friedrich von Gagern was killed early in the fighting, but the rebels were routed. Hecker, disguised as a peasant, fled into Switzerland, as did many of his supporters. One by one, the bands of republican volunteers were quickly crushed. Freiburg, a rebel stronghold, was taken by the government's troops in short order. Offenburg gave up the rebel cause, and the troops of Hesse and Nassau quelled outbreaks of violence in Mannheim. By early May the republican uprising was defeated throughout Baden, and charges of treason were brought against some thirty-five hundred participants. The German revolutions would not be taken over by democratic republicanism. The liberal advocates of constitutional monarchy, as much as the conservative supporters of absolutism on the run, had stopped this course—at least for the moment.[10]

To many German revolutionaries, suppression of the Baden republic by forces of the German Confederation accentuated the need to create a German state with a democratic central government. Liberals were just as anxious to unite Germany under a government that would be representative, but not fully democratic. So both groups participated in the creation and work of a national constituent assembly in the spring of 1848—men of divergent political views held together by a common nationalism.

The demand for greater unity and more representative government for the German Confederation had grown rapidly during the year before revolutions broke out. A revolt among Russia's Polish subjects in 1846, the successful struggle for more democratic and centralized government in Switzerland in 1847, and increasing indications that Denmark would absorb the largely German inhabitants of Schleswig and Holstein unless prevented by a strong Germany—all these events had stimulated the desire for national unity among the Germans. The liberal merchant of Mannheim, Friedrich Bassermann, as early as February 12, 1848 —before the revolution in France—had attracted national attention by calling in Baden's parliament for the creation of an assembly of state parliamentarians alongside the Federal Diet to achieve "more common legislation and more unified national institutions." At the end of February, Heinrich von Gagern had been moved by Bassermann's initiative to introduce a similar motion in the state parliament of Hesse-Darmstadt. Speaking a few days after the revolution in Paris, Gagern vaguely cited external dangers to Germany to justify vigorous steps toward unity. The leadership of affairs, he said, should be placed in the hands of a national cabinet. The chief minister would govern in cooperation with a council of princes and a representative "council of the people."

Because of the wide publicity given the Bassermann and Gagern proposals and the responsive chords they agitated, the creation of a parliament for Germany as a whole was a common demand of liberals in all the state revolutions, and several rulers indicated their approval. Even before the revolutions made much progress, the first step was taken by Friedrich Römer to achieve a national representative body. The fifty-four-year-old lawyer—leader of Württemberg's liberals—arranged a meeting of fifty-one liberals and democrats in Heidelberg on March 5. At this early stage of the revolution and on into early April, liberals and democrats made common cause in the movement for national unification as they had done in March to force concessions from the frightened princes of the German states. Thus the Heidelberg meeting included the Baden radicals, Hecker and Struve—whose ill-fated republican revolution was then more than a month in the future—as well as Baden's liberal leaders Welcker and Bassermann. The meeting also included Adam von Itzstein—still trying at seventy-three to bridge the gap between liberals and radicals, Heinrich von Gagern from Hesse-Darmstadt, Johann Dietrich Dresel from Nassau, David Hansemann from Rhenish Prussia, and other veteran liberals from western and southern Germany.

The group that assembled in Heidelberg on March 5 agreed that early elections to a national assembly should be held. Beyond this it could not agree. Hecker and Struve foresaw the creation of a German republic. Gagern and the majority in Heidelberg wanted to create a union of princely states under a limited monarch. A committee of seven was designated to arrange for a large meeting of representatives from all the German states in Frankfurt, there to make definite plans for the election of a national constituent assembly. Men who favored monarchy were in a majority in the committee, and it was this committee that decided whom to include in the proposed meeting. It invited all former and present members of state parliaments and other corporative bodies in Germany, plus selected additional persons.

On March 31 the much larger group met for the first time in Frankfurt. The timing was auspicious. Liberalism was triumphant in most of the German states by the end of March, and the Federal Diet itself—left over from the Metternich era but with altered membership—on March 30 asked the state governments of the German Confederation to facilitate the election of a national constituent assembly. The 574 participants in the meeting that began on March 31 had been called together independently of the Diet, but their function was to plan for just such elections. Their meeting thus came to be called the "Preliminary Parliament" (Vorparlament). Representatives came from all the German states and included 141 Prussians but only two Austrians.

The Vorparlament had been called to the election of a constituent assembly, but its radical wing at first tried to persuade it to decide at once several basic questions about Germany's future. Gustav von Struve presented the radical program during the first meeting. He realized the necessity of permanently disarming the forces of conservatism throughout Germany before they could recover from the March revolutions. Thus he aimed the first of his fifteen demands at the most crucial institution of all, the standing armies of the German states, and proposed that they be dissolved. His second was pointed at the next most important institution of the traditional governments, the professional bureaucracies, and these too he would disband. As a good German-Catholic, he also proposed the separation of church and state, believing that the traditional churches would continue to be on the side of conservatism.[11]

Struve also would abolish the existing tax structure, remove all established privileges, and remedy the distress of the lower classes by social reform. Then, striking directly at the institution he was trying to undermine in several of his other demands, Struve's fifteenth point called for: "Elimination of hereditary monarchy and its replacement by freely elected parliaments, led by freely chosen presidents, all united in federative constitution after the pattern of the North American free states."

One can only speculate about the course of German history if the Vorparlament had adopted Struve's program. Germany might have become a democratic republic at that time. It seems more probable, however, that adoption of such a program would have precipitated an immediate, desperate, and successful counterrevolution. For the moment, the monarchs of Germany were not put to such a test because a majority in the Vorparlament opposed Struve's program. Heinrich von Gagern spoke of realism for the majority; knowing the power still inherent in the old order, he urged the assembly not attempt the impossible. He accurately pointed out that the majority was "true to the principle of monarchy." From the voting on a related issue, it would seem that no more than some 150 of the 574 participants were republicans. Thus the Vorparlament finally agreed that a "National Assembly should be elected on May 1; that the suffrage could vary according to the systems in effect in the separate states; and that in each state one representative was to be chosen for every fifty thousand inhabitants." The Vorparlament adjourned on April 4. Delegates such as Gagern returned home to consolidate liberalism. Others—most notably Struve and Hecker—two weeks later were trying in Baden to build a democratic republic by force; by the time elections to the National Assembly were held, their Baden republic had gone down in defeat.

The German states held elections on or about May 1, each in its own way. In five of the states almost all adult males were permitted to vote, but more commonly suffrage was restricted by property or tax requirements. In six states voting was direct; in all the others, including Prussia, the voters chose electors who in turn elected the delegates. There is reason to believe that the combination of official restrictions and their own apathy kept a majority of the adult males of Germany from casting votes; for those who did go to the polls, secret balloting prevailed in several of the states, while voting in others was public. A majority of those chosen were middle-class and aristocratic liberal monarchists. Seventy electoral districts of the Habsburg monarchy failed to choose any delegates at all.[12]

But for the national-minded liberals and democrats of the German states, spring had never come with as much hope as in

1848. It might well have reminded them of a happy stanza in Heine's *Germany: A Winter's Tale* about an earlier May.

> There was bud, then, and blossom on bush and on bough,
> The sunbeams were laughing and winking,
> The birds were all singing and yearning in song,
> And the people were hoping and thinking. . . .

About 380 of the delegates chosen to the National Assembly (Nationalversammlung) convened on May 18 in Frankfurt, where Habsburg emperors of the Holy Roman Empire had been crowned from 1562 until Napoleon's time. From all directions they converged on the old city of fifty-eight thousand inhabitants, through the valleys of the Neckar, the Tauber, and the Saale, up the Rhine and down the Main. Some made their way by the rattling new railroad cars, some by carriage, some by river steamer, still others by combinations of these conveyances. For those from neighboring Nassau, Hesse-Darmstadt, and Hesse-Cassel or the nearby districts of northern Bavaria the trip was short and familiar; for others, the convening of the Nationalversammlung meant long journeys from Holstein in the north, the country of the Inn and the Isar of the south, or the far-off eastern provinces of Prussia—a world away—to meet in a strange place with strange men.

Catholics came who had known few but fellow Catholics before: from bustling Rhineland parishes, sleepy Danubian dioceses, and the Oder uplands of Silesia. Protestants came to whom Catholicism was still the hereditary foe: from the Elbe-drained lands of middle Germany, from Lutheran strongholds in Pomerania and the Mecklenburgs. Many of these men were from cities that exceeded Frankfurt in size or trade or even historical tradition; others, knowing nothing and caring less for city ways, were soon homesick for thinly populated heaths and hills, for undulating stretches of rye or wheat, or for shadowed stands of beech and oak, spruce and pine. Different men from varying environs they were, speaking sundry dialects; but a strong if nebulous sense of being Germans provided a common bond for most of them, and the shared will to create a German political community gave them a high sense of calling. They constituted the first elected parliament ever to meet for Germany as a whole. Their convening in Frankfurt in 1848 was for most the greatest adventure and the supreme challenge of a lifetime.

Altogether, more than eight hundred persons became members of the Nationalversammlung, some as replacements for original members who resigned. These men were not professional and salaried politicians, and many could not attend regularly. Those who arrived in time assembled for the first meeting on May 18 in Frankfurt's old town hall (the Römer). From there they soon filed in ceremonial procession into St. Paul's Church, where most subsequent meetings were held. Attendance in the *Paulskirche* meetings thereafter increased, ranging much of the time from four to five hundred members.

The delegates were well-educated, 81.6 percent having attended universities. Several noted liberal professors were among them, including Dahlmann, Jakob Grimm, Welcker, and Robert von Mohl. A majority of the members were men of what might be called the intelligentsia; no fewer than 92 were former *Burschenschafter*. But this was not a parliament of "professors" as is still sometimes suggested; among the 812 delegates there were 49 university professors and approximately 75 other teachers. There were 43 writers (including Julius Fröbel, Arnold Ruge, and the poet Ludwig Uhland); some 39 clerics (about equally divided between the Catholic and Protestant faiths); and 26 medical doctors. At least 216 lawyers and judges (106 *Rechtsanwälte*, 110 *Richter* and *Staatsanwälte*) were elected. All in all, 325 members and substitutes were officers and civil servants of one sort or another, and the number of persons in the service of the state and municipal governments is increased to at least 436 if the professors, teachers, and librarians thus employed are included. Some 153 members were noblemen. Agrarian interests were represented by many of the bureaucrats and noblemen and by the 46 who were most specifically identified as independent farmers. While 49 merchants and factory owners were included (Friedrich Bassermann among them), only 4 craftsmen (and no factory workers or small peasants) sat in the National Assembly. Hundreds of thousands of workers and peasants had voted, but they had cast their ballots for men they recognized by custom as their "betters."

In the absence of organized political parties, members of the National Assembly grouped themselves into clubs according to their political views, taking the names of hotels and restaurants where they held meetings. (The main ones, ranging from left to right, were the *Donnersberg*, the *Deutsche Hof*, the *Württembergische Hof*, the *Casino*, and the *Café Milani*.) Because middle- and upper middle-class representatives held a solid majority in the assembly, it is scarcely surprising that in political orientation —if we summarize the political groupings that were formed and reformed during the months of debate—liberals rather than democrats held the upper hand. This was strongly suggested from the beginning in two emotionally related actions: while choosing Heinrich von Gagern as its presiding officer, the National Assembly denied a seat to Friedrich Hecker, whose republican rebellion in Baden had cost the life of Gagern's brother a month earlier. Republicans formed a tenacious, vigorous, and sizable minority. When the National Assembly voted on a provisional chief executive for Germany, 171 ballots were cast for a republican candidate, 355 against.[13]

While the majority of delegates in Frankfurt clearly wanted a united German monarchy, in May 1848 there was the possibility that the country might become democratic as well. For in addition to the delegates who wanted to create a democratic republic, a large group hoped that Germany would become democratic within a monarchical framework.

The men who were to lead the fight for democratic government in the Nationalversammlung during the next year reflected in their persons all the forces that had created a movement for democracy during the *Vörmarz*. Jakob Venedey represented the living French tradition of 1789. This radical lawyer, son of a Rhenish republican of the 1790's, had been imprisoned for participating in the Hambach Festival in 1832, had escaped to France, and had not returned to Germany until 1848. Ludwig Simon— another democratic spokesman from the Rhineland— was a lawyer from Trier who was blessed with a keen and logical mind and with a resounding voice that he used to good advantage in the *Paulskirche*. Moritz Mohl, like Venedey, had lived for a long time in France. An economist and political scientist who had served as a state official in Württemberg during a score of years before 1848, he stood to the left of his liberal brother, Robert von Mohl, and dropped the aristocratic "von" from his name.

The role of science in the growth of German democracy is reflected in the fact that 26 of the delegates—3.2 percent, or 1 of every 31—were medical doctors and that only 4 of the 26 appear to have joined conservative political clubs at Frankfurt. The tendency of science to give rise to political progress was reflected also in the careers of four of the leading democratic delegates in the Frankfurt Assembly. Wilhelm Löwe, a physician from Calbe in Prussian Saxony, was only thirty-four in 1848. The parliamentary career he then began would, with one major interruption, last until his death in 1886. Karl Vogt, three years younger than Löwe, was a nephew of Karl Follen and the son of a professor of pharmacology. Vogt had known Georg Büchner as a fellow student of medicine in 1833–34 at Giessen; subsequently he had collaborated with Louis Agassiz in Switzerland in research that Charles Darwin would use in the development of his theory of evolution; had lived in Paris from 1844 to 1846; and had been called back to Giessen as a professor in 1847 at the age of thirty. Science also figured in the pre-1848 career of Emil Adolph Rossmässler, author of published studies of iconography, botany, and zoology while holding a professorship in an academy of forestry at Tharandt near Dresden. In the mid-1840's Rossmässler had joined the dissident German-Catholic movement. So had Franz Wigard. Like Löwe, Wigard in time became a physician; and like Venedey, Vogt, and many other democrats, he was an admirer of the United States. He wanted a united German republic with an elected president on the American pattern. He performed an important service to the National Assembly by serving as the editor of the stenographic minutes of the debates, in which he himself was an active participant.

Several of the democrats in the Frankfurt Assembly were academicians. As a professor of economics at Marburg, Bruno Hildebrand had antagonized government authorities by his vigorous defense of academic freedom and had been dismissed from the faculty in 1846 for criticizing the ruler of Hesse-Cassel.

Karl Mittermaier was a well-known professor of jurisprudence at Heidelberg and a seasoned parliamentarian who had sat since 1831 in Baden's Chamber of Deputies and had served several terms as its president. Mittermaier was an admirer of American government. So was Karl Nauwerck, who had found his way into politics through a crisis over academic freedom at the University of Berlin. As a young instructor Nauwerck had been told in 1843 that he must abstain from lecturing on political subjects, whereupon he had resigned his instructorship; in the first municipal elections after the incident, he had been elected to the City Assembly of Berlin.

Economic self-interest appears to have played little if any part in making democrats of these men of the middle class. Its part in shaping the political attitudes of Bernhard Eisenstuck was ambiguous. Nephew of Christian Gottlob, a liberal leader of the Saxon Landtag since 1830, Eisenstuck was apprenticed in a Chemnitz factory at fourteen, rose to become part owner, but never lost his sympathy for the workers. As a co-founder of an association of artisans, he had advocated prolabor legislation through the bleak 1840's.

There were many other supporters of democracy in the National Assembly, but these men were fairly representative of the others in background and were its most vigorous spokesmen during the crucial debates on the suffrage system. The dynamic Robert Blum would have been among them but for his untimely death. On the franchise issue the democrats would get help from a number of other delegates who normally did not support democratic measures but who had specific reasons for favoring universal and equal suffrage. These part-time supporters of democracy would include such opposite types as Gabriel Riesser, the Jewish liberal from Hamburg, and old Friedrich Ludwig Jahn, who had founded the Turnvereine in 1810 to whip up pride in Germandom against Napoleon.[14]

The election of such men to a National Assembly testified to the sudden major alterations in political conditions in the German states in March and April 1848. The collaboration of liberal and democratic leaders—supported by middle-class, working-class, and peasant demonstrators and at times by armed rebellion—had effected changes that otherwise could not have

been won so early. In May, notwithstanding the obvious differences that had arisen between them in the various state
revolutions, liberals and democrats remained hopeful that they
could work together to unify their country. No one could yet say
whether Germany would settle for the partial achievement of
liberal goals or become democratic. The survival of monarchy
and aristocracy in the German states during the turbulent spring
weeks offered a strong indication of the outcome unless democrats could mobilize greater power than they had assembled in
Baden in April. But outbreaks of violence were sporadically
continuing, and neither democracy's advocates nor its enemies
could be certain in mid-May whether 1848 would mark its solid
foundation or only a dramatic failure.

V.

THE FRUSTRATION OF
DEMOCRATIC UNITY,
1848–1849

As much as the democrats of Germany desired political equality in their separate states, a democratic government for a unified German nation was an even more compelling goal in 1848. Many liberals agreed that national unity was all-important. A full year was to pass after May 1848, however, before the final showdown occurred between the forces of democratic and liberal unification and their conservative and particularist foes. But in several skirmishes along the way within individual states, the inability of liberal and democratic nationalists to stand together became increasingly apparent, foreshadowing their ultimate failure to realize their far-reaching national ambitions.[1]

In the summer of 1848 the National Assembly acted as if German unity were an accomplished fact. While beginning work on a constitution, the assembly functioned as a provisional all-German parliament. On June 29 it created a provisional executive for national affairs in the form of a regency. Bidding for Austrian participation in German unity, the assembly elected Archduke Johann, uncle of the Habsburg emperor, as regent of the Reich (*Reichsverweser*). Johann had won considerable popularity among rank and file Germans by opposing Napoleon, by marrying a commoner in 1827, and by supporting German unity in 1848. To aid the sixty-six-year-old chief executive, the assembly set up a provisional Ministry of State. Somewhat hesitantly, the old Diet of the German Confederation turned over its affairs to the Habsburg *Reichsverweser*.

If the new regime was to act as a genuine national government for a united Germany, it could not be content with the functions the Diet had performed. If, on the other hand, it tried to exert greater central power than the Diet, it was almost certain to encounter opposition from the major German states, for revolution had not put an end to particularism. The first conflict between the new central authority and the old sovereign states occurred during the opening weeks of Archduke Johann's regency and on an issue of fundamental importance. Moving against the very core of particularism—the military forces—the Frankfurt Assembly on June 28 declared that the regent was to be endowed with the supreme command of all armed forces. On July 16, the very day after taking office, the minister of war instructed the armies of the separate states to consider themselves at the disposal of the *Reichsverweser*. Particularism responded with undininished vigor. Austria took issue with the declaration. The Prussian government announced that it would retain sole control of its troops. Other states made it equally clear that they would not surrender command of their separate armies.[2]

In short, a Reich army depended on a voluntary transfer of command by the state governments. No major state was likely to curb its own sovereignty except to preserve the new liberal-conservative governments against efforts by democrats to win power by force. The different governments therefore cooperated with the regent and the Frankfurt Assembly only to intervene collectively in several states in the summer and fall of 1848. The first after Baden to experience intervention was Nassau.

In March the revolution had seemed to be developing in Nassau in much the same way as in other German states. In April a liberal leader and former *Burschenschafter*, August Hergenhahn, became head of the ministry in the capital city of Wiesbaden. Supported by the liberal majority in the state parliament, Hergenhahn resisted radical legislation and sought to suppress further unrest. But this did not suit Nassau democrats, who were energetically led by a watchmaker, Georg Böhning. Böhning had fought against Napoleon, served with the Greek rebels in the 1820's, participated in the Hambach Festival in 1832, and helped plan the ill-fated uprising in Frankfurt the following year. When the revolution created a Nassau militia in March 1848, Böhning became its commander. The liberal ministry in Wiesbaden, recognizing in him an effective radical leader, arrested him in July, whereupon the militia mutinied and set him free. At this point Archduke Johann, using the remaining military apparatus of the German Confederation, answered a request for help from Hergenhahn. Austrian and Prussian troops in the service of the German Confederation had been garrisoned for years in Mainz, across the Rhine from Wiesbaden. On July 18 they intervened to uphold Nassau's liberal ministry. Böhning quickly discovered that liberalism as well as the Metternich system could turn democrats into refugees; he fled to Strasbourg. Within a week, the troops of Austria and Prussia had suppressed the democrats of Nassau and returned to their barracks.[3]

The pattern soon repeated in nearby Frankfurt, one of four sovereign city-states within the German Confederation and the seat of the Diet. A few patrician families controlled the Senate, the dominant body of the republic; in March they conceded freedom of association and assembly, but continued to resist the demand for equal political rights. The democrats then took to the streets; after an outbreak of violence on July 6–7 the city government attempted to arrest some of their leaders, but was prevented by popular resistance. In September revolution threatened to go out of control.

The grievances of Frankfurt's democrats focused on the National Assembly. In earlier months the nationalistic assembly had cheered German rebels in the duchies of Schleswig and Holstein and approved the intervention of Hanoverian and Prussian armies to help them win independence from the Danish king. Then, bowing before international pressures, Prussia had signed a truce with Denmark on August 26 without consulting the National Assembly. If Prussia was not overruled, the duchies would be lost, and a *German* defeat would compromise the authority of the assembly. But the Nationalversammlung had no military power of its own, and there was no way to coerce Prussia. After acrimonious debates and a first vote repudiating the armistice, a vote on September 16 upheld the Prussian truce by 257 to 236. To many radicals, the assembly, already suspect for lack of democratic fervor, now appeared wanting in national zeal. Frankfurt's democrats fully shared the chagrin and alarm of their brethren throughout Germany. Almost as soon as the vote had been taken clusters of indignant people began roaming the city, threatening supporters of the armistice and vandalizing their homes. On the seventeenth, twelve thousand persons gathered on Frankfurt's Whitsun Meadow where the radical Germain Metternich (no relation to the exiled Austrian statesman) called for a new revolution.

Though the central authorities were unable to force Prussia to fight Denmark, they quickly demonstrated that they could suppress the democratic outbreaks. In the early hours of September 18 some two thousand Prussian and Austrian troops from Mainz, veterans of the battle of Wiesbaden, moved into Frankfurt, strengthened by artillery units from the army of Hesse-Darmstadt. Workers were especially active in the democratic resistance, but many middle-class citizens were among the five hundred to a thousand participants. By evening the uprising was dispersed, leaving about 60 rebels and soldiers dead and more than 150 wounded. The National Assembly had been saved and its dependence upon the states demonstrated. Radical democracy had suffered another setback.[4]

The Frankfurt uprising in September was the signal for a second attempt in Baden to create a democratic republic. The liberal authorities there had found it easier to scatter Hecker's republicans in April than to eliminate their agitation. Outside Baden's borders—from Switzerland and from France—the revolutionary émigrés of April had regrouped their forces and maintained contact with supporters inside the country. News of the Frankfurt uprising encouraged Gustav Struve to return. On September 21 he crossed the Swiss frontier into the little Baden town of Lörrach, where he and his followers were welcomed with great enthusiasm. From the town hall he proclaimed all of Germany a republic and himself the head of its provisional government. A good many armed Swiss citizens joined the uprising, and Struve was supported by all kinds of German radicals; one of his lieutenants was the young Wilhelm Liebknecht, later to be a leading German Marxist. Both socialist and nonsocialist republican refugees prepared to return from France and Switzerland to participate in the new revolution. But this time the rebellion was crushed before it could get underway. Troops of the Baden government met the rebels at the town of Staufen on September 25 and defeated them after two hours of fighting.

Both sides counted dead and wounded; Struve and his wife were made prisoners.[5]

The September uprisings in Frankfurt and Baden provoked the counterrevolution. Middle-class citizens in all parts of Germany recoiled at the news that Struve had not only threatened confiscation of monarchist property, but at once endeavored to carry out his threat in Lörrach and the surrounding communities. The democratic cause also had been tarnished by the cold-blooded killing of two conservative members of the National Assembly during the Frankfurt uprising. Both events disenchanted middle-class liberals and cemented their alliance with the traditional powers within the several states of Germany.

The liberal central government shared the widespread anxiety about the revolutionary outbreaks in Frankfurt and Baden. As minister of the interior in the provisional national government, Anton von Schmerling expressed to the ministries of the various states his concern about the "democratic associations and popular assemblies." Garrisons in southern, western, and central Germany were instructed to take quick action against "anarchic movements and uprisings," and liberal members of the National Assembly were sent to supervise the suppression of democratic rebels in trouble spots.[6]

The central authorities in Frankfurt showed a continued readiness to employ the armies of the larger states in defense of liberal-conservative arrangements. In the fall, troops from Prussia, Hanover, and Saxony—all of which had liberal ministers—restored order and princely rights in Saxe-Altenburg in central Germany. The liberalized governments of Bavaria, Saxony, and Weimar supplied troops to reestablish the authority of the duke and his liberal ministry in nearby Saxe-Meiningen.[7]

At this point, in November 1848, the restoration of traditional authority in the most powerful states, Austria and Prussia, lessened the chances for national unity and generated new power to suppress the democratic movement throughout Germany. Habsburg emperor and Hohenzollern king had been intimidated in March, but not overthrown; their feudal nobles had been temporarily pushed into the background, but not seriously weakened; and most significant, their armies, though humiliated in March, had been preserved intact. Furthermore, in each of

the two great states of Germany as in the lesser ones, democratic agitation had alienated many liberals. In both Vienna and
Berlin, counterrevolution scored decisive victories in November.

In the fall of 1848, Austria was still fighting revolts of Hun-
garian and Italian nationalists, but Bohemia had been subdued
in June when the artillery of Prince Alfred von Windischgrätz
leveled the barricades in Prague. A new revolution won control over Vienna in the first week of October, again forcing
Emperor Ferdinand to flee the city and putting weapons in the
hands of tens of thousands of rebels. The army that had restored Habsburg power in Prague now turned its guns upon the
capital city of the empire. By October 31, after five days of
bombardment and street fighting, Vienna was under martial
law. Revolutionary leaders were either imprisoned or killed.
Among those who were put to death was Robert Blum, one of
the ablest democratic members of the National Assembly. Under
the autocratic ministry of Prince Felix zu Schwarzenberg, liberal
concessions made earlier were retracted. The weak-minded
Emperor Ferdinand was compelled to abdicate on December 2—
not by revolutionaries, but by the royal family and Schwarzenberg. His eighteen-year-old successor, Franz Joseph, would
not be bound by Ferdinand's promises to the revolutionaries.
Thus began a Habsburg reign that would be a major obstacle
to German unification in 1849, deny autonomy to the Slavic
minorities of Austria, and last until after the death of the emperor
sixty-eight years later; 1918, not 1848, was to be the year of
collapse for the Habsburg monarchy.[8]

After November 1848, Prussia, too, was free to take a firmer
stand on the side of counterrevolution because of changes in its
internal affairs. One element in the shift to the right was the
town and city working class, whose assertiveness alarmed many
middle-class liberals. Prussian workers—primarily artisans—
continued into the autumn to agitate for better wages, shorter
hours, and state guarantees of jobs for all, but their revolutionary
spirit diminished as the supplies of foodstuffs increased and
food prices declined. Many leaders of the newly created organizations of workers in 1848 favored political democracy, but
they tended to give even higher priority to the preservation or
restoration of the guilds' right to regulate access to the various

trades. Socialists and communists were able to win few of the workmen except in Cologne.

Marx (and Engels) had returned to Germany in the spring of 1848, arriving in Cologne on April 11. Marx and the Communist League wanted Germany to become a unitary republic. In the newspaper that he published for the better part of a year, the *Neue Rheinische Zeitung*, Marx concealed his socialist leanings because he needed the subscriptions of many nonsocialists in order to continue to publish this *Organ der Demokratie*, as the paper called itself. Indeed, in June 1848 he even proclaimed the dissolution of the Communist League. By this time, however, middle-class Germans had come to fear the radicalism of Marx and his Cologne associates. After visiting the Rhineland in April, the famous chemist Justus von Liebig wrote to a close friend that Germany was headed toward a total revolution; that "Communism, under the banner of the republic, will swallow us all up."

No such threat really existed. Marx and Engels knew in 1848 that they could win few followers by openly demanding a proletarian revolution. Recognizing their own weakness, they continued to call for a common front and urged workers and peasants to join the democratic cause. But the *Neue Rheinische Zeitung* itself won little support among city workers, even those of Cologne, because its aims lacked clarity and its style presumed an educated audience. It was not easy for unsophisticated men to understand a newspaper (if they read it at all) that called for cooperation among democrats of all types one moment and for the downfall of the bourgeoisie the next; that insisted at the same time upon bourgeois victory in the Revolution of 1848 as an essential fulfillment of the "laws" of historical progress; that denounced the "barbarism" of the craft guilds, which many workers in 1848 wanted to revive. As the organ of Cologne's large Workers' Society commented on July 25, "the music is pitched so high we, unfortunately, can't whistle the tune."

The spirit of Prussia's artisans after the spring of 1848 was better reflected by labor spokesmen who met in Berlin from August 23 to September 3 under the leadership of a Berlin typesetter, Stephan Born. Though democratic, they declared: "We, the workers, are by nature the support of calm and order." This meeting marked the creation of the first all-German working-class association, the General German Workers' Brotherhood (Allgemeine deutsche Arbeiterverbrüderung). Led by Born, the Verbrüderung in the following months strove to bridge the gap between workers in various trades and regions. Its aims were better working conditions, improved living standards, and full rights of citizenship for the individual working man in Germany. In Prussia as in other states, it called for equal suffrage for all men and vigorously supported the democratic movement. But it represented a mere twelve thousand workers, and they were only loosely linked to its central committee, which was established in Leipzig in September 1848.[9]

In Prussia as in other German states in 1848, the divisions among middle-class citizens operated as decisively against the attainment of democracy as did the weaknesses of labor. Differences between liberals and democrats had become apparent even before the election of the Prussian Constituent Assembly on May 1, and they became more troublesome thereafter. The body of 402 delegates that met in Berlin was divided into a left wing, determinedly democratic and inclined to favor a republic; a right wing of moderate conservatives and conservative liberals; and a sizable center that had trouble making up its mind. All in all, the Constituent Assembly was substantially more democratic in outlook than the liberalized Prussian ministry headed by Ludolf Camphausen, which presented its draft for Prussia's first constitution to the opening meeting of the assembly on May 22.

Reflecting the March demands of the liberals, the ministry's draft constitution would leave the king with command over the army, the right to appoint ministers of his own choice, and the authority to veto legislation. The aristocracy and other propertied classes would be given special representation in an upper house, equal suffrage would be provided for all adult males, but balloting would be indirect. This draft constitution provoked prolonged discussion in May, June, and July—punctuated by sporadic outbreaks of violence in the streets of Berlin. A wild demonstration of workers, students, and other radicals on June 14—waving red flags and calling for creation of a republic—culminated in the most serious outbreak since March, an attack on the Berlin armory, and it was calmed only with difficulty. King Frederick William IV blamed the debacle on Camphausen and replaced him with a liberal bureaucrat, Rudolf von Auers-wald, and a cabinet really led by David Hansemann.[10]

Ministry and assembly continued to go different ways. On July 26 the constitutional committee of the latter, led by Franz Benedikt Waldeck, a Westphalian Catholic and a democrat of personal warmth and organizational ability, produced its own constitution. This Waldeck Charter was more democratic than the ministry's draft in several ways. It proposed to supplement and check the standing army by a national militia, most of whose officers would be elected by the men. It would eliminate the monarch's absolute veto; bills passed unchanged three times by both houses of parliament would become law even if the king opposed them. Both houses would be elected by universal and equal manhood suffrage, as the democrats wished. At the same time, the Waldeck committee made concessions to the liberals. It proposed that the suffrage be indirect, and it would not give the proposed parliament the power to bring down a ministry by a vote of "no confidence." The Waldeck Charter thus provoked additional lengthy and acrimonious debates. Too democratic to suit the ministry, it was not democratic enough to satisfy the radicals. Conservatives found it altogether intolerable.

The weaknesses of the working class and divisions between liberals and democrats revived confidence among the conservatives. At the royal court unregenerate nobles such as the brothers Leopold and Ludwig von Gerlach urged the king to reassert his power and dissolve the Constituent Assembly. The noble landlords of Prussia sought to influence popular opinion by starting a newspaper of their own, the *Neue Preussische Zeitung*; appealing to the religious instincts of Prussia's Protestants, it carried a cross on its masthead and was soon known as the *Kreuzzeitung*. Seeking to play off the craftsmen against the liberal industrialists, it condemned "anarchic industrial freedom" and called for the revival of craft guilds. The conservative aristocrats also promised significant concessions to the peasantry; they offered to give up the collection of manorial dues and to surrender the police and judicial powers that they had exercised on their estates. The Prussian War Ministry, meanwhile, denounced the idea of electing officers, as proposed for the militia by the Waldeck committee, and in November made explicit in the title of a pamphlet what it privately had been preaching all along: "Against democrats only soldiers help."

The possibility that the army might be put to work to restore royal authority and noble privilege in Prussia caused continuing concern among the democrats. As early as August they attempted to lessen the danger by demanding a purge of all army officers who could not reconcile their political convictions with the new constitutional order. But when the Constituent Assembly on September 7 reasserted this demand, the Auerswald-Hansemann ministry resigned. It appeared that Prussia's monarch now must either accept genuine parliamentary control of the military or defy the Constituent Assembly. But Frederick William still wavered. As a concession to the reactionaries, he appointed one of their own, General Friedrich von Wrangel, as commander of the armed forces between the Elbe and the Oder rivers. But the king balanced the naming of Wrangel with another partial concession to the assembly. The new ministry was headed by Ernst von Pfuel, an army officer of liberal reputation; and Pfuel in his additional capacity as minister of war issued a vigorous condemnation of reactionary attitudes within the officer corps.

For democrats in Prussia, the last days of October were pivotal. In an attempt to counteract the federal collaboration of the liberals and conservatives, radicals from several German states held a second Democratic Congress in Berlin from October 26 to 31. (A preliminary congress had met in Frankfurt in June.) In the Berlin gathering Stephan Born, Arnold Ruge, Wilhelm Weitling, and a host of other socialists and liberal democrats— 234 altogether, representing 140 towns and cities—pledged themselves to work for a republic and the rights of man, but they could not agree on a specific course of action. The congress was most united in support of Ruge's unrealistic demand that Prussia intervene on behalf of the Viennese revolutionaries, who were being crushed by the imperial artillery during the very days the democrats met in Berlin. The members appealed for mass support, and on the morning of October 31 a thousand persons made their way to the Prussian Constituent Assembly to watch while Waldeck presented a motion calling on the government to support the Viennese revolution. The assembly decisively voted down Waldeck's motion and everybody went home again. That same day the Democratic Congress adjourned, having shown clearly that it was unable to unleash a second revolution in Prussia.

The Berlin meeting of the democrats had revealed their divisions and their weaknesses. Prussia's Constituent Assembly, meanwhile, had provoked the king and the aristocracy by resolving that the Prussian monarch should no longer be said to rule "by the grace of God" and by abolishing on October 31 all titles except those of public office. When news reached the Hohenzollern court on November 1 that the Viennese revolution had ended in a Habsburg victory, the mood was right for the reassertion of royal authority.

The gauntlet was thrown before the Constituent Assembly the very next day. Informed that the king was recruiting a new ministry under the leadership of Count Friedrich Wilhelm von Brandenburg, a general and an uncle of the monarch, the assembly protested and demanded instead the creation of a representative ministry. The king refused. A week later the new minister-president informed the Constituent Assembly that it was adjourned until November 27, at which time it would meet in the town of Brandenburg. Knowing that they would thus be robbed of the support of Berlin's democratic workers and students, the delegates continued their meeting on November 9 and agreed to reassemble the next day in clear defiance of the royal will.

"Against democrats, only soldiers help," the generals had said. The army that had been removed from Berlin in March returned. Early in the afternoon of November 10, General Wrangel marched into the city with thirteen thousand men. Giving the Constituent Assembly fifteen minutes to evacuate the theater in which its sessions had been held, he kept an eye on his watch while the members, acknowledging their powerlessness, marched out together. Two days later a state of siege was proclaimed in Berlin and its environs. Wrangel ordered the closing of all political clubs, prohibited meetings of more than twenty persons, and reimposed censorship on all publications. The more persistent delegates to the Constituent Assembly repeatedly tried to meet in Berlin, but were prevented from doing so. A few sporadic outbreaks in the provinces were immediately put down by the army.[11]

Force broke the limited power of Prussian democracy in November, and on December 5 a royal decree adjourned the Constituent Assembly in Brandenburg *sine die*, but the Prussian conservatives avoided unqualified reaction. On December 6 the monarch, at the urging of his ministers, promulgated a draft constitution which gave the state a central parliament. The upper house would be elected by men of property who had reached the age of thirty, the lower house by equal, secret, and virtually universal manhood suffrage. In the parliament elected on January 22, 175 of the deputies at first supported the king and his ministry against 158 members of the divided opposition.

Having granted the suffrage to many craftsmen and peasants as well as to the middle class, the government granted other favors to the lower orders to win their loyalty to the crown. Peasants were pleased by renewed assurances that manorial dues would be elimianted and that the tax exemptions and police powers of the nobility would end. In February the artisans rejoiced over the restoration of guild monopolies in some seventy trades. Democrats in the lower house continued to press for more radical reforms, but by May 30, 1849, the king issued a revised constitution—and then he felt strong enough to abandon equal suffrage in favor of a highly undemocratic three-class voting system.[12]

In retrospect, it can be seen that the victory of counterrevolution in Austria and Prussia doomed the movement for democratic unity in Germany, but in November 1848 this was not yet apparent.

The Frankfurt parliament had, from the outset, faced thorny problems and had itself aggravated some of them. For example, it had hoped at first to bring into the German nation all territories that had been embraced by the German Confederation—though Limburg was also part of The Netherlands, Bohemia and Moravia were largely populated by Slavs, and many South Tyroleans were Italians. Although Holstein alone among the king of Denmark's provinces belonged to the Confederation, the Frankfurt Assembly wanted the new German nation to include Schleswig as well. Many delegates were unwilling to leave out Prussia's

eastern territories, although these were heavily Polish in population and had not been included in the Confederation. The
desire to bring these diverse but unattainable areas into the new
German Reich heightened disunity and frustration within the
assembly; abroad it collided with Britain's support of Denmark,
France's fear of a German advance into the Low Countries, and
Russia's extensive interests in Poland. As a consequence, the
assembly was disappointed in its hope for quick diplomatic
recognition by its neighbors. Only the United States and a few
of the smaller nations of Europe established relations with the
emerging government in Frankfurt.

In October the National Assembly's helplessness in the face of
the Viennese revolution and counterrevolution demonstrated
anew that the power of the central government in Frankfurt was
not equal to its pretensions. The authoritarian coup d'état in
Prussia in November brought about another confrontation between the Frankfurt authorities and the forces of particularism.

Until the October events in Vienna, majority sentiment in
the Frankfurt Assembly had favored the inclusion of Austria in
the united German nation and even accepted its leadership.
This was the "Greater German" (*grossdeutsch*) way to unity. But
Viennese radicalism, the way it was suppressed, and the realization that Austria's non-German populations made it impossible
for the Habsburgs to rule Germany caused rising sentiment
in favor of unification under the king of Prussia. This "Small
German" (*kleindeutsch*) way to unification had been handicapped
earlier by Prussia's size, which caused fears that it would dominate in its own interest a Reich without Austria. It had been
handicapped, too, by Prussia's August truce with Denmark in
Schleswig-Holstein. Adjournment of Prussia's Constituent Assembly on November 9 outraged all democrats. Angry speeches
were made and defiant resolutions passed in Frankfurt; but
no amount of anguish in Germany's provisional capital could
undo the armed victory of conservatism in Prussia. Protests and
gestures of intervention only confirmed the impotence of the
Frankfurt government.

Nevertheless, in its preparation of a national constitution the
Frankfurt Assembly continued to act as if its voice would be
obeyed in all the German states. For six months the delegates had

amply discussed a statement of basic constitutional principles for the protection of individual rights. The United States had given the world its Declaration of Independence and its Bill of Rights, and the France of 1789 had issued its Declaration of the Rights of Man. The Frankfurt Assembly borrowed from these pronouncements and reflected special German conditions in putting together its own Declaration of Fundamental Rights (*Grundrechte*). Just before Christmas, a fifty-paragraph document passed by a standing vote after a second reading.

The Declaration of Fundamental Rights admirably embodied those principles on which both liberals and democrats could agree. Proclaiming the *Grundrechte* to be norms "for the constitutions of the German states," the assembly declared that a representative legislature should be created in each state. Every public office was to be "open equally" to all who were qualified, and military duties were "the same for all." The right to form associations and freedom of person, speech, and assembly were proclaimed. Equality before the law and trial by jury were to be implemented throughout Germany. Corporal punishment and the death penalty were abolished. The equal rights of non-German minorities were guaranteed.

The liberal spirit was also reflected in the cultural provisions of the *Grundrechte*. Abolition of all state churches highlighted the provisions separating church and state. Religious associations were to be formed freely and to manage their own affairs. No individual was to be forced to participate in any religious ritual against his will. The repressive measures of the Metternich era were repudiated. Education was to be guaranteed to all through schools and universities freed from the restraints of censorship. Doctrinaire rationalists wanted to purge the schools of religious instruction, but in this they failed; religious instruction was to be permitted in the public elementary schools under the supervision of churches, but otherwise the schools were to be "freed from supervision of the clergy."

Economic liberalism triumphed through the abolition of noble privileges, in the proclamation that "every relationship of bondage or serfdom is ended forever," in the guarantee of the inviolability of property, and in the provisions for freedom of emigration and of movement of the individual to "any part of the territory of the Reich." (The last-mentioned clause confirmed one of the few freedoms embraced by the Germanic Confederation.) Liberalism's victory was finally buttressed by the declaration that every person was free to enter any economic activity he chose; with this *Gewerbefreiheit* one of Adam Smith's central ideas was written into the national constitution, much to the chagrin of thousands of Germany's guild craftsmen.

Aware, however, that particularism was far from dead, some delegates wanted to compromise with it by consulting the state governments before promulgating the *Grundrechte*; others would have none of this. A thirty-one-year-old democratic leader from Württemburg, Adolf Schoder, was among the most aggressive, able, and indefatigable proponents of civil rights. When more conservative delegates on December 21 moved to consult the state governments, Schoder was quick to oppose them, and the motion to negotiate with the states was defeated by a vote of 334 to 69. The assembly resolved on December 23 to publish at once one hundred thousand copies of the Fundamental Rights, without waiting for completion of the constitution; state laws not in harmony with them were to be changed accordingly or be abolished.[13]

Differences of opinion, volubly expressed, on the *Grundrechte* had been thoroughly aired since October 19 in the debates on the structure of government. Agreement was reached on the most important issues, but only after the turn of the year.

The constitution for the new Reich completed on March 27, 1849, represented relatively little compromise with states' rights. It provided that the German states should continue to exist, but under a strong central government. Laws would be made by a German parliament (Reichstag); they would require approval by both an upper house representing the states (Staatenhaus), and a popularly elected lower house (Volkshaus), modeled upon the United States House of Representatives. Half of each state's delegation in the Staatenhaus would be appointed by the state government, half would be chosen by the state parliament. The ministry for the Reich was to be "responsible," but as the liberals wished, no provision was made for "ministerial responsibility" in the English sense; the parliament was not authorized to overthrow a ministry by a vote of "no confidence." The liberals planned a special law to provide for judicial proceedings against ministers who might act unconstitutionally, but it was never enacted. The chief of state was left free to select whatever ministers he pleased; and by January 26 it had been settled that the nation was to be headed by a hereditary monarch, to be called "Emperor of the Germans" (*Kaiser der Deutschen*). After long debates, the assembly decided that the emperor should have only the right to delay legislation, not to wield an absolute veto against measures the parliament might propose. To the satisfaction of the democrats, measures passed by three separate sessions of the parliament would become law without the approval of the emperor.

The democrats, predominantly *grossdeutsch*, had favored a unicameral, popularly elected parliament and had opposed making the head of state hereditary. The liberals defeated them on these issues, but finally yielded to insistence from the left that the lower house should be elected democratically.

The liberal opposition to democratic suffrage did not capitulate without a struggle, for it was led by men who had proved their courage and tenacity many times during the Metternich era—men such as Dahlmann, Welcker, Mathy, Bassermann, Friedrich von Raumer, and Heinrich von Gagern. These men had worked hard for a freer Germany, but they had registered their opposition to democracy well before 1848, and it was hardly surprising that the liberal-controlled constitutional committee on February 15 proposed an undemocratic Reich Election Law. It would deny the vote to domestic servants, apprentices in the crafts, factory workers, and everyone else who was paid by the day. It goes without saying that the committee also sought to disfranchise recipients of public relief funds. The draft of February 15 also provided for open rather than secret balloting. It stipulated direct election of representatives, though a number of liberal members of the assembly—including Heinrich von Gagern—favored the indirect process. Several liberals were opposed to making even the restrictive suffrage equal, proposing instead a system of voting in which each man's ballot would be weighted according to the amount of taxes he paid. The draft presented by the liberal-controlled constitutional committee thus had failed to satisfy either the most conservative of the liberals or the democrats, and by February 19 more than sixty motions to amend it had been submitted.

French and American practices frequently were cited by both the liberals and their democratic opponents in the subsequent debates on the Election Law, as they had been in discussions of the Fundamental Rights and on the issue of a federal versus a unitary state. Some delegates pointed out that not even all Americans voted. The democrats, on the other hand, cited foreign experience (for example, that of France before 1830 and again before 1848) to show that suffrage restrictions perpetuated and aggravated dissent. Another scientist-revolutionary, Karl Vogt—associate of Liebig and Agassiz and a graduate of and professor of medicine in the University of Giessen, alma mater of many German democrats—put the arguments for restricted suffrage in Germany on a level with the defense of slavery in America.

The Frankfurt Assembly included not a single factory worker, craft apprentice, or day laborer, but the right of the workers to equal suffrage was defended as tenaciously as any proletarian could have wished. In the decisive debates of February and March 1849 the argument for a democratic franchise was presented with eloquence and in detail by thirteen middle-class delegates: Eisenstuck, Hildebrand, Jahn, Löwe, Mittermaier, Moritz Mohl, Nauwerck, Riesser, Rossmässler, Ludwig Simon, Venedey, Vogt, and Wigard. Though not present in the assembly, workers did what they could outside the *Paulskirche* to influence the decision. The executive committee of Stephan Born's General Workers' Brotherhood—hearing of the proposed suffrage restriction—distributed ten thousand copies of a protest in all parts of Germany, asking local associations of workers to endorse them with appropriate signatures and send them to Frankfurt as quickly as possible.

Pressures outside the assembly may have swayed some liberals to support equal suffrage. Many shared the democratic distaste for aristocratic rule. Some were moved by a desire to make a unified nation an appealing cause for all Germans. Others, like Max Duncker, went further and accepted concessions to democracy for the sake of unity. "We fought against universal suffrage with every means, but to give up national unity on that ground seemed to me scarcely justified." Though numerically stronger, liberals were so divided on specifics that they could not contain the monolithic advocacy of universal manhood suffrage. When the democrats finally agreed to support offering the German crown to the king of Prussia a bargain was sealed in which they obtained substantially what they wanted. The assembly on February 20 agreed that virtually all males who had reached their twenty-fifth birthday should have the right to vote. The approval of universal manhood suffrage caused conservatives and liberals to renew their efforts for oral and public voting and for indirect elections, but on May 1 they were defeated on these issues by votes of 249–218 and 264–202. The first reading was concluded on March 2. On March 27, immediately after the constitution was finally accepted, the delegates gave a standing vote of approval to the democratic draft of the Election Law. Manhood suffrage was to be equal, secret, direct, and universal.

With these difficult issues settled, the democrats were ready to vote on a head for the new state. On March 28 each delegate was asked to designate orally the German ruler he wished to make emperor of the Germans. Freedom of decision was severely limited. Austria had indicated its unwillingness to join a united Germany that would exclude its non-German territories. The candidacy of the Habsburg ruler was thus out of the question, and Prussian participation could be won, if at all, only by making the Prussian monarch the hereditary ruler of Germany. As the roll call slowly proceeded on March 28, it was soon apparent that many delegates—particularists as well as democrats—could not bring themselves to endorse Frederick William IV. Only a handful of diehard republicans declared that they would endorse no hereditary emperor, but altogether 248 (111 of them from Habsburg lands) withheld their votes; among the abstaining democrats were Eisenstuck, Moritz Mohl, Rossmässler, Ludwig Simon, Venedey, Vogt, and Wigard. However, 290 delegates voted to offer the emperorship to the Prussian king, and this number included many men who had supported democratic suffrage (Löwe-Calbe, Jahn, Hildebrand, Mittermaier, and Riesser among them).

"God be with Germany and its newly chosen Emperor." With

these words the presiding officer, Eduard Simson, announced the results of the voting on March 28 to a cheering National Assembly as bells were rung and cannon salvos fired. Both democrats and liberals had bent their principles to create a constitution for Germany. The resulting framework of government also represented a complex of compromises between practices of foreign states—especially those of the United States—and unique German conditions. But neither the *Grundrechte* nor the constitution reflected the traditional powers of the German aristocracy or the particularistic preoccupations of the monarchs of the larger German states. On March 28 it remained to be seen whether the king of Prussia would be as ready to make compromises of his own for the sake of German unity as the assembly had finally shown itself to be.[14]

On April 3, Frederick William IV hesitated while tentatively refusing the imperial crown. He indicated that only the approval of "the crowned heads, the princes, and the free cities" could make him consider the invitation, and he gave no assurance that even this would cause him to accept. By mid-April the proposed constitution was rejected by the rulers of four of the strongest German states: Austria, Bavaria, Saxony, and Hanover. Austrian delegates were instructed to take no further part in the affairs of the Frankfurt Assembly. But to the surprise of Frederick William IV, on April 14 the governments of twenty-eight of the smaller and middle-sized states, while suggesting certain changes, gave the constitution and the Hohenzollern headship of the German Empire their approval. On April 24 the king of Württemberg—hard-pressed by public sentiment and his parliament—added his recognition of the constitution. Meanwhile, on April 21 the lower house of the Prussian parliament spoke in favor of the proposed Reich constitution; the upper house also indicated approval. Obviously there was widespread popular support for German unity in the spring of 1849, even for relatively democratic unity.

If Frederick William had been content to reign over Germany as a limited monarch under the terms of the Frankfurt constitution, most of Germany might have been formed into a nation. Austria, still fighting to reassert its power in Hungary and in northern Italy, could not have prevented unification under

Prussia's leadership, although the Russian czar, Nicholas I, might have been able to do so. In any case, Frederick William IV had to think of international complications that would arise from his attempt to lead Germany to unity. He was inclined to oppose the Frankfurt conditions, and the vote for acceptance by his own parliament only made him more stubborn. On April 27 he dissolved the Prussian lower house. The next day he sent to Frankfurt his definitive rejection of the offer of the German crown and the proposed constitution; his note indicated that the democratic provisions made it unacceptable. In May the Prussian delegates were told to withdraw from the Frankfurt Assembly. The Prussian government henceforth regarded what was left of the National Assembly as an illegal body. [15]

The frustration of national aspirations by the Prussian monarch triggered the last of the German revolutions of 1848–49. In Prussia scattered rebellions in late April and early May were suppressed quickly. In Saxony, when the king, encouraged by Berlin, refused to accept the Frankfurt constitution and appointed a reactionary ministry, a revolt was proclaimed in Dresden on May 3 by an assorted group of radicals. They were led by the labor organizer Stephan Born, the composer Richard Wagner, the Russian anarchist Michael Bakunin, and a few members of the Frankfurt Assembly. The king was forced to flee his capital city. But his salvation was close at hand; Prussian troops marched into Saxony. By May 9, after four days of severe street fighting, the rebels—some ten thousand strong—were overwhelmed; twenty-five had been killed and four hundred wounded. The Wettin dynasty was restored to power. [16]

In western Bavaria, meanwhile, another revolt had broken out. In the Bavarian Palatinate, where the Hambach Festival had been staged in 1832, a group of democrats met at Kaiserslautern on May 1 and resolved to resist their government and to support the Frankfurt Assembly. Some Bavarian troops joined the rebellion. By May 17 virtually all of Bavaria west of the Rhine was under rebel control. Yet here as in Saxony the initial success did not last. Without waiting to be asked, Prussian contingents marched into the Palatinate and by June 15 had quelled the revolution.

In Württemberg, attempts to support the Frankfurt Assembly

took a different form, but ended with no greater success; in the capital city of Stuttgart the assembly itself faded into history.

Since late May, republican and other democratic delegates had attempted to carry on the work of the National Assembly. Although Saxony and Hanover had followed the Austrian and Prussian examples and ordered the withdrawal of their delegates, on May 26 the rump Assembly in Frankfurt had issued a call for help to the people of Germany over the heads of their governments. This appeal to revolution caused a number of additional secessions from the body. Remembering that Austrian and Prussian troops were in nearby Mainz, several of the remaining delegates suggested that they should transfer their meeting to the greater safety of Württemberg. Karl Vogt's logic carried the day when he told the delegates: "The troops hostile to the constitution are here, we are sitting in the middle of them." By a vote of 71 to 64 on May 30 the remaining delegates decided to move to Stuttgart.

What was left of the National Assembly—about one hundred delegates—held its next meeting in the Württemberg Chamber of Deputies on June 6. After several ballots the democratic rump Assembly chose its own provisional government for the German nation—a five-man regency, dominated by Franz Raveaux, the son of a French immigrant, and now a Cologne businessman and newspaper editor who had embraced a host of republican and democratic causes since his expulsion from a gymnasium at the age of fourteen. Despite Raveaux's experience, charm, and eloquence, this last radical experiment lit no bonfires of enthusiasm. By mid-June the Prussian government, victorious in the Palatinate, was putting pressure on Württemberg to give the rump assembly the *coup de grace* and was offering to help in the execution. The Württemberg government decided to do the job itself. On June 16 the rump was prohibited from meeting in the parliament building. Two days later the ministry used troops to disperse the persistent democratic parliamentarians.[17]

The last act of the German Revolution of 1848–49 was played out violently in Baden, where Hecker and Struve in April 1848 had attempted to found a German republic through force. Baden's Grand Duke Leopold had recognized the Frankfurt constitution, but in the spring of 1849 the demands of his own

tenacious and numerous democratic subjects remained unfulfilled. Throughout the country, republican clubs continued to
try to win the support of Baden's soldiers. Indeed, the third revolution in the grand duchy began as a mutiny in the regular army.
On May 12 the rebels gained control of the important fortress
of Rastatt, southwest of Karlsruhe where the Rhine separates
Germany from France. Next day a group of local democrats met
with revolutionary leaders from the Bavarian Palatinate and the
Rhineland in the town of Offenburg to coordinate their action.
The ostensible aim was to conquer state power in Baden and use
it as a base from which to force acceptance of the Frankfurt constitution by the other states of Germany. But Friedrich Hecker's
true intention to create a social republic surfaced at once.

At first success came easily. On the night of May 13–14 the
grand duke fled his capital city and the liberal ministry followed
him. A central revolutionary committee immediately created a
provisional government in Baden, which at first was supported
by most of the grand duchy's bureaucrats and judges and even
by a number of army officers. The new government's head and
one of its more moderate members was Lorenz Brentano, the
son of a wealthy Mannheim merchant. Brentano had become a
lawyer and, after 1845, a democratic member of the parliament
of Baden; he had served in the Frankfurt Assembly but had not
participated in the two previous revolutions there. Another merchant's son, the twenty-nine-year-old socialist Amand Goegg,
became minister of finance in the revolutionary regime. For
Goegg, this was the third Baden revolution within a year. In
June the new government was joined by Franz Raveaux when
the provisional regency of the rump assembly was chased out of
Stuttgart.

Radicals from all parts of Germany—including many members
of the General Workers' Brotherhood—rallied to support the
revolution in Baden in May and June with enthusiasm and considerable confidence. Military command was assumed first by
Franz Sigel when this officer of Hecker's revolution returned
from exile in Switzerland, and later by Ludwig von Mieroslawski,
who had led a revolt among fellow Poles in the spring of the
previous year. Johann Philipp Becker, socialist veteran of the
April 1848 revolt, crossed the Swiss frontier once again in an

endeavor to salvage his dream of German freedom. Otto von Corvin, a renegade Junker who had abandoned the uniform of a Prussian officer in 1835 to marry the daughter of a Frankfurt tobacco dealer, had fought in the April revolt; now he returned from France to become a colonel in the revolutionary militia. Friedrich Engels briefly led revolutionary troops. From Switzerland also came Karl Heinzen, who offered to become a leader but returned to exile when he was only assigned the role of a private in the ranks. Gottfried Kinkel, a professor of art history came bearing the scars of an abortive democratic revolt in Bonn; he was accompanied by his twenty-year-old lieutenant, Carl Schurz. Finally Struve, freed from prison by the rebels, for the third time took part in an attempt to make Baden a republic.

The revolutionary government in Karlsruhe quickly organized elections to a constitutional assembly, to which the voters sent democratic delegates. Had there been no intervention from outside, at least one German state surely would have emerged from the turmoil of 1848–49 as a democratic republic. But none of the other German governments would let this happen. The liberalized ministries of Hesse, Nassau, and Württemberg sent troops to aid Baden's grand duke and the Prussian army, acting independently, formed the decisive legion of counterrevolution in Baden as it had elsewhere.

The reconquest of Baden moved slowly at first, for the revolutionaries found far-reaching public support against the hated Prussians; but there was never much doubt about the outcome. Twenty thousand armed revolutionaries put up a tough struggle, but they faced four or five times that number of regular troops. The Prussian army occupied Mannheim on June 15 and by early July had entered south Baden. The first fortress conquered by the insurgents was the last to be wrested from them; some six thousand starving troops at Rastatt capitulated on July 23. Several of their leaders were executed and large numbers fled the country. About eighty thousand Badeners—one out of every eighteen or nineteen inhabitants—emigrated in 1849–50, providing evidence of the extent of revolutionary sentiment, the thoroughness of counterrevolution, and the continuing economic attractions of the New World.[18]

In the summer of 1849 the dull thud of fallen expectations

echoed in thousands of hearts. As calm returned, Germans could count the costs and gains of the Revolution of 1848–49, while trying to assess the reasons for its failures.

As many as five thousand lives had been lost during the events of 1848–49. Much property had been destroyed, and, more significant, the democratic movement suffered lasting damage in that many of its strongest supporters were forced to flee the country. Friedrich Hecker became a farmer in Illinois, fought with the Union army in the Civil War, and died in St. Louis in 1881. His lieutenant, Franz Sigel, was appointed a general in Lincoln's army after 1861. Karl Heinzen became a crusading editor in the United States, and Lorenz Brentano ended his days a Republican congressman. Young Carl Schurz served successively as American minister to Spain, a general for the North in the Civil War, a Republican senator, and secretary of the interior. Struve, Löwe-Calbe, and several other revolutionaries went to the United States, but later returned to Europe. Some of the defeated rebels never crossed the Atlantic. Eisenstuck, Hildebrand, and Venedey lived for a time in neighboring European countries and then were allowed to return to Germany. Franz Raveaux died in Belgium, Ludwig Simon and Karl Vogt in Switzerland. Among the socialist revolutionaries, Karl Marx found his way to London in August 1849, where he lived out the remaining half of his life. Within Germany the democratic movement had suffered from the execution in 1848 or 1849 of such leaders as Robert Blum and Georg Böhning.[19]

While the revolutionary leaders were penalized by the counterrevolution, in their own brief moments of power they had set up no Terror. No guillotines had been put into bloody operation, no kings or princes beheaded. The revolutions had forced several abdications, but not a single German dynasty was successfully dethroned. Clearly, then, an underlying reason for the failure of the democratic movement in 1848–49, was the deeply embedded respect for traditional authority, which had been instilled in Germans for too many centuries, by too many rulers, and by too many nobles, pastors, and teachers. The old values of obedience, duty, and gratitude for small favors could not be thrown off all at once.

Before concluding that the German people were uniquely unsuited for democracy, it is well to remember that efforts to achieve democratic government elsewhere in 1848 also resulted in failure. English democrats were given no concessions. In France a conservative reaction was evident in the provinces within a few weeks after the Second Republic was proclaimed in Paris—well before the radical workers frightened the bourgeoisie during the "June Days." In the Bouches-du-Rhone, the department that included France's second largest city, Marseille, the voters in April 1848—by secret ballot—elected an equal number of monarchists and moderate republicans to represent them in the Constituent Assembly. In Marseille, as in several of the German states, liberal authorities were telling dissident workers, "do not trouble the city with your clamorous demonstrations"; and there, too, force was used against those who refused to heed the warning. The fact is that all of Europe's democratic experiments of 1848 were failures.[20]

If the German revolutions are viewed against their national background and in their European context, the great surprise of 1848–49 is not the respect the German people showed for authority, but the considerable extent of their disrespect and their willingness to challenge it. Though German democracy was a young movement, it demonstrated that it possessed an ambitious leadership and a surprising number of shock troops. By March 31, 1849, many were organized in twelve regional associations affiliated with the so-called "March Society" (named in honor of March 1848), and there were some nine hundred branch organizations. Nevertheless, the persistent democrats spoke for a small minority within the population. Absolutely reliable statistics are not available, but an official estimate made in Bavaria in 1849 is suggestive; it reported 32,900 "resolute" (*entschiedene*) democrats in that state as against 755,500 "resolute" conservatives. In any case, the numbers of the determined democrats were insufficient.[21]

Furthermore, the democratic leaders had made a fundamental mistake in strategy. In 1848 they strongly believed that their first priority was the achievement of national unity under a democratic central government. If this could only be won, they thought, democracy and freedom within the states would follow. The chances for democracy were not good in 1848, but surely they would have been improved if the priorities had been reversed—if a concerted effort had been made by Germany's democrats to achieve their aims in the individual states without simultaneously trying to unite. Many experienced and respected democrats in each state went off to Frankfurt in May 1848, collectively spending tens of thousands of man hours of work that might have been invested instead in expanding their grass-roots power bases. Trying for democracy within the states and for national unity at the same time, German democrats failed to achieve either.

While democrats divided their leadership between the state capitals and Frankfurt, the leaders of the traditional forces remained at home. Undistracted by demanding work in the National Assembly, conservatives and reactionaries could concentrate upon mending fences behind which democracy could be contained. Above all, the armies of Austria and Prussia were kept intact and under the control of the ruling houses. The ability of the conservatives to divide the revolutionaries of March 1848 by concessions and their readiness to use military power against democratic rebels sealed the fate of German democracy in 1848–49.

Concern about property and order in 1848 won the conservatives many middle-class allies against the democrats, and that concern helped to make the reaction the following year tolerable to large numbers of liberals. Democracy thereafter was widely associated with the threat of social revolution. Furthermore, from then on middle-class Germans tended to see in democratic government a demagogic threat to the very rationalism, freedom, and orderly progress for which German liberalism was striving. As early as April 11, 1848, a Berlin cousin of Johann Jacoby was writing to him that five-sixths "of all respectable people in Prussia—the bourgeoisie and the propertied classes—would willingly donate five bottles of champagne each if the whole business of liberty had remained where it used to be." David Friedrich Strauss, elected to the Württemberg parliament as a supposed radical in the late spring of 1848, wrote in February 1849: "Under Russian despotism, I could at least exist, to be sure with clipped wings; but the rule of the masses would destroy me. Therefore I hate whatever leads to that." In Giessen, Justus von Liebig in June 1849 welcomed news of Prussian victories over the Baden revolutionaries. Clearly, the anxieties of the liberals about order, property, and rationalism helped to thwart the democrats, but the cause of historical understanding is not served by accusing them of a "betrayal of the interests of the people and of the revolution," as communist historians have done. Most of the leading liberals were true to the principles for which they had always stood. Few had ever pretended to be democrats before 1848.

Moderate and conservative liberals in 1849 could find considerable satisfaction, however, in the results of the revolutions within their individual states. It is true that few liberals gained a lasting hold on state power; but many policy concessions granted by the traditional authorities survived. Most of the prominent liberals (and the upper middle class generally) had desired recognition and favors more than the responsibility and power of office. In 1848–49 they got a considerable degree of what they had wanted. Henceforth, therefore, upper middle class liberals would be reluctant to demand that representatives of all the people gain genuine power over the state. Seen in this light, the movement for democracy may not have suffered in the long run as much from liberal failures in 1848–49 as from liberal successes.

For those liberals who did want genuine parliamentary government, partial and noteworthy gains could be counted. Parliamentary control over ministries and monarchs had not been achieved, but even Prussia now had a parliament of limited influence where there had been none before. The suffrage systems in effect after 1849–50 were not democratic, but more Germans could vote than ever before. Other changes that liberals had wanted before 1848 had been achieved: constitutions in states where they had not existed earlier; trial by jury; freedom of religion; abolition of the legal basis of noble privilege; and a larger if not fully satisfying amount of economic freedom.[22]

The revolutions of 1848 marked an especially important turning point in the history of Germany's Jews. At least 9 of the 255 revolutionaries who were killed in the fighting in Berlin on March 18 and 19, 1848, were Jews. Jews fought in the republican uprisings in Baden, Frankfurt, Bavaria, and Saxony. Many were

active as liberal or democratic journalists. Five sat in the Prussian
Constituent Assembly, and Jews were elected to the parliaments
of at least seven other German states in 1848. Nine Jews and
ten Christianized Jews were elected to the National Assembly
(five of the nineteen from Austria). Gabriel Riesser served as a
vice-president, and when Heinrich von Gagern gave up the
presidency of the Assembly, Eduard Simson, a Christian of Jewish parentage, was elected to the post. Riesser and Simson were
members of the delegation that offered Frederick William IV
the emperorship of Germany. "We have participated in the
German development in its light and shadow, in its good and
evil, we have the German essence and German spirit in us";
thus Rabbi Ludwig Philippson of Magdeburg summarized Jewish
involvement in the events of 1848.

When the revolutions were over, Jews were guaranteed legal
and political equality in most of the German states. (Some of
these gains were to be lost during the decade of reaction that
followed, but won again in the 1860's.) And although social and
even administrative discrimination continued to run in currents
that were strong and deep, the way had been opened for Jews to
enter the universities, to rise slowly in the professions, and to
play an increasingly active part in Germany's cultural life.[23]

Whether Jews or Gentiles, middle-class Germans derived the
greatest benefits from the government changes of 1848–49,
but this group embraces more than what Marx designated as
"bourgeoisie." In describing this "mad year" as a revolution of
the "liberal bourgeoisie," the father of modern communism and
his disciples termed its results a partial victory for capitalism.
But it was more than that: its lasting political gains reached the
German middle class at large—intellectuals and professional
men as well as the then small number of capitalists.

Factory workers failed to win any lasting class advantages in
1848–49 because they lacked three essential qualities for revolutionary success: large numbers, a widespread revolutionary
spirit, and established organizations. No one could suddenly
give them the first; improvement of economic conditions in
the spring and summer of 1848 worked against the second;
and too many tried all at once to give them the third. The result was many separate local or occupational organizations

with small memberships and no coordinated aims or strategy. Born's Verbrüderung was a notable early attempt to create an all-German organization of labor, but it did not have time to consolidate before the revolution was over. Many artisans exerted themselves for the revolution; in October 1849 the magazine of the cigar workers estimated that three hundred in this industry alone had been forced to flee to Switzerland.[24]

For German democrats—whether workers or from the middle class—the revolution left little immediate consolation. In a few states democrats retained large representation in the parliaments, but reactionary changes in the suffrage systems soon ended that. While large numbers emigrated, others remained in Germany smoldering in helpless rage, succumbing to weariness, or wallowing in self-pity. But the long-range results of the revolution were not altogether negative. To be sure, those who worked for democracy after 1849 knew better than to try to create a republic. They also knew the futility of resorting to revolutionary violence. But their effort did not cease. Indeed, large numbers of Germans, especially workers, had for the first time been jarred from their political apathy and had fought for a political cause: social and liberal democracy. Defeat failed to discredit it. The goals of 1848–49 would remain the basic goals of German democrats until the eve of World War I.

Most positively, the revolutions dramatically demonstrated that a movement for democracy did exist in Germany. Its goal remained out of reach, but the quest had become an indigenous part of the German political tradition. In this light Bismarck's policies, the ambiguous character of the empire he was able to unite, the mass movement for democratic objectives that developed within that empire after 1890, and the creation and character of the Weimar Republic, all assume a logic of their own.

VI.

REACTION AND A NEW CRISIS,
1850–1866

In March 1850, Hoffmann von Fallersleben reflected the despair of German democrats amidst reaction as he wrote about "power without justice and justice that lacks power":

> Was sollen wir hoffen?
> Die Zeit ist zu schlecht:
> O weh, die Macht ist rechtlos,
> Und machtlos ist das Recht. [1]

The counterrevolution lasted for a decade, in which liberals and democrats were reluctant to work together. By 1859, however, common hatred of authoritarian government and concern about international dangers brought the allies of 1848 together again. In the 1860's they would jointly build the first genuine political parties in Germany in order to press their state governments for reforms at home and for steps toward national unity. Many would look to Prussia for leadership. But in the years 1861–66 Prussia was in the grip of a grave internal crisis that severely tested the new coalitions of liberals and democrats while jeopardizing the major achievement of the revolution—the Prussian constitution.

The decade of counterrevolution opened in 1849–50 with the revival of Austrian power within a resurrected German Confederation. For more than a year the king of Prussia tried to block the Habsburg resurgence by proposing a closer German union under his rule, and the plan that Frederick William IV set forth won the support of many liberals by incorporating their desires for a national parliament. Representatives (elected by unequal suffrage in some of the states) met at Erfurt in March and April 1850 and approved its basic provisions. This "Erfurt Constitution" stipulated that the lower house of a national parliament would be elected through an indirect and three-class system of voting; any bills it might pass would be subject to veto either by the head of the state or by a committee of six rulers of the component states. Since this constitution obviously would enhance Prussian power, Austria opposed it. The showdown came in a conference at Olmütz in Bohemia on November 29, 1850, when Prussia was forced by Austria to renounce its plans. Meanwhile, in the absence of real unity, the Diet of the German Confederation had been revived under the presidency of a Habsburg envoy. In April 1851 the king of Prussia also rejoined.

Although the Habsburg monarchy thus checkmated the hopes of many liberal nationalists and the Hohenzollern aspirations to political leadership in Germany, Vienna's exertions for economic predominance were frustrated by Prussia. For more than two years the Austrians sought to replace or combat the Prussian-led Zollverein with a customs union of their own, but in February 1853 the pact was renewed for twelve more years under Prussian direction. Thus, while the Habsburg monarchy reasserted its formal political headship over the German Confederation, Prussia retained and strengthened its economic leadership.

The restored Diet of the German Confederation in Frankfurt reflected the Prussian-Austrian standoff. Count Arthur de Gobineau, assigned to the city on the Main as a French secretary of legation, in 1854 called it "the central point in Germany where the negative and positive electrical forces neutralize each other." The Diet opposed national reform, and it prodded and helped the state governments to carry out counter-revolutions. In July of 1851, under the combined pressure of Austria and Prussia, it ordered all the states to repudiate the Fundamental Rights (*Grundrechte*) that the National Assembly had adopted in December 1848. The press of the Germanies was again restricted, and a special committee of the Diet urged several states to revise their constitutions of 1848.[2]

Reaction in the individual states, meanwhile, had grown directly out of the suppression of the democratic revolutions. In Baden, Grand Duke Leopold was able to return to his capital in

August 1849, and Prussian troops remained until November 1850, while the state's own army was being reorganized. Baden's liberal traditions limited the reactionary ministers during the 1850's, but even moderate liberals were not to regain government power until the end of the decade. In Württemberg no Prussian invasion suppressed revolution for the sovereign. Instead, in three successive elections the unflinching democrats of Württemberg—led by a former member of the Frankfurt Assembly, Adolf Schoder—gained an impressive number of votes. But each of the three assemblies with liberal-democratic majorities was dissolved, and in November 1850 the king ordered the suffrage of 1849 replaced by the undemocratic system of 1819. By the mid-1850's the authoritarian policies of the government were reviving criticism even among the liberals of Württemberg.

Only Bavaria preserved and implemented the achievements of 1848. Ludwig von der Pfordten, as minister-president from 1849 to 1859, tried to follow a moderately liberal policy, although sometimes he lacked the strength to overcome resurgent conservatism in the upper house. The policies he urged on a responsible king, Maximilian II, whose own unpretentious disposition accepted limited royal authority, slowed but did not arrest the pace of reform. Notably in education, the years after 1848 closed the gap between backward Bavaria and her northern neighbors. Developments in Hesse-Darmstadt were more typical of the decade of counterrevolution. Elections in December 1849 gave democrats a majority in the lower house, but the grand duke soon dissolved it, appointed a conservative ministry, and restricted freedom of the press and of association. In October 1850 an executive decree replaced the democratic suffrage with a system of weighted and indirect voting. The repressive domestic measures of the 1850's provoked even the liberals, who increasingly favored the unification of Germany under Prussian leadership.

Developments to the north further reflected the methods and results of reaction. The Diet of the German Confederation intervened militarily in Hesse-Cassel on behalf of the ruler in October 1850; thus supported, the elector in 1852 limited the suffrage to those who owned property. In Hanover the parliament successfully opposed a reactionary revision of the constitution in

1853, but two years later, supported by the Federal Diet, the Hanoverian monarch substantially restored the constitution of 1831. As in other states, the reactionary policies provoked the reemergence of liberal-nationalist opposition. By 1859 the liberals were finding a highly effective organizer and spokesman in Rudolf von Bennigsen, lawyer and the son of a Hanoverian general and statesman. Meanwhile, Mecklenburg-Schwerin was restored as the prize exhibit of counterrevolution. The liberal constitution of 1849 was withdrawn with the help of the neighboring kings of Prussia and Hanover, and the Constitutional Inheritance Compromise of 1755 (*Grundgesetzliche Erbvergleich*) restored. This government by feudal estates survived until 1918. In Saxony the king and his conservative ministry dissolved the Chamber of Deputies on June 1, 1850, suspended freedom of the press, restored the constitution of 1831, and dismissed protesting liberal professors from the University of Leipzig.[3]

In Prussia the conservatives who gained power in November 1848 made some compromises with liberalism through 1850 and then took a more reactionary course for a full decade. The constitution of 1849–50 was the most important result of their compromises. It provided two advantages to those who wanted to organize liberal-democratic reform movements: the creation of a parliament finally legalized the existence of some local political associations, and universal male suffrage was guaranteed in elections to the lower house. But universal suffrage for men was rendered undemocratic in three ways: voting was not secret; it was indirect, the voters choosing electors who in turn selected the members of the Chamber of Deputies; finally, voting was flagrantly unequal.

The three-class suffrage divided Prussian voters within each electoral district into groups according to their payment of direct taxes. The richest men—those who contributed a third of the district's taxes—elected one-third of the electors of the district. The small group of taxpayers who contributed the next highest third of the tax revenue chose another third of the electors. The poorer population—men who paid no direct taxes and those who contributed the lowest third of the total in their district—chose another third. These electors then met and by majority vote named the district's member or members in the Chamber of Deputies. (Some districts were assigned one, some two, and some three members.) By standing together, the electors chosen by the first and second classes (two-thirds of all electors in each district) could control the choice of the district's representative(s) in the Chamber of Deputies, although these electors themselves were chosen by only 15 to 20 percent of the district's voters. With the elections thus controlled by conservative landowners and the upper middle class, few third-class voters bothered to go to the polls. This suffrage system maddened democrats, but it checked their ability to elect enough representatives to achieve further reforms.

While the Prussian constitution created an undemocratic lower house, it renounced the elected upper chamber of December 1848 in favor of an aristocratic house; and it failed to provide for genuine parliamentary government. The House of Lords, as defined by the monarch in 1854, included about thirty representatives of designated cities, one representative from each of the Prussian universities, ninety aristocrats chosen by the hereditary nobles, and notables who might be appointed for life by the king. Legislation required approval by the House of Lords as well as by the lower house, and the king retained power of absolute veto over legislation. Ministers were appointed and dismissed at the pleasure of the monarch. The Prussian army was not under parliamentary control; after 1850 as before, army officers took a personal oath of allegiance to the king, not an oath to uphold the constitution.

For Prussia's ultraconservatives, even the constitution of 1850 was too "democratic." Time after time during the 1850's they urged Frederick William to renounce it, but Otto von Manteuffel, the Prussian minister-president from 1850 to 1858, advised the monarch to uphold the basic law as a means of preserving the centralization of authority in Prussia. The Manteuffel ministry itself was conservative and prevented a resurgence of the democratic movement in the 1850's.

During election campaigns the government in Berlin instructed district officials, pastors, and teachers to work for progovernment candidates, and controls over the press prevented the appearance of any appeals for revolutionary action. Furthermore, after March 1850 the police once again were empowered to prevent any gathering that they believed might disturb public order, and they kept careful watch on all persons suspected of subversive activities.[4]

In all the German states, attempts to reenergize the movement for democracy were handicapped by the lack of political parties and by cultural reaction, economic recovery, the prohibition of labor organizations, the presence in Prussia of a large non-German minority, and a diminution in inspiration from abroad.

Local political associations were now allowed in the German states, but they were still new and lacked cohesion in the 1850's. Official policies inhibited the growth of any genuine political parties, and no organization by democrats was permitted. For example, although the democratic association in Stuttgart had only three to four hundred members in 1850 in a city of forty-six thousand inhabitants, city officials regarded it as a danger to "the existing order," and it was outlawed in 1852 under a new Württemberg law regulating associations. The associations law of 1850 in Prussia, typical of the laws adopted in the other states, required local organizations to register their statutes and the names of their members with the local police. Organizations that aimed to change "the existing order" were banned, and those that cut across state lines were disallowed.

Improved means of communication in time made possible greater cohesion within the political groups that were permitted to exist. The postal system was improved in the 1850's. Telegraphy gradually facilitated contacts among political leaders after the first major line (Berlin to Frankfurt am Main) was opened to public use in October 1849. In the next year Austria, Prussia, Bavaria, and Saxony formed a German-Austrian Telegraph Union, which had 545 stations in operation by 1861; but telegraphy would only slowly come into common use.

For many years, Germany's "political parties" continued to be merely loose collections of male prima donnas. Candidates sometimes identified themselves with one group during a campaign only to join another after taking their seats in parliament. None of the features of modern parties—discipline, ideological solidarity, a coordinated press, administrative organization, provision for physical facilities, centralized leadership, and a sense of being bound to a constituency—existed in the political associations of Germany in the 1850's, and they would come into being only slowly thereafter.[5]

The schools' curricula, meanwhile, had been altered by the counterrevolution in order to inhibit the spread of liberal and democratic ideas. Frederick William in 1849 bluntly blamed the superintendents of teacher-training seminaries "for all the misery which was last year brought upon Prussia." The schools, he said, had "eradicated religious belief and loyalty" from the hearts of his subjects. In December 1850 he named Karl Otto von Raumer, a professional civil servant, as minister of cultural affairs, and for the next eight years Raumer managed schools and churches in a conspicuously reactionary fashion. In other states, as in Prussia, efforts were made to purge the schools of Pestalozzi's humanistic pedagogy and to make sure once again that children learned to fear God and to honor state authorities.

Similarly, in the reaction that followed 1849 the governments of Prussia, Saxony, Hesse, and other states cooperated with officials of their established churches to repress religious dissent, especially when it had political overtones. German-Catholic groups and congregations of Protestant Friends that had supported the Revolution of 1848 were forced to disband, and their leaders were jailed or compelled to flee. Johannes Ronge found refuge in London until he was allowed to return to Germany in 1861. Gustav Adolf Wislizenus went to the United States, subsequently returning to Europe to live in Switzerland until his death in 1875. Leberecht Uhlich continued his work as best he could in Germany. A few small Free Congregations persisted here and there, and in 1859 a national merger of these radical Protestants and German-Catholics was carried out. Ronge, Uhlich, Rupp, Edward Balzer, and others were free to speak in the 1860's, but few followers were won for their League of Free Religious Congregations of Germany. In Nuremberg, a city of seventy-seven thousand inhabitants, there were only 129 members in 1867. The leaders were encouraged in their efforts to spread a purely rational ethic by the publication of Ludwig Büchner's *Kraft und Stoff* (1855), which popularized scientific materialism while incidentally declaring the superiority of democratic government over one based upon aristocratic privileges. The book enjoyed large and continuing sales, going through twenty-one printings by 1904. Its wide influence indicated that officialdom could not eliminate criticism of traditional theology, but the prompt dismissal of Büchner from the Tübingen faculty illustrates the repressive policies of the 1850's.

Many Germans who could no longer be won for reaction by the churches were more susceptible after 1849 to the ideas of Arthur Schopenhauer. Against the Kantian and Hegelian view of man as the master of Reason, Schopenhauer portrayed man as the captive of innate urges that he called the "Will." The "Will," irrational and purposeless, could not be satisfied; always taking new forms, it set man on a restless search for "becoming" which had no final goal. Thus, the striving for "progress"—the effort to build a better world—was only an illusion, dooming its advocates to disappointment. Such views had enjoyed little favor even among intellectuals before 1848 (Schopenhauer had published them as early as 1819), but the disillusioning failure of the revolution seemed to add new validity to this interpretation of human nature.

Antidemocratic arguments were set forth at length in the 1850's by a number of writers. From his post at the University of Berlin, his seat in the Prussian House of Lords, and the columns of the conservative *Kreuzzeitung*, the jurist Friedrich Julius Stahl condemned democracy as wrong-headed and sinful. Many liberals differed with him only by degrees. Men such as Rudolf Haym, Robert von Mohl, Heinrich von Sybel, and Karl Theodor Welcker also attacked democracy in their publications after 1848. Gervinus was one of the few democrats among the liberal intellectuals.[6]

Economic improvement, meanwhile, kept many Germans satisfied. As a result of their successes in 1848, the upper bourgeoisie were better able to influence economic policies than before, thus accelerating commercial and industrial development. The discovery of gold across the Atlantic in California in 1849 put more money into circulation and stimulated an international economic upswing which the German states shared. These changes, plus the activities of the Zollverein and the initiative of the ambitious entrepreneurs themselves made German industrial growth one of the most significant features of Europe's economic history between 1850 and 1870. Railway lines were expanded from 5,900 to 19,000 kilometers; output of hard coal rose from 5,000,000 to 26,000,000 tons; production of pig iron increased from 212,000 to 1,400,000 tons. Smokestacks "sprouted from the earth like mushrooms" in Saxony, the Rhineland, and Westphalia during the boom of the 1850's. Investment opportunities were abundant, and commerce flourished. Thus, until the international depression of 1857–59, the chief unrealized aim of the increasingly numerous capitalists was German unity, which they felt would help business by providing larger markets. Some, but by no means all, also favored free trade.[7]

The lower classes enjoyed little of the profits of these years, but even their lot was better than in the crisis years just before the revolution. In Prussia low-interest loans from state banks permitted three times as many peasants to become free proprietors during the fifteen years after 1850 as during the thirty-seven years before. If such new yeomen were satisfied with the political order, other elements of the rural population were in no position to express any grievances, for the great majority of farm workers and peasants, though legally free, remained economically dependent upon the noble landowners. Lorenz von Stein, professor of philosophy and law in Kiel, could describe the peasantry as "an unconquerable conservative force" and "a natural barrier among the lower classes of society." In 1850 he called for government policies that would benefit the industrial workers—declaring social reform from above the only means to prevent social revolution. But his hope for "a monarchy of social reform" did not materialize. The Prussian government in 1853 forbade the employment of youngsters under twelve in factories, but greater numbers of boys and girls under fourteen were employed in Germany in 1861 than in the 1840's. Money wages increased, but so did prices. Real wages were lower in 1856 and 1857 than at the beginning of the decade, but throughout those years they were higher than before the revolution.[8]

Those workers who were not satisfiied with existing political conditions were unable to make their discontent felt. No socialist press was allowed to exist, and the rare worker who somehow was exposed to the post-1848 polemics of Marx did not become a prospective ally of middle-class democrats by the experience. From London, Marx denounced "the petty bourgeois democratic party" of Germany and argued that it was "far more dangerous to the workers than the previous liberal party." The leaders of the General Workers' Brotherhood remained true to the principles of democracy, but could say little about them in print or in public speeches. Because of police restrictions they agreed in February 1850 to deemphasize the political interests of the organization, calling instead for the creation by workers of consumer cooperatives, worker-owned workshops, and mutual health insurance agencies. Occasionally leaders of the Brotherhood revealed their commitment to political democracy. After an article in the *Verbrüderung* in March 1850 spoke of the need for a "democratic republic," all the German state governments ordered the dissolution of the workers' associations. On the rare occasions when workers engaged in street demonstrations—as did several thousands in Berlin on the third anniversary of the Revolution of 1848—the police used force to scatter them. Thus, Germany's workers could do almost nothing to revive a democratic movement in the 1850's.[9]

As before the revolution, the presence of a large and self-conscious Polish minority in Prussia posed a special problem for Germans who wanted to make that state democratic. Entire districts in the east contained Polish majorities. The nationalist tenor of the Polish uprisings in the following decade alarmed many liberals and divided German democrats. The persistence of Polish nationalism in the 1850's and a revolt of the Polish subjects of Russia just across the frontier in 1863 kept German anxieties alive. Only a handful of radical democrats in Germany —including Johann Jacoby—expressed sympathy for the cause of Polish nationalism in 1863. To conservatives and to many Prussian liberals, the large Polish minority would provide a powerful argument against the introduction of equal and secret suffrage in Prussia until 1918.[10] Meanwhile the flaws of democracy abroad may have discouraged German acceptance of Western political values as much as did the emphasis of German Romanticism upon authoritarian traditions.

Germans increasingly were esposed to news about the United States as 1,700,000 migrated between 1850 and 1869, but much of the news in the 1850's was not inspiring. The federal structure of government that many Germans had envied in 1848 was in

obvious trouble. German democrats who fled to America contributed to the mounting criticism of the United States. From
Boston, Gustav Adolf Wislizenus attempted to discourage his
compatriots from migrating because of his objection to slavery.
Friedrich Kapp, a republican of 1848, returned to Germany after
a few years in the United States, and wrote: "Politically, from
the year 1789 to the present, Europe has taken just as many
steps forward as the Union has taken backward." Karl Theodor
Griesinger, another revolutionary who had crossed the Atlantic
in 1851, published a two-volume account of America in 1862,
concluding that "the Congress in Washington consists of drunk-
ards and gamblers, if not of something still worse. . . . God
save the Union!" Antidemocratic Germans publicized the flaws
in American democracy to prove that popular sovereignty would
bring only evil to any country. Schopenhauer in 1851 listed a
whole catalogue of American horrors: "suppression of the free
blacks, lynch law, frequent and often unpunished assassinations,
duels of unheard-of-brutality, along with the open scorning
of justice and the laws, repudiation of public debts, . . . ever
increasing mobocracy." He concluded that "this test case of a
constitution embodying abstract justice on the opposite side of
the planet" did not "speak well for republics."[11]

In Europe there was no country whose institutions could
inspire great enthusiasm among German democrats. Even the
image of Switzerland was tarnished in the eyes of working-class
democrats when the government in Bern—worried about socialistic agitation among émigré German workers in Geneva and
elsewhere—in March 1850 ordered the dissolution of thirteen
organizations and expelled many of their members.[12]

London's great World Exhibition of 1851 drew German visitors
and excited their admiration, but England's government in the
1850's seems to have provided less stimulus to reform among
Germans than it had inspired between 1832 and 1848. Some
continued to write favorably about English political practices
in order to urge reforms in Germany, as did Gervinus who
commented in 1856 on the "many natural outlets" in England
for the "desires and complaints of the people." On the other
hand, German democrats were bound to find British government
in the 1850's insufficiently representative. The suffrage that had

seemed progressive in 1832 now reflected a stodgy status quo. The outstanding liberal interpreter of the British Constitution was Rudolf von Gneist, professor of law at Berlin and a member of Prussia's Chamber of Deputies from 1858 to 1893. Like several other German liberals who continued to admire British government, Gneist portrayed it in a more conservative light than reality warranted. Reflecting his own preference, the British past, and theory rather than practice, Gneist regarded the rising power of parliament as a mistake and attributed much greater influence to the crown than it actually possessed in early Victorian Britain. His views were not without practical consequences. In January 1869, for example, the chief minister of Baden would resist demands for full parliamentary government in his state by arguing that it did not exist in England.[13]

France also had ceased to provide an example of genuinely representative government. In 1851, German democrats in exile had hoped and believed that a new revolution in Paris would soon open new chances for them at home. Instead, by 1852, Emperor Napoleon III was consolidating an authoritarian rule that he maintained until 1869. His use of democratic suffrage in climbing to power only strengthened the conviction of many German liberals that it inherently fostered Caesarism. Julius Fröbel, the one-time radical who had returned from America, now denounced "democratic absolutism with its *suffrage universel.*" The Prussian liberal historian, Heinrich von Sybel, asserted that "the introduction of the general, direct, and equal franchise has always been the beginning of the end for any form of parliamentarism."[14]

All this notwithstanding, Napoleonic France, not by its domestic institutions but through its foreign policy, prompted liberals and democrats in Germany to join in the first genuine political parties and national associations in their history. Concern about France caused several of the German princes to favor these new and clearly anti-French organizations. Indirectly, French policy also called forth developments in Prussia that led to the greatest political crisis in Germany since 1849.

German anxieties about the expansion of French power were first aroused when Napoleon III took his empire into the Crimean War in 1854. Many Germans were convinced that the

French emperor coveted the Rhineland, as had his famous uncle. These fears were greatly aggravated in the spring of 1859, when Napoleon sent his army into Italy to help Piedmont-Sardinia defeat Austria, the leading German power. Though no French troops crossed the Rhine, Prussia mobilized its army during the international crisis and—thought many—prevented such an invasion.

A good many German nationalists had long since concluded that Austria would not take the lead in unifying Germany, nor could Austria be relied upon even for protection against the supposed danger west of the Rhine. Simultaneously, the Habsburg defeat made possible the first steps toward the unification of Italy. Both the Italian example and the fear of France aroused powerful desires for German unity. Increasing numbers of liberal nationalists and even some democrats began to look to Prussia for leadership, though many south Germans resented her failure in 1859 to assist Austria against France.

This vigorous revival of liberal nationalism coincided with the end of a decade of unprecedented economic growth. The Prussian-led Zollverein had helped to create the larger markets necessary for business expansion, but many barriers to intra-German trade remained, and small states such as the Mecklenburgs and the Hanseatic cities refused to join. The German states still maintained separate systems of coinage, weights, and measures; differing laws regulating industry, banking, commerce, and patents; separate bureaucracies to enforce the laws; and separate postal and telegraphic systems. To maintain growth, still greater unity was needed, as was demonstrated after the onset of the depression of 1857. An association of German economists, founded in 1857–58, made national unity its larger aim, though its ostensible purpose was the establishment of free trade. The Cologne Chamber of Commerce flatly stated four years later that unification was "the fundamental condition for successful creative activity by Germany in the economic sphere," and it unabashedly sounded the call for "a representative assembly of the German people."

Meanwhile, Napoleon III's military intervention in Italy in 1859 and the establishment of the Kingdom of Italy the next year had done what the economic leaders alone could not have managed. National unification south of the Alps reinvigorated the urge for unity among large numbers of Germans not primarily concerned with the economic advantages of unification, and prompted the founding of the first political associations after 1849 that included democrats and cut across state lines.[15]

On July 17, 1859, some thirty democratic spokesmen—including several who had served in the Frankfurt Assembly—met in Eisenach in Saxe-Weimar, site of the Wartburg festival of 1817, and proclaimed that "the current world political situation" held "great dangers for the independence of our German Fatherland." Such dangers, they asserted, required the calling of a new national assembly to create a "strong and lasting central government" under the leadership of Prussia. Two days later a meeting of liberal politicians in Hanover chaired by Rudolf von Bennigsen likewise pointed to "the threatening military preponderance of France" and called for Prussian initiative in creating "a common constitution for the Fatherland"—one that would assure justice and the free development of the individual as well as the independence of the nation in the international arena. The next step was to bring the Hanoverians and the Eisenachers together. Representatives of both met in Eisenach for three days in mid-August and announced plans to create "a German national party," inviting "patriots of all factions from north and south Germany"—democrats and liberals—to join. The proposed association—the first that can be called a genuine German political party—was established as the Nationalverein (National Society) on September 15–16, 1859, in a meeting at Frankfurt am Main. Bennigsen became its chairman. Its business manager until 1865 was Fedor Streit of Coburg, a follower of Struve in 1848 and a combatively democratic publisher.

The founders of the Nationalverein quickly discovered that it was easier to announce the creation of a new party than to make it an effective instrument of political action. The Austrian government, recognizing that the Nationalverein was basically pro-Prussian, denounced it and urged the other state governments to prohibit it. The two Hessian states and Hanover did so with special vigor by attempting to prevent the organization of local branches and by branding it as a front for subversion. Thus the Hanoverian ministry in 1861 warned: "Behind the liberals press the democrats and behind these the socialists and communists."

That even moderate liberals were confronted by such allegations tells a great deal about the restricted conditions of German politics in the early 1860's; that they persisted in working with democrats, notwithstanding such smear campaigns, speaks for their courage as well as for their pragmatism. Their determination to move toward national unity, and the benevolence of a few of the state governments, enabled them to expand membership in the Nationalverein to five thousand by May 1860, to seventeen thousand by the fall of 1861, and to twenty-six thousand in September 1862. This organization could have obtained a much larger following if its middle-class leadership had made a vigorous attempt to organize the working class. Fedor Streit and a number of the other democratic leaders wanted to do so, and the issue was debated repeatedly; but the liberals—disapproving the political and social demands of the workers—prevailed. When spokesmen for a group of Leipzig workers sought in 1862 to join the Nationalverein, its executive committee rejected the overture. Repeated efforts by democratic leaders to lower the dues to attract worker-members were obstructed.

The middle-class members who were admitted gave the Nationalverein a tighter unity than had any previous German political association. To escape persecution its local branches pretended to be independent, but issued membership cards provided by the national office. Dues were collected by the chapters but were sent to the Verein's headquarters in Coburg. Each member was required to endorse the statutes of the national organization, which also provided propaganda guidelines to be followed in local agitation. Although the Nationalverein restricted its formal program to the achievement of German unity, many of its members campaigned locally for liberal or democratic candidates in state elections. In a number of areas the first organized opposition after 1849 to the reactionary policies of the state governments was organized by local leaders of the Nationalverein.

Given its geographical scope, the Nationalverein did not demand reforms in the individual states, and, indeed, for some time it was hesitant to endorse completely democratic suffrage for the projected national parliament. On this issue, however, it was difficult to settle for anything less than the ill-fated Frankfurt constitution of 1849 and still keep the support of the democrats. The Nationalverein finally went on record in favor of that constitution—including the bill of rights and democratic suffrage—in its national convention of October 1862. One of its motives in doing so was the desire to win greater support in the south German states, where many democrats had been reluctant to join because of its previous equivocation on these matters and because its leaders were known to favor unification under Prussian leadership.[16]

In the south as in the north of Germany, Napoleon III's short war against Austria in 1859 had aroused emotions and political awareness to a pitch unknown for a decade, and it prompted both liberals and democrats to organize their first significant political associations since 1849. Demanding more unified German action in the face of foreign dangers, they disagreed, however, over the form it should take. Some, believing that only Prussia could lead Germany to unity, were particularly active in creating local branches of the Nationalverein. Others were moved by the events of 1859 to renew the old demand for *grossdeutsch* unification under Habsburg rule. Many, prizing the independence of their own states, simply called for aid to Austria by the separate governments of the German Confederation and sharply criticized Prussia for failing to provide it. The rulers and ministers of the south, knowing that they would need popular support if their states should become involved in war, showed increasing tolerance toward liberal and democratic political activity. Amnesties granted between 1859 and 1862 permitted revolutionaries of 1848–49 to return to their homelands, where they invigorated the new political associations. The Austrian government, needing whatever help it could get in Germany now that it had been weakened in Italy, actually gave financial support to a few who supported the *grossdeutsch* movement. Foremost among these was Julius Fröbel.[17]

Whatever their position on the question of national unity, liberals and democrats in southern Germany pressed vigorously in the 1860's for reforms at home. In Baden, as in other German states, a decade of reaction ended with the Austrian defeat at

Solferino in June 1859. Together with the revival of the liberal movement, the cry for Prussian initiative to unify Germany rose here with greater force than in any other south German state. The liberals at the grand-ducal university of Heidelberg, Carl Theodor Welcker, Karl Mittermaier, and August Ludwig von Rochau, had been among the founders of the National-verein. Their influence and positions attracted many of their fellow Badeners to its ranks, especially since Grand Duke Frederick himself hoped for a Prussian initiative. As it happened, other problems facing the government worked for the liberal cause. A prolonged conflict with the Catholic minority, led by the archbishop of Freiburg, had resulted in an impasse. Forced to choose between satisfying the Roman hierarchy or a Protestant and liberal majority among his people and in parliament, the grand duke opted for the stronger and appointed August Lamey, the chief parliamentary spokesman of the liberals, to head a new ministry in 1860.

This unprecedented appointment of the leader of a parliamentary majority inaugurated five years of rapid domestic reform. The public was given the right to nominate local administrative officers; the court system was separated from the general state administration; the principles of public proceedings and trial by jury were more widely implemented than before; and full legal equality for Jews was enacted. Only in the troublesome matter of church-state relations did Lamey disappoint a significant number of his liberal supporters. Chiefly over this issue, the left-liberals in 1865 finally formed a separate organization of their own, the Baden Progressive party (Fortschrittspartei). Though they continued to support him, the anticlerical Progressives in the Chamber of Deputies insisted upon many more restrictions against the church than Lamey was willing to see enacted. There was little difference between the Progressives and the more restrained liberals on the question of national unity; some in each group opposed Prussian leadership, while a majority tended to favor it. If the Progressive leaders gradually pressed for more political reforms than the moderates were ready to approve, they did so in part to compete with Baden's democrats for popular support.

Democrats had been far from satisfied by Lamey's reforms,

and they did not share the enthusiasm for Prussia that many liberals felt. Well before the creation of the Progressive party, democrats in Baden had attempted to form their own party. The chief impetus was given by a returning émigré, Ludwig Eckardt. Having participated in the Viennese and Dresden uprisings in 1848 and 1849, Eckardt had found refuge in Switzerland in the 1850's. Back in Baden, he joined the Nationalverein in 1862, but soon left it because its majority favored a Prussian-led Germany. In January 1864 he joined with several other returned revolutionaries—including Amand Goegg and Jakob Venedey—to correspond with men in other states who disliked Prussia and hoped to create a united Germany through a democratically elected national assembly.[18]

Elsewhere in southern Germany, liberals and democrats collaborated better than in Baden, though disagreements over internal reforms and Prussia's role in Germany would disrupt their common fronts by 1866.

In Bavaria the leader of the liberals was the lawyer-publisher Karl Brater. Early in the decade of reaction, Brater had been squeezed out of his office as mayor of the ancient town of Nördlingen, and by 1855 he had become a well-known critic of the government. In 1858, at thirty-nine years of age, he was elected to the Bavarian Landtag to represent Nuremberg. Here the discontent of the lower middle class caused many voters to support liberals and democrats. A co-founder of the Nationalverein, Brater sat on its central committee with the leader of Bavaria's democrats, Karl Crämer von Doos. A year older than Brater, Crämer had worked his way up from mill hand to factory owner. His sympathy for the workers caused him to support the innovation of cooperatives and helped him win a political following. With other liberals and democrats, he and Brater in March 1860 founded a "club" in Munich to discuss and loosely coordinate efforts for reform in Bavaria. Three years later, to prepare more effectively for the approaching Landtag elections, these men created the Bavarian Progressive party. In 1864 and 1865 they perfected its organization, expanding it into active local associations notably in Munich, Nuremberg, Fürth, Dinkelsbühl, and Rothenburg.

The Progressive party's program favored German unity, but

left members free to prefer either Austrian or Prussian leadership. More directly, the new party stepped up pressure for reforms in Bavaria. For too long, the local branch in Nuremberg declared, only the "potentates" had formulated policy—"and a bad one at that." The Progressives promised to change the character of the Bavarian House of Lords or eliminate it altogether, increase the powers of the lower house, and restrict the government by decreasing the intervals for parliamentary approval of budgets from six years to no more than two. Like similar organizations in southern Germany, the Bavarian Progressive party was predominantly Protestant and anticlerical. Its own liberalism as well as its resentment of Catholic influence in a largely Catholic state caused it to demand freedom of religion and the elimination of church influence from the public schools. While showing some concern for social welfare measures, it was basically a laissez-faire party.

On a number of principles, therefore, the leaders of the Bavarian Progressives could agree, but their incompatibility on others eventually led to schism. One basic matter on which the liberal and democratic leaders disagreed was reform of the suffrage. The liberals were willing to call for more frequent elections, but they refused to recognize the right of all adult males to vote equally, secretly, and directly. This caused considerable anguish among democratic members of the party, and their disaffection increased in the fall of 1865 when Brater and other liberals explicitly called for Prussian leadership in a united Germany. On October 30, 1865, Crämer pulled out of both the Nationalverein and the Progressive party. He joined the anti-Prussian Volkspartei (People's party) then emerging in Württemberg, taking with him the former local branches of the Progressive party in Nuremberg and Fürth in Franconia. In the Bavarian Palatinate, other branches of the Progressive party followed Georg Friedrich Kolb—a democratic Landtag deputy closely associated with Crämer since 1860—into the Württemberg-led Volkspartei. Other Bavarian democrats stayed with the Progressive party. This organization finally endorsed universal manhood suffrage in 1869, but even then it could not agree to a fully democratic suffrage reform.

Having divided among themselves and antagonized a great

many of the kingdom's Catholics, the liberals and democrats were unable to achieve any significant reforms in Bavaria. But they had laid down foundations for the continuity of liberal and democratic political agitation throughout the remaining decades of the nineteenth century.[19]

In Hesse-Darmstadt, too, a Progressive party was created early in the 1860's in close conjunction with the local branches of the Nationalverein. The organizers of the Nationalverein in the grand duchy did not disguise their desires for internal changes as well as for German unity. As the new chapter in Offenbach informed the grand duke, their aim was to prevent revolution through the achievement of timely reforms. In the state as a whole the pro-Prussian liberals followed the lead of a vigorous Darmstadt attorney, August Metz, one of the founders of the Nationalverein and a member of its central committee. Democrats rallied around Ludwig Büchner in Darmstadt or the equally anti-Prussian Alexis Dumont of Mainz. With both liberals and democrats supporting it in 1862 the new Progressive party won a majority of the seats in the lower house of the parliament. There the pro-Catholic policies of the ministry of state preserved liberal solidarity. But in 1866 schism would come to the Progressive party of Hesse-Darmstadt as it had to the Progressives in Bavaria. Here, too, the breakup of the reform coalition would be precipitated by the refusal of the democrats to preserve their alliance with the pro-Prussian liberals.[20]

Because of their widespread dislike of Prussia and traditional love of independence, Württembergers gave the Nationalverein less support than had Badeners. Yet, both liberals and democrats desired the election of a national assembly that would guarantee "the unity of Germany conjointly with its development toward freedom." They made this the first principle in their program when they founded their Progressive party in 1861. The second plank emphasized the need to reform Württemberg's own constitution. They further demanded introduction of voting by secret ballot, public and oral proceedings in the law courts, greater administrative autonomy for the municipalities, and freedom of the press and association. They called on the Württemberg ministry to recognize unreservedly "the constitutional principle" and to conform to the will of the state's parliament.

Thus Württemberg's liberals in the Progressive party agreed on a considerably more democratic program than the Progressive parties in the other states adopted, but their democratic allies were not content with it. Some continued to hope for the eventual creation of a republic. They wanted equal, direct, and universal suffrage as well as the secret ballot. Many feared that the Progressive program opened the way for recognition of Prussian leadership in Germany, or that it endorsed too much centralization for the future united Germany. In 1863 these Württembergers welcomed two returning veterans of the revolution. Karl Mayer, a charismatic "man of the people" who had served in the Frankfurt Assembly, returned to Stuttgart from Switzerland. Ludwig Pfau, editor in 1848 of a revolutionary newspaper, came back to Stuttgart from a prolonged stay in France. With Julius Haussmann—a Stuttgart republican of 1849 who had subsequently served a prison term for his revolutionary acts—Mayer and Pfau set to work to create a new and distinctly democratic party. Taking over direction of the Stuttgart newspaper, *Der Beobachter*, in February 1864, the three men used it to rally Progressives who wanted democratic reforms without delay and who opposed unification of Germany under Prussia.

Unlike its counterparts in Bavaria and Hesse-Darmstadt, the Progressive party in Württemberg never coalesced; like them it came apart over the issue of Prussia. In January 1866 the new Volkspartei was formally organized in Stuttgart by Mayer, Pfau, and Haussmann. In response, liberals among the former Progressives founded a new German party in August 1866, expressly endorsing the unification of Germany by Prussia. But in creating their new party the Württemberg liberals faced stronger competition from the Volkspartei than liberals elsewhere had met from democrats. They needed to take a more radical position than did liberals in the other south German states, accepting the central principle of the democrats as their own: direct and secret suffrage for all adult males in state elections. With both Volkspartei and Deutsche Partei supporting this, Württemberg's parliament soon enacted reform legislation.

From the outset, the men who organized the Volkspartei favored a federal union of the German states as well as reform in Württemberg. Even before they formally announced the birth of the new party in their homeland, Mayer, Pfau, and Haussmann had begun to line up supporters in other states. As noted above, Crämer and Kolb in Bavaria were among the earliest to join in the effort to provide the movement with an all-German following. Leopold Sonnemann, leader of Frankfurt's liberal democrats, joined together with his followers. Other allies were won here and there in Baden, Saxony, and even in Prussia (where Johann Jacoby was the best known among them and Guido Weiss was an active publicist for the cause). Meeting in Stuttgart in September 1868, representatives of many of the local branches adopted a program for what henceforth would call itself the German People's party (Deutsche Volkspartei). Notwithstanding its new name this organization won little strength outside of south-western Germany. But its aims, its devotion to them, and its large following in Württemberg made it the first democratic party to achieve significance in any German state.[21]

Support for Prussia in southern Germany had arisen from the conviction that German unity could be achieved in no other way and that it was a goal worthy of the sacrifice of some political ideals. Opposition to Prussian leadership had flowed originally from traditional south German sympathies toward Austria and from living memories that Prussia had frustrated efforts for democratic unity in 1849. That opposition had been enormously invigorated in the period 1861–66 by events in Prussia. Throughout these years, the powerful northern kingdom was embroiled in the most serious internal political struggle it experienced between 1849 and 1918—one in which the Hohenzollern ruler and his ministry earned the condemnations of both liberals and democrats, north and south, by their unconstitutional rule. Authoritarian and antiauthoritarian Germans agree on little, but have recognized the Prussian constitutional crisis of 1861–66 as a fundamental turning point in the struggle for representative and democratic government in Germany.[22]

In one of the ironies of German history, the crisis was precipitated under a new Prussian ruler and a new ministry that at first had aroused the hopes of liberals. In 1857 the physical and mental health of King Frederick William IV broke, whereupon his brother, Prince William, took over state affairs. When William officially became regent in October 1858, he swore to uphold the constitution, and he soon dismissed Manteuffel, appointing to the new cabinet three conservative liberals who had served in the ministry with David Hansemann in 1848. Prince William, hoping in this way to achieve greater popular support, thus inaugurated what came to called—expectantly—the "New Era."

The regent had been trained as an officer, and as a boy of seventeen he had served briefly at the front in Prussia's 1814 campaign against Napoleon. Regarded as a reactionary in 1848, he had been sent to England by Frederick William until the excesses in Berlin were calmed. But he had not opposed the granting of the conservatively liberal constitution in Prussia, and in the 1850's he had been critical of reaction. His chief attention had been given, as before 1848, to the army. When he became regent William decided to expand the Prussian military forces and to improve their effectiveness so Prussia could assert its influence more vigorously in German affairs.

The regent's goals were suggested in 1858 by the vague announcement of the policies of the new ministry, which proclaimed that "Prussia must make moral conquests in Germany." This had caused Germans who hoped for unity to look to Berlin with new interest. Prussia's voters also had responded favorably to the modest shift to the left. When a new Chamber of Deputies was elected in November 1858, moderate conservatives, liberals, and a few liberal democrats formed a majority for the first time since the revolution; stand-pat conservatives and reactionaries suffered a sharp loss. But what seemed to be an electoral endorsement for the regent in November 1858 threatened to become his nemesis when he sought to implement his military program.

In December 1859, William appointed General Albrecht von Roon minister of war. Both feared Napoleon III's foreign policy. Both had been distressed by shortcomings of organization and administration in the army that had shown up during Prussia's brief mobilization in response to the war in Italy. They were determined to create a highly professional army that would be utterly dependable in war and a solid support for the crown in domestic troubles. In 1860 they proposed to extend the length of compulsory service from two years to the three-year term already legally authorized but not practiced. The size of the Prussian standing army would be increased from 150,000 to about 220,000 men; reorganization of the reserve forces would make it more responsive to royal command. An appropriation bill to finance more barracks, training facilities, and schools for officers was presented to the Chamber of Deputies.

The liberals were much concerned about the costs of the program, and they were upset by the proposal to make the army more professional. They made it clear that they did not like the plan to reduce the independence of the reserves and the militia from the regular army. They opposed the extension of the active duty period, believing that the longer period of service would return citizens to civilian life unduly accustomed to authoritarian discipline. Assuming that the ministry would not ignore the views of the liberal leaders, the Chamber of Deputies approved a provisional appropriation for one year.

In January 1861, Frederick William IV died, and the regent inherited the throne in his own right at sixty-three as King William I. In that same month it became clear that the government was going ahead with its reorganization of the army. In the spring, increasing public concern was expressed. What had begun as a calm discussion in the chamber was becoming a disturbing political issue. At this stage of the controversy Karl Twesten, a liberal writer in Berlin who had been a republican in 1848, published a polemical pamphlet against the government's plans. When he was challenged to a duel and shot through the arm by a reactionary general, the issue became heated. Twesten was elected to the new Chamber of Deputies in December 1861, as were Franz Benedikt Waldeck, Julius Rupp, Rudolf Virchow, and a number of other democrats of 1848–49. The Prussian elections of December 1861 thus showed that not even the three-class voting system without secret ballot could prevent the revival of opposition when the middle-class voters rose to defend the constitution. In the new chamber a strong majority opposed the ministry. It included 91 conservative liberals, 50 moderate liberals, and—most surprising—109 members of a new organization of liberals and democrats, the Progressive party. Founded only in June, the Progressive party was the largest group in the new house.

The more radical parliament, as expected, opposed the plans of Roon and William I. In March 1862 it refused to appropriate additional funds for military expansion and reorganization. The monarch and the Prussian military leaders were alarmed by what they seriously believed to be a recrudescence of the revolutionary spirit. Roon talked at times of the need to abolish the Chamber of Deputies altogether, and military plans were made for holding Berlin in the event of an uprising. These were only to be last-resort measures, but then the king dissolved the chamber, called for new elections, and dropped liberals from the cabinet. Roon remained minister of war in the conservative government that was announced on March 14. What had begun as a disagreement about military matters was becoming a test of strength between the Hohenzollern dynasty and Prussia's thirteen-year-old parliament.[23]

In the campaign leading up to the new elections on May 6, 1862, the liberals and liberal democrats were better organized than they had ever been. Many of the twenty-six thousand members of the Nationalverein were organized into local branches throughout Prussia, and these included the most influential of the government's critics. Their contacts with liberals and democrats from other German states made them aware that the latter would not accept Prussian leadership in the unification of Germany unless constitutional government were upheld in Berlin. In its annual convention of October 1862, the Nationalverein criticized the government of Prussia while praising both the Prussian people and their resisting Chamber of Deputies.[24]

The opposition of the Prussian chamber to government policy had been even more directly strengthened in June 1861 when the German Progressive party (Deutsche Fortschrittspartei) was organized. The inclusion of "German" in its title indicated a desire for counterpart organizations in other German states. Its pledge to work for national unity and support of parliamentary government in Prussia did, in fact, help inspire the formation of the separate Progressive parties in southern Germany, but the "German" Progressive party remained Prussian.

The leadership and membership of Prussia's Progressive party and of the Nationalverein were overlapping; eight members of the central committee of the Fortschrittspartei in 1862 were among the twenty-five members of the central committee of the latter. In many places the existing organization of the

Nationalverein created the local branch of the new party. Like the Nationalverein, the Progressive party included both liberals and democrats, and many Prussian Progressives—like those in the south—did not wish to include the masses. The prospects of gaining much support from the common folk were not cheering, for most third-class voters in Prussia continued to stay away from the polls on election days, and conservatives won as many class-three votes as did their opponents in the three elections of 1861–63. Thus the program of the Fortschrittspartei did not call for equal suffrage; though many of its leaders favored it, others were strongly opposed, arguing that equal and public voting would bring increased power to conservatism and that equal and secret suffrage would facilitate the growth of an independent labor movement. Much internal debate in the Progressive party centered on the suffrage issue, but in its official public pronouncements the party stressed other objectives on which most of its members were agreed.

The Progressive leadership was largely middle class but heterogeneous in occupational interests. The principal occupations of the 135 Progressive deputies elected in May 1862 are shown in the following table:

Principal Occupation	No. in Progressive Party (and % of Total Progressive Party Delegation)	No. in Chamber as a Whole (and % of Chamber Total)
Judicial officials	34(25%)	90(26%)
Administrative officials	9(7%)	44(13%)
Retired officials	11(8%)	18(5%)
Agricultural landowners	26(19%)	82(23%)
Merchants & industrialists	13(10%)	21(6%)
Lawyers	12(9%)	16(5%)
Persons of independent means	6(4%)	12(3%)
Educators	6(4%)	13(4%)
Physicians	5(4%)	6(2%)
Journalists	3(2%)	4(1%)
Craftsmen	3(2%)	5(1%)
Clergymen	1(1%)	19(5%)
Others	6(4%)	22(6%)
Totals	135(99%)	352(100%)

Business and the professions were more dominant among the Progressives than among other parties. Still, merchants and industrialists made up only 10 percent of the Progressive deputies elected in May 1862. If any social or occupational group can be said to have been predominant in the leadership of the Progressives, it was the municipal, district, and state officials, who accounted for 40 percent of the deputies. On a major economic principle—free trade—numerous large farmers, as exporters of grain to England, could agree with middle-class liberals; thus one out of every five of the Progressive deputies was, by primary occupation, a landowner. Indeed, a number of East Prussian landlords had taken the lead in organizing the Progressive party in 1861. But only 7 percent of the Progressives were members of the nobility, whereas noblemen constituted 21 percent of the chamber as a whole.

Among the democrats who led the Progressive party were several men who had been leaders in the 1848 revolution. They included Franz Benedikt Waldeck; the physicians Johann Jacoby and Wilhelm Löwe-Calbe; and Hermann Schulze-Delitzsch, who had won a large following in the 1850's as the organizer of workers' cooperatives. Among the sympathizers of that unsuccessful national and democratic movement who had not been active in it were the East Prussian aristocrat Leopold von Hoverbeck, the chief organizer of the party, and the physician Rudolf Virchow who now became one of its leading spokesmen. These liberal democrats shared leadership with liberals such as Karl Twesten, Max von Forckenbeck (a lawyer from a Westphalia), the energetic historian Theodor Mommsen, and Hans Viktor von Unruh (a manufacturer of railroad equipment who, for a time, had presided over the Prussian Constituent Assembly in 1848). With both democratic and liberal spokesmen, the Progressives would disagree on many issues, but they were united in favoring German unity, free trade, and defense of the Prussian constitution.[25]

The conservative ministry appointed in March 1862 had hoped the elections would return a Chamber of Deputies more friendly to Roon and the king, but it was bitterly disappointed by the voters on May 6. The conservative and Catholic factions supporting the government declined from 68 seats to 39. The conservative "Old Liberals," wanting to protect parliamentary rights but inclined to be conciliatory, were reduced from 91 to 65 seats. The election gave the part-liberal, part-democratic Fortschritts-partei 135 seats; the Progressives thus formed the largest group in the new house as they had in the previous one. Another 96 liberals remained outside the Progressive party but were will-ing to cooperate with it. Altogether, therefore, 231 of the new chamber's 352 members could be counted upon to oppose the government's military policy.

Under these conditions, a few of the king's ministers began to suggest compromise with the parliament on the army reorgani-zation. The minister of finance stated that to rule without parlia-mentary approval of the budget would not be in harmony with the constitution. Roon himself at one point was ready to bargain with the parliamentary liberals. But the possibilities of compro-mise were ended on September 17 when King William insisted that the term of active duty must be increased as planned. Convinced that the Prussian army had built the Prussian state and that the Hohenzollern dynasty rested upon its support, William was not prepared to have his rights as supreme com-mander of that army diminished. He argued that money could be raised without parliamentary approval, and he precipitated a sharp cabinet crisis by threatening to abdicate unless the ministry supported him.

General von Roon, who had been inclined to compromise, was equally ready to march with his monarch once the king an-nounced his will, but he knew that to do so required a minister-president who would be similarly sturdy in implementing the will of the crown against the protests of liberals and democrats. Roon knew where to turn. For months he had been in close touch with Otto von Bismarck, the stormy Junker who had supported counterrevolution in 1848. For months Roon had been suggest-ing that he be brought into the ministry. On September 18, Roon telegraphed his friend—since May, Prussia's ambassador to France—that the awaited crisis was at hand. Early the next day Bismarck left Paris by train.

By the time Bismarck arrived in Berlin, two ministers had resigned rather than fly in the face of the Prussian Chamber of Deputies. On September 22, after assuring the king that he was ready to push through the desired military reorganization against the will of the chamber, Bismarck was authorized to form a new ministry. No one at the time could know whether the new minister-president would be able to cope with the crisis. The king himself knew that it was a gamble to resist the chamber. Neither he nor anyone else expected the new chief of government to hold his position for the next twenty-eight years.[26]

The new minister-president of Prussia was forty-seven years old in 1862 and powerfully self-assertive: "I want to play only the music which I myself like, or no music at all," he had written when twenty-three. Independent of Darwin, he had developed an earthy sort of Darwinian outlook on life. "It is the destiny of the weak to be devoured by the strong," he commented on one occasion. But Bismarck's determination and his competitive spirit were checked by flexibility. He shrewdly sensed that it was more useful to play opponents against one another than to destroy them, and he proved himself to be adept at applying this insight. His economic and political philosophy was shaped by devotion to the interests of his fellow Junkers, to his monarch, and—above both—to the increasing power of the Prussian state; but in serving all these he insisted upon room for opportunistic maneuver. "If I had to go through life with principles," he once remarked, "I would feel as though I had to walk a narrow path in the woods . . . [with] a long pole in my mouth."

As Prussia's envoy to the Diet of the German Confederation from 1851 to 1859, Bismarck had become a bitter foe of Austrian influence in German affairs. His anger had not subsided during his years as Prussian ambassador to Russia (1859–62) and France (since May 1862). By 1859 he had become a confirmed advocate of Prussian leadership in the unification of Germany—motivated not by ideological commitment to nationalism but by his desire to magnify the power of Prussia. Although his motives were quite different from theirs, Bismarck had adopted the national objective of the Prussian liberals and democrats.[27]

Tactics guided his first dealings with liberals in the Prussian chamber in 1862. In an attempt to split the opposition, he held out the possibility of ministerial appointments to Baron Carl von Vincke, Heinrich von Sybel, and Eduard Simson. Unfortunately for Bismarck, his promise to the king to stick by the army reform did not permit him to strike a real compromise with the moderates. During the next several months, therefore, he fought the parliamentary opposition without scruple. The constitution, he told parliament on January 27, 1863, assumed compromise on legislation between the chamber, the House of Lords, and the crown. The "doctrinaire absolutism" of the chamber, he said, had made compromise impossible; authority must be exercised in such a situation, because the life of a state allowed no interruption.

The Chamber of Deputies did not let so sweeping a declaration of authoritarianism go unchallenged. Support mounted for a bill aimed against Bismarck by Hermann Schulze-Delitzsch. Based on the 1848 concept of juridical rather than parliamentary responsibility of ministers of state, the legislation would authorize the chamber to bring charges of unconstitutional behavior against a minister, which could result in his dismissal if the charges were upheld in a judicial trial. The Chamber of Deputies adopted the measure on April 27, 1863. There was no chance that either the House of Lords or the monarch would allow it to become law, but the vote of 249 to 6 demonstrated how fully Bismarck had outraged the chamber.

The minister-president struck back hard. On June 1, 1863, a sweeping edict provided that newspapers could be banned by administrative rather than court action for encouraging a "general attitude" considered "dangerous to the public welfare." Legal scholars declared this ukase unconstitutional, a new association for defense of freedom of the press quickly won twenty-five hundred members, and the decree was publicly criticized by the king's own son, Crown Prince Frederick, who thus acquired a lasting reputation as a liberal. Under heavy public pressure, the decree was withdrawn in November. It had been imposed to assure the election of a new chamber that would cooperate with the government, but it had boomeranged; when the elections were held on October 28, 1863, Bismarck's foes were stronger than ever. Liberals increased their representation to 106, the Progressive party won its greatest victory with 141 seats—40 percent of the total.[28]

It was clear in the fall of 1863 that the voters were standing behind the opposition majority in the chamber, but the Prussian government continued to hold trump cards that had once before guaranteed its success. There were surpluses of state revenues in 1862–64, as income from state railways increased and the bureaucracy collected taxes without the approval of the parliament. Furthermore, the Prussian army stood ready to put down any revolt that might break out; and remembering its effectiveness against German revolutionaries in 1849, the opposition leaders did not expect a new revolt.

Other circumstances also sharply restricted the radicalism of the chamber. One was its sensitivity to foreign dangers in the era of Napoleon III. Thoughts of revolt were stifled, too, by belief that only Prussia could lead Germany to unity. The Fortschrittspartei itself declared that the unification of Germany could not be conceived "without a strong central power in the hands of Prussia." And another kind of hope worked against thoughts of revolution: Bismarck's opponents could tell themselves that, after all, the voters had stood more and more firmly behind them since 1861; that, in time, Bismarck would either fall from power or bend to the will of parliament. Thus, both despair and some degree of optimism counseled legal rather than revolutionary resistance to the minister-president's high-handed measures. Liberals such as Johann Jacoby called upon the Prussian voters to refuse to pay taxes; but Jacoby was jailed for doing so, and the leadership of the Progressive party refused to adopt this line of civil disobedience. The task of the majority of the Progressives, as Leopold von Hoverbeck defined it in February 1863, remained the same throughout the conflict: to avoid either "ignominious capitulation" or "radical excess."

Bismarck's foes were further handicapped because they remained internally divided. Throughout the four-year crisis there was no more agreement in the Progressive party on positive aims of fundamental importance than there had been when the party was founded in 1861. It was unwilling to encourage the development of independent organizations of factory workers; it remained silent on the issue of democratic suffrage, because a declaration for equal and secret suffrage would have split the party; and it was unable to take a positive stand on other constitutional questions. While insisting that budgets must have the approval of the Chamber of Deputies, it could not agree that the lower house should be able to force the fall of a ministry by a majority vote of "no confidence." Only a few Progressives dared suggest that the king should be required to select new ministers from their own ranks. The party's dilemmas sprang from its origin as a coalition of liberals and liberal democrats. This alone was enough to paralyze it.

But if Bismarck's parliamentary foes could not agree on war aims, they were tenacious in their defensive struggle in support of parliamentary rights. Repeatedly the liberal and democratic allies in the chamber resisted and condemned the government with their votes, their speeches, and their press. When the chamber on February 22, 1866, once again defeated a motion to legalize the state budget, the government entered a fifth year of operating on funds that had not been approved by parliament. The end of the constitutional crisis was not in sight, much less the character of its outcome. [29]

What had happened since 1859 is clear above all the details of day-to-day political conflict. During the 1850's it had become generally apparent that Austria, while supporting reaction in the individual German states, could not bring them into a unified nation. Increasing numbers of liberals and democrats who longed for unification had begun in 1859–60 to look to Prussia for leadership. To awaken popular enthusiasm for unity and to bring pressure upon the state governments for internal reforms, they and pro-Austrian associates had created the first political parties in German history. The regency of William I had reawakened enthusiasm for Prussian leadership, but it was checked by the onset of the constitutional crisis in Berlin. To liberals and democrats, it seemed that only a parliamentary victory in the constitutional struggle could open the way for Prussia to lead Germany to unity. Thus those who watched outside the Chamber of Deputies cheered the stout resistance of the opposition majority to Bismarck's ministry from 1862 to 1866. But the limitations under which Bismarck's foes carried on their resistance—some of them self-imposed—promised no early end to the struggle. The initiative remained with the minister-president throughout. The gambles he made in 1866 would decide not only the prospects for German unity but the outcome of the internal crisis in Prussia as well; and they would also greatly influence the chances for democracy in Germany as a whole during the remaining decades of the nineteenth century.

VII.

UNIFICATION: BISMARCK'S TRIUMPH OVER THE LIBERAL DEMOCRATS

In the *Communist Manifesto*, early in 1848, Marx and Engels had predicted that the "bourgeois revolution" in Germany would be "but the prelude to an immediately following proletarian revolution." In April 1850, Marx had announced that a new revolution was "imminent." Subsequent events showed, however, the error of these reckless prophecies, and what happened after 1866 differed even more strikingly from their author's youthful expectations. Germany was to become a nation, but consolidation would leave the established social fabric intact. The accomplishment was not Marx's, but that of another Prussian, Otto von Bismarck. Bismarck's instrument was the Prussian army, the power of which he had enhanced by flaunting the will of the Prussian parliament. Important concessions to democratic principle, too, were to find a place in his statecraft of 1866–71, but ironically Prussia's liberal democrats would suffer a decisive setback as part of the process of unification. By 1879 the democratically elected parliament of the new Reich would appear to be severely circumscribed by institutional bulwarks against popular sovereignty and by Bismarck's proclivities for authoritarian government.[1]

The enlarged Prussian army first fought with Austria for a cause favored by many liberal nationalists. The revolutionaries of 1848 had been powerless to bring either Schleswig or Holstein, largely German in population, into the closer union they aspired to build. Since then, the Danes had incorporated these provinces into their own kingdom, which the Diet of the German Confederation was powerless to prevent. Though locked in economic and political rivalry, Austria and Prussia shared a common interest in preventing the absorption of the duchies by Denmark. In a short war in 1864 they took Schleswig and Holstein from Denmark once and for all.

Bismarck saw collaboration with Vienna as a temporary expedient. In 1864 and 1865, through tough bargaining, he reasserted Prussian economic leadership against Austrian pretensions, renewing the Zollverein for a period of twelve years. Meanwhile, he repeatedly provoked disputes with Austria over plans for the future of the duchies. A truce was reached by the Convention of Gastein in August 1865: for the moment, Prussia was to administer Schleswig, Austria Holstein. But again Bismarck was only marking time, and tension grew. In April 1866 he prepared for an armed showdown with the Habsburgs by forming an alliance with the new kingdom of Italy, which hoped to wrest Venetia from Austria. British and Russian neutrality was assured. To keep France on the sidelines Bismarck hinted that Napoleon III might be allowed to annex Belgium and even territory along the Rhine at Prussia's expense.

On June 12, 1866, Bismarck provoked his war with Austria by sending Prussian troops into Holstein. He was widely condemned in Germany for this aggressive action. Two days later the Diet of the Confederation approved Austria's request that member states mobilize their forces against Prussia. Prussia declared war against Electoral Hesse, Hanover, Saxony, Frankfurt, and the south German states, all of which had taken Austria's side. Swift victories followed. Hesse-Cassel was completely occupied by June 18; Hanover's army surrendered eleven days later. The decisive engagement in a decisive war was not long in coming. Moving into Bohemia from Saxony, Lusatia, and Silesia, the Prussian armies fell upon the main Austrian force on the rainswept fields and hills around Sadowa (near Königgrätz) on July 3. After an all-day struggle involving almost half a million men, the Austrians were routed, and before their collapsing lines could stabilize, they agreed to an armistice. Politically the Prussian victory assured much more—the end of the German Confederation, the end of Habsburg predominance among the German states, and the beginning of Prussian mastery over a German nation.

When the Diet in Frankfurt had taken its stand on June 14, Prussia had declared the German Confederation to be dissolved, and its military success guaranteed that there would be no revival. Therein lay Austria's chief setback. Territorially, she lost little; Venetia was ceded to Italy, but Bismarck restrained the Prussian generals and King William from taking more. Similar reserve characterized the settlement with Saxony and the south German states, which had mobilized on the side of Austria. These were required to enter into treaties of alliance with Berlin, to revamp their armies on the Prussian model, and to guarantee mutual support in the event of attack by another power. In case of war, their armies were to pass under the command of the Prussian king.

The idea that Bismarck showed great moderation amidst victory in 1866 is a myth, for Prussia directly expanded at the expense of the city-state of Frankfurt, the large kingdom of Hanover, the electorate of Hesse-Cassel, and the duchy of Nassau. All these had sided with Austria, and all, like Schleswig-Holstein, were annexed to Prussia. The Hohenzollern kingdom now sprawled across all of northern Germany from the Russian frontier in the east to France in the west; it had gained five million new subjects. With the Prussian army Bismarck had managed to accomplish in Hesse-Cassel, Nassau, and Hanover what the revolutionaries of 1848 had been unable to—the overthrow of three established dynasties, the only German ruling families to be deprived of their thrones by force between 1815 and 1918.[2]

On August 18, 1866, Prussia and fifteen other states of northern Germany entered a compact to create a new German union. Soon twenty-three states north of the river Main, most of them very small, joined to build a government under Prussian dominance. This was indirect annexation, made possible by the fear of Prussian military power. In creating this North German Confederation, Bismarck made use of democratic procedures as well as military force. The new federation's Constituent Assembly was elected on February 12, 1867, on the basis of the Frankfurt Assembly's democratic suffrage of 1849, with voting being equal, secret, direct, and universal for adult males. Yet the majority of the members elected to the Constituent Assembly were moderate liberals and liberal conservatives, not democrats. Eduard Simson, the liberal who had presided over the Frankfurt Assembly in 1849, was chosen to chair the gathering in Berlin while it deliberated over a draft constitution. Bismarck had considered the constitutional proposals of Max Duncker and other liberals and had already negotiated the basic terms of the draft with the participating governments, but the liberals won significant additional concessions. After formal approval of the new constitution by the state governments the North German Confederation became an accomplished fact on July 1, 1867. Thus was born a state of some thirty million inhabitants, of whom twenty-five million were citizens of the enlarged state of Prussia.

Prussian power and liberal demands made this Confederation much more centralized than the German Confederation had been. The federal union was headed by the Prussian king as president. He held supreme command over the armies of the union and was empowered to name the chief minister (chancellor) of the state; to this office he appointed Bismarck who continued to serve as minister-president of Prussia. The participating states preserved a large measure of autonomy, with their dynasties and governing institutions remaining intact. Furthermore, a Bundesrat (Federal Council)—resembling the Diet of the German Confederation of 1815–66—represented the governments of the states within the North German Confederation, which appointed and controlled its delegates. Measures could not become law without the approval of this upper house of ambassadors. Thus the structure fully protected the interests of the states, but it guaranteed the predominance of Prussia by placing the executive power in the hands of its king and his chief minister. Executive authority, checked by the Bundesrat, was also limited by the popularly elected parliament. This Reichstag was a major concession by Bismarck and the Prussian king to the spirit of 1848–49.

The democratic Reichstag was the joint product of Bismarck's disenchantment with Prussia's three-class suffrage during the constitutional struggle and of his opportunistic maneuvers in 1866 to win liberal and popular support against Austria. On April 9, 1866, he had issued a call for election of a German assembly through universal suffrage, and on June 10 he had made it clear that he intended to accept in large measure the democratic system that the revolutionaries adopted in Frankfurt. This was so radical that the king balked at first. "Why that is revolution you're proposing to me," William objected. Bismarck left no doubt that his motives were not revolutionary. "Until the victory in foreign affairs," he later explained, "I was ready, if necessary, to pay *'black mail'* to the Opposition." Thus he "had no hesitation whatever in throwing into the frying pan . . . the most powerful ingredient known at that time to liberty-mongers, namely, universal suffrage." It was designed not only to pacify his domestic opponents, but to rob foreign enemies of any chance to play public opinion against the Prussian government during the war and after; in Bismarck's own words, it would "frighten off foreign monarchies from trying to stick a finger into our national omelette."

What had been offered in 1866 to mobilize support against Austria could hardly be repudiated in 1867 because the parliaments of the sourthern states were yet to be won for German unity under Prussia. Indeed, Bismarck even found it expedient to accept for the North German Confederation the democratic principle that he had not promised in 1866 and did not want in 1867—the secret ballot. A great many liberals in the Constituent Assembly had not wanted equal suffrage, but virtually all were opposed to public balloting, knowing that this would enable conservative landlords to control the voting of peasants dependent upon them. Thus the liberals insisted that the suffrage be secret, and Bismarck finally agreed.

While the democratic suffrage was achieved for the North German Confederation, democratic government was not, for the powers of the Reichstag were carefully limited. The veto right of the Bundesrat protected Prussia and the other state governments against Reichstag interference in their internal affairs and against the passage of laws that were contrary to vital conservative and particularistic interests. (For example, limited suffrage continued in all states.) In addition, the Reichstag could not control the appointment of the chancellor.

His purpose, Bismarck had told the envoy of Saxony, was "to overthrow parliamentarism with parliamentarism," and indeed he had succeeded in preventing the Reichstag from ruling the North German Confederation. But the constitution required parliamentary approval of budgets by the Reichstag as well as the Bundesrat—thanks to the pressures exerted by the liberals in the Constituent Assembly. This must be viewed as an important gain in the long struggle for representative government in Germany.[3]

In Prussia, however, the emergence of the North German Confederation brought defeat for the liberal democrats, which would have lasting consequences in Germany's future.

Bismarck's parliamentary foes in Prussia had, under increasingly difficult conditions, continued to criticize his rule; as late as February 1866 the Chamber of Deputies had rejected the government's budget proposals. Then the war against Austria had weakened their will to resist Bismarck and had undermined their public support.

The voters of Prussia, having given the parliamentary opposition increasing support from 1861 through 1863, registered their new sentiment at the polls in the summer of 1866—confirming Bismarck's dictum that "a battle won . . . strangely alters men's minds." The public balloting occurred on June 25, three days after Prussian troops had moved into Hanover, Hesse-Cassel, Saxony, and Austria. In the new chamber the conservatives, who had supported Bismarck and the army, quadrupled their representation from 35 to 136. The Progressive party, the chancellor's toughest domestic foe, was a heavy loser, declining from 141 to 95 seats; and some of the Progressive deputies were now ready to support the government. Other liberals declined in strength from 106 to 53 seats. In the previous chamber the anti-Bismarckian liberals and Progressives had commanded a strong majority. In the new one they were a minority.[4]

Flushed with victory in the Prussian elections and in the war against Austria, Bismarck astutely offered peace to the more moderate opposition leaders in the new Chamber of Deputies. Thus he proposed that the king open the new session of parliament on August 5 by asking the chamber to vote retroactive approval of all expenditures since the last budget had been passed by parliament in 1861. Moderates could view this request as recognition of the chamber's constitutional budget powers. At the same time, the policies of William I and Bismarck—previously so loudly, persistently, and rightly condemned by the parliamentary opposition as unconstitutional—would be justified before public opinion in Prussia and in the other German states by parliamentary approval of the "bill of indemnity." The king was not easily won to this stratagem because he regarded such a request as an admission of past errors." Finally, however, William assembled the parliament in the White Hall of the royal palace in Berlin to make the desired overture. His description of what had been done as an "unavoidable necessity" could be interpreted to mean that it might be done again. But he then expressed the hope that "recent events" would cause the deputies to grant an indemnity and end the conflict between crown and parliament.

The indemnity bill provoked anguished conferences among those who had stood up for the rights of parliament since 1860. Many of the liberals—never democratic, strongly nationalistic, and believing that the rights of parliament had now been acknowledged—could accept Bismarck's olive branch with no sense of surrender. Karl Twesten had quietly approved the basic idea of an indemnity bill as a way out of the impasse even before Königgrätz strengthened Bismarck's arm. Now, in the Chamber of Deputies, he said bluntly what many other liberals were thinking: "No one may be criticized for giving precedence to the issue of power at this time and maintaining that the issues of freedom can wait, provided that nothing happens which can permanently prejudice them."

Still others, including many liberals outside Prussia, were fatalistic, or—as they preferred to consider themselves—realistic. It was said that one must accept the "moral power of the facts" or the "law of history"—phrases widely used to explain the "inevitability" of Prussia's success. The famed chemist Justus von Liebig, though he lived in defeated Bavaria, called it a triumph for "science," for "intelligence and knowledge." For none was acceptance of Prussia's victory seemingly easier than for August Ludwig von Rochau. A *Vormärz* radical, Rochau had shared the national disillusionment of the early 1850's. In 1853 he had added a new word to the vocabulary of liberal politics with a book on *Realpolitik* (policy [or politics] of realism). "The law of power," said the author, "dominates political life just as the law of gravity dominates the physical world." It was actually irrational, he concluded, to try "to subordinate might to right." In 1853, Rochau had wanted the liberal and democratic nationalists to act accordingly, but in 1866 he could only advise his friends to adapt themselves to the *Naturgesetz* ("law of nature") that he saw at work in Bismarck's successes.

Voices of dissent were still heard, though in diminished numbers. "Beware of the fetishism of success," Rudolf Virchow warned his fellow liberal democrats in Prussia's Chamber of Deputies. Virchow, the scientist, refused to recognize that the "laws of nature" had determined the events of 1866; he left such playing with science to others. Torn between nationalism and democratic principles and worried by the sharp decline in their public support, a number of Progressive deputies were ready to approve the indemnity bill, but more than half refused. Waldeck, who had endorsed Bismarck's foreign policy, could not bring himself to support the indemnity. To do so would mean, he stated, the "betrayal of all that the opposition has fought for during the time of conflict." In the chamber, Virchow declared that he and his colleagues could not approve the policies the government had pursued since 1861, that "no government in the world should be justified for denying a people its constitutional rights."

Virchow and his supporters in the Progressive party were the best democrats the Prussian parliament had in 1866, but this Chamber of Deputies in September was no longer the parliament that had taken its stand against the government. When the votes on the indemnity bill were cast on September 3, only 75 members of the house voted against it; 230—including 43 of the 95 Progressives—gave it their votes. And when the king in September proposed a bonus to generals who had distinguished themselves in the campaign against Austria, the chamber modified the request only to include Bismarck (at his own suggestion); his share was 400,000 thalers.[5]

It would be wrong to regard these developments as a total victory for authoritarianism in Prussia. To the great disappointment of reactionaries, the constitution had been preserved; thus the compromise of 1866 did not mark the "unconditional surrender" of the liberals. It reaffirmed what they had gained in 1848–50 and much of what they had advocated from 1862 to 1866.[6]

Yet the outcome of the constitutional crisis set back Prussia's democrats; the cooperation with the liberals that had existed before and during March 1848 and again in the early 1860's ended; and they became an isolated minority. In the winter of 1866–67, 34 of the 95 Progressives in the Prussian Chamber of

Deputies broke with the democrats and joined other liberals in Prussia and throughout Germany to establish the National Liberal party. Forckenbeck, Gneist, Lasker, Twesten, and Unruh were among Bismarck's former foes who played major roles in the new party. The Progressive faction left behind failed to hold the remaining ground; in the Prussian parliamentary elections of 1867, only 48 of its 61 members were returned, and the 1870 elections brought a gain of only one seat. [7]

Between 1867 and 1871, Bismarck was able to complete the unification of Germany by continuing to mix money, iron, and blood with concessions to representative government. The task was to bring the south German states into union with the rest of Germany. The chief obstacle was traditional south German particularism. The chief foreign obstacle was the Second French Empire of Napoleon III, whose military adventure in Italy in 1859 had done so much to influence German desires for unity.

Bismarck's knowledge that France would oppose the full unification of Germany had caused him in 1866 to settle for the treaties of alliance with the south German states. Besides, he knew that Baden's grand duke wanted eventually to bring his state into the Prussian-led union and the other states closer to Berlin. Financing the war had strengthened Prussia's great banking firms while weakening the states that had supported Austria. Industrial and railway concerns in the south, hitherto looking to Frankfurt for loans, turned increasingly after 1866 to Berlin; and Frankfurt itself was now a part of Prussia. In 1867, Bismarck extended democratic suffrage in the south German states in an attempt to bind their economies more closely to Prussia's. Believing that elected representatives from the south would be more pliable than the state governments, he put pressure on the latter to agree in July to the creation of a parliamentary assembly within the framework of the German Customs Union. This Zollparlament would consist of members of the North German Reichstag plus deputies elected for terms of three years by the southern states through direct, secret, and equal manhood suffrage.

The initial result appeared to brake the momentum toward national union. When the voters of the southern states elected their representatives to the Zollverein parliament in February

1868, they clearly understood that the central issue was not the economic union itself but their eventual complete integration into a German polity. Both the advocates and the opponents of unity under Prussian leadership staged vigorous campaigns, and the southern nationalists suffered defeat. In Hesse-Darmstadt they won three of six seats, and in Baden a majority of eight out of fourteen; but in Bavaria the supporters of German unity under Prussian rule captured only twenty-one of forty-eight seats, and in Württemberg their opponents won all seventeen. Thus in February 1868 the prospects for unity seemed dim. "To attain with one blow a homogeneous structure for Germany," Bismarck commented, "is only possible in the event of war." But he insisted that Prussia must do nothing to provoke one.[8]

Against the continued growth of Prussian power and the possibility of conflict, Napoleon III of France was increasingly vigilant. But—humiliated by foreign policy failures and troubled by growing opposition within France—he was still searching for allies when he learned in July 1870 that a Catholic member of the Hohenzollern family had accepted an invitation to fill the vacant throne of Spain. It is impossible to say with certainty how early Bismarck became a supporter of Leopold's candidacy for the Spanish throne, or what his precise purposes were at the outset. But he pushed it from the end of February 1870 on, though he knew the French would not tolerate a Hohenzollern "encircle-ment." A biographer of Bismarck reasonably concludes that he "deliberately set sail on a collision course with the intent of provoking either war with France or a French internal collapse."[9] The result of his provocations and of folly in Paris was that the French government declared war on Prussia on July 19.[10]

The French declaration of war alienated European opinion, automatically put the entire North German Confederation into the conflict, and delivered Prussia the support of the south German states. The war that followed was a brilliant success for German arms and a debacle for the Second French Empire. By late August the German forces directed by Helmuth von Moltke had driven through Lorraine and cornered Napoleon III and his army at the Belgian and Luxembourg frontiers. At Sedan—while William I, Bismarck, Moltke, and Roon watched from the hills above the battle—the Germans scored their decisive triumph against the outnumbered French; Napoleon III and more than one hundred thousand troops surrendered on September 2. The debacle at Sedan unseated the imperial government in Paris. The new provisional government, in the face of public pressure but against the judgment of many of its members, continued the war, but finally capitulated on January 28, 1871. By the Treaty of Frankfurt, France was to remain under occupation until it paid an indemnity of five billion francs, and, with the full approval of many German liberals and some democrats, was to surrender Alsace and Lorraine. Meanwhile, capitalizing on the exaltation produced by a popular and successful war, Bismarck created the German Empire.[11]

Even before the Battle of Sedan, Bismarck had begun to draw the south German states into a larger union with the North German Confederation. During September 1870 the governments of Baden and Württemberg indicated their desire to become part of a "German Empire," but Württemberg as well as Bavaria held out for a looser framework than that of the North German Confederation. Eduard Lasker, a revolutionary of 1848 and now a leading National Liberal in the North German Reichstag, volunteered to help stir up popular pressures in southern Germany against the recalcitrant governments. But Bismarck preferred to achieve his goal through negotiation; he prompted the National Liberal press to demand greater speed in the achievement of unity and, finally, even offered concessions to the government in Munich. By November 23 he had Bavaria's agreement to participate in the union, and that of Württemberg was given two days later. With few changes, the constitution of the North German Confederation was to become the constitution of the new empire.

Having patiently negotiated with the particularist governments of the south, Bismarck also acknowledged the right of the democratically elected representatives of the North German Confederation to share in the founding of the empire, though their roles in the drama were carefully restricted. When a special session of the Reichstag of the Confederation considered the treaties for unity that Bismarck had negotiated, several deputies criticized the methods and form of unification. Only a socialist, August Bebel, called for the creation of a republic, but many

Progressives argued that an all-German constituent assembly should be elected to draft a new constitution. The National Liberals, wanting a tighter union, nevertheless decided to settle for the attainable: "the girl is ugly," said Lasker, "but she has to be married anyhow." On the crucial issue the Reichstag voted 195 to 132 on December 9 to approve the arrangements Bismarck had made with Bavaria. Seventy members absented themselves rather than vote, but most of the Progressives voted with the large majority. The Reichstag then sent a delegation to German military headquarters at Versailles to urge William I to accept the leadership of a united Germany.

When the parliamentarians arrived in Versailles, William I threatened to spoil their limited participation in the achievement of unity. Bismarck remarked: "the King . . . believes . . . that the Sovereigns of Germany *alone* can give him the Imperial crown, and that therefore the deputation from the Reichstag . . . are a pack of revolutionists who are encroaching on the rights of the Minor Sovereigns of Germany and should therefore not be received at all." Bismarck finally convinced the king, but William refused to receive the Reichstag delegation until after the rulers of the German states had approved his assumption of the imperial title. This done, the liberal president of the Reichstag, Eduard Simson, delivered a moving address to the king on December 18, and the sovereign indicated that he would accede to the wishes of the other princes *and* the German people.

On January 18, 1871, the official ceremony to proclaim the German Empire was held in the Hall of Mirrors of the great palace Louis XIV had built at Versailles in the seventeenth century—at a time when the Hohenzollerns ruled a small patrimony of scattered territories within the Holy Roman Empire. The ceremony involved only princes and generals. The liberal and democratic forces that had initiated the movement for German unity were not represented; neither north German nor south German parliamentarians were allowed to participate in the formal birth ritual of the united nation.[12]

The men who controlled the massive new state in central Europe proved to be as undemocratic in practice as was the ceremony that celebrated its creation, but to win popular support they perpetuated the democratically elected parliament of the North German Confederation. Left-liberals and democrats thus won a national forum for the decades to come. Meanwhile, during the years liberal democrats were defeated in Prussia, democratic principles succeeded in southern Germany.

In Württemberg, Bismarck's war with Austria in 1866 had helped the democratic Volkspartei of Karl Mayer, Ludwig Pfau, and Julius Haussmann win backing among their anti-Prussian countrymen. The war aided the Württemberg democrats in other ways. Having supported the losing side, their king now had to seek parliamentary approval of increased appropriations and public acceptance of the unpopular treaty of alliance with Prussia that Bismarck had forced upon him as part of the peace settlement. Bismarck also made the Württemberg government more vulnerable to democratic pressures by giving the North German Confederation a democratically elected Reichstag and by insisting in 1867 upon the election of southern representatives to his Zollverein parliament on the basis of democratic suffrage.

Mayer, Pfau, and Haussmann capitalized on the opportunities these events offered them. In 1867 their Volkspartei collected forty-three thousand signatures for a petition asking the king that a state constitutional assembly be elected to complete the unfinished work of 1849–50. Rather than risk that, the government proposed to the regular parliament a draft law for suffrage reform. Thus on March 21, 1868, one month after the Zollparlament elections were held, universal secret manhood suffrage was adopted in Württemberg to choose the seventy elected members of the Chamber of Deputies. The twenty-two dignitaries who sat in it as representatives of privileged corporate groups would continue to do so for three more decades. As a result of this mixed system Württemberg began to acquire the reputation it would enjoy in imperial Germany as a "people's monarchy."

In neighboring Baden, too, Bismarck indirectly and unintentionally helped left-liberals and democrats score new successes after 1866. Grand Duke Frederick I, King William I's son-in-law, entered the war against Prussia with great reluctance. He and his army deserted the Austrian cause with what many considered indecent haste at the first opportunity. The grand duke then appointed a new ministry, whose members were politically less skilled than their immediate predecessors. The tasks they needed to perform could not increase their popularity—to win parliamentary approval of the new treaty of alliance with Prussia, which required increased appropriations to carry out expensive army reforms on the Prussian model. Relations with the Catholic hierarchy, disturbed since the 1850's, were aggravated by the new ministry. Furthermore, in Baden as in Württemberg, the democratic election of representatives to Bismarck's customs union parliament in February 1868 stimulated public agitation for electoral reform at home. Dissident Catholics as well as democrats raised a clamor for both direct and secret suffrage in state elections.

Partly to compete with their democratic and Catholic rivals, partly out of conviction, a faction of the liberal parliamentarians now raised reform demands of their own. August Lamey, no longer in office, was among their leaders, working closely with Karl Eckhard, Johann Caspar Bluntschli, and Friedrich Kiefer. The driving force among the left-liberals was Kiefer, an official in the Ministry of Justice. He passionately threw himself into the campaign for reform, warning up and down the land that liberalism, to survive, must be converted from a loose association of the educated and propertied middle class into an organized mass movement.

Most liberals refused to join these critics of the government, but with the country in ferment the ministry wanted the support of as large a majority in the Chamber of Deputies as possible. By June 1869 the leading minister, Julius Jolly, was beginning to reach an understanding with the left-liberal leaders. He rejected their demands for annual parliamentary approval of budgets, for reorganization of the upper house, and for direct election of the Chamber of Deputies, but he would support some other changes. Thus, between September 1869 and April 1870 wide-ranging reforms were enacted by the Baden Landtag with the approval of the ministry. The secret ballot was introduced. The right to vote, enjoyed by most men since 1818, was extended to all adult males. The terms of deputies were reduced from eight years to four, making the chamber more responsive to changes in public sentiment. And the government formally acknowledged the right of the chamber to elect its own presiding officer, control its own agenda, and initiate legislation. Thus in the winter of 1869–70 aims of Baden liberals and democrats since the days of Rotteck were fulfilled at last. The state was not yet a full-fledged monarchical democracy, but it was on its way to becoming one.[13]

The new German Reich that emerged in 1870–71 contained, besides its democratically elected Reichstag, two states of the southwest in which liberal and even democratic impulses were strongly rooted. Württemberg and Baden together had only one-seventh of the population of Prussia, but supporters of popular sovereignty could hope that they, like a small cake of yeast in a large bowl of dough, would move and change the politics of the empire. Yet, as the Reich was consolidated in the 1870's, such hopes remained unfulfilled. No new advances toward democracy occurred; Bismarck opposed them, the most influential parties did not press for them, and democracy remained an impotent minority movement.

In the 1870's the National Liberal party—the largest in the Reich—proved itself a loyal prop of the new empire. It was led by men who for twenty years or more had pushed for representative government and German unity; but theirs was an elitist spirit. The left within the National Liberal party after 1871 found an effective spokesman in Eduard Lasker, a hard-working judge and founding member of the party. Lasker had directed sharp words against Bismarck in the Prussian constitutional conflict of the 1860's, and after 1871 the animosity remained alive as Lasker strove for a freer and more centralized Reich. But even this formidable Jewish orator did not demand equal suffrage for Prussia. Many right-wing National Liberals, meanwhile, rallied around Johannes Miquel. A revolutionary socialist in 1848 and a founder of the Nationalverein in 1859, Miquel had announced in 1866 that politicians should no longer ask for "what is desirable, but for what is attainable." After 1871 he had became a director of one of Germany's largest banks (the Diskonto-Gesellschaft), and he held seats in both the Reichstag and the Prussian Chamber of Deputies. Rudolf von Bennigsen, who had presided over the Nationalverein, was the logical mediator between the left-wing and the more conservative National Liberals. The acknowledged leader of the party, he stood closer to its right wing than to Lasker. He frankly argued that the National Liberals should defend the interests of industry, foreign and domestic commerce.

The National Liberals commanded sufficient strength in the Prussian Chamber of Deputies to elect Bennigsen president in 1873, when they also reached their height in popular backing and in influencing the national government. When the first Reichstag was elected in 1871 the National Liberals won more votes than any other party to capture 125 seats—twice as many as the next largest faction. They held 155 seats from 1874 to 1877. As the largest group in the parliament, their support was indispensable during the early years of Bismarck's chancellorship.

Since both Bismarck and the National Liberals agreed to strengthen the new federal government, they collaborated to create the institutions of the new Reich. An Imperial Bank, an office to coordinate and supervise Germany's railroads, and a national system of justice were among the results of their cooperation. Partly to please the National Liberals, Bismarck followed a policy of free trade and agreed in 1874 to a Reich Press Law that afforded considerable freedom of expression. But on many matters the National Liberals, not Bismarck, made the concessions. In 1874, Lasker courageously argued for the annual review of military expenditures by the Reichstag against Bismarck's attempts to deprive the parliament of control over the size of the army; but he was sharply criticized by many members of his own party. In the end the National Liberals supported a compromise worked out by Friedrich Miquel and the chancellor. By the terms of this arrangement (the *Septennat*), the size of the standing army was to be debated and approved by the Reichstag, but only once every seven years. Only in 1878 did the National Liberal leaders once again attempt to strengthen the influence of the Reichstag and their own party over Bismarck's policies. The result was the opposite of their intentions: Bismarck whipped them into line by raising the specter of socialist revolution and calling new Reichstag elections that reduced the National Liberals to two-thirds of their 1874–77 representation; by the following year he had found other parliamentary supporters.

During their alliance with Bismarck, National Liberals in the Prussian Chamber of Deputies continued to oppose universal manhood suffrage. The party whose 1867 program claimed credit for the Reichstag suffrage could have joined with the Progressives to form a majority in the Prussian chamber from 1873 to 1879, but it made no effort to introduce equal, secret, and direct suffrage into Prussia. Events of the 1870's showed that the National Liberal party would not exert itself to democratize the new German Empire.[14]

By 1879 it was equally clear that no effective thrust for democracy could come from Prussia's Progressive party. This group had made important contributions to Germany's slow advance toward popular sovereignty, but had been drastically set back by Bismarck's combination of authoritarianism, nationalism, and timely conciliation. In 1863 the Progressives had won 40 percent of the seats in the Prussian Chamber of Deputies, but in the elections to that body after 1871 they and kindred left-liberals never won more than 16 percent, a peak reached in 1873. In the Reichstag the Prussian Progressives and liberal democrats from southern Germany seldom occupied more than 14 percent of the seats. Bismarck had won a decisive victory over the Prussian liberal democrats in the process of unifying Germany, and those in the south were not heavily represented in the Reichstag. The liberal democrats might have helped to achieve democracy in the German Empire, if they had possessed the will, but some other party would have to provide the necessary mass following.[15]

The one party other than the National Liberals that won such a following in the 1870's was the Catholic Center. Containing democratic as well as conservative elements, in the first decade of unity it was the major national party of opposition. Yet by 1879 the Center party was becoming a supporter of the constitutional status quo rather than a force for democratic reform.

Tentative steps to organize Catholics politically had been taken in the period from 1848 to 1867, but the Center emerged as an organized party only in the year that German unification was completed. Its leaders were inspired by pro-Austrian sentiments, a strong sense of states' rights, devotion to a papacy whose ecclesiastical and territorial status was threatened by various crises throughout western and southern Europe, and a distinct awareness of the minority status of Catholicism in Prussia and in the emerging empire. Catholics had formed a slight majority in the old German Confederation, led by the Catholic dynasty of Austria, but in the new Reich, headed by Protestant Prussians, they were outnumbered: 15,000,000 Catholics found themselves in an empire containing 25,550,000 Protestants. Defensive anxieties prompted a ready Catholic response to the new Center party. With 58 seats when its caucus was organized in December 1870, it was the third largest group in the Prussian Chamber of Deputies. Winning 63 seats in the first Reich elections of March 1871 it became the second largest party in the Reichstag of the German Empire.[16]

Prussian Catholics had tended to support Bismarck and the crown in the constitutional struggle, but the attitude of the Prussian and Reich governments toward the new party and the Catholic church after 1870 quickly altered the relationship. The official restrictions against the church, and Catholic resistance to them, came to be designated the *Kulturkampf*, or "struggle for civilization." The conflict originated in the tragic chronological juxtaposition of three important events: (1) the completion of German unification without Catholic Austria; (2) emergence of the Center party; and (3) the promulgation by the Vatican Council in July 1870 of the dogma of papal infallibility, which decreed that when the pope spoke officially on matters of faith and morals he could not err. Obedient to a supranational authority in Rome, the Catholic majorities in Baden and Bavaria and the Polish Catholics in Prussia's eastern provinces were now supplemented by anti-Prussian Alsace-Lorraine, where 76 percent of the population was Catholic. In the east, the west, and the south, Catholics were concentrated on the sensitive borders of the Protestant-ruled Reich. Just across these frontiers the new Germany faced Catholic Austria and Catholic France, both suspected of harboring thoughts of revenge against Prussia. Thus both international and domestic considerations made Bismarck view Catholicism in Germany with concern and the Center party as its offensive spearhead in politics.[17]

In restricting the Catholic church in Germany, Bismarck hoped to force it and the Center party to submit to the sovereignty of the new German Empire and of the Prussian state within that empire. His backers in this instance included liberals and progressives, who as Protestants or as secularists or as nationalists, viewed a confessional party with distrust and disdain. The iron chancellor's liberal and democratic adversaries shared this aversion. Under their stimulus, in November 1871 the Reichstag made preaching opposition to the state a penal offense. In July 1872—again with Reichstag approval—the Society of Jesus was banned in Germany. By laws of May 1873, fully approved by the Prussian Chamber of Deputies, the education of priests and pastors in Prussia was to be supervised by the state and required to include secular studies; state authorities were empowered to veto the appointment of clerics to church positions; and the right of the papacy and the church hierarchy to discipline Prussian priests and laymen was restricted. In December 1874, Bismarck formally broke off diplomatic relations with the Holy See. He interfered freely in the appointive powers of the hierarchy, naming Catholics loyal to him to church offices. Those loyal to Rome who attempted to fill church positions against the orders of German public authorities could be deported and denied citizenship according to a law approved by the Reichstag in April 1874. Ending centuries-old exclusive privileges of the churches, civil marriage was made compulsory. The state also took over the registration of births and deaths. In Prussia all Catholic religious orders except those engaged in nursing were dissolved.[18]

The Catholic church in Germany suffered severely under Bismarck's *Kulturkampf*, but the struggle consolidated the Center as a mass party. In the Reichstag elections of 1874 its representation increased from 63 to 91 members. Crossing all levels of German society, it included industrialists and workers, landed aristocrats and landless peasants, and large numbers of middle-class Catholics. Priests were active leaders of its municipal, provincial, and state committees. In Ludwig Windthorst the Center found an effective and able leader. His determination and parliamentary eloquence were constant irritations to Bismarck, who once exclaimed: "My life is preserved and made pleasant by two things —my wife and Windthorst. One exists for love, the other for hate." Windthorst insisted that neither Rome nor the German bishops instructed the Center how it should speak and act, but the church had no more clever or tenacious defenders anywhere than this diminutive Hanoverian lawyer and the powerful party he led.

Overlooking no means of countering Bismarck's thrusts with pressures of their own, in 1873 Center representatives in the Prussian Chamber of Deputies came out in favor of equal suffrage. Ironically, the Center proposals were defeated with the help of men who claimed to be liberals and democrats and enemies of Catholic reaction. Prussia's Progressives and her National Liberals solidly backed the *Kulturkampf* and had initiated some of its measures; they were in no mood in 1873 to give equal suffrage to lower-class voters who might not share either their liberalism or their anticlericalism. The Center's advocacy of democratic suffrage in Prussia may have been simply tactical—an attempt to win popular support for the party and to put Bismarck on the defensive. But the negative attitude of the liberal parties prevented the testing of the Center's commitment to democratic principle at a time when it was emphatically a party of opposition.

By 1878 both the Center and Bismarck were weary of the conflict. The great majority of German Catholics had proved their loyalty to the church, but they could not prevent substantial disruption of its work. All the Prussian bishoprics were without regular incumbents, and some 1,400 of 4,600 parishes had no priests. Other states had adopted restrictive measures similar to those in Prussia. Furthermore, the Center's votes in Reichstag elections had slightly declined from 28 percent in 1874 to 25 percent of the total in 1877. The relative steadiness showed that Bismarck had not been able to discredit the Center, but it seemed increasingly obvious to thoughtful Catholics that they could not win the *Kulturkampf* either.[19]

At this point diverse considerations made Bismarck ready for reconciliation between church and state and for an understanding with the Center party. Eager to restrict the powers of the Reichstag in general and the National Liberal party in particular, he could achieve the latter objective by winning the support of the Center. Concern about the socialist movement, still small but growing rapidly, further prompted him to settle the conflict with the church. His endorsement in 1878 of a protective tariff, then being demanded by agrarian interests in both the Center and the Conservative parties, was a signal to both groups that they might replace the National Liberals as Bismarck's parliamentary allies. Death also played a part in the reorientation of German policy, for the passing of Pope Pius IX in February 1878 made it easier for Bismarck to compromise with the church. The new pontiff, Leo XIII, agreed to consult Berlin before making appointments to church offices in Germany, and Bismarck agreed to restore bishops and priests to their charges. By July 1879 reconciliation had progressed far enough that Bismarck's tariff—a major landmark in both the economic and political history of imperial Germany—was passed by the Reichstag with votes from the Center and over the opposition of liberal democrats and a majority of the National Liberals. The National Liberal party, born from the split of the Progressives in 1866 over Bismarck's indemnity bill—now suffered schism over the chancellor's tariff legislation.

Catholic support thus enabled Bismarck to put his "liberal" policies of 1866–78 behind him and to inaugurate the more authoritarian policies of the remaining decade of his stewardship. Much of the anticlerical legislation of the 1870's remained in effect, and many Catholics continued to feel only hatred for Bismarck; but the *Kulturkampf* had convinced their leaders that the interests of the church in a Protestant-dominated Reich could best be safeguarded under a benevolently conservative government. Bismarck's gradual retreat from the *Kulturkampf* further reduced the chances that the Center party might attempt to democratize the Hohenzollern monarchy. So did rising Catholic concern about the spread of socialism, which appeared to threaten church and monarchy alike. Windthorst could honestly proclaim in 1879 that his party would "never pursue its special grievances, its special purposes, when throne, fatherland, and the most vital interests of the nation were at stake."[20]

The complex developments which embrace the founding and consolidation of the Reich support no facile assessments of their contribution to the nature of German government between 1848 and 1914. Ulysses S. Grant, a contemporary of the events described, provided one of the most misleading judgments when he celebrated the creation of the German Empire as "an attempt to reproduce in Europe some of the best features of our own

Constitution."[21] Since Grant's time the unification of Germany has more commonly been interpreted as an authoritarian victory for Bismarck, iron, and blood. This verdict contains obvious, but only partial, truth. One of the major goals of German democrats —national unity—had been achieved. A second major aim—a national parliament elected by democratic suffrage—had also been realized. Several democratic reforms had been effected in Württemberg and Baden. The years 1866–71 stand, therefore, as an important stage in the political modernization of Germany. But Bismarck, while conceding a democratically elected Reichstag, had carefully built dikes around it. In fact, he had created a Reich dominated by Prussia, and while reaffirming the budgetary power of the Prussian Chamber of Deputies, he had unmistakably defeated those of his countrymen who believed that government policies should be not only limited by parliamentary majorities but determined by them.

The net result of Bismarck's statecraft in the years 1866–71 was an improvised Prussian empire rather than a rationally planned German nation. It was what German scholars tend to call a "constitutional" state, an incomplete synthesis in which traditional monarchical powers were definitely limited, but in which popular sovereignty was not yet won. After 1878, Bismarck himself attempted to alter the internal balance of power that his compromises of 1866–71 had established and to guide Germany more explicitly by conservative and reactionary principles.

Clearly much remained to be done before firm direction from above would give way to democracy in Germany, and no large movement to accomplish such a change was available in 1879. Significant movement toward democracy would depend in the future upon the growth of a new left—one that was only slowly gaining cohesion during the decade of German unification.

VIII.

A NEW LEFT:
SOCIAL DEMOCRACY,
1863—1890

Marx and Engels agreed that the unification of Germany would hasten the growth of a centralized international socialist movement. By 1874, when he estimated that the Bonapartist character of the new polity would protect "all propertied classes against the onslaught of the working class," Engels predicted that future historians would consider the battles of 1870 less important than "the unpretentious, quiet, and constantly forward-moving development of the German proletariat."[1]

This prophecy is not confirmed even in the most recent scholarly reappraisals of the Bismarck era. But the socialist founding father hit the mark in one respect: the Social Democratic movement organized in the 1860's was slowly becoming the major force of democratic opposition, official efforts to repress it (especially after 1878) notwithstanding.

In the decade it was organized, Social Democracy stood for no single ideology. Its varied principles, never fully synthesized, were taken from the liberal-democratic movement, from the Judeo-Christian conscience (grieved by the social injustice of the nineteenth century), from English economic theory, and from the utopian socialists of the earlier nineteenth century. From Hegel it borrowed a modified dialectical philosophy, which contributed a method of reasoning, an inflated terminology, and a sense of certainty about the future.

Marx and Engels have been justly celebrated for giving the German socialist movement a foundation in economic theory, but a number of other men made important contributions. Karl Rodbertus was educated in the law, economics, and philosophy at Göttingen, Berlin, and Heidelberg before settling on a Pomeranian estate. In 1847 he sat in the United Diet and the following year, voicing democratic principles, he was elected to Prussia's Constituent Assembly; for two weeks he served as minister of education in the Auerswald-Hansemann cabinet. In 1849 he defended the Frankfurt constitution, then withdrew from political activity to protest three-class suffrage in Prussia. Though backing Bismarck against the liberals during Prussia's constitutional conflict, Rodbertus continued to pursue his economic program, first announced in 1842, whose goal was to provide the worker with a larger share of the national income. Workers, he insisted, must receive more than the bare subsistence to which capitalism confined them. Independently of Marx, Rodbertus explained the exploitation of the proletariat in terms similar to the theory of surplus value. His cure, however, differed drastically. Rather than urge the workers to overthrow the existing state, he asked that state to legislate a higher return on the efforts of labor. By calling on established authority to grant social justice he made socialism politically and socially respectable. His doctrines attracted to the socialist movement Germans of moderate and peaceful disposition, even after his death in 1875.

The program of Marx and Engels, basically established by 1848, never was to be fully endorsed by all German socialists; but by the 1870's, in varying degrees, it influenced the thought of all the leaders of the movement. While only a few grasped the intricacies of its economic theory, even rank and file socialists were beginning to accept Marxism as a secular faith. In it the Judeo-Christian conception of the world as an arena of struggle between God and the devil for the souls of men was sublimated to the concept of struggle between classes for material mastery. Private property became the Marxian forbidden fruit, the cause of all subsequent social troubles. The assumption of "surplus value"—Marxism's economic "sin"—justified the ultimate extinction of the capitalist class, the bourgeoisie. The inevitable victory of the proletariat displaced Judgment Day in the new eschatology. Calvinism's belief in salvation after death was scrapped, but the dogma of a sainthood of the elect was retained in a modified version: the socialist faithful believed that the newly discovered laws of social evolution predestined them to inherit an earthly paradise of proletarian solidarity and individual fulfillment. Thus, while condemning all religious faiths, Marxism provided a new faith of its own, a temporal religion for an age of materialism.

The harsh Marxist talk of class struggle did not entirely exclude old democratic liberalism from the new movement. Social Democracy became a mixture of violence, a program of reform challenged by sermons of revolution, love of freedom, and talk of a "dictatorship of the proletariat." A major reason for the mixed aims of German socialism was its dual character of labor movement and school of determinism. Just as the economic interests of the middle class compromised the ideals of liberal democracy, so the desire of industrial workers for modest but immediate economic gains modified Marx's revolutionary dogmas in the socialist movement.[2]

The grievances of workingmen in the Bismarckian era were numerous and real. While the tempo of industrialization in Germany had increased since 1850, working conditions had remained oppressive. Unemployment had risen during the depression that began in 1857, was only briefly alleviated by the boom in 1871–72, and rose again during the prolonged economic stagnation which began the following year. Both national income per capita and real wages increased once again after 1881, but at severely disparate rates; the former doubled during the next twenty years, while the latter only rose by one-third. The divergence would have been even larger but for the pressure exerted by labor organizations in the 1860's. In those years adult males commonly worked fourteen hours a day, and there was little regulation of child labor. In Baden, for example, the employment of children under twelve years of age was allowed before 1870, and the law passed in that year authorized a twelve-hour working day for youngsters between twelve and sixteen. Mothers commonly worked at factory jobs too. Families were crowded into miserable housing in the grimy industrial sections of Germany's mushrooming cities.

The conditions of the industrial workers improved after 1890, but remained unenviable. Meanwhile, their numbers grew from five million in 1871 to nine and a half million in 1910. Urbanization proceeded apace: almost two-thirds of the forty-one million

Germans in 1871 still lived in rural areas; two-thirds of the sixty-eight million in 1914 lived in towns of over ten thousand. The population of Berlin, for example, increased by six times between 1871 and 1918. The industrial workers in the great metropolitan centers were flocking to Social Democracy, attraced by the promise of immediate improvements in their existence rather than by the theoretical constructs of "scientific" socialism.[3]

Industrialization accentuated grievances among many Germans who were not members of the factory proletariat. The cheaper manufactured products slowly but inexorably were crowding out of local markets the wares that had for centuries been produced by craftsmen in small workshops. The master artisans and the journeymen they employed, like the many small merchants who were being squeezed by the competition of large enterprises, came to form the lower middle class. By 1850, Marx had formulated the basic attitude his followers were to take toward this group throughout the next century. While recognizing that many petty bourgeois spokesmen favored political democracy and even social reforms, he had argued that they did so only "to bribe the workers"—"to break their revolutionary strength by making their position more bearable for the moment." In a revolutionary crisis, he expected that the lower middle class would be a reactionary force and must be opposed by the "workers," After 1870, Engels judged it only slightly less harshly; he agreed that it tended to be reactionary in a crisis, though he acknowledged that "there are good elements among it, who, of their own accord, follow the workers."

Actually the lower middle class produced not only followers but leaders of the proletariat; for the psyches and political actions of men are shaped by more than the economic interests of a class as defiined by Marx. Neither Marx nor genuine proletarians achieved the organization of Social Democracy in the 1860's. Rather, it was artisans like those who had fashioned labor brotherhoods in 1848—tailors, bookbinders, cigarmakers, carpenters, and shoemakers. Several craftsmen who had participated in the Verbrüderung between 1848 and 1852 helped to revive the local workers' associations after 1861, when some relaxation in the enforcement of the association laws once again made such efforts possible. Other leadership came from middle-class democrats, veterans of 1848, including Hermann Schulze-Delitzsch in Prussia, Emil Adolf Rossmässler in Saxony, and Ludwig Büchner in Hesse-Darmstadt. In the 1860's these men led the vain struggle to create a democratic mass party representing many interests. Few liberal democrats were willing to pledge themselves to socialism or to drastic social reform; to that extent, Marx had been right about them. The idea of cooperation between workers and liberal democrats lingered on through the 1860's, but as early as 1863, Ferdinand Lassalle—like Marx a member of the middle class—denounced it as humbug and organized Germany's first socialist workers' party.[4]

Lassalle, born in 1825, was raised in a Breslau merchant household that knew no poverty, but as a Jew he knew legal and social discrimination. From the personal experiences of a sensitive childhood emerged two lasting personality traits: identification with the underdog and an almost boundless personal ambition for social acceptance and fame. Lassalle grew into young manhood impartially indulging his twin passions for radical scholarship and women. He developed his political philosophy through reading Hegel, Heine, and Börne, but he became an activist only after meeting Countess Sophie von Hatzfeldt—a woman twenty years his senior who had been cast out by her husband without adequate financial support. In 1847 and 1848 he achieved considerable notoriety as the Countess' attorney and intimate friend. Though his first "underdog" was a noblewoman, he dramatized his defense of her rights into an indictment of class privilege.

Lassalle joined the socialist republicans of the Rhineland who rallied around Marx in 1848–49. Jailed as the leader of strikes against unauthorized taxes, he was out of circulation when the revolution in Prussia was broken, and so was not forced to join his comrades in exile. During the 1850's he nourished his radical philosophy and achieved some success as a writer. During the decade of reaction he corresponded with Marx and became a Marxist of sorts. In April 1861, during a brief stay in Berlin, Marx spent ten days in Lassalle's apartment, and Lassalle returned the visit while in London the following summer. Soon master and disciple clashed over fundamentals, and in November 1862 they ceased exchanging letters.

Lassalle, according to Marx, was "infected with superannuated French liberalism." He was a German nationalist who hoped for unification under Prussian leadership and was as assiduous as the most self-conscious Marxists in his defense of the interests of labor. To the state-socialist Karl Rodbertus he wrote late in April 1863 that the abolition of private ownership of land and capital had been "the inner kernel" of his conviction ever since he "began to think about economic matters." To achieve socialism, he proposed what the Verbrüderung had called for in 1848—state credit to workers' industrial cooperatives. But how was the state to be persuaded to provide this? Repeatedly, Lassalle told audiences of workers that they must win political power. This conviction caused him to advocate universal, equal manhood suffrage as "the most fundamental and important" of all the demands of labor. In 1863, having failed to win the Progressives and other liberal democrats to his ideas, his program of political equality for all men produced an invitation to lead a group of workers in Leipzig.

The result was the General German Workers' Union (Allgemeine Deutsche Arbeiterverein), founded on May 23, 1863, with Lassalle as its president. A few days before, Lassalle had met Bismarck, at the latter's initiative, for the first of several talks, and he clearly hoped the Prussian minister-president might inaugurate both social legislation and equal suffrage. But Bismarck went away unconvinced, and Lassalle continued to champion an organized workers' push for political rights. The progress of his new movement was uneven. Existing local associations were suspicious of his authoritarian poses, while the hitherto unorganized workers in the Rhineland received him enthusiastically. Optimistically, he wrote to Countess Hatzfeld that the atmosphere at these meetings was like "the founding of new religions" must have been in the past. On the threshold of great events, private entanglements ended Lassalle's career. A love affair with the daughter of a Bavarian diplomat earned him the challenge to a duel with the young woman's fiancé. The aggrieved rival was quicker on the draw, and on August 31, 1864, his bullet killed the working-class dictator. By the time he was struck down, only 6,400 had rallied to his banner. Nevertheless, he had—as Marx later grudgingly admitted—"reawakened the laboring movement in Germany" after fifteen years of slumber.

Whatever Lassalle's ultimate personal ambitions may have been, the German workers who followed him believed his promise to lead them under "the banner of democracy." In the decades that followed his death thousands, in Austria as well as in northern Germany, were attracted to Social Democracy by Lassalle's speeches and writings long before they read Marx. Each year on August 31 hundreds of them would gather in Breslau to place red ribbons on his grave.

Although disputes broke out among Lassalle's successors, membership in the German Workers' Union grew to 9,421 by the end of 1865. The growth could be attributed mostly to the party's new newspaper, the *Social-Demokrat*, whose editor, Johann Baptist von Schweitzer, gradually consolidated his leadership over the organization. Like Lassalle, he called for Prussian leadership in Germany and hoped Bismarck would grant equal suffrage. The *Social-Demokrat* openly took Bismarck's side against the Progressives, who had refused to endorse either equal suffrage or social legislation. "Parliamentarianism," Schweitzer wrote in January 1865, "means empty wordiness . . . whereas Caesarism at least means masterful initiative."[5]

Many of Germany's artisans had not been able to stomach the Prussian sympathies of Lassalle and cared just as little for those of Schweitzer. One of these was August Bebel. Born near Cologne in 1840, the son of a Prussian noncommissioned officer who died when the boy was four, Bebel was left an orphan at thirteen. A journeyman lathe operator at eighteen, he settled in Leipzig two years later, unacquainted with socialism. In an educational society for workers he improved upon his meager education and rounded out those qualities of character that early marked him as a leader. Patience, tenacity, and a sober understanding of the world as he found it remained his style until death on the eve of World War I. In Leipzig, he discovered, and at first rejected socialism, partly because he disliked Lassalle. In 1863 he was still unwilling to endorse the fully democratic suffrage advocated by the great charmer of workers and women, warning his fellow toilers that they were "not yet ready for it." Two years later, at twenty-five, Bebel had established himself as a labor leader in Saxony and was beginning to work with Ludwig Eckardt and other liberal democrats of the anti-Prussian Volkspartei movement in south Germany. In that year he met Wilhelm Liebknecht.⁶

Liebknecht was fourteen years Bebel's senior. In 1849, as a young veteran of the revolutions, he had fled Baden for Geneva, where he met Friedrich Engels. In his next exile, London, he was in frequent contact with Marx during the next twelve years. Returning to Germany in 1862, he joined the General German Workers' Union; like Bebel, he rejected Lassalle's and Schweitzer's readiness for a pact with Bismarck. More a true "forty-eighter" than a Marxist, he preached the right of all to vote in direct, equal, and secret elections; demanded that parliament have power over questions of war and peace; called for the abolition of all privileges based on birth, position, or religion; and argued that standing armies should be replaced by a "people's militia."

In the fateful summer of 1866, Liebknecht and Bebel became the leading personalities in the newly created Saxon People's party (Volkspartei), through which they attempted to mobilize both workers and middle-class citizens against Prussia, just then completing its defeat of Austria. Continuing the next year to capitalize on anti-Prussian sentiment in Saxony, Austria's most faithful ally in the war of 1866, Bebel was elected to the constituent Reichstag of the North German Confederation; a few months later Liebknecht joined him in the first regular Reichstag, to which Schweitzer was also elected.

Through Liebknecht, Bebel had approached Marxism, but neither man rigidly accepted the full doctrine. Both had been so preoccupied with other issues that—to the disgust of the exiled father of scientific socialism—they had done little to recruit support for the International Working Men's Association, which had been founded in 1864. For Liebknecht the bitter memories of 1849 remained vivid; as late as December 1867 he was writing to Engels that "the fall of Prussia equals the victory of the German revolution." (Engels agreed.) Furthermore, he acknowledged the practical political circumstances in which he worked. "I am not dealing here with well-trained communists, but with recruits for communism, who still have certain prejudices which must be considered," he wrote. Marx, corresponding secretary for Germany within the General Council of the International, had no sympathy for such undogmatic explanations.

While tending the affairs of the Volkspartei, Bebel and Liebknecht began to strengthen both the organization and the class-consciousness of a previously loose-knit and nonpolitical confederation of labor organizations in which Bebel had been active, the League of German Workers' Associations (Verband deutscher Arbeitervereine). Bebel became its president in October 1867. Several circumstances the following year facilitated his efforts to give the Verband a definite political program. Economic hardships provoked numerous strikes and made many of the workers more receptive to socialist ideas. Johann Philipp Becker—the aging but inveterate revolutionary who had participated in the Hambach Festival in 1832 and led troops in the Baden revolt in 1849—since the end of 1865 had been propagandizing from Geneva for the first International Workingmen's Association. German workers desired to join it in growing numbers. Further, the newly published first volume of Marx's *Das Kapital* was widely publicized in Germany early in 1868. Few read the difficult book, but news about it strengthened socialist convictions among many spokesmen for German labor; Becker described it as "this Bible of socialism, this testament of the new Gospel," and Schweitzer, the leader of the Lassalleans, publicly praised it. In August 1868 the national congress of the Lassallean party declared its solidarity with the International. The next month the national congress of Bebel's Verband adopted as its own program some statements Marx had written in 1864 as a preamble to the International's statutes.[7]

At the same time sharp competition had developed between Bebel and Liebknecht on the one hand and the Lassallean party on the other for the leadership of Germany's workers. In the summer of 1869 the rivalry intensified; Bebel, Liebknecht, and a number of dissident Lassalleans—publicly denouncing Schweitzer as a traitor to the socialist movement—called on "all the Social Democratic workers of Germany" to send delegates to a convention to create a united movement.

Meeting at Eisenach in August 1868 some 260 delegates, including several former Lassalleans, proclaimed the creation of what was soon regarded as Germany's first "Marxist" party, the

Social Democratic Workers' party (Sozialdemokratische Arbeiterpartei). By announcing their intention to affiliate with the International, the "Eisenachers" loosely established the allegiance of the new party to Marx, though Marxism was not a part of their program. The Partei did not demand a dictatorship of the proletariat; rather, it called for the creation of a *freier Volksstaat* (which could be translated either as a "free democratic state" or a "republic," but meant the latter to the Eisenach leaders). Only popular government, based on equal manhood suffrage, the program flatly announced, could solve social problems.

As leaders of the new party and as bitter foes of Prussia, Bebel and Liebknecht were reluctant to sever their ties to the liberal-democratic Volkspartei in the south German states, but late in 1869 they had to choose sides. In September the congress of the International, notwithstanding Liebknecht's opposition, went on record in favor of nationalization of landed property. The Volkspartei in the south, drawing much support from small farmers, brought pressure on the Eisenachers to disavow the International. Liebknecht and Bebel refused. By the next spring the break between the Eisenachers and the Volkspartei leaders in the west and south was largely complete.[8]

German workers could now choose between two socialist labor organizations, the Lassallean General German Workers' Union of Schweitzer or the newer Social Democratic Workers' party of Liebknecht and Bebel. Both parties had at least vaguely identified themselves with the International, and their behavior in the Franco-Prussian War of 1870–71 raised new questions about their patriotism. Hatred of Prussia, not Marxist dogma, caused Bebel and Liebknecht to abstain from voting when the Reichstag approved war credits; but the Lassalleans and many Eisenachers supported the German war effort as long as it appeared to be purely defensive. Then, with the smashing Prussian victory at Sedan and the proclamation of the Third French Republic in September 1870, German socialists concluded that the war had become one of Prussian aggression. The leaders of both parties opposed continuation of the war, and some openly hoped for a French victory. They opposed the annexation of Alsace-Lorraine, and in 1871 they declared their sympathy for the Paris Commune.[9]

While the unification of Germany thus reduced the differences between the two socialist parties, it left them isolated and discredited. Bebel and Liebknecht, arrested in December 1870, subsequently served prison sentences for their opposition to the war, and Bebel was the only man in either party to win a seat in the new Reichstag in 1871, when the socialists polled a mere 124,000 out of 3,888,000 votes.

The desirability of joining forces became increasingly apparent to both groups, and the retirement of Schweitzer in 1871 removed the major obstacle. When three Lassalleans and six Eisenachers were elected to the second Reichstag in 1874 they coordinated their parliamentary tactics. The Bismarck ministry in Prussia inadvertently provided new incentives for fusion by intensifying repressive measures against the Lassalleans. In June 1874 they were ordered to close their central office in Berlin and many local branches. If the Eisenachers had possessed any significant organization in Prussia, they, too, would have been hard hit, but their strength was largely concentrated in Saxony. In July their party congress voted to join the Lassalleans. After considerable jockeying for position, representatives of the two factions gathered in May 1875 at Gotha in Thuringia. There seventy-one Lassalleans and fifty-six Eisenachers agreed to form a single organization, the Socialist Workers' party of Germany (Sozialistische Arbeiterpartei Deutschlands). After 1890 it would be called the Social Democratic party of Germany (Sozialdemokratische Partei Deutschlands)—better known by its German initials as the SPD.

Marx and Engels read a draft of Liebknecht's program of the Socialist Workers' party before it was approved at Gotha, and both bluntly indicated their displeasure. Liebknecht and Bebel agreed that they must compromise with Lassallean ideas if the merger was to last; their program must fuse the diverse strains of German Social Democracy. Its pledge that the united party would be "conscious of the international character of the labor movement" while struggling against "all exploitation" paid lip service to Marx. The Gotha program sounded vaguely Marxist, too, in its demand that the means of production be transformed into "the common property or society." But it became explicitly Lassallean when it promised to work "at first" within a national framework and called for the creation of "socialist productive cooperatives with state help" as a step toward destruction of "the iron law of wages." The Gotha program did not recognize the need to create a "dictatorship of the proletariat." Rather, its constitutional principles resembled those of liberal democracy. It plighted to strive for a "free state," which meant what it had at Eisenach, and it demanded "universal, equal, direct electoral and voting rights with secret and obligatory voting by all citizens of twenty years of age or more for all elections and votes in state and community." Finally the new party pledged to pursue its objectives "by all legal means."[10]

If the Gotha program was far too moderate to satisfy Marx, it was sufficiently revolutionary to cause widespread concern in Germany. There was no mistaking the intention of the Socialist Workers' party to further political democracy, and if that had been its sole objective it could have drawn strength from the Progressives. But its intention to work for the elimination of private ownership of the means of production was clear and repelled many liberal democrats, generating among them an antisocialist concern which held back their own reformist activities. Patriotic Germans remembered that the leaders of the party had not fully shared in the national enthusiasm of 1870; religious Germans knew that some socialist spokesmen were openly atheists. Without engaging in a single revolutionary act, the socialists were feared and rejected as a party of violence and disorder.

Even before 1875, Bismarck had become concerned about Social Democracy, and his alarm increased as the united movement gained strength at the polls. Almost half a million votes sent twelve Social Democrats to the Reichstag in 1877. The party was then only the fifth largest in Germany, but it was pulling up with the Conservatives (fourth largest) and the Progressives (third largest). With forty-two socialist newspapers claiming a circulation of one hundred fifty thousand copies, the party was certain to gain support in years to come; the geographic concentration of its vote prompted additional fears. In Saxony, the most densely populated and most extensively industrialized German state where anti-Prussian sentiment remained strong, the socialists won more popular votes in 1877 than any other party, capturing seven of twenty-three Reichstag seats. Visiting

Leipzig in 1877, the young Karl Kautsky found not only artisans and factory workers in the party organization, but physicians, lawyers, journalists, and students. Social Democracy captured a large percentage of the votes in Berlin, Hamburg, and several other cities. At this point Bismarck decided it must be crushed.

In 1878 the chancellor found the pretext he needed to propose repressive legislation against Social Democracy. On May 11 a mentally unbalanced youth, Max Hödel, attempted to assassinate Emperor William I. Hödel's tenuous relationship with the Socialist Workers' party had been brief, and he had been expelled just two days before making the attempt on the emperor's life. Nevertheless, Bismarck blamed the act on the socialist movement and insisted that drastic measures be taken against it. The bill he proposed was so sweeping and so loosely worded that it was decisively rejected by the Reichstag. On June 2, Dr. Karl Nobiling made the second attempt within little more than three weeks to kill the kaiser, seriously wounding the popular octogenarian monarch. Although Nobiling had never been a member of the Socialist Workers' party, Bismarck at once saw a chance to cripple it and at the same time to set back liberal opposition to his first antisocialist bill. He reported that Nobiling was a socialist, dissolved the Reichstag, called new elections, and suggested that the kaiser would not have been wounded if the National Liberals had approved his proposal following the first attempted assassination. Fearing repudiation at the polls, many National Liberals now announced that they favored antisocialist legislation, but this did not prevent their party's sharp defeat in the voting on July 30. The Conservatives gained significantly, and the Social Democrats lost three of their Reichstag seats.

When the new parliament was convened, Bismarck had the majority he needed. This time his proposal was more carefully drawn, and he accepted a number of Reichstag amendments; on October 19 it was passed by a vote of 221 to 149. The National Liberals joined with the two Conservative parties, one Center deputy, and one Progressive to approve the "exceptional" law, which went into effect at once. Thus, within three years after its creation, the Socialist Workers' party was confronted by an attempt to legislate it out of existence.[11]

The antisocialist law of October 1878 was enacted for a period of two and a half years, but it was renewed repeatedly. It won substantial support from left-liberals in 1884 and from the Center in that year, in 1886, and in 1888. Social Democracy had to fight for its life until 1890.

The repressive legislation authorized the state governments to abolish associations that aimed at "the undermining of the existing state and social order through Social Democratic, socialistic, or communistic endeavors." This definition was sufficiently broad to allow the states to act at times against trade unions as well as the socialist party, though the legislation was not primarily intended to crush the unions and was never as rigorously enforced against them as against explicitly political organizations. The new law authorized the prohibition or restriction of periodicals and books. It empowered the government to prohibit and dissolve socialist meetings, to inspect party records, and to seize party funds. In cities where Social Democracy was particularly strong, state authorities could proclaim "a minor state of siege" for one year, during which persons who were considered dangerous to public order could be banished. The Berlin police president was instructed to prepare periodical "surveys of the general situation of the Social Democratic and anarchist movement," and copies were sent to authorities in other federal states to facilitate repression. Between 1878 and 1890 the "exceptional" laws legitimized dissolution of 352 socialist associations, 1,500 arrests, 893 expulsions from the empire, and the banning of 1,299 publications. [12]

In the 1880's Bismarck fitted a second arrow to his bow. While unrelentingly striking at the socialists, who claimed to speak for labor, the chancellor bid for labor's support by sponsoring a pioneering social welfare program. As early as 1879 he had written that "the most effective way in which the governments can combat the socialist danger, threatening from all sides, is the way of economic and practical reforms"; these, he suggested, were necessary complements to the repressive legislation. The antisocialist laws could only achieve "partial and transitory" results against socialist activities because "the evil lies deeper than these manifestations." In 1881 he laid before the Reichstag the first of his major proposals for social insurance. Laws providing for compulsory insurance against sickness and on-the-job accidents were passed by the Reichstag in 1883 and 1884, with support from the Conservative, Center, and National Liberal parties. These were rounded out in 1889 by a system of pensions for workers who reached the age of seventy or who became incapacitated earlier. Benefits were variously financed by contributions from the workers, their employers, and—in the case of old-age pensions—partially by the Reich government.[13]

Neither Bismarck's stick nor his carrot was able to check the growth of Social Democracy, but the party suffered severely during the first years of repression. On October 19, 1878, the socialist leaders, seeking to forestall state action, voluntarily dissolved the formal administrative organization of the party for the duration of the antisocialist legislation. Liebknecht and Wilhelm Hasenclever, the editor of *Vorwärts* (*Forward*) announced on October 21 that they would avoid the promotion of ideas and actions forbidden by the exceptional law, but their attempt to save the party's central newspaper failed. Within a few days *Vörwarts* and the other two most important socialist newspapers were closed. Only the Reichstag faction was left to give informal leadership to the movement as a de facto executive committee, and it was handicapped by internal dissension as well as by occasional imprisonment of its leading members. Party congresses had to be held sub rosa in Switzerland or Denmark.

Fully aware of the need for a central newspaper if the movement was to be sustained and given direction, Bebel and Liebknecht struggled to create one published outside Germany. In September 1879 the new *Sozialdemokrat* began to appear in Zürich, edited by the Bavarian, Georg von Vollmar, until January 1881, and subsequently by Eduard Bernstein.

The nephew of a liberal revolutionary of 1848 and son of a Jewish railroad engineer, Bernstein had been attracted to socialism by the ideas of Lassalle. He was a member of the committee that organized the Gotha conference to unify the German socialist movement in 1875, when he was only twenty-five. In the mid-1870's, he was much influenced by Eugen Dühring, a radical instructor at the University of Berlin whose writings then enjoyed widespread popularity. Like a number of other young socialists of intellectual promise who had rallied around the

Berlin instructor, Bernstein was won over to Marxism in 1879 after reading an effective criticism of Dühring's doctrines by Friedrich Engels. For some months, Bernstein's Marxism continued to be suspect among the orthodox because he worked as an assistant to Karl Höchberg, a wealthy young Jew whose socialism was based upon ethical idealism rather than upon economic determinism. Höchberg was tolerant of diverse socialist impulses, he generously used his money to support them, and he helped make possible the publication of the *Sozialdemokrat*. After Bernstein succeeded Vollmar in the editor's chair, he quickly sought and won the confidence of the masters of Marxism. He frequently wrote to London for the advice and criticism of Engels, who was generous and specific in his responses; and in February 1884 he spent eight days in London as Engels's house guest. Engels thus significantly influenced the ideological line and style of the new central-organ-in-exile, and if he was an orthodox Marxist in the 1880's, so was Bernstein.

To distribute the *Sozialdemokrat* in Germany, Julius Motteler, its business manager, improvised a clandestine organization with great skill and patience. A clothmaker and merchant by trade, Motteler was a close friend of Bebel and had sat in the Reichstag from 1874 to 1878. With the help of a courageous rank and file, at the peak of his success Motteler smuggled some ten thousand copies of the newspaper every week to subscribers in Germany. In 1887 bundles of copies—frequently sent in luggage on fast trains across the Swiss frontier—were reaching and being distributed in Berlin (1,285 copies), Hamburg (765), Leipzig (800), and several other cities. Sometimes copies were taken to Belgium and Holland, thence into the Reich. At other times the plates were sent to a socialist printer in Germany and there run off.[14]

The Marxist orientation of the *Sozialdemokrat* provoked frequent criticism from more moderate members of the socialist caucus in the Reichstag; for even under the impact of Bismarck's blows, the Social Democrats continued to disagree among themselves about both theory and tactics. Gradually the main division came to be between those who wanted to work for reforms within the existing order and those who insisted upon a totally negative attitude toward the German state until it could be over-

thrown by revolution. Socialists involved in practical organizational and political work under the repressive legislation tended
to favor the first course of action; the theorists—particularly
those living abroad—held out for the uncompromising position.
The earlier division between Lassalleans and Eisenachers became
blurred in the process. Some Lassalleans were more revolutionary than most Marxists; the latter had to subordinate their
abundant concern for fine theoretical distinctions to the practical
tasks of survival. Though inconsistent, party leaders tended to
talk in Marxist terms more than before, if only to keep the
workers on guard against the paternalistic lures of the Bismarckian state on the right and the inflammatory appeals of the
anarchists on the left. Thus from 1878 to 1890 party members
became more, if superficially, familiar with Marxist writings and
concepts. Marxist principles were echoed by Bernstein in the
Sozialdemokrat and more profoundly by a theoretical magazine,
Die neue Zeit, which appeared in Stuttgart at the beginning of
1883, the year Marx died. It was edited by the Austrian socialist
Karl Kautsky, who had joined his German comrades in their
Swiss exile in 1880. Kautsky grew up in Prague and Vienna. As
the teenage son of a theater painter, he first embraced Czech
nationalism and democratic republicanism in the German-
dominated Habsburg Empire. Having identified with one oppressed group, he found it easy to sympathize with others. His
interest in socialism was aroused by the Paris Commune of 1871
and quickly strengthened by avid reading. Religion was no
barrier; his formally Catholic parents were pantheists, and his
discovery in 1871 of Charles Darwin's *Descent of Man* confirmed
his materialist outlook. In 1875 the twenty-one-year-old student
joined the Social Democratic movement in Vienna. Soon he was
struggling through Marx's *Das Kapital*, which transformed his
hitherto purely ethical attachment to socialism into one based
upon "scientific" economic analysis. By 1880 he was known to
the leaders of the German socialist movement by his obvious
dedication to the cause and by his scholarly writings for socialist
publications. He spent the spring of 1881 in London and had
several discussions with Marx and Engels. He was not quite
thirty when he founded *Die neue Zeit* with the blessings of
Liebknecht and Bebel. Writing to Engels about the journal's

purpose, he declared that it would show no sympathy for any kind of "utopianism and toleration of reformism." Within months the journal had 2,200 subscribers. Kautsky was to guide it for thirty-four years, making it the world's most respected intellectual journal of "orthodox" Marxism.[15]

Most German socialists increasingly called themselves Marxists, but concentrated pragmatically on immediate accomplishments rather than on mastering Marxist theory or engaging in revolutionary action. Because participation in elections had not been denied them and because only the Reichstag could rescind the antisocialist laws, party leaders after 1878 devoted much of their effort to electioneering and to achieving the traditional objectives of liberal democracy. The election campaign of Wilhelm Hasenclever in Halle in 1884 was typical. Presenting himself as a candidate who knew "where the shoe pinches the workers," Hasenclever promised dedication to "universal, equal, direct, and secret suffrage" in state and municipal elections; tuition-free schools; tax relief; reduction of terms of military service; election of judges by democratic suffrage; freedom of press, association, and assembly; elimination of Sunday work and of child labor; legal limitation of the length of the working day; and state support for cooperatives. While radically democratic, not one of the nine planks in his platform was specifically socialistic. This was also true of the socialist candidates' platforms in Berlin electoral districts in 1884. The first demand of all of them was for "universal, equal, direct suffrage with secret balloting for state and community."

Partly because of the limitations imposed by the antisocialist laws, and partly because of their own inclinations, even those Marxists who defined Social Democracy as a revolutionary program tended in practice to put greater emphasis upon parliamentary activity. Liebknecht refused to disavow revolution, but in his conception it differed little from evolution. "All of human history is a continuous revolution," he wrote on one occasion, and on another he declared that "the revolutionary demands . . . can be achieved by way of reform."

No single individual could speak for Social Democracy as a whole in the period 1878 to 1890, but the most commanding figure was August Bebel. Caught between theory and practical tasks, between the left and the right wings of the party, at times he was almost as inconsistent as Liebknecht. He insisted that Social Democracy must be revolutionary, yet he too shrank from acts of violence. Bebel harmonized this apparent contradiction by insisting that revolution must not be attempted before conditions were ripe for its success; and he, like Engels, remained convinced that revolutionary opportunities would not be long in coming. Sometimes he wrote scornfully of "the parliamentary comedy," but he led the party's Reichstag delegation through most of the 1880's and was quick to defend the parliament against reactionary attempts to make it less representative. Speaking in November 1885, Bebel avowed that the Social Democrats strove for "parliamentary rule" and thus wanted to see the Reichstag become "the decisive factor in the German Empire." He worked incessantly for greater socialist representation in the Reichstag, optimistically expected throughout the 1880's to win increasing numbers of votes, and was even willing to cooperate with the left-liberals in elections in order to win more seats for them and for his own party.[16]

The effort to expand Social Democratic strength in the Reichstag often seemed frustrating after 1878. In the elections of 1881 the party regained the three seats it had lost after the two attempts on the emperor's life, but its popular vote was only about three-fourths as large as it had been in 1878. Twenty-four socialists were elected in 1884 (eighteen of them representing a moderate position within the party), only to be cut back to eleven in 1887. But the popular vote for the party steadily grew after 1881, bolstering the confidence that many socialists placed in the ballot box. The semiannual reports by the Berlin police repeatedly and accurately noted the continued growth of Social Democracy; the report of July 1886 pointed out that the party had spread over the whole empire and was well organized.

A whole complex of circumstances assured the survival and growth of Social Democracy. Probably the most important was the rise of socialist trade unions. Antisocialist legislation used against the unions irritated them without checking their expansion. Furthermore, election organizations were allowed to function in the major cities, even though party leaders frequently were expelled from them. The possibilities of electioneering are suggested by a letter from Liebknecht to Kautsky during the 1884 campaign: "In the last six days," he wrote on October 10, "I had nine meetings, one conference, and twenty-five hours of railroad and stage-coach travel." The socialist press was vital in preserving the movement. The vigor of the repression varied from place to place and from year to year, but socialist newspapers, legal or illegal, were never fully eliminated as a means of rallying support for socialist candidates; in 1890 the socialists were publishing sixty newspapers instead of forty-two as in 1877.

While the Social Democrats in the Reichstag provided central direction, survival depended upon local initiative. In towns and districts front organizations were created in the form of singing clubs, smoking societies, scientific study groups, or gymnastic associations. As soon as one of these could be determined to be socialistic and was banned, the police complained, it would reappear as a new organization with a new name. Monetary support was obtained from a few wealthy donors, dues of party members, left-liberal sympathizers, socialists in foreign counries, and various money-raising activities; pictures of party heroes were sold, and other income was raised by sponsoring lotteries, concerts, and theatrical performances. Agitation was partially driven underground, but never eliminated. Women carried leaflets in their blouses to avoid detection while distributing them. Red flags mysteriously appeared atop towers, telegraph poles, and factory smokestacks. Secret meetings were held in forests or small villages near large cities, while others were open picnics attended by hundreds of persons wearing red ribbons or carrying red flowers. Funerals of party leaders became political demonstrations; the police estimated that twenty thousand of the Hamburg faithful turned out in August 1879 for the most impressive one, that of a former Reichstag deputy, August Geib.

Technological development must have helped to subvert the repressive legislation: bicycles and electric street railways, first used widely during the 1880's, facilitated contact among Social Democrats and the dissemination of their propaganda. In Berlin, for example, the number of fares carried annually on the streetcar lines tripled from 13,200,000 in 1882 to 38,200,000 in 1890.

Industrialization and urbanization were on the side of the socialist movement; in 1880, Germany had only fifteen cities with
populations of one hundred thousand or more; in 1890 there
were twenty-six. As urban centers grew and wages rose after
1886, emigration declined sharply; more and more, dissident
Germans who earlier might have taken passage abroad remained at home to vent their discontent at the polls.

All these circumstances made the Social Democratic vote in
Reichstag elections rise from 312,000 in 1881 to 550,000 three
years later and to 763,000 in 1887 (although in that year Bebel
and several other leaders were serving prison terms).[17]

Repression had not prevented the growth of Social Democracy, but Bismarck stubbornly insisted that it be continued. In
February 1888 the Reichstag extended the antisocialist legislation
to September 30, 1890, despite increasing criticism. When William II became emperor in June 1888, he favored new social
welfare measures, but Bismarck opposed any further concessions. In October 1889 the chancellor proposed to the parliament that the repressive measures be made permanent, and he
looked to his Reichstag majority of Conservatives and National
Liberals for approval.

This time, however, Bismarck encountered difficulties. Even
though they had supported the repressive legislation, the National Liberals had long expressed misgivings about its harsher
provisions. They would not vote to make it permanent unless
the authority to banish socialist agitators from the cities to the
smaller towns was eliminated. The Conservatives, wishing to
retain repression against Social Democracy, informed Bismarck
that they would support the watered-down version only if the
government signified in advance that it would not be relaxed
further. By early 1890, therefore, it appeared that there would be
no antisocialist law at all after September unless Bismarck approved the compromise bill.

At a tense crown council on January 24, 1890, the kaiser
indicated that the government should endorse the limited antisocialist legislation that the National Liberals were willing to
support, but the chancellor disagreed. If the full law was not
passed, Bismarck argued, the government could manage without it. A sharper draft could be put before the next Reichstag;

and if, during the lapse of repressive legislation, the socialists became violent, armed force could be used against them. Bismarck warned that the longer the government postponed "resistance" to the socialists the more powerful it would have to be when finally exerted. William II was confronted with what had always been the chancellor's trump card—his threat of resignation. The kaiser backed down. The government failed to urge the Conservatives to support the compromise bill proposed by the National Liberals, and the next day they voted against it because they considered it too weak. The Center, the Progressives, and the Social Democrats opposed it because it was too repressive. It failed to pass.

The stage was thus set for the important Reichstag elections of February 20, 1890, and—unlike previous elections—under conditions favoring Bismarck's opponents. With the antisocialist law due to expire on September 30 and the kaiser himself calling for prolabor legislation, it was more difficult than before to convince working-class voters that Social Democracy was a threat to the Reich. In high spirits on election eve, Engels in London wrote Bebel of his hopes that the party might win as many as 1,200,000 votes. But when they were counted, the Social Democrats had won 1,427,298—one out of every five and more than any other party received. The movement that Bismarck had tried to eliminate—the constant proponent for democratization of the empire and all of its component states— was now, by popular vote, the largest in Germany. Because the government refused to redraw Reichstag districts in line with increasing population, the Social Democrats captured only thirty-five seats, but even this number constituted a sharp increase over the eleven mandates they had held from 1887 to 1890. Within a month after the socialist victory at the polls the hated Bismarck was dismissed by William II.[18]

Thus the era of Bismarck ended with the first major victory at the polls of a party more determined than any other to change the shape of the empire the Iron Chancellor had built. Lagging behind its Western neighbors and rivals in progress toward democracy, Germany alone had produced a united socialist party with a large following. Its emergence pushed the German movement for democracy into a radically new phase.

The liberal democratic movement had produced ideas and sacrifices that testify to the wisdom and the civic courage of the individuals who had kept it alive in a generally apathetic society. Furthermore, liberal democracy was an essential forerunner—both parent and schoolmaster—of the Social Democratic movement. The liberal democratic movement, however, always was a weak force in the total context of German society. One source of weakness was the large gap between its egalitarian political values and the material interests of is propertied proponents. This discrepancy had weakened the will to work for the democratic government to which their principles should have committed them.

Many Progressives and other left-liberals had been hesitant to push for fully democratic political reform because they feared that it would lead to social, economic, and cultural leveling. They had something to lose under a democratic government. The Social Democratic party and the workers who backed it were not bothered by such contradictions. They stood to gain by democratic reform in general and by their own eventual accession to state power in particular. Workers could not know with certainty that their interests would be well served by socialization, but obviously no amount of leveling could harm them. For Social Democrats, therefore, the principles of political democracy were not merely abstract ideals; they were practical means toward the achievement of social justice. To support such principles required on their part no sacrifice, but only a frank recognition of self-interest.

Free to work for political democracy without the reservations that held back the liberals, Social Democrats also possessed a significantly stronger potential power base. Every challenge of governments by liberal reform movements in nineteenth-century Germany ultimately faced the military power of the state. Since 1848 the liberals had been able to throw growing economic power into the scale, and this had enabled them to win some political concessions. But in the power clashes of the 1860's the liberal-democratic movement had been weakened by the liberal willingness to come to terms with the state and had been transformed into a precarious residual force of ideas and verbal suasion. It even lacked the power inherent in tight organization.

Attempts to create a genuine "movement" of liberal democracy always had been handicapped by its highly individualistic ideology; liberal democrats had been better as individual thinkers, speakers, and writers than as organizers. In contrast, Social Democracy had an ideology highly compatible with the needs of a mass movement; indeed its central principle *was* organization. It also held two other potential sources of strength that liberal democrats never had won; by 1890 it had the support of a large and growing body of voters; and it soon would wield, through its affiliated labor unions and their ability to strike, both economic and physical muscle that might be used to win political concessions.

If Social Democracy brought significant new assets to the movement for democratic government in Germany, it also brought liabilities. One of the most fundamental intellectual liabilities lay in the Marxist refusal to accept political democracy in a capitalistic society as an end in itself. A democratic republic was viewed as only an intermediate stage that must give way to proletarian dictatorship. Socialist theoreticians disagreed about the role of democratic polity in the socialist future. For those who accepted the idea of even a temporary dictatorship, democratic reforms and fidelity to Marxist dogma might, at some point in the future, create a crisis of will for the party. But in 1890 this highly abstract and esoteric issue fermented well below the surface. The organizers and day-to-day leaders as well as most followers were committed to the achievement of political democracy; the future would determine whether they would treat it in fact as a goal in its own right or only as a means to other ends.[19]

Social Democracy in 1890 suffered from other, more immediately troubling contradictions—scars it would bear for decades from its struggle for survival under Bismarck. Having favored the unification of a democratic German nation before 1866, some Social Democrats had only loathing for the Prussian-dominated empire in which they lived. Though functioning as a parliamentary party, Social Democracy since 1878 had grown distrustful of parliamentary processes and of the bourgeois political parties that had supported Bismarck's repressive measures. Opposing acts of violence, it nonetheless used a

revolutionary rhetoric. Conservatives and liberals alike, therefore, accepted its revolutionary pronouncements at face value
and ascribed its peaceable conduct to the overwhelming physical
superiority of the established order. Needless to say, no party in
parliament considered joint action on any issue with the Social
Democrats.

Frightened by the SPD's socialism and detesting its internationalism, the National Liberal party had moved farther to the
right. The avowed atheism of Social Democracy prevented collaboration even with democratic elements in the Center party.
The longing of Bebel and Liebknecht's followers for political
equality and for genuine parliamentary government gave them
much in common with many middle-class democrats, but their
talk of revolution closed the door to the formation of a democratic bloc. Thus the rise of Social Democracy in parliamentary
isolation divided as much as it buoyed the partisans of popular
sovereignty in Germany.

IX.

OBSTACLES TO DEMOCRACY IN
STATE AND SOCIETY AFTER 1890

In 1894—four years after the Reichstag refused to renew the antisocialist laws—Grand Duke Ernst Ludwig of Hesse, son of Queen Victoria's second daughter Alice, married young Victoria of Saxe-Coburg-Gotha, daughter of the British Queen and empress' second son, Albert. For a few days the heads of Europe's most powerful dynasties converged on the sprawling, verdant garden city of Darmstadt to stage a social spectacle that briefly eclipsed the mounting threats to the order safeguarding their inherited eminence. For a festive moment the observer was as if carried back to the days of the Congress of Vienna.

Though seventy-five years of age, the imperial grandmother of bride and groom came from England to bless the union. Russia's Czarevitch Nicholas, on the eve of his own elevation to the throne, hastened by to press his suit with another of Victoria's granddaughters, the bridegroom's sister Alix. Finally the British ruler's most famous and controversial descendant, Emperor William II of Germany, son of her eldest daughter, welcomed the august gathering both as kinsman and as lord of the German Empire. He knew how to headline such a display of monarchistic strength and solidarity, which seemed to confirm that kingship was destined to repulse all assaults by democratic and socialist enemies, and, in Germany at least, even to preserve the social and political dominance of the aristocracy over the new grandees of expanding industrial capitalism.[1]

After 1871 the Hohenzollern rulers of the German Empire and their chancellors were among the major obstacles to democratization. Bismarck's compromises with democratic principle, first proposed on the eve of the war with Austria, seemed in jeopardy under his successors.

The first emperor, William I, had accepted and observed the constitutions of Prussia and the Reich as immutable features in an imperfect world. He died at almost ninety-one in March 1888. It is just possible that his son and successor, Frederick III, might in time have ushered in genuine parliamentary government. Thirty years earlier Frederick had married Queen Victoria's oldest daughter, who reinforced her husband's admiration for English traditions and institutions. Since the 1870's, liberals and liberal democrats had optimistically looked forward to the time when the crown prince would come to power, but Bismarck had repeatedly expressed undisguised fears that he might form a "Gladstone Ministry." When he inherited the throne in March 1888, Frederick was too ill with cancer of the throat to walk down the cold streets of Berlin in the funeral procession for his father. As emperor, he saw that several left-liberals were conspicuously decorated, and he secured the dismissal of Robert von Puttkamer, Prussia's reactionary minister of the interior. But he did not turn out Bismarck, and he made no effort to inaugurate constitutional reform. On June 15 he died, after a reign of only ninety-nine days. The old chancellor then faced the task of adjusting a third emperor to his methods and policies.[2]

Since 1878, Bismarck had hinted repeatedly that he was prepared to change the constitution without Reichstag approval—in other words, to carry out a royal coup d'état. How seriously he himself took these threats is impossible to know with certainty. He did exploit them to accomplish less drastic political aims, and the strategy worked at times. Whether or not Bismarck wanted to resort to an illegal modification or abrogation of the constitution, clearly he regretted his concession of democratic suffrage at the federal level. A month before the electoral campaign of 1890 he had spoken in the crown council of the possible use of violence against the socialists. His threats availed nothing, for on February 20 the Social Democrats won their greatest victory yet.

Did the chancellor in fact wish to carry out a coup in March 1890? Opinions among experts will continue to differ because they depend upon inconclusive evidence. Possibly Bismarck sought only to prepare the Protestant kaiser, his Protestant fellow ministers, and leaders of the Conservative and overwhelmingly Protestant parties to accept another unpalatable but far less drastic way to create a seemingly unassailable government majority by gaining the Catholic Center as a parliamentary ally. As a matter of fact, neither recourse was tried. The kaiser sharply upbraided Bismarck for negotiating with Ludwig Windthorst, the Center leader in parliament, and he also rejected presentation of provocative new antisocialist measures to the Reichstag. Tension between the old chancellor and young William II reached the breaking point on March 15 over several issues. When Bismarck finally offered his resignation three days later, it was accepted immediately. Within a few days he went off to his country estate, whence his oracular pronouncements of discontent emanated at irregular intervals until his death in 1898.

Virtually every aspect of Bismarck's chancellorship was important for its influence on Germany's subsequent development. For this volume, the most important fact is that the man who had been remarkably able to compromise with changing times before 1871 had after that used his power to block the implementation and survival of the parliamentary system in the German Empire.[3]

After dropping the chancellor whose domestic policies had demonstrated his growing incapacity to grapple with contemporary problems, William II quickly revealed the inadequacy of his own judgment by trying to take his place. The new emperor's philosophy of government was no less authoritarian than Bismarck's but rested, so it is generally agreed, not on a record of success but on a personal sense of insecurity. Worst of all, it was accompanied by frequent boastful and tactless public pronouncements. As early as 1882, William had decided that "democratic principles can only create weak and often corrupt pillars of society." In May 1891 he declared before the Landtag of the Rhineland Province: "One man alone is master in the land, and it is I. I will tolerate no one else next to me." Though outwardly sympathetic to the material demands of labor, he was bitterly critical of the party most workers supported. He professed an ambition to be a kaiser of the people, but lacked the ability to hurdle the barriers between monarch and masses. Thus in November 1891 he told military recruits at Potsdam: "If Socialist agitations continue as they are doing, I may have to order you to shoot down your relatives—God forbid!—but even then you must obey my commands without murmuring." By 1891, William II himself was talking of resorting to the kind of coup d'état that he had refused Bismarck. In 1895 he privately complained to the czar of Russia that the Reichstag oscillated between the Social Democrats and "the ultramontane Catholics," adding that both parties would soon be ripe "for hanging, together and separately."

"In short, His Majesty has no political judgment." Thus Baron Friedrich von Holstein, a councillor of the Foreign Office and a loyal monarchist, privately summed up the shortcomings of the new emperor. At heart William II wanted to be an enlightened despot, a Frederick the Great; but under Bismarck the German people had grown accustomed to the emperor as a venerable national patriarch, not as an active author of day-by-day policy. Even at its outset the reign of William II fell far short of an actual dictatorship, but for thirty years, from 1888 to 1918, the kaiser impulsively and irregularly interfered in government decisions at various levels and invested both the domestic and foreign course of German statecraft with an air of the unpredictable which shook confidence at home and abroad. At the same time he left no doubt that he would never permit even the most minute expansion of parliamentary authority.[4]

Much depended after 1890 upon the wisdom and strength of the men who headed the government. Relieved of Bismarck, William II appointed Leo von Caprivi as imperial chancellor and minister-president of Prussia. A general, Caprivi had served since 1883 as chief of the imperial admiralty. Although not an innovator by temperament and a conservative by inclination, he felt uneasy in an atmosphere in which government's main purpose seemed to be the circumvention of the state's fundamental law. He was ready to seek accommodation with the parliamentarians rather than to defy them. Under his aegis a progressive income tax passed in Prussia; German trade treaties with Russia were negotiated, reducing protective tariffs on grain by almost one-third; Bismarck's diplomatic alliance with the czar was allowed to lapse. Finally, he liquidated another one of Bismarck's prejudices with the legislation in 1891 of guaranteed Sunday rest and limited working hours for women and children.

By 1892, however, the former chancellor's firm, if arthritic, grasp on the wheel of empire was missed openly. The great landowners suffered from the reversal of Bismarck's protectionism. Social Democrats, Progressives, and National Liberals were angered when the Caprivi ministry also courted the Center party by proposing a bill to restore a large measure of church control over elementary education. William II, finding that his political enemies shared his own prejudices against Catholicism, undercut the chancellor by withdrawing the school bill. Now the Center also had cause to sulk. Unable to control imperial whims, the well-meaning Caprivi failed to win liberal confidence, alienated the Catholics, and offended the Conservatives. To appease the latter, William in 1892 separated the office of chancellor from that of Prussian minister-president. He appointed an avowed reactionary, Count Botho zu Eulenburg, head of the Prussian cabinet.

By May 1894, Eulenburg was demanding the passage of a new antisocialist law, even if several dissolutions and a change in the Reichstag suffrage should be necessary. It was Bismarck's rumored monarchical coup d'état under new management. In opposing Eulenburg's proposal, Caprivi offered his resignation on the one hand, while on the other arranging to consult the state governments. On October 25 the minister-presidents of the more important states met in Berlin and counseled against the introduction of repressive federal legislation, but for Caprivi this was a Pyrrhic victory. On October 26 the kaiser accepted his resignation, and dropped Eulenburg at the same time.[5] It was not much easier to find a suitable successor to Caprivi than to Bismarck. Philipp Eulenburg, a cousin of the retired Prussian minister-president, sketched the ideal candidate as "a man who is neither conservative nor liberal, neither ultramontane nor progressive, neither ritualist nor atheist." After two Prussian chancellors, appointment of a south German would soothe the aggravated particularism of Germans below the Main. Eulenburg, a close friend of the kaiser, proposed a solution to the quandary. Prince Chlodwig zu Hohenlohe-Schillingsfürst was named chancellor and head of the Prussian government. As minister-president of Bavaria from 1866 to 1870, Hohenlohe had favored union under the Hohenzollerns. In 1871 he became vice-president of the first German Reichstag, and he served as Germany's second ambassador to France from 1874 to 1885. At the time he succeeded Caprivi he was imperial administrator of Alsace-Lorraine. Born in 1819, the year of the Carlsbad Decrees, this septuagenerian lacked energy and resolution. August Bebel described him to Friedrich Engels as "an old, worn out little man who makes a miserable impression."

William had no intention of tailoring future policy to the pattern indicated by the choice of a south German chancellor. As if convinced that gestures of good will could substitute for actions, he sought to pursue his favorite course of centralization and extension of Prussian control over the Reich. Both he and Hohenlohe agreed that the Reichstag must be kept in check. Otherwise the chancellor's conservative prescriptions diverged from those of his sovereign. He sought to preserve, even to expand, the role of the states in the affairs of Germany. In addition to raising the voting age for Reichstag elections, for instance, and limiting workers' suffrage by a three-year residence requirement, he advocated that one-fourth of the German parliament be elected by the state legislatures.

In December 1894, Hohenlohe proposed to the Reichstag a bill which sought to repress Social Democracy by amending the regular penal law of the Reich. In the guise of defending the state against revolution, the draft legislation would have authorized new police and court action. But to win support, Hohenlohe incorporated Center party stipulations to outlaw criticism of religion, marriage, and the family, and this was too much for the anticlerical National Liberals. In May 1895 the measure was defeated. Two years later the Prussian Chamber of Deputies, by a close vote, rejected a proposal that would have allowed the police to dissolve associations which, in the opinion of the authorities, endangered public peace or the security of the state.

After 1897, when William II succeeded in placing his own men in key offices against the opposition of the chancellor, Hohenlohe's powers were even more severely limited. The monarch imposed his will upon both the chancellor and the Prussian ministry from 1897 until the close of the century, but he was unable to overcome the Reichstag. In the elections of June 1898 the Conservatives and National Liberals declined in strength.

The Center picked up six seats, and the Social Democrats made their best showing yet. They still were not strong enough to form a dominant bloc with the liberal democrats, but the government could no longer overlook them. In November 1899 the Reichstag rejected yet another imperial attempt to curb Social Democracy. This was the so-called *Zuchthausvorlage* (Penitentiary Bill) that the kaiser had pushed since 1897. The measure would have imprisoned anyone who urged workers to engage in a strike that endangered life or property and was subject to such broad interpretation that it could have been used to cripple Progressive and Catholic as well as Social Democratic unions. Even some National Liberals opposed the bill, arguing that it would merely increase labor support of the SPD.

Instead of adopting antilabor laws, in December the Reichstag pursued the opposite course. Until then, the right to associate had been regulated by the states. Existing laws frequently prohibited organizational activity across state lines. Rigid enforcement could have meant prosecution of bourgeois parties. Thus demands for uniform and liberal national legislation had gained ground in the Reichstag. For two years the kaiser held out against Hohenlohe's desire to compromise, but the expenses occasioned by his favorite project, a large navy, brought William II around. On December 7, 1899, the Reichstag adopted, and the Bundesrat endorsed, a simple two-sentence law permitting all-German "domestic associations of every kind."

In internal affairs, the Hohenlohe administration demonstrated repeatedly that the emperor's romantic absolutism had to yield to the need for parliamentary compromise. As monarchs had known since the Middle Ages, a powerful state needed funds to preserve and augment its stature and therefore must adjust its policies to the wishes of those who paid the bill.[6]

The Reich structure provided effective means to resist reactionary modifications, while the closely interrelated government structure of Prussia gave it an equally formidable barrier against efforts toward democratic reform.

The empire was an improvised union of twenty-five federal states plus the "Imperial Territory" (*Reichsland*) of Alsace-Lorraine. Within it, the federal states retained their separate dynasties, constitutions, and bureaucracies. Most of the state governments remained undemocratic from 1871 to 1918, and each retained exclusive control over its own police, schools, and most taxes.[7]

The Reich constitution made the king of Prussia hereditary head of the Reich and conveyed upon him the title of "German Emperor." In theory the emperor was a limited monarch; any decree he issued was legal only if it bore the countersignature of the chancellor, and the constitution gave him neither an absolute nor a suspensive veto over legislation passed by the Reichstag. But he was assigned broad administrative powers. A Bundesrat Committee on Foreign Relations, created chiefly to satisfy Bavaria, remained without influence. The emperor's command of the military forces of Germany gave him powers potentially greater than the routine ones set by the constitution. The constitution authorized the kaiser to declare martial law (*Kriegszustand*) in any part of the German Empire in which public security might be threatened.

The day-to-day leadership of civilian affairs was the function of the imperial chancellor. The constitution asserted that by countersigning the emperor's decrees the chancellor "thereby assumes responsibility." But responsibility to whom? By giving him the presidency of the Bundesrat and the leadership of business there, it implied responsibility to that body; by requiring Reichstag approval of legislation, it implied some responsibility to the elected deputies of the nation. But the constitution gave the emperor complete freedom to appoint this official, who would, nevertheless, be called upon to serve three rivals: his sovereign, the representatives of the states, and the representatives of the German people. Only one of the three—the emperor—could dismiss him.

Like the kaiser, the chancellor owed most of his influence over the Reich to Prussian sources of power. With the exception of two brief periods (1873 and again from 1892 to 1894), the same man served simultaneously as minister-president of Prussia, foreign minister of Prussia, and chancellor of the Reich. As minister-president he was empowered by his king to direct the affairs of the largest state in the Reich—about two-thirds of the entire German Empire. The numerous, omnipresent, and conservative Prussian civil servants loyally implemented his policy.

As Prussia's foreign minister, he instructed and led the Prussian delegates in the Bundesrat (over which he presided as chancellor of the Reich). Limitations as well as powers came with the chancellor's Prussian offices. As minister-president he stood or fell by the choice of the king of Prussia, but he also had to show sensitive regard for the Prussian Chamber of Deputies. Because this body was always much more conservative than the Reichstag, it was difficult for any chancellor to follow policies that satisfied both parliaments, which met only a few blocks apart in Berlin. All in all, however, the chancellor's positions of power made him the pivotal figure in the government of Germany—as long as he avoided the mistake that had brought even Bismarck low, that of losing the support of his royal master.[8]

Only by placing themselves under the control of the Reichstag could the chancellors who followed Bismarck have freed themselves of dependence upon William II. But such a changeover to genuine parliamentary government was blocked not only by the emperors and chancellors themselves but by the failure of the Reichstag to demand it.

The Reichstag had been for Bismarck both a concession to democratic principle and an instrument for combating it. The parliament had been more independent than he liked. It formulated its own agenda, chose its own presiding officer, opened its meetings to the public, and published its debates. Its members could not be arrested for their parliamentary statements and votes; until 1890 they were elected for three-year terms, thereafter at five-year intervals. Since 1873, when Alsace-Lorraine was allowed to elect fifteen deputies, the Reichstag had consisted of 397 members chosen from single-member districts in which voting was equal, direct, and secret for all adult males. As a consequence, although only 30 to 35 percent of the eligible voters of Prussia ever cast ballots for their Chamber of Deputies; 71 percent participated in the Reichstag elections of 1890; 84 percent did so in 1907 and 1912. Some who felt constrained to vote for Conservative candidates in the open balloting for the Prussian parliament regularly cast secret ballots for Progressive or even socialist candidates in Reichstag elections.

The constitution allowed the Reichstag to be more than a mere "fig leaf" of absolutism. Whenever it was dissolved by the emperor, new elections were required within sixty days. The Reichstag could not force the emperor to dismiss a chancellor, but it could call on the chancellor to explain and justify his policies and actions, criticize him freely, and refuse to cooperate with him. The annual budgets (and the special seven-year budgets for the army) required Reichstag approval. As the yearly expenses of the Reich increased tenfold from 350,000,000 marks in 1872 to 3,500,000,000 in 1913, the nation's parliament was offered many opportunities to modify government policies.

The representatives' power to *influence* the government of imperial Germany is indisputable, but several factors prevented them from achieving *control* over policy that democratization required. One was the number of parties, and a second was the antagonisms that separated them. No one party could win a majority of the seats, and factional differences prevented the formation of majority coalitions for reform. Finally, even at the national level, democratic suffrage was ineffective because of failure to reapportion seats in a time of unprecedented human mobility. People left rural areas for the city, but the distribution of seats in the Reichstag remained the same. In 1900 the vote of a Prussian democrat in Berlin's sixth Reichstag District with a population of 697,000 counted only one-twelfth that of a Prussian conservative in the constituency of Löwenberg with 60,000 inhabitants.[9]

A much more fundamental obstacle to the establishment of genuine parliamentary government was the federal structure of the empire. The Bundesrat institutionalized particularistic opposition against the centralization that Reichstag control of the executive would bring. The Bundesrat consisted of fifty-eight representatives (sixty-one after Alsace-Lorraine was allowed three in 1911), appointed by the various state governments. Each delegation could only vote as a bloc in accordance with instructions from its government. The Bundesrat could veto any legislation proposed by the popularly elected Reichstag because the constitution required that all legislation must be approved by both chambers. Changes in the constitution could be blocked by fourteen negative votes in the Bundesrat. With seventeen delegates, the Prussian government alone thus was empowered to preserve the constitution against changes it did not want.

Combinations of other states also could obstruct constitutional change: Bavaria had six delegates, Saxony and Württemberg four each, Baden and Hesse three each; Braunschweig and Mecklenburg-Schwerin two each; the remaining states each had one delegate. The Reichstag could be made the supreme instrument of government only by depriving the Bundesrat of its veto power. Such a major constitutional change, however, would diminish the influence of the state governments over Reich affairs, would curtail their ability to control their own internal policies, and would make their reigning families superfluous. Because parliamentarization would also mean centralization, it is hardly surprising that all state governments, working through the Bundesrat, alertly opposed it. None did so more continuously than the government of Prussia. The strongest official declaration of the particularist argument against Reichstag control had been presented in the Bundesrat by Bismarck in April 1884—in words that underscored the potent threat to his own accomplishments of 1866–71:

> The Royal Prussian Government would see in such a shifting of the center of gravity of governmental power a great danger for the continuance of the new-born unity of Germany. . . . The idea of the establishment of a responsible Reich Ministry. . .is, therefore, in the conviction of the Royal Government,. . . to be combatted . . . because this kind of excess, if it were to succeed, would, in the conviction of the government, bring about a new dissolution of German unity. [10]

If Prussia's delegation alone could block constitutional reform in the Bundesrat, the one practical hope for achieving genuine parliamentary government for the Reich lay in the internal democratization of Prussia. Prussia's three-class suffrage system was both the target of reformers and a massive obstacle to their efforts. Laws of June 1891 and June 1893 only tinkered with details, leaving the basic suffrage system of 1849 intact. As before, the status quo gave comfortable majorities to the landed aristocrats and their upper-middle-class allies in the Chamber of Deputies. Controlling both houses of parliament, the nobles also dominated the Prussian bureaucracy. As late as 1910 all but one of the twelve heads of provincial administration (*Oberpräsidenten*) in Prussia were members of the aristocracy, as were twenty-three of the thirty-seven heads of regional administration (*Regierungspräsidenten*). Germany's democrats knew they could achieve no fundamental reform of the Reich government until the government of Prussia was altered. Only a democratized Prussian suffrage could produce a Chamber of Deputies as democratic as the Reichstag; and only such a chamber could eventually bring about the appointment of the sort of Prussian minister-president who, as *Reichskanzler*, might assist in the democratization of the empire.[11]

Knowing that equal suffrage in Prussia and other democratic reforms would hurt their own interests, four of the major political parties stoutly defended the constitutional status quo during most of the Wilhelmian era (1888–1918). Together National Liberals, the Center, the Free Conservatives, and the Conservatives could muster majorities in the Reichstag until the election of 1912, in which voters gave to these establishment parties only 48.4 percent of the seats. They virtually monopolized the Prussian Chamber of Deputies. The men who led each of these parties resisted the democratization of Germany, though the National Liberal and the Center parties contained many members who favored it. Significantly, each of these parties of preservation reached a different segment of the German population. The Center was strong in the Rhenish, Silesian, and Polish provinces of Prussia and in southern Germany. It exercised no influence in Protestant Saxony, which was a stronghold of the National Liberals, though to a lesser degree than Prussia. The Conservatives, almost nonexistent south of the Main, were very strong in the eastern and central provinces of Prussia. Similarly, each party drew its strength from well-defined socioeconomic elements in the population. Thus—by one party or another— Germans in every geographical area and in all walks of life were admonished to uphold the existing social and political order.

The unity of the National Liberal party, seriously strained in the 1870's, did not survive Bismarck's protective tariff of 1879. In 1880 those who agreed with Eduard Lasker in favoring free trade and a greater measure of parliamentary power followed him out of the party. The conservative remainder kept the conservative faith. The party drew votes primarily from middle-class Protestants, and some of the rank and file supporters favored a greater measure of popular sovereignty; positions on public issues were determined, however, by parliamentary delegations, drawn from the upper middle class and powerfully influenced by politically conservative business lobbies.[12]

The policies of the National Liberals in the 1870's had alienated whole blocs of German voters. One-third of the population—German Catholics—could not forgive the party's support for Bismarck's *Kulturkampf*, and many industrial workers were antagonized when it supported Bismarck's antisocialist legislation. Chancellor and kaiser subsequently redeemed themselves with many Catholics by dropping the anti-Catholic laws and with some industrial workers through adoption of the social welfare program; National Liberalism, which had supported neither change, of course, could not recover the lost ground. Though Social Democrats, the Center, and even the Progressives developed close affiliations with labor organizations, National Liberalism remained a party of employers.

Fearing both the Catholic and the socialist masses, the National Liberals consistently opposed moves to introduce the secret ballot in Prussia; the employers they represented stood to benefit most if every man's vote was known. The left fringe of National Liberalism had some predisposition to replace three-class suffrage with multiple votes for the wealthy and the educated; on the right some National Liberals openly suggested in the early 1890's that equal suffrage in Reichstag elections should be abandoned. Neither extreme represented or moved the party.[13]

The NLP paid a considerable price for its rigidity. From an all-time high of 152 seats in the Reichstag in 1874, it dropped to 45 in 1881, never to reach as high as 60 again. Symptomatic of its character as a party of upper-middle-class interests, National Liberalism fared better under Prussia's unequal suffrage than in the democratic elections to the Reichstag. On the eve of World War I, one out of eight Prussian deputies, but only one out of ten Reichstag members, was a National Liberal.

In 1914 the National Liberal party claimed 283,711 members. Originally founded by German patriots distrustful of Prussia, its major strength now resided in the Hohenzollern kingdom, where it had 64,800 members in the Rhine Province, 43,100 in Westphalia, and 26,500 in Hanover. In Baden the party had 31,200 members and in the kingdom of Saxony 21,200. Since the founding of the empire its voting strength had dwindled from 30 percent in 1874 to 14 percent in 1912. Only by forming a coalition with Conservatives and Free Conservatives could the National Liberal party continue to exert a significant influence in the politics of the German Empire. But in so doing it also enabled its one-time enemies to preserve a disproportionate influence on government policy.[14]

Leadership of the National Liberals was a trying task, for the party included mixed elements even after the secession of 1880. The job was managed well, however, by a Baden lawyer, Ernst Bassermann, who became chairman of the National Liberal caucus in the Reichstag in 1899 and general party chairman in 1904. His second in command was the leader of the Prussian National Liberals, Robert Friedberg, a member of the Prussian Chamber of Deputies from 1886 through 1918. Friedberg rivaled Bassermann in the management of the party while serving after 1904 as its deputy chairman and as head of the executive committee.[15]

Germany's Catholics followed another party that struck few blows for democratic reform and generally supported the status quo. Conservative like the NLP, the Center party nevertheless exercised a wider appeal. It addressed itself in fact to three large Catholic constituencies: the industrial workers of Silesia, the Rhine, and the Ruhr valleys, property owners of the faith, including the factory owners in the same regions, and landed aristocrats and farmers throughout the Reich. Keeping such diverse elements in harmony required skillfull leadership. The great Windthorst died in 1891 leaving a gap no one could fill. Francis Lieber was only partly successful before his passing in 1902, and the head of the Center's Reichstag caucus from 1893 to 1909, Count Alfred von Hompesch, was even less so. Georg von Hertling, a former professor of philosophy in Bonn and Munich and a considerable orator, stood out among Catholic Reichstag deputies, thanks to political longevity (with the exception of six years in the 1890's he had sat continuously from 1875 to 1912) and his widely recognized talents. Called to the minister-presidency of Bavaria in 1912, he controlled the strong branch of the party in his jurisdiction. But unlike Windthorst, Hertling remained a civil servant rather than becoming a parliamentarian. He symbolized the dilemma of a caste called upon to lead in a system of which it fundamentally disapproved. After the turn of the century Hertling was increasingly overshadowed by Peter Spahn. A tall Rhenish judge who lacked personal charm and oratorical brilliance, Spahn talked less and worked harder than his rival and succeeded him as chairman of the Center's Reichstag delegation in 1912. Adolf Gröber, a former judge, in 1895 founded the Württemberg branch of the Center party and soon joined the inner circle of party leaders in Berlin. Most of the time he, Hertling, and Spahn were on the side of the Catholic nobles, landowners, and businessmen whose interests carried great weight in the party. Karl Trimborn, a Rhenish lawyer closely linked with Catholic labor, also participated in the national leadership of the Center. The Bachem family in Cologne, publisher of the *Kölnische Volkszeitung*, wielded extensive influence; Carl Bachem sat in the Prussian Chamber of Deputies from 1889 to 1904 and in the Reichstag from 1889 to 1907. A younger man of great energy and political skill, Matthias Erzberger, was then rising in the left wing of the party, but his full weight would not be felt until after 1914.[16]

The party's generally conservative leaders stood on powerfully fortified political ramparts. By 1914 the Center was supported by 446 newspapers reaching 2,625,000 readers; a significant labor movement; a youth movement with 350,000 members; some 2,000,000 voters in Reichstag elections; 91 members of the Reichstag (51 from Prussia, 29 from Bavaria, 6 from Baden, 4 from Württemberg, and 1 from Oldenburg); and 103 members of the Prussian Chamber of Deputies. About 60 percent of the seats in the Bavarian Landtag were held by Center deputies on the eve of World War I.[17]

By 1900 it was obvious that the Center was a Catholic party; but should it seek to retain or to broaden its character? During the decade before 1914 an often bitter controversy simmered over this question. Was it to be a fighting arm of the church in the political arena or an instrument to express the broad secular interests of Catholics and other Christians? Hoping to attract as many workers as possible to the antisocialist unions affiliated with the Center, the Bachem family and its supporters worked through the *Kölnische Volkszeitung* to open the unions and the party to Christians of all denominations. They represented what was called the "Cologne Orientation," though ironically a Cologne jurist who sat in the Prussian Chamber of Deputies, Hermann Roeren, became the spokesman for their opposition, the so-called "Berlin Orientation." Stressing the confessional character of the party, Roeren and his lay allies were supported by a number of high-ranking clerics.

Papal politics entered the controversy over the nature of the Center as a Christian party, for in advocating an end to its "splendid isolation," Julius Bachem sought to keep alive the spirit of Leo XIII during the antimodernist pontificate of Pius X (1903–14). The controversy had an equally basic political dimension, for fundamentally at issue was the relationship between the party and the Protestant-dominated Reich and its state-citadel, Hohenzollern Prussia. The Cologne faction emphasized the broad, Christian character of the Center in hopes of covering the remaining scars of the *Kulturkampf*. Roeren's emphasis on Catholic exclusiveness, on the other hand, preserved the *Kulturkampf* tradition of the Center party opposition in the Bismarckian empire. The debate over confessionalism was not laid to rest until the death of Pius X. In the end, Roeren failed to gain control, and the Center remained officially interdenominational, while de facto confessional because few non-Catholics joined it.

For the same reason the Center remained, for the most part, conservative. Notwithstanding internal disagreements, the persecution of the 1870's inspired political caution among Center leaders, who usually avoided actions that might antagonize the state authorities; for, as the *Kulturkampf* had shown, in a country that was two-thirds Protestant, Catholics as such could not challenge monarch or administration. This consideration was set forth confidentially in 1900 by the leading Center party members of the Reichstag and the Prussian Chamber of Deputies in a carefully prepared message to the pope. "It is obvious," they warned, "that defenders of Catholic interests in our country must proceed only with the greatest prudence in order not to rekindle a new Kulturkampf through incautious actions."

These memories and apprehensions narrowly circumscribed

the political freedom of the Center, which reckoned with (and strongly reciprocated) the hatred of the left-liberal parties and kept up an unrelenting attack against the Social Democrats. Like the National Liberals, the Center could only turn right, whether in the Reichstag or in the Prussian Chamber of Deputies. In the latter the Conservatives, though Protestant, could be counted on to help protect the Catholic church as part of their efforts to uphold religion and the respect for established authority. In return this political alliance limited the options of the Center on reform issues. [18]

Political arithmetic after 1890 made it obvious that the imperial government and the Conservative parties needed the Center. Conservatives, Free Conservatives, and National Liberals were able to preserve a majority in the Prussian Chamber of Deputies. In the Reichstag they occupied 34 percent of the seats following the election of 1890. Thereafter their share declined steadily. Without Catholic votes the German government majority could not count on passage of its legislative proposals.

Thus, while no love was lost between them, William II and the Center party nevertheless became allies. As were the leaders of other political parties, the Center's guiding spirits at times were alarmed by William's behavior. But to give expression to their apprehensions, they feared, would only increase the kaiser's prejudice against the Catholics. As the largest generally conservative party in the Reichstag after 1890, the Center sometimes withheld its support on specific issues in attempts to win concessions, but its leaders were anxious to prove the loyalty of the party and of Catholicism to the German Empire and its ruler. [19]

A small democratic impulse survived in the Center party after 1890 among Catholic laborers. The church hierarchy in Germany had long shown a keen if patriarchal interest in improving the welfare of the industrial workers, but they did not sponsor real trade unions until after Social Democracy and its unions began to win Catholic as well as Protestant workers in significant numbers. To counter this threat was the central task of a new organization founded in 1890 to promote social welfare, the Catholic People's Union (Volksverein für das katholische Deutschland). Growing rapidly, the Volksverein claimed five hundred thousand members in 1906, eight hundred thousand by 1914. [20]

In 1901 the General Association of Christian Trade Unions of Germany (Gesamtverband der christlichen Gewerkschaften Deutschlands) was founded, with headquarters at Cologne. Johann Giesberts became the editor of its central newspaper, the weekly *Westdeutsche Arbeiterzeitung*. Adam Stegerwald, born in 1874 of a peasant family near Würzburg and a cabinetmaker by trade, assumed executive direction in January 1903. Under Stegerwald's energetic stewardship the Christian unions sought support among all denominations. Nevertheless, they were justifiably called Catholic rather than "Christian," for as late as 1913 some three hundred thousand of their three hundred forty-two thousand members were Catholics. While outnumbered seven to one by the socialist unions in Germany as a whole, the Christian Trade Unions represented the majority of workers in Catholic urban parishes, with 45 percent of all the organized workers in the Rhineland-Westphalia area as members. Their leaders upheld the democratic Reichstag suffrage against its critics, and some energetically demanded the vote for all adult males in Prussia.[21]

Catholic labor leaders were not able to turn the Center into a party of democratic action before 1914, but after the turn of the century their influence slowly grew. Johann Giesberts was elected to the Prussian Chamber of Deputies and, in 1905, to the German parliament. Five of the ninety-one Centrists in the Reichstag of 1912 and six of about one hundred Center members of the Prussian Chamber of Deputies from 1908 to 1918 were trade-union men. This was no great victory for labor, but concern for the loyalty of rank and file Catholic workers made the Center leaders increasingly sensitive to their desires. In a February 1904 memorandum for Pope Pius X the party chiefs emphasized that their unions had proved useful in the struggle against Social Democracy and that they had brought the Center "extraordinary support" in German elections. Looking ahead, the party's leaders wrote: "If the Center party as such is to be sustained, if it is not to be driven back [destroyed, according to an earlier draft] in the large cities and industrial districts and be restricted to the purely rural districts, then the Center party must want the Christian Trade Unions to develop well in the future."[22]

The challenge of Social Democracy and the organization of Catholic labor to meet it made the Prussian suffrage issue increasingly difficult for Center leadership. All along the party had favored introduction of the secret ballot in Prussia as protection for Catholic peasants east of the Elbe River and for workers in the western districts against the prying eyes of Protestant landlords and industrialists. But the contrary interests of aristocratic landowners and wealthy businessmen in the party and the party leadership's perpetual reluctance to challenge their conservative allies in parliament silenced the Center's advocates of electoral reform.

As a consequence, the Center was inconsistent about suffrage reform. In 1904, Carl Bachem, echoed approvingly by *Germania*, the party's central newspaper, spoke generally in the Prussian Chamber of Deputies in favor of "a real reform," but insisted that "to make proposals . . . in a fundamental question of that kind was not the business of the parliament or of a single party but rather the business of the government." On the other hand, when the government was hostile, party leaders were ready to use the suffrage issue to demonstrate their indispensability. In the Reichstag elections of 1907 the government, angered because the Center had voted against colonial appropriations, attempted to smear the party as unpatriotic. Center leaders later that year retaliated by introducing a motion in the Prussian Chamber of Deputies in favor of equal suffrage. They could do so in full knowledge that their radical feint would discomfit king and ministers, but fail in the face of Conservative and National Liberal opposition.

On the whole, the existing three-class suffrage in Prussia benefited the Center party. In the equal secret balloting of Reichstag elections the party slipped from a peak strength of 106 seats in 1890 (26.7 percent) to 91 in 1912 (22.9 percent); meanwhile, the Prussian franchise allowed it to do slightly better than maintain its representation in the Chamber of Deputies (22.7 percent of the seats in 1888, 23.2 percent in 1913). Still, pressures within their own ranks and a desire to forestall the continued growth of Social Democracy—which was capitalizing on the issue of suffrage reform—caused party leaders to give lip service to equal suffrage without pushing the matter enough to disturb their good relations with the Conservatives. At times they tried to hide their actual indifference to electoral reform by criticizing proposals of other parties as inadequate; at other times they argued that it would be unrealistic to make a great issue of equal suffrage. Given the makeup of the Chamber of Deputies, a Center election leaflet of April 1913 explained, a proposal for "universal, equal, secret, and direct suffrage . . . does not have the slightest prospect of realization." The party could not make equal suffrage a central issue, the leaflet continued, because it was necessary to work with the Conservatives against "all parties of the left" in order to prevent the possible outbreak of another *Kulturkampf*. [23]

While the Center party did not exert itself for equal suffrage in Prussia, neither did it strive for genuine parliamentary government in the Reich; even Adam Stegerwald of the Catholic trade unions insisted that neither the English nor the French system of control by parliament was desirable for Germany. As a party that included influential south German particularists, the Center could not favor the greater centralization that would have resulted from making the Reichstag supreme. Furthermore, as a minority party it could favor neither royal absolutism under a Protestant monarch nor dominance by anti-Catholic parliamentary majorities. Thus the Center became exactly what its name implied—neither a party of reaction nor a party of democratic reform. If judged by its actions rather than by an occasional pronouncement aimed at keeping the support of Catholic workers, the party was often as conservative as were the factions which traditionally bore that label. [24]

Two political parties of imperial Germany were conservative in title as well as in action. One faction of the old Prussian Conservative party, supporting Bismarck's unification of the Reich, had split off in 1866 to form the Free Conservative party. (In the Reichstag it called itself the Imperial party [Reichspartei].) Industrial magnates and landed aristocrats led it. As supporters of Bismarck, the Free Conservatives reached their peak strength in the Reichstag of 1878; thereafter they lost votes to the rejuvenated mother party, which had been reorganized in 1876 as the German Conservative party (the DKP) and grudgingly accepted the Reich as an accomplished fact.

The two Conservative parties remained tremendously influential because of their close relations with the Hohenzollern dynasty and their power within the Prussian Chamber of Deputies, but they steadily declined in strength in the Reichstag. The Free Conservative party had 14 percent of the Reichstag seats in 1878, but never filled more than 7 percent of them after 1890 (3.5 percent in 1912). The rise of democratic forces likewise took its toll on the DKP in Reichstag elections. From a high of eighty seats in 1887 (20 percent of the total), the DKP dropped to fifty-six in 1898 and to forty-three in 1912 (11 percent). Furthermore, only four of its forty-three deputies elected in the last prewar campaign represented constituencies outside Prussia. In popular votes, meanwhile, the two parties had declined from a combined strength of 27 percent of the total in 1878 to 12 percent in 1912. With 1,493,000 votes in 1912, the two then mustered less public support than either the National Liberal or Center parties; and their net catch was only a third as large as that of the dreaded Social Democrats.[25]

In Prussia, meanwhile, the Conservative parties not only persisted but flourished because of the three-class suffrage. Together they won 161 seats in the Prussian chamber in 1879, 209 in 1893, 212 in 1908, and 202 in 1913. The DKP dominated. In 1893 it alone won 145 seats (33 percent), and it had a powerful bloc of 148 deputies in the Prussian chamber of 1913–18. Agrarian Prussia east of the Elbe River gave the DKP its great strength: 74 percent of the deputies it elected in 1880 and 87 percent of those elected in 1912 came from these "old Prussian" [pre-1815] areas. East Elbia was the stronghold of feudal mores in Germany. There many peasant voters voluntarily supported Conservative aristocrats at the polls, identifying their own agrarian interests with those of their "betters." In other districts, as Hellmut von Gerlach later recalled from personal observation, the landlords marched their farm workers "straight from the fields" to the polls to vote under close supervision. Because of these conditions and the refusal of many urban and democratic Prussians to cast third-class ballots, the DKP repeatedly won about 12 percent of the votes of the poor (class three votes) in Prussian elections.

While the Conservative parties commanded popular support among the peasants, their leadership was of the aristocracy. Of the 43 DKP Reichstag deputies of 1912–18, 24 were noble estate owners (*Rittergutsbesitzer*). In the Prussian Chamber of Deputies elected in 1913, 76 of the 148 Conservative party members were men of the nobility. Aware that both economics (declining grain prices) and politics were against them in the long run, they fought changes with gritted teeth. A leader of the DKP, Baron Ernst von Heydebrand und der Lasa, spoke for his colleagues when he told a Progressive deputy about 1900: "The future belongs to you to be sure. The masses will make their weight felt and rob us, the aristocrats, of our influence." "However," Heydebrand added ominously, "we will not voluntarily sacrifice our position." The aristocrats were determined to continue to dominate German society and polity as long as possible, and they set the tone for both as long as the German Empire existed. Commanding the army and leading the Prussian Chamber of Deputies, Prussia's nobles also won a larger share of the top administrative and diplomatic positions than they had held at any time since the era of Hardenberg and Stein. Yet they remained unsatisfied. The novelist Theodor Fontane recognized their problem while denouncing their behavior. The more the nobles became convinced of their superfluity, he wrote a friend in 1894, "the more unbearable they become in their demands." Responsive to these demands, the two Conservative parties fought against all efforts at substantial reform in the Prussian suffrage system, and many of them would have done away with equal votes in Reichstag elections if they had possessed the power to do so.[26]

From the 1870's into the twentieth century the Reichstag leadership of the Free Conservatives was shared by the founder of Germany's heavy industry lobby, Wilhelm von Kardorff, and by the largest employer of industrial labor in the Saar, Carl Ferdinand von Stumm, both of whom wanted to see all socialists denied the right to vote. The chairman of the DKP from 1892 to 1911 was Baron Otto Karl Gottlob von Manteuffel, son of the reactionary Prussian minister-president of the 1850's. But the man who determined Conservative policies more forcefully than anyone else after 1900 was Baron Ernst von Heydebrand und der Lasa, a Silesian landowner, member of the Prussian Chamber of Deputies throughout the reign of William II, and a member of the Reichstag from 1903 to 1918. Because of his influence, he was popularly nicknamed "the uncrowned king of Prussia."

Some 60 newspapers speaking for the Free Conservative party and 214 for the DKP (including much of the "nonpartisan" press) continued to influence the political thought of hundreds of thousands of voters throughout the Wilhelmian era. Because of the Conservatives' position of power in the Prussian Chamber of Deputies, the Center and National Liberal parties needed their help and frequently were forced to reciprocate in the Reichstag. In their opposition to democratization, therefore, the Conservative parties were both inflexible and effective.[27]

A smaller group, the Christian Social party, never became as effective a foe of democracy as the larger parties of the status quo, but it assisted in upholding the constitutional structure while explicitly introducing anti-Semitism into German politics. Founded in 1878 by the Conservative chaplain to the Hohenzollern court, Adolf Stoecker, the new party favored paternalistic social welfare legislation, urged the workers to love both "King and Fatherland," and repudiated Social Democracy as "impractical, un-Christian, and unpatriotic." Anti-Semitism, which had been inflamed by the depression of the 1870's, was incorporated in a campaign manifesto for the Reichstag elections of 1878: "We respect the Jew. . . . But we firmly believe that no Jew can be a leader of Christian workers in either a religious or an economic capacity." Neither the call for moderate social reform nor the anti-Semitism achieved significant results in Berlin, but Stoecker—running in Westphalia as a Conservative—won a seat in the Reichstag in 1881 and held it, except for the five years 1893 to 1898, until 1908.

Stoecker's anti-Semitism had a religious rather than a racial basis and was quickly secularized by different extremist splinter groups. In 1890 a Berlin school administrator, Hermann Ahlwardt, proposed that Jews be treated as foreigners, and he was elected to the Reichstag three years later. The small anti-Semitic parties in 1893 placed sixteen deputies in the Reichstag, eleven of whom represented the German Reform party, whose strength was concentrated in industrial Dresden and among the rural districts of Hesse. They declined to ten deputies in 1903, but captured sixteen seats in 1907. Christian Social candidates could take only three seats in the elections of 1912, which gave seven more to other explicit anti-Semites. It appeared that political anti-Semitism was fading slowly. But in that same year a book by Heinrich Class, *If I Were the Kaiser*, unwittingly heralded the "Third Reich" while defending the Second. Frankly calling for authoritarian action by the emperor, Class demanded that Jews be disfranchised and barred from all public offices and from the professions. He would allow them to remain in Germany only as "aliens," paying double the taxes that "Germans" should pay.

Several of the Jew-haters for a time combined prejudice with demand for more democratic and compulsory suffrage and a graduated income tax. By 1907, however, they were again lined up with the Conservatives in defense of the status quo. Meanwhile, they had steadily hurt the movement for democratization by denouncing the groups that most constantly demanded it— the left-liberal and Social Democratic parties—as parties of Jewry. They may have held back the expansion of democratic demands even more basically by diverting the dissatisfactions of some workers in Berlin and Dresden and of farmers in Hesse away from the social and political structure toward anti-Semitism. Failing in their attempts to win sizable parliamentary representation, the anti-Semitic splinter parties nevertheless achieved some successes. After 1893 all the larger parties except Social Democracy showed a strong tendency to nominate and elect only "Christians." At times the Conservatives openly endorsed anti-Semitism. In its Tivoli Program of 1892 the DKP—normally more discreet—pledged itself to fight against "the multifarious and disruptive Jewish influence upon our national way of life."[28]

Behind the major parties that upheld undemocratic government stood a number of related pressure groups. Among the most significant were the Pan-German League, the Farmers' League, and two other economic associations—the League of Industrialists and the Central Association of German Industrialists. Through overlapping memberships, they coordinated their activities well.

The Pan-German League (Alldeutscher Verband), led after 1908 by the anti-Semitic Heinrich Class, was founded in January 1891 by Karl Peters, who had won fame as an explorer of Africa. The new organization was created to mobilize popular support for German expansion. It favored incorporation of German-

Austria, German-Switzerland, and The Netherlands into the Reich and demanded that the government promote Germandom throughout the world. It defended monarchical institutions against parliamentary encroachments and was convinced that only a powerful monarch could carry out the imperialistic policies it desired. The Pan-German League never became a mass movement, but its seventeen thousand members, mostly from the upper middle class, exerted an influence out of proportion to their numbers. About one-third were teachers in schools or universities.[29]

Several economic organizations of the imperial era stood ready to help finance the right-wing political parties, to win votes for them, and to influence them as best they could. The economic pressure group that was most publicly active and most influential was the Farmers' League (Bund der Landwirte). Created in 1893, it showed signs of becoming a political party and was viewed as a threat by the Conservative parties until they found that it effectively mobilized peasant votes for them. Its chairman, Baron Conrad von Wangenheim, sat in the Reichstag as a Conservative from 1898 to 1903. Vice-Chairman Gustav Roesicke was elected both to the Prussian Landtag and the Reichstag as a Conservative. The Bund helped to elect 157 supporters to the Prussian Chamber of Deputies in 1903, 150 in 1913. By 1907 persons supported by the Bund filled 138 of the 397 mandates to the Reichstag. (All DKP Reichstag deputies elected between 1898 and 1914 were pledged to its program.) As early as 1894 it could claim almost two hundred thousand members, and its rolls swelled to three hundred thirty thousand by 1914—most of them small farmers and most in Prussia. Control was exercised by some two thousand owners of large estates, a high percentage of whom were aristocrats. Antiliberal, antidemocratic, antilabor, antisocialist, and anti-Semitic, the Bund der Landwirte powerfully revitalized the DKP in the 1890's and provided it with a mass base thereafter.[30]

The Farmers' League agitated in public, but its operations behind the scenes were more complex, especially those involving the business lobbies that developed in the German Empire.

The Central Association of German Industrialists (Central-verband Deutscher Industrieller) was founded in 1876 when some ninety leaders of industry gathered in Berlin at the call of Wilhelm von Kardorff, leader of the Free Conservative party. The Centralverband attempted to coordinate and represent the several regional or specialized industrial associations that financed its activities—the most important being the Association of German Iron and Steel Industrialists. Together, the two organizations waged the campaign for tariff protection from 1876 to 1879. In 1878 they created a joint central election committee, through which they supported one hundred candidates for Reichstag seats—men of "unconditional devotion to industry"— and opposed with equal zeal the election of fifty free-trade candidates.

From its beginnings the Centralverband vigorously fought Social Democracy and favored state control of labor unions. Strongly supporting Hohenlohe's *Zuchthausvorlage* in 1898–99, it spent twelve thousand marks to agitate on behalf of the antilabor measure. In 1904, spurred into action by a great strike of textile workers at Crimmitschau in Saxony, it established the Main Office of German Employers' Associations to coordinate the antilabor activities of several separate employer associations. The light-industry Union of Industrialists (Bund der Industriellen), organized in 1895, created a similar agency in 1904, the Union of German Employers' Associations. Though the two parent groups competed on tariff questions and other issues, they merged in 1913 into a common Union of German Employers' Associations, the better to direct industry's defenses against the demands of the trade unions.

The men who led the Centralverband opposed political as well as social reform. Some were content merely to oppose further democratization, but others were outright reactionary. One of the latter was Henry Axel Bueck, a founder of the Centralverband and its business manager from 1886 to 1911. Ernst Bassermann privately noted in 1908 that Bueck favored "the removal of universal suffrage, the sooner the better."[31]

Throughout the Wilhelmian era several officers of the Centralverband were active in the Conservatice, Free Conservative, and National Liberal parties. These parties shared the campaign contributions the Centralverband urged industrialists to make. In 1907, for example, at least six hundred thousand marks

($150,000) were collected. The money was managed in Berlin by Paul von Schwabach, director of the Bleichröder banking firm, who passed it on to Baron Octavio von Zedlitz-Neukirch, a leader of the Free Conservative party. He in turn distributed the funds among the parties and pressure groups he trusted. In 1912 the Centralverband had more than a million marks in its election fund, which was administered by a National Liberal. Instead of distributing funds through the central offices of the political parties, the Centralverband itself then gave direct support to 120 carefully chosen candidates, at least three-fifths of whom were National Liberals; 41 of those candidates were elected.

On a less lavish scale the Union of Industrialists (Bund der Industriellen)—liberal rather than reactionary on constitutional issues—supported candidates of its choice for public office. A significant part of the campaign expenses in 1907 of the rising young National Liberal, Gustav Stresemann, were provided by this organization, with which he was closely linked as a professional lobbyist for small industry in Saxony. The light-industry interests of the Bund were often at odds with those of the Centralverband, and by 1912, Stresemann was complaining to the chairman of the National Liberal party that the rival Centralverband was buying the whole party and shaping its policies.[32]

Disagreeing over tariffs and constitutional issues, the two major industrial associations had a common interest in supporting politicians who opposed democratization. Most of the great merchants and shippers of Germany shared this interest, but they favored liberal economic policies. Thus in 1909 leading merchants, shippers, industrialists, and bankers formed a new business lobby, the Hansabund. The avowed purpose of this pressure group was to elect Reichstag deputies whose views on tax and tariff questions were in line with those of commerce and light industry and in opposition to the protectionist Farmers' League. In 1913 the chairman of the National Liberal party acknowledged that money from the Hansabund was indispensable in its election campaigns. Otherwise, German businessmen tended to back candidates who opposed democratic constitutional reform. The richest of them were increasingly linked with the landed aristocracy of Prussia in business ventures, through purchase of East-Elbian estates, entry of their sons and nephews into the Prussian bureaucracy, and intermarriage. Some obtained patents of nobility, but for the most part they absorbed the political values of the aristocracy without gaining social acceptance. Opposing democratization, Germany's upper bourgeoisie had abundant means to support opposition by others.[33]

The opposition to democracy of the conservative parties and of the aristocracy and upper bourgeoisie that stood behind them should not be surprising. Meanwhile, powerful social institutions helped to preserve a conservative spirit among the German masses. The most important of these were the bureaucracy, the press, the churches, the schools, and the army. To the extent that "the mind of Germany" remained undemocratic after 1890, these institutions deserve much of the credit or the blame.

The various states had developed centralized bureaucracies before they created genuine parliaments, and even after 1871, Germany was not so much governed by politicians as administered by bureaucrats, and it was these—not leaders of political parties—that the heads of state called to serve in their cabinets. Bureaucrats in high positions commonly were drawn from the nobility or admitted to it; those in lower posts usually came to them from experience as noncommissioned officers in the army. The bureaucracy constituted no small caste, and, as Max Weber noted, it was growing. In 1907 there were 390,000 civil servants in the administrative and judicial agencies of Germany—more than the total membership any political organization could claim except the Social Democratic and the Center parties. These constituted the bureaucracy only in the narrowest sense. Some 420,000 others held civil service positions in the postal service, state railways, and other public agencies. Disregarding the teachers and military officers who also held public employment, approximately one out of every seventy-five inhabitants (or the head of one out of every fifteen to twenty families) was a member of the bureaucracy in 1907. This hierarchy ranged in distinction from the imperial chancellor down to railwaymen and mail carriers.

The vast social gaps that divided the civil servants were spanned by a shared sense of duty that was deeply ingrained and—for the majority—an awareness that their livelihood depended directly upon the state. The very concepts of duty and pride in state service were sufficient to make most members of the bureaucracy loyal supporters of the status quo. To these incentives were added the desire for secure careers, advances in salary and rank, and acquisition of official titles. In a hierarchical society, it meant much to be designated a *Geheimrat* and a great deal more to win the distinction of a *Wirklicher Geheimer Ober-regierungsrat*. Civil servants exchanged political and economic independence for a sense of participation in the power structure of the state. Though a few lower-ranking officials were sympathetic with Social Democracy, joining that party could mean dismissal and to strike was unthinkable.

The fact that civil servants permeated all layers of German society helps to explain the pervasiveness of conservative political habits and attitudes in Germany before 1914. That there was a large bureaucracy in middle-class Germany helps to explain the relative disinclination of that class to embrace either liberal-democratic ideals or socialism before 1914. The bureaucrats, as the historian Otto Hintze pointed out in 1911, formed a strong bridge between the rulers and the ruled in imperial Germany. So, in large part, did another social institution, the press.[34]

In Metternich's Germany the press had provided an important if restricted mechanism for the spreading of liberal ideas. In the German Empire, too, newspapers were essential instruments of propaganda for those who demanded political reform, but only a very few called for fundamental alterations. No more than 2 percent of all of Germany's newspapers and periodicals (altogether about four thousand in 1914) were Social Democratic, and none of the mass-circulation newspapers was socialistic. Liberal democratic and left-liberal newspapers were considerably more numerous (about 10 percent of the total) and enjoyed a larger circulation. But both the left-liberal and the Social Democratic newspapers had to operate within the limitations of imperial press regulations. The Reich Press Law of 1874, which remained in effect throughout the imperial era, required no censorship in advance of publication, but the government reserved the right to arrest editors and to ban newspapers that incited readers to treason or other illegal activity. Criticism of monarchy and of specific monarchs was punishable by imprisonment, and such punishment was repeatedly levied against offenders. For the most part, however, the government relied upon positive rather than negative measures to influence public opinion in a conservative direction, once the antisocialist laws were dropped in 1890. Control of news supply was a significant part of the technique. The largest of the central agencies that supplied news to German newspapers, the Wolffsche Telegraphenbüro, was an official agency.

Much press support for the status quo was freely volunteered. For example, daily supplies of progovernment news were provided by the great press firm of the newspaper and magazine publisher August Scherl. The first German press magnate to capitalize on advertising to finance the publication of cheap newspapers for great numbers of readers, Scherl started his *Berliner Lokal Anzeiger* in 1883, soon made it a daily, and could rejoice in a circulation of 150,000 copies by 1885. By 1912 he had built this and other journals into a publishing empire worth twelve million marks. When he then decided to retire, the Prussian government prevented the purchase of Scherl's enterprise by the left-liberal firm of Rudolf Mosse. On January 20, 1914, the Prussian minister of agriculture, Baron Clemens von Schorlemer, could assure the chancellor that purchase of Scherl's concern by men of conservative political views had been arranged through official mediation.[35]

The press in imperial Germany included advocates of democratic reform, but its overall political impact was considerably more conservative than progressive. And with great unanimity, the Christian churches of Germany positively fostered respect for monarchical and authoritarian government throughout the imperial era.

Each of the federal states was autonomous in the regulation of the churches; ultimate sovereignty was vested in the ruler of each state, who delegated the task of supervising church affairs to his minister of culture. The king of Prussia powerfully influenced church policies even after reforms in the period from 1873 to 1876 introduced a system of lay and clerical representation in synods paralleling the state-appointed church bureaucracy at all levels in the Evangelical church of Prussia. Thus, when William II in 1890 called for social reform, the church leaders followed; as

William's enthusiasm for the workers cooled, so did that of the leaders. In December 1895 the Supreme Consistory warned clergymen against neglecting their spiritual duties in favor of "purely economic interests," cautioning them that their proper task was to preach in such a way as to foster "fear of God, loyalty to the King, and neighborly love." The lower classes should be taught that happiness was to be found through faithful adaptation to "the secular order and the secular government ordained by God" (*Gottes Weltordnung und Weltregierung*).[36]

Protestants made up 62 percent of the population of the German Empire; almost a third were Catholics. The Catholic church was administered under the papacy by fourteen bishops and five archbishops (Munich, Bamberg, Freiburg, Posen, and Cologne). Only in Bavaria, Baden, and Alsace-Lorraine did Catholics constitute a majority; but in terms of absolute numbers, Prussia, though two-thirds Protestant, held 60 percent of Germany's Catholics. This majority's support for the established order had been put to a severe test during the *Kulturkampf*, but not even Bismarck's repression had broken the respect for state authority that had been instilled in priests for many centuries.

Kaiser William II at times lectured Catholic clergy as well as Protestant pastors, calling upon both to support his efforts "to preserve religion for the people and to increase their respect for both Throne and Altar." The Catholic hierarchy sometimes outdid Protestant leaders in pledging help against political radicalism. Cooperation between Rome and the kaiser "becomes all the more important as the spirit of negation, destructiveness and subversion spreads more widely in our Fatherland," pleaded the archbishop of Cologne in 1903. Persecution under Bismarck had had the same effect on the priesthood as on the lay leaders of the Center party, rendering it particularly anxious to prove its devotion to the ruling Protestant dynasty. "We are loyal to the Imperial house because we are loyal to the House of God," vowed one priest who spoke at the General Assembly of German Catholics at Aachen in 1912; the audience responded with "prolonged, thunderous applause" when he continued: "If the time should come when thrones totter, then everyone will see that we Catholics are not second-class but first-class patriots."

Clerical authority began to slip in the imperial era, as science, materialism, and urbanization produced insights and conditions undermining the traditional rapport between priest and parishioner. But men of the cloth continued to enjoy respect, hence their views still carried weight, and their conservative attitudes were widely accepted as models of conduct.[37]

Where the influence of the churches waned, the power of the schools and universities filled the ideological gap. Unfortunately for the cause of democracy, teachers and professors, as well as priests, fostered conservative social and political values.

By the turn of the century illiteracy virtually disappeared from most sections of Germany because of the elaborate systems of obligatory schooling in the federal states. In 1905 the German governments maintained almost 60,000 elementary schools with 9,000,000 pupils, served by some 150,000 full-time teachers, trained in 208 teachers' colleges. After completing eight years of elementary school, most students went to work. About one in thirty—including only a few sons and daughters of workingmen—left primary institutions after only four years to enter several types of middle schools or preacademic gymnasia. The twenty universities that existed in 1871 enrolled 13,068 students. Twenty years later this figure had more than doubled, rising to 28,077. Just before the outbreak of war in 1914, university enrollment stood at 60,853.

In the elementary schools the pupils were taught to read and write and were introduced to history, geography, and arithmetic. Religious instruction was a standard part of the curriculum in each grade. Stiff discipline was maintained at all times, and pupils were taught the virtues of hard work, punctuality, and obedience. Learning by rote discouraged individualism. Though the secondary schools placed greater emphasis on speculative thought, their social composition was bound to encourage acceptance of the existing order.

Occasionally, a teacher might publicly protest the undemocratic values the schools instilled in their pupils, but such an act would end or, at best, endanger his career. One of the most vocal critics of Prussia's schools in the imperial era was Eduard Sack. Dismissed from his teaching post in Königsberg in 1864, Sack had been forced to stop publishing a newspaper for teachers started in 1861. He joined the editorial staff of the liberal-democratic *Frankfurter Zeitung* in 1872 and for three decades kept up in its columns a running attack on the Prussian schools. "All schools must be people's schools," he wrote in 1874; "that is, they must be open to each child regardless of class or wealth and special privileges." Stack demanded that all traces of militarism and clericalism be removed from the schools; in fact, he argued in 1886, the "purpose and goal of all education" should be to teach "freedom, equality, and brotherhood." But when Sack retired from journalistic activity in 1905 the schools of Prussia were as undemocratic as ever.

In both the lower and higher schools, "patriotic history" occupied an especially important part in the curriculum. Its emphasis on the state as the embodiment of the highest secular values reflected a proud tradition among Germany's nineteenth-century historians. The emphasis was freely offered by the teachers of history as their own special contribution to national culture, but it was intensified after William II came to the throne. In 1890 the Prussian Ministry of State ordered greater emphasis on the lives of the Prussian rulers and on their concern "for the welfare of the people." Finally, students should be taught "the perniciousness of Social Democracy." The Revolution of 1848 was portrayed as a foolish aberration, reflecting foreign rather than German ideals. The eleventh edition of a widely used manual for Prussian history instructors informed them in 1910 that history, properly presented, "teaches various forms of government, and shows that ours is the best, namely a strong monarchy, limited in legislation by the representatives of the people, but supreme in administration."[38]

The universities of imperial Germany, while justly celebrated for their scholarship, did little more than the schools to accept democratic ideas. They, too, were public institutions. Professors were officials of the federal states, appointed by the ruler upon nomination by the state minister of education and religious worship. The university faculties made recommendations for professorial appointments that were often followed, but exceptions were numerous. From 1815 to 1848 a number of academicians had been leaders in the movement for national unity and constitutional government, notwithstanding this system, but the liberal and national successes of 1848–71 had left most professors satisfied with the constitutional structure of the Reich.

The conditions of society were a different matter, at least for imperial Germany's foremost academic economists. In the 1860's the impact of Marxism and the rise of socialism had focused attention on the grievances of the working class, and several professors of economics joined in the call for regulatory and social welfare measures. Adolf Wagner and Gustav Schmoller were among their most influential spokesmen. In 1872 they joined with other academicians, civil servants, businesssmen, and journalists to create the Association for Social Policy (Verein für Sozialpolitik) to promote reform by sponsoring careful studies of social problems. The reforms they demanded required intervention by the state in economic affairs, contrary to the Manchesterian doctrine of laissez-faire. As a consequence, Wagner, Schmoller, and their associates were stigmatized as "academic socialists" (*Kathedersozialisten*) by many contemporary liberals. The label was misleading. Hoping to conserve and strengthen the existing order, they believed that timely reforms would convert the workers (as Schmoller put it in 1872) into full members of state and society. The rise of Social Democracy would be checked and the potential for revolution eliminated. By the 1880's, Bismarck had accepted the basic premise of the *Kathedersozialisten* as state policy. Meanwhile, they had lent no support to the movement for parliamentarization, and Schmoller did not criticize the three-class suffrage in Prussia until 1910.

Most of imperial Germany's university professors were more socially complacent or apathetic than those who joined the Verein für Sozialpolitik. Their prevailing attitudes toward politics were rooted in their intellectual values as well as in their favorable socioeconomic status. The very concept of their educational mission was profoundly elitist; their aim was not to raise mass man but to assist in the inner growth of small numbers of cultivated individuals for whom the spiritual and mental dimensions of life were expected to be of high importance. To most academicians, therefore, the movement for democracy seemed worse than politically mistaken; it was a threat to civilization as they understood it. Furthermore, most of them considered involvement in political activity to be incompatible with the emphasis on scholarly objectivity. In 1848 forty-nine professors had been elected to the Frankfurt parliament, but only five held seats in the Reichstag of 1912–18.

Those professors who were inclined to join political parties were aware that the liberal-democratic groups were not fully respectable and that the Social Democratic movement was off limits. The widely publicized case of Leo Arons confirmed the latter contention. Arons, an able physicist connected by marriage to the Bleichröder banking house, was recommended in 1892 by the faculty for a professorship at the University of Berlin. But he was also a Social Democrat. His appointment as professor was rejected by the Prussian Ministry of Culture, which then repeatedly tried to persuade the faculty to terminate his position as an instructor (*Privatdozent*) in the university. When the faculty resisted these invasions of academic freedom, William II himself entered the matter, proclaiming in 1897: "I tolerate no socialists among . . . teachers in the royal institutions of higher education." Empowered by a special law passed in 1898 to take disciplinary action against instructors, the Prussian Ministry of State in January 1900 denied Arons the right to lecture thereafter.

Most of the professors who joined any party at all were Conservative, Free Conservative, or National Liberal. Catholic faculty could join the Center. These parties were acceptable. So was public speaking on behalf of the imperial government. Thus in 1897 the kaiser could write to a friend: "In the great university towns all over the country the professorial class has met us willingly and is going to cooperate by speaking, writing and teaching Germany's need to possess a strong fleet." The most famous scholars of the time were among those who propagandized for the navy. A partial list would include the names of Lujo Brentano, Hans Delbrück, Otto Gierke, Ernst Haeckel, Adolf von Harnack, Georg Jellinek, Karl Lamprecht, Gustav Schmoller, Werner Sombart, Adolf Wagner, Max Weber, and Wilhelm Wundt.[39]

From these men and from their less famous colleagues, German university students in the imperial era could learn a great deal. The universities could equip students with much technical knowledge, intellectual independence in their specialized academic fields, and patriotic attitudes along with the prized dueling scars they won in their fraternities. But the handful of academicians who emerged after 1900 as spokesmen for democratic reforms were exceptions to be noted later.

In its early decades of growth, the movement for democracy in Germany had drawn heavily upon the intellectual climate of the eighteenth-century Enlightenment—upon the optimistic belief that men were fundamentally social and rational and thus capable of self-government; in the last decades of the nineteenth century, by contrast, the most widely discussed development in science—the Darwinian theory—seemed to challenge this faith with its implication that men, like other animals, were selfish and irrational. The theory's emphasis on the struggle of species for survival and on natural selection of the fittest denied democratic assumptions in the political sphere. Both the natural and social sciences produced new arguments that elites were necessary to manage the political affairs of mankind. This belief was reinforced at the turn of the century through the writings of Gaetano Mosca and Vilfredo Pareto in Italy, Lord John Acton and Graham Wallas in England, Henri Bergson in France, Max Weber and Robert Michels in Germany. Michels, though a Social Democrat, significantly helped to undermine the assumptions that had made a functioning democracy seem possible. "The majority of human beings," he wrote in his famous volume on the sociology of political parties, are "predestined by tragic necessity to submit to the domination of a small minority." In Germany, furthermore, elitist fused with racial theories. The world-famous Darwinian biologist, Ernst Haeckel, was among the first to prepare their merger. In his best-seller of 1899, *Die Welträthsel*, Haeckel produced a veritable bible for atheists, resting his arguments upon the latest findings of science. But he declared that Christ's anthropological characteristics were "decidedly not Semitic," that they were, rather, the features of a "higher Aryan race." In that same year a physician-delegate to the annual congress of the SPD, Ludwig Woltmann, published a book in which he attempted to synthesize Darwinism, racism, and Marxism. Woltmann pointed the way toward a form of racial socialism not unlike that proposed by Hitler after World

War I. Meanwhile, though he was a liberal on immediate issues, Haeckel endorsed euthanasia for the incurably ill or mentally defective. So did many fellow members of the Monist League, founded by Haeckel in 1906; among these was his successor as head of the league, Wilhelm Ostwald, an internationally respected physical chemist. Though Ostwald called himself a democrat, he would do away with political parties and have the state of the future governed by "great men" in accordance with scientific principles.

Many lesser scientists simply accepted the status quo of imperial Germany. The physicians who were elected to the Reichstag in the period from 1867 to 1918 can serve as a political barometer (even if somewhat imprecise) of German science. Those who had been elected to the Frankfurt parliament in 1848 had, with few exceptions, stood left of center. Of the forty-three who joined German party caucuses in the Reichstag after 1867, only fifteen belonged to left-liberal groups and only two were Social Democrats. No physician was elected as a Social Democrat after 1874. It appears that science, which had tended to foster liberalism in the 1840's, supported the status quo in imperial Germany, and, when it did not, often advocated even more rigorous regimentation than did the government in power.[40]

The army itself was a mighty educational agency. The schools, Helmuth von Moltke told the German Reichstag in 1874, accompanied the majority of German youth only a short distance in their journey through life; fortunately, he added, the educational services of the army began where school instruction left off. In speech after speech, the chief of staff of the Prussian army echoed the lecture he had given the Constituent Reichstag of the North German Confederation: "Military service . . . constitutes the school in which to train the rising generation in order, punctuality, cleanliness, obedience, and loyalty."

The idea that the army should be not only an instrument of war but the educator of the nation, though resisted by left-liberals as well as by the Social Democrats, became one of the most important social doctrines of the German Empire. True or not, it came to be accepted in Germany and—with baneful effect—about Germany by friend and foe alike. Throughout the imperial era, at least one year of military service was required of all able-bodied males, and most served longer. As Germany and her neighbors developed the first mass peacetime armies in European history (having some four hundred thousand troops on active duty in 1874, Germany expanded her peacetime standing army to seven hundred thousand by 1914) wave after wave of recruits were called up and then returned to the civilian reserves after exposure to strict discipline and to the sociopolitical attitudes of their officers.

Expansion of the Prussian army after 1871 made it increasingly necessary to draw officers from the middle class; by 1913 only 30 percent of the army officers were members of noble families. But, even then, 52 percent of the generals and colonels were aristocrats, and these leaders of the Prussian army set the tone for all the military forces of imperial Germany. While the commanders prided themselves upon being "above politics," most were conservative. When they bothered to acknowledge Germany's domestic politics at all, it was to express scorn for the Reichstag. As one officer of the 1890's later recalled, they thought it was unpatriotic of the parliamentarians to reveal Germany's internal discord "for the nation and the world to see." Hating Social Democracy, every officer tried to prejudice recruits against it; and they constantly stood ready to suppress any attempt the socialists might make to put revolutionary theory into action. Well aware of this, even Friedrich Engels could only advise the Social Democratic leaders in Germany that they must not attack until the military "ceases to be a force against us."

Engels staked his hopes for the future on converting the agricultural laborers—"the cream of the Prussian army"; but such a possibility did not appear bright when he died in 1895. Because of its role in unification and of the international tensions of the imperial era, the army had come to be widely respected as the most important secular institution in the Reich. As early as May 1870 the future imperial chancellor, Prince Hohenlohe, while watching a parade in Berlin, had noted the change since 1848: "No trace of the former animosity...which used to be noticeable among the lower classes." By 1900 military mores permeated German society. Decades later, Gerhard Ritter cogently recalled the results of the emphasis on military values in civilian life during the Wilhelmian era: "The notions 'sharp' or 'soft,' originating from military drill . . . , were also used to judge political conditions. . . . The idea of 'standing smartly,' of 'resolute behavior' and of a 'plucky tone' did a great deal to confuse the political ideas of the German citizenry."[41]

The barricades against democratization that had been built into the constitutions of Prussia and the Reich, although carefully safeguarded by the rulers of imperial Germany, would have been more vulnerable if they had simply protected the narrow interests of a small elite. In fact, however, the conservative indoctrination provided by the bureaucracy, the press, the churches, the schools, and the army convinced most Germans that there was no alternative to the status quo.

At the same time the psychological divisions among Germans comprised one of history's most profound legacies to the new Reich and were mirrored in antagonisms between states, religions, and classes. Important new developments only aggravated them when they should have been soothed. The rise of capitalism and socialism made class divisions more acute than ever, and Bismarck's antisocialist legislation sharpened this tension. The crises accompanying the burgeoning of capitalism intensified fear and hatred of Jews among German Protestants and Catholics, and in turn the anti-Semitism heightened the anxieties of German Jews. The growth of socialism and, more basically, of materialism put German Catholicism on the defensive as did Bismarck's *Kulturkampf*. The steady growth of federal power kept alive south German suspicions and hostilities against the north (particularly Prussia). The divisiveness within the Reich sustained and intensified individual and group feelings of anxiety and insecurity that had existed earlier within the separate German states. The sense of individual and group alienation was strong and prevalent from 1871 to 1914. Not trusting one another, great numbers of Germans felt the need for strong government to superimpose order upon their historically rooted heterogeneities.

If history caused Germans to look at one another as something less than brothers, it also made them view the external world with distrust; and Bismarck's portrayal of post-1871 Germany's vulnerability in the midst of jealous neighbors did not allay popular anxieties. The deep sense of inferiority and insecurity created before 1870 in small-state Germans amidst a Europe dominated by great powers could not suddenly be eradicated by unification, though the Reich made Germany herself a great power and a potential threat to others. If the Germans continued to subordinate humane and democratic domestic aspirations to the demands of foreign policy—internal freedom to the struggle for national freedom in the international arena—it was because the experiences of history made this seem the only rational priority (*Primat der Aussenpolitik*). If they showed an abiding reverence for the state as an abstraction and for the imposing state they had achieved at last, it was because they had been made to feel by history the need for a powerful, if confining, political structure, both to bridge their internal divisions and to protect them in a hostile international environment.[42]

Fearing internal and external enemies, both real and imaginary, great numbers of Germans felt a strong state to be a necessity and believed that one could not exist on democratic foundations. How could popular sovereignty be trusted if the German people spoke with no sovereign consensus, but in a cacophony of voices? How could government by the people be risked when the people were psychically divided and surrounded by a world of potential foes? The enemies of democracy in Germany kept asking these questions throughout the imperial era. By way of response millions of Germans continued to accept the pronouncedly hierarchical structure of their society and rejected democratic experimentation with the political order. Heinrich Mann perceptively captured a widespread sentiment when, in his novel about the early years of the reign of William II, he had his hero Dietrich Hessling say: "I believe that in these hard times we need order as never before, and therefore we need a strong government like our young Kaiser runs."[43]

Social Democracy and the liberal democrats, facing a phalanx of entrenched popular and hostile institutions, had to democratize the German mind before they could capture a majority of German votes.

X.

THE GROWTH OF SOCIAL DEMOCRACY,
1890–1914

On May 1, 1889, Emperor William II ordered Prussian school-teachers to help combat "the spread of socialist and communist ideas." Pupils, the kaiser advised, should be shown "how constantly during the present century the wages and living conditions of the working class have improved under the guiding care of the Prussian kings."[1] In the quarter-century that followed, the teachers tried and failed. Industrialization enormously augmented the huge army of factory workers, and to keep them docile the imperial government introduced new social reforms. Yet every year additional legions of workers—and even middle-class Germans—arrayed themselves behind the red banners of Marx and Engels, Bebel and Liebknecht. After 1890 the rechristened Social Democratic party (SPD) grew rapidly, and by 1913 it received more than a third of the votes and occupied more Reichstag seats than any competitor. The constant and prodigious swelling of its ranks was the most significant development in the internal politics of the Reich during the reign of William II. For the first time Germany had produced an indigenous democratic mass movement.

Industrialization, already impressive in the Bismarck era, continued at high tempo after 1890. The production of raw iron rose from 4,000,000 tons in 1886 to 17,800,000 in 1911. Steel production mounted from 2,200,000 tons in 1890 to 18,300,000 in 1913. In the newer industries, particularly in the manufacture of chemical, electrical, and optical products, Germany achieved not only preeminence in Europe—as she had in steel production—but global leadership. Rising demands for labor in industry and commerce, plus the inability of agriculture to absorb the burgeoning population, wrought radical demographic changes.

Between 1882 and 1907 the population of the cities increased by 8,500,000, while the number of rural inhabitants declined by 400,000. Thousands of peasants moved each year to Berlin alone. In 1890 the capital had 1,578,794 inhabitants; in 1913, 4,200,000 —one out of fifteen Germans—lived in metropolitan Berlin. In 1890, 26 cities had populations of 100,000 or more, but by 1910 almost twice as many (48) had passed that mark.

Amidst rapid economic development Germans found more opportunities to advance from the ranks of farm laborers or factory hands into the lower middle class or even higher. At the same time the percentage of the population dependent upon industrial wages increased. By 1914 some 9,500,000 of Germany's 68,000,000 inhabitants could be broadly defined as industrial workers, though not all were employed in large factories. They and their families made up 30 to 40 percent of the total population.[2]

Marxists at the turn of the century could generalize more glibly about the class consciousness of the workers than can today's scholar, for the sciences of the human mind—Freudian and otherwise—were then only beginning to develop. The millions of industrial workers of 1914 obviously included diverse personality types. Some undoubtedly took pleasure from oppressing others and, having no lower class to dominate, found victims among their own comrades, wives, and children. Some, instead of rebelling against class discrimination and economic exploitation, probably derived a kind of psychic gratification from being oppressed. A good many factory workers were content with their conditions, having recently left behind even poorer ones in the country, but a growing minority felt deeply disgruntled.[3]

The imperial government knew that Bismarck's social legislation had not silenced all opposition, and events of the 1890's clearly indicated that the government was not ready to supplement paternalistic welfarism with the granting of political equality to the lower classes. The kaiser and his councillors realized that there was no way to enact democratic constitutional changes without increasing the political power of the masses; social reform, however, was a different matter because social benefits for industrial and agricultural laborers did not change the conservative government structure. This knowledge had motivated Bismarck's program to insure workers against sickness, accidents on the job, invalidity, and old age, which gave Germany's proletariat unprecedented state protection without responding to its political demands.

In 1890 the leading authorities of Germany recognized that the social ills connected with industrialization required not only social security measures but new state regulatory action. William II sponsored the first international conference for the protection of industrial labor by government regulation. His reform-minded minister of commerce in Prussia, Hans Hermann von Berlepsch, drafted statutes prohibiting work in factories on Sunday and other holidays, night work by women and children, working days in excess of eleven hours for women, female labor in mines, and employment of children under thirteen years of age. After the enactment of such laws on June 1, 1891, children of thirteen and fourteen could still work in factories, but no more than six hours per day; fifteen-year-olds could and did work up to ten hours per day.[4]

Since these additional welfare measures failed to slow the growth of political opposition, the imperial and Prussian governments suspended further social reforms in the later 1890's. Instead they attempted to enact legislation thwarting the activities of unions and of the SPD. When these efforts failed under Hohenlohe, Count Arthur von Posadowsky-Wehner, an experienced bureaucrat who served as Reich secretary of the interior from 1897 to 1907, once again attempted labor reform. His comments to Bundesrat delegates in January 1904 illustrate his reasoning. "The hope of Bismarck to be able to keep the masses in check through universal suffrage has not been fulfilled," he said, but he warned that elimination of equal suffrage "would be impossible without enormous catastrophes for which no one could assume responsibility." One must attempt, therefore, "to lead the Social Democratic movement into more reasonable paths" and try to make "the workers politically more mature, as they are in England." Other statements show that Posadowsky did not so much hope to moderate Social Democracy as to break it—to check its rise by turning the other cheek and satisfying some of the economic demands of the nonsocialist workers.[5]

Several of the new measures initiated by Posadowsky and carried through by his successor, Theobald von Bethmann-Hollweg, extended the regulatory authority of the government. Working conditions of seamen were codified in 1902, and those of Prussian miners were improved by state legislation three years later, though neither act established maximum working hours. The iron and steel industry, in which the twelve-hour day was common, was required in 1908 to allow rest periods during each shift. That same year the working hours for women were reduced to ten a day, a step affecting some 1,900,000 members of the labor force. But no attempt was made before 1914 to set a general maximum workday or workweek for adult males in German industry.

By other legislation, meanwhile, the imperial government endeavored to improve the social security of the proletariat along lines pioneered by Bismarck. After the turn of the century it began to use public funds to construct housing for workers. Accident insurance was extended in 1900 to cover all toilers in agriculture and industry; and a law enacted in the spring of 1902 provided similarly comprehensive sickness coverage. A social insurance bill, passed in 1911, introduced pensions for widows and orphans of both factory and farm workers. By 1913, over 14,500,000 persons were protected by state-sponsored sickness insurance, nearly 16,500,000 received old age and invalidity benefits, and almost 25,000,000 enjoyed insurance protection against accidents.

Nevertheless, Germany's laboring men and women remained unprotected against another ravage as certain as old age—periodic unemployment. Insurance against temporary loss of income was unknown anywhere in the industrial universe. Another immediate concern—better pay—also went unattended. Germany, like other nations before 1914, enacted no minimum wage legislation. Average real wages in agriculture and industry increased about 30 percent between 1900 and 1913, but even in the latter year it was a rare factory worker who earned more than fifteen hundred marks; the average was about eleven hundred. Farm income was far less.

In Munich a petition of the "workers of the Royal Bavarian Artillery Shops," marked by a notable lack of polemic intensity, contrasted the income of a skilled munitions worker in 1898 (1,314 marks) with a minimum subsistence budget for a family of four (1,874 marks). A model household of the same size in Berlin in 1907 with an income of 1,300 marks spent just under 60 percent, or 735 marks, on food; 210 marks on rent; 55 marks on heat, fuel, and lighting; and 110 marks on clothes. This left 190 marks per annum to cover taxes, insurance deductions, medical and educational expenses, and recreation. The conclusion is inescapable that such an average family dreaded illness, never saw the inside of a theater or concert hall, bought no books or magazines, abandoned all hope of improving its children's future through education, and took no vacations.[6]

The goods and services listed on a typical working-class budget could rarely be purchased in sufficient amounts. In 1895, 40 percent of the unskilled workers in Munich occupied tenement apartments with only one heated room. In 1913, six hundred thousand Berliners lived in quarters that housed four or more persons per room. In the German capital at that time a one-room apartment with kitchen cost 250 to 270 marks per annum. It was rare for a working-class family to enjoy running water or an inside toilet; in the older buildings a single outhouse served all occupants. Poor sanitation caused tuberculosis and other contagious diseases which claimed many victims each year.

Unskilled migrants from the country might at first accept such conditions as being no worse than those they had just left behind. But to the city-born, experienced factory hand these surroundings were constant reminders that his government's highly touted social reforms were insufficient. Some drowned their disappointed expectations in strong drink, but increasing numbers sought to improve their lot by joining labor unions, and of these the majority opted for socialism.[7]

These new associations taught growing numbers of workers that improved pay and working conditions could only be won through demonstrative actions such as strikes. With the coming of the twentieth century, German law became less antagonistic to the workers' plans and aspirations, though the thrust of its provisions and their enforcement could hardly be termed pro-labor.

The Industrial Code of Germany acknowledged the right to

organize local unions. Existing restrictive associations laws were not enforced so workers could be organized regionally and even nationally. Yet unions above the local level survived precariously until the Imperial Associations Law of 1899 at last legalized their existence. (State laws forbidding union recruitment of women and male workers under twenty-one, together with police inspection of membership lists, only disappeared with the enactment of the second Imperial Associations Law in 1908.)

The Industrial Code recognized the right to strike, but also permitted lockouts. Furthermore, factory owners had the legal right to dismiss strikers, to refuse to hire workers who had struck against previous employers, and to import workers to replace strikers, and they freely availed themselves of these opportunities. Labor leaders could develop countervailing pressures during a strike only by coercing all workers in a plant to participate and by preventing "scabs" from entering the premises; and they made free use of these methods.

Strikes frequently became violent, whereupon local police and judges almost automatically aided the proprietors by insisting upon the maintenance of order and the arrest and punishment of strikers who disrupted it. Army units were called in at times to safeguard laborers who continued to work in struck factories. Even when there was no violence, strikes were handicapped by Paragraph 153 of the Industrial Code. Decried as infamous by all labor leaders, this clause authorized prison sentences of up to three months for anyone who by threats or insults brought pressure on another to join a strike; some judges considered it an insult (and assigned penalties accordingly) if one worker merely called another a "strikebreaker."[8]

Initiative in organizing labor had been provided by the parties of the left, and the major unions formed between 1890 and 1914 continued to be closely linked with political parties. In 1868, Max Hirsch and Franz Duncker of the Progressive party had organized unions that would attract workers to their party while vigorously demanding better conditions within the capitalistic system. Leading personalities in the Catholic church and the Center party pursued similar objectives with religious overtones, particularly after 1890. By 1913, 107,000 workers belonged to the Hirsch-Duncker or Progressive unions, 342,000 to the

"Christian" (largely Catholic) unions. Both groups, however, were increasingly overshadowed by the socialist labor movement.[9] During the period of Bismarck's repressive measures, SPD and socialist labor organizations remained separate, on paper at least, and the latter called themselves "Free Unions" to escape the stigma of illegality. But political and economic leadership overlapped from the beginning, and the party insisted that it was the senior partner. To socialist politicians the function of the unions was to win recruits to the movement. The unions accepted this subsidiary role by concentrating on bread and butter issues, yet they actually provided the major impetus for the impressive growth of the movement. In 1877, on the eve of Bismarck's repressive campaign, they counted 49,000 members; by 1891, a year after the chancellor's fall, they had a membership of 277,659. During the next decade they grew at an average rate of 39,000 a year. After the turn of the century, this rate more than tripled, and in 1908 the army of card-carrying socialist workers approached 2,000,000. After the enactment of the Imperial Associations Law of that year, conversions to socialism continued at an even higher rate so that in 1913 the total union membership stood at 2,548,763. Women, who constituted only 2 percent of the total membership of the Free Unions in 1892, now made up 9 percent of this number.[10]

Alarmed by the rise of the socialist-led unions, some factory owners after 1900 encouraged the creation of rival organizations that opposed strikes while supporting the monarchy and espousing nationalism. The employer-sponsored groups—most of which functioned only within a single plant or company— were castigated as "yellow unions" by the more combative organizations. Some of them merged in 1907 to form the Union of Patriotic Workers Clubs (Bund vaterländischer Arbeitervereine). Three years later a broader agreement loosely linked a number of them under the Main Committee of National Workers Associations (Hauptausschuss nationaler Arbeiterverbände). By 1914 these and other antisocialist "yellow unions" may have recruited as many as 281,000 members, most of whom tended to vote for National Liberal candidates.[11]

Counting those who belonged to "yellow unions" as part of

the labor movement (though their apathy makes doing so questionable), as many as 3,700,000 workers in Germany may have been organized by 1914. With more than 2,500,000 members, the Free Unions enrolled at least 68 percent of the organized workers, though only about 26 percent of the industrial labor force. Their enormous growth in membership after 1890 was matched by mounting success in strikes and by growing financial resources. The Free Unions won 30 percent of their strikes in 1890–91, 45 percent in 1895, and more than 60 percent from 1911 to 1913. With incomes of less than 2,000,000 marks in 1891, the forty-seven Free Unions in 1913 had a treasury of 82,005,580 marks.

Some of the socialist-led unions recruited workers in a single craft or trade, while others attempted to organize whole industries. The organizations varied greatly in strength as well as in character. Because of their separate origins and differing purposes, the socialist unions could not easily unify their efforts; that was a major reason why the SPD could maintain its primacy. But common problems and interests made cooperation among the unions increasingly desirable, and in 1890 the leaders created a General Commission of the Labor Unions of Germany (really only of the socialist-led unions) to give loose coordination to their separate activities. Although each of the affiliated unions preserved its autonomy (the Book Printers Union, the Metal Workers Union, and so on), the General Commission gradually increased its influence over them. Furthermore, it insisted that they be regarded as important in their own right and that their interests were not always the same as those of the SPD. Through the commission, the unions by the late 1890's were beginning to challenge the party's tutelage.

These tendencies were championed by Carl Legien, who became in 1890 the first chairman of the General Commission. Though only twenty-nine, Legien already had served several years as head of the lathe operators' union. He gradually put his personal stamp upon his new position, which he was to hold until his death in 1920. He was born in Marienburg (East Prussia), reared in an orphanage, and then apprenticed to a cabinetmaker. During his compulsory military service, he was assigned as an orderly to a general. These experiences neither brightened his prosaic personality nor remedied his cultural deficiencies. His interests were narrow; he knew nothing about the arts and had little use for theories, even those of socialism. A union official before he joined the SPD, Legien remained preoccupied with union affairs even after he was elected to the Reichstag as a Social Democrat in 1893. Intelligent and aggressive, he made the General Commission and the affiliated unions his almost exclusive concern. "Organization is everything," he told his fellow unionists in 1896, and this laconic utterance might well stand as his motto.

While Legien and his associates increasingly refused to take orders from the SPD, they preserved close cooperation between organized labor and the party. All the leaders of the Free Unions were prominent in the party, and they urged their followers to join it. Because a significant percentage did so, the mushrooming growth of the unions was the most direct cause of the rapid augmentation of SPD membership.

Statistics on the membership of the unions are readily available, as are those showing the growth of the SPD, but it is impossible to determine with precision how many union members also belonged to the party or what percentage of party members belonged to unions. The separate sets of data make it possible, however, to state with certainty that a majority of the unionists did not join the SPD; if every one of the SPD members of 1913 (1,085,905) had belonged to the Free Unions, they would have accounted for only 42 percent of the membership. Yet, it is clear that only a minority of the union members, even though a sizable one, simultaneously belonged to the party. A study of overlapping participation in Stuttgart in 1900 showed that about 30 percent of the members of the Free Unions also held party membership and formed 70 percent of total party membership there. Probably this local ratio mirrored the national situation rather accurately. If, in fact, 30 percent of the 2,548,763 unionists in 1913 belonged to the SPD, they accounted for 764,629 members. And if there were 764,629 union members among the SPD's 1,085,905 in 1913, the unionists made up 70.4 percent of the party's total rank and file. Without arguing for the exactness of these trial percentages, it is clear that vast numbers of union members had joined the SPD by 1914, thus making certain that it would remain a party of organized labor, whatever else it might become. [12]

The growth of the unions gave the SPD a major opportunity to expand. During the 1880's the party's only surviving central agency was the Reichstag caucus, and its members scattered to their respective homes between parliamentary sessions. Even after the end of the antisocialist legislation state laws concerning associations technically forbade central organization and administration of a nationwide political party, but they were not regularly applied. In 1890, SPD leaders, gambling on lax enforcement, established headquarters in Berlin for a five-member national executive committee (Vorstand) to direct the affairs of the party. This committee normally met twice a week and could assemble quickly on other occasions if necessary. Bebel and its other members moved their households to Berlin in the autumn of that year.

There were few disagreements between the new executive committee and the Reichstag caucus because for many years the same men led both. Bebel and Paul Singer were co-chairmen of the new Vorstand, and both belonged to the steering committee of the Reichstag delegation. Singer normally chaired the meetings of the caucus, but here—as in the Vorstand—it was Bebel who acted as the first among equals.

Bebel was no longer a young man. (In 1892, Engels congratulated him on the "silver anniversary" of his entry into the Reichstag.) By 1894, he complained of the need for fresh air and rest and of recurrent stomach and intestinal ailments that occasionally put him to bed. But he continued to give intelligent leadership to the party through the better part of two more decades. It was a leadership that balanced his own sense of what was right with keen appraisals of the readiness of the majority to follow his lead. He was, as Philipp Scheidemann noted, "half lion, half fox." His years of service to the party, his attractive personality, and a clear, sharp voice compounded a charisma that no other party leader possessed.

Co-chairman Paul Singer was born into a Jewish family in Berlin in 1844. Orphaned four years later, the youngster knew hard times. In 1869 he and his brother established a women's wear factory that made him moderately wealthy. Having become politically active in the 1860's as an associate of the aging Johann Jacoby, Singer followed Jacoby into the socialist movement in the 1870's when Bebel's leadership was well established. During the next decade he concentrated on organizational work, used his financial resources to support the movement, and achieved great popularity among Berlin workers. Following his election to the Reichstag in 1884 and his selection as chairman of the SPD caucus, he decided to devote his undivided energies to the party and withdrew from business in 1887. Though he was not particularly effective as a speaker, he was an expert on parliamentary procedure and a skilled tactician. His direction of SPD parliamentarians continued until his death in 1911.

Both Bebel and Singer were practical men, and the executive secretary of the Vorstand, Ignaz Auer, was ready to compromise with reality in order to build a large and effective political organization. Elected to the Reichstag at thirty-one in 1877, Auer sat for the same district in Saxony from 1880 until he died in 1907. He had become the leader of the saddlemakers union while still in his twenties, and his style as a party leader remained that of a pragmatic union administrator. Though he opposed Legien's moves to make the unions independent of the party, he possessed neither head nor heart for theory and steadily resisted Kautsky's efforts to make Marxism the party's official ideology.

Other veteran Social Democrats shared in the direction of the growing and legal party in the 1890's, and new men became particularly important after 1900; but it was primarily Bebel, Singer, and Auer who charted its course through the first decade of the twentieth century. Wilhelm Liebknecht sometimes helped to make important decisions, but although generally identifying himself as a Marxist, he was most essentially a democrat of the 1848 vintage. Bebel, at this time the most orthodox Marxist of the leadership, sent Engels frequent complaints in the early 1890's about what he described as Liebknecht's lack of understanding of issues. Liebknecht in turn complained that Engels saw issues "through Bebel's highly colored lenses." By 1894 relations between the two founders of the party were strained, though Bebel continued in public to sing Liebknecht's praises until the old man died in 1900 at seventy-four.

Notwithstanding their popularity among rank and file comrades, the top leaders of the SPD were not dictators either in ideology or in tactics. Their work was reviewed and they were continued in office or voted out by the supreme body of the SPD, the party congress. Beginning in 1890, party congresses could again be held on German soil and thus could meet annually. This alone greatly improved the nationwide coordination of SPD affairs. Consisting of delegates elected by the local organizations of the party and sent at their expense, these conventions constituted the highest court of appeal in SPD affairs. Each congress held vigorous and lengthy debates on many issues before handing down its rulings in the form of resolutions. The party congresses reviewed the work of the leaders and determined which ones should remain in office.

Financial problems also limited the power of the national executive committee. Through the 1890's it was largely dependent upon the voluntary contributions of the local organizations and their statewide associations, some of which sent almost nothing to Berlin. In this period the Berlin and Hamburg branches provided the Vorstand with 23 percent of its operating capital. Later the Vorstand improved its finances, after the party congress adopted a rule whereby each local organization was expected to send Berlin 20 percent of its membership dues. Though not rigidly enforced, this requirement in combination with rapid increases in members sharply boosted the income of the national executive committee. From a total of only 258,326 marks in 1892–93, annual income was raised to 1,357,762 marks by 1910–11. With growing means to aid the local organizations when they needed help for their publicity, campaigning, and other activities, the national leaders were increasingly able to influence them.[13]

Central coordination of the party and its propaganda were helped by technology. The telephone may partly explain the survival and growth of Social Democracy in the 1880's. It surely enabled the party to function more effectively within a hostile political environment. Instruments had been placed in German postal and telegraph offices as early as 1877—within a year after Alexander Graham Bell demonstrated their practicality in Philadelphia. By the 1890's Berlin had more telephones than any city in Europe, and a four-hundred-mile long distance call in Germany cost only one mark. By the end of 1905, more than twenty-one thousand communities in the empire had telephone service. The number of instruments in use increased from about 93,000 in 1893 to 1,420,000 in 1914—one for every fifty persons. From the early 1890's, at the latest, Social Democrats regularly used telephones in their work. Writing to Engels in September 1891, Bebel routinely mentioned a call he had received that day from Auer regarding a party election. Contrary to some reports that allow the SPD executive committee no telephone as late as 1905, it seems to have had two instruments more than a decade earlier. Certainly one was in use in the editorial office of the party's central newspaper by November 1894, and at that time telephones seem to have been in general use in the SPD press. The potential political effects of such instant communication were not lost on officialdom. Recommending in 1899 that larger associations of local political parties be legalized, Count Posadowsky pointed out that the existing laws of association had been made unenforceable by the development of "commerce, the telegraph, and the telephone."[14]

Besides facilitating dialogue between party officials, the technology of the late nineteenth century enabled the SPD to build an elaborate press network, which in turn helped bring in new members and provide greater cohesion among them.

From its beginnings, Social Democracy had recognized the need for newspapers if it was to grow into a mass party; as early as 1890 the SPD was publishing sixty newspapers, but only nineteen were dailies and their total circulation was only 260,000 per issue. Seven years later the dailies numbered thirty-nine, and by 1914 vendors hawked ninety socialist papers every day and sold about one and a half million copies. These constituted the primary line of communication between the leadership, the ranks, and grass-roots opinion.

Founded in 1890, the daily *Vorwärts* did double duty as the organ of the large and radical Berlin branch of the party and as the chief organ of the entire movement. Until his death in 1900, Wilhelm Liebknecht occupied the uncomfortable post of chief editor. Day by day his work was supervised by a press commission elected from the Berlin leadership, but it also had to satisfy the executive committee of the national party and the caucus of its Reichstag delegation. Liebknecht was therefore caught in a constant cross fire between the radical Marxists and the more moderate elements. Nevertheless *Vorwärts'* readership grew, reaching a circulation of 161,000 in 1914. A provincial daily, the *Leipziger Volkszeitung*, also exerted a national impact on the socialist movement. Its chief editor, Paul Lensch, was a plain-spoken, effective Marxist polemicist, who turned his paper into the favorite organ of the left wing. Other significant regional party dailies included the *Hamburger Echo*, the *Chemnitzer Volksfreund*, the *Karlsruher Volksfreund*, and the *Münchener Post*.

As the example of the *Vorwärts'* many guides and masters indicates, the press operations of German Social Democracy lacked systematic central direction, though the executive committee as well as the Reichstag caucus occasionally took issue with a specific editor. In an attempt to make socialist newspapers more independent of the sources which fed news to their bourgeois counterparts rather than to impose upon them uniform editorial policies, the party in July 1908 opened its own news service, the Sozialdemokratisches Pressebureau in Berlin. Besides mailing daily releases to all SPD newspapers, the Press Bureau transmitted more urgent items by telephone to the nineteen largest socialist papers. But local editors and their committees continued to determine what their publications would actually print.

A number of additional socialist publications were designed to appeal to specific segments of the movement. Legien's General Commission of the Free Unions issued its own *Correspondenzblatt*, and even in the early 1890's almost every one of the affiliated unions published its own newspaper. *Die Gleichheit* (*Equality*), a journal for women, was started in 1892. Nine years later, Albert Südekum initiated *Kommunale Praxis*, a special magazine on municipal government. For those interested in theoretical and scholarly expositions of Marxism, there was Kautsky's *Die neue Zeit*, while SPD readers critical of such dogma favored the *Sozialistische Monatsheftet*. Easily the most successful party periodical, however, was the oldest, *Der wahre Jakob*, which offered literary material, political cartoons, and folksy humor with a socialist bite. Founded in 1884, its circulation rose to 366,000, while the learned, scriptural *Neue Zeit* never appealed to more than an earnest elite of 10,500 subscribers. Finally, in 1909 a journal for the young, *Arbeiter-Jugend*, began regular publication. This extensive and diversified press apparatus addressed a public which had little cash to spare. Its ability to distribute information cheaply owed much to the technological revolution of late nineteenth-century journalism, for the inventions of that time that laid the basis for the "yellow" press also made possible its socialist counterpart. The linotype machine, the steam-driven rotary press, the typewriter, and the newly available wood-pulp paper all enabled socialists as well as capitalist press lords to turn out daily newspapers quickly and inexpensively. By the 1890's the telephone speeded the collection of the news, and the bicycle accelerated the journey of the finished product from the press room to the street vendors.

The sale of newspapers, magazines, and books, produced and marketed in the most up-to-date fashion, accounted for half of the entire income of the SPD. The newspapers alone administered a capital of 21,500,000 marks by 1914, and employed more than 11,000 persons, ranging from 267 editors and 89 business managers to 7,600 delivery men.[15]

The ultimate test of the party's ability to expand had to be met by direct agitation and electioneering from precinct to precinct. In this, too, the socialist journalists performed yeoman services. As editor of an SPD weekly paper in Giessen in the late 1890's, Philipp Scheidemann wrote campaign leaflets, set them in type, and distributed them by bicycle, between speeches at party meetings. Soon he emerged as his party's candidate in city, state, and Reichstag elections. During these same years, Wilhelm Keil doubled as an editor of the SPD newspaper in Stuttgart and was a tireless speaker during election campaigns. Keil was elected to the state parliament in 1900, but continued to serve as an editor. Human workhorses such as these won converts to their party in the 1890's by working a great deal harder at grass-roots agitation than did their political rivals.

The socialists also developed systematic and detailed plans for getting out the vote on election day. In Bremen, for example, careful lists of eligible voters were prepared for every campaign in each district. The lists were arranged by streets and by houses. On election day, two party members were stationed at the polling places to check off the expected voters as they made their appearance. At regular intervals the poll watchers sent a runner with their newest information to SPD district headquarters. There the voters were once again checked off on the prepared lists. From time to time during the day, names and addresses of persons who had not voted were forwarded by messenger to door-to-door canvassers. These *Schlepper* ("tugboats") in turn called on recalcitrants and urged them to cast their votes. The local organizations of the SPD, by making more systematic efforts than rival parties to round up the voters in their territories, could take a great deal of the credit for the electoral growth of Social Democracy.[16]

At the same time, from the national leadership down to the smallest precincts, party activities continued to be circumscribed by police restrictions and incursions. While the failure of the Reichstag to renew the antisocialist "exceptional" legislation in 1890 clearly took the worst pressures off SPD campaigners, plenty of regular statutes could be used to inhibit their efforts. At one point in 1895, the police, acting under Prussia's law forbidding mergers of local political groups, closed the central office that coordinated the operations of the party's branches in Berlin. Members of the national SPD executive committee as well as local leaders were fined by the court of first instance, which also ordered the dissolution of the national executive committee. These decisions were appealed to the Supreme Court of the empire and were not upheld, but it was March 1897 before the fines against Bebel and others were dropped and the ban against the SPD Vorstand was lifted.

The failure of these legal proceedings spurred on the efforts of Hohenlohe and the kaiser during the next ten years to secure enactment of new antisocialist legislation. During this interim the SPD operated under constant difficulties. Even after the Imperial Associations Law of 1899 legalized the existence of nationwide political parties, local police filed voluminous and frequent reports on SPD assemblies and on major and minor officers of the party. Friedrich Ebert, then still under thirty and only known locally, was kept under government surveillance in

Bremen throughout the 1890's. And when delegates came to town for the SPD's national congress in 1904, the police recorded its own complete transcript of their lengthy debates. Laws concerning libel and the respect due the monarchy and its institutions were applied with particular vigor to socialist newspapers. "If only we had French freedom of the press," Bebel sighed in a letter of 1895. SPD editors were not required to submit copy to a censor in advance of publication, hence their papers rarely pulled punches. But issues of their publications that transgressed the legal limits could be and were confiscated by the police, and a publication guilty of repeated offenses could be banned altogether. Furthermore, the responsible editor of a newspaper was subject to fines and imprisonment if he criticized monarchical government or published remarks that could be interpreted as likely to incite readers to violate the laws. In 1900, Paul Löbe, as editor of the SPD newspaper in Breslau, was sentenced to a year in prison, after publishing a call for public demonstrations against Prussia's three-class electoral law. Over a seventeen-year period SPD attorney Hugo Haase was called upon to represent a single party editor, Otto Braun, in no fewer than sixty-four court trials. *Vorwärts* estimated in 1913 that Social Democrats and unionists had been assessed 1,188 years of imprisonment and fines of 556,000 marks since 1890. Violations of press restrictions accounted for a major part of both totals.[17]

While the laws and the police of Germany constantly inhibited many Social Democrats and punished others who did not restrain themselves, the SPD continued to agitate. The party concentrated its major effort upon winning the workingmen, but it also sought the support of other special-interest groups. Particularly after 1900 it intensified its bid for members among women, youth, middle-class citizens generally, and the farm population. With all but the last group, it scored substantial successes.

In endorsing the demands of German feminists the SPD applied its own egalitarian principles on behalf of victims of discrimination. In the 1890's about one-fourth of Germany's women held full-time jobs of some sort, and one-third of these were in industry where they were paid substantially lower wages than men doing the same work. Denied the right to vote in federal, state, and local elections, they did not win the right to join political parties and attend public meetings until passage of the Association Law in 1908. In imperial Germany, as everywhere else except Australia, New Zealand, and Finland, women were second-class citizens; and, as elsewhere, they were organizing in the 1890's to alter their centuries-old position of social and political inferiority.

Even before 1848 a few German women had raised the cry for equal rights as part of the movement for liberal democracy. A pioneer was Louise Otto, who was born in Saxony in 1819—the same year as Chancellor Hohenlohe. Her father, a liberal democrat, taught her that men and women should possess the same civil rights. In poetry and novels, the daughter began voicing this conviction, but even the revolutionary males at St. Paul's in Frankfurt generally disregarded her. From 1849 to 1852 she published a democratic newspaper, the *Frauenzeitung*. She expanded her name to Otto-Peters in 1858 by marrying a democratic journalist, who left her a widow in 1864; in that year she founded an organization to foster the education of women, until then neglected even at the secondary school level. The next year, to mobilize support for occupational equality and broader rights for women, she called into existence the Allgemeine Deutsche Frauenverein. Thus the feminist movement in Germany began to take form in the same decade as the organization of the Lassallean and Eisenach socialists. Well before her death in 1895, Frau Otto-Peters had won a widespread following among middle-class women.

The young August Bebel had attended the foundling congress of the Allgemeine Deutsche Frauenverein, but neither his Eisenacher party nor the Lassalleans put great emphasis upon women's rights. The Gotha Program of the united socialist party in 1875 demanded equal suffrage for "all citizens," but did not stress the implication that this would include voting privileges for women. In 1879, Bebel published the first edition of his most widely read contribution to socialist literature—a book that became a powerful weapon in the socialist campaign to win women to the party. In *Die Frau und der Sozialismus*, the author contended that the exploitation of women was as essential an element of capitalism as was exploitation of the proletariat; that neither could be emancipated except through the overthrow of the existing economic structure. He urged women to take jobs in industry and the professions in order to win an economic basis for independence and equality and argued that they should have the same sexual freedom as men. He portrayed the woman of the future, under socialism, as a worker whose family cares would be eased by communal nurseries, kitchens, and laundries; only then would woman become "a free being, the equal of man." Bebel's book made simultaneous converts for feminism and socialism. By 1891 women were coming in large numbers to meetings at which Bebel was scheduled to speak; sometimes they formed as much as a third of his audience.

"In the next revolution," Bebel wrote Engels in September 1891, women would play "a gigantic role." Many of his male comrades did not share this conviction and had little sympathy for the contemporary women's liberation movement, but when the SPD in 1891 adopted a new program at Erfurt, it explicitly called for equal suffrage for all citizens "without distinction of sex." During the 1890's the SPD stepped up its campaign for women's rights. Besides demanding that women be given the ballot, it agitated for stiffer regulation of their working conditions in industry. The SPD insisted that laws preventing them from joining political parties be changed; pending that, it created ostensibly nonpolitical clubs and unions for women in order to draw them closer to the party. Where state laws permitted women to join political parties, local branches of the SPD offered them membership for half the dues paid by men.[18]

A number of male Social Democrats did organizational work among females, but major leadership came from their own ranks. One of the first was Clara Eissner Zetkin, like Louise Otto-Peters born in Saxony in 1857. When she was sixteen her mother, a member of the middle-class Allgemeine Deutsche Frauenverein, sent her to a Leipzig teacher-training school run by another member. At twenty-one Clara gave her affections to a Russian émigré, Ossip Zetkin, then living in Saxony, and under his influence became a Marxist. When her lover was expelled from Germany in 1880, Clara went with him to Austria, then to Switzerland, and in 1883 to France; in Paris, in the year of Marx's death, the couple finally married. Clara became a Paris correspondent for German socialist publications and in 1889 participated in the founding of the Second International. That same year she was widowed; she was thirty-two. Returning to Germany, she threw herself into the work of organizing women for the SPD. In 1892, she took over editorship of *Die Gleichheit* and saw its circulation grow to 28,700 copies per issue by 1905, then to 125,000 by 1914. Frau Zetkin was to become a leader of left-wing socialism and after 1918 of the Communist party. Born five years before Bismarck became minister-president of Prussia, she died, once again an exile, in Moscow five months after Hitler became chancellor of Germany.

Three women who worked closely with Zetkin in the 1890's— Emma Ihrer, Ottilie Baader, and Luise Zietz—did not move as far to the left as she did. The first-named, the wife of a Berlin pharmacist, also attended the founding congress of the Second International in 1889. Though Zetkin's journalistic activity made her much better known, Frau Ihrer did more pathbreaking organizational work. She successfully began to organize working women in Berlin during the 1880's and in 1890 became one of the seven charter members of the General Commission of the Socialist Unions. She persuaded the SPD party congress in 1890 to start a newspaper for women, and she preceded Zetkin as its editor.

While Ihrer directed the organization of women for the unions, Ottilie Baader mobilized women for the party in the 1890's. Born in 1847, daughter of a Silesian factory worker, she moved to Berlin when she was thirteen. There she joined the socialist cause. In 1900 she was named the SPD's central coordinator for women's work.

Luise Zietz also came from lowly origins and reached the highest level of party leadership. Her father was a Holstein weaver, her husband a Hamburg dockworker. Before her marriage she worked as a domestic servant. Through her Social Democratic husband, she became active in the party at the age of twenty-seven. In 1897, Frau Zietz attended the SPD party congress as the leader of Hamburg's socialist women. After eleven more years of untiring work she was elected an associate member of the SPD executive committee. She held this position for many years, gradually becoming more influential than Zetkin in the inner circle of party leaders. After the revolution of 1918, when Germany would finally permit the election of the first women to its parliament, Zietz was among them.

Two other women attracted large followings for the SPD. Lily Braun's background differed vastly from that of the women who won the leading organizational positions. Her father, Hans von Kretschman, was a general in the Prussian army. Through Ludwig Büchner's newly founded Society for Ethical Culture and the bourgeois feminist movement, Lily Braun was led to political commitment on the moderate left in the early 1890's. Soon she became one of the first of her sex in Germany to demand publicly that women be given the right to vote. Following the death of her first husband, she fell in love with a Social Democratic editor, Heinrich Braun. Breaking with her family and the bourgeois feminists in 1896, she married Braun and became a socialist herself. Great beauty and a capacity for passionate oratory—plus, perhaps, a certain charisma that came from being a general's daughter in the socialist movement—made her one of the most popular women speakers in the party in the late 1890's. Braun was, however, more interested in feminism than in socialism. She never rose high in the party's councils and left the SPD in 1906.

The rise of women in and through socialism was exemplified most tellingly by Rosa Luxemburg. Born in Poland, she occupied a leading position in that divided country's socialist movement when she decided to move to Germany and contribute her energy to furtherance of the strongest party of the Second International. Luxemburg became a dogmatic advocate of the class struggle. Only intermittently interested in the cause of her suppressed nation and not at all in that of her suppressed sex, she put her considerable intelligence in the service of the proletariat and by 1914 had gained recognition as a leader of the SPD's left wing.[19]

While these half-dozen personalities held center stage, many anonymous women devoted long hours of essential but unpublicized work to the socialist cause. They did secretarial work in party offices, helped publish and distribute newspapers, passed out leaflets, joined and supported strikes, and carried placards in socialist demonstrations. Grateful for their increasingly effective contribution, the SPD party congress in 1909 voted that each local branch of the party should include at least one woman on its executive committee. While not all local organizations followed these instructions, 936 women held positions on local committees in 1914. The number of women delegates to the party congresses was increased from four in 1890 to thirty-two in 1908, and about that number attended each subsequent congress before the outbreak of the war.

The number of women in the SPD was sharply increased after the Associations Law of 1908 was adopted. In that year the ratio of men to women in the party was fourteen to one. By 1914, it had increased to eight to one. No other party had so strongly and completely endorsed the equalization of women in German society and politics, and no other had won so many women as members. [20]

SPD recruitment of youth was hampered even more by legal restrictions than was that of women, but it, too, developed after 1900. Until 1908 several states denied persons under twenty-one the right to join unions or political parties, and the Association Law of that year legalized participation only for youths of eighteen or older. Yet, at that time some nine hundred thousand youngsters from the ages of fourteen to eighteen held jobs in industry; one industrial worker out of every seven was in this age group. Larger numbers held nonindustrial jobs. Altogether, about four million youths were employed in some capacity in Germany in 1908, most of them receiving for their labor barely more than the cost of a poor bed and scanty meals.

Partly because of the legal limitations that ruled out any major campaign to recruit youth, partly out of concern for their own organizations, many union leaders opposed creation of separate associations for working youths. SPD leaders themselves took notably less initiative in the organization of a youth movement than they had shown in setting up clubs for women. But young workers did not wait for initiative from above, for the impatience with the older generation that spawned a bourgeois youth movement at the turn of the century stirred teenage workers as well. In Berlin two dozen apprentices founded a local association of working youths in October 1904. When it began to publish its own newspapers in 1905, it had five hundred members. By the next year similar organizations had been formed in Halle, Königsberg, and other industrial centers in northern Germany. A conference of their representatives was held in Berlin in December 1906 and formed the Association of Free Youth Organizations of Germany. Max Peters (no relation to Luise), not yet nineteen and leader of the Berlin group, was chosen to coordinate the association's work. Local groups all over northern Germany affiliated. By 1908, notwithstanding disruptions by local police, they enrolled 3,789 members, and the newspaper Peters edited for working youths had ten thousand subscribers.

To avoid prosecution, these groups tended to avoid overt political action. Many concentrated upon the specific job problems of apprentices and young factory workers. All fostered the education of their members through lectures, discussion evenings, and visits to museums and art exhibitions. Wanting members to focus their energies on self-improvement as well as on the class struggle, they waged campaigns against smoking, drinking, and pornography. But while tending to avoid current political issues, the leaders groomed their comrades for subsequent membership in the Free Unions and the SPD.

Meanwhile, in 1904 another association of socialist youths had sprung up in Baden and other southern states. Its initiator was Ludwig Frank of Mannheim—a thirty-year-old Jewish attorney and SPD deputy in the parliament of Baden. Youth in other cities organized and looked to Frank for leadership and inspiration. In February 1906 representatives of the southern youth groups, meeting in Karlsruhe, established the Association of Young German Workers (Verband junger Arbeiter Deutschlands). They also founded a monthly journal, *The Young Guard* (*Die junge Garde*), edited by Frank.

Led by a socialist parliamentarian and operating in states with relatively liberal laws, Frank's groups did not conceal their socialist character. Their attractive and popular leader's program combined democratic political reforms with condemnation of militarism, a radical stand at that time in Europe. By May 1908 the south German socialist youth movement had 85 chapters with 4,500 members (250 of them girls), and *Die junge Garde* had a circulation of 9,000.

When laws were changed so persons of eighteen could join

the SPD, the Central Association of Youth Organizations disbanded, though many local youth groups continued their educational efforts. But the youngest segment of labor, boys and girls between fourteen and eighteen, still could not become members of any political or professional associations. Union and party leaders, careful not to challenge the law, but equally anxious to extend their influence among young people, adopted a new youth program at the party congress of 1908. They authorized each local organization to create a special committee consisting of party, union, and youth representatives for the promotion of ostensibly nonpolitical teenage activities. At the same time the SPD executive committee established a central youth office in Berlin, supervised by a twelve-member management board which would also direct the party paper for the young, *Arbeiter-Jugend*. This board included four prominent party leaders, four union officials, and four youths. Carl Legien, Luise Zietz, and Emma Ihrer were among the members. Friedrich Ebert, of the SPD executive committee, served as chairman until November 1918. In 1912, Max Peters became national secretary for youth affairs. Though only twenty-four, he was given a position of power which no other party would have accorded a person of his age. Meanwhile, Ludwig Frank continued to win youths to the socialist cause, as did Wilhelm Liebknecht's son Karl, like Frank a vocal foe of militarism. By 1914, 837 local branches supported the socialist youth program; 391 of these maintained modest youth centers. At the same time the *Arbeiter-Jugend* was reaching over one hundred thousand subscribers, and each year thousands of its readers found their way into the SPD.[21]

In its agitation on behalf of women and youth, the SPD broke virgin political soil and initiated a new stage in the struggle for democracy. The support it gained contributed significantly to the party's growth after 1890. All women and youths, regardless of origin, occupied legally and socially inferior positions. As the first to take a stand on their behalf, the SPD rose above its traditional status of a class party.

Meanwhile Social Democracy expanded as an intellectual influence through its enthusiastic endorsement of new scientific ideas and its negative attitude toward religion. Germany, together with other western nations, stood in the vanguard of scientific development. The SPD was in part a political reflection of this tendency. Socialist leaders insisted that their interpretation of history and economics was scientific, that the changes they demanded were not merely ethically desirable, but were essential to bring social relationships into harmony with scientific truth. Young socialists and prospective recruits were urged to study Ludwig Büchner's *Strength and Substance* (*Kraft und Stoff*) or his *Conception of God* (*Der Gottesbegriff*), Arnold Dodel-Port's *Moses oder Darwin*, or the writings of Ernst Haeckel. In *Die neue Zeit*, Karl Kautsky attempted to demonstrate that Darwinism and socialism were compatible. *The Perception of Nature in the Light of Darwinism* (*Die Naturerkenntnis im Lichte des Darwinismus*), a popular treatise by Emanuel Wurm, was in a third printing by 1891, enhancing the reputation of its socialist author. Wurm held a seat in the Reichstag from 1890 to 1907 and was reelected in 1912.

Social Democracy's endorsement of the latest developments in science led almost inevitably to a challenge of traditional religious practices. The party assailed church leaders for consistently siding with established authority. Above all, it maintained that church and state should be separated and that public schools be completely secularized. On matters of belief it stood for personal independence and privacy. It favored no confession and no sect and maintained that church and party membership were compatible. Yet the thrust of German socialism was unmistakably hostile to religion. Adolf Hoffmann's best-selling tract, *The Ten Commandments and the Propertied Classes* (*Die Zehn Gebote und die besitzenden Klassen*) crudely attacked the Judaeo-Christian ethic as a conspiracy of privilege. This treatise made him immensely popular among fellow socialists and predictably enraged the clergy of all confessions. "Ten Commandment Hoffmann" was elected to the Reichstag in 1904 and to the Prussian parliament four years later. His party colleagues in both bodies shared his views. Among the 110 SPD deputies elected to the Reichstag in 1912, 69 identified themselves as "free thinkers" or as "dissidents." Of the remainder none were known as active church members.[22]

The prevailing opposition to religion in the SPD at first alien-

ated many middle-class Germans, but after 1890 it became congenial to increasing numbers. A good many bourgeois recruits
joined the party or gave it their votes after personal revolts
against Protestantism, Catholicism, or Jewish orthodoxy.

The SPD did little to attract Jewish sympathizers before the
mid-1890's. Marx had offended many Jews by denouncing their
religion along with others. Engels had taken much the same
line, and Lassalle, though born of Jewish parents, occasionally
had given vent to anti-Jewish sentiments. As late as 1892, Bebel
privately complained about the growing concentration in Berlin
of Jews from the eastern provinces; the next year, at his suggestion, the SPD party congress adopted a resolution that this
population movement might help to radicalize the petty bourgeoisie and the peasantry. But many Social Democrats knew
that anti-Semitism was inconsistent with their democratic principles; others soon recognized that it was not bringing recruits
to them but to small reactionary parties that made Jew-baiting
their chief stock-in-trade.

After the mid-1890's Bebel, Liebknecht, and other leaders
forcefully and repeatedly denounced anti-Semitism, and demands that Jews receive full equality of rights found frequent
and resounding echoes in the SPD press. The party also provided Jews with opportunities for political leadership. While no
bourgeois party in 1898, 1903, and 1907 elected a single candidate for the Reichstag who openly identified himself as a Jew,
the SPD elected several. In the 1870's the liberal parties had
attracted virtually all the votes cast by Jews, and these parties
continued to win a majority of them; but by 1903, 20 to 25
percent of the Jewish vote in the Reichstag elections was cast for
the SPD. Because Jews then formed barely more than 1 percent
of the German population, this meant only thirty to forty thousand ballots—barely 1 percent of the SPD totals. But more important than either Jewish votes or money was the Jewish talent
that the SPD harnessed. Between 8 and 14 percent of the SPD
deputies in each Reichstag session in the period from 1890 to
1914 identified themselves as Jews or were of Jewish background; so were several of the party's leading theorists and
many of its attorneys and journalists. The SPD was not the
"Jewish party" that anti-Semites liked to contend it was; but its

members among secularized middle-class Jews contributed skills the working class could not provide, which were needed to bring in more working-class members and to complete their ideological indoctrination.[23]

In winning the support of women, youths, dissidents from the Christian religions, and Jews, Social Democracy was recruiting the underprivileged. But other bourgeois Germans who did not suffer from discrimination also joined or supported the SPD.

Lassalle had dismissed the bourgeoisie as "a reactionary mass," and both Marx and Engels at times had described it in almost equally negative terms. Yet these three men, as well as Bernstein, Kautsky, Luxemburg, and many other prominent personalities had all come to the German socialist movement from the middle class. Bebel wrote Engels in 1886 that the middle-class German was "the greatest coward and weakling on the broad face of the earth" and exclaimed in 1892: "What wretched people are these German bourgeois!" But he knew that the SPD could not hope to achieve majorities without some bourgeois support, which it gathered in the counting houses, in the university lecture halls, in the salons, and most important at the ballot box.

In short, the SPD could not offer the bourgeoisie any promises that catered to specific class interests, but it would not spurn members of the middle class who might be attracted to it. The party's uncompromising demands for broad constitutional reforms, its criticism of militarism, and its internationalism appealed to a good many educated middle-class Germans who were otherwise indifferent, if not hostile, to socialism. The moment the onus of illegality had been removed, Bebel and his associates were finding friends among "scholars, officials, teachers, merchants, technicians, etc." Never, he reported to Engels in 1891, had he received so many letters and oral comments from such professional people giving advice, making proposals, sending money, and offering their personal services. He concluded that if capitalistic society were to be replaced by a socialist regime at an early date—and he then thought this possible by about 1898—the party would have the help of many men who hitherto had served the Hohenzollern dynasty.

Bebel noted, however, that many persons who fully sympathized with the SPD were prevented by social and economic pressures from joining the party. Fear of economic and social retaliation may also have prevented many middle-class citizens from voting for the SPD in state elections where the secret ballot had not been introduced. But balloting in Reichstag elections was secret. The votes cast for the SPD in these elections so far exceeded the total number of union members (and by four to ten times the total membership of the party) that the importance of middle-class support at the polls could not be challenged. The number of such voters varied from election to election, and the percentages they formed of the totals for the SPD cannot be determined precisely. But an investigation in 1905 yielded an estimate that between 20 and 25 percent of the SPD ballots in the three Reichstag elections of 1893–1903 came from the middle class. Gerhard A. Ritter has suggested that this estimate was too high, but it would appear about right for the Reichstag elections of 1903 and 1912. Statistically, even if all members of the Free Unions voted for the SPD in socialism's triumphal breakthrough on the eve of World War I, they accounted for no more than 60 percent of its total. If the votes of many unorganized workers in urban and rural areas were among the remaining 40 percent, at least 20–25 percent of the votes for the SPD in the last election before the war probably were cast by middle-class voters. The SPD, though primarily a party of labor, was no longer exclusively that. After 1900 it had to give attention to the wishes of growing numbers of middle-class members and voters.[24]

The party received little rural support, and the moving spirit for a socialist search for rural votes was Georg von Vollmar, leader of the Bavarian branch. He was seconded by Eduard David in Hesse, where Otto Boeckel's anti-Semitic movement had won a large following among the peasants. In 1895, Vollmar and David prepared a draft program for consideration by the annual party congress. To win support among the owners of small farms, Vollmar wanted the SPD to endorse state credit aid to save them from bankruptcy. This, however, would mean the perpetuation of private ownership, and—so Marxists argued— inefficient production units. When the program came to a vote it was opposed by Kautsky and rejected by the party congress.

This debate was the first and last attempt for a nationwide alliance between peasants and socialism. Bebel wrote in 1895— with gratuitous sarcasm, for he initially had been indifferent to a socialist farm program—that the SPD had preserved the purity of its socialist principles and thus delayed the possibility of coming to power in rural areas by at least ten years. After 1895 the party directed its rural agitation primarily toward farm laborers, but no great victories could be celebrated. The SPD offered the rural worker no real hope of improving his miserable lot in life until after the collapse of the capitalistic system. Besides, the farm owners usually dominated their hired hands sufficiently to prevent them from turning to socialism. Thus the only region in which the SPD scored significant success in rural areas was Mecklenburg; there it won more votes in 1898 than did any other party. Elsewhere the pickings were slim. In 1912 not a single Social Democratic Reichstag deputy was elected from a predominantly rural district.[25]

Failing to win the peasantry, the SPD could console itself with the knowledge that this was numerically a declining element in the population of Germany. The overall trend in membership and electoral strength could cause only optimism. By 1907 there were 2,704 local branches in all parts of the Reich, and seven years later almost twice that number. When revolution broke out in Russia in 1905, the German Social Democrats had 384,327 members. The Associations Law of 1908 made it easier to win more, and another three-quarters of a million joined during the next decade. When the war broke out 1,085,905 citizens of the German Empire belonged to the SPD. The party that most scathingly criticized the Reich had enrolled far more members than any other.

Hundreds of thousands of Germans who did not formally join the SPD supported it at the polls as the party counted larger voting totals in every single Reichstag election of the Wilhelmian era. After polling 1,427,000 votes in 1890, the SPD won 1,787,000 in 1893; 2,107,000 in 1898; and then—in its most powerful jump forward—3,011,000 in 1903. By this time it had become a truly nationwide party. Twenty-five years earlier, 207 of 397 Reichstag election districts had failed to give it any votes. In 1903 it totally failed in only three of the 397 districts; in 56 it won absolute majorities. In cities the SPD was particularly powerful at the polls. In 1903 it won 67 percent of the ballots in the Berlin districts, about the same percentage in Hamburg and in Chemnitz (Saxony), 57 percent in Solingen (near Cologne), 55 percent in Stuttgart (Württemberg), 51 percent in Bremen, and 48 percent in Mannheim (Baden). Even in a Munich district where the population was 89 percent Catholic, the socialists took 56 percent of the votes in 1903; in Cologne (80 percent Catholic), they won 38 percent. Königsberg—though surrounded by rural, conservative East Prussia—gave the SPD 49.5 percent of its votes in 1903.

Though the government made an all-out effort to arouse the electorate against the SPD in the election of 1907, the party slightly increased its national total to 3,259,000. Finally, with another mighty lunge, Social Democracy won 4,250,000 votes in the Reichstag election of 1912.

In every Reichstage election after 1887 the SPD won a larger percentage of the votes than any other party, and only in 1907 did it fail to increase its lead over the other parties. Capturing 19 percent of the national total in 1890, it won 32 percent in 1903, 29 percent in 1907, and 35 percent in 1912. In that year it again won more than 50 percent of the votes in many Reichstag districts, including those of Berlin (76 percent), Potsdam, Hamburg, Bremen, and 22 of the 23 districts in the kingdom of Saxony.

Nevertheless, the SPD had trouble turning votes into Reichstag seats. In runoffs it generally faced a solid phalanx of the other parties. There was no reapportionment after 1867, thus the disparity between the impact of rural and urban votes increased. Even in the Prussian province of Saxony, for instance, where cities did not grow at the pace of Berlin, Hamburg, Munich, or Frankfurt, the conservative member from Salzwedel-Gardelegen, elected in 1912, represented 29,400 eligible voters while his socialist colleague from Magdeburg spoke for a constituency of 61,400. The more sparsely populated rural districts that normally returned conservative candidates enjoyed a disproportionate per capita representation, both in the Reichstag and in state parliaments. The size of socialist parliamentary contingents always lagged behind its percentage of the popular vote. Yet though many more votes were needed to elect a socialist to parliament, the SPD's Reichstag caucus increased from 35 deputies in 1890 to 81 by 1903. After the setback of 1907, the party's electoral triumph in 1912 mandated 110 deputies. Thus, on the eve of World War I, 28 percent of the deputies in the imperial Reichstag represented the empire's most radical party. [26] Even that total did not come up to the SPD's 35 percent share of the popular vote. In the Prussian Chamber of Deputies, however, a vastly different situation prevailed. Even in Reichstag elections, the SPD had more trouble in Prussian districts. With 32 percent of the popular vote in the Hohenzollern kingdom in the Reichstag election of 1912, the SPD carried only 22 percent of the Prussian Reichstag districts as compared with 39 percent of the vote in the remainder of the empire. The uphill battle in Prussia in national elections was nothing like the challenge presented by the three-class suffrage in Prussian Landtag elections. In most districts the party did not even bother to campaign. The annual congress of the SPD in 1900 resolved that party members throughout Prussia henceforth should take an active part in elections for the Chamber of Deputies. But its first efforts were barren; though they won 19 percent of the votes in the election of 1903, the three-class suffrage plus the combined opposition of other parties prevented it from winning a single seat. With 24 percent of the vote in 1908, it finally placed 7 deputies in the Prussian parliament, and these were increased to 10 (out of a total of 443 seats) in 1913. On the eve of World War I, the empire's most popular party could claim only 2 percent of the seats in the lower house of Prussia—the state that dominated the empire.

In the parliamentary elections of the other federal states, the SPD scored earlier victories, but its scope was reduced by the class discrimination of most state suffrage laws. In addition to the separation of voters into income classes, as in Prussia, state, municipal, and communal voting codes granted plural suffrage to persons of means and education and withheld votes from those who failed to meet requirements of home ownership, payment of direct taxes, and minimum levels of income. In 1895, 36 Social Democrats sat in the parliaments of 11 of the federal states. By 1913 the party had won entry to the parliaments of 22 of the 26 states (including Alsace-Lorraine), and it had increased its total representation to 231. In several of the tiny principalities, the SPD by 1914 held more parliamentary seats than any other party. Of the larger states, it occupied 26 of 91 seats in Saxony, 20 of 73 in Baden, 17 of 92 in Württemberg, and 30 of 159 in Bavaria. Meanwhile, particularly between 1909 and 1913, the Social Democrats won increasing representation in municipal assemblies. For example, the SPD captured its first seat in the City Assembly of Frankfurt am Main only in 1901, with the election of Max Quarck, but it filled almost one-third of the 71 seats by 1914. From 1910 to 1914, Social Democrats won 109 of the total of 511 seats in the city assemblies of Berlin, Breslau, Cologne, Dresden, Frankfurt, and Munich, Germany's six largest cities.[27]

The largest party in the empire by 1890–1914, the SPD constantly debated its goals. Even in its socially homogenous beginnings, it had embraced members of widely diverging viewpoints concerning the means and ends of power. During the 1880's the uncompromising Marxists had slowly gained in influence vis à vis the pragmatists who sought through evolutionary means to give Germany a reformed society and a democratic state. The balance of power between these quite different elements—and thus the work and aims of the SPD—were inescapably affected by the increasing magnitude and heterogeneity of its following.

XI.

MARXIST THEORY AND REVISIONIST PRACTICE IN THE SPD

The Social Democratic party grew into a massive political army between 1890 and 1914, but was constantly engaged in an internal debate over its identity and its aims. Although large in 1890, it remained a minority party. As such, it faced three alternative routes into the future. It could become an out-and-out party of revolution and seek to impose its will as a minority; but this choice would repudiate the political democracy it favored. It could concentrate on political and social reform and thus win political allies; but this would require it to abandon its socialistic goals. Finally, it could continue to advocate evolutionary change, but to eschew compromising parliamentary alliances with bourgeois factions, putting its faith in eventually attracting an absolute majority of the voters. In that case the party would have to rise above and beyond its original working-class character, while not betraying the proletariat. The whole character of the movement to democratize Germany and its chances for success were dependent upon the way in which the SPD would resolve the struggle for power in its ranks between theoretical Marxists and pragmatic social democrats.

Marxism had won increasing numbers of adherents within the movement under the repressive legislation of the 1880's and seemed to emerge as its dominant element during the months that followed Bismarck's fall. The feeling of release and exuberant optimism that captured German socialists in 1890 was followed in 1891 by the adoption of the Erfurt program, which was much more uncompromisingly Marxist than the statement drafted at Gotha sixteen years earlier. Since this party platform lasted as long as the empire, its radical verbiage continued to shock, frighten, and arouse resistance among bourgeois Germans both in and out of government. It exaggerated out of all proportion both the danger and the promise of German socialism. Foes felt more threatened, friends came to expect more than Social Democracy ever seriously tried to accomplish. Actually, the fine print of the Erfurt program revealed the party's predilection for revolutionary slogans wrapped around reformist action. Fierce words dominated the section devoted to theoretical principles and final goals; the list of immediate demands continued to stress the aims of political democracy and economic equalization that the socialists had pressed since the 1860's, adding to the earlier call for universal, equal, direct, and secret suffrage the cardinal political principle of proportional representation. In practice, after 1891, the party supported not revolutionary violence but evolution, and at a rate sanctioned by the voters.

The SPD was turning into a movement of reformist procedure while continuing to claim faithful adherence to Marxist theory. One might say of its flamboyantly publicized Marxist slogans what George Bernard Shaw wrote of Wilhelm Liebknecht: they covered "every compromise by a declaration that the Social Democrats never compromise."[1] Liebknecht's own words at Erfurt revealed this divergence between pretense and reality: "If so far we have not achieved results in the Reichstag, that is not the fault of parliamentarism: it is simply the consequence of our not having yet in the country, among the people, the necessary power. If we had behind us as many votes, and as much force, as the bourgeois parties have, the Reichstag would be for us as fruitful as it is now for them. . . . To say this is not to maintain that every question can be solved by legislation; but let someone show me any other road that leads to the goal! I know there is another which, in the view of a few among us, is shorter—that of violence . . . but that road leads to Anarchism."[2]

No stronger warning against violence could have been given in 1891, the word "anarchism" was the most derogatory and sinister in the SPD vocabulary. Many of the best Marxists as well as Social Democrats who knew little of Marxist theory repudiated revolutionary violence while continuing to give lip service to the goal of a socialist revolution. Friedrich Engels was among them. Throughout the 1880's he had cautioned against attempts at revolution. Shortly before his death in 1895 he wrote that any "revolutionary" must be mad who "of his own accord" would provoke "a barricade fight in the new workers' districts of Berlin."[3] Thus despite its red flags and its Marxist theory the new, mass democratic movement had not attempted revolution during its formative years and was evolving away from such tendencies by 1890. But it was not moving in unison. Though the SPD never succumbed to sectarian fragmentation, as did French socialism before, during, and after the 1890's, it witnessed factional quarrels and all the tensions inherent in dogmatic controversy.

Radical Marxists in the SPD gathered around an elder statesman of the party, the able historian and journalist Franz Mehring, but looked for dynamic leadership to Karl Liebknecht and Rosa Luxemburg. Liebknecht, born in 1871, was a sensitive youth, loving music and poetry. He studied at the universities of Leipzig and Berlin and at Würzburg, where he took his doctorate in law and economics. In 1893–94 he served his compulsory term in the army, then returned to civilian life imbued with a burning hatred for the uniform and everything it symbolized. Whatever that year inflicted on him, he later recalled that he "bore it all with pride, contempt, and pity." Before long he became famous for his polemics against "the brutality of the barracks and the cruel degradation" that accompanied the soldier's regimented existence.

Civilian life for Karl Liebknecht turned out to be no bed of roses. He married in 1900, shortly after death had taken the father he respected and admired. His wife died ten years later, leaving him three children. His second marriage remained childless. By the time he had passed through these trials Liebknecht had become a respected but notorious public figure. Following his studies he had opened a law practice in Berlin with his brother Theodor and had risen quickly as one of the most skillful and sought-after defenders of socialists who had run afoul of authority. Following his conspicuous stint as defense counsel of the striking streetcar workers of Berlin, the voters of the capital's 45th Ward (*Kommunalbezirk*) elected him to a seat on the city council.

Liebknecht's role as the SPD's prime polemicist against militarism everywhere gained him both fame and an indictment for "preparing a treasonable undertaking." Though he was convicted and condemned to serve a prison sentence of eighteen months, his Berlin constituency sent him to the Prussian Landtag in 1908 and elected him to the Reichstag four years later.

Liebknecht frankly told the court that tried his case in 1907: "The aim of my life is the overthrow of the monarchy, as well as the emancipation of the exploited working class from political and economic bondage." Antimilitarism would free the citizen from a state which "tamed him as one tames animals." Once that capacity to regiment had been wrested from the hands of monarchic authority, "the duke, too, must go." But Liebknecht's words and actions supported a revolution without violence. He also insisted at his Leipzig trial that he was merely engaging in a labor of public enlightenment designed to engender widespread revulsion against military institutions. "Every action I undertake, exhausts itself in the dissemination of reason and is of itself legal, quite evidently legal!" he added. In February 1910 he flatly stated in the Prussian Chamber of Deputies that his faith was not in "Browning pistols, machine guns and sabres," but in intensive agitation and the mass strike. At the end of his rainbow beckoned democracy, the independent, concerted action of a free people, the liberty so often promised and so often withheld from the German working classes. While his uncompromising antimilitary pacifism remained a minority sentiment among prominent SPD members, his espousal of political liberty and equality earned him a strong public following and the respect of the more pragmatic, less outspoken party leadership.[4]

Far more cool, consistent, and systematic in Marxist theory was Liebknecht's feminine but not feminist colleague, Rosa Luxemburg. Born near Lublin in the same year as Liebknecht, she was the daughter of a liberal-minded Jewish merchant. Rosa was the youngest of five children, a sickly girl who once remained bedridden for a full year because of a hip disorder which ever after handicapped her movements. At fifteen she joined a revolutionary group that hoped to achieve Polish freedom in collaboration with the Russian revolutionary movement. While a student in Switzerland she married the son of a German émigré, settled in her husband's country in 1897, and gained German citizenship. By the time the marriage was dissolved in

1903, Rosa was widely known to German socialists through her articles in *Die neue Zeit* as a proponent of Marxist orthodoxy.

A genuine internationalist, Rosa Luxemburg retained some traces of a socialist type of Polish nationalism. The two attitudes were entirely compatible. Capitalism as it existed in the Polish provinces stood and fell with the dominant foreign presence, whether Russian, Austrian, or German. German capitalism was the most vigorous of the three and the target of her most persistent attacks, but she never forgot the broader context. She attended the London congress of the Russian Social Democratic party (RSDLP) in May 1907 as a Polish delegate and spoke at the Stuttgart congress of the International in 1907 as a representative of Russian Social Democracy. As late as July 29, 1914, she attended an emergency session of the International Socialist Bureau as a representative of her Polish countrymen. A little woman with a limping gait, Luxemburg was equally energetic as agitator, journalist, teacher, and scholar.[5]

The left-wing members of the SPD celebrated the outbreak of the Russian Revolution in 1905, but the manner and the intensity of their rejoicing were far from uniform. A police report tells that Liebknecht and Clara Zetkin addressed a rally of "men, women, and girls" in Berlin on February 9, 1905, which adopted a smug resolution expressing solidarity with those subjects of Nicholas II who were endeavoring "to raise Russia into the ranks of the modern states." Then the crowd gave "three cheers for the speaker, Liebknecht" and "went its way without any disturbance."

Rosa Luxemburg meanwhile celebrated the sequel to Bloody Sunday as a new phase in the class struggle. She told the readers of the *Sächsische Arbeiter Zeitung* on April 29 that the Russian proletariat had risen to the occasion and writ large on its banners not just the republic, "which could just as well be postulated by the bourgeoisie" but "the realization of Socialism." The urban proletariat had risen in the spirit of "political enlightenment, proletarian consciousness, in response to *Social democratic education.*" Far from merely raising the Russian people laboriously from inferiority to a par with the masses of central and western Europe, the events of 1905 revealed how irresistible a movement devoted to political and social liberty could be, precisely because of the formidable entrenchments behind which the established order responded to the attack. Thus "the Russian Revolution becomes at the same time . . . a reminder to those of little faith, the timid calculators in our own ranks, as well as a *warning* to our ruling classes . . . whose military budgets likewise summon to the surface powers which they one day shall not know how to control."

This frank admiration of Russian revolutionary courage by Luxemburg and other left-wing SPD members does not confirm the thesis of present-day East German hagiographers of communism who seek to claim the Liebknecht-Luxemburg wing as disciples of the Russian movement that ultimately stormed and held the present German bridgehead. The German socialist left was excited and stimulated by the Russian events, but the revolution of 1905 did not convert even Rosa Luxemburg into a disciple of the Russian movement. If anything the "Red Rosa" of those days might well have felt that Lenin's centralist organizational ideas were cast in the same mold as those of the "timid calculators" in the German SPD, whom she repeatedly took to task in editorials and speeches. Both she and Lenin were orthodox Marxists, both believed that a great war was in the making to be followed by intense and destructive social upheavals. The collapse of capitalism was inevitable and not far off. But Luxemburg refused to accept Lenin's disregard for democracy. She insisted that the SPD should lead the workers in mass strikes to prepare them for the coming revolution. She emphasized the ultimate necessity of spontaneous mass revolt and rejected the Leninist plan of salvation by a small band of tightly organized professional revolutionaries. In the final analysis, while Lenin believed in an absolutist dictatorship of the proletariat she put her trust in a democratic one.

Today, six decades after the revolution of 1917, it occasions no surprise that neither Liebknecht nor Luxemburg, posted as they were in splendid isolation in a vast no man's land between Marxist-Leninism and Reformism, garnered an extensive following. Their supporters were zealous, and their unhampered access to the socialist press and their inexhaustible penchant for writing and orating gave them a disproportionate exposure in discussions of doctrine and strategy, but their influence never moved the party. Many of their disciples were young, however, and as a result both leaders of the left wing hoped to gain from the future whatever the present denied them.[6]

Also on the left, but not as extreme, was the "Kautsky Center," which followed fairly consistently but with occasional variations the theories set forth in the writings of Karl Kautsky. Kautsky prided himself upon his fidelity to Marxism, and he neither abandoned the revolutionary predictions of the master nor tried to anticipate prematurely the promise that the masses would be ripened for revolution by capitalism itself. His ambiguous position was defined as exactly as possible in his resolution that was adopted by the Paris congress of the Second International in 1900: "The winning of political power by the proletariat in a modern democratic state cannot be the result of a *coup de main*, but can come only as the conclusion of long and patient activity for the political and industrial organization of the proletariat, for its physical and moral regeneration, for the gradual winning of seats on municipal bodies and legislative authorities."

The resolution fitted Kautsky's personality. No organizer, he frankly confesses to his friend Viktor Adler that he always felt uncertain of himself "in practical and tactical matters." Beneath the benign and at times helpless appearance was a vindictive and often bitter soul; but a profound distaste for violence in any form caused him to shrink from any vigorous expression of his inner sentiments. When it came to action, therefore, he stood on the right, while his theory tended to place him with the left. Only in this sense did he form a "Center." Kautsky in 1902 could agree with Luxemburg that the party must not renounce the winning of power by "force." To do so, he wrote, would condemn it to mere "parliamentary cretinism and statesmanlike craftiness." He believed: "Only the parliamentary republic—whether with or without a monarchic apex in the English style—can . . . form the basis from which the dictatorship of the proletariat and the socialist society can emerge. This republic is the state of the future for which we must strive." And when Kautsky translated "force" (*Gewalt*) into practical terms, he sounded like Legien, whose influence he deplored. "*Gewalt*," he wrote to Victor Adler, is "every instrument of power" that might enable the movement to force its will upon its opponents; he continued, "Organization is also a *Machtmittel*" and synonymous with the "force" which he himself approved. His radicalism evidently constituted a highly scholastic exercise of an introspective mind and an easily depressed temperament. As a professed leftist he smarted in particular under Rosa Luxemburg's repudiation, but consoled himself that if the "Rosa demagoguery" should ever be put to the test, "the great majority of the party" would be on *his* side. Since his own position was obscure, these reflections may have provided only limited comfort, but his observation to Adler in October 1913 that it was "not people from the 'masses' but almost exclusively intellectuals" who preached "aggressive action" demonstrated his capacity for lucid insight. Indeed, the call to violence issued more often from the salon than from the workbench. Between jousts with the militant left, Kautsky found as much controversy when facing a larger and ultimately far more representative faction to the right, the "revisionists" led by Eduard Bernstein. [7]

The name of this group derived from the insistence by some articulate Social Democrats that Marxist doctrine had to be revised in the light of actual developments since Marx's formulation of socialistic theory. Many of the basic ideas of "revisionism" were developed by a Bavarian socialist leader, Georg von Vollmar. Born in 1850, Vollmar was trained as an officer and served in the papal guard at Rome. He ended his military career after suffering a leg wound in the Franco-Prussian War, and from then on got about only painfully on crutches or by wheel chair. He became a Social Democrat in the early 1870's, much influenced by the speeches of Bebel and Wilhelm Liebknecht. In 1879 he went to Zürich to edit the *Sozialdemokrat* for a year. Back in Munich, he began as early as 1884 to embrace arguments of moderation and to display a willingness to cooperate with the bourgeois left. By 1890, Vollmar was urging concentration upon "the immediate tasks" of Social Democracy, not upon the ultimate objectives. He had become a "revisionist" before the term existed, and until his death in 1918 he was a major force in turning the SPD away from Marxism. Unable to curb Vollmar (whose Munich organization shared the particularist proclivities characteristic of all Bavarians), the national leaders, Engels, Bebel, and Kautsky, vocally disapproved of the "Royal Bavarian

Social Democrat" but could not change his views or reduce his regional influence.[8]

The leading theorist of revisionism was Eduard Bernstein. As editor of the *Sozialdemokrat* from 1881 to 1888 he had followed a strong Marxist line and sharply criticized all deviationists. As a result of his prominence as a particularly unyielding party propagandist, a standing order for his arrest prevented him from returning to Germany even after Bismarck's antisocialist laws had expired. Bernstein moved to England whence he maintained a vigorous correspondence with German party leaders, who soon had cause to wonder about the curious and disturbing impact of exile in London on this middle-aged Marxist stalwart. With every letter he sounded less like the Bernstein of old and more like the troublesome Vollmar in Munich. Was it "English influence," as Bebel and Kautsky charged? Bernstein denied that observation of and association with the Fabians had affected his theoretical views. Whatever the cause, he changed from a revolutionary into an evolutionary socialist during his years in England. His new dogmatic pronouncements, written there and published by Kautsky in *Die neue Zeit* (1896–97) document time and place of his conversion.

Bernstein finally returned to Germany in 1901 and was elected to the Reichstag the following year. He now addressed a larger forum than Kautsky's coterie of political philosophers. In the halls of the national parliament his blend of democratic pragmatism, trade unionism, pacifism, and patriotism, all held together by a spirit of evolutionary moderation, spoke to Germany and received a response that accelerated the growth of the SPD.

Bernstein sought to develop his theory of socialism empirically, without the "labor theory of value," the theory of "surplus value," and the gloomy belief in a necessary revolutionary "catastrophe" before socialism could be achieved. Whatever some socialists thought of it, revisionism became a significant contributor to the growth of German democracy.[9]

In 1899, Bernstein expanded the *Neue Zeit* essays into a book.[10] "Unable to believe in finalities at all," the author wrote, "I cannot believe in a final aim of socialism. But I strongly believe in the socialist movement, in the march forward of the working class." He saw no indication that capitalism was nearer collapse than it had been more than half a century earlier when, in the *Communist Manifesto*, Marx and Engels prophesied its demise. The middle class, far from getting smaller, seemed to be increasing with the growth and broadening of corporate ownership. Bernstein, moreover, was concerned about the welfare of German society as a whole, not just that of a single class. He even endorsed acquisition of Kiaochow Bay as a means of safeguarding "the future interests of Germany in China." His domestic program would make the government more responsible to the people by instituting ministerial responsibility, reform of the Prussian franchise, and women's suffrage. He called also for increased social insurance, graduated taxation, and certain government regulation of industry. All these reforms he hoped to see achieved without violence—by propaganda, education, and organization of the voters for peaceful pressure.

Privately, Bernstein had long repudiated Marxism even more emphatically than in his published works: "Do not forget," he wrote to Bebel on October 20, 1898, "that *Das Kapital*, its scientific character notwithstanding, was in the last analysis a tendentious work and remained uncompleted, uncompleted in my opinion because the conflict between scientific knowledge and political opinion made the task increasingly difficult for Marx. From this viewpoint, the fate of the great work is almost symbolic and in any case a warning." On October 31, 1898, Rosa Luxemburg wrote to Bebel, urging that Bernstein should henceforth be regarded by the party much as it viewed Gustav Schmoller or any other bourgeois "social reformer."[11]

Events outside Germany soon added to the symptomatic importance of Bernstein's new positions. In June of 1899 the French socialist Alexandre Millerand stirred the entire Second International by joining a bourgeois cabinet in Paris. Not only was Millerand the first socialist to succumb to the blandishments of ministerialism, but the minister of war in this cabinet was the same general who had directed the bloody suppression of the Paris Commune in 1871. Millerand's action seemed to many socialists everywhere an overture to corruption and the end of class consciousness and class solidarity. German Marxists could see in Bernstein another potential "traitor" to the cause of "revolutionary" socialism.[12] From 1899 to 1901 the controversy grew in intensity, revealing increasingly that Bernstein had powerful friends as well as adamant critics within the SPD. While Ignaz Auer and Georg von Vollmar swung the Bavarian branch of the party behind him, Kautsky, by May 1901, was advocating the excommunication of Bernstein, his former close friend of eighteen years. "I am rid of the last remnants of my sympathy for him, [and] hate him as our worst enemy," Kautsky wrote to Viktor Adler. "As long as Bernstein is in the party, there will be no peace."

Bebel, meanwhile, who had for some years felt that Bernstein's position no longer represented German Social Democracy, saw a need for factional restraint. He knew that Bernstein's most violent critics also had enemies in the party. If every group started to read every ideological adversary out of the congregation, the SPD would collapse, he reasoned. "You wouldn't believe how much animosity against Parvus [Alexander Helphand] and also against Rosa [Luxemburg] pervades the party," Bebel wrote Kautsky on September 4, 1901, warning of the domino effect any major exclusion would activate. Kautsky resigned himself to Bernstein's continued presence in the movement, though it depressed him and made him scornful of the compromisers who maintained the nervous stalemate. The solid establishment of revisionism in the SPD and in the Second International made something of an opportunist of Kautsky himself. "Where we can shake off the revisionists only by splitting the party, we must tolerate them," he wrote in 1904 to Adler; "where we can isolate them, however, we must do it."[13] Lukewarm Marxist comrades were censured and threatened, but they were never isolated or expelled. The revisionists slowly inherited the commanding positions in the SPD. Their increasing influence prompted a deepening bitterness among the extreme left-socialists, but this did not retard their rise.[14]

The decline of revolutionary Marxism within the SPD and a corresponding increase in revisionist strength could be ascribed also to some auxiliary elements. Under party sponsorship, a Central Union of Consumers' Societies gradually evolved in the 1890's from local organizations. The consumers' societies were led by Adolf von Elm (1857–1916), a cigarmaker who had worked in the United States for a time before returning to

Germany in the early 1880's. Theoretically, Elm's cooperatives were independent of the SPD, but recruited party members whose unrevolutionary interests in self-improvement under capitalism had to be considered in party councils. Elm, as a member of the Reichstag, as a trade union leader, and as an outspoken critic of socialist radicalism forcefully represented these autodidactic elements. He did not press the demands of the masses for full democracy, contending that "a powerful educational work is still necessary in order to make them able to govern themselves." Like the party as a whole, he nevertheless considered himself to be a "revolutionary" and defined the term in 1911 much as the SPD lived it: "A revolutionary is one who promotes the building up of the organizations of the workers, for without it a revolutionizing of conditions is impossible. . . . To want to create lasting results in economic affairs with revolver in hand is the folly of fanatical, immature minds."[15]

Elm exemplified a type of socialist whom we have already encountered in Carl Legien and whose massive armies of quickly expanding trade unions contributed more than any other development of the Wilhelmian era to put Marxist theories on the back burner. In addition to his post as chairman of the General Commission of the Free Trade Unions (as the socialist labor movement in Germany called itself), Legien represented the SPD in the Reichstag from 1893 to 1898 and again from 1903 to 1918. As a socialist he was conservative, more than fulfilling Kautsky's gloomy prophecy of 1892 that the pragmatic and economic preoccupations of the union leaders would be "the grave of revolutionary thought processes." Speaking to union representatives in 1899, Legien flatly declared that organized labor in Germany wanted no upheaval. "We want conditions of peaceful development."

The practical successes of moderation further dampened socialist radicalism. The militant speeches of the ideologues found a scant response, and the gradual rise in real wages bolstered Legien and the Free Trade Unions. Similarly, while Bismarck's accident, sickness, and old age pensions could not overcome the theoreticians' objection to the system that introduced them, they moved the unions to appreciate the state and aroused pride in its industrial successes. Thus, Gustav Bauer, deputy chairman of the unions under Legien, expressed the will of the majority of Free Union leaders in 1913: "There remains no issue in Germany" that could be viewed as "a question of life and death to the proletariat."[16]

Worker dissent against this undramatic pursuit of bread and butter issues—though militant—remained small, and most of its supporters quit both the party and the unions in 1908. Led by Fritz Kater, some twenty thousand wage earners renounced all political parties and proclaimed their adherence to revolutionary syndicalism. This movement played no significant role in German politics. Its struggle for a precarious existence confronted two disparate enemies. The authorities closely watched its meetings and publications and outlawed both in 1914. The Free Trade Unions succeeded in discrediting Kater's organization to the point where the anemic syndicalist press felt constrained to admit that even in Berlin, the center of the sect's modest strength, "not a few" workers "knew nothing of our existence." Thus Legien's Free Trade Unions monopolized socialist labor strength, and more radical tendencies in the working classes remained both weak and—thanks to their secession in 1908—outside the SPD.[17]

At the same time the Free Trade Unions retained a certain independence from party control. Especially in the Ruhr, socialist trade unionists thought it essential to deemphasize political and ideological goals. Addressing a population predominantly Catholic, the Socialist labor organization competed with the Christian (Catholic) Trade Unions for members, while seeking their support for joint strike actions. By 1912 the Christians had recruited 78,000 miners in the Ruhr, two-thirds the strength of the Free Trade Unions' regional membership of 114,000. When the socialists called a miners' strike in February of that year and the Christians refused support, it fell far short of its goal—a 15 percent increase in wages. Setbacks such as this convinced Otto Hue, chief of the socialist Miners' Union, that ideological differences within organized labor must be minimized and common economic objectives stressed. At a higher level, Legien had long adamantly opposed using the unions as political shock troops. When Rosa Luxemburg pressed for the general strike as a gesture of solidarity during the Russian Revolution of 1905,

Legien warned that this would begin a revolution in Germany as well. "Once the masses take to the streets, there is no turning back. Then the motto will be: Bend or break." He insisted that the times were not ripe for such a showdown.

This confrontation between ideological radicalism in the party and pragmatic moderation in the unions brought about a showdown at the 1906 SPD congress held in Mannheim, which turned into an encounter of unequal forces. On the left Rosa Luxemburg reflected her own Polish-Russian experience derived from a sphere in which labor was poorly organized and incapable of systematic negotiation with employers, so that concerted action depended on spontaneous uprisings and politically oriented work stoppages. Her agitation within the SPD for similar tactics had no significant impact. Karl Kautsky assumed a more representative stance. To him the party constituted the vanguard in the struggle for a socialist society, and once that goal had been reached, he assumed that its leaders would form the government. Thus the party, to him, was supreme and must preserve that supremacy. He recognized the indispensable role assigned to the unions but insisted that all party members in their ranks must be guided by party decisions. Bebel finally joined Legien's opposition to the mass strike. He merely insisted that when and if such a movement should occur, it must be controlled by the party.

Legien himself, a pragmatist, seized upon the resulting opportunity to avoid a destructive and divisive battle. He and Bebel fashioned the compromise that saved everybody's face. If in the future the party leadership accepted the need for a general strike, it was to meet with the leadership of the union "and take all steps needed to carry out this action successfully." Such consultation must occur before work stopped. Thus the unions ostensibly recognized the general strike as a necessary and acceptable weapon, but—more significantly—the party surrendered to the unions the right to veto *any* strike action.[18]

The growing power of the unions and dependence of the party on union support, as documented by the Mannheim resolution, was paralleled by a gradual change in the quantitative balance of power between the two. Socialist ideologues had begun to organize labor in the 1860's and thereafter had become accustomed to leading the workers. By the early twentieth century that state of affairs was being reversed. In 1893 union membership accounted for only one-eighth of the SPD vote; in 1898 it could claim one-fourth, by 1907 one-half, and by 1912 60 percent. Union membership was two and a half times as large as party membership in 1913. Trade unionists became increasingly powerful and numerous among the SPD's Reichstag deputies: 11.6 percent in 1893, 23.5 percent in 1903, and 32.7 percent in 1912 were labor leaders. Eight of the twelve top party officials who sat in the Reichstag of 1912–18 were veterans of the labor movement. This union predominance in the highest councils of the SPD as well as in the membership redounded to the benefit of revisionism. The Mannheim meeting had been a clear setback for the left wing. The unions had emerged and would continue to represent the decisive element of power in the revisionist controversy within the SPD between 1890 and 1914.[19]

Two claims may be made about the post-Mannheim SPD. The coexistence of Marxist theorists and revisionist trade unionists did not split the party nor brake its growth. The cooling of revolutionary ardors, whether manifested by the drift away from orthodox Marxism or by the reluctance of some trade unionists to strike for equal suffrage, did not reduce the party's role as the most consistent organized force for democracy in imperial Germany. If anything, it became even more single-mindedly democratic between 1907 and 1914.

The party concentrated its domestic combative energies on the fight against Prussia's three-class suffrage system. On this issue total party harmony prevailed. Even Karl Liebknecht agreed with the SPD as a whole in these years that democratic suffrage must be its major positive demand. The SPD freely used the firebrand of the extreme left to address the mass demonstrations it officially sponsored, and Liebknecht even invited bourgeois support.

No such unity, however, prevailed on the question of what form of government best suited a future German democracy. The party seldom spoke of creating a *Republik*, but talked instead of a *Volksstaat*, which might mean democratic parliamentarism wedded to a limited monarchy. Some socialists denounced republican government as tending to support "the class dominance of moneyed aristocracy." Bebel probably represented the great majority of Social Democrats when he addressed these words to imperial and Prussian authorities in 1903: "You only need guarantee the same rights and freedoms that are guaranteed the working class in the bourgeois republics, and the longing for the republic will vanish of its own accord." And he confessed to his French comrades: "How ever much we may envy you French your republic, and wish we had one, we don't intend to get our heads smashed in for its sake. Monarchy or republic—both are class states."[20]

With the acceptance of limited monarchy went a slowly increasing disposition to tolerate socialist expressions of patriotism. The Reichstag elections of 1907 played into the hands of the national elements within the SPD. Branded as a "red menace" in the campaign because of its criticism of Germany's colonial policy, the SPD was isolated and dealt a sharp setback. Its representation fell from the high of 81 in 1903 to 43. Even Bebel, who had previously defended the Kautsky Center in public utterances, tended to align himself with the moderate revisionists.

After this reverse Social Democratic attachment to the German national cause showed more and more plainly through internationalist rhetoric. The French socialists in the Second International tried in 1907, 1910, and 1912 to win agreement among the national sections that a great general strike would be called if war should threaten, but on each occasion the SPD obstinately opposed such a commitment. One historian has concluded that the internationalism of the SPD on the eve of World War I "had in fact more kinship with the Wilsonian ideal for the League of Nations than with the *Communist Manifesto.*" It is premature to speak of a triumph of nationalism in the SPD prior to 1914; but there is no gainsaying the marked rise of patriotism.[21]

Max Schippel in the revisionist *Sozialistische Monatshefte* had justified SPD support for a Reichstag military budget under certain conditions as early as 1897, and in the following year Wolfgang Heine developed his idea of trading socialist support for a *Revolution von oben*: "We give military credits to the Government; the Government thereupon grants us new liberties. . . . The 'policy of compensations' has worked advantageously for the Catholic Centre, why not for Social Democracy?" After the disastrous elections of 1907, Heine intensified his campaign, insisting that the Social Democrats must be prepared to defend "German civilization," and warning that in a war crisis it would be "hardly possible to enter upon nice distinctions between aggressive and defensive wars." He found increasingly outspoken support. On April 25, 1907, Gustav Noske openly told the Reichstag that the Social Democrats, too, recognized the duty of national defense and would resist with the rest if Germany should be "pressed to the wall by any other nation."

During the years that followed, Noske took a keen interest in armaments questions, became a party expert on naval affairs, and supported Germany's colonial policy. By 1912 he had converted at least one prominent member of the left wing. Paul Lensch, the editor of the *Leipziger Volkszeitung*, had earlier been a leading critic of the revisionists; now he emerged as the scourge of colonial expansion championed by the "English bourgeoisie" and strongly suggested that Germany must face it down. The views of Schippel, Heine, Noske, and Lensch were not formally endorsed by party leaders, but the fact that they and other nationalists could comfortably remain in the SPD speaks for itself.

On one national question virtually all Social Democrats were agreed, for it harmonized their opposition to autocracy with support for the fatherland: if war should break out between Germany and Russia, they must fight for their country. Even Marx had sanctioned this, and it had been reaffirmed on many occasions by Engels and by Bebel. Partly because of enduring enmity against czarism, partly because of the rising tide of patriotism in general, and partly as a means of securing the adoption of a graduated tax on income, property, and inheritance, the large SPD Reichstag delegation in 1913 approved an increased military budget. This action created a furore, but was endorsed by a vote of 336 to 140 at the party congress in September 1913.[22]

In party assemblies and mass demonstrations the Social Democrats still sang the stirring strains of the "Internationale," prophesying ever anew "*la lutte finale!*" Lustily they shouted in halls decked with red banners: "no more tradition's chains shall bind us." But each time the music ended, the ensuing silence found them still bound—and each time a little more bound—by national traditions. The radicalism of the socialist left was gradually limited by the same force that had restricted bourgeois movements for liberalism and democracy in the nineteenth century. In World War I radicals would be on the side of the German state, convinced that they must protect it against the barbarism of a threatening Russia. Nationalism and socialism, the two great ideological waves which Friedrich Meinecke saw rising separately out of the nineteenth century, not only criss-crossed but gradually began to flow together during the last decade of peace in Europe's optimistic era.[23]

But the moderate left was not altogether cut off from power within an SPD which during these years refused to excommunicate anyone. The contest between factions was fought out between 1911 and 1913 at the highest echelon in the party. When Paul Singer, a co-chairman of the SPD, died in 1911, Carl Legien proposed that Friedrich Ebert, since 1905 a member of the executive committee, be named as his successor. Ebert, for tactical reasons or in the interest of party unity, refused to stand for the office. Instead, Hugo Haase was chosen, against the opposition of leading trade unionists, to serve as co-chairman with Bebel during the aged founder's last years. A smallish man of rational mind and great idealism, Haase had won practical experience as a successful lawyer. Kautsky, pleased by the election, wrote Adler that Haase was "a splendid person and a highly able head, a very good leader, in whom I place the greatest confidence." But he added with equal truth that Haase lacked authority and was neither a brilliant writer nor a "thrilling" speaker. His election as co-chairman of the party seemed superficially to tip the sensitive balance within the party leadership in favor of the left, but Ebert's presence on the executive committee guaranteed that the interests of the unionists and party revisionists would not suffer.[24]

In the same year that Haase was named co-chairman, Ebert's chief rival among the rising men in the party, Philipp Scheidemann, was elected along with Otto Braun to the SPD executive committee. Both of these new members were firm believers in a policy of gradualism, convinced that the steady rise of the socialist vote in Reichstag elections would eventually give the party the power it needed to realize its program. In 1912, Scheidemann gained another position of prominence when the 110 Reichstag deputies of the party elected him their chairman. He held this key position throughout World War I. Scheidemann, like Ebert, was a man of humble origins. He talked at times a more radical policy than Ebert's, perhaps for tactical reasons, or because he lacked Ebert's poise. "The most banal speaker I ever heard," was Bülow's unkind verdict: "His speeches, pretentiously delivered, were like small change that had worn down in passing through hundreds of greasy fingers." Scheidemann was a dapper and officious man who looked anything but the part of a revolutionary. The American newspaperman and playwright, Ben Hecht, interviewing him at the end of World War I, was understandably reminded of the mature Buffalo Bill: "He had the same dandyish goatee and mustachio." Scheidemann, like many union leaders, was content to strive for the attainable, trusting that the future eventually would secure the final aims of socialism. [25]

Friedrich Ebert found his reward for patience when he was chosen co-chairman of the SPD upon Bebel's death in 1913. The man who six years later would become the first president of a German republic was born, like his bitter opponents Liebknecht and Luxemburg, in the year the empire was founded. His father was a master tailor in Heidelberg, a busy and upright Catholic who had no time for politics. The Protestant mother was annoyed when an uncle from Mannheim introduced young Ebert to socialism during the years of Bismarck's antisocialist laws. Quick of mind and interested in books, the boy wanted to study at the university. Family circumstances, however, decided that he would become an apprentice in some craft, and he learned the trade of saddler. At eighteen he settled briefly in Mannheim where his Marxist uncle introduced him to the writings of Lassalle. The next year, 1890, found Ebert blacklisted by a Hanoverian employer because of his support for the SPD in the Reichstag elections. In Kassel he was dismissed again after organizing a saddlers' strike. In the Bochum area he was beaten up for his socialist activities. Shortly thereafter, in Bremen, he found a more congenial atmosphere for his activities. He was

elected to the parliament of the city-state in 1899 and at about
the same time was named to head a central labor office created
by the socialist unions of the great Weser port.

Ebert gained national recognition within the SPD when he
organized the annual party congress of 1904, which met in
Bremen. Election to the executive committee at thirty-six began
an important career for him in Berlin the following year. With
the close support of Legien and other revisionist friends, Ebert
rose steadily in influence. A quiet, deliberate man of firm will
and sober judgment, he won grudging respect even from some
socialists who hated his policies. In 1912 he won election to the
Reichstag. The following year the party congress at Jena chose
him as Bebel's successor, giving him 443 votes out of a total
of 473. His elevation confirmed once again the ascendancy of
reformism, though it goes too far to say that in either 1911 or 1913
absolute dominance of the party passed into Ebert's hands.²⁶
Haase would not be dominated by anyone, even Ebert, and the
natural balance representing diverse trends in the party could
not be destroyed; for the party was held together by an equi-
librium of tensions within it.

Both the left and the right managed to have their way in the
SPD until 1914. The left on the eve of the war was as always
chiefly interested in following a revolutionary and internation-
ist line and in holding propaganda posts of significance within
the party. The right, as earlier, was mainly interested in preventing any attempt to use the masses in a general strike for
revolutionary and internationalist political purposes. Neither
group was satisfied, but each had much to gain by staying in
the party and little to win by leaving it. Despite infiltration
by revisionists, the press continued to reflect the ideas of the
moderate (Kautsky) left. Konrad Haenisch, a prewar leftist,
complained that increasingly the editorial staffs of party newspapers were homogeneously revisionist, but he was named by
the executive committee in 1911 to create and direct a "Central
Office" that would prepare broadsides and pamphlets for use in
agitation and propaganda.²⁷ Meanwhile, the right, controlling
the trade unions and much of the SPD's organizational structure,
saw that the party did not translate revolutionary principles into
practice.²⁸

Both the left and the right hoped to preserve the SPD, to control rather than to wreck it. The chief change in the party in 1913 was that Ebert sounded even less like a Marxist than had Bebel. His emerging leadership honestly reflected the true character of German Social Democracy. Even so, the division of labor and the balance of forces within the SPD continued to uphold revolutionary theory in a party which on the eve of 1914 was no longer really revolutionary.[29]

The SPD worked vigorously for democratic objectives from 1890 to 1918. Was the party democratic? Did it foster democratic attitudes among its members? Did its very collectivist principle and the discipline of its organization and that of the labor unions cause members simply to follow as a matter of habit? The evidence yields mixed answers to these questions.

Social Democracy did not initiate the German tendency to subordinate the individual to the whole, but it did not correct and even cultivated it. Lassalle wrote in 1863 that the German workers were "instinctively inclined to dictatorship, if they can be fully convinced that this dictatorship is exercised in their interests."[30] Forty-six years later Kautsky complained to Viktor Adler: "In Germany the masses are drilled to wait for the command from above."[31] Bülow and Ernst Troeltsch both noted the discipline of German Social Democracy. Friedrich Naumann worried about centralization within it, and Hugo Preuss, a leading Progressive, wrote that except for the Prussian army there was "nothing more Prussian than Prussian Social Democracy."[32] To these and certain other bourgeois contemporaries, the great failing of the SPD was its unwillingness to foster a spirit of individualism. With both socialism and capitalism in mind, Max Weber commented in 1906: "Everywhere the house is ready-made for a new servitude. . . . Those who constantly fear that in the world of the future too much democracy and individualism may exist and too little authority, aristocracy, esteem for office, or such like, may calm down."[33]

The tragic toll of historical legacy and contemporary circumstance was levied in these years upon the SPD. Bebel had glimpsed it when he wrote that a party cannot freely choose its weapons: "It is influenced by the way of battle and tools of the opponent, which force the attacker to fight not as he would wish but as he must."[34] The SPD insisted upon disciplined solidarity because the undemocratic environment of Germany seemed to offer a democratic movement no choice but this or failure.

This alternative became no more palatable when one considered the most obvious by-product of rigidity: organizational regimentation. In 1911, Bebel sadly confessed that "few traces of the old willingness to sacrifice are left in the party; today every service must be paid for and indeed paid for well." He traced it all back to "the trade union attitude . . . which recognizes no such thing as a free service." A vast bureaucracy of hundreds of professional functionaries—business managers, publishers, secretaries, and editors—had been created to sustain a growing party and to hold together a membership which by 1914 exceeded one million men and women. Made up of cool, sober, and experienced veterans of party life, "this private hierarchy rejected all daring enterprise and theoretical fanaticism." It is not surprising, therefore, that half of the socialist Reichstag spokesmen of 1912–18 were professionals rather than amateurs, men who had made careers as party or union officials, not as workers or independent intellectuals. It was also noteworthy that the socialist contingent in the national parliament was getting older: 62 of the 110 members had previously served in the Reichstag; 64.5 percent of these veterans had been under forty when first elected, but of the 48 newcomers in 1912 only slightly more than one-fourth were under middle age. These aging pros buttressed reformist domination. Their sentiments prevailed in the twelve-members executive committee and in the party committee established in 1912, consisting of elected regional leaders and providing disproportionate representation to the less highly urbanized centers of party strength.[35]

The intentions of both leftists and rightists, of hacks and idealists, of professionals and amateurs within the prewar SPD remain, from a democratic viewpoint, thoroughly admirable. Even those who talked most radically of force and violence were men and women who dreamed of an age of socialist brotherhood in which the Golden Rule and democratic principles would prevail. Nor can the democratic impact of the SPD upon German society before 1914 be doubted. Conservatives were hardened against democratic reform by socialist pressures, but they would have opposed concessions anyway. The party shook hundreds of thousands of Germans out of political apathy and gave them an education in the aims and practices of democracy. It made many other Germans who did not join the movement aware that democratic reforms were needed.

More than any force in Germany the SPD prepared the people for whatever acceptance the Weimar Republic received in 1918–19. The chief legitimate grievance democrats can harbor against pre-1914 Social Democracy, therefore, is that it neither used the revolutionary spirit it engendered to realize its own ideals nor joined with bourgeois democrats to accomplish more moderate reforms peaceably.

Historical background, faith in evolutionary growth, concern for the organization, and, above all, minority status combined with democratic allegiance to the principle of rule by the majority, all made it impossible for German Social Democracy to attempt to win power by force. But its adherence to the myth of class revolution often prevented the SPD from seeking or even welcoming alliances with bourgeois democrats; at other times it prevented such alliance even when the party wanted them. Thus, while furthering democracy in imperial Germany, the rise of the new left before 1914 by no means ensured its early triumph.

One of the historical functions of the SPD was to cause a number of leaders of the bourgeois, "middle" parties to move to more democratic positions. The rise and challenge of Social Democracy goes far to explain the residue of democratic principles that remained in the programs of bourgeois reformers in Wilhelmian Germany.

XII.

BOURGEOIS DEMOCRATS
IN WILHELMIAN GERMANY

Many middle-class Germans supported democratic reform and joined the rising chorus of discontent in the Wilhelmian era without allying themselves with Social Democracy. They opposed the status quo, but often faltered when they were asked for clear alternatives. Perhaps it could not be otherwise. As the left-leaning faction of the great liberal mainstream, these bourgeois critics of the Second Empire shared the handicap of liberalism's basic paradox. Its demand for individual freedom meant that the liberal faith sprouted in relatively uncomplicated societies; sparse populations living on and from the land had initiated its rise. But as liberal freedom generated industrial and commercial expansion, it transformed the uncomplicated agrarian scene into a complex technological and urban one. The resulting communities with their increased numbers of dynamic and divergent interests demanded a curtailment of individual liberty and exacted social regulation for the sake of individual survival. In terms of this dialectic, liberalism was self-defeating.

In addition to this inherent weakness, German liberalism, meeting the tumult of an industrial revolution, suffered from a lack of effective evangelists. Germany in the eighteenth century had produced a profound philosopher of liberalism in Immanuel Kant, indeed one so profound that his message eluded a broad public. Hegel had absorbed part of that liberal strain, adding his own camouflage of verbal obscurity and separating the message even more effectively from general comprehension. Nineteenth-century Germany produced no great lay prophet of liberalism, no Alexis de Tocqueville, no John Stuart Mill, who could adapt the creed to the rising democratic current and balance intellectual power with a talent for popularization. Nor did Germany in the nineteenth century feel the moral, intellectual, and political spur of a Giuseppe Mazzini, who fused freedom with nationalism and convinced his generation that progress toward popular sovereignty was the veritable will of God. The most impressive moral force generated in *Mitteleuropa* between 1815 and 1914 turned out to be Marx and his postulates of socially egalitarian collectivism which condemned politically egalitarian liberalism as anachronistic and unworkable. At the very moment when Marx began to make an imprint on the popular mind, Germans were being swept off their feet by their country's prime practitioner of a dynastically led state collectivism, Otto von Bismarck. In this new climate—which included, of course, the persistence of traditional conservative attitudes—the wonder was not that the democratic advocacy declined after 1866, but that it survived at all as a school of thought and as a political movement.[1]

But survive it did, and its bourgeois supporters found their political home in one of the Progressive parties. Throughout the 1870's and 1880's many Progressives contented themselves to play a waiting game until Crown Prince Frederick would supplant William I as well as his Iron Chancellor and democratize the nation from above. After they had been forced to bury this hope in 1888, Germany's bourgeois democrats instituted democratic initiatives from below, modified by an unfailing opposition to social revolution. Just as did their forerunners in the Revolution of 1848 and during the Prussian constitutional conflict of the 1860's, liberals of the left suffered from an instinctive fear of the masses, whose political conversion and salvation they were forced to leave to the Social Democrats. The Progressives' dilemma suggested that democracy's flame burned unevenly among them. They remained factionalized and hence often paralyzed because in essence they wished to democratize Germany while keeping "the mob" at bay. Nowhere was this Faustian indecision more apparent than among the oppositionist intelligentsia, which included a core of stalwart Progressives plus a peripheral and changing group of snobs who rejected the empire because some of its nationalist supporters exuded the sweat of the uncultured, and of sensitive as well as alienated spirits who decried what they considered the exclusively materialist ethos of Wilhelmian Germany.

On the political stage the German bourgeois democratic movement expended a disproportionate amount of its energies just trying to stay together or to unite after periodic schisms. The Prussian Progressive party (Fortschrittspartei) split after the war of 1866 when its right wing supported the Bismarckian coalition, then dominated by the National Liberals. In the 1871 Reichstag, Progressivism was reduced to a shadow of its vigorous image of a decade earlier and captured only forty-five seats. Its parliamentary spokesmen generally supported Bismarck's foreign and domestic policies, despite the party's honest concern for genuine parliamentarism.

A major recovery seemed to impend when the elections of 1881 returned 105 left-liberals (59 Progressives and 46 secessionists from the National Liberal party), making that bloc for the first and last time the largest group in the Reichstag. Two dramatic policy decisions had contributed to this result. The antisocialist laws initially—and very temporarily—reduced the SPD's strength at the ballot box, while Bismarck's abandonment of free trade had left wide merchant discontent. Between 1881 and 1884 the traffic flow of 1867 was reversed as the Progressives were joined by left-wing dissenters from the National Liberals. These schismatics included some great names, such as Eduard Lasker and Ludwig Bamberger, but they were men past their prime, worn out by numerous unsuccessful parliamentary battles. They constituted a host of old chiefs commanding few Indians. "There is not a one among them," Gustav Freytag wrote to a friend in September 1880, "who could give the [liberal] cause a new élan."

Three years later these consolidated left-liberal forces, now merged into the Deutsche Freisinnige Partei, suffered a drastic setback, as both Conservatives and Social Democrats recovered. Though operating under one management they returned only sixty-seven members to the Reichstag. But their popular vote of close to one million held through the remainder of the 1880's as did their delegate strength (down by one to sixty-six after the election of 1890).

Schism continued to dog left-liberalism. In 1893, disagreement over whether to support the military budget prompted many of the former National Liberal secessionists to form the Liberal Association (Freisinnige Vereinigung) which backed the government. The Progressive majority under Eugen Richter's leadership, which these deviationists left behind, reorganized into the Liberal People's party (Freisinnige Volkspartei). The combined Reichstag strength of the two left-liberal groups dropped to thirty-six in 1893, where it remained through the election of 1907. In 1910 the Liberal Asssociation in turn lost a portion of its small following to a short-lived Democratic Association (Demokratische Vereinigung).

Beyond these self-generated factions left-liberalism could count on a small group of Reichstag deputies (ten in 1890, eight in 1898, seven in 1907) who represented the German People's party (Deutsche Volkspartei), which assumed the succession of Haussmann's, Mayer's, and Pfau's Württemberg Democratic People's party. Though the new name adopted in 1867 proclaimed the ambition to seek support throughout Germany, this party's most conspicuous convert outside the southern kingdom remained Leopold Sonnemann (1831–1909) and his *Frankfurter Zeitung*. About 30 to 35 percent of its total vote came from beyond Württemberg, almost wholly from constituencies in Bavaria and Baden. At most, therefore, a southern regional party, the DVP, constituted the strongest single bloc in the Württemberg Landtag between 1895 and 1905, a clear indication that democratic liberalism represented a major political force in only one state of the federal empire.

In 1910 the Liberal Association and Liberal People's party, together with the DVP, tried to arrest the decline of bourgeois democracy by merging once more under their original common label. They called the result the Progressive People's party (Fortschrittliche Volkspartei). The venture barely succeeded. The joint effort garnered forty-two Progressive seats in the Reichstag of 1912–18, fewer than the Progressives had occupied after the election of 1871, seven less than the three constituent parties had conquered separately in 1907. Their share of the popular vote actually increased from 9.9 to 12.3 percent, but this total, which represented 1.5 out of 12.25 million votes, still fell short of the Center's 2 million (91 seats), and the National Liberals' 1.7 million (45 seats). It did not come close to the 4.25 million ballots marked for the SPD, which enlarged its Reichstag contingent from 53 to 110. The returns indicated in addition that the new Progressive People's party had failed to recoup the staggering left-liberal losses suffered during the past half-century in sections of record population growth such as the Rhineland, Berlin, Silesia, and Saxony. In these highly industrialized regions it could not match the socialist appeal. If the area also included a Catholic majority, Progressive ranks were further reduced by losses to the Center party. Even in conservative strongholds such as East Prussia and Pomerania where Progressives, rather than the SPD, had long represented opposition elements, it barely held its own, or even lost ground. Only in Hesse-Nassau, Schleswig-Holstein, and some of the small principalities did the new party markedly improve on the performance of its predecessors.

For all its limited appeal and the changing social composition of its membership, the Progressive movement marched in unison on many issues, and its different factions recognized the kinship of their purposes. The Fortschritt spoke for democracy on behalf of a middle-class coalition which steadily became less "grand" and more "petit." As late as 1890 its representatives in the Reichstag included nine bankers and factory owners, but none remained by 1912; eleven estate owners sat for the Progressives in 1874, but only three in 1912. In the course of this transformation its social attributes came to include an inordinately high number (over 50 percent) of degree-bearing university graduates and a growing shift among leaders and representatives toward professional men ranging from university professors and physicians to lawyers, writers, newspaper editors, and schoolteachers. One artisan reached the Reichstag on the Progressive ticket in 1912; workers did not penetrate into the highest councils. The forty Progressives elected to the Prussian Chamber of Deputies in 1913 reflected the socioeconomic profile of their movement's notables: they included seven merchants and manufacturers, seventeen lawyers, teachers, and journalists, nine civil servants and clergymen, three artisans, and four "others."[2]

Despite William I's apprehension that the Progressive Party harbored secret republican sympathies, a misconception opportunistically abetted by Bismarck, who would hurl at his Progressive enemies any epithet from "republican" to "Girondist," the lawyers, doctors, professors, teachers, and civil servants who constituted the backbone of this loyal opposition could be called anything but republicans or revolutionaries.

Their chosen label "Progressive" fitted their character, an amalgam of idealism, inertia, and opportunism. They approved of progress, without ever explaining what it was. Did it signify service to a set of categorical imperatives, or merely the pragmatic pursuit of the attainable? Conflict between these two faces of political programming was no stranger to the socialist camp, but the SPD did have its scriptures, lip service to which could and did endow the working class movement with a unity which no intrusion of reality could destroy. Progressivism advocated a program of political reform similar to the immediate political aims of Social Democracy, but pressed it with far less determination and consistence and without comparable ideological fervor or militant rhetoric. From the time of the constitutional conflict of 1862 to the eve of World War I, *Fortschrittler* of every description carried the banner for freedom of expression, freedom of assembly, free trade, representative government, and equal and secret suffrage. This implied a parliament chosen by universal manhood suffrage which participated fully in all legislation, including the vote on war and peace, and unlimited budgetary control with annual reconsideration of military expenditures. Yet throughout the 1870's the Progressives in Prussia made no attempt to revise the three-class electoral system. Only in the last decade of the Bismarckian era did they gradually and hesitantly come to favor full democratic suffrage for Prussia and all federal states. They did so, as did their increasingly more successful socialist competitors for the democratic vote, because they fared so much better in Reichstag than in Prussian Landtag elections. Their year of triumph in the federal campaign of 1881 gave them 28 percent of all Prussian constituencies in the German parliament, but only 13 percent of the seats in the Prussian Chamber of Deputies. From that moment on the Prussian Progressives pushed for the secret ballot. In every subsequent session they introduced a bill favoring its enactment, and after 1893 they expanded these regular efforts to include abolition of the three-class electoral system. Even after their short-range gains among class three voters were lost to the SPD, the Progressives maintained this position. They really had no choice, for after

1898 they received almost no support from voters of the first and second classes.

Similar reasons of expediency prompted the Progressives to favor reapportionment of parliamentary constituencies to reflect the growth of cities, from which they, like the Social Democrats, drew much support. Had they prevailed on this issue and earned in the Prussian Chamber of Deputies in 1903 a number of seats commensurate with their popular vote, the total would have been 46 instead of 26.

The Progressives also favored proportional representation. Experience with this system in the selection of industrial courts, of worker representatives in the Bismarckian social insurance system, and in municipal elections caused many of them to conclude that it was the key to their survival. Through proportional representation, the Progressives could continue to elect representatives even from urban electoral districts that gave most of their votes to the SPD. One of the more enthusiastic bourgeois supporters of this reform argued in 1909 that the Progressives and National Liberals together would have had "a liberal majority in the Reichstag today had we possessed the proportional representation system." He added, "The goal of a majority [bloc] composed of the left-liberals and the Social Democrats still may be realized most quickly with the system of proportional representation."[3]

This generally hard-nosed confidence in the benefit of electoral reform suffered a setback in the form of a surprisingly good Progressive showing in the Prussian Landtag elections of 1913. For once the forty seats conquered in that state campaign approximated left-liberal strength in the 1912 Reichstag election. All of a sudden the Progressive movement appeared to be gathering new strength under a system of qualified voting. The outbreak of World War I, however, prevented a new trend and terminated an era during which the pressures of industrialization and urbanization had slowly aligned the political objectives of left-liberalism with those of the Social Democrats.

At no time did the two democratic elements converge on social policy issues. The bourgeois democrats considered the SPD a class party, while viewing their organizations as potential havens for all supporters of political equality. Progressivism rejected any diminution of property rights, and its major nineteenth-century leader, Eugen Richter, repeatedly warned that a socialist state could turn Germany into a "great national penitentiary."[4] If Germany was to be spared such a fate, according to left-liberalism, the empire must be democratized excluding socialism and inroads must be made on the SPD's labor constituency. Pursuit of the working-class vote had moderated the dogmatism of organized Marxism; the same goal drove the Progressives farther to the left. Throughout the imperial era they encouraged the growth of patriotic, procapitalist, Progressive unions to counter the socialist labor movement. This effort began in 1868 when the liberal economist Max Hirsch, and Franz Duncker, a publisher and the co-founder of the Progressive party, established the German Worker Associations (Deutsche Gewerkvereine), which came to be known as the "Hirsch-Duncker" (H-D) unions and chiefly attracted Protestant workers. Like the larger Catholic and Social Democratic labor organizations, the Progressive union claimed to be completely independent of any political party, but as their chairman admitted, their leaders had affiliated with one of the left-liberal parties. Their general aims were set forth in 1908 by a conference of chiefs of branch unions. The Gewerkvereine pledged themselves to work for "the raising of the working class [through self-help] on the foundation of the existing social order," and they accepted the aims of "social justice" and "political freedom and [local and provincial] self government." The H-D or Progressive unions claimed 122,000 members in 1910.

The general improvement of labor conditions was also advanced by another bourgeois organization, the Social Policy Association (Verein für Sozialpolitik). This group of social reformers, founded and led in the 1870's by the academic socialists, subsequently attracted Lujo Brentano, Max Weber, and a good many other Progressive intellectuals sympathetic to left-liberalism. Both components of its membership wavered between a deep interest in public policy and a reluctance to compromise their academic "objectivity" by active involvement in politics. They were reluctant, too, to commit the Verein für Sozialpolitik to a partisan cause. "Discussion," as Gustav Schmoller pointed out, was to be its "major concern." Yet a spokesman for German manufacturers correctly assessed the results of their work, if not their motivation, when he wrote in 1912 that these "academic socialists" had "for forty years . . . stirred up the German workers and encouraged them to blackmail German entrepreneurs."

Among the economists in the Verein für Sozialpolitik, none did more to provide an intellectual justification for the organization of trade unions and collective bargaining than Lujo Brentano. In his memoirs he stated his motivation clearly: "Because I wanted our economic life protected from all attempts of revolutionary change . . . , I demanded that the principle of freedom which governs contemporary economics be extended to the workers and thus be logically, honestly and consistently completed." Greatly influenced by sojourns and study in Great Britain, Brentano began his tireless crusade for bourgeois acceptance of organized labor in 1870 and continued it until after the Second Empire had ceased to exist. The commitment of so noted an academician helped to make the cause of labor respectable in the eyes of many other middle-class Germans. In the 1890's a few liberal Protestant theologians and pastors took an active interest in labor affairs and organized several Protestant educational associations for workers (Arbeitervereine).[5]

The most noted of these pastors was Friedrich Naumann, a Progressive who saw the impending dangers and potentialities of Germany's domestic situation in the Wilhelmian era with a clairvoyance unmatched by more professional politicians. Even unfriendly critics of Germany have acknowledged Naumann's nobility of character. What he wanted in essence was the merging of the "two great waves" of the nineteenth century to meet the needs of the twentieth. Bourgeois nationalism would be fused with proletarian socialism by embracing political reform and social welfare to make a great community of all Germans. Naumann certainly had his limitations, the most striking of which was his narrow and anti-Catholic Protestantism, which automatically alienated the sympathies of one-third of the people of Germany. Equally impractical was his persistent belief that the National Liberals might yet join the left for democratic reform. His prolonged tendency to rely upon the kaiser for the initiative in creating a "people's monarchy" was unrealistic, as he himself came to realize. Only in 1908 did he exchange parliament for Caesar as the savior of German nationality, but even that shift did not diminish his support for a German navy and colonial expansion, which made joint action with Social Democracy difficult. But his ultimate failure was most basically rooted in the problem he tackled; the very divisions among Germans which he deplored made it impossible for them to rally behind the common program he offered. Naumann addressed a working class that ignored or distrusted him and his organization. Instead of fusing bourgeois nationalism and social democracy, his National Social Society, which could not even agree whether to label itself national social or national socialist, remained a small club of pastors and professors with only 22,704 members in 1902. At their most successful, the Naumannites won 30,322 votes in the Reichstag election of 1903 and one deputy, Hellmut von Gerlach, who was elected by a predominantly agrarian constituency in Hesse. After that debacle Naumann prevailed on his organization to join the Liberal Association. Despite some grumbling most members followed him, and subsequently joined the reconstituted Progressive People's party of 1910.[6]

The immediate effect of Naumann's venture eludes quantification. The National Social Society was only one chapter in his life. He survived its failure, went on to a Reichstag seat, grew in stature as a spokesman of democratic, rather than social, nationalism, and retains a reputation as a German prophet of liberty whose words have meaning for his countrymen across half a century of tumult and failure. Friedrich Meinecke has suggested that the bridges the former pastor wanted to build could have enabled Germany to cross without violence into the democratic era, thus avoiding the Nazi experience. Such hero worship, however, distorts cause and effect in politics. Democracy is not irreversible, nor a cure for every social, economic, and political ill. How a Naumannite Germany would have faced defeat in 1918 remains a matter for speculation, as does the supposition that it would have been immune to the crises that racked and destroyed the Weimar Republic.

Friedrich Naumann filled the eighteen years between the founding of the short-lived National Social Society and the outbreak of World War I with hundreds of speeches, essays, and books in the service of democracy. He favored equal suffrage, the creation of a bloc of democratic and nationalist parties in the Reichstag so that the parliament might actually rule, redistribution of Reichstag seats according to population density, increased social welfare legislation in the interest of labor, the right to strike, profit-sharing and "co-determination" in industry, and a balance of federal and state power in the Reich.

The Naumann program won a number of able and enthusiastic young middle-class supporters. Theodor Heuss, who after two world wars was to become the first president of the German Federal Republic, was weaned from Marx and Nietzsche to fight with Naumann for democratic reforms. Max Weber, the famed sociologist, intermittently worked with Naumann as a capricious but prestigious "brain trust." The democratic ideas of both Naumann and Weber were powerfully motivated by considerations of national power. Most important for German democracy, both men sincerely and energetically embraced its principles and popularized them as spokesmen for the Progressive party. Both overcame conservative inclinations to work for reform. It confuses the issue, therefore, to say that they were "in the best sense of the word, conservative."[7] Some of the Naumannites indeed appeared conservative because of their naive confidence in monarchy, but it was not conservatism in Naumann that made him inspire and win the collaboration of the noted feminist Gertrud Bäumer, of the Progressive party leader Theodor Barth, or of the Progressive industrialist Robert Bosch. Nor was it a conservative message that made Albert Schweitzer read the National-Social weekly *Die Hilfe* from the day it began publication.

So much greater the pity, therefore, that Social Democracy was almost as unresponsive to Naumann's thesis of class fusion as was the kaiser. At the Lübeck congress of the SPD in 1901 the moderate social Democrat Ignaz Auer repudiated, to the accompaniment of "stormy applause," the proposal by Adolf von Elm that the party join in a bloc with "Pastor Naumann." Most members were convinced that Naumann's overtures were contrived to sabotage their own political rise.[8]

At the time Naumann tried to break down the barriers between classes, the first platform of the National Social Society drafted under his direction in 1896 began the left-liberal quest for sup-

pressed minorities by announcing his partisanship for equal
women's rights. It was a drastic departure, for hitherto even the
left-liberal call for "universal suffrage" had invariably meant the
vote for men only. Given the numerical preponderance of women
in Germany (31.3 million to 30.4 million men in 1907) democratic
advocacy of electoral reform excluded, except by the socialists,
more than half the country's adult population; and except for
Finland, where women secured the vote in 1906, and Norway
which enfranchised them in 1913, this attitude and condition
prevailed throughout the Continent and substantially throughout the world.

Women were, of course, less easily excluded from many economic and cultural sectors of activity. Their role as breadwinners,
had been rapidly magnified by the Industrial Revolution, but
left-liberals appealed largely to office workers, to the one out of
thirty who claimed professional status in law, medicine, and the
like, and to the many women (about 25 percent) in the teaching
profession.

Largely as the result of this female preeminence in the class-
room, the hitherto male bastions of higher education lost their
unisexual status during the reign of William II. In 1891, twenty-
four years after neighboring Switzerland had first admitted
women to universities, Grand Duke Frederick I of Baden opened
Heidelberg to students of both sexes. By 1914 all German universities had followed (even Prussia surrendered in 1908), and
among the German student body of 60,853 (less than 1/1,000th
of the total population) a sprinking of 4,156 young ladies,
generally from affluent and relatively enlightened families, pursued advanced degrees. Concurrently the number of academic
preparatory schools for girls rose to 38 in 1909 and to 50 by the
time the war broke out.

Other barriers proved more durable. The Civil Code of 1896
perpetuated the social and economic enserfment of woman by
delegating unqualified control of her dowry as well as her children to the husband. Marianne Weber, herself notably emancipated, described this humiliating condition as it had applied to
her mother-in-law. In the fifth decade of her life Helene Weber
had "at her disposal neither a fixed household allowance nor a
special sum for her personal needs." She was subjected to her

husband's "continued control" and to his "frequent criticisms" of what he considered to be her spendthrift ways.[9]

Most German wives in the century's last decade still accepted this condition as part of the natural order. The 1890 edition of *Meyer's Konversations Lexikon* stated flatly in its article on the "Frauenfrage" that in Germany, unlike Britain and the U.S.A., "a political feminist movement has so far been entirely absent." If women resented their inferior status they probably took their troubles to the Lord or found ways inside the home to vent their frustration and resentment. Only late in the nineteenth century did a few educated, middle-class women found a feminist movement to change the legal and social dependency of their sex on men. The 1908 edition of another German encyclopedia, *Brockhaus'*, acknowledged that a viable feminist movement seeking political as well as economic and legal equality had taken root in the empire, although it added with obvious relief that the enfranchisement of females was only advocated by its "radical elements."

Germany's bourgeois *Frauenbewegung*, or feminist movement, was older than these encyclopedists realized. It was started in 1865 by Louise Otto-Peters, whose husband had been one of the 1848 revolutionaries, and it made rapid gains during the 1890's. Helene Lange, another pioneer, born in 1848, and a teacher, began as a feminist leader by organizing the women teachers of Germany. From 1893 she published the leading periodical for women in German, *Die Frau*, in an effort to awaken their professional ambitions and mobilize their strength. Young Gertrud Bäumer in 1898 became Lange's assistant and close associate and quickly won recognition as one of Germany's foremost feminists. In 1901, Bäumer and Lange began to edit an annual feminist handbook (*Handbuch der Frauenbewegung*). By that time, German girls who enjoyed reading were finding the literature of the feminist movement readily available in their city libraries. The democratic ideas of feminism were "in the air," and they were powerfully attractive to intelligent young women in the decade before the outbreak of World War I. Membership in occupational or regional associations grew. The nonpartisan Federation of German Women's Clubs (Bund deutscher Frauenvereine), founded in 1894, represented 850 member associations by 1908. Ten years later it represented almost one million members.

Most middle-class feminist associations were primarily concerned with increasing educational, cultural, or occupational opportunities for women and did not feel that equal legal and political rights constituted the essence of their quest. In 1896 the Federation of German Women's Clubs received a lecture by Clara Zetkin and Lily Braun about the gulf that separated their bourgeois world from the revolutionary, class-conscious pursuit of human equality; and not without reason. As late as the 1898 congress of the Federation its presiding officer, Auguste Schmidt, urged an associate that the suffrage issue be soft-pedaled, in order not to "repulse many timid souls." Mona Lauer, who founded the Women's Welfare Association (Verein Frauenwohl) in 1888 and soon branched out into journalism as editor of *Die Frauenbewegung* and into unionism as organizer of the Hirsch-Duncker union of female sales clerks in Berlin, was the first bourgeois activist to espouse a sweepingly egalitarian program.

Before long, however, nonsocialist and nonunionist German womanhood joined the pursuit of political equality. In 1901 a new German Association for Women's Suffrage (Deutscher Verband für Frauenstimmrecht) held its constituent conclave in Berlin. The following year it affiliated with a new German branch of the International Women's Suffrage Alliance charted in Hamburg, where local association laws allowed women to join political clubs. The Federation of German Women's Clubs could no longer lag behind, and at its 1902 annual meeting it vowed to foster "understanding for the idea of woman suffrage" as the only means by which its general efforts could succeed.

That was six years after Naumann's National Social Society had seconded the women's movement and well after even more representative segments of Progressivism had expressed their sympathy for that cause. In 1899 the Progressive Women's Federation (Fortschrittlicher Frauenverband) became the first nonsocialist party organization to press for equality. Successor to the Women's Welfare Association, it also advocated the recruitment of female workers into the H-D unions with increased energy. Naumann appointed Gertrud Bäumer co-editor of his magazine *Die Hilfe*, the first time a woman moved from the humble status of contributor (which Progressive political organs such as *Nation* had accorded them since the 1880's) into a policy-making position.

The next unequivocal Progressive commitment on behalf of organized womanhood followed in the wake of the new Association Law of 1908 which permitted women to join political organizations throughout Germany and converted some bourgeois liberals to bid for feminine support. In April 1908 the Liberal Association, that independent-minded faction which had formed to support the 1893 military budget, but had since steadily drifted leftward, faced a motion at its annual congress endorsing women's suffrage. At Friedrich Naumann's urging the proposal was toned down to a mere recognition "in principle" of the need for equal political rights, and then was passed. Next the Association elected Else Lüders, a left-liberal suffragist, to its national executive committee, the first party, other than the SPD, to accord such recognition to a woman. (But left-liberals would not have been left-liberals if this historic occasion had not been marred by the secession from the party of three of its strongest advocates of female equality, Rudolf Breitscheid, Theodor Barth, and Hellmut von Gerlach, who refused to stomach the party's support of imperialism.) After the fusion of all Progressive factions, their 1912 congress listened to Gertrud Bäumer's argument that left-liberalism's future might well depend on the tapping of Germany's richest lode of dormant votes and that legal and social discrimination on sexual grounds constituted a perpetual wholesale violation of the rights of more than half of Germany's population. The delegates responded by endorsing the view that increased participation of females in the nation's economic life and in public affairs would, "in the opinion of wide party circles," lead to their political equality, but they neither proposed nor endorsed a plan for action. Many more prominent Progressives, like their socialist counterparts in the early 1890's, were in no hurry to recognize their mothers, wives, and sweethearts as political equals. Once again progress was allowed to remain a desideratum, the implementation of which was entrusted to fate and the mute and abstract dynamics of the future. When war came, not one of the German states allowed women to vote in their parliamentary elections, and the

Reichstag (like most other European parliaments and the United States Congress) continued to represent only men.[10]

Left-liberals played the genteel echo to socialism not only in women's rights, but as opponents of anti-Semitism. Despite the achievement of legal equality and their overwhelming and demonstrative loyalty to the German Empire (in the 1870's 70 percent of all Jewish voters supported the National Liberals, only 2 percent the Social Democrats), discrimination against Jews had continued. They attended the universities out of proportion to their share of the population and were more active in municipal politics and government than ever before, but it remained virtually impossible for a Jew to obtain a judicial appointment or a place in the administrative bureaucracy of Prussia. The officer corps of the Prussian army was likewise closed to non-Christians.

Imperial Germany knew no pogroms such as those in Russia, and it experienced no Dreyfus Affair; but as early as 1878 the slogan "vote for no Jews" was heard in election campaigns, and in every national election after that year the new anti-Semitic political groups won a sprinkling of votes. Their propaganda made the established parties increasingly hesitant to nominate Jewish candidates for office. As anti-Semitism increased in the 1880's, unbaptized Jews disappeared from the Prussian Landtag, and the number of Jews and converts who held seats in other state parliaments and in the Reichstag declined. For tactical reasons and anti-Semitism within its ranks, the National Liberal party after 1878 nominated few Jews for Reichstag seats. No Jew or convert represented the National Liberal party in the Reichstag from 1881 to 1914, though a few baptized Jews found leadership positions in the party.

Confronted by the rise of anti-Semitism, numerous Jews converted to Christianity; Leopold Ullstein had all five of his sons baptized because, as one of them later wrote, "the state we were destined to serve was Christian." As a result, Jews declined from 1.2 percent of the population in 1871 to just under 1.0 percent (615,000) in 1910. But those who in the 1880's preferred to resist discrimination rather than abandon their faith tended to transfer their political allegiance from the National Liberals to the Progressives. Before 1878, it appears, only about 20 percent of Jews voted Progressive, but in the following decade approximately 65 percent did. The Progressives opposed anti-Semitism and continued to nominate Jews for office. Max Hirsch, the cofounder and guiding light of Progressive unionism, remained to his death in 1903 a practicing Jew. Left-liberal leaders such as Theodor Barth and Rudolf von Gneist founded in 1890 the Association against Anti-Semitism (Verein zur Abwehr des Antisemitismus). The two leading newspapers of liberal democracy were owned by Jews: the *Frankfurter Zeitung* of Leopold Sonnemann and Theodor Wolff's *Berliner Tageblatt*. Of the fourteen Jews and converts who held Reichstag seats between 1881 and 1892, five were Social Democrats, but eight were Progressives.

Social Democracy, which did everything more dogmatically and emphatically, opposed the anti-Semites even more consistently than did the Progressives, and its ideology appealed to many educated Jews, alienated from their religion in this period of rising materialism. During the 1890's and after the turn of the century, the majority of a small band of Jewish politicians were Social Democrats. Of the twenty-five Jews and converts who sat in the Reichstag between 1893 and 1914, sixteen represented the SPD and five were Progressives. The rank and file Jewish voters, on the other hand, opposing atheism and socialism, continued to distrust Social Democracy and turned to the SPD only slowly and hesitantly. Their gradual conversion came less from changing conviction than from growing dissatisfaction with left-liberal timidity toward rising political anti-Semitism. Conservatives whispered or openly charged that Progressivism represented Jewish interests, but many Jewish leaders by 1900 complained that left-liberal opposition to anti-Semitism remained half-hearted and that bourgeois democrats on occasion allied with Jew-baiters in order to defeat Social Democrats. Except for left-liberal support of an anti-Semite in the Berlin municipal election of 1899, there is no hard evidence to sustain that charge, nor much indication that Jewish voters took it to heart. Jacob Toury has estimated that the Social Democratic share of the Jewish vote increased from 6 percent in the 1880's to no more than 20 to 25 percent in the prewar decade, chiefly at the expense of the National Liberals. Sixty percent of the Jewish vote continued to go to the Progressive until 1914, and Jewish socialists were largely alienated from Jewish as well as capitalist society.[11]

Many progressives joined another controversial and risky battle when they supported the vocal but minority criticism of German militarism and its arch symbol, Kaiser William II. Apart from Eugen Richter, Bismarck's tireless critic before 1890 on this issue, the Progressive who acquired the greatest fame and notoriety in this connection was the historian and Bavarian Landtag deputy, Ludwig Quidde. An editor of the *Deutsche Reichstagakten des 14. und 15. Jahrhunderts*, author of several seminal monographs describing other political institutions of the Holy Roman Empire, one of the founders of the *Historische Vierteljahrsschrift*, and secretary of the Prussian Historical Institute in Rome, Quidde made his political debut with a polemic against German militarism in 1893, and the following year became a best-selling author with his *Caligula*. Readers quickly recognized in the Roman emperor who promoted a horse to the consulate their own kaiser who had a habit of raising equine mentalities to high position. The book was both acclaimed and condemned as an attack on a hitherto sacrosanct office and personage. It sold tens of thousands of copies, and thereafter a growing number of bourgeois pacifists recognized Quidde as their spokesman.

German pacifism as an organized movement owed much of its initial impetus to an energetic Austrian woman of letters, Berta von Suttner, the daughter of a soldier, the Austrian Field Marshal-Lieutenant Count Francis Kinsky. Her two-volume novel, *Lay Down Your Arms!*, (*Die Waffen nieder!*), published in 1889 (the year of Hitler's birth), chronicled the sufferings of an aristocratic Austrian belle who lost her first husband on the battlefield of Solferino in 1859 and whose second spouse was executed during the siege of Paris in 1870–71, after being mistaken for a German spy. Suttner portrayed war as a senseless tragedy of errors rather than as a feast of heroism. In 1891, "Friedensberta" as her detractors called her, organized the Austrian Society of the Friends of Peace, and the following year she began publishing in Dresden a monthly journal to promote the pacifist movement (entitled, like her famous novel, *Die Waffen nieder!*). In that same year the German Peace Society (Deutsche Friedengesellschaft) was founded in Berlin by the Viennese bookseller and journalist Alfred Fried, who also edited its organ *Rampart of Peace* (*Die Friedenswarte*). While Suttner sought to attain her goals through moral transformation and viewed a peaceful world as an ethical end, Fried has been called a "free trade pacifist." He attempted to further international harmony by appealing to practical considerations of economic interdependence between sovereign states, echoing the dictum of Norman Angell that "the capitalist has no country." The late Eckhart Kehr, in fact, has accused him of espousing peace in Europe so that the resulting saving of national energies could be applied to overseas expansion. Be that as it may, Progressives such as Hellmut von Gerlach, the pedagogue Friedrich Wilhelm Foerster, and the Württemberg *Fortschrittler* Conrad Haussmann gave qualified support to Fried's movement.

Other left-liberals considered even Fried's practical pacifism too emotional and utopian and sought to foster understanding among nations by the organized promotion of small single steps in the international arena. To that end Progressives like Max Weber, Friedrich Naumann, Ernst Troeltsch, and Adolf Harnack added their signatures to the first manifesto of the Association for International Understanding (Verband für internationale Verständigung) founded in 1910. They believed that a piecemeal approach to problems of power politics would render pacifism more respectable in Germany, where until 1914 the movement was more likely to be suspected of subversion than in any other major European country. In order to avoid being confused with the Friedensgesellschaft, the association strongly emphasized its differences with Fried. It sought to be in international affairs what the Verein für Sozialpolitik was on domestic questions by disseminating information rather than proposing modes of action. Eventually it attracted a small, eclectic membership, including even a member of the Prussian upper house. But this very sobriety and moderation paralyzed it in the long run, and when war broke out Progressivism had nothing to show for this effort but good intentions.[12]

Progressive criticism of German militarism was often muted and indecisive. Men such as Naumann continued to call for a strong navy and an energetic foreign policy, especially after the elections of 1907; and for every Quidde who rebuked the kaiser, there were many more Progressives who shied away from radical action for democratic reform lest they be called antimonarchical. Because of these differences among themselves, the Progressives as a whole suffered from an "anaemia of spiritual force" on the eve of World War I, as noted by William H. Dawson, a perceptive British student of Germany. Finding it very difficult to act in unison, they all too commonly distinguished themselves by an "attachment to abstract political principles" and by preoccupation with fringe reforms rather than fundamental renovation of the German state structure. [13]

One of the major difficulties confronting the Progressives lay in their inherent respect for human individualism. A party of minor prima donnas, they never achieved solidarity behind firm central leadership. Naumann spoke for a large faction of the group, especially after the death of Theodor Barth in 1912. Hellmut von Gerlach carried his own following through his outspoken newspaper, *Die Welt am Montag*. A more conservative but equally anticlerical Munich deputy, Ernst Müller-Meiningen, led the nationalistic Bavarian branch of the party. Conrad Haussmann shared leadership of the Württemberg wing with Friedrich von Payer. Payer, who slowly emerged as the "grand old man" of the Progressive movement after 1912, was first elected to the Reichstag at twenty-nine years of age in 1877, just in time to vote against the antisocialist laws. Subsequently, he served for eighteen years as presiding officer of the lower house of the Württemberg parliament. He helped to unify the Progressives in 1910 and 1912 and played an even bigger role in holding them together during the war. [14]

If the individualism of its leaders and members handicapped the Progressive party, it did not suffer from a lack of publicity. On the eve of 1914 it had the support of more newspapers (about 270) than any other party in Germany except the Center. Oldest and most distinguished of these organs was the moderate *Vossische Zeitung* of Berlin. It appealed to a group of influential readers so small that it failed to meet its costs of publication. Bought in 1913 and maintained as a "prestige" piece by the famed Ullstein publishing family, it was placed under the editorial direction of an active left-liberal, Georg Bernhard. "It was a rare day," one of the owners later recalled, "that did not find him lunching with some government minister, a secretary of state, an ambassador or university professor," and, he might have added, one of the Social Democrats with whom Bernhard had considerably sympathy. The Ullstein profits meanwhile rolled in from the two-million-copy sales of the *Berliner Illustrierte Zeitung* and from the most popular early afternoon daily in Germany, the *Berliner Zeitung am Mittag*. Whether the heart of the owner dwelled on the editorial page of the *Vossiche* or in the latest news releases of the *BZ* was never clear. Certainly Ullstein's support did not turn Progressivism into a mass army recruited from readers of the firm's mass media. Years afterward, when Hitler had destroyed the publishing fortunes of the family, one of its scions in emigration would speculate belatedly: "Yes, perhaps we also have to share the blame for not having made sufficient use of the power we ourselves had created."[15]

The *Berliner Tageblatt*, another important Progressive newspaper, was more radically democratic than the *Vossische Zeitung*. Under its vigorous editor, Theodor Wolff, it also sharply criticized German foreign policy. The *Frankfurter Zeitung* was equally democratic and critical. Its founder, Leopold Sonnemann, was only twenty-five and Frankfurt had only 64,316 inhabitants when he started the newspaper in 1856. It grew with the city in size and cosmopolitan outlook and reputation. In 1914 greater Frankfurt claimed 445,000 citizens and the *Zeitung* enjoyed a worldwide reputation for intelligent and liberal journalism of integrity. Its editors, despite bourgeois affiliations, sympathized with the demands of labor and strongly supported freedom of speech for Social Democrats. By 1906, when it celebrated its first half-century of publication, the *Frankfurter Zeitung* could boast that it was "the foremost fighting organ of German democracy."[16]

"The first master-symptom of revolution is the 'transfer of the allegiance of the intellectuals,'" wrote Lyford P. Edwards in his study of the "natural history" of revolutions.[17] Crane Brinton in his volume on the "anatomy" of revolutions agreed: "No ideas, no revolution."[18] Both as symptoms and as partial causes of revolutions, the disaffection of intellectuals has played a part in all the great European upheavals of modern times. Eugen Schiffer, the National Liberal leader of the Wilhelmian era, acknowledged this in his postwar memoirs, but he contended that no intellectual movement systematically advocated the revolution that came in 1918.[19] A recently published history of German liberalism agrees with Schiffer.[20] Specifically revolutionary political literature was indeed not common in imperial Germany, but literature and journalism in the Wilhelmian era do reflect discontent and disaffection as indicated by the growth of the socialist movement and the demands of left-liberalism.

The great Progressive-oriented newspapers gave space to leading intellectual, predominantly academic, spokesmen for political reform in pre-1914 Germany. Most of these men believed that change would strengthen state and nation and that an overhauling of the existing order constituted a fundamental postulate of patriotism. Believers in the monarchical institution, they wanted to win all classes to its continued support but knew that this could not be achieved through social legislation alone (although men like Naumann never doubted the compatibility of monarchy and social justice), but only by enlisting every citizen as participant in the continuous drama of politics. In a series of articles and speeches, Hugo Preuss campaigned for a genuine system of local self-government patterned after the English mode. Gerhard Anschütz, professor of law at Berlin and author of the authoritative commentary on the Prussian constitution of 1850, saw "democratic institutions as means to the end of strengthening state power." Democracy and patriotism, in his opinion, "were not only compatible, but nothing short of interdependent." This dialectic also persuaded Friedrich Meinecke to cast off from his conservative moorings and embrace Friedrich Naumann's Patriotic Democracy (*Vaterländische Demokratie*), embodied in a projected merger of Prussia and the Reich, or a "full organic community of the German national state."[21]

Weber, a colleague of Anschütz's after the latter returned to Heidelberg in 1916, underwent a similar metamorphosis. Born in 1864, the fourth of eight children, Weber was the son of a National Liberal member of the Prussian Chamber of Deputies. From his mother, a southwest German Protestant, the youngster acquired a strong social conscience which reacted early against the father's cold bureaucratic liberalism. The youthful scholar's emergence as a distinctive political thinker was attended by a complex and traumatic struggle for emancipation from parental authority. In 1898, Weber suffered a nervous breakdown. The following year he married and left home, on the threshold of his thirtieth year. During his crisis he had become increasingly depressed by the realization that Bismarck's political success had destroyed among Germans the habit of independent political thought and had tempted William II to fuse in his own regime the ways of "Boulanger and Bonaparte."

Weber's personal emancipation initiated his odyssey which began in the Pan-German Union and ended with the founding of the German Democratic party in 1919. It mirrored an inconclusive struggle within himself between his aspiration to excel as an objective student of society and his sense of duty which demanded personal involvement in politics. His search for a position and a program acceptable to his heart and his intellect pushed Weber gradually left of center, but his addiction to social analysis always paralyzed his capacity for political action. Convinced that a declining aristocracy could not and should not retain its disproportionate share of political authority, he feared that neither bourgeoisie nor proletariat possessed the political maturity to assume its share of responsibility. Like many of his fellow academics he found intermittent consolation in a blend of nationalism and democracy. The shortcomings of William II would eventually convert him to equal suffrage and parliamentary government. Both Reichstag and Prussian Landtag, he came to insist, must take up the intellectual and programmatic slack resulting from executive drift and irresponsibility by exercising an unceasing check on kaiser and bureaucracy. His advocacy of control of the government by a strong parliament, backed in turn by a clear public mandate, was Weber's way of seconding Anschütz's view of the "interdependence" of patriotism and democracy because the resulting unity of nation and state would increase the thrust of national power.

Weber became another apostle of national union under a democratic system, but like Naumann's utopia of classless national solidarity, his vision was doomed to remain "gray theory." The regime resisted reform, the strongest opposition party continued to travel the road of class conflict, and Weber, as well as the lesser left-liberal professorial idealists of the Wilhelmian era, vainly waited until 1918 for a merger of the national and democratic elements in the National Liberal, Progressive, and Social Democratic parties.[22] Nonacademic writers of twentieth-century imperial Germany struck more iconoclastic poses and used more uncompromising language than did these noted scholars. Older critics whose adolescence had been impressed by the experience of 1848 were succeeded by the firebrands raised in the smug, muscle-flexing atmosphere of the 1870's and 1880's.

The patriarchs uttered the more gentle reproofs, but they laid the foundations for what eventually grew into a monumental anthology of discontent. In Brunswick, for instance, the popular novelist Wilhelm Raabe (1831–1910) commiserated as early as 1875 with Germany's "poor boys" whom the Bismarckian system consigned to a life dominated by drillmasters of every description. Reminiscing late in life, after Bismarck's death, about the founding of the Nationalverein, the novelist compressed his generation's disappointment into a dozen trenchant words: "Those were the days! Then we had hope—and what have we now?"[23]

The present, Raabe and many of his contemporaries agreed, demanded a battle of Sedan in reverse to teach the jobbers and subalterns of the Reich that there was more to life than killings, either on the battlefield or at the stock exchange. That was the message of Conrad Alberti's *Die Alten und Jungen* (1889); of Friedrich Spielhagen's best-selling novels of the 1880's, whose ensemble at its most incisive recalled the venom, if not the vigor and spice of Balzac's *Human Comedy*; and of Hermann Sudermann's fiction and drama, populated by the stock figures of Reich society—old aristocracy and nouveaux riches.[24]

But one of the most striking defections from the Hohenzollern establishment involved a creative genius genuinely "disinherited" by the disappointments following the achievement of national unity—Theodor Fontane (1819–1898), like many sterling Prussians a descendant of Huguenot immigrants. From 1860 to 1870, Fontane had written for the *Neue Preussische Zeitung*; as correspondent of this mouthpiece of conservatism he covered the wars of 1864, 1866, and 1870. After final victory he changed camps and, literally, existences. For the next twenty years he covered the Berlin theater for the *Vossische Zeitung*. More important, his emancipation from political conservatism was followed by a late flowering as a novelist. In 1878, when he was almost sixty, he published *Vor dem Sturm*, a novel about the war of 1813–14, while his greatest work, *Der Stechlin*, appeared posthumously in 1899.

In contrast to many other converts, the change of political front did not prompt Fontane to deny his own or his country's past. He continued to portray the virtues, as well as the faults, of the Junker of Brandenburg, and nowhere more movingly than in the central character of his last novel, old Dubislav von Stechlin. This salty, honest squire confirmed Fontane's persisting attachment to some of the canons of the *Kreuzzeitung*. Even as critic on the staff of a liberal paper he shared the conservative abhorrence of Bismarck's Bonapartism, as its editorialists of the 1860's had called it; he warmly embraced its nostalgia for a restoration of Prussia's simple virtues.

Much as he questioned Bismarck's greatness, Fontane despised William II even more. The young emperor's public masquerades poisoned the author's declining years. "Everything," he wrote in 1892, "[he does and says] is wind in the sails of Social Democracy, and the best circles [of society] are dominated by an attitude comparable to that of 44 years ago in February '48: 'This cannot go on, something must give.' " In one of his last letters he drew ominous comparisons with England's last Stuart kings. The kaiser's "lapses into attitudes which resemble those . . . of James II scare me to death."[25]

But while the master of *Stechlin* put his faith in the accessible antidotes of equal suffrage and a strong parliament, the most influential critic of Wilhelmian Germany among the writers who were adults in 1871, Friedrich Nietzsche pronounced Germany's ills all but incurable. His cultural despair, rather than Fontane's reformism, guided the young rebels who grew up in the shadow of World War I. More than any "thinker and writer before him he presumed to make [a] clean sweep of all values professed by other men" and "dared to claim a comparable freedom from all traditional authority, whether divine or human."[26] Though most of his condemnations of German philistinism were penned before William II began his reign, Nietzsche first began to affect a generation of German elite minds during the administration of the last Hohenzollern. Antikaiser and antichrist, he condemned both past and present and wrote off a future whose leaders, he warned, were being stunted by the mindless *scientia gratia scientiae* writ large over every German university curriculum. His strident accents of value-defying irrationality, however, appealed not only to the post-Bismarckian generation which, finding Germany united, despaired of discovering in life a purpose of comparable grandeur, but they also strengthened the existing order. "Vitality and instinct" served established authority better "than excessive doses of intellectuality." As had been true of Rousseau and Marx, Nietzsche's large and diverse audience read him "partially" and therefore "misunderstood him completely." His popular image was that of a bold destroyer without redeeming creative features. He was condemned to survive as everyone's favorite master of verbal violence, who provided quasi-scriptural authority to every species of barbarity from simple verbal carping to the burning of books and ultimately of men.[27]

Nietzsche's nihilistic pronouncements first stirred explosive discontent among those born on the eve of or after unification. This "generation behind schedule" not only grieved over disappointed expectations, as had Raabe and Fontane, but recoiled from the materialistic vulgarity of the world surrounding it. Besides committing its favorite doomsayer's most popular aphorisms to heart, it rediscovered Georg Büchner and worshipped such house gods of rebellion as Ibsen, Zola, Tolstoi, and Dostoevski. It joined every patrol dispatched to feel out the weakness of the prevailing powers: aristocracy, capitalism, and bureaucracy. The strength and number of its enemies heightened its bitterness, spurred desperation, and reduced the chances of victory. The rebellion of Wilhelmian intellectuals anticipated the German penchant for inviting destruction by attacking superior adversaries, which ran riot in two world wars.

Several of the most radical and politically alert critics gathered around the Munich magazine *Simplicissimus*. This journal, often banned from newspaper stands at railway stations and other public places, amplified part-Nietzschean and part-socialist criticisms of current bureaucratic and military conventions, of bourgeois morals and manners, social inequalities, and the philistinism of officially sponsored art. By 1908 it had a circulation of one hundred thousand, rivaling the SPD's *Vorwärts*. Its symbol, a ferocious bulldog loose from its chains, portrayed its purpose to do "a job of destruction without parallel." Its favorite target was William II, the anecdote ridiculing the sovereign its favorite theme. *Simplicissimus' Kaiserwitze* were repeated with relish even by the judges who banned the magazine for *lèse majesté*.

At another juncture of culture and politics in Prussia, Maximilian Harden published his highly personal and remarkable Berlin journal, *Die Zukunft*, which had more than twenty thousand readers at times from 1900 to 1914. Harden's viewpoint, like that of *Simplicissimus*, was chiefly negative. Born in 1861 as Felix Ernst Witkowski, sixth son of a Jewish silk merchant, he adopted the name by which he is best known during a career on the stage that ended in his twenty-eighth year. Praising Bismarck after 1890, Harden was bitterly disappointed by William II. He was a monarchist at heart, but believed the monarch should remain aloof from the tempests of politics. He insisted that the kaiser must acknowledge constitutional limitations. "Where the belief is fed that the monarch is the source of all power," Harden warned in 1900, "there some sick mind will conceive the folly that his violent removal would be a heroic deed, conducive to the welfare of the people." In this year, as in 1893 and 1898, he wound up behind prison bars for his criticism of William II. Before World War I he was noncommittal on the move to introduce equal suffrage in Prussia, but he generally favored government by a cabinet with responsibility to the Reichstag as a means of curbing the kaiser. Although no opponent of expansionism, he characterized the present regime as a harbinger of German decline because it failed to pursue consistent goals of national interest. The shapelessness of Wilhelmian policies frightened him. Far from opposing monarchy as an institution, Harden and *Die Zukunft* nevertheless shook public confidence in and undermined the prestige of dynastic government.[28]

Many major literary figures of the imperial era remained, of course, outside the circle of *Simplicissimus* and *Die Zukunft* because their work touched only the fringes of political controversy. At the same time this army of rebellious individualists should lay to rest the myth of a uniquely German predilection for conformity. Our arbitrary, random tour of literary landmarks confirms the opposite. [29] Benjamin Franklin ("Frank") Wedekind's [30] iconoclastic plays shook the theatrical world, while his satiric poems about William II enriched the pages of *Simplicissimus*. Richard Dehmel's sensuous, middle-class humanitarianism, while never singlemindedly dedicated to proletarian liberation, at least established the workingman's yearning for the good life as a legitimate literary theme. Gerhard Hauptmann chronicled society's oppression of the humble, particularly in his plays *Before Dawn* and *The Weavers* which depicted the corruption of village life by the inroads of industrialization. [31] The rifle fire of such skirmishers became inaudible, however, when Heinrich Mann leveled his heavy guns on the enemy and when the prophetic thunder of his prose reduced William II's image to a pitiful shadow of Victor Hugo's *Napoléon le petit*. In 1913, Mann, in his great essay on Zola, explained the fall of France's Second Empire when he maintained that it had been governed by contempt for the individual and for mankind; but his readers knew that he was really prophesying the doom of Germany's Second Empire. In the following year, only a month before the outbreak of World War I, he finished his mighty obituary of the Wilhelmian era, the novel *Der Untertan*, describing the German scene of power and prosperity as mere staging and the garrulous omniscience of its ruler as a charade depending for effect chiefly on "frequent costume changes." [32]

Germany's intellectual rebellion constituted a rich and varied chaos. Its bourgeois apostles attacked, exhorted, denigrated, and warned. Their efforts prompted a biographer of Heinrich Mann to admit after the novelists death in 1950, and after his prophecies of 1914 had been vindicated twice: "We cannot claim that our poets slept; it was we who did not know how to read." Their diversity renders any discussion of their work in the context of this volume and this chapter a more than questionable undertaking. Still, if the literary outsider, the *Einzelgänger*, the rebel of the mind, had any fixed political anchorage, it was among the sophisticated utopians of left-liberalism. If his work strayed into the pages of political journals, at least before 1914, it would represent most often a marriage of minds such as represented by Theodor Fontane's twenty-year association with the *Vossische Zeitung*. And it was Richard Dehmel who expressed

the liberal essence of Wilhelmian Germany's intellectual individualism when he wrote to a bewildered friend after the outbreak of revolution in 1918: "To your question—what shall we
do?—I can really retort only this: What we should always do!
Begin mankind's improvement with our own persons.' "³³ He
also illuminated the roots of liberalism's failure as a political
mass movement. Great causes have flourished on castigating
the wickedness of others, rather than on purifying morals in
their own ranks. From Christianity to Bolshevism revolution has
been inquisitorial rather than uplifting.

Yet no such sense of inevitable failure permeated the leadership of left-liberalism. It rejected the Wilhelmian order with
growing intensity, but it presented no alternatives; it was constantly offering the enemy a negotiated peace. Left-liberals
understood what a nationalist era exacted of them in matters of
principle. Though they were willing to support controversial
and unpopular causes, they sought to survive by modifying the
solutions potential allies among the avant garde of social and
political reform tried to press on them. After Bismarck had
called them antinational because they opposed authoritarian
government, militarism, and protectionism, they were constrained to formulate an aggressive patriotic message of their
own.

While it cannot be proved that the struggle for political survival in a hostile environment alone explains the liberal imperialism of a Naumann or a Weber, the liberal reclamation of the
national cause undoubtedly constituted a step in that direction.
But in arguing that the nation could be preserved and strengthened only by reinforcing the political and economic rights of the
lower classes, left-liberals were also reconciling nationalism and
democracy and painting opponents of change with the same
antinational brush Bismarck had used on them.

In retrospect we know that the liberal imperialists must share
responsibility for the course in foreign policy that brought Germany to disaster in 1918; that the priority they assigned to the
achievement of national solidarity, transcending class barriers,
helped to feed the historical currents that flowed ever more
rapidly downhill to 1933. But from the perspective of 1900 their
ideals constituted a sound strategy. There was no other way to

recapture the national idea that their precursors had helped to create before 1871; no other way to resurrect respect for democratization, both political and social, among Germans of the middle class.

This mixture of ideals and strategy confronted the Weber-Naumann liberals with two major tasks. Naumann's experience showed that utopia and reality could not be reconciled simply by founding a new party. They sought to reach their goal by the expedient of a merger of the left-liberal parties. The Richter tradition among left-liberals and the particularism of the Württemberg Volkspartei reduced the success of that approach. But even if regional differences could have been compromised, the remaining obstacles in the path of a national democratic mass movement remained formidable.

The last twenty years of imperial Germany's history demonstrated that a bourgeois democratic movement could not build a majority constituency at the expense of its four larger, if mutually hostile enemies: Conservatism, National Liberalism, political Catholicism, and Social Democracy. An alliance with one of them would constitute the price of admission to the pantheon of political power, and if democracy was the one principle which left-liberalism could not compromise, then an entente with Social Democracy remained the only possibility. But the Weber-Naumann justification of imperialism also blocked that exit, all fervent invocations of the classless nation-state notwithstanding. On the other hand, surrender of the imperialist justification of democracy risked the loss of most middle-class backing. Hellmut von Gerlach's Democratic Association might then have remained the microscopic residue of German liberal democracy.

Like Richard Dehmel's protagonist in one of his famous poems, *Der Arbeitsmann*, the bourgeois left needed only one boon in order to be "as free as the birds are: only time."[34] Time to make its case for free trade and the interdependence of national economic interests, time to bring about and prosper from the egalitarian franchise and the enfranchisement of women, time to build bridges across the chasm that separated bourgeois democracy from Social Democracy, and time, finally, to impregnate left-liberalism itself with a discipline that would neutralize internal disputes before they degenerated into an atom spray of more and more smaller and smaller splinter parties.

This need highlights the promise of German bourgeois democracy and confirms its fateful shortcomings. Time ran out in 1914, before democracy on any terms had permeated German politics and society. The last battles on behalf of representative and popular government will be described in the following chapter.

XIII.

PUBLIC POLICY AND THE DEMOCRATIC IMPULSE IN A DECADE OF INTERNATIONAL CRISIS, 1904–1914

Shortly after the twentieth century began, the swelling of the democratic movement and the intensification of foreign dangers broke down the boundaries separating foreign from domestic questions and merged them into one problematic complex. The mass force of the movement for democratic reform in modern Germany was unmistakably felt at last in the elections of 1903, when the SPD won eighty-one seats in the Reichstag. One of every three ballots was marked for the Social Democratic party, while another 10 percent of the electorate voted for one of the several left-liberal factions. With more than three million votes, the SPD's popular support surpassed by more than one million that given to any other political party. Up to that time Bismarck's successors had been able to excuse their failure to sponsor constitutional reform by pointing to the relatively weak demand for change among the German people; but public apathy could no longer be an alibi.

Imperial Germany's precarious eminence in world affairs also rendered domestic reform more urgent than before. The Franco-Russian alliance of 1895 had been disturbing, but it was counterbalanced by Germany's Triple Alliance, which had provoked it. However, when Britain drew near to France in the Entente Cordiale of 1904 and to Russia in 1907, Germany and her allies faced a potential bloc of superior strength, and the public interest began to dictate measures of domestic reform to bolster national solidarity. Yet throughout the ensuing critical decade the empire witnessed no systematic effort along those lines. The decisive tragedy of imperial Germany's last peaceful decade undoubtedly remains her passivity in July 1914 when history thrust upon her government the opportunity to arbitrate between war and peace. At the same time, the indifference of Prussian and imperial leadership to the rising demands for political change at home looms as a comparable misfortune.

After 1903, German conservatives continued to oppose democratic reform on grounds of "state interest" (approximately what Americans after 1945 called "national security"). Many opponents of governmental and social transformation contended and seriously believed that the growing vote for Social Democracy was proof that the lower classes were incapable of self-government. Prussia's three-class suffrage system was defended by patriots as a vital counterweight to the radicalism of the Reichstag. The continued allegiance of Social Democracy to revolutionary Marxist slogans confirmed many middle-class Germans in the prevailing view that the SPD placed material class interests above those of the nation. Some conservatives sincerely feared, therefore, that genuine parliamentary government would place Germany under the control of men who would betray her. Others, anticipating correctly that the democratic left would restrict their traditional economic and class privileges, invoked the national interest to promote their continued well-being.

The vested interests of kaiser and cabinet, of course, were served by whatever strengthened the state. For the imperial government, historical experience counselled a new revolution from above. Frederick the Great had prepared the Prussian state for the strains of the Seven Years' War by his reforms as an enlightened despot. Success against Napoleon had been prepared by Stein's unprecedented unleashing of popular enthusiasm. Not blood and iron alone, but the Prussian constitution of 1850 and the revolutionary expedient of equal suffrage in the North German Confederation had hastened the unification of Germany.

As heirs of these precedents German leaders could justify rejection of the new demand for democratic reform only if one of two conditions prevailed. If they were not bent upon expanding German economic and political power in Europe and abroad, they might afford the debilitating luxury of widespread and growing discontent at home. Second, if an expanding Germany faced no neighboring rivals anxious to limit or even diminish German power, its leaders might hold in check a people whose majority chafed under the restriction of second-class citizenship. Between 1904 and 1914 the empire enjoyed neither of these conditions.

But Germany did possess a chancellor who of all incumbents of that difficult office since Bismarck promised to maneuver most successfully between a kaiser whose morbid penchant for quick, thoughtless decision placed government before a succession of distasteful faits accomplis, a Reichstag in which the ideologically divided Catholic Center formed the indispensable core of every majority, a Prussian Landtag dominated by the two conservative parties, and an electorate almost evenly divided between supporters and opponents of his government. Born in 1849, the son of Bernhard Ernst von Bülow, Bismarck's secretary of state for foreign affairs from 1873 to 1878, young Bernhard was an experienced diplomat, having served at Rome, St. Petersburg, Vienna, Paris, and Bucharest, and capped his career with three years (1897–1900) in the position held by his father. In 1886 he had married Maria Beccadelli di Bologna, Principessa di Camporeale, the stepdaughter of Italy's former premier, Marco Minghetti. A man of urbane charm, intelligent, tolerant, well-read, he was equally free from illusions and from firm convictions. He conformed closely to Eulenburg's model of a government leader, being "neither conservative nor liberal, neither ultramontane nor progressive, neither ritualist, nor atheist."

Bülow aroused great expectations, despite his inexperience in domestic affairs. As early as 1895, William II had touted him as "my Bismarck" with whom he would "clean up the filth of parliamentary and party machinery." The Bavarian plenipotentiary to the Federal Council, Hugo von Lerchenfeld-Köfering, praised the chancellor to his own new minister-president, Klemens von Podewils, as the first of Bismarck's successors to master Reich and Prussian affairs as Germany's founding father had, and as a man moderate in his objectives, conciliatory but firm and intelligent in his actions. The new government leader's conception and management of the Tariff Act of 1902 went far toward reconciling agrarian and industrial interests, divided since Caprivi's chancellorship. The act's passage appeared to confirm the kaiser's high expectations as it would place a stable majority coalition of Conservatives and National Liberals in charge of German parliamentary politics.

Over a long view, however, Bülow's personal assets and liabilities portended the continuation of conservative policies associated with the undistinguished stewardship of his predecessor Hohenlohe. His administration displayed merely a greater capacity to roll with the punches delivered by the expanding phalanx of his adversaries, and it survived by maneuver instead of leadership. While Bülow, never harried by excessive self-doubt, took pride in his "natural elasticity," contemporaries labeled him the "rubber chancellor." Albert Ballin, the managing director of the Hamburg-American shipping line, feared that it was not the chancellor's Bismarckian stature, but his capacity for "completely spoiling the Kaiser" by "constantly telling him the grossest flatteries" that kept him in office. Year after year the emperor trusted the handsome, articulate cajoler as did the greatest part of the educated classes and the middle class whose courtship took up much of Bülow's time when he was not truckling to his sovereign's fragile vanity. Satisfying petty interests on all sides, the diplomatic *routinier* lacked any creative drive as a policy maker. It was characteristic of him that the one parliamentary reform associated with his administration provided salaries and free travel to members of the Reichstag, a transparent attempt to purchase their support. Convinced that the German people were far from ready to govern themselves, he rejected genuine constitutional change.[1]

Throughout all but the last year of Bülow's chancellorship, events seemed to confirm, if not his opinion of the German nation's low level of political maturity, at least the practicality of his general policies. Despite the electoral results of 1903 his popularity remained high. Thus fortified, his government faced down two major challenges, the first emanating from the revolution in Russia, the second, in 1907, from the uprising of the Herero tribes in German Southwest Africa.

It has been observed in an earlier chapter that Russia's upheavals in 1905 had not prompted German Social Democracy to adopt more aggressive revolutionary programs. Even the party's left wing viewed the demonstrations in St. Petersburg as an example of working-class capacity to extract concessions from tyranny rather than as a model for present or future action. The influence of refugees from the Russian Empire, like Rosa Luxemburg and Alexander Helphand, generated in the SPD no more than a warm sympathetic interest in the fate of the Russian movement. The numerous demonstrations, thirty-one in Berlin alone, on the German labor movement's observance of the first anniversary of the Russian uprisings, advocated reform of the Prussian suffrage system, not social revolution.

Accordingly, both Reich and Prussian governments decided to allow these activities to proceed. The Prussian minister of the interior believed that the SPD would always work within the law, and Minister of War Karl von Einem doubted that the workers were disposed to imitate their Russian brothers. Bülow and his deputy Arthur von Posadowsky wanted to avoid all actions that would endow Social Democracy with the halo of martyrdom. The kaiser, to be sure, in a letter to his chancellor written at the end of 1905, complained that he could not afford to send a single soldier out of the country "without putting into the most extreme jeopardy life and property of its citizens." Before dealing with her enemies abroad, therefore, he advised that Germany "first shoot down, behead or [otherwise] render harmless the socialists . . . if necessary by a blood bath." But this epistle merely constituted an especially strident illustration of the difference between imperial words—forever militant— and imperial actions—forever dilatory. Actually the one determined foe of socialism at the highest level remained Admiral Alfred von Tirpitz, who did not advocate shooting all Social Democrats, but dissolving the Reichstag and calling new elections, which he expected would return a majority favoring new special antisocialist legislation, and, incidentally, grant him a long-range commitment to naval expansion. As the kaiser, meanwhile, did not insist on drowning socialism in its own blood, posterity might do better to judge him by his speech from the throne (delivered five weeks before his raging New Year's Eve letter to Bülow) in which he called for further social legislation as "the main duty of the Reich."[2]

Since his position seemed secure Bülow could ignore both the emperor's impulsive call for an antisocialist St. Bartholomew's massacre, and Tirpitz's summons to a new election. His executive independence was limited only by the growing centrifugal forces within both the National Liberal and the Center parties, mainstays of the government majority in the Reichstag. The Reich Association of Young National Liberals increased its influence in high party councils and pressed for increased cooperation with left-liberals and even, on occasion, the SPD. At the same time the Center left wing, led by Matthias Erzberger, turned in 1906 against Germany's colonial policy, forcing the chancellor to solicit left-liberal votes in support of imperialist measures.

In order to attract Progressive backing Bülow was at last compelled to yield some ground to the reform forces. He began with token changes in the Prussian electoral law. The measure he offered did not modify the three-class system, but increased by ten the total number of deputies elected from urban districts. Even the conservatives approved this modest alteration, and the bill became law at the end of May 1906. This trifling concession gained the Social Democrats seven seats in the Prussian lower house in the ensuing elections, but did not appease the advocates of democratic suffrage. It merely provided another specimen of Bülow's conception of public policy; whenever pressures threatened to overwhelm the government, its leader bent a little, but as he boasted in his memoirs, "During my long term of office, [I] had . . . no difficulty whatever in rejecting all proposals [of reapportionment] from the outset."[3]

Before the end of 1906 other events forced the chancellor to continue on the course of further reform or to accept a showdown. When during that year open war broke out in southwest Africa between imperial forces and the native Hereros, the left wing of the Center party joined the Reichstag opposition. In December liberal Catholics and the SPD, usually at loggerheads, joined to defeat supplementary appropriations for the colonial war. Determined to have the money, to teach both of Bismarck's old foes a lesson in patriotism, and perhaps to divert the public interest in domestic reform, Bülow now took Tirpitz's advice, dissolved parliament, and launched an electoral campaign with devotion to flag and country as the government's single issue. The Center was attacked as it had not been since the *Kulturkampf*. Nor did Bülow spare the Social Democrats. He enlisted the state governments in the battle against party socialism as well as federal agencies such as the navy and the colonial and post office departments. Private lobbies also joined the crusade. In Berlin the Imperial Union for Combating Social Democracy, founded in 1904 to unite "all Germans regardless of religious and political distinctions . . . [for] Kaiser and Reich," mobilized its 144,000 members. The union's printing presses distributed millions of leaflets warning the nation that "revolutionary. . . Social-Democracy ranges itself with Hottentots and Hereros against its own motherland." The "yellow" (nationalist) labor unions urged members in Catholic Bavaria to reject candidates presented by antipatriotic socialism and Centrism. A National-Liberal pamphlet, circulated in East Prussia, pleaded with voters "to throw out the Poles and destroy Social Democracy."

As a result of such efforts the rapid rise of the SPD (which had begun in 1887) was suddenly checked and the party suffered a setback in the elections held on January 25, 1907. Its share of the popular vote declined only slightly, from 31.7 to 29 percent, and remained the largest in the country. But because no other parties supported its candidates in the runoffs, its Reichstag contingent shrank from 81 to 43, falling behind the Progressives, as well as National Liberals and Conservatives. The Center party seemed to have held its own; it won 105 seats, as compared to 100 four years earlier, and its popular vote declined only from 19.7 to 19.4 percent. But the experience of 1907 heightened a sense of vulnerability among its leadership, which for the next ten years faithfully echoed government policy and silenced within its ranks the voices of Erzberger and his liberal following.[4]

Once more Bülow had finagled a victory. The parties of reform had been contained by minor concessions and then skillfully discredited. Socialist parliamentary opposition had been reduced, the Center brought back into the government coalition, left-liberal imperialism enlisted to support the campaign against democratic government, while Conservatives and National Liberals had scored palpable gains. But the chancellor was to be granted little time in which to savor his triumph. During the spring of 1907, Maximilian Harden's journal *Die Zukunft* began publication of a series of attacks against Prince Philipp von Eulenburg, a close friend and confidant of the kaiser, accusing him of abetting the monarch's autocratic tendencies and revealing in sensational detail evidence of his homosexual predilections. (Some information concerning the favorite's indiscretions on the latter account appear to have been leaked to the magazine by Bülow himself.) Many individuals in all camps took the stories at face value; courtiers and officers at once avoided the accused lest they be tarnished with the same brush of perversion. In May the crown prince brought the case to his father's attention, and the kaiser ordered Eulenburg to take steps to clear his name. When he failed to make such a move, and when one of his rumored consorts lost a libel suit against Harden because the judge ruled that the editor of *Die Zukunft* had proved his allegations, the stain spread. The kaiser now rallied to his friend, a second trial sentenced Harden to four months in jail, but the tough journalist succeeded in shifting the case to a Bavarian court at the bar of which a fisherman and a former valet recounted personal experiences which confirmed Eulenburg's homosexuality. In May 1908, the former imperial intimate was arrested and indicted for perjury. His physician confined him to bed, and the unsavory litigation dragged on for another year before Prince Philipp at last appeared before a judge, but the trial had to be suspended when the accused collapsed after an hour of testimony. (When Eulenburg died in 1921 his guilt had still not been established, nor his reputation restored.) Meanwhile, his associate, General Kuno von Moltke, won a third libel action against Harden, but when the latter threatened another appeal, the government quietly paid his fine and the court cost in return for his agreement to pursue the matter no further. The scandal at last disappeared from the judicial calendar as well as from the pages of the daily press. Its most important historic result was the wave of unrestrained criticism of the kaiser's government which it unleashed and the resultant damage to the prestige of monarchic institutions.[5]

The Eulenburg affair, therefore, exacted not only financial but also political sacrifices from the government. In 1906, Bülow certainly had not intended to pay more than a nominal price for

Progressive support in parliament. After his vindication by the elections of 1907 he continued to argue that the German nation was not seriously interested in Prussian suffrage reform. But by the following year Social Democratic and Progressive pressure had been revived by the invigorating currents of the Eulenburg scandal, and the "rubber chancellor" grew more conciliatory. On April 19 the Reichstag enacted a new government-sponsored Association Law which was viewed as a considerable step forward even by the Social Democrats. This legislation inaugurated a *federal* civil right of association across state boundaries and invalidated all state-sponsored restrictions on that civic prerogative. At the same time the government retained substantial functions of surveillance: political meetings had to be registered with the police twenty-four hours in advance, the use of any language other than German was prohibited, and juveniles under eighteen continued to be denied the right to join political organizations. Social Democrats, Progressives, and some Centrists assailed these restrictions and voted against the bill, but a socialist historian later admitted that the measure came as a boon to party activity, ranking in importance with the cancellation in 1890 of Bismarck's antisocialist legislation.[6]

Next Bülow sought to paper over the resurgence of disagreements in the government bloc on suffrage reform, notably between Center and Progressives. At his suggestion William II's opening speech to the newly elected Prussian Chamber of Deputies on October 20, 1908, came close to echoing Friedrich Naumann without specifically promising a democratic franchise. The address vaguely favored "an organic development" of the Prussian election code to meet "economic development, the spread of education and patriotism, as well as the strengthening of the sense of responsibility to the state." This *Thronrede* was too general to win the support of democratic reformers, but it upset the Conservatives.[7]

This Prussian-based party of established privilege already had many causes for anger at Bülow in October 1908. Outraged by the Eulenburg affair, its members had been even more incensed by a tax proposal outlined in the semiofficial press in late September. The measure proposed a levy on all inherited property worth more than twenty thousand marks. By mid-October 1908,

Conservatives began to rally against this "death duty," condemning it as a political kowtow before the Progressives.[8] The Bülow-inspired *Thronrede* of October 20 had added to the ferment of issues. There were growing signs of a reform crisis in Germany when suddenly, eight days later, the *Daily Telegraph* crisis broke. In the public outcry over the latest follies of Kaiser William II, which temporarily overshadowed the suffrage and tax issues, Bülow momentarily gained a new lease on political life.

The passion engendered by the *Daily Telegraph* incident can be understood only against the background of the Eulenburg scandal, Bülow's proposed tax policy, SPD and Progressive pressure for reform, and the promise of suffrage revision in the speech from the throne of October 20. On the other hand, these domestic landmarks alone do not explain it all. Their significance was now enhanced by an episode which highlighted failures of foreign policy.

Public anxieties over Germany's international position had been mounting for several years, and the public airing of the kaiser's foolish indiscretions only brought them into the open. When Bülow took over at the Wilhelmstrasse in 1897, France and Russia had already achieved what Bismarck had feared but managed to forestall—an alliance countering his own masterful alignments. In 1893 czardom and the Third Republic had concluded a binding military accord which would end only with Lenin's seizure of power. This rapprochement, however, did not lessen the partners' alarm at the growth of German influence in Turkey. The German penetration of the Middle East aroused even greater concern in England, whose interests had been predominant there. The British and the Russians were equally disturbed by German colonial expansion in the Far East after the Sino-Japanese War (1894–95). Still more disconcerting to the former was the rapid growth of a German navy after 1898. Commercial rivalry and the recklessly belligerent speeches of the kaiser only aggravated the mounting tensions. The British Foreign Office's "gray eminence," Sir Eyre Crowe, whose mother and wife were German, became the most influential spokesman of a growing grave distrust of the German system of government which placed no check on avowedly aggressive preferences of the monarchic establishment. By 1904, Germany's multiple thrusts on three continents had laid the foundation for a fateful "diplomatic revolution" in Europe. England and France, previously arch rivals, began a close collaboration. The Entente Cordiale, concluded that year, was at first no more than a friendly understanding, not an alliance, but its basic purpose was to coordinate resistance against the assertive policies of their powerful neighbor to the east. Bülow, Holstein, and the kaiser determined in 1905 to break this entente, but their challenge of the French advance into Morocco only tightened it. Meanwhile, the pressure of Germany in the Middle East made it seem that England and Russia could no longer afford the unrestrained rivalry that had embroiled them in that theater since the 1820's. In 1907, acting in part on the premise that it was better for them to share domination of Persia than to face Germany on the Persian Gulf, Petersburg and London in turn converted hostility into cautious partnership. The Triple Entente was thus complete. Great Britain modified her policy of isolation, which had been punctuated in the past by short-range wartime commitments to one European bloc or another. Now she became in time of peace a full-fledged participant in the mainland alliance structure.

Fears of German aggressiveness had produced the entente that heightened anxieties in Berlin. Germany was not encircled by enemies who lay in wait for a favorable moment to attack her, but by 1908 fears of such encirclement were at an all-time high in the capital. Nor was the southeast reassuring, where Austria-Hungary had proved an unqualified liability as an ally. Germany's alienation from Russia in the 1890's had derived from Berlin's bows to Vienna, but now Austria was less ready to confront future crises. The Danubian ally spent less for arms than any other European great power and produced fewer of the sinews of war—less steel for instance—than any of her primary rivals. Yet Austria-Hungary followed a militant foreign policy in the Balkans, even threatening to involve herself in a war with Russia; and Germany under Bülow encouraged her. On October 5, 1908, the Habsburg monarchy precipitated a new international crisis by announcing the annexation of Bosnia and Herzegovina, provinces still claimed by Turkey and coveted by

Russia's protegé Serbia. The month before, a second Moroccan crisis had developed, and on October 30, Bülow warned France of the seriousness of the situation in northwest Africa. The combined domestic and foreign policy issues clearly meant trouble for the chancellor.[9]

In this setting, filled with domestic and international tension, Germans read the London *Daily Telegraph*'s famed "interview" with their kaiser published on October 28. The monarch's statements momentarily threatened completely to disrupt Anglo-German relations. They came, Bülow later recalled, like a "sudden slap in the face," arousing the entire nation to a sudden awareness of twenty years of political mismanagement.[10] The kaiser's folly was especially disturbing to those many conservative Germans who considered good relations with Britain the major antidote to their own diplomatic "encirclement." It shocked even more deeply many anglophile Germans who had long supported constitutional reforms. Grievances over foreign and domestic policies thus merged almost completely in November 1908 under circumstances more favorable for the attainment of parliamentary government than any that had existed since 1848.

In view of its disturbing effect upon Anglo-German relations, the most ironic feature of the *Daily Telegraph* crisis was its origin: it grew out of the kaiser's own attempts to convince the English that he was John Bull's true friend. In an "interview"—actually not a question and answer session but merely a policy statement— to be published in the prominent London newspaper, William II claimed that he and his general staff had worked out the winning campaign plan that the British had used in the Boer War of 1899–1902. Nothing could have been more insulting to the English public than this remarkably condescending appeal to its friendship. The kaiser's foolishness was made worse by his assertions that he could be counted upon to restrain Germany's allegedly anglophobe public opinion.

Such pronouncements were surely deplorable, but the kaiser had not sinned alone. Before publication William II sent a draft of his statement to Bülow. The chancellor, vacationing at the time, carelessly forwarded it to the Foreign Office for advice and early return, certainly a cavalier manner in which to handle proposed comments by an indiscreet emperor. After the diplomats had scanned it with equal superficiality the draft again passed through Bülow's hands, doubling his personal responsibility, and reached the kaiser with only minor suggestions for change. When the interview appeared, the words attributed to William II seemed so amazing that many Germans questioned its authenticity. All doubts—and hopes—were dispelled, however, when the semiofficial *Norddeutsche Allgemeine Zeitung* on October 31 admitted that the text was genuine and that the chancellor himself had seen—but not read—the draft. Bülow's excuse seemed lame and ungallant in 1908, and the passing years have failed to revise that impression. But the October 31 announcement also indicated that his offer to resign had not been accepted by the kaiser, and public outrage thenceforth concentrated on William II.[11]

The governments of the federal states shared in the public alarm. The Bundesrat's committee on foreign affairs assembled in Berlin, and members urged that the emperor should learn to control his words. To ward off formal joint representations by the federal princes, Bülow assumed full responsibility for persuading William II to behave henceforth in a "more seemly fashion." The staid Prussian council of ministers even contemplated advocating greater restraints on the emperor "in the interests—nay, it might even be for the salvation—of the Prussian Crown."

Conservatives joined in the general criticism, despite the efforts of some of their leaders to preserve a unanimous stance in support of the emperor. In the Reichstag they adopted a declaration on November 5 urging the kaiser to be moderate in his future public comments, thinking probably as much of the *Thronrede* of October 20 as of the *Daily Telegraph* interview. But the party of the landed aristocracy was not willing to support any parliamentary limitation of the powers of the monarch. Neither were the Centrists; anxious to reestablish themselves as a loyal party and to break the liberal-Conservative bloc, they acted with more restraint than any other party during the crisis. One of their chief spokesmen, Count Georg von Hertling, openly deplored the public debate of the kaiser's shortcomings.[12]

The National Liberals revealed again the limits of their "liber-

alism" during the November furore. Characteristically, they
sought to preserve liberal appearances while acting in a firmly
conservative manner. When the Reichstag debate over the affair
finally opened, their leader Ernst Bassermann led the oratorical
attack against the vagaries of "personal government." But he
was firing blank bullets. The National Liberals in the Reichstag
agreed that the honor of the empire must be salvaged and that
respect for the monarchy must not be endangered. Their subsequent interpellation, formulated with great foresight, merely
asked if the chancellor was prepared to take responsibility for
the kaiser's expressions as published in the *Daily Telegraph*. It
did not hint at the desirability of significant political change, and
Bassermann on November 10 explicitly disavowed interest in
ministerial responsibility.[13]

The crisis confronted the Progressives with a supreme test.
They had cast their lot with the Bülow government in the expectation of reforms and had been disappointed. Could they
continue to support such a government after the revelation of
imperial irresponsibility and ministerial carelessness? Max Weber
and Friedrich Naumann were prepared to make radical demands. Naumann advocated that the Progressives in the Reichstag propose a bill decreeing joint responsibility of the chancellor
to the Reichstag and to the Bundesrat. The measure would also
require that imperial selection of future chancellors follow formal
discussion of candidates with the standing committees of both
chambers. Some south Germans, such as Müller-Meiningen
and Payer, seconded Naumann's proposals, but they were voted
down in their own party caucus. Progressive Reichstag deputy
Otto Wiemer revealed why, when he spoke of the need for
ministerial responsibility, but added that he and his colleagues
did not want "this question to become a test of power between
crown and parliament." Another Progressive leader told the
Reichstag: "We want no parliamentary regime for the simple
reason that it is not possible as long as the constitution of the
German Empire exists." Ministerial responsibility, he added,
could not be reconciled with the powers of the Bundesrat.[14] The
Progressives continued, therefore, to support the Bülow government, partly because they still hoped for reform, partly because
the only alternative—while the Bülow coalition yet lived—would

be an alliance with the SPD. At the same time Max Weber's despairing judgment that imperial dilletantism would eventually become the major obstacle to Germany's world role failed to influence even the most aggressive left-liberals during the *Daily Telegraph* crisis.[15]

This episode clearly revealed the weakness of the bourgeois parties and the lack of firm will in the prewar Reichstag to favor effective representative government. Only the SPD really wanted a parliamentary state, and even its members exercised great restraint and displayed little inclination to exploit their emperor's revealed nakedness. Social Democratic speakers did not call for abdication as many bourgeois opponents expected them to. Even Georg Ledebour's proposal for a party proclamation to the people, castigating the kaiser's personal regime was ultimately rejected by the Reichstag *Fraktion*.[16] In short, the parties were angry but not ready to translate indignation into a program. Bülow, the second culprit, remained in command of the situation. He made the crisis seem even more exclusively the fault of the kaiser than it had originally appeared. The oily chancellor told the Reichstag on November 10 that the emperor realized the unfortunate effect of his words and would henceforth maintain greater reserve. Then he added his famous hint that he would assume personal responsibility for William II's future good behavior, but with the qualification that neither he nor any successor could accept the responsibility of office unless the kaiser lived up to his promise of oratorical self-discipline. This seemed to satisfy the Reichstag, proving again that it was easily satisfied.

The kaiser emerged hurt, but unreconstructed. He promised to respect his constitutional obligations in the future—a vague undertaking in view of the uncertainty as to how he defined such a commitment. Maximilian Harden saw through the contrite pose when he wrote in mid-November to Friedrich von Holstein, with characteristic ruthless clarity: "I no longer have any confidence in promises . . . this monarch will *never* change." Even as Germany's premier muckraker was venting his unbounded pessimism, the object of his skepticism was consoling himself hunting near Donaueschingen on the Fürstenberg estates. On November 15 the German nation learned that this excursion had been marred by the sudden death from a heart attack of the imperial chief military aide General Dietrich von Hülsen-Haeseler, who was stricken while dancing in a ballet costume (shades of Eulenburg!), a divertissement designed to restore the emperor's flagging spirits.[17] But even this embarrassing and degrading tragedy failed to extract from imperial Germany's greatest peacetime domestic crisis a threat to the authority of a single *Amtmann*, nor did it change a comma in a constitution that needed reform rather than respect. The *Daily Telegraph* affair did, however, alienate William II from his favorite chancellor and aggravated the political and institutional isolation and irresponsibility of the monarch. More than ever after 1908 his decisions were formulated in the remote and autocratic sanctuaries occupied by his civil and military personal staffs.[18]

But there remained the question of suffrage reform that had been promised in the *Thronrede* of October 20. The Progressives in January and February of 1909 once again pressed for a far-reaching reform of the voting system as a means of deflating the Social Democrats. But their Conservative "allies" in the Bülow bloc opposed anything of the sort. The National Liberals favored secret and direct balloting and a redistricting of representation, but persisted in rejecting equal voting rights. Only the Center stood with the bourgeois left on secret and direct suffrage, but its joint votes fell short of victory in a close vote, 165 to 168. When Progressive leaders the following month sought Bülow's promise to bring in a new reform bill with full government support, they were told that it must wait. This fulfilled Max Weber's gloomy prediction of November 5, 1908, that no new electoral law was to be expected and that the coalition of the Progressives with the National Liberals and Conservatives had lost its justification. Domestic developments in the spring of 1909 gave no new promise of peaceful reform in Prussia. By June, Karl Liebknecht was greeted only with repeated outbursts of laughter as he tried to impress upon the Prussian Chamber of Deputies the serious need for a classless suffrage bill.[19]

Slight though it was, Bülow's support for minor reforms of the suffrage system now, by the spring of 1909, made the Conservatives anxious to bring him down, and his continuing sponsorship of financial reforms only increased their determination.

The artful dodger of the Wilhelmstrasse tried hard to sweeten the pill of the graduated, federal inheritance tax by pointing out that four-fifths of the five hundred million marks in increased revenue he sought would be paid by average citizens in the form of excise taxes on utilities, such as electricity, and on staples, such as beer. He finally overplayed his hand when he threatened to resign if the Reichstag failed to pass the tax measure. The Conservatives considered this anything but a threat and remained adamant in their opposition. This gave the Center party, especially its agrarian leaders, the chance it had awaited to break the Bülow bloc and regain the good graces of the kaiser. A majority combination of Conservatives and Catholics defeated the government proposal on June 24, 1909, by a mere eight votes (194 to 186). So determined were the Conservatives to kill the inheritance tax proposal that they accepted support on the issue from Polish, Danish, and Alsatian minority representatives —men they usually scorned as unpatriotic—in order to carry the motion. The kaiser, outraged by parliamentary defiance of "his" government at first, declared his readiness to impose the tax bill which he believed was favored by a majority of his subjects. But Bülow, true to his public promise, offered his resignation, and the kaiser, always less belligerent than his words implied, accepted both defeat and fall of the cabinet.

The departure of the wily improviser over an issue in which his support came from National Liberals, Progressives, and Social Democrats garnered him an undeserved popularity that lasted on into World War I. Bülow retired in response to a parliamentary defeat suffered not long after winning an overwhelming victory in a federal election. In that respect 1909 constituted a replay of 1890. The kaiser's secondary role in this overturning of a government seemed to indicate a shift in the domestic balance of strength in the Reichstag's favor. Bülow counted on a return to power with the help of liberal and democratic forces and in his memoirs strongly suggested that he would have "brought the proletariat into full, harmonious political equality" if he had remained "at the helm a few years longer," thus avoiding the November 1918 revolution.[20] But the actual facts of his nine-year record as chancellor offer no evidence to sustain this claim. In any case, his fall constituted no substantial advance toward parliamentary government. To make it clear that he was not bowing to the parliamentary majority in dismissing Bülow, the kaiser named the new chancellor without consultation with Reichstag or party leaders. What happened in Germany in July 1909 gave every indication that "constitutionalism had not yet become parliamentarism."[21]

Bülow's successor, Theobald von Bethmann-Hollweg, assumed office on July 14, 1909, and remained imperial chancellor for eight years to the day. Arthur Rosenberg's harsh verdict on his stewardship has been accepted by many critics of the Wilhelmian era: "The severest charge that can be brought against the *ancien régime* in Germany is that such a man . . . was Imperial Chancellor in July 1914."[22] A contemporary Progressive assessment gave a more ambiguous verdict, concluding that Bethmann "was the best of all ministers who led their nation on the road to ruin."[23]

Bethmann was the grandson of a prominent Protestant political leader and Prussian minister of education of Frederick William IV's declining years. The family had made its money in Frankfurt's most prestigious private bank, but the future chancellor was born and raised on his father's estate of Hohenfinow in Brandenburg. He studied law and then chose an administrative career which he pursued with dazzling success. At twenty-nine he was a *Landrat*; in 1899 he became *Regierungspräsident*, and later in the same year provincial governor of Brandenburg, the youngest incumbent of such high office in Prussia at the time. In 1901 he declined the post of Prussian minister of the interior, but accepted when it was offered again four years later. Knowledgeable observers then began touting him as a future chancellor.

From 1905 to 1909, Bethmann-Hollweg worked at the center of domestic political controversy. His "reforming conservatism" spawned Prussia's small reapportionment in favor of urban constituencies, which antagonized Conservatives and left-liberals alike. The measure indicated what electoral reforms could be expected from a statesman who had lost confidence in the Prussian system, but who could not accept the universal manhood suffrage laws governing Reichstag elections. Yet at this point Bethmann-Hollweg's isolation from all major parties failed to slow his career. Following the elections of 1907 the more reformist Vice-Chancellor Posadowsky resigned and Bethmann-Hollweg succeeded him. In his new post he contributed the Association Law of 1908 and insisted that the promise of electoral reform be added to the speech from the throne of October 20. After Bülow's resignation the vice-chancellor worked out a compromise tax bill that dropped the death duties but lengthened the catalog of federal excise taxes and added imposts on dividends. Bethmann had become the Lykurgus of Wilhelmian compromise, while his emperor searched with flailing desperation for a successor other than this dutiful civil servant who, as William complained to his cabinet chief, "is always lecturing and pretends to know everything better." Four weeks passed before the kaiser reluctantly elevated the peerless administrator to the chancellorship.

Bethmann-Hollweg accepted this promotion as reluctantly as he had every elevation since his days as a *Landrat*. To an old friend, the Prussian minister in Karlsruhe, Karl von Eisendecher, he wrote: "Only a genius or a man driven by ambition and lust for power can covet this post. And I am neither." Yet the years ahead would exact precisely the kind of drive and creative ability which the new chancellor confessed to be lacking. Bülow's replacement was to constitute a kind of final opportunity for the empire. No one in 1909 greeted Bethmann's nomination with jubilation or rejected it with horror. Conservatives viewed him with more favor than the record might seem to justify; the SPD agreed that his appointment to the highest government post constituted a Conservative victory. Friedrich Naumann, overrating the strength of Bethmann's liberal impulses, welcomed his succession, while National Liberals more realistically viewed it with glum indifference. A courtier offered the most penetrating judgment when he explained Bethmann's choice for the chancellorship as an indication that "the Emperor wants to rule himself."

A variety of observers recognized that the new chancellor's handicaps derived from his positive qualities of character. The Lübeck representative in the Federal Council credited him with a strong sense of duty and a lack both of self-righteous rigidity and of tenacity in the pursuit of policy goals. James W. Gerard, the United States ambassador from 1913 to 1917, remembered

Bethmann as a likeable man who had "none of the military class' singlemindedness and inflexibility" and "nothing of the German habit of trying to overwhelm one with his personality." Albert Ballin noted sympathetically that he possessed "all the qualities which honor the man but ruin the statesman."[24]

The imperial system of government under William II evidently would not allow an independent and strong personality of decided views to become chancellor in 1909. The kaiser wanted above all a loyal servant who would bow before the royal will. Bülow had proved an unreliable tool. Bethmann, on the other hand, turned out to be more pliable; he might offer advice, but he never directly opposed the monarch. Bülow's fate had reinforced the lesson presented by Bismarck's fall that no chancellor survived without the support of William II, Bethmann knew that should he fall from favor, others stood ready to take his place, among them such powerful rivals as Admiral Tirpitz. Before long, therefore, the last Hohenzollern ruler was talking almost as freely as he had before the *Daily Telegraph* affair, boasting that he was an instrument of divine providence and therefore not responsible to the nation.

The political situation Bethmann inherited also limited his freedom of action. The Progressives turned from him because their hopes of reform from above had been disappointed repeatedly, and the Conservatives were aroused to a pitch of unprecedented vigilance by his predecessor's attempt to tax their wealth. The latest internal upset, however, left the latter and the Center in control of the Reichstag. The two parties constituting Bethmann's majority worked together much more easily than did the defunct Bülow bloc because the vulnerable Catholic partner in the new coalition had no other wish than to repair political fortunes damaged by the unsuccessful 1907 campaign against colonialism. The nature of his parliamentary support reinforced Bethmann's own disposition to shun controversy. Attired as a major in the reserves, he told the Reichstag in his maiden speech as government chief that the people did not want to be disturbed by experiments in domestic or foreign policy. Commenting on the address, the *Kreuzzeitung* observed that nothing in it pleased or angered anyone, from which judgment it was only a short step to the reaction of the *Berliner Tageblatt* which summed up the personality that emerged from the performance as "dry and uninspiring."[25]

The course Bethmann pursued until 1914 was initiated by his attempt to cooperate with the parliamentary majority he found in 1909. He hoped that the resulting partnership could expand into an eventual "Bethmann bloc" of all nonsocialist parties. As had his predecessors, the last prewar chancellor viewed the SPD as an "un-German" party, and like them he would leave the chamber when a socialist rose to speak. Yet he hoped to make the prevalent majority responsive to the needs of those segments of the population which he, too, wanted to immunize against socialist appeals. He continued Bülow's effort to obtain conservative acceptance of some taxation of agrarian property, and he favored Germany's slow but steady expansion of social legislation. In the first issue he failed. Even the appeals of national interest would not move the self-appointed guardians of patriotism on the right. In 1913 he was forced to meet a defense budget, which had risen from 1.3 to 2.1 billion marks since his accession, by a new income tax, and for that measure's passage he was forced to accept Social Democratic votes. In the second sphere, however, Bethmann-Hollweg's government could point to a number of achievements. In the mining industry a law drafted and passed in 1905 on the heels of a massive strike and providing for worker committees to negotiate with management on hours and working conditions was expanded in 1909 to include worker participation on safety boards. The extension of sickness benefits from thirteen to twenty-six weeks during the Posadowsky era was overshadowed by the Reich Insurance Law of 1911, drafted by Bethmann's new interior minister Clemens Delbrück. It extended sickness insurance to agricultural and domestic workers and made survivors eligible to receive a deceased breadwinner's workman's compensation and old age benefits. A supplementary bill extended all existing social legislation to white-collar workers.[26]

Reform of Prussia's three-class suffrage remained Bethmann's most critical challenge as well as opportunity in his search for a broader parliamentary majority. Before a Bethmann bloc could coalesce, Prussia must be freed from the stranglehold exercised by the Conservatives in the Chamber of Deputies. Once that was accomplished the new chancellor hoped to persuade National Liberals to join a government coalition in the federal as well as the Prussian parliament. Working with an overwhelming majority on both levels would enable him to govern with independence from day-by-day parliamentary vagaries which he often naively described as standing "above the parties." Guided by the limited and imprecise promises of the 1908 imperial address, Bethmann therefore presented to the Prussian chamber a draft bill in February 1910 which proposed that future elections be direct, that the representation of first-class voters be reduced while that of the second and third classes be raised by allowing holders of university diplomas to vote one class above their property status. At the same time the measure introduced plural voting on the basis of age and wealth and—for the first-class constituents—on the basis of educational qualifications.

Some features of the bill satisfied each of the nonsocialist parties, but as a whole it satisfied no one. Conservatives rejected direct elections; the Center deplored the failure to grant the secret ballot. Industrial pressure groups, ranging from moderate conservatives to National Liberals, came closer than any element to supporting the reform, although even they demanded additional plural votes for individuals holding responsible positions in management. The National Liberal leadership, more disabled than usual by a simmering Young Liberal revolt within its ranks, exerted no significant pressure to equalize suffrage or to support the government. Conservatives and Catholics, commanding a majority of roughly 250 of the chamber's 433 seats, finally agreed to back each other's pet provisions. The right would accept the secret ballot and the Center would join them in insisting on the preservation of indirect elections. Thus a majority for a reform bill emerged which rejected the major provision of the government proposal while adding a substantial proviso which the government, in turn, declined to countenance.

It is impossible to estimate what the passage of Bethmann-Hollweg's small package of change would have contributed to Germany's future or to know how such passage could have been assured. There can be no doubt that the chancellor's inept approach to the Prussian parliament killed whatever chance of adoption existed. Though he strongly believed that the controversy over electoral reform must be terminated because it demoralized the public spirit, he did nothing, beyond sermonizing, to lift this political burden from Germany's back. He failed to consult the parties in advance. The voting reform bill was simply handed down from the sacrosanct precincts of the Prussian Ministry of the Interior to the parliamentary committee, with the unequivocal indication that speedy acceptance was expected. After that autocratic procedure, which Conservatives resented as much as did Progressives, no amount of exhortation from monarch or from ministers could rescue the doomed enterprise. Bethmann could find no majority for his bill, and he would accept no amendment that would have assured its passage. The single most constructive proposal—addition of the secret ballot—the chancellor rejected because he thought it undermined civic responsibility. As a result, the chamber once more turned down electoral reform and the government abandoned the cause altogether until 1918.[27]

The net effect of Bethmann's weak attempt at partial concessions was to send Social Democrats into the streets in 1910 in the mightiest demonstrations for equal suffrage that Germany had ever witnessed. They began their mass protests in January, even before Bethmann's "reform" proposals became known. In one day in February forty-two public demonstrations occurred in Berlin. These protests became almost chronic throughout the early months of the year, despite strong-arm police intervention against even peaceful demonstrations; conversely, they only hardened the resolve of the authorities to reject all concessions. The Prussian Chamber of Deputies was unmoved by Liebknecht's revelations of police brutality against the Social Democratic marchers in February 1910. Only with difficulty did Bethmann dissuade William II from decorating forty Berlin policemen for bravery against SPD demonstrators, and on April 15 the kaiser unsuccessfully importuned his chancellor to dismiss the Berlin prefect of police for dereliction of duty because he had licensed some of these SPD parades.

Official hostility did not stay the SPD. On March 6, 150,000 persons assembled in the Tiergarten to demand equal suffrage. In April crowds of 200,000 to 250,000 persons, most of them well dressed, marched in Treptow Park and other parts of Berlin for the same purpose. By April, Rosa Luxemburg was calling insistently for a great general strike for equal suffrage. Union leaders successfully opposed her, and theorists like Kautsky cautioned against violent excesses. Party leaders representing all shades of opinion agreed with Liebknecht that equal suffrage was, from the socialist point of view, "the most burning, pressing, central political question in Germany." So why endanger such unanimity by needless militancy?

Conditions remained troubled throughout the summer. The campaign for universal suffrage augmented the SPD's following. Albert Ballin noted with alarm that "the situation is desperate. . . . In my opinion, we are today in the midst of a great upheaval." The wife of the Württemberg plenipotentiary to the Federal Council agreed that Germany was experiencing a state of latent revolution. Some desperate Conservatives prayed for an early public uprising which would justify total repression, and SPD leaders in 1910 publicized instructions from the commanding general of the VIIth Army Corps for the arrest "of all persons known to be [revolutionary] leaders and agitators, without taking any notice of the immunity of Reichstag members."[28]

A measure of calm seemed to be returning to domestic politics in 1911 as government and opposition began to gird for a more conclusive confrontation of their differences in the Reichstag elections to be held in January of the following year. Bethmann and his secretary of state at the Foreign Office, Alfred von Kiderlen-Wächter, recognized the usefulness of an aggressive foreign policy to divert public opinion from domestic grievances. In 1907, Bülow had capitalized on the colonial issue; now apparent French intentions to strengthen the Third Republic's grip on Morocco promised to provide an equally attractive opportunity to repeat that performance. About three weeks before the French marched into Fez (May 21), Kiderlen proposed seizure of the Atlantic port of Agadir to obtain a pawn to exchange for territorial concessions elsewhere. Germany's senior diplomat viewed this coup as Germany's last opportunity to extend its overseas empire without resorting to war. Failure to stage it would disaffect patriots, while prompt action might help the government in the coming elections. But by the time the gunboat *Panther* anchored at Agadir on July 1, a step sanctioned with great misgivings by a reluctant kaiser, the French had made their move. Nevertheless, at this juncture the projected scenario appeared successful. Germany demanded the French Congo in return for abandoning her interests in Morocco, and the German public—the SPD alone excepted—applauded the maneuver. When Berlin had to compromise its original demands, however, and accept an agreement on November 4, which yielded merely two strips of land connecting the German Cameroons with the Congo and Ubangi rivers, the general dissatisfaction deepened. Press organs of heavy industry and commerce castigated the kaiser's "personal regime" as being responsible for the disappointing results of the second Moroccan encounter. The *Hamburger Nachrichten* editorialized on New Year's Eve that the government had failed to rally a patriotic majority for the coming election. "Germany's position as a rising world power must be maintained with iron dice," the paper thundered. Kaiser and chancellor clearly had lacked the recklessness needed to play for such high stakes; Bethmann-Hollweg confided to his diary the dismay he felt after watching the frivolous unconcern with which a majority of the nation faced the eventuality of war. Yet his own readiness to follow Kiderlen's course displayed an equal and far less excusable irresponsibility.[29]

The African diversion of 1911 had not strengthened the government's hand for the forthcoming contest. A poor harvest in 1911 and higher food prices increased grumbling and, in the cities especially, rallied additional support to the SPD. The situation was tailor-made for a Social Democratic campaign that assailed government tax policy and associated the rising excise burden on the average voter with the rising war danger in the wake of the second Moroccan crisis. At the same time the SPD denied that it sought to overthrow the government, but advocated democratization of government and army, additional social reform, including the eight-hour day, and free trade, especially on imports of fodder and food products. This program once again pointed toward increased collaboration with congenial Progressivism; it appealed to selected National Liberal groups. Jakob Riesser, the leader of the Hansa Bund, an association designed to defend all industrial and commercial interests against agrarian lobbies, was not deterred in his effort to draw the free-trading SPD into "constructive collaboration" by the indignant withdrawal of such industrial representatives as Emil Kirdorf. Signs multiplied that an unalloyed opposition to Social Democracy would continue only among Conservatives and Centrists and such stand-pat pressure groups as the Agrarian and Industrialist Leagues.

Balloting was preceded by a ruthless competition for votes. Parties sought to misrepresent one another's aspirations by issuing forged pamphlets and appeals over the false signatures of opponents. Wholesale attendance at rival meetings and the silencing of speakers by noisy demonstrators, a standard tactic during campaigns of the Weimar era, were "pioneered" in 1912. Conservatives in East Prussia and Catholics in Bavaria would rent all meeting facilities, regardless of need, to assure that they would not be available to socialist and liberal groups. Economic and social sanctions were used to eliminate competitors. Landowners in the Silesian town of Sagan, for instance, induced the resignation of a Progressive mayor by threatening to boycott town merchants. Parties sought to increase their support in crucial districts by a host of ingenious subterfuges. In Leipzig the SPD took surplus voters from safe districts and had them register new and spurious residences in the hitherto National Liberal downtown district. (A watchful police clerk, noting a succession of fifty registration blanks, all completed in the same handwriting, unmasked that scheme.) Progressives, fighting to retain control of Berlin's First District, used students and hotel employees, notoriously mobile elements, to swell the rolls and in the runoff succeeded by a ten-vote margin over the Social Democrats. In Saarbrücken the Center party persuaded three thousand commuting mine workers to change registration from their rural domiciles to the downtown rooming houses that sheltered them during the work week in order to defeat the incumbent National Liberal leader Ernst Bassermann. After they failed to unseat their prominent foe, these shock troops attacked his party's victory parade.

After such epic efforts, 84.9 percent of all eligibles cast votes on January 12, exceeding ever so slightly the record 84.7 percent vote of 1907. This high rate of participation extended uniformly across Germany. Mecklenburg-Schwerin, whose inhabitants could only vote in federal elections, witnessed a record participation of 90.1 percent. Oldenburg, three-quarters of whose inhabitants still lived in communities of less than two thousand, registered the smallest turnout with 76.4 percent. Throughout Germany the quantitative difference between rural and urban voting was negligible, 84.6 percent in the country, 85.2 in cities over one hundred thousand.

The record turnout decided little. Out of a total of 397, an unprecedented 191 districts required runoffs. After the first contest each party, except the SPD, had won fewer seats than at a comparable point in the preceding campaign. While Bebel's party brought home 64 safe seats in 1912 as compared to 29 in 1907, the Progressives at the other extreme remained the only major party unable to translate their popular vote gains into a decisive majority in a single constituency. The second round, however, confirmed a leftward trend. The parties that had consistently supported the government suffered a clear defeat. Although Conservatives and Center took care not to compete in any undecided district, the former won only 35 out of 81, the latter 12 out of 28 runoffs. Liberals, Progressives, and Social Democrats discussed collaboration, but achieved little agreement. SPD support undoubtedly contributed to Bassermann's victory in Saarbrücken, but it presaged no alliance in other areas; socialists of the Saar had simply picked a liberal over a Catholic as the lesser evil. National Liberals won 27 of 42 runoff victories at the expense of the SPD, and 12 against Center and Conservative opposition, while Progressives in turn gained 42 out of 56 contested constituencies, 21 over SPD and 19 against Conservative and Center competition. Clearly the two wings of liberalism also did their best to stay out of one another's fire. Yet National Liberal district organizations remained free to make their own bargains, and this freedom included occasional alliances with Conservative candidates. In southern Germany this stance drove some defectors into Progressive ranks. But by and large, the party of Lasker and Bamberger remained internally divided, and indecision (rather than any crafty opportunism trying to play both ends against the middle) left it short of the 1907 performance.

Despite an identity of policy goals, no demonstratively effective major collaborative effort took shape between Progressives and SPD. In 31 districts left-liberals threw their weight behind the forces of labor, but only 13 out of the 110 elected SPD representatives owed all or part of their victory to such support. On balance, the Progressives, seeking and gaining the vote of disgruntled National Liberals and an occasional Centrist defector, could not risk the loyalty of such new recruits by asking them to vote for a socialist. The SPD, on the other hand, found it easy to support Progressives against Conservatives. Left-liberalism won 19 out of 23 such races, 10 of them with decisive SPD backing. The two parties helped one another where local exigencies left them with no alternative. Quantitatively, Progressives reaped greater benefits, inasmuch as almost one-fourth of their Reichstag delegation had depended on socialist votes, while only slightly more than 10 percent of the large SPD contingent could be said to owe its mandate to Progressive runoff strength. Over the long haul the election results of 1912 portended no respective opening either to the left or to the right.[30]

After all votes had been counted and all contests validated, everyone had lost seats except the SPD. Conservative groups mourned a deficit of thirty-nine despite an increase in the popular vote for the Conservative party. The Center had lost nine representatives and fared worse as a government supporter than it had in opposition. It returned the smallest delegation since 1874. National Liberals gave up thirteen mandates, and Progressives, while increasing their popular vote by close to 20 percent, fell seven seats short of their previous election total. Minorities like the Poles, Alsatians, and Danes, as well as Hanoverian particularists, held their own. The SPD increased its Reichstag contingent by sixty-seven, more than twice its actual 30 percent gain in popular votes. For the first time it was cutting deeply into the Catholic voting bloc, only 54.5 percent of whose members still opted for the Center, while about eight hundred thousand of its working-class constituents had defected to socialist unions. In sum, 4.5 million voters had backed government parties, 7.5 million had cast a ballot for the opposition.

But the clear language of the returns proved deceptive. The elections of 1912 changed little, and Germany's future remained beclouded. The Conservative-Catholic bloc had been shaken but not undermined. Conservative opposition to democracy and parliamentarism had hardened even as it suffered reduction. The *Kreuzzeitung* concluded after the ballots had been counted that Bismarck, in conceding universal manhood suffrage had overestimated the rationalism and patriotism of the German people. In the face of a rising democratic tide the right increased its lobbying for military preparedness, an issue which attracted the support of liberals. (A new organization promoting increased armaments, the Wehrverein, recruited two hundred thousand members within a year and counted Friedrich Meinecke among its charter members.) Pan-Germans entered the lists on behalf of electoral elitism in conjunction with kindred groups such as the Farmers' League. One of the league's partisans, the retired General Konstantin von Gebsattel, proposed in 1913 that the vote be confined to males who had performed their military service, while suggesting plural suffrage on the basis of property and education. If his program could not be enacted by constitutional means, Gebsattel urged that it be imposed by decree.

Simultaneously anti-Semitism girded its loins to recover the ground lost by its splinter parties in the *Judenwahlen* of 1912. Following the bankruptcy of its electoral effort, this movement fell into the hands of the fanatic Theodor Fritsch, who eschewed future parliamentary contests, favored abolition of the Reichstag, replacement of the kaiser by a "constitutional dictator," and vigilantist assassination of Jews and radicals in case of a revolution. Fritsch founded the Reichshammerbund which preserved the hard core of German anti-Semite racism, even as "respectable" politicians, such as the editors of the *Kreuzzeitung*, decided to play down that issue henceforth. Big agriculture and big business increased their effort to contain democracy and labor unions. But the magnates of farm, finance, and factory all too often embraced laissez-faire liberalism, as the split between the Industrialist League and the Hansa Bund on the eve of the election demonstrated. The conservatism of big money became diluted, and its capacity to act suffered accordingly.[31]

The convergence of conservative and liberal aspirations and the uncertainty of what kind of a Germany the meeting of these two opposites would produce focused in the career and importance of the rising National Liberal politican Gustav Stresemann. Born in 1878 as the son of a brewery owner, Stresemann served as lobbyist for the Association of German Chocolate Manufacturers and the Association of Saxon Industrialists and finally found larger outlets for his talents in the German Industrialist League as well as the Hansa Bund. He joined the National Liberal party in his mid-twenties and advanced rapidly as the spokesman of its moderate left, winning a Reichstag seat in 1907. Two years later he moved to Berlin and continued to lobby for industry, while his own success as an investor gave him sufficient financial independence to allot more and more of his time to the promotion of his political career. Financial independence also enabled him to return to certain idealistic assumptions first formulated in his student days. The first major political influence in his life had been exerted by Friedrich Naumann, and the mature Stresemann—always predisposed to consider National Liberalism the heir of the 1848 constitutional program —returned to this mentor of his youth when he urged his party to "seek the support of all classes, of handicraftsmen and workers." But though he espoused the social and economic policies of left-liberalism, he opposed electoral reform in Prussia. As did other liberals of all shades, this precocious managerial and political entrepreneur supported German imperialism and the promotion of the empire's military and naval strength. In 1912 both he and his protector Bassermann stood ready to collaborate with the victorious SPD, but not until the Social Democrats dropped their opposition to increased appropriations for preparedness. The elections, in Stresemann's optimistic view, had made this issue the touchstone of German socialism's future. The SPD, he believed, could rally 'round the flag and subsequently forge a majority with liberalism or stagnate and decline in continued isolation. Given the National Liberals' inauspicious performance at the polls, these conclusions smacked not only of delusions of grandeur, but also represented a distinct minority viewpoint within National Liberal ranks, where the returns of January 1912 had nipped the potential flowering of maneuver and experiment. In a spirited meeting of the party's steering committee on March 24, the failure of Bassermann's leadership was frankly exposed, "many bitter words were spoken," and all notions of a leftward commitment firmly rejected. Bassermann retained his post, but the more conservative Robert Friedberg was elected co-chairman, and Stresemann lost his seat on the executive committee. In a letter dated March 28, the party's treasurer warned Stresemann that the NLP could not survive financially without the contributions of its prosperous right wing. At the annual congress in May a National Liberal majority again recorded its opposition to democratic suffrage and social legislation, and Friedberg spoke out against bargains with SPD and the Progressives.[32]

In the Center party the election had created the opposite situation. Unlike the National Liberals it could blame its setback on a leadership drawn from the party's conservative elements. The ensuing internal shifts yielded a seat on the executive committee for the Swabian schoolmaster Matthias Erzberger, the spokesman for south German petty bourgeois and workingclass Catholicism. But in his new position Erzberger was not dominant nor were his views sufficiently reformist to alter the course of the Center or the political direction of the German nation. He remained an energetic and outspoken foe of socialism. Center and SPD now had 201 seats in the Reichstag, constituting a clear majority-in-waiting. But instead of seeking allies on the left, all elements in organized political Catholicism combined to keep it on a traditional course. When the party's conservative leader, Georg von Hertling, became minister-president of Bavaria, his place was taken by Peter Spahn, a leader of identical convictions.

The elections of 1912 therefore left those who favored democratic reform in a minority and the potential reform forces too divided to form a majority bloc. Left-wing Centrists and National Liberals remained minorities in their own parties. Until an emergency would enable them to swing their associates, or persuade them to defect to the Progressives or Social Democrats, reform through parliamentary processes remained unlikely in Germany, and Friedrich Naumann's exultant diagnosis that the election of 1912 signified a new era—was merely a harbinger of further disappointments. When the new Reichstag convened, the SPD indicated willingness to participate responsibly in its business by allowing Philipp Scheidemann to become one of the parliament's new vice-presidents. But the new speaker, Peter Spahn, refused to serve with a socialist, and venomous protracted wrangling became the first order of business of the newly elected house. Nothing illustrated better how little the elections had changed than Bethmann-Hollweg's address on February 16 which paid lip service to the unexceptionable purpose of healing internal divisions while ruling out further democratization.[33]

The Prussian elections of May 1913 drove the final nail into the coffin of prewar electoral reform. The SPD gained only 10 seats with its 775,000 votes, while the Conservative party, with only 400,000, won 148. In the face of the inevitable distortions of the three-class suffrage, voting was apathetic: 50 percent of the first-class voters, a little more than 40 percent of those in class two, and only about 30 percent of those in class three bothered to go to the polls in Prussia in 1913, a far cry from the record turnout in the Reichstag elections of the previous year.[34] The Prussian Chamber of Deputies offered no forum for their aspiration.

Angered by the elections of 1913, even SPD revisionists were ready to gird for mass strikes in favor of suffrage reform, but once again trade union leaders exercised a decisive moderating influence. The SPD congress of 1913 voted down the general strike, 335 to 142, and even on the far left reformist restraint won over activism. But SPD impatience continued to rise. When on May 18, 1914, a new Prussian minister of the interior, Friedrich Wilhelm von Loebell, flatly told the Chamber of Deputies that he envisioned no proposal of suffrage reform, the Berlin *Vorwärts* called for new protest demonstrations. In mid-June a general assembly of SPD leaders in the Berlin area approved Rosa Luxemburg's view that equal suffrage could not be attained without a mass strike. The government's refusal to sponsor democratic reform was playing directly into the hands of the radicals within the SPD.[35]

Two weeks later the assassination in Sarajevo of the heir to the Habsburg throne raised more pressing foreign policy issues, preventing a new rash of Social Democratic demonstrations that surely would have erupted if war had not come in the summer of 1914.

The year 1914 found many other citizens of the Reich nursing grievances as fundamental as those of the Social Democrats. Those inhabitants (about 3.5 million in all) who spoke Polish,

Lithuanian, Danish, and French, as well as the 1.75 million inhabitants of Alsace-Lorraine remained aliens within the empire. The constant activity in the Reichstag of their spokesmen, one Dane from Schleswig, as many as ten deputies from Alsace-Lorraine, and eighteen to twenty Poles, testified to the persistence of a substantial, unamalgamated population bloc within the Bismarckian nation-state.

The agitation of these minorities further confirmed the conservative argument that democracy would only increase their centrifugal impact. At the same time the conservative reaction to their demands underlined that the right, notably in Prussia, had long abandoned it traditional dependence on dynastic loyalty and embraced National Liberal political and cultural chauvinism. The minority positions in parliament were, however, equally inconsistent. At times ethnic and regional splinter factions sought the support of the Social Democrats and the Progressives. More often, however, they lined up with the Center, since 90 percent of the Poles and more than 80 percent of Alsace-Lorraine's population worshiped at Catholic altars. Thus ethnic minority positions on the political spectrum remained unpredictable, and they contributed disproportionately to the chaotic instability of the Reichstag.

The policy of imperial Germany did very little to win the friendship of any of the minority groups, the Poles least of all. "Unworldly dreamers, without any sense of reality, were the only Germans who could advocate compromise with the Poles," Bülow later recalled. And this reflected the attitude that guided his policy toward some three million persons in Prussia. Three-class suffrage relegated these Polish citizens, most of them agricultural workers or very small landowners, to the third class of voters, and thus reduced their political weight. The use of their language, previously allowed in elementary schools in Polish districts, was largely forbidden in 1873 and even further restricted in 1900. After the turn of the century Polish could not be spoken in public meetings except in districts in which 60 percent of the population was Polish. The Prussian government in 1886 began to purchase land owned by Poles in order to resettle the eastern areas with Germans, and this program was expanded in the 1890's by Reichstag appropriations. The measures proved to be ineffective, however: the Polish birth rate exceeded the German, and government encouragement of German settlers failed to close the population gap. Oppression only strengthened the national spirit of the Poles. The realists and moderates among their leaders demanded full autonomy within Prussia, while a minority of radical nationalists soon would settle for nothing less than reunification in a resurrected Poland. Prussia would hear of neither solution. The conflict simmered on, and the German majority could only take comfort from the more cooperative conduct of the Protestant Masurian and Lithuanian minorities (about two hundred thousand each), whom their authorities treated more generously, either because they were less troublesome, or vice versa—no one could be quite sure which.[36]

The story was repeated on a smaller scale in northern Schleswig which, with a Danish population of about 140,000, had been taken from the king of Denmark in 1864. There, as in the Polish provinces and in Alsace-Lorraine, only German could be spoken in public meetings except where at least 60 percent of the people were non-German. Schools were closely supervised, and the Danish-language press was subjected to special censorship. The Germans continued to believe that the Danes in northern Schleswig favored secession and reunion with Denmark, and in fact many did. The minimum demand among the Schleswig Danes was for a large measure of autonomy and like other ethnic minorities in Prussia, they also supported the demand for equal suffrage. So little had the German government accepted them as trustworthy citizens that when war came in 1914 their one Reichstag deputy, Hans Peter Hanssen, was arrested immediately and the Danish-language newspaper he edited suspended even after he had been released. Except for Friedrich Naumann, Hans Delbrück, and a few other bourgeois politicians, only the Social Democrats protested against the harsh German policy in Schleswig and tried in vain to change it. Bülow, whose own father's career had begun in the service of the king of Denmark, nevertheless repeated the policy of land expropriation and German colonization which was failing to dampen the Polish spirit.[37]

Alsace-Lorraine was assigned a special place in the German Empire after 1870. Prussia would not allow any other German federal state to incorporate the captive provinces, and the south

German governments continued to oppose their absorption by Prussia. Because of their location on the French frontier and the sympathies which even the German ethnic majority retained for France, Germany did not dare give Alsace and Lorraine full self-government as enjoyed by all other states of the empire. A compromise arrangement was tailored to suit the demands of German security and particularism. The provinces were organized together as an "Imperial Territory." They were administered by a civilian viceroy (*Statthalter*), appointed by the German emperor and directly responsible to him rather than to the chancellor. Military authority was exercised by the Prussian army which occupied such key fortresses as Metz and Strassburg and the commander of which also reported directly to the head of the house of Hohenzollern—who wore in this case his other crown, that of Prussia. In the eyes of the military command, through which William II tended to view it, Alsace-Lorraine served only as an outpost against the dreaded French. The interests of the civilian inhabitants were always subordinated to the demands of military necessity. Since 1.3 million of the 1.5 million inhabitants of the area were Catholics, the *Kulturkampf* left the two provinces with bitter memories. French propaganda and German tactlessness joined to keep ill will alive.[38]

The representatives of the people of Alsace-Lorraine demanded at least full autonomy within Germany, and a few lived only for reunion with France. Almost all were unhappy with the status quo. In 1911, in an attempt to please the Center party and to quiet unrest, Germany granted the provinces a constitution. The Reichstag insisted that it provide equal suffrage for all men twenty-five years of age or more in elections to the lower chamber of a provincial parliament. Half of the upper house was to consist of men of property indirectly elected; the other half would be German residents appointed by the kaiser. The positions of the governor and the commanding general of the Prussian forces, both appointed by the kaiser as before, continued unchanged. Henceforth Alsace-Lorraine would send three representatives to the imperial Bundesrat, and these would be appointed and instructed by the imperial *Statthalter*. Since the federal states feared that their presence would merely increase the Prussian voting bloc from seventeen to twenty, the new law stipulated that the Alsace-Lorraine votes would not be counted if they provided a majority for Prussia.[39]

How little the constitution of 1911 changed the circumstances and the attitudes of the people of Alsace-Lorraine quickly became apparent. Hans Delbrück confessed publicly in 1913 that "politically they refuse to belong to the German people." The famous Zabern incident of that year offered the most dramatic evidence yet of the real relationship between the provinces and the German government.

The crisis of 1913 began with the instructions of a young lieutenant in Zabern (Saverne) to German recruits that they should use their weapons if attacked by local civilians. According to reports that quickly spread among the town's nine thousand predominantly French-speaking, Catholic inhabitants, the officer promised to pay ten marks to any man who, under provocation, carried out this order. Angered by the rumors, the *Savernois* took to the streets. On November 28 the German commander, Colonel von Reuter, arrested twenty-eight Alsatian demonstrators. This free use of police power by the garrison forces, in total disregard of the new state constitution, caused an outburst of rage in the German Reichstag as well as in Alsace-Lorraine. Bethmann-Hollweg tended to sympathize with the civilian viewpoint, but the kaiser insisted that the army be supported unwaveringly in the affair and forced the resignation of the civil governor, Karl von Wedel. The chancellor swallowed his own convictions and defended the army commander before the Reichstag, which responded with an overwhelming vote of no confidence (293 to 55) against him.

Though National Liberals and Centrists joined with Progressives and Social Democrats in this censure, their demonstration produced few results. The conservative Prussian minister of the interior Hans von Dallwitz succeeded Wedel in Strassburg, a measure of Bethmann's designed to pacify Conservatives on the Zabern issue, while removing an opponent of reform from the Prussian cabinet. But the Reichstag, having relieved its collective conscience, failed to pursue the Alsatian issue, thereby reducing pressure on the government and passing up once again a favorable chance for a showdown on consitutional government in peacetime Germany. Early in 1914 the German commander who had arrested the twenty-eight Alsatians was decorated by the kaiser after a court-martial board found that he had only done his duty in keeping order, alleging that the civilian police had failed to do so. The failure of German policy to achieve Germanization of Alsace-Lorraine was obvious on all sides on the eve of World War I. Bethmann himself admitted as much to the Bavarian minister-president in December 1914. So bitter was anti-German sentiment in the western border provinces that a good many of the inhabitants would serve the Allies in war, either abroad or in subversive activities at home. (Many would help the Allies distribute German-language propaganda in favor of democratic and republican revolution in Germany.) A young German recruit later recalled the tense relations that prevailed between citizens and overlords: "Before our departure the C.O. addressed us. Where we were going, he said, we would still be on German soil, but the place was alive with suspicious persons, enemies almost, against whose machinations we must guard ourselves. We would be billeted in private homes, but we must not trust the householders; we must lock our doors at night and sleep with our weapons beside us. The C.O. referred to Alsace-Lorraine, which for forty-three years had been part of Germany."[40]

The minority problems of imperial Germany had to be corrected before the country could become a genuinely democratic state. Yet distrust of the nation's alien subjects made solutions difficult to foresee. Imperial Germany knew few critics in any of the German parties as bitter as the minorities and no reformers who called so insistently for radical alterations of the Second Reich.

Meanwhile, as the debates over Alsace-Lorraine revealed, particularist grievances in Germany had not disappeared during the years of unification. Institutionally, imperial Germany became more highly integrated with every passing decade; psychologically, federal frictions were as bothersome in the last decade of peace as in the 1880's, and perhaps even more so. Almost all non-Prussian Germans felt a strong attachment to the Reich, but very few had any affection for the dominant dynastic state or for their emperor, the Prussian king. The old *Zerrissenheit* failed to heal, and William II's efforts to force the pace of unity only slowed the mending process. Bethmann's excellent personal relations with such state government leaders of congenial views as Georg von Hertling of Bavaria, Karl von Weizsäcker in Württemberg, Alexander von Dusch in Baden, and Christoph Vitzhum von Eckstädt in Saxony did not stabilize the erosion wrought by public disaffection. Had the state sovereigns not feared to encourage Germany's foreign enemies, and therefore swallowed most of the anger and frustration generated by William's posturing as *pater familias* of the German dynasties, the open quarrels between the conservative elements of the empire's historic components would have become much more overt and threatening to the status quo.[41]

Refusal to equalize the Prussian suffrage further increased anti-Prussian sentiment, notably in the south where reform of the lower houses of parliament moved toward democratization and to that degree widened the institutional and spiritual isolation of Prussian conservatism. In 1906 election of the Bavarian Chamber of Deputies became direct, equal, and secret. Every male inhabitant twenty-five years of age who possessed Bavarian citizenship and who paid direct taxes could vote.[42] Württemberg's most recent constitutional changes wrought comparable revisions. Although elections to the lower chamber of the Landtag had been direct since 1867, twenty-three members of that body continued to represent such restricted categories as knights (thirteen), Protestant and Catholic churches (nine), and the University of Tübingen (one). Among the popularly chosen members numerical inequities were likewise rife. By the turn of the century the representative from Stuttgart stood for a constituency of two hundred fifty thousand, while his colleague from Ellwangen represented only five thousand inhabitants. Several innovations during the thirty-year stewardship of Minister-President Hermann von Mittnacht (1870–1900) had foundered on opposition by the upper house or a lack of the requisite two-thirds majority in the lower chamber. In January 1905, however, the government of Mittnacht's successor, Wilhelm von Breitling, shepherded a new law through both chambers which added the corporate members of the lower assembly to the membership of the lords and transformed the representative branch of the Landtag into a gathering elected by direct and secret suffrage of all male citizens twenty-five or over. Urban representation was increased by giving Stuttgart six Landtag members and to the remaining five urban and sixty-three country constituencies were added seventeen new seats elected proportionally from the entire kingdom, the first German experiment with proportional representation.[43]

Baden's new law on universal manhood suffrage, adopted in 1904, only transformed the electoral process from the indirect to the direct mode. The members of the lower house had been chosen by all male resident citizens over twenty-five since 1869. Hesse-Darmstadt adopted the direct and secret ballot in 1911, but continued to limit voting to those who paid direct taxes while granting all voters over fifty years of age a second ballot.[44]

At the same time some dams of privilege withstood every assault. Important aristocratic bastions, such as the upper houses of the state parliaments, remained practically untouched by reform. Illustrative of the composition of these bodies was the Bavarian Reichsrat which in 1912 consisted of eighteen Wittelsbach princes, four church dignitaries (three Catholic bishops and the president of the Protestant consistory in Munich), seventeen *Standesherren* (descendants of imperial vassals of the Holy Roman Empire), thirty-two additional hereditary members from old noble families, and seventeen life members appointed by the king. Characteristic of the atmosphere prevalent in such gatherings—even one considered as open-minded as the Bavarian upper house—was the fact that a speech by a member warning the government against polarizing Bavaria into socialists and nonsocialists elicited unanimous ringing indignation.

In Bavaria and Württemberg the suggestion that enactment of universal manhood suffrage gave parliament a representative scope which justified ministerial investiture by its members was roundly denounced by both ministries in power; in Baden and Hesse no hint of such a suggestion ever ruffled the collaboration between parliament and executive. Monarchs retained control of ministers at all levels of German government life.

Prussia was not the only state to reject even limited democratization as enacted by the south German parliaments. In the city-state of Hamburg the electoral reform of 1896 had decreed that one-fourth of the 160-member Bürgerschaft was to be elected by the "Notables" (active and retired judges and civil servants), one-fourth by owners of landed-property, 8 by the inhabitants of outlying villages, and 72 by the direct vote of all "citizens" twenty-five or over (male inhabitants with an annual taxable income of twelve hundred marks or more). The law, furthermore, gave the privileged as many as three votes. Public officials could also vote as property owners, and both groups cast ballots to elect the 72 members representing the citizenry at large. Under this regimen only 69,000 Hamburg denizens voted in local as compared to 200,000 in Reichstag elections, but the SPD, which had remained unrepresented until the turn of the century, nevertheless elected 13 members in 1904. This sudden increase, combined with the fear and unrest generated by news of the Russian Revolution of 1905, prompted the introduction early in 1906 of a constitutional amendment that divided the citizenry into two classes, those who paid taxes on an income of twenty-five hundred marks or more (28,479) to whom the proposal alloted 48 Bürgerschaft seats, and those whose income fell below that minimum (48,000) who could choose the remaining 24 members. The 954 notables and 8,731 landowners would continue to elect the 80 upper-class representatives. Despite the virtual declaration of a general strike on January 16 and 17, accompanied by demonstrations in which over a hundred persons suffered injuries, the proposition passed overwhelmingly on January 31. How effective it was can be gathered from the fact that while all three Reichstag seats from Hamburg continued to be safely socialist, as they had been since 1890, only 20 of the 160 mandates in the city-state's legislature had become SPD preserves by 1914.[45]

In Saxony the holding action against democratic suffrage rested on similar legislative strategies. Since 1868 the "red kingdom" had chosen the members of the Landtag's lower house directly, restricting suffrage to male citizens owning a house or paying a minimal direct tax of three marks per year. Here, as in Hamburg, the rising tide of Social Democracy prompted in 1896 the enactment of a three-class electoral system which divided the voters into taxpayers paying less than thirty-eight, less than three hundred, and more than three hundred marks respectively. In contrast to Prussia, the inequities resulting from establishing separate registers in each constituency were avoided; on the other hand, persons paying no direct taxes remained disfranchised. The gambit succeeded, and by 1901 the SPD had been completely eliminated from the Landtag, at a time when it carried twenty-two out of twenty-three Saxon Reichstag districts. For a state 60 percent of whose population toiled in industry, while only 15 percent pursued agricultural endeavors, it had succeeded rather too well. The government quickly realized that silencing the working-class majority only played into the hands of the most radical elements of socialism. (This was especially noticeable after the massive textile workers' strike in Crimmitschau of 1903–4.) But universal manhood suffrage would have resulted in an SPD majority in the lower house of the Landtag and would have paralyzed parliament, since a chamber dominated by socialists would remain perpetually deadlocked with an aristocratic upper house. The dilemma resulted in a compromise passed in May 1909 by the Conservative and National Liberal majority which at that moment held seventy-seven out of eighty-two lower house seats. Every male citizen twenty-five or over cast one vote, two votes after his fiftieth birthday. Direct taxpayers were granted additional ballots, as many as three if their income exceeded twenty-eight hundred marks per year. A secondary school diploma also conferred supplementary voting rights. No one, however, could cast more than four votes. The system contained the SPD, though perhaps less completely than hoped. The 1909 Landtag, destined to sit until 1918, the representative character of which had been further distorted by assigning forty-eight seats to rural, but only forty-three to urban constituencies, still contained a Conservative-National Liberal majority of fifty-three. But the SPD, supported by 341,000 of the 635,000 individual voters, did elect twenty-six deputies. Population growth (13 percent from 1904 to 1914) and an even more spectacular rise in taxable income (31 percent for the same period) probably invested more working-class adults with additional votes than had been anticipated. In any case Saxony's electoral law of 1909 reflected not only the established elite's unwillingness to permit the election of a socialist majority, but also revealed the limits within which any effort to suppress majority preferences had to maneuver.[46]

Mecklenburg finally presented the one instance of total constitutional stagnation. Divided into two grand duchies (Schwerin and Strelitz), it remained subject to the legislative authority of joint estates. A seat and a vote depended on ownership of land and office, since estate membership consisted of the owners of 622 *Rittergüter* and the mayors of 32 privileged towns. From 1870 to 1914 liberal Reichstag members from Mecklenburg, the only representatives their fellow citizens had an opportunity to choose, unsuccessfully demanded federal intervention. These men claimed that this system, going back to the sixteenth century, violated the German constitution. But the Federal Council vetoed every such proposal because its constituent governments wanted to avoid any act that would create a precedent for Reich meddling in the internal affairs of a German state. The Mecklenburg estates themselves had no intention of surrendering their prerogatives, and the grand dukes in Schwerin lacked the energy, and in Strelitz the inclination, to lead a local reform movement. The introduction of representative government had to await the revolution of 1918.[47]

Mecklenburg's constitutional immobility thus reflected the retarding effect which anti-Hohenzollern particularism exercised on the democratic movement. Anxious to preserve the vestiges of dynastic and state sovereignty, not even the federal states of the south supported the reformist proposals of the Reichstag. Supremacy of the popularly and nationally elected parliament on any issue raised the specter of centralization, a development equally repugnant to Baden liberals, Hamburg's conservative patricians, and Mecklenburg's reactionary landlords.

As a result of a multiplicity of such unresolved controversies, Germany on the eve of World War I resounded with rhetoric prophecies of revolution. It has been said that people "never seem to expect revolution for themselves, but only for their children. The actual revolution is always a surprise."[48] In 1914, Germany constituted a qualified exception to the general rule. Whatever the actual chances of revolution might have been, fear of it was a constant topic of conversation, and a perpetual theme of extremist oratory. Prince Ernst Hohenlohe, after a trip to the capital city in the campaign year of 1912, wrote: "I found in Berlin a very pessimistic mood, which a serious Conservative gentleman of my acquaintance expressed with the words: 'In ten years we will have no monarchy!'"[49] Indeed, Conservatives and princes had every right to feel that a revolution was in progress around them, and Social Democaratic rhetoric even gave them some basis for their forebodings about the future. On the festive twenty-fifth anniversary of the kaiser's reign in 1913, the Berlin *Vorwärts* rudely shattered the splendor of the occasion, greeting the monarch in the name of millions of German socialists with the cry: "Long live the republic!"[50]

In that same year the reactionary Count Ernst zu Reventlow, chief diplomatic correspondent of the Agrarian League's *Deutsche Tageszeitung*, added his word of caution in a booklet entitled *Der Kaiser und die Monarchisten*, warning that in the world at large, "the so-called current of the times is of an anti-monarchical nature." To counter this momentum Reventlow sought to move the kaiser to drastic action against the rising democratic movement. "Nothing is more dangerous," he wrote, "than when monarchs seek to please Demos." Like many other vocal pessimists, the conservative journalist put his trust in a possible revolution from above to prevent a revolt of the masses.[51]

One could cite many another purposeful or neurotic *Schwarzseher* who warned in the Wilhelmian era that the days of monarchy were numbered. And untold thousands of Germans would remember after 1918 with the certainty of historical hindsight that they had known in 1914 that revolution and republic were near at hand. But volumes of such evidence would prove at most that William II had personally alienated great numbers of his people, not that the principle of monarchical government was losing support in imperial Germany.

Writers who cannot be accused of uncritical affection for William II have agreed that he might well have continued to reign for many years if Germany had not gone to war in "that fatal summer of 1914."[52] As for the kaiser himself, he never bothered to acknowledge the gift of Reventlow's booklet in 1913. When the conservative journalist went to see William's chief civilian aide, Rudolf von Valentini, he was told that his concern about the monarchy was unnecessary, that the German people were monarchist at heart.

Certainly the Social Democratic leaders lacked the zeal for a republican coup. Their party remained too divided to become the vanguard of social or political revolution. The predominant right wing continued to long for an evolution toward political democracy in eventual unison with bourgeois elements embracing the same purpose. Symbolically, Ludwig Frank, one of the younger advocates of that policy and a socialist Jew, volunteered for front-line service in 1914 and became the first Reichstag member to die in action. Hellmut von Gerlach accurately recalled in his memoirs that "before the war [only] Social Democracy and a few South German democrats demanded the republic. But really only in principle." Adalbert Wahl, the conservative chronicler of the era, concluded: "It required a complete collapse as a result of the lost war to make [the republic] possible."⁵³

Germans took too much pride in their empire to join in any revolution to change its constitution. Theirs was a state of sixty-eight million people in the heart of Europe. Beyond its boundaries their flag waved over a colonial realm of 1,135,000 square miles, won since 1884. Stretching from northeastern China through part of New Guinea to the east coast of Africa (present-day Tanzania), the overseas possessions contained thirteen million native inhabitants, supervised by twenty-four thousand Germans. The country's foreign investments totaled $6 billion in 1913, and a growing international trade was then valued at about $4 billion annually. To protect colonies, investments, and trade, Germany had spent between 1898 and 1914 some $800 million for the most modern navy in the world. An efficient peacetime army of 870,000 men protected the homeland from attack and stood ready to uphold its system of government against domestic rebellion. Imperial Germany was easily the most powerful and most prosperous state on the continent of Europe.

The kaiser, celebrating the twenty-fifth anniversary of his reign in 1913, shared in the credit for his country's power, progress, and prosperity. German communities in such distant centers as Guatemala City and Capetown celebrated the jubilee enthusiastically, as did many foreign notables. Six days after the Carl Schurz Memorial was unveiled on Morningside Heights in

New York, on May 16, 1913, the New York *Times* published a congratulatory address to the German emperor in which several dozen distinguished Americans, led by Andrew Carnegie, Frank B. Kellogg (president of the American Bar Association), William A. Dunning (president of the American Historical Association), and Nicholas Murray Butler (president of Columbia University) joined with others to felicitate William II upon "a reign notable in countless ways, in none more so than in the maintenance of twenty-five years of unbroken peace." Butler, in a special section of the New York *Times* devoted to the kaiser on June 8, wrote: "If the German Emperor had not been born to monarchy, he would have been chosen monarch—or Chief Executive—by popular vote of any modern people among whom his lot might have been cast."[54]

Great numbers of William's subjects would have expressed themselves less extravagantly; but all in all, the German people were then enjoying the best years they had every known in history. Despite the growth of democratic demands, millions of them could still agree with Adolf Grabowsky's words of 1907 in the *Zeitschrift für Politik*: "In the common interest everybody keeps his place, because he knows that the common trust will be returned to him a hundred fold."[55] The war that began in the summer of 1914 was to prove the loyalty of reformers and conservatives alike. Only the resistance to their domestic demands and more than four years of hardships would finally break their patience, preparing them to accept revolution.

The crisis of 1914 had been anticipated by Eduard David of the SPD on December 2, 1912, when he explained to the Reichstag how German diplomats could avoid involvement in a future Balkan war: "If Austria attacks Serbia and Russia comes to the latter's assistance, we are not obligated by the alliance to take up arms. This is exceedingly important, for it is our sole guarantee of peace against the military party in Vienna."[56] Unfortunately, Germany had no guarantee against the kaiser's whims and "the military party" in Berlin in 1914. The kaiser on July 5 pledged support for Austria against Serbia, and Bethmann-Hollweg, as was his wont, acquiesced in the royal will. The kaiser could well afford to tell the Austrian Ambassador on July 5 that "he did not doubt at all that Bethmann-Hollweg would agree with him completely."[57]

The kaiser subsequently made no attempt to frustrate the will of his generals. Though his chancellor fundamentally desired peace, he was willing to risk a general war to uphold the power position of Germany and Austria-Hungary. His conduct of German policy in July 1914 was determined by considerations that were defined by the leaders of the army. These were set forth in a military plan that the chief of the general staff, General Alfred von Schlieffen, had begun to develop in the 1890's, first drafted in 1904–5, and again revised during the remaining four years of his life.

The "Schlieffen Plan," as it evolved after 1905, was a great gamble, based upon closely timed troop movements which only extravagant good fortune could keep on schedule. Success depended on a host of unlikely assumptions. It assumed that Germany would be threatened by France and Russia and required that in such a war Germany would quickly defeat France. Invasion of neutral Belgium became the prerequisite for this speedy victory. The plan also dictated that operations in the west must precede full Russian mobilization.[58]

The Russian government in 1914 asserted that the call to arms of its millions was aimed only at Austria. The German generals discounted this claim as a ruse, and their anxieties over their country's encirclement were shared by many civilians. At a central committee meeting of the National Liberal party in February 1913, Ernst Bassermann complained that Germany was "surrounded by enemies" and that "the friends we possess are in part at any rate lukewarm friends on whom we shall not be able to count in all political eventualities." At the same time Maximilian Harden was leading a chorus of journalistic warnings against the Russian danger. The Catholic Center, traditionally sympathetic to the Austrian Habsburgs, was singularly united in its hostility to czardom, and one foreign enemy Social Democrats hated was the government of Nicholas II. Average Germans, less committed to specific causes, quoted with increasing frequency an old saying that perfectly captured a mood of rising desperation: "Better a fearful end than fear without end."[59]

Under the impact of this amalgam of anxieties, delay was rejected by generals and civilians alike. Together they pressed

Austria-Hungary to break with Serbia. Not because they were bound by the Dual Alliance with Austria to help the Habsburg ally (they were not), but because they had lost their balance and were bound to the doctrinaire timetable of the Schlieffen Plan, the generals at the end of July 1914 insisted that Germany must have the initiative in what they prematurely assumed was a developing war among the great powers and that the only way it could obtain that initiative was to take it. This in turn demanded offensive diplomatic action against Russia and France and culminated in a precipitous declaration of war against both. The "machine," as the kaiser is said to have acknowledged many years later, "ran away" with him.[60]

Many nations joined in preparing the way for World War I, but two hard facts overshadow all others in the immediate crisis of 1914. Berlin encouraged Vienna to make war against Serbia, hoping for a limited conflict, but resigned to risk a general one. When the contest still might have been localized, the ultimata delivered to Russia and France closed the door on peace as a result of Germany's belligerent haste. The case in favor of a concomitant deliberate German bid for world power is less open and shut. Fear rather than confidence dictated the Reich's action. Fear of the eventual military superiority of Germany's neighbors (and the inclination to view them all indiscriminately as enemies) became coupled with fear of internal unrest. As early as December 1912 the conservative *Ostpreussische Zeitung* advocated a "brisk, jolly war" to reduce the growth of the SPD's electoral support. Deployment of military power constituted the most obvious response to both threats, and the constitutional and parliamentary leaders of imperial Germany, from kaiser to deputy, entrusted her destinies to her military chieftains, narrowly trained technicians in the craft of war. If democracy had not been tested in peace, its time would not arrive on the eve of war.[61]

By the decade of 1904 to 1914 a century of slow maturing and the votes of millions stood behind the movement for democratic reform in Germany. Whether genuine parliamentary government could have overcome the obstacles to unity and political harmony, posed as much by particularist impulses and institutions as by overt conservatism, eludes a summary answer. But reform of Prussia's three-class suffrage system was a likely first step, and its accomplishment would have done a great deal to prepare the people for the strains of self-government and of war. Democracy could not have staved off defeat, but reforms before 1914 almost certainly would have guaranteed a smooth constitutional transition, making revolution as unnecessary in 1918 as it appeared unlikely in the years before 1914. Seen in this light the years from 1904 to 1914 constitute a decade of missed opportunities.

The responsibility for the failures of these years must be assumed by a great variety of individuals and groups. The bourgeois political parties must be assigned a sizable share of it. The failures of the two chief advisers of the kaiser in this period, Bülow and Bethmann-Hollweg, were obvious and significant. Either for crass self-interest or in noble deference to the common good, William II should have pressed for reforms as a means of winning the full personal and material loyalty of the German people, including the millions of Social Democratic voters who could have been won by a genuinely democratic system. The last emperor might have fused the plebiscitary monarchical system inaugurated by the Bonapartes and the constitutional dynasticism even then associated with kingship in Great Britain and Scandinavia. But he preferred the road taken by Charles X (whom, to be sure, he never acknowledged either as precursor or as example). What had become impossible in nineteenth-century France turned out to be quite as insupportable to twentieth-century Germans, especially after William had led "my army," "my navy," and "my people" into total military disaster. Republican revolution, a mere specter of words in 1914, was to become reality four years later.

NOTES

I THE BEGINNINGS

1. The bishop's remarks are quoted from the impressive study by Klaus Epstein, *The Genesis of German Conservatism*, p. 266. See also: Adolf Rapp, *Der Kampf um die Demokratie in Deutschland seit der grossen französischen Revolution*, pp. 1–25 (sensible but out-of-date); Herbert A. L. Fisher, *The Republican Tradition in Europe*, pp. 1–57 (still suggestive); and the following works of basic importance for the situation before 1789: R. R. Palmer, *The Age of the Democratic Revolution*, vol. 1; Fritz Valjavec, *Die Entstehung der politischen Strömungen in Deutschland 1770–1815*, pp. 15–145.

2. See, for example, Michael Demiaskovich, *The National Mind*, pp. 337–83; Friedrich Wilhelm Foerster, *Erlebte Weltgeschichte 1869–1953*, p. 213; William J. Bossenbrook, *The German Mind*, and other works cited in John L. Snell, *Wartime Origins of the East-West Dilemma over Germany*, pp. 1–13. Rebuttals to the anti-German interpretations are offered by Gerhard Ritter, *Das deutsche Problem*.

3. G. P. Gooch, *Studies in German History*, p. 1; Eugen Diesel, *Germany and the Germans*, pp. 13–63, 145–69; Franz Schnabel, *Deutsche Geschichte im neunzehnten Jahrhundert*, 1:81, 88 (fundamental); Hajo Holborn, *A History of Modern Germany: The Reformation*, pp. 3–14.

4. Harold C. Deutsch, *The Genesis of Napoleonic Imperialism*, pp. 43–45, 64, and passim.

5. See the essay by Theodor Schieder in Werner Conze et al., *Staat und Gesellschaft im deutschen Vormärz 1815–1848*, pp. 9–38; the less useful work by Frederick Hertz, *The Development of the German Public Mind*, p. 224; and Leonard Krieger, *The German Idea of Freedom*, p. 74 (for the 1788 quotation). For an excellent short account of the wars of the period 1648—1815 and their effects on the Germans, see Hajo Holborn, *A History of Modern Germany: 1648–1840*.

6. Schnabel, *Deutsche Geschichte*, 1:84, 105; Friedrich Meinecke, "The Year 1848 in German History," p. 482.

7. See the work by Mary Alice Gallin, *German Resistance to. . .Hitler: Ethical and Religious Factors*, rev. ed. (Washington, 1961), pp. 26–35; Guenter Lewy, *The Catholic Church and Nazi Germany* (New York, 1964); Holborn, *The Reformation*, p. 152 and passim; Georg Iggers, "Heinrich Heine and the Saint-Simonians," pp. 289–308; Ritter, *Das deutsche Problem*, pp. 13–22.

8. The following are suggestive: Epstein, *German Conservatism*, pp. 112–75, 266, and passim (treating both Catholic and Protestant attitudes); Robert H. Lowie, *Toward Understanding Germany*, p. 102; Friedrich C. Sell, *Die Tragödie des deutschen Liberalismus*, pp. 14–17 (a useful work based largely upon literary sources); W. H. Bruford, *Germany in the Eighteenth Century*, pp. 1–43, 45–129.

9. For additional detail see Robert E. Dickinson, *Germany*; Walter Prescott Webb, *The Great Frontier*, p. 69; two treatments by Dietrich Gerhard: "The Frontier in Comparative View," pp. 218–23, and *Alte und neue Welt in vergleichender Geschichtsbetrachtung*, pp. 130–133; Heinrich Heffter, *Die deutsche Selbstverwaltung im 19. Jahrhundert*, p. 168 (insights and an encyclopedic array of information); and Helen P. Liebel, "The Bourgeoisie in Southwestern Germany, 1500–1789," pp. 283–307.

10. On the Enlightenment in Germany see the excellent brief survey by Gooch, *Studies in German History*, pp. 37–74; Valjavec, *Die Entstehung der politischen Strömungen*, pp. 15–145; and Fritz Hartung, "Der aufgeklärte Absolutismus," pp. 15–42 (which elaborates on an idea developed earlier by Otto Hintze) Helen P. Liebel's, *Enlightened Bureaucracy versus Enlightened Despotism in Baden, 1750– 1792*, pp. 5–12, 22, and passim is the best English treatment of Karl Friedrich; Chester V. Easum, *Prince Henry of Prussia*, p. 315; W. F. Reddaway, *Frederick the Great and the Rise of Prussia*, pp. 155–88, 301–21, and passim; Gerhard Ritter, *Friedrich der Grosse*, pp. 183–224 and passim (for a defense of Frederick); G. P. Gooch, *Frederick the Great* (a more critical appraisal), are among the standard works on Prussia's greatest monarch.

11. Reinhart Koseleck, *Preussen zwischen Reform und Revolution*, pp. 62, 23–149; Gordon A. Craig, *The Politics of the Prussian Army*, 1640–1945, pp. 2, 14–20; Hans Rosenberg, *Bureaucracy, Aristocracy, and Autocracy*; Gerhard Ritter, *Staatskunst und Kriegshandwerk*, 1:13–59 passim; Ritter, *Friedrich der Grosse*, pp. 158–82, 257–60, and passim.

12. F. L. Carsten, *Princes and Parliaments in Germany from the Fifteenth to the Eighteenth Century*, esp. pp. 123–48; Epstein, *German Conservatism*, pp. 260–64 and passim; Walter Grube, *Der Stuttgarter Landtag 1457–1957*, esp. pp. 379–449.

13. Liebel, *Enlightened Bureaucracy versus Enlightened Despotism*, pp. 107–8 (Schlosser quotation); Ismar Elbogen and Eleonore Sterling, *Die Geschichte der Juden in Deutschland*, pp. 11–171; F. G. Dreyfus, *Sociétés et mentalités à Mayence dans la seconde moitié du XVIII siècle*, pp. 278–320 (a superb study).

14. For German views of Britain before 1789, see W. B. Robson-Scott, *German Travellers in England, 1400–1800*, p. 149 and passim; Heffter, *Selbstverwaltung*, pp. 49–55, 76–109.

15. Paul Ben Baginsky, ed., *German Works Relating to America, 1493–1800*, pp. 64–93 and passim, listing items held by the New York Public Library; Paul C. Weber, *America in Imaginative German Literature in the First Half of the Nineteenth Century*, pp. 2–42 passim; Thomas D. Clark, ed., *Travels in the Old South*, 1:186; Otto Vossler, *Die amerikanischen Revolutionsideale in ihrem Verhältnis zu den europäischen untersucht an Thomas Jefferson*, p. 2n; Henry M. Adams, *Prussian-American Relations, 1775–1871*, pp. 4–25; Ernst Fraenkel, ed., *Amerika im Spiegel des deutschen politischen Denkens*, (for Klopstock and Forster quotes) pp. 16–24, 49–77; Eugene Edgar Doll, *American History as Interpreted by German Historians from 1770 to 1815*, (for Schlözer quote) pp. 423–501; Elisha P. Douglass, "German Intellectuals and the American Revolution," pp. 200–218; Thomas Paine, *Geschichte der Revolution von Nord-Amerika vom Abt Raynal*.

16. Jacques Droz, *L'Allemagne et la révolution française*, esp. pp. 27–28, 80, 83, 105, 109, 135–49, 249, 371–92; Sydney Seymour Biro, *The German Policy of Revolutionary France*, 1:31n, 36; Palmer, *Democratic Revolution*, 2:432–37; Otto Tschirch, *Geschichte der öffentlichen Meinung in Preussen vom Baseler Frieden bis zum Zusammenbruch des Staates (1795–1806)*, 1:11; Reinhold Aris, *History of Political Thought in Germany from 1789 to 1815*, pp. 37–62; Valjavec, *Entstehung der politischen Strömungen*, pp. 153–243, 437, 454, and passim (pertinent to the paragraphs that follow as well as to those above, as is Epstein, *German Conservatism*, pp. 434–594 and passim).

17. Hans Kohn, *Prelude to Nation-States*, pp. 134–35; Aris, *Political Thought*, pp. 44–47; Palmer, *Democratic Revolution*, 2:62, 329–30, 437–44; Biro, *Revolutionary France*, 1:94, 99, 125, 127–28, 2:900; Jakob Venedey, *Die deutschen Republikaner unter der französischen Republik*; Dreyfus, *Sociétés et mentalités à Mayence*, pp. 546–59

Notes to Pages 13–20   [385]

(for Forster quote); Robert B. Holtman, *Napoleonic Propaganda*, p. 83; Gordon Craig, "Engagement and Neutrality in Germany," pp. 1–16.
18. Herbert A. L. Fisher, *Studies in Napoleonic Statesmanship*, pp. 173–384; Enno E. Kraehe, *Metternich's German Policy*, 1:20–53; Owen Connelly, *Napoleon's Satellite Kingdoms*, pp. 15–16, 176–222; Palmer, *Democratic Revolution*, 2:344, 444–56; Walter Grab, *Demokratische Strömungen in Hamburg und Schleswig-Holstein zur Zeit der ersten französischen Republik*; Georges Lefèbvre, *The French Revolution from 1793 to 1799*, p. 359 and passim; Droz, *L'Allemagne et la révolution française*, pp. 115–32. Considerable detail on the impact of France, 1792–1813, is offered by Agatha Ramm, *Germany, 1789–1919: A Political History* (London, 1967), pp. 22–102.
19. Tschirch, *Geschichte der öffentlichen Meinung*, 1:294; Droz, *L'Allemagne et la révolution française*, p. 109; Rosenberg, *Bureaucracy*, pp. 161, 201; Rudolf Olden, *The History of Liberty in Germany*, pp. 35–36.
20. Schnabel, *Deutsche Geschichte*, 1:339; Krieger, *German Idea of Freedom*, pp. 141–45 (perceptive throughout).
21. See Gerhard Ritter's summary of his larger work on Stein, in *Lebendige Vergangenheit*, pp. 84–100; Walter M. Simon, *The Failure of the Prussian Reform Movement*, pp. 4, 6–37 (deemphasizes the accomplishments of the reformers); Ernst Rudolf Huber, *Deutsche Verfassungsgeschichte seit 1789*, 1:118–34, 183–98 (a systematic and basic reference work); Heffter, *Selbstverwaltung*, pp. 76–109; the older work by Guy Stanton Ford, *Stein and the Era of Reform in Prussia, 1807–1815*; (from which the quote is taken) and the detailed analysis by Koselleck, *Reform und Revolution*, pp. 487–559.
22. Koselleck, *Reform und Revolution*, pp. 560–86; R. C. Raack, *The Fall of Stein*; Kraehe, *Metternich's German Policy*, pp. 272–76; Aris, *Political Thought*, pp. 136–65 (on Humboldt); Otto Vossler, "Humboldts Idee der Universität" pp. 251–68; Craig, *Prussian Army*, pp. 37–57; Ritter, *Staatskunst und Kriegshandwerk*, 1:67–105; William O. Shanahan, *Prussian Military Reforms, 1786–1813*, which now must be supplemented by Peter Paret, *Yorck and the Era of Prussian Reform, 1807–1815*, pp. 117–90; Simon, *Prussian Reform Movement*, pp. 145–93; and the perceptive essay on Humboldt in Georg G. Iggers, *The German Conception of History*, pp. 44–62.
23. Koselleck, *Reform und Revolution*, pp. 163–332; Simon, *Prussian Reform Movement*, pp. 69–70; Elbogen and Sterling, *Juden in Deutschland*, pp. 172–83; Rosenberg, *Bureaucracy*, p. 212; Ernst Klein, *Von der Reform zur Restoration*, p. 317 and passim.
24. Simon, *Prussian Reform Movement*, p. 119 and, more generally, pp. 51–66, 105–42, 240; Schnabel, *Deutsche Geschichte*, 1:356–58, 458–78, 2:282–91; Krieger, *The German Idea of Freedom*, pp. 158–59.
25. For the growth of nationalist thought see Friedrich Meinecke, *Weltbürgertum und Nationalstaat*, chaps. 1–8; Aris, *Political Thought*, esp. pp. 207–359; Kohn, *Prelude to Nation-States*, pp. 120, 259, and 133–300 passim; Jacques Droz, *Le Romantisme allemand et l'état*.
26. There is a large body of literature on the events of 1812–15. See Kraehe, *Metternich's German Policy*, pp. 147–323; Gordon A. Craig, *War, Politics, and Diplomacy*, pp. 22–45; Paret, *Yorck*, pp. 191–96; Hellmuth Rössler, *Österreichs Kampf um Deutschlands Befreiung*, 2:111–258 (a song of praise, based on archival research, on the theme "Ein Volk, ein Reich, ein Führer"); Heinrich von Srbik, *Metternich*, 1:146–229. Among the many older works that place greater emphasis on Prussia's role, see Heinrich von Treitschke, *Deutsche Geschichte im neunzehnten Jahrhundert*, vol. 1, whose treatment of Humboldt is corrected on some points by Gordon A. Craig, "Wilhelm von Humboldt as Diplomat," pp. 81–102. See also studies mentioned by Andreas Dorpalen, "The German Struggle against Napoleon, The East German View," pp. 485–516.

II REPRESSION AND NEW IMPULSES

1. On the settlement of 1814–15 and Metternich's policy regarding the German Confederation see: Richard Metternich, ed., *Memoirs of Prince Metternich*, 3:286–329; Ernst Rudolf Huber, ed., *Dokumente zur deutschen Verfassungsgeschichte*, 1:90–102, 117–40; Enno E. Kraehe, *Metternich's German Policy*; Enno E. Kraehe, "Raion d'état et idéologie dans la politique allemande de Metternich (1809–1820)," pp. 181–94; Paul W. Schroeder, *Metternich's Diplomacy at Its Zenith, 1820–1823*. Metternich was both Kraehe's opportunist and Schroeder's reactionary. See Heinrich von Srbik, *Metternich*, 1:193–206, 350–420. The literature since Srbik's two-volume biography appeared in 1925 is reviewed in his third volume—posthumously published—and by Paul W. Schroeder, "Metternich Studies since 1925," pp. 237–60.

2. Gagern's comment on the aims of the *Burschenschaften* is from Paul Wentzcke and Wolfgang Klötzer, eds., *Deutscher Liberalismus im Vormärz*, pp. 57–61. Follen's "Great Song" is quoted from Leonard Krieger, *The German Idea of Freedom*, pp. 269–70. See also: Paul Wentzcke, *Geschichte der deutschen Burschenschaft . . . bis zu den Karlsbader Beschlüssen*; Srbik, *Metternich*, 1:588–98; Ernst Rudolf Huber, *Deutsche Verfassungsgeschichte seit 1789*, vols. 1–2; Werner Conze et al., *Staat und Gesellschaft im deutschen Vormarz 1815–1848*, esp. pp. 207–69; Henry A. Kissinger, *A World Restored*, pp. 191–246.

3. For Metternich's comments on the granting of constitutions see Schroeder, *Metternich's Diplomacy*, p. 46. The thinking of the nobility in this period is treated by Sigmund Neumann, *Die Stufen des preussischen Konservatismus*. See also: Hans Rosenberg, *Bureaucracy, Aristocracy, and Autocracy*, p. 227; Conze et al, *Staat und Gesellschaft*, pp. 89–93, 117; Otto Ernst Schüddekopf, ed., *Die deutsche Innenpolitik im letzten Jahrhundert und der konservative Gedanke*, p. 23 (a useful documentary compilation); Theodore S. Hamerow, *Restoration, Revolution, Reaction*, pp. 19, 54; and Reinhart Koselleck, *Preussen zwischen Reform und Revolution*, pp. 337–447, 680–90.

4. Huber, *Verfassungsgeschichte*, 1:442–72, 2:185–281, 345–71; Hans Schneider, *Der preussische Staatsrat 1817–1918*, pp. 169–70; William O. Shanahan, *German Protestants Face the Social Question*, esp. pp. 37, 49, 193, 301 (a careful study); Fritz Fischer, "Der deutsche Protestantismus und die Politik im 19. Jahrhundert," pp. 473–518; Hajo Holborn, *A History of Modern Germany: 1648–1840*, pp. 485–509; Robert M. Bigler, "The Rise of Political Protestantism in Nineteenth Century Germany," pp. 423–44; Annette Kuhn, *Die Kirche im Ringen mit dem Sozialismus 1803–1848*; Karl Kupisch, *Die deutschen Landeskirchen im 19. und 20. Jahrhundert*, pp. 51–56 (thin but encyclopedic handbook); Jerry F. Dawson, *Friedrich Schleiermacher*, pp. 132–37; and—for the Gutzkow quotation—E. M. Butler, *The Saint-Simonian Religion in Germany*, p. 298.

5. On "liberalism" and "democracy" in the period 1815–48 see: Erich Brandenburg, *Die Reichsgründung*, 1:118–26; the critical comment on Brandenburg's interpretation by Friedrich Meinecke, "Zur Geschichte des älteren deutschen Parteiwesens," pp. 46–62; Brandenburg's rebuttal, "Zum älteren deutschen Parteiwesen," pp. 63–84; John H. Hallowell, *The Decline of Liberalism as an Ideology, with Particular Reference to German Politico-Legal Thought*, pp. 1–50; Fritz Valjavec, *Die Entstehung der politischen Strömungen*, pp. 180–206; Hartwig Brandt, *Landständische Repräsentation im deutschen Vormärz*, pp. 160–281. See also: Ludwig Bergsträsser, *Geschichte der politischen Parteien in Deutschland*, pp. 43–94 passim; Heinrich Heffter, *Die deutsche Selbstverwaltung im 19. Jahrhundert*, p. 353 and passim; Huber, *Verfassungsgeschichte*, 2:371–414; Krieger, *German Idea of Freedom*,

pp. 268–76; Joachim H. Knoll, *Führungsauslese in Liberalismus und Demokratie*, pp. 123–25 (of limited value); the suggestive essay on the problem of revolution in the nineteenth century by Theodor Schieder, *Staat und Gesellschaft im Wandel unserer Zeit*, pp. 11–57; Theodor Schieder, "Die Theorie der Partei im älteren deutschen Liberalismus," pp. 183–87; and Ernst-Wolfgang Böckenförde, *Die deutsche verfassungsgeschichtliche Forschung im 19. Jahrhundert*, pp. 42–134 and passim. On the development of nationalism see: Friedrich Meinecke, *Weltbürgertum und Nationalstaat*, pp. 1–315 passim, which perceptively and clearly surveys the developing victory of nationalistic over more universal, humanistic ideals among German intellectuals, as does Georg G. Iggers, *The German Conception of History*, pp. 3–123, and Friedrich C. Sell, *Die Tragödie des deutschen Liberalismus*, pp. 70–71 and passim. On these and virtually all other matters in Germany between 1800 and 1840, I owe a major debt to the suggestive and informative work by Franz Schnabel, *Deutsche Geschichte im neunzehnten Jahrhundert*, such as, on liberalism, 2:62–214 passim.

6. The thirteen states that granted constitutions between 1814 and 1820 were, in chronological order, Nassau, Schwarzenburg-Rudolstadt, Lippe-Schaumburg, Waldeck, Saxe-Weimar, Bavaria, Baden, Liechtenstein, Württemberg, Hanover, Brunswick, Hesse-Darmstadt, and Saxe-Coburg-Saalfeld.

7. For the paragraph above see: Brandt, *Landständische Repräsentation*; Huber, *Verfassungsgeschichte*, 1:314–34; Huber, ed., *Dokumente*, 1:141–200; Richard K. Ullmann and Stephen King-Hall, *German Parliaments*, pp. 37 ff. (thin); Walter Grube, *Der Stuttgarter Landtag 1457–1957*, pp. 499–524; Thomas Ellwein, *Das Erbe der Monarchie in der deutschen Staatskrise*, pp. 40–93; Lothar Gall, *Der Liberalismus als regierende Partei*, pp. 6–57; Conze et al., *Staat und Gesellschaft*, pp. 126–29, 145–56; Krieger, *German Idea of Freedom*, pp. 229–42, 256–61; Schnabel, *Deutsche Geschichte*, 2:78–86, 226; Metternich, ed., *Memoirs*, 5:433–34.

8. Huber, *Verfassungsgeschichte*, 1:336–86, 2:30–46; Grube, *Stuttgarter Landtag*, pp. 499–524; Conze et al., *Staat und Gesellschaft*, pp. 129–36.

9. James K. Feibleman, *The Two-Story World*, p. 112; C. E. Black, *The Dynamics of Modernization*, p. 24.

10. Krieger, *German Idea of Freedom*, pp. 86–138, 323–24; Reinhold Aris, *History of Political Thought in Germany from 1789 to 1815*, pp. 65–105; William Archibald Dunning, *A History of Political Theories*, pp. 131–32, 154–69; Guido de Ruggiero, *The History of European Liberalism*, pp. 218–20, 229–40; essential excerpts from Kant's *Principles of Political Right* (1793) and *The Philosophy of Law* (1796) and Hegel's *The Philosophy of Right* (1821) in Margaret Spahr, ed., *Readings in Recent Political Philosophy* (New York, 1935), pp. 164–206; John Bowle, *Politics and Opinion in the Nineteenth Century*, p. 39. For Gagern's linking of Reason and freedom in 1833, see Wentzcke and Klötzer, eds., *Deutscher Liberalismus*, p. 123. A number of other "practical-minded" liberals appear to have been little influenced by Hegel. See Wolfgang Hock, *Liberales Denken im Zeitalter der Paulskirche*, pp. 6–17.

11. A thorough study is needed of the relationship between German scientists and politics in the period 1815–48. State repressive measures against those who favored political changes are emphasized in the overly brief and sometimes inaccurate sketch by W. H. G. Armytage, *The Rise of the Technocrats*, pp. 76–85. The paragraphs above draw upon: R. Hinton Thomas, *Liberalism, Nationalism and the German Intellectuals (1822–1847)* pp. 20–50, 120 (thin); Huber, *Verfassungsgeschichte*, 2:165, 411, 487; Brockhaus' *Konversations-Lexikon*, 14th ed., 17 vols. (Leipzig, 1908), 14:587–88; *Allgemeine deutsche Biographie*, 56 vols. (Leipzig, 1875–1912), 32:315–19 (Schönlein); Erwin H. Ackerknecht, *Rudolf Virchow*, pp.

16, 18, 164n, 165, and passim; Kurt Koszyk, "Carl D'Ester als Gemeinderat und Parlamentarier (1846–1849)," pp. 43–60; and two articles by Douglas D. Hale, Jr.: "Gustav Bunsen," pp. 129–39, and "Friedrich Adolph Wislizenus," pp. 260–85.
12. See: Otto Döhner, Jr., *Georg Büchners Naturauffassung*, pp. 21–63 and passim; Pier Westra, *Georg Büchner dans ses rapports avec ses contemporains*; Anton Büchner (grandchild of Wilhelm Büchner), *Die Familie Büchner: Georg Büchners Vorfahren, Eltern und Geschwister* (Darmstadt, 1963), esp. pp. 9, 18, 33, 42; Karl Viëtor, *Georg Büchner*, pp. 9–22, 256; Herbert Lindenberger, *Georg Büchner*; Ludwig Büttner, *Georg Büchner, Revolutionär und Pessimist*, pp. 8, 10, 36–44, 48–49, 62–76; Franz Mehring, *Geschichte der deutschen Sozialdemokratie*, 1:83–85, 222, 2:232–33, 246, 3:12, 67–77, 236; and, for the much more voluminous literature, Werner Schlick, *Das Georg Büchner-Schrifttum bis 1965*. On Ludwig B., see: the useful sketch of him in Charles Coulston Gillespie, ed., *Dictionary of Scientific Biography*, 3:563–64; Jutta Dreisbach-Olsen, *Ludwig Büchner*, pp. 33–62 and passim.
13. Edward H. Reisner, *Nationalism and Education Since 1789*, pp. 121–50; Andreas Flitner, *Die politische Erziehung in Deutschland*, pp. 87–149 and passim; Adalbert Rang, *Der politische Pestalozzi*; William Setchel Learned, *The Oberlehrer*, pp. 44–63.
14. Horst Ehmke, *Karl von Rotteck, der "politische Professor"*; Hans Zehntner, *Das Staats-Lexikon von Rotteck und Welcker*, pp. 14, 36, and passim; Inge Schliepper, *Wurzeln der Demokratie in der deutschen Geschichte*, pp. 163–64 (Rotteck on democracy); Koppel S. Pinson, *Modern Germany*, p. 60 (quotation of Dahlmann); Waldemar Röhrbein, *Hamburg und die hannoversche Verfassungskonflikt 1837–1840*, pp. 42–184; Huber, *Verfassungsgeschichte*, 2:93–115; Karl-Alexander Hellfaier, "Die politische Funktion der Burschenschaft von ihren Anfängen 1814 bis zum Revolutionsjahr 1848 an der Universität Halle-Wittenberg," pp. 103–49; Rolland R. Lutz, "The German Revolutionary Student Movement," pp. 215–41 (interesting accent on the elitism of the *Burschenschafter*); Federico Federici, ed., *Der deutsche Liberalismus*, pp. 104–25 (on the Göttingen Seven). The generally conservative function of higher education is emphasized by Lenore O'Boyle, "Klassische Bildung und soziale Struktur in Deutschland zwischen 1800 und 1848," pp. 584–608. Cf. her essay on "The Problem of an Excess of Educated Men in Western Europe, 1800–1850," pp. 471–78.
15. Kurt Koszyk, *Deutsche Presse im 19. Jahrhundert*, pp. 13–104 passim; Aris, *Political Thought*, pp. 288–341; Hans Kohn, *Prelude to Nation-States*, pp. 289–96; and, for one of several translations of Görres's "Germany and the Revolution," Mack Walker, ed., *Metternich's Europe* (New York: Harper Torchbook, 1968), pp. 48–63. For the paragraphs above, see further: Metternich, ed., *Memoirs*, 3:288; Huber, *Verfassungsgeschichte*, 2:32–184 passim; *Brockhaus' Konversations-Lexikon*, 4:494–96 (on Cotta and his press); Lenore O'Boyle, "The Image of the Journalist in France, Germany, and England, 1815–1848," pp. 302–12; and Gregor Richter, "Der Staat und die Presse in Württemberg bis zur Mitte des 19. Jahrhunderts," pp. 393–425. The quotation from the *Deutsche Tribüne* and the statistics on the *Press-und Vaterlandsverein* are from Douglas D. Hale, Jr., "The Press and Fatherland Society in 1832."
16. For the development of railroads see A. Sartorius von Waltershausen, *Deutsche Wirtschaftsgeschichte 1815–1914*, pp. 98–106. See the suggestive remarks on the social repercussions of technological development by Schnabel, *Deutsche Geschichte*, 3:381–91; Hamerow, *Restoration*, p. 7. A concise treatment of the development of the Zollverein may be found in Huber, *Verfassungsgeschichte*,

2:282–305, and a longer account is provided by W. O. Henderson, *The Zollverein*, pp. 29–189. Heinrich von Gagern was one of many liberals who hoped for Prussian leadership in the unification of Germany and was greatly encouraged by the development of the Zollverein—as is shown by Wentzcke and Klötzer, eds., *Deutscher Liberalismus*, pp. 83–84, 90–91, 110, 115–16, 155–56. The Württemberg liberal, August Schott, favored the Customs Union while other leading liberals—Ludwig Uhland, Paul Pfizer, and Friedrich Römer—in 1833 voted against participation by their state in the Zollverein. (See Grube, *Stuttgarter Landtag*, p. 518). On the impact of the early railroads see Manfred Riedel, "Vom Biedermeier zum Maschinenzeitalter," pp. 101–23.

17. J. H. Clapham, *The Economic Development of France and Germany, 1815–1914*, pp. 82–103, 150–56, 283; Wolfgang Köllmann, *Friedrich Harkort*, 1:56–186; W. O. Henderson, *The State and the Industrial Revolution in Prussia, 1740–1870*, pp. 43–193; Ilja Mieck, *Preussische Gewerbepolitik in Berlin 1806–1844*; three works by Richard Tilly: "The Political Economy of Public Finance and the Industrialization of Prussia, 1815–1866," pp. 484–97, "Germany (1815–1870)," pp. 156–60, 169, and *Financial Institutions and Industrialization in the Rhineland, 1815–1870*; Conze et al., *Staat und Gesellschaft*, pp. 115–19, 134–39, 167–70; Fritz Redlich, "The Leaders of the German Steam-Engine Industry during the First Hundred Years," pp. 121–48; Dietrich Eichholtz, *Junker und Bourgeoisie vor 1848 in der preussischen Eisenbahngeschichte*, pp. 12–183 (a well-researched study, notwithstanding its Marxist-Leninist bias); three excellent studies by Wolfram Fischer: *Der Staat und die Anfänge der Industrialisierung in Baden 1800–1850*, pp. 307, 309, 313, 329, and passim, "Soziale Unterschichten im Zeitalter der Frühindustrialisierung," pp. 415–35, and "Government Activity and Industrialization in Germany (1815–70)," pp. 83–94; Walther G. Hoffman, "The Take-Off in Germany," pp. 95–117.

18. Jacques Droz, *Le Libéralisme rhénan, 1815–1848*, pp. 165–79 and passim; Rudolf Stadelmann, *Soziale und politische Geschichte der Revolution von 1848*, pp. 9, 13–14, 22; Wilhelm Treue, "Dagobert Oppenheim," pp. 145–75; Helmuth Croon, *Die gesellschaftlichen Auswirkungen des Gemeindewahlrechts in den Gemeinden und Kreisen des Rheinlandes und Westfalens im 19. Jahrhundert*, pp. 7–13, 61–63, and passim.

19. Marxist historians, of course, continue to identify the liberal movement of the period 1815–48 with the economic interests of the bourgeoisie. See, for example, Siegfried Schmidt, "Zur Frühgeschichte der bürgerlichen Parteien in Deutschland," pp. 973–91. Occupational statistics are from Hale, "Press and Fatherland Society."

20. Varnhagen von Ense, quoted by Riedel, "Vom Biedermeier zum Maschinenzeitalter," p. 105.

III FOREIGN MODELS AND DOMESTIC AGITATION

1. *Allgemeine Zeitung* (Augsburg), May 13, 1832 (Ausserordentliche Beilage, Nos. 185–86).

2. Ernst Rudolf Huber, *Deutsche Verfassungsgeschichte seit 1789*, 2:48–62, 126–49, 175; Heinrich Heffter, *Die deutsche Selbstverwaltung im 19. Jahrhundert*, pp. 161, 247, 276–80.

3. Karl-Georg Faber, *Die Rheinlande zwischen Restauration und Revolution*, pp. 312–25; Federico Federici, ed., *Der deutsche Liberalismus*, pp. 140–46 (excerpts from writings of participants in the Hambach Festival); Kurt von Raumer, "Das Hambacher Fest," pp. 207–17; Leonard Krieger, *The German Idea of Freedom*, p. 265; Richard Metternich, ed., *Memoirs of Prince Metternich*, 5:241; F. Gunther

Eyck, "English and French Influences on German Liberalism before 1848," pp. 313–41; Kurt Koszyk, *Deutsche Presse im 19. Jahrhundert*, pp. 66–77. For the coverage of the Hambach Festival by a major liberal newspaper, see the *Allgemeine Zeitung* (Augsburg), particularly May 15-June 8, 1832 (pp. 542–640 plus supplements and special supplements; the quotation in the text above appeared in Ausserordentliche Beilage, No. 202, May 25, 1832).
    4. Reinhart Koselleck, *Preussen zwischen Reform und Revolution*, pp. 114–15n.
    5. Erich Brandenburg, *Die Reichsgründung*, 1:138; Heinrich von Srbik, *Metternich*, 1:679–83; Huber, *Verfassungsgeschichte*, 2:151–84; Douglas D. Hale, Jr., "Gustav Bunsen," pp. 129–39.
    6. Klara Kautz, *Das deutsche Frankreichbild in der ersten Hälfte des 19. Jahrhunderts nach Reisebeschreibungen, Tagebüchern und Briefen*, pp. 35–81; Wolfgang Schieder, *Anfänge der deutschen Arbeiterbewegung*, pp. 14–28, 45–61, 98–100, and passim.
    7. J. G. Legge, *Rhyme and Revolution in Germany*, pp. 191–219; Heinz-Otto Sieburg, *Deutschland und Frankreich in der Geschichtsschreibung des neunzehnten Jahrhunderts*, pp. 104–32, 241–73; Koppel S. Pinson, *Modern Germany*, pp. 65–71; Hans Kohn, *The Mind of Germany*, pp. 99–127; Golo Mann, *Deutsche Geschichte des neunzehnten und zwanzigsten Jahrhunderts*, pp. 143, 163–64; Oscar J. Hammen, "The Failure of an Attempted Franco-German Liberal Rapprochement, 1830–1840," pp. 54–67; Georg G. Iggers, "Heinrich Heine and the Saint-Simonians," pp. 289–308; Federici, ed., *Der deutsche Liberalismus*, pp. 161–71 (excerpts from writings of Heine and Börne); Hans-Joachim Schoeps, ed., "Metternichs Kampf gegen die Revolution," pp. 541–52.
    8. Karl Löwith, *From Hegel to Nietzsche*, pp. 63–89; Beatrix Mesmer-Strupp, *Arnold Ruges Plan einer Alliance intellectuelle zwischen Deutschen und Franzosen*, pp. 83–86 and passim; (for Ruge quote) Walter Naher, *Arnold Ruge als Politiker und politischer Schriftsteller*, pp. 1–161; Fritz Schlawe, "Die junghegelische Publizistik," pp. 30–50; Hans Rosenberg, *Rudolf Haym und die Anfänge des klassischen Liberalismus*, pp. 11–39.
    9. An excellent brief account of developments in Switzerland, 1830–48, and their impact on Germany is offered by William L. Langer, *Political and Social Upheaval, 1832–1852*, pp. 133–37. See also: Franz Schnabel, *Deutsche Geschichte im neunzehnten Jahrhundert*, 2:194–95; Heinrich Schmidt, *Die deutschen Flüchtlinge in der Schweiz 1833–1836*, pp. 20–21, 49–56, 118–19, 140–41, and passim; Naher, *Arnold Ruge*, pp. 133–61; Koszyk, *Deutsche Presse*, pp. 80–86; Paul Wentzcke and Wolfgang Klötzer, eds., *Deutscher Liberalismus im Vormärz*, p. 204; Wilhelm Mommsen, "Julius Fröbel, Wirrnis und Weitsicht," pp. 497–532; Friedrich C. Sell, *Die Tragödie des deutschen Liberalismus*, pp. 70–71; F. Gunther Eyck, "Mazzini's Young Europe," pp. 368–73, 377; Schieder, *Anfänge der deutschen Arbeiterbewegung*, pp. 29–44, 66–81, 97, 123–25, and passim.
    10. Rondo Cameron et al., *Banking in the Early Stages of Industrialization*, pp. 130, 145; Hermann von der Dunk, *Der deutsche Vormärz und Belgien 1830/48*, pp. 126–330.
    11. Theodor Wilhelm, *Die englische Verfassung und der vormärzliche deutsche Liberalismus*; Charles Edgar McClelland, "The German Historians and England," pp. 1–122; C. W. Hasek, *The Introduction of Adam Smith's Doctrines in Germany*, p. 397 and passim; Jacques Droz, *Le Libéralisme rhénan, 1815–1848*, pp. 227–91, 425–55, and passim; Dietrich Eichholtz, *Junker und Bourgeoisie vor 1848 in der preussischen Eisenbahngeschichte*, pp. 12–183 passim; Heinz Boberach, *Wahlrechtsfragen im Vormärz*, pp. 55, 62–77, 99, 103–4; Heinrich von Treitschke, *Deutsche Geschichte im neunzehnten Jahrhundert*, 3:702 and passim; Eyck, "English and

French Influences," pp. 313–41; Oscar J. Hammen, "Economic and Social Factors in the Prussian Rhineland in 1848," p. 829; Schnabel, *Deutsche Geschichte,* 2:175–79, 190–92, 3:393–94; Douglas D. Hale, Jr., "The Making of a Liberal Leader," pp. 34–51; Wentzcke and Klötzer, eds., *Deutscher Liberalismus,* pp. 68, 78, 81, 148, 159, 162, 183, 409, and passim; Schoeps, ed., "Metternichs Kampf," p. 535; Werner Conze et al., *Staat und Gesellschaft,* pp. 190–205, 242; Erich Angermann, *Robert von Mohl 1799–1875,* pp. 19–58 and passim; Donald G. Rohr, *The Origins of Social Liberalism in Germany,* pp. 78–157 passim; Friedrich Zunkel, *Der rheinisch-westfälische Unternehmer 1834–1879,* pp. 44–46, 93–98, 133–69, and passim; Ludwig Puppke, *Sozialpolitik und soziale Anschauungen frühindustrieller Unternehmer in Rheinland-Westfalen;* Schieder, *Anfänge der deutschen Arbeiterbewegung,* p. 101; Ernst Schraepler, "Der Bund der Gerechten," pp. 5–29.

12. The daily *Allgemeine Zeitung* (Augsburg) carried numerous and rather detailed reports about America throughout the period for which it has been selectively examined (1822–48). The paragraphs above are based largely upon: Ernst Fraenkel, ed., *Amerika im Spiegel des deutschen politischen Denkens,* pp. 24–28; Henry M. Adams, *Prussian-American Relations, 1775–1871,* pp. 33–63; Paul C. Weber, *America in Imaginative German Literature in the First Half of the Nineteenth Century,* pp. 43, 44, 47, 53, 72, 73–75, 85, 102–19, and 43–277 passim; Thomas D. Clark, ed., *Travels in the Old South,* 2:23, 35, 50, 58, 67, 142, 241, 3:17–25, 35–60, 84–86, 97, 115, 133–43, 173–92, 256–82, 330–35; Henry A. Pochmann, *German Culture in America,* pp. 67, 77, 115–22, 125–27; Wentzcke and Klötzer, eds., *Deutscher Liberalismus,* pp. 169–70, 279; Bernhard, Duke of Saxe-Weimar-Eisenach, *Travels through North America during the Years 1825 and 1826,* 2:57, 58, 238, and passim, of which excerpts appear in Oscar Handlin, ed., *This Was America,* pp. 155–68; Thomas Sergeant Perry, ed., *The Life and Letters of Francis Lieber,* pp. 8–71; Frank Friedel, *Francis Lieber: Nineteenth-Century Liberal* (Baton Rouge, 1947), pp. 1–62; Drake De Kay, "Encyclopedia Americana, First Edition," pp. 201–20; Henry Steele Commager, ed., *America in Perspective,* pp. 36–39; John A. Hawgood, *The Tragedy of German-America,* pp. 21–200; Mack Walker, *Germany and the Emigration, 1816–1885,* pp. 1–133 passim; Alfred Vagts, *Deutsch-Amerikanische Rückwanderung,* pp. 154–68; Max Freund, ed., *Gustav Dresel's Houston Journal.*

13. Walker, *Germany and the Emigration,* facing pp. 1 and 131 for *Allgemeine Zeitung* quotations.

14. Friedrich Schmidt, *Versuch über den politischen Zustand der Vereinigten Staaten von Nord-Amerika,* 1:vii–xii, 2:1–101; Angermann, *Robert von Mohl,* pp. 25–27 and passim; Handlin, *This Was America,* p. 179 (quoting Tocqueville); J. P. Mayer, ed., *Alexis de Tocqueville,* 1:8, xvi–lxvii (for the discussion by Theodor Eschenburg of Tocqueville's reception in Germany); Fraenkel, ed., *Amerika im Spiegel,* pp. 78–113; Federici, ed., *Der deutsche Liberalismus,* pp. 67–75, 178–206, 209–11 (excerpts from the writings of Rotteck and Welcker); Bruno Siemers, "Die Vereinigten Staaten und die deutsche Einheitsbewegung," pp. 176–205; Eckart G. Franz, *Das Amerikabild der deutschen Revolution von 1848/49,* pp. 3–98 passim; Friedrich von Raumer, *Die Vereinigten Staaten von Nordamerika,* esp. 1:vi–viii, xiv, 129, 131–49, 217–78, 312, 536, 2:268–339.

15. Carl Wittke, *Against the Current,* pp. 1–57 (for Heinzen quote); Veit Valentin, *Geschichte der deutschen Revolution von 1848–1849,* 1:286; Mommsen, "Julius Fröbel," pp. 510–11; Hans Blum, *Die deutsche Revolution 1848–1849 mit 256 authentischen Faksimilebeilagen,* facing p. 96 (for the leaflet of March 1848); Walker, *Germany and the Emigration,* p. 63 (on the Prussian order of 1836); Metternich to Nesselrode, Jan. 19, 1824, quoted by Dexter Perkins, *Hands Off,* p. 27.

16. Rolf Engelsing, "Zur politischen Bildung der deutschen Unterschichten 1789–1863," pp. 337–63; Schieder, *Anfänge der deutschen Arbeiterbewegung*, pp. 51–53, 245–87, and passim; Schraepler, "Der Bund der Gerechten," pp. 5–29; P. H. Noyes, *Organization and Revolution*, pp. 34–54; Franz Mehring, *Geschichte der deutschen Sozialdemokratie*, 1:103–15, 140–222, 328–74, 2:90–97 and passim; Edmund Silberner and Werner Blumenberg, eds., *Moses Hess: Briefwechsel* pp. 79–80, 95, 105–8, and passim; Edmund Silberner, *Moses Hess*, pp. 125–66; Gustav Meyer, *Friedrich Engels*, pp. 3–91. For the origins of Marx's socialism and his development as a revolutionary one may begin with the following, which suggest additional literature: George Lichtheim, *The Origins of Socialism*; Isaiah Berlin, *Karl Marx*, pp. 23–157; Oscar J. Hammen, "The Young Marx Reconsidered," pp. 109–20, and Hammen, *The Red '48ers*, pp. 3–193, 411–12.

17. Jürgen Kuczynski, *Die Geschichte der Lage der Arbeiter unter dem Kapitalismus*, 1:220–341 (valuable notwithstanding the polemically Marxist interpretations); Oscar J. Hammen, "The Specter of Communism in the 1840's," pp. 404–20; Faber, *Die Rheinlande*, pp. 334–47; Ilja Mieck, "Das Berliner Fabriken-Gericht (1815–1875)," pp. 249–71; Wolfram Fischer, *Der Staat und die Anfänge der Industrialisierung in Baden 1800–1850*, 1:72–83, 331–42, 362–80, 385–87; Theodore S. Hamerow, *Restoration, Revolution, Reaction*, pp. 29, 31–35, 77–86, 104, 181; Wentzcke and Klötzer, eds., *Deutscher Liberalismus*, pp. 282, 342, 368, 369, 399 (for Gagern quote); Hansjoachim Hennig, "Preussische Sozialpolitik im Vormärz?" pp. 485–539; Carl Jantke and Dietrich Hilger, eds., *Die Eigentumslosen*; Helmut Bleiber, *Zwischen Reform und Revolution*, pp. 121–200 and passim.

18. R. Hinton Thomas, *Liberalism, Nationalism and the German Intellectuals (1822–1847)*, pp. 1, 20–50, 84–85, 100, 104–19, 122–31; for two recent centennial appreciations of Gervinus, see Jonathan F. Wagner, "Georg Gottfried Gervinus," pp. 354–70; and Charles E. McClelland, "History in the Service of Politics," pp. 371–88; Wolfgang Hock, *Liberales Denken im Zeitalter der Paulskirche*, pp. 34–68 and passim; Valentin, *Revolution*, 1:37–51, 55–57, 161, and passim; Droz, *Le Libéralisme rhénan*, pp. 353–61; Hartwig Brandt, *Landständische Repräsentation im deutschen Vormärz*, pp. 160–281; Wentzcke and Klötzer, eds., *Deutscher Liberalismus*, 115–17, 121–28, 292–94, 355–58, 361–79, 382–83, 388–90, 399–402; Koszyk, *Deutsche Presse*, pp. 111–12; Fischer, *Der Staat und die Anfänge*, pp. 72–83, 387–90, and passim; Rohr, *Origins of Social Liberalism*, pp. 78–157 passim; Zunkel, *Der rheinisch-westfälische Unternehmer*, pp. 44–46, 93–98, 133–69, and passim; Reinhard Höhn, *Die Armee als Erziehungsschule der Nation*, pp. 33–76, which sums up matters treated in greater detail in Höhn's *Verfassungskampf und Heereseid*. Itzstein is the subject of a Ph.D. dissertation by Josef Rosskopf, (Johannes Gutenberg University of Mainz, 1954) that I have not consulted.

19. Catherine Magill Holden, "A Decade of Dissent in Germany;" Annette Kuhn, *Die Kirche im Ringen mit dem Sozialismus 1803–1848*, pp. 86–93 and passim; *Brockhaus' Konversations-Lexikon*, 14th ed., 17 vols. (Liepzig, 1908), 7:137–38, 13: 991–92, 14:28, 16:41, 781–82 (brief factual articles on the dissident movements and their leaders); William O. Shanahan, *German Protestants Face the Social Question*; Frolinde Balser, *Sozial-Demokratie 1848/49–1863*, 1:30, 347. Robert M. Bigler, "The Rise of Political Protestantism in Nineteenth Century Germany," p. 423.

20. Ernest Hamburger, *Juden im öffentlichen Leben Deutschlands*, pp. 10–20; Jacob Toury, *Die politischen Orientierungen der Juden in Deutschland*, pp. 1–46 (quotations from pp. 19, 38, 40); Ismar Elbogen and Eleonore Sterling, *Die Geschichte der Juden in Deutschland*, pp. 194–234; R. Adam, "Johann Jacoby's

Notes to Pages 73–77   [393]

politischer Werdegang 1805–1840," pp. 48–76 (quotation from p. 66); Arnold Heinz Schuetz, "Johan Jacoby—A Prussian Democrat," pp. 2–4, 10–12. A biographical study of Aaron Bernstein (1812–1884) would throw light on the development of Reform Judaism, the democratic movement in Germany, and the German press. (He was editor of the *Berliner Volkszeitung* during the last quarter-century of his life.) Basic data are provided in *Brockhaus' Konversations-Lexikon*, 2:813.

21. For state policy and increasing political criticism in Prussia see: Koselleck, *Reform und Revolution*, pp. 337–97, 680–93, and passim; Droz, *Le Libéralisme rhénan*, pp. 314–45 and passim; Boberach, *Wahlrechtsfragen im Vormärz*, pp. 38–42, 103–14; Huber, *Verfassungsgeschichte*, 2:435–60, 477–98; Hans Schneider, *Der preussische Staatsrat, 1817–1918*, pp. 148–205; the essay by Walter Bussmann on Frederick William IV in Konrad Repgen and Stephan Skalweit, eds., *Spiegel der Geschichte*, pp. 711–26; Wentzcke and Klötzer, eds., *Deutscher Liberalismus*, pp. 35–36, 232–412 passim, esp. pp. 382–87; Otto von Bismarck, *Bismarck, the Man and the Statesman, Being the Reflections and Reminiscences of Otto, Prince von Bismarck*, 1:19–21, 44, 309; Valentin, *Revolution*, 1:28–100; and Eichholtz, *Junker und Bourgeoisie*, pp. 119–24. For thoughtful and well-informed brief accounts of these matters see Hajo Holborn, *A History of Modern Germany: 1840–1945*. .

22. Schuetz, "Johann Jacoby," p. 29.

23. Thomas, *Liberalism*, p. 12 (for both quotations).

IV 1848

1. The *Allgemeine Zeitung* (Augsburg), February 27, published the news that Louis Philippe had abdicated. A special supplement on February 28 announced the creation of a republic in France. More details followed in the leap-year edition of February 29, which reported preoccupation in Munich with news of the events in Paris and widespread speculation about their repercussions in Germany.

There is a large body of literature on the revolutions of 1848–49 in Germany. An excellent detailed survey is offered by Ernst Rudolf Huber, *Deutsche Verfassungsgeschichte seit 1789*, 2:309–935. A mine of information is provided by the most exhaustive study available, the work by Veit Valentin, *Geschichte der deutschen Revolution von 1848–49*, the rich and colorful but inadequately organized product of three decades of careful research and devotion to the cause of democracy; Valentin's historiographical essay is indispensable (2:595–613). The single-volume abridgment in English sacrifices detail, but reasonably well reflects Valentin's interpretation and style: *1848: Chapters of German History*. A more reserved account from a National Liberal viewpoint is offered by Erich Brandenburg, *Die Reichsgründung*, 1:175–297. Among newer works, the following are especially useful: Jacques Droz and Ernest Tonnelat, *Les Révolutions allemandes de 1848*, including the historiographical survey, pp. 11–22; Rudolf Stadelmann, *Soziale und politische Geschichte der Revolution von 1848*; and Theodore S. Hamerow, *Restoration, Revolution, Reaction*. See also the survey of literature in Theodore S. Hamerow, "History and the Germany Revolution of 1848," pp. 27–44, which can be valuably supplemented by the bibliography in the work of an East-German historian: Gerhard Schilfert, *Sieg und Niederlage des demokratischen Wahlrechts in der deutschen Revolution 1848/49*, pp. 322–36. See further Andreas Dorpalen, "Die Revolution von 1848 in der Geschichtsschreibung der DDR," pp.324–68. For the most important documents, see Ernst Rudolf Huber, ed., *Dokumete zur deutschen Vergassungsgeschichte*, 1:261–450. Examples of the cartoons and leaflets of the revolution may be found in the work by the son of a leading revolutionary of 1848, Hans Blum, *Die deutsche Revolution 1848–1849 mit 256 authentischen Faksimilebeilagen;* see also W. A. Coupe, "The German Cartoon and the Revolution of 1848," pp. 137–67.

2. Hans Krause, *Die demokratische Partei von 1848 und die soziale Frage;* Stadelmann, *Revolution,* pp. 12–14, 26, 50, 78–80,155–73; Droz and Tonnelat, *Les Révolutions,* pp. 97–99, 513–91; Hamerow, *Restoration,* pp. 107–9, 140–6, 156–72; Schilfert, *Revolution,* pp. 39, 80; Lenore O'Boyle, "The Democratic Left in Germany, 1848," pp. 374–83. Brandenburg's thesis that the "democrats" were solidly united in favor of the "German Republic" (*Die Reichsgründung,* 1:227) has not withstood subsequent research. The role of the artisans in the Revolution of 1848—emphasized by Stadelmann, Droz-Tonnelat, and Hamerow—has been explored more recently in greater depth by two valuable monographs: Frolinde Balser, *Sozial-Demokratie 1848/49–1863;* and P. H. Noyes, *Organization and Revolution.* For a Marxist interpretation see Rolf Weber, "Die Beziehungen zwischen sozialer Struktur und politischer Ideologie des Kleinbürgertums in der Revolution von 1848/49," pp. 1186–93. Friedrich Zunkel, *Der rheinisch-westfälische Unternehmer 1834–1879,* pp. 170–82, portrays the shift of bourgeois liberals to more conservative positions under the impact of the revolutions of 1848–49.

3. Valentin, *Revolution,* 1:115–40, 385–98, 504–6; Werner Conze et al., *Staat und Gesellschaft im deutschen Vormärz 1815–1848,* pp. 115, 134–42; Noyes, *Organization and Revolution,* pp. 376–80 and passim; Paul Wentzcke, "Bayerische Stimmen aus der Paulskirche (Juni–Juli 1848)," pp. 485–99. For more on Lola, see the bibliographical references in William L. Langer, *Political and Social Upheaval, 1832–1852,* p. 389n.

4. Walter Grube, *Der Stuttgarter Landtag 1457–1957,* pp. 525–27; Karl-Johannes Grauer, *Wilhelm I. König von Württemberg,* pp. 286–88, 291–95, the work of a Srbik epigone.

5. Heinrich von Srbik, *Metternich,* 2:247–99; R. John Rath, *The Viennese Revolution of 1848,* pp. 34–153.

6. Ernst Kaeber, *Berlin 1848,* pp. 35–100 (colorful and accurate); Erwin H. Ackerknecht, *Rudolf Virchow,* p. 133 (for sanitary conditions in Berlin as late as 1870); Noyes, *Organization and Revolution,* pp. 62–78; Valentin, *Revolution,* 1:84–88, 410–58, 538–43; Hamerow, *Restoration,* pp. 99–100; Gordon A. Craig, *The Politics of the Prussian Army, 1640–1945,* pp. 92–106; Priscilla Robertson, *Revolutions of 1848,* pp. 110–26; Huber, *Verfassungsgeschicte,* 2:571–86; Otto von Bismarck, *Bismarck, the Man and the Statesman, Being the Reflections and Reminiscences of Otto, Prince von Bismarck,* 1:35; Hans Schneider, *Der preussische Staatsrat 1817–1918,* pp. 205–9; Frank G. Weber, "Palmerston and German Liberalism, 1848," p. 134. On the mode of election of the Prussian Constituent Assembly, see Donald T. Mattheisen, "Voters and Parliaments in the German Revolution of 1848," pp. 5–6.

7. Hellmut Kretzschmar and Horst Schlechte, eds., *Französische und sächsische Gesandtschaftsberichte aus Dresden und Paris 1848–1849,* pp. 45–98 passim, for reports from Dresden by the French chargé, Baron Eugène de Méneval; Valentin, *Revolution,* 1:216–29, 368–71; Huber, *Verfassungsgeschichte,* 2:526–29; and the interesting East German study by Rolf Weber, *Die Revolution in Sachsen 1848/49,* pp. 15–50.

8. Wöhler to Liebig, March 21, 1848, in Robert Schwarz, ed., *Aus Justus Liebigs und Friedrich Wöhlers Briefwechsel in den Jahren 1829–1873,* pp. 182–83; Huber, *Verfassungsgeschichte,* 2:530–44; Valentin, *Revolution,* 1:196–216, 229–31, 362–68; Otto Vitense, *Geschichte von Mecklenburg,* pp. 447–53.

9. Percy Ernst Schramm, *Neun Generationen*, pp. 140–81, 284–93; Huber, *Verfassungsgeschichte*, 2:514–16, 519–22, 544–47; Paul Wentzcke and Wolfgang Klötzer, eds., *Deutscher Liberalismus im Vormärz*, pp. 381–415; Valentin, *Revolution*, 1:167–80, 184–96, 231–39, 353–56, 359–62, 371–72, 2:386–90; Philipp Losch, *Geschichte des Kurfürstentums Hessen, 1803 bis 1866*, pp. 228–47.

10. Conze et al., *Staat und Gesellschaft*, pp. 166–71; Huber, *Verfassungsgeschichte*, 2:509–13; Valentin, *Revolution*, 1:152–67, 342–48, 482–504; Georg Trübner, "Johann Philipp Becker und die Revolution 1848," pp. 410–27; Kretzschmar and Schlechte, eds., *Französische und sächsische Gesandtschaftsberichte*, pp. 55–82 passim (on the organization and arming of Germans in France by Herwegh).

11. The work by Droz and Tonnelat gives more attention to religion in the Revolution of 1848 than most accounts, finding Protestant churchmen generally conservative and some Catholic clerics on the side of democracy. *Les Révolutions*, 127–46, 481–512, and passim; see also Jacques Droz, "Religious Aspects of the Revolutions of 1848 in Europe," pp. 134–49. The Droz thesis is partially confirmed by Eberhard Amelung's dissertation, *Die demokratischen Bewegungen des Jahres 1848 im Urteil der protestantischen Theologie*. Some members of the lower clergy favored democracy, and many Catholics who were theologically and politically conservative actively worked for separation of church and state. (Huber, *Verfassungsgeschichte*, 2:610, 685–87, 703–5). A number of German Catholics were energetic democrats in 1848 (see Balser, *Sozial-Demokratie*, 1:30, 347). The religious spirit of the common people appears to have justified their acts of rebellion in some cases. When Berliners carried their dead to the royal palace following the fighting of March 18 they sang "Jesu, meine Zuversicht" ("Jesus, My Assurance"), and this became a kind of "hymn of the revolution" (Noyes, *Organization and Revolution*, p. 69). There is valuable information on the political activity of the Catholic clergy in Konrad Repgen, *Märzbewegung und Maiwahlen des Revolutionsjahres 1848 im Rheinland*. The whole question of religion and the churches in the Revolution of 1848 warrants the thorough study it has not yet received.

12. For the steps toward unification through May 1, 1848, see Frank Eyck, *The Frankfurt Parliament, 1848–1849*, pp. 37–90; Wentzcke and Klötzer, eds., *Deutscher Liberalismus*, pp. 413–15; Huber, *Verfassungsgeschichte*, 2:400–401, 587–608; Eckhart G. Franz, *Das Amerikabild der deutschen Revolution von 1848/49*, p. 104; Repgen, *Märzbewegung und Maiwahlen*, pp. 32–36, 138–308, and passim; Valentin, *Revolution*, 1:374–77, 466–79; Krause, *Die demokratische Partei*, pp. 35–59 (for Struve quote); Theodore S. Hamerow, "The Elections to the Frankfurt Parliament," pp. 15–32.

13. Mack Walker, ed., *Metternich's Europe* (New York, 1968), p. 189, offers a translation of Heine's verse from *Germany: A Winter's Tale*. I have partially modified the most commonly given summaries of occupational identities of the members of the National Assembly in the light of data presented in Max Schwarz, ed., p. 8, and Eyck, *Frankfurt Parliament*, pp. 90–101. For the paragraphs above see also: Valentin, *Revolution*, 2:1–22; Huber, *Verfassungsgeschichte*, 2:608–22; Gilbert Ziebura, "Anfänge des deutschen Parlamentarismus," pp. 185–236. Data and historical street plans for Frankfurt and other cities involved in the Revolution of 1848 may be found in E. A. Gutkind, *Urban Development in Central Europe*, p. 270 and passim.

14. The essential data are available in Schwarz, ed., *MdR*. He reports 23 physicians in his text, but identifies 26 medical doctors in his biographical sketches. Though this volume is not free of errors, it is an invaluable work of reference for students of German history, 1848–1933. The biographical sketches

presented above on Jahn, Riesser, Rossmässler, Simon, and Wigard are based on the *Allgemeine deutsche Biographie*, 13:662–64; 28:586–89, 29:268–71, 34:377–79; 42:458–59. See the appropriate volumes of *Brockhaus' Konversations-Lexikon*, 14th ed. (Liepzig 1908), for biographies of all the others except Nauwerck, who is mentioned by neither of these reference works nor in present-day German encyclopedias. On Rossmässler, see also the memoirs of the Dutch-born radical scientist Jacob Moleschott, in1848 a lecturer in Heidelberg, *Für meine Freunde*, p. 228; on Nauwerck: Kaeber, *Berlin 1848*, pp. 21, 22; Valentin, *Revolution*, 1:572, 2:20–21, 129, 178; Franz, *Das Amerikabild der deutschen Revolution*, pp. 119–21, 125–28, 139; and—of some peripheral interest—Karl· Nauwerck, *Statistisches Wörterbuch über die Vereinigten Staaten*. See also Herman Misteli, *Carl Vogt*; Dieter Wittich, "Zur Geschichte und Deutung des Materialismus von Karl Vogt, Jakob Moleschott und Ludwig Büchner," pp. 389–402, and Otto Döhner, Jr., *Georg Büchners Naturauffassung*, p. 45 (for information on Vogt and Büchner as medical students at Giessen in 1833–34).

V FRUSTRATION OF DEMOCRATIC UNITY

1. This chapter draws heavily upon: Ernst Rudolf Huber, *Deutsche Verfassungsgeschichte seit 1789*, 2:309–935; Veit Valentin, *Geschichte der deutschen Revolution von 1848–49*; and other works cited in the first footnote of the previous chapter.
2. Valentin, *Revolution*, 2:1–41, 42–94 passim, esp. 91–92; Gordon A. Craig, *The Politics of the Prussian Army 1640–1945*, pp. 113–14; Huber, *Verfassungsgeschichte*, 2:622–33, 647–55. See also Paul Wentzcke, "Bayerische Stimmen aus der Paulskirche (Juni–Juli 1848)", pp. 485–99; Frank Eyck, *The Frankfurt Parliament, 1848–1849*, pp. 113–205 passim (a survey of the National Assembly through March 1849, based largely on the debates).
3. Huber, *Verfassungsgeschichte*, 2:516–19; Valentin, *Revolution*, 1:180–84, 356–59. For a good concise recent account of events in Nassau, see Wolf-Heino Struck, "Das Streben nach bürgerlicher Freiheit und nationaler Einheit in der Sicht des Herzogtums Nassau," pp. 170–75.
4. Huber, *Verfassungsgeschichte*, 2:697–9; Valentin, *Revolution*, 1:239–45; 372–74, 2:159–66; Eyck, *Frankfurt Parliament*, pp. 254–384. For the background on German nationalism in the northern duchies see W. Carr, *Schleswig-Holstein, 1815–48*, pp. 21–293.
5. Valentin, *Revolution*, 2:169–82. See also Paul Neitzke, *Die deutschen politischen Flüchtlinge in der Schweiz 1848–49*, pp. 17–28.
6. Valentin, *Revolution*, 2:164–69; Huber, *Verfassungsgeschichte*, 2:699–701; and, on Schmerling's concern, the report of September 30 by the Württemberg minister in Frankfurt, cited from the Württemberg archives by Frolinde Balser, *Sozial-Demokratie 1848/49–1863*, 1:246.
7. Huber, *Verfassungsgeschichte*, 2:532–33, 535–36; Valentin, *Revolution*, 2:300–301, 383–84.
8. R. John Rath, *The Viennese Revolution of 1848*, pp. 317–65; Huber, *Verfassungsgeschichte*, 2:710–23; Valentin, *Revolution*, 2:183–226. For the nationality problems in the Habsburg lands see Robert A. Kann, *The Multinational Empire*, 1:58–84, 118–26, and passim.
9. Liebig to Wöhler, May 5, 1848, in Robert Schwarz, ed., *Aus Justus Liebigs und Friedrich Wöhlers Briefwechsel in den Jahren 1829–1873*, p. 187; Oscar J. Hammen, *The Red '48ers*, pp. 185–410; P. H. Noyes, *Organization and Revolution*, pp. 81–261; Balser, *Sozial-Demokratie*, 1:11–65 and passim and supporting documents

in vol. 2. Noyes and Balser treat Born and the *Verbrüderung* favorably, Noyes in greater detail for 1848, Balser thereafter. See also: Theodore S. Hamerow, "1848," pp. 147–52; Theodore S. Hamerow, *Restoration, Revolution, Reaction*, pp. 67, 78, 123, 137–55; Rudolf Stadelmann, *Soziale und politische Geschichte der Revolution von 1848*, p. 74; Jacques Droz and Ernest Tonnelat, *Les Révolutions allemandes de 1848*, pp. 127–46, 481–512; Gerhard Schilfert, *Sieg und Niederlage des demokratischen Wahlrechts in der deutschen Revolution 1848/49*, pp. 55–85 and passim (valuable, with Marxist-Leninist slant); Walter Schmidt, "Der Bund der Kommunisten und die Versuche einer Zentralisierung der deutschen Arbeitervereine im April und Mai 1848," pp. 577–614; John Weiss, "Karl Marlo, Guild Socialism, and the Revolutions of 1848," pp. 77–96.

10. Friedrich Meinecke, "The Year 1848 in German History," pp. 480, 488, 489; Huber, *Verfassungsgeschichte*, 2:724–30; Valentin, *Revolution*, 2:42–74.

11. Hans Krause, *Die demokratische Partei von 1848 und die soziale Frage*, pp. 109–202 passim; Donald T. Mattheisen, "Voters and Parliaments in the German Revolution of 1848," pp. 6–22; Walter Naher, *Arnold Ruge als Politiker und politischer Schriftsteller*, pp. 201–6; Noyes, *Organization and Revolution*, pp. 265–85; Valentin, *Revolution*, 2:227–75; Huber, *Verfassungsgeschichte*, 2:641–47, 683–89, 705–9, 729–56; Craig, *Prussian Army*, pp. 112–24; Heinz Boberach, *Wahlrechtsfragen im Vormärz*, pp. 115–27.

12. The three-class voting system that was to remain in effect from 1849 to 1918 is discussed in the next chapter. For the above paragraphs see: Hamerow, *Restoration*, pp. 186–92, 215; Huber, *Verfassungsgeschichte*, 2:756–66, 854–56, 3:35 –53; Valentin, *Revolution*, 2:275–96, 344–47, 469–75; Leonard Krieger, *The German Idea of Freedom*, pp. 338–44; Craig, *Prussian Army*, pp. 120–24; Schilfert, *Revolution*, pp. 267–316; Boberach, *Wahlrechtsfragen im Vormärz*, pp. 127–50, and cf. pp. 35–38, 92–103. Interesting case studies of the election campaigns of the democrats and the liberals in January 1849 in the Bonn and Trier areas (where the democrats won) are available in the careful works by Renate Kaiser, *Die politischen Strömungen in den Kreisen Bonn und Rheinbach 1848–1878*, pp. 47–66, and Hansjürgen Schierbaum, *Die politischen Wahlen in den Eifel-und Moselkreisen des Regierungsbezirks Trier 1849–1867*, pp. 40–60.

13. John A. Hawgood, *Political and Economic Relations between the United States of American and the German Provisional Central Government at Frankfurt-am-Main in 1848–1849*, pp. 8–21 and passim; W. E. Mosse, *The European Powers and the German Question, 1848–71, with Special Reference to England and Russia*, pp. 15–25; Frank G. Weber, "Palmerston and German Liberalism, 1848," pp. 125–36; on the failure to win French diplomatic recognition, Hellmut Kretzschmar and Horst Schlechte, eds., *Französische und sächsische Gesandtschaftsberichte aus Dresden und Paris 1848–1849*, pp. 117–262 passim (which also documents the refusal of the German states to surrender their separate diplomatic representation to the Frankfurt Assembly and refusal by the cabinet of Saxony to publish the *Grundrechte* in January 1849); Rudolf Buchner, *Die deutsch-französische Tragödie 1848–1864*, pp. 19–36. Friedrich Meinecke's factual and speculative treatment of the implications of the events of November-December 1848 in Prussia for the possibilities of *kleindeutsch* unification of Germany are now readily available in a translation (basically of the 7th [1928] edition) of his *Weltbürgertum und National-staat*. See his *Cosmopolitanism and the National State*, pp. 271–324. For other matters treated in the paragraphs above, see: Huber, *Verfassungsgeschichte*, 2:619–81, 756–61, 767–83; Noyes, *Organization and Revolution*, pp. 315–37; Valentin, *Revolution*, 2:1–182, 297–329 passim; Franz Wigard, ed., *Stenographischer Bericht über die Verhandlungen der deutschen constituirenden Nationalversammlung zu*

Frankfurt am Main, vols. 1–6, esp. 2:786–87, 6:4301–81; Ludwig Bergsträsser, *Die Verfassung des deutschen Reiches vom Jahre 1849*, pp. 72–96; Eckhart G. Franz, *Das Amerikabild der deutschen Revolution von 1848/49*, pp. 119–20, 122, 126; Krause, *Die demokratische Partei*, pp. 70–78; Eyck, *Frankfurt Parliament*, pp. 206–53, 314–43.

14. For the wording of each clause in the constitution as initially proposed by the constitutional committee, changes made in the first reading by the National Assembly, revisions made by the committee, and the version finally approved by the National Assembly, see Bergsträsser, *Die Verfassung*. See also, for the above paragraphs: Eyck, *Frankfurt Parliament*, pp. 343–82; Huber, *Verfassungsgeschichte*, 2:783–841; Carl J. Friedrich, *The Impact of American Constitutionalism Abroad*, pp. 26, 52–54, 81–82; Franz, *Revolution*, pp. 107, 115–33, 139, 141; Krause, *Die demokratische Partei*, pp. 78–93; Valentin, *Revolution*, 2:329–51; Balser, *Sozial-Demokratie*, 2:629; Wigard, ed., *Stenographischer Bericht*, vols. 7–9, esp. 7 (Jan. 19–26, 1849):4779–4888 (on hereditary monarchy), 7 (Feb. 15–March 2, 1849):5217–5559 (first reading of the Election Law), 8 (March 17–27, 1849):5792–6069 (final debates and voting on the constitution), 8 (March 27, 1849):6069–70 (final vote on the Election Law), 8 (March 28, 1849):6084–95 (voting to designate the hereditary ruler). Theodor Schieder has rightly pointed to the pivotal importance of the suffrage debates of February 15–20, 1849: "At no hour of the Frankfurt Parliament's history were the social questions . . . so much brought into the foreground as here" (*Staat und Gesellschaft im Wandel unserer Zeit*, Munich, 1958, pp. 67–69). For a cogent, up-to-date treatment in English, see Carol Rose, "The Issue of Parliamentary Suffrage at the Frankfurt National Assembly," esp. pp. 140, 143, 145–49.

15. The reports of the French chargé in Dresden had accurately reflected the persistence of particularism. See especially Méneval to Foreign Ministry, May 5, 1848, and Jan. 5, 1849, in Kretzschmar and Schlechte, eds., *Französische und sächische Gesandtschaftsberichte*, pp. 93–94, 259–62. Other matters discussed above are treated by Huber, *Verfassungsgeschichte*, 2:842–56; Valentin, *Revolution*, 2: 351–447 passim.

16. Rolf Weber, *Die Revolution in Sachsen, 1848/49*, pp. 327–55; Michael Doeberl, *Bayern und die Deutsche Frage in der Epoche des Frankfurter Parlaments*, pp. 181–86, and *Entwicklungsgeschichte Bayerns*, 3 vols. (Munich, 1931), 3:230–34, treats the uprisings in the Palatinate without mentioning their suppression by Prussian troops. Huber redresses this omission, *Verfassungsgeschichte*, 2:868–72.

17. Walter Grube, *Der Stuttgarter Landtag 1457–1957*, pp. 529–31; Wigard, ed., *Stenographischer Bericht*, 9 (May 30, 1849):6781–98 (decision by the assembly to leave Frankfurt), 9 (June 6, 1849):6820–22 (election of the provisional Regency), 9 (June 6–18, 1849):6819–86 (for the final meetings of the assembly in Stuttgart).

18. Huber, *Verfassungsgeschichte*, 2:856–84; Valentin, *Revolution*, 2:410–544; Johann Philipp Becker and Christian Esselen, *Geschichte der süddeutschen Mai-Revolution des Jahres 1849*; Carl Wittke, *Against the Current*, pp. 57–78. On Kinkel and Schurz, see Kaiser, *Politische Strömungen*, pp. 12–74 passim. Participation by members of workers' associations in the revolt is noted by Balser, *Sozial-Demokratie*, 2:632–34. See also Gustav Meyer, *Friedrich Engels*, pp. 116–18; Neitzke, *Die deutschen politischen Flüchtlinge*, pp. 31–55.

19. Carl Wittke, *Refugees of Revolution*, pp. 43–373; Eitel Wolf Dobert, *Deutsche Demokraten in Amerika*; Mack Walker, *Germany and the Emigration, 1816–1885*, pp. 153–57; Valentin, *Revolution*, 2:545–93; Huber, *Verfassungsgeschichte*, 2:411–13, 509, 511–12, 515, 519, 520, 701, 875, and passim (for comment in text and notes on the careers of German revolutionaries after 1849); Eberhard Kessel, "Carl

Schurz and Gottfried Kinkel," pp. 109–34; Eberhard Kessel, ed., *Die Briefe von Carl Schurz an Gottfried Kinkel*, pp. 23–45 and passim; Alfred Vagts, *Deutsch-Amerikanische Rückwanderung*, pp. 168–90; and Neitzke, *Die deutschen politischen Flüchtlinge*, pp. 56–86.

20. Thomas Rodney Christofferson, "The Revolution of 1848 in Marseille," pp. 112–16, 124. For the larger perspective see William L. Langer, *Political and Social Upheaval, 1832–1852*, pp. 319–512 passim and (for an extensive review of other relevant literature) pp. 615–55; William L. Langer, "The Pattern of Urban Revolution in 1848," pp. 90–118; and Félix Ponteil, *Les Classes bourgeoises et l'avènement de la démocratie, 1815–1914*, (Paris, 1968).

21. See, for example, Balser, *Sozial-Demokratie*, 1:251 (citing a report of 579 *Vereinsorte* and 355 connected *Zweigvereine* affiliated with the *Central-März-Verein* as of March 31, 1849); Günther Müller, *König Max II. und die soziale Frage*, pp. 37–38; Schierbaum, *Die politischen Wahlen*, pp. 21–32 and passim.

22. For the paragraphs above see: Arnold Heinz Schuetz, "Johann Jacoby—A Prussian Democrat," p. 61 (for the comment by Jacoby's physician-cousin, Julius Waldeck, of April 11, 1848); Adolf Rapp, ed., *Briefwechsel zwischen Strauss und Vischer*, 1:224 (see also pp. 213, 228), 2:30; Liebig to Wöhler, June 24, 1849, in Schwarz, ed., *Aus Justus Liebigs und Friedrich Wöhlers Briefwechsel*, p. 200; Hans Rosenberg, *Rudolf Haym und die Anfänge des klassischen Liberalismus*, pp. 164–65 and 116–79 passim; Krieger, *German Idea of Freedom*, pp. 371–93; Walter Bussmann, "Zur Geschichte des deutschen Liberalismus im 19. Jahrhundert," pp. 527–57; Valentin, *Revolution*, 2:545–93; and Huber, *Verfassungsgeschichte*, 3:1–223 passim. For an example of communist arguments and the "betrayal" quotation given above, see Gustav Seeber, *Zwischen Bebel und Bismarck*, p. 168. The conflict of liberals and democrats is treated more dispassionately by Wilhelm Mommsen, *Grösse und Versagen des deutschen Bürgertums*, pp. 122–30 and passim.

23. Adolf Kober, "Jews in the Revolution of 1848 in Germany," pp. 135–64, though generally valuable, is corrected on some points and supplemented by Jacob Toury, *Die politischen Orientierungen der Juden in Deutschland*, pp. 47–99. P. G. J. Pulzer, *The Rise of Political Anti-Semitism in Germany and Austria*, pp. 7–13, provides a brief survey. See also Josef Fraenkel, ed., *The Jews of Austria*, pp. 83–88, 285–87, 429–30; Felix Hirsch, "Eduard von Simson," pp. 261–77; Ismar Elbogen and Eleonore Sterling, *Die Geschichte der Juden in Deutschland*, pp. 235–39; and Ernest Hamburger, *Juden im öffentlichen Leben Deutschlands*, pp. 21–30, 170–209, and passim. One of the most prominent Jews among the democrats of 1848–49 was Jacoby. See Schuetz, "Johann Jacoby," pp. 89–92 and passim.

24. For the estimate reported above from *Concordia*, organ of the Cigar Workers' Union, see Balser, *Sozial-Demokratie*, 1:67. The basic Marxist interpretation of the Revolution of 1848 was laid down by Marx himself in April 1850. See Max Eastman, ed., *Capital, the Communist Manifesto, and Other Writings by Karl Marx*, pp. 355–58. A fuller but similar treatment, perceptive on many matters but doctrinaire in its economic-determinist generalizations, was offered in 1851–52 by Friedrich Engels in *Germany: Revolution and Counter-Revolution*—most recently made available in an edition introduced by Leonard Krieger for Phoenix Books. East German interpretations after World War II are reviewed by Andreas Dorpalen, "Die Revolution von 1848 in der Geschichtsschreibung der DDR," pp. 324–68.

VI REACTION AND A NEW CRISIS

1. Published in the newspaper of the General Workers' Brotherhood, *Verbrüderung*, March 19, 1850; reprinted by Frolinde Balser, *Sozial-Demokratie 1848/49–
1863*, 2:669. I have used the terms "counterrevolution" and "reaction" inter-
changeably in this chapter and elsewhere. Though the counterrevolutionaries of
the 1850's were very real, it would be impossible to apply to them the narrow
and abstract definitions offered by Arno J. Mayer, *Dynamics of Counterrevolution
in Europe, 1870–1956*, pp. 59–64 and passim.

2. Arnold Oskar Meyer, *Bismarcks Kampf mit Österreich am Bundestag zu Frankfurt (1851 bis 1859)*; Heinrich von Srbik, *Deutsche Einheit*, 2:17–122; Ernst Rudolf
Huber, *Deutsche Verfassungsgeschichte seit 1789*, 2:885–926; Helmut Böhme,
Deutschlands Weg zur Grossmacht, pp. 19–50; Gobineau to Tocqueville, July 12,
28, 1854, in Alexis de Tocqueville, *"The European Revolution" and Correspondence
with Gobineau*, pp. 242, 246. The repressive measures taken by the Confederation
and by individual state rovernments are discussed in detail by Balser, *Sozial-
Demokratie*, 1:226–33, 239–336; for documents, 2:542–46, 595, and passim.

3. For the reaction of the 1850's outside Prussia see: Huber, *Verfassungsgeschichte*, 3:54–134 passim; Lothar Gall, *Der Liberalismus als regierende Partei*, pp.
58–112 (which emphasizes the limited successes of Baden's reaction, ignoring
the suppression of democrats and left-liberals); Walter Grube, *Der Stuttgarter
Landtag 1457–1957*, pp. 531–40; Balser, *Sózial-Demokratie*, 1:239–440, 2:562–63
and passim (esp. 1:354–57, for the data on the Württemberg elections of 1849–
50); Leonhard Lenk, "Revolutionär-kommunistische Umtriebe im Königreich
Bayern," pp. 555–622; Adalbert Hess, *Die Landtags-und Reichstagswahlen im Grossherzogtum Hessen 1865–1871*, pp. 21–49; Karl Pagel, *Mecklenburg, Biographie eines
deutschen Landes*, pp. 97–98; Rudolf Kötzschke and Hellmut Kretzschmar, *Sächsische Geschichte*, pp. 341–48.

4. For the reaction of the 1850's in Prussia see Huber, *Verfassungsgeschichte*,
3:159–223; Hans Schneider, *Der preussische Staatsrat 1817–1918*, pp. 209–47;
Eugene N. Anderson, *The Social and Political Conflict in Prussia, 1858–1864*, pp.
18, 219, 237, 243–54; Heinrich August Winkler, *Preussischer Liberalismus und
deutscher Nationalstaat*, pp. 3n, 5n; Adalbert Hess, *Das Parlament das Bismarck
widerstrebte*, pp. 15–25; Hansjürgen Schierbaum, *Die politischen Wahlen in den
Eifel-und Moselkreisen des Regierungsbezirks Trier 1849–1867*, pp. 63–113; Renate
Kaiser, *Die politischen Strömungen in den Kreisen Bonn und Rheinbach 1848–1878*,
pp. 75–134; Karl Obermann, "Zur Geschichte der deutschen Arbeiterbewegung
nach der Revolution von 1848/49 zu Beginn der fünfziger Jahre," pp. 842–69;
Heinrich Neu, "Bismarcks Versuch einer Einflussnahme auf die 'Kölnische
Zeitung,'" pp. 221–33.

5. Theodor Schieder, *Staat und Gesellschaft im Wandel unserer Zeit*, pp. 110–71
passim; Theodor Schieder, "Die Theorie der Partei im älteren deutschen Liberalismus," pp. 183–96; Thomas Nipperdey, "Die Organisation der bürgerlichen
Parteien in Deutschland vor 1918," pp. 550–602; Huber, *Verfassungsgeschichte*,
3:l09–10, 171–74; Balser, *Sozial-Demokratie*, 1:339–45, 2:542–43, 547–49, and passim. The interrelationships of technology and domestic politics in nineteenth-
century Germany invite research. On telegraphy one might begin with Winshaw
(no other name given), "On the Present State of Electro-Telegraphic Communication in England, Prussia, and America," pp. 198–99; Ludwig Galle, *Katechis-
mus der elektrischen Telegraphie*, 4th ed. (Leipzig, 1870), p. 366; Richard Hennig,
Die älteste Entwickelung der Telegraphie und Telephonie, pp. 129, 131, and 67–133
passim. The earliest telegram of a political organization to which I have seen
reference was sent by a leader of the Nationalverein (see below) on February 27,

1862; quoted from D.D.R. archives by Gerhard Eisfeld, *Die Entstehung der liberalen Parteien in Deutschland 1858–1870*, p. 46. Indicative of the political utility of the new medium, this telegram urgently asked for the quick dispatch of a thousand membership cards to Berlin.

6. Edward H. Reisner, *Nationalism and Education since 1789*, pp. 161–71; Andreas Flitner, *Die politische Erziehung in Deutschland*, pp. 165–79; Robert C. Binkley, *Realism and Nationalism, 1852–1871*, pp. 62–63; Theobald Ziegler, *Die geistigen und sozialen Strömungen Deutschlands im 19. und 20. Jahrhundert*, pp. 252–312; Karl Kupisch, "Der Deutsche zwischen 1850 und 1865," pp. 108–42; Friedrich Wilhelm Kantzenbach, "Zur geistig-religiösen Situation der christlichen Konfessionen zwischen 1850 und 1860," pp. 193–219; Joachim Rohlfes, "Staat, Nation und evangelische Kirche im Zeitalter der deutschen Einigung (1848–1871)," pp. 593–616; Catharine Magill Holden, "A Decade of Dissent in Germany," pp. 433–35; Hugo Eckert, *Liberal-oder Sozialdemokratie*, pp. 141–51 (on the Free Congregations); the useful chapter on Ludwig Büchner in Niles Robert Holt, "The Social and Political Ideas of the German Monist Movement, 1871–1941," pp. 62–100; Ludwig Büchner, *Kraft und Stoff, oder Grundzüge der natürlichen Weltordnung, nebst einer darauf gebauten Moral oder Sittenlehre*; Andrew Lees, "Revolution and Reflection," kindly made available by the author, demonstrates the continued vitality of liberal intellectuals during the 1850's; K. B. Beaton, "Der konservative Roman in Deutschland nach der Revolution von 1848," pp. 215–34. There is a large body of literature on Schopenhauer. See the continuing volumes of the *Schopenhauer-Jahrbuch* (Kiel, 1912–).

7. A. Sartorius von Waltershausen, *Deutsche Wirtschaftsgeschichte 1815–1914*, pp. 141–87; Hans Rosenberg, *Die Weltwirtschaftskrisis von 1857–1859*, pp. 72–74, 87, 98, and passim; George M. Kren, "Gustav Freytag and the Assimilation of the German Middle Class," pp. 483–94; J. H. Clapham, *The Economic Development of France and Germany, 1815–1914*, pp. 278–322 passim; Richard Tilly, *Financial Institutions and Industrialization in the Rhineland, 1815–1870*; Wolfgang Zorn, "Wirtschafts -und sozialgeschichtliche Zusammenhänge der deutschen Reichsgründungszeit (1850–1879)," pp. 318–42; Rondo E. Cameron, "Founding the Bank of Darmstadt," pp. 113–30; Friedrich Zunkel, *Der rheinisch-westfälische Unternehmer 1834–1879*, pp. 99–127, 182–205; Walter Bussmann, "Zur Geschichte des Liberalismus im 19. Jahrhundert," pp. 527–57; Theodore S. Hamerow, *Restoration, Revolution, Reaction*, pp. 207–9, 219–22, 234–36; also Hamerow's *The Social Foundations of German Unification, 1858–1871*, 1:3–13; Böhme, *Deutschlands Weg zur Grossmacht*, pp. 57–82; Leonard Krieger, *German Idea of Freedom*, pp. 338–44.

8. Hans Hübner, "Die ostpreussischen Landarbeiter im Kampf gegen junkerliche Ausbeutung und Willkür (1848–1914)," pp. 552–69; Hamerow, *Social Foundations*, 1:69–77; John Weiss, "Dialectical Idealism and the Work of Lorenz von Stein," pp. 75–93; Dirk Blasius, "Lorenz von Stein und Preussen," pp. 339–62; Günther Müller, *König Max II und die soziale Frage*, pp. 42–89; Jürgen Kuczynski, *Die Geschichte der Lage der Arbeiter unter dem Kapitalismus*, 2:129, 152, and 127–211 passim, 18:101–64 passim.

9. Werner Blumenberg, "Zur Geschichte des Bundes der Kommunisten," pp. 81–122; Schlomo Na'aman, "Zur Geschichte des Bundes der Kommunisten in Deutschland in den zweiten Phase seines Bestehens," pp. 5–82; Georg Eckert, "Aus der Korrespondenz der Kommunistenbundes (Fraktion Willich-Schapper)," *Archiv für Sozialgeschichte*, 5 (1965): 273–318; Stanislaw Schwann, "Die Neue Oder-Zeitung und Karl Marx als ihr Korrespondent," pp. 59–90; Peter Stadler, "Wirtschaftskrise und Revolution bei Marx und Engels," pp.

113–44; Lenk, "Revolutionär-kommunistische Umtriebe," pp. 555–622; Isaiah Berlin, *Karl Marx*, pp. 165–205; Max Eastman, ed., *Capital, the Communist Manifesto, and Other Writings by Karl Marx*, p. 358; Fritz Mehring, *Geschichte der deutschen Sozialdemokratie*, 2:177–236; Balser, *Sozial-Demokratie*, 1:62–65, 72–479, 2:504–24, 539–65, 577, 616–22, 644–48; Obermann, "Zur Geschichte der deutchen Arbeiterbewegung," pp. 842–69.

10. Winkler, *Preussischer Liberalismus*, pp. 34–41; Rolf Weber, *Kleinbürgerliche Demokraten in der deutschen Einheitsbewegung 1863–1866*, pp. 69–71; Krieger, *German Idea of Freedom*, p. 220. See Erwin Gugelmeier, *Das schwarze Jahr (1917–1918)*, p. 17.

11. John A. Hawgood, *The Tragedy of German-America*, pp. 57–58, 227–66; Mack Walker, *Germany and the Emigration, 1816–1885*, pp. 157–74; Henry A. Pochmann, *German Culture in America*, p. 77; Thomas D. Clark, ed., *Travels in the Old South*, 2:195; 3:238–40 (Fröbel), 217–18 (Busch), and, for other accounts published in the period 1849–61, 3:203, 204, 210–17, 227, 238, 244, 252–66, 282, 291–314, 327, 366, 377; G. A. Wislizenus, *Aus Amerika*, 1:5–10, 81–82, 97, 2:42–43; Theodor Griesinger, *Freiheit und Sclaverei unter dem Sternenbanner oder Land und Leute in Amerika*, 1:150, 2:524–46, 678–79; Ernst Fraenkel, ed., *Amerika im Spiegel des deutschen politischen Denkens*, pp. 28–33, 114–15 (quoting extract from Schopenhauer's *Parerga und Paralipomena*); Carl J. Friedrich, *The Impact of American Constitutionalism Abroad*, pp. 30–34; Rudolf Ullner, *Die Idee des Föderalismus im Jahrzehnt der deutschen Einigungskriege dargestellt unter besonderer Berücksichtigung des Modells der amerikanischen Verfassung für das deutsche politische Denken*, pp. 17–18 and passim; Carl Wittke, *Refugees of Revolution*, pp. 58–373; Eitel Wolf Dobert, *Deutsche Demokraten in Amerika*, pp. 120–30 (Kapp) and passim; Alfred Vagts, *Deutsch-amerikanische Rückwanderung*, pp. 118–19 and passim.

12. Balser, *Sozial-Demokratie*, 1:259–68.

13. Charles Edgar McClelland, *The German Historians and England*, pp. 116–17, 123–212 (especially valuable for the period 1850–70). A penetrating study of Gneist and a few other German liberals is provided by Reinhard J. Lamer, *Der englische Parlamentarismus in der deutschen politischen Theorie im Zietalter Bismarcks (1857–1890)*. Both of these works valuably supplement the older study by Raymond James Sontag, *Germany and England*, pp. ix, 61–89, and passim. For the Prussian ministry's memo of Aug. 12, 1849, mentioned in the text, see Hellmut von Gerlach, *Die Geschichte des preussischen Wahlrechts*, pp. 14–15; and for a summary of Julius Jolly's article in the *Karlsruher Zeitung*, Jan. 30–31, 1869, "Über englischen Parlamentarismus," see Gall, *Der Liberalismus als regierende Partei*, p. 446.

14. Rudolf Buchner, *Die deutsch-französische Tragödie 1848–1864*, pp. 41–84, 107–20; H. Gollwitzer, "Der Cäsarismus Napoleon III. im Widerhall der öffentlichen Meinung Deutschlands," pp. 23–75; Eberhard Kessel, ed., *Die Briefe von Carl Schurz an Gottfried Kinkel*, pp. 54–106 iassim; Binkley, *Realism and Nationalism*, pp. 124–56; Andreas Dorpalen, *Heinrich von Treitschke*, pp. 139–44, 147; Heinrich Heffter, *Die deutsche Selbstverwaltung im 19. Jahrhundert*, pp. 352, 358, 372–403; Hamerow, *Social Foundations*, 1:165–66.

15. Böhme, *Deutschlands Weg zur Grossmacht*, pp. 86–183; Hamerow, *Social Foundations*, 1:96–112, 135–180; Eisfeld, *Die Entstehung der liberalen Parteien*, pp. 15–24; and, for the international aspects, Lynn M. Case, *French Opinion on War and Diplomacy during the Second Empire*, pp. 15–123; W. E. Mosse, *The European Powers and the German Question, 1848–71, with Special Reference to England and Russia*, pp. 49–109.

16. Rudolf Schwab, *Der deutsche Nationalverein, seine Entstehung und sein Wirken*, pp. 3–79; Julius Heyderhoff and Paul Wentzcke, eds., *Deutscher Liberalismus im Zeitalter Bismarcks*, 1:26–68; Eisfeld, *Die Entstehung der liberalen Parteien*, pp. 52–53 (which quotes the Hanoverian denunciation of the Nationalverein in 1861) and 25–57; Lenore O'Boyle, "The German Nationalverein," pp. 333–37; Shlomo Na'aman, *Demokratische und soziale Impulse in der Frühgeschichte der deutschen Arbeiterbewegung der Jahre 1862/63*, pp. 31–76.

17. On the ill-fated efforts to achieve a Greater Germany under Habsburg leadership in the early 1860's, see: Enno Kraehe, "Austria and the Problem of Reform in the German Confederation, 1851–1863," pp. 274–94; Huber, *Verfassungsgeschichte*, 3:393–435; Willy Real, *Der Deutsche Reformverein*; and the illuminating material made available by Hans Rosenberg, ed., "Honoratiorenpolitiker und 'grossdeutsche' Sammlungsbestrebungen im Reichsgründungsjahrzehnt," pp. 155–233.

18. Gall, *Der Liberalismus als regierende Partei*, pp. 114–375; Weber, *Kleinbürgerliche Demokraten*, pp. 9–30.

19. Theodor Schieder, *Die kleindeutsche Partei in Bayern in den Kämpfen um die nationale Einheit 1863–1871*, pp. 11–40 and passim; Eisfeld, *Die Entstehung der liberalen Parteien*, pp. 29, 41, 125–35, 214–15.

20. Eisfeld, *Die Entstehung der liberalen Parteien*, pp. 33, 51, 147–51; Hess, *Die Landtags-und Reichstagswahlen im Grossherzogtum Hessen*, pp. 21–94.

21. Eisfeld, *Die Entstehung der liberalen Parteien*, pp. 136–43, 153–58, 203–4; Weber, *Kleinbürgerliche Demokraten*, pp. 9–30; Arnold Heinz Schuetz, "Johann Jacoby—A Prussian Democrat," pp. 234–79.

22. See Carl Schmitt, *Staatsgefüge und Zusammenbruch des zweiten Reiches*, p. 10 (a long title for a short pro-Nazi essay by a prominent political scientist); Ludwig Bergsträsser, *Die Entwicklung des Parlamentarismus in Deutschland*, p. 12.

23. Huber, *Verfassungsgeschichte*, 3:269–95; Gordon A. Craig, *The Politics of the Prussian Army, 1640–1945*, pp. 136–56; Gerhard Ritter, *Staatskunst und Kriegshandwerk*, 1:152–85; Heyderhoff and Wentzcke, eds., *Deutscher Liberalismus*, 1:69–87; Hans Rosenberg, ed., *Die nationalpolitische Publizistik Deutschlands vom Eintritt der neuen Ära in Preussen bis zum Ausbruch des deutschen Krieges*, 1:177–90, 2:509 (a most valuable abstract of pamphlets, journals, and newspapers); and Schuetz, "Johann Jacoby," pp. 194–95 and passim. Relatively little scholarly attention has been focused upon William I. For a superficial account written shortly before his death, see G. Barnett Smith, *William I and the German Empire*, pp. 1–37 (for his life to 1857). See also Erich Marcks, *Kaiser Wilhelm I*, pp. 1–200 (thin and generally respectful), and the popular biography by Paul Wiegler, *Wilhelm der Erste*, pp. 7–270. For details on the election campaigns of 1858 and 1861 and the results in two Prussian districts, see Kaiser, *Die politischen Strömungen*, pp. 134–56; Schierbaum, *Die politischen Wahlen*, pp. 115–50.

24. Schwab, *Der deutsche Nationalverein*, pp. 72–112; Schieder, *Die kleindeutsche Partei*, pp. 11–40 and passim; Weber, *Kleinbürgerliche Demokraten*, pp. 30–47; Eisfeld, *Die Entstehung der liberalen Parteien*, pp. 27–158 passim.

25. Heyderhoff and Wentzcke, eds., *Deutscher Liberalismus*, 1:26–94 passim; Winkler, *Preussischer Liberalismus*, pp. viii, 8–15, and passim; Eisfeld, *Die Entstehung der liberalen Parteien*, pp. 71–110; Anderson, *Social and Political Conflict*, pp. 215–16, 227–33, 236–38, 255–351, 412–13, 418; Krieger, *German Idea of Freedom*, p. 400; Walter Gagel, *Die Wahlrechtsfrage in der Geschichte der deutschen liberalen Parteien 1848–1918*, pp. 26–37, 177–79 (a valuable monograph); Hess, *Das Parlament das Bismarck widerstrebte*, pp. 53–54, 65–69 (for the occupational data presented above). For the election of April 28–May 6, 1862, in specific

districts, see: Kaiser, *Die politischen Strömungen*, pp. 163–91; Schierbaum, *Die politischen Wahlen*, pp. 150–65.

26. Huber, *Verfassungsgeschichte*, 3:294–303; Otto Pflanze, *Bismarck and the Development of Germany*, pp. 156–70; Otto von Bismarck, *Bismarck, the Man and the Statesman, Being the Reflections and Reminiscences of Otto, Prince von Bismarck*, 1:264–97. The principal documents on the Prussian internal conflict may be found in Ernst Rudolf Huber, ed., *Dokumente zur deutschen Verfassungsgeschichte*, 2:31–89.

27. Bismarck, *Reflections and Reminiscences*, 1:80, 193, 196; Pflanze, *Bismarck*, pp. 17–155 passim; Meyer, *Bismarcks Kampf mit Österreich*, esp. pp. 399–482, 492; L. Raschdau, ed., *Die politischen Berichte des Fürsten Bismarck aus Petersburg und Paris (1859–1862)*, 1:55, 184, and passim; Gustav Adolf Rein, *Die Revolution in der Politik Bismarcks*, pp. 45–132 passim; Otto Becker, *Bismarcks Ringen um Deutschlands Gestaltung*, pp. 158–210. Representative of the many biographies, see Charles Grant Robertson, *Bismarck*, pp. 1–119; Erich Eyck, *Bismarck*, 1:11–418; Arnold Oskar Meyer, *Bismarck*, pp. 9–168; A. J. P. Taylor, *Bismarck*, pp. 9–52; Ludwig Reiners, *Bismarck*, 1:1–340; Werner Richter, *Bismarck*, pp. 11–76. For additional material see Karl Erich Born, ed., *Bismarck-Bibliographie*.

28. The standard work in English by Anderson, *Social and Political Conflict*, should be supplemented by Winkler, *Preussischer Liberalismus*, Hess, *Das Parlament das Bismarck widerstrebte*, and Eisfeld, *Die Entstehung der liberalen Parteien*, pp. 106–22. See also, for the paragraphs above: Otto Pflanze, "Juridicial and Political Responsibility in Nineteenth-Century Germany," Pflanze, *Bismarck*, pp. 171–212; Huber, *Verfassungsgeschichte*, 3:305–20; Bismarck, *Reflections and Reminiscences*, 1:298–387; Eyck, *Bismarck*, 1:421–510 passim; Irene Fischer-Frauendienst, *Bismarcks Pressepolitik*, pp. 16–20, 54, 147–52; Rosenberg, ed., *Die nationalpolitische Publizistik*, 2:475–558; Heyderhoff and Wentzcke, eds., *Deutscher Liberalismus*, 1:116–70; Erwin H. Ackerknecht, *Rudolf Virchow*, pp. 170–76; Erich Brandenburg, *Die Reichsgründung*, 1:418–34, 2:3–197; Kaiser, *Die politischen Strömungen*, pp. 191–213; Schierbaum, *Die politischen Wahlen*, pp. 167–82.

29. Anderson, *Social and Political Conflict*, pp. 126, 235, 236, and passim; Hellmut Seier, *Die Staatsidee Heinrich von Sybels in den Wandlungen der Reichsgründungszeit 1862/71*, pp. 106 and 91–124 passim; Schuetz, "Johann Jacoby," pp. 190–224; Ackerknecht, *Rudolf Virchow*, pp. 176–77; Winkler, *Preussischer Liberalismus*, pp. 16–99; Hess, *Das Parlament das Bismarck widerstrebte*, pp. 30–150; Hamerow, *Social Foundations*, 1:14, 148–80, and 269–307 passim; Krieger, *German Idea of Freedom*, pp. 361–62; Huber, *Verfassungsgeschichte*, 3:320–48; Eyck, *Bismarck*, 2:114–18, 198–205; Pflanze, *Bismarck*, pp. 262–83; Craig, *Politics of the Prussian Army*, pp. 160–74; Rosenberg, ed., *Die nationalpolitische Publizistik*, 2:858–80, 953–76; Heyderhoff and Wentzcke, eds., *Deutscher Liberalismus*, 1:132–33, 149–50, and 70–334 passim; Weber, *Kleinbürgerliche Demokraten*, pp. 78–80 and passim; Johannes Hohlfeld and Klaus Hohlfeld, eds., *Dokumente der deutschen Politik und Geschichte von 1848 bis zur Gegenwart*, 1:110–12 (excellent documentation); Kaiser, *Die politischen Strömungen*, pp. 213–18.

VII UNIFICATION

1. For the quotations see Max Eastman, ed., *Capital, the Communist Manifesto, and Other Writings by Karl Marx*, pp. 355–57. A useful survey of the changing German interpretations of unification is provided by Elisabeth Fehrenbach, "Die Reichsgründung in der deutschen Geschichtsschreibung," pp. 259–90 (article in

a collection of scholarly essays acknowledging the hundredth anniversary of the founding of the empire). For another recent interpretive attempt both thought-provoking and unconvincing, see Robert H. Berdahl, "New Thoughts on German Nationalism," pp. 65–80.

2. Otto von Bismarck, *Bismarck, the Man and the Statesman, Being the Reflections and Reminiscences of Otto, Prince von Bismarck*, 1:202–3, 269, 2:1–80; Helmut Böhme, *Deutschlands Weg zur Grossmacht*, pp. 135–83; Otto Becker, *Bismarcks Ringen um Deutschlands Gestaltung*, pp. 108–57; Otto Pflanze, *Bismarck and the Development of Germany*, pp. 213–310. Chester Wells Clark, *Franz Joseph and Bismarck*, esp. pp. 55–472; Hermann Oncken, ed., *Die Rheinpolitik Kaiser Napoleons III von 1863 bis 1870 und der Ursprung des Krieges von 1870/71*, 1:19–36; Herbert Geuss, *Bismarck und Napoleon III*, pp. 112–71; Willard Allen Fletcher, *The Mission of Vincent Benedetti to Berlin, 1864–1870*, pp. 22–76; E. Ann Pottinger, *Napoleon III and the German Crisis, 1865–1866*, esp. pp. 60–184, 210; Lynn M. Case, *French Opinion on War and Diplomacy during the Second Empire*, pp. 177–215; Richard Millman, *British Foreign Policy and the Coming of the Franco-Prussian War*, pp. 6–96; W. E. Mosse, *The European Powers and the German Question*, pp. 146–250; Heinrich von Srbik, *Deutsche Einheit*, 4:118–484 (a valuable work, marred by its unrestrained tribute to the Third Reich, 4:483–84); Wolfgang v. Groote and Ursula v. Gersdorff, eds., *Entscheidung 1866*, pp. 76–195; Margaret Sterne, "The End of the Free City of Frankfurt," pp. 203–14; Gordon A. Craig, *The Battle of Königgrätz*.

3. Becker, *Bismarcks Ringen*, pp. 211–455, is at its best on these matters and provides the most useful single account available. See also: Bismarck, *Reflections and Reminiscences*, 2:62–63, 65; Ernst Rudolf Huber, *Deutsche Verfassungsgeschichte*, 3:641–80, together with his *Dokumente zur deutschen Verfassungsgeschichte*, 2:223–40; Julius Heyderhoff and Paul Wentzcke, eds., *Deutscher Liberalismus im Zeitalter Bismarcks*, 1:331–81; Erich Eyck, *Bismarck*, 2:325–41; Pflanze, *Bismarck*, pp. 337–63; George G. Windell, "The Bismarckian Empire as a Federal State, 1866–1880," pp. 291–99; also Windell's *The Catholics and German Unity, 1856–1871*, pp. 71–75; Hellmut Seier, *Die Staatsidee Heinrich von Sybels in den Wandlungen der Reichsgründungszeit 1862/71*, pp. 177–78; Renate Kaiser, *Die politischen Strömungen in den Kreisen Bonn und Rheinbach 1848–1878*, pp. 228–41; and the excellent monograph by Walter Gagel, *Die Wahlrechtsfrage in der Geschichte der deutschen liberalen Parteien 1848–1918*, pp. 38–72.

4. I have used the election statistics given by Gagel, *Wahlrechtsfrage*, pp. 61, 176, and by Huber, *Verfassungsgeschichte*, 3:93n, 352. For other material on the transformation of 1866 see: Heinrich August Winkler, *Preussischer Liberalismus und deutscher Nationalstaat*, pp. 34–99; Wolfgang Hock, *Liberales Denken im Zeitalter der Paulskirche*, pp. 138–70; Seier, *Die Staatsidee Heinrich von Sybels*, pp. 168–69, 124–67; Hans Rosenberg, ed., *Die nationalpolitische Publizistik Deutschlands vom Eintritt der neuen Ära in Preussen bis zum Ausbruch des deutschen Krieges*, 2:925–52; Pflanze, *Bismarck*, pp. 262–83, 310–23; Kaiser, *Die politischen Strömungen*, pp. 218–27; Hansjürgen Schierbaum, *Die politischen Wahlen in den Eifel und Moselkreisen des Regierungsbezirks Trier 1849–1867*, pp. 186–201.

5. Karl-Georg Faber, "Realpolitik als Ideologie," pp. 10–28 and passim—an outgrowth of the following indispensable work by Faber: *Die national-politische Publizistik Deutschlands von 1866 bis 1871*, 1:24–140 passim; Robert Schwarz, ed., *Aus Justus Liebigs und Friedrich Wöhlers Briefwechsel in den Jahren 1829–1873*, p. 326; Karl Heinrich Höfele, "Königgrätz und die Deutschen von 1866," pp. 393–416; Winkler, *Preussischer Liberalismus*, pp. 99–107; Andreas Dorpalen, *Heinrich von Treitschke*, pp. 34–35 (on Rochau); Heyderhoff and Wentzcke, eds.,

Deutscher Liberalismus, 1:338–46; Bismarck, *Reflections and Reminiscences*, 2:76–79; Huber, *Verfassungsgeschichte*, 3:352–69; Erwin H. Ackerknecht, *Rudolf Virchow*, pp. 177–81; Johannes Hohlfeld and Klaus Hohlfeld, eds., *Dokumente der deutschen Politik und Geschichte von 1848 bis zur Gegenwart*, 1:174–81; Pflanze, *Bismarck*, pp. 215, 323–31; Eugene N. Anderson, *The Social and Political Conflict in Prussia, 1858–1864*, pp. 270–72; James Fremont Harris, "Eduard Lasker, 1829–1884," pp. 52–55, 204, and passim; Stanley Zucker, "Ludwig Bamberger and the Crisis of German Liberalism," pp. 64–86.

6. Compare the views offered by Conze in Groote and Gersdorff, eds., *Entscheidung 1866*, p. 210, and by Craig, *Prussian Army*, pp. 174–79, with the "unconditional surrender" phrase in Pflanze, *Bismarck*, p. 331.

7. For the breakup of the Progressives, the creation of the National Liberal party, and the 1867 elections in Prussia see: Gerhard Eisfeld, *Die Entstehung der Liberalen Parteien in Deutschland 1858–1870*, pp. 161–97; Winkler, *Preussischer Liberalismus*, pp. 107–13; Pflanze, *Bismarck*, pp. 331, 354–55; Eyck, *Bismarck*, 2:315–24; Huber, *Verfassungsgeschichte*, 3:367–72; Gagel, *Wahlrechtsfrage*, pp. 45–72, 176; Dorpalen, *Heinrich von Treitschke*, pp. 126 27; Heyderhoff and Wentzcke, eds., *Deutscher Liberalismus*, 1:331–86; Kaiser, *Die politischen Strömungen*, pp. 247–77.

8. Becker, *Bismarcks Ringen*, pp. 550–612; Böhme, *Deutschlands Weg zur Grossmacht*, pp. 213–21, 236–51, 264–77; W. O. Henderson, *The Zollverein*, pp. 304–29; Wolfgang Zorn's concise essay in Schieder and Deuerlein, eds., *Reichsgründung 1870/71*, pp. 196–225; Bismarck, *Reflections and Reminiscences*, 2:47–62; Pflanze, *Bismarck*, pp. 367–403; Windell, *The Catholics and German Unity*, pp. 84–115 and passim; Adolf Rapp, *Die Württemberger und die nationale Frage 1863–1871*, pp. 258–88; Theodor Schieder, *Die kleindeutsche Partei in Bayern in den Kämpfen um die nationale Einheit 1863–1871*, pp. 173–92; Lothar Gall, *Der Liberalismus als regierende Partei*, pp. 419–26; Adalbert Hess, *Die Landtags-und Reichstagswahlen im Grossherzogtum Hessen 1865–1871*, pp. 67–74.

9. The quotation is from Pflanze, *Bismarck*, p. 449. For the debatable view that Bismarck did not seek war with France *before* July 1870, see the scholarly study by Lawrence D. Steefel, *Bismarck, the Hohenzollern Candidacy, and the Origins of the Franco-German War of 1870*. Jochen Dittrich is not convincing in his effort to prove that Bismarck did not want war even in July; for a synthesis of Dittrich's booklength study, see his essay in Schieder and Deuerlein, eds., *Reichsgründung*, pp. 64–94. A more recent German examination emphasizes the thrust toward war in Bismarck's policy: Josef Becker, "Zum Problem der Bismarckschen Politik in der Spanischen Thronfrage 1870," pp. 529–607; for the diplomacy of 1867–70 see also, among many other works: Pflanze, *Bismarck*, pp. 403–49; Bismarck, *Reflections and Reminiscences*, 2:57–62; Case, *French Opinion*, pp. 215–40; Oncken, ed., *Die Rheinpolitik Kaiser Napoleons III*, 1:36–96 plus (for documents) all of vol. 2 and 3:3–352; Geuss, *Bismarck und Napoleon III*, pp. 172–250; Fletcher, *The Mission of Vincent Benedetti*, pp. 108–83, 282–86; Mosse, *European Powers*, pp. 253–302; Hans A. Schmitt, "Count Beust and Germany, 1866–1870," pp. 20–34; for the subsequent exhaustive and solid review of this question, see Heinrich Potthoff, *Die deutsche Politik Beusts von seiner Berufung zum österreichischen Aussenminister Oktober 1866 bis zum Ausbruch des deutsch-französischen Krieges 1870/71*.

10. Bismarck, *Reflections and Reminiscences*, 2:87–103; Steefel, *Hohenzollern Candidacy*, pp. 94–219; Pflanze, *Bismarck*, pp. 449–57; Case, *French Opinion*, pp. 241–69; Oncken, ed., *Die Rheinpolitik Kaiser Napoleons III*, 1:91–114, 3:355–459; Geuss, *Bismarck und Napoleon III*, pp. 250–76; Mosse, *European Powers*, pp. 302–5, 382–88; Fletcher, *Vincent Benedetti*, pp. 241–58.

11. Millman, *British Foreign Policy*, pp. 162–218; Mosse, *European Powers*, pp. 350–58; Schieder, *Die kleindeutsche Partei in Bayern*, pp. 254–61; Gall, *Der Liberalismus als regierende Partei*, pp. 474–96; Pflanze, *Bismarck*, pp. 411, 458–62, 480–81; Michael Howard, *The Franco-Prussian War*; Eberhard Kolb, "Bismarck und das Aufkommen der Annexionsforderung 1870," pp. 318–56 passim (plus the articles sim (plus the articles by W. Lipgens and L. Gall cited by Kolb); Jean-Baptiste Duroselle, "Die europäischen Staaten und die Gründung des Deutschen Reiches," pp. 386–421; and Robert I. Giesberg, *The Treaty of Frankfort*, pp. 17–176.

12. Becker, *Bismarcks Ringen*, pp. 687–767; Bismarck, *Reflections and Reminiscences*, 1:392–93, 2:126–34; Eyck, *Bismarck*, 2:540–67; Russell to Granville, Dec. 18, 1870, in Paul Knaplund, ed., *Letters from the Berlin Embassy, 1871–1874, 1880–1885*, p. 29; Fritz Hartung, *Deutsche Verfassungsgeschichte vom 15. Jahrhundert bis zur Gegenwart*, pp. 273–97; Heyderhoff and Wentzcke, eds., *Deutscher Liberalismus*, 1:470–93; Erich Eyck, *Auf Deutschlands politischem Forum*, pp. 18–25 (a lively sketch of Lasker); Schieder, *Die kleindeutsche Partei in Bayern*, pp. 264–93; Huber, *Verfassungsgeschichte*, 3:724–65. The more important documents may be found in Huber, ed., *Dokumente*, 1:198–227. See also Faber, *Die national-politische Publizistik*, 2:556–660 passim.

13. Rolf Weber, *Kleinbürgerliche Demokraten in der deutschen Einheitsbewegung 1863–1866*, pp. 107–283 passim; Rapp, *Die Württemberger*, pp. 77–92 and passim; Walter Grube, *Der Stuttgarter Landtag 1457–1957*, pp. 541–43; Gall, *Der Liberalismus als regierende Partei*, pp. 407–65 passim.

14. Erich Brandenburg, *Fünfzig Jahre Nationalliberale Partei 1867–1917*, p. 32 and passim; Eisfeld, *Die Entstehung der liberalen Parteien*, pp. 161–97; Heyderhoff and Wentzcke, eds., *Deutscher Liberalismus*, 1:331–86, 2:3–223 and passim; Hohlfeld and Hohlfeld, eds., *Dokumente*, 1:228–32; Gerhard Stoltenberg, *Der deutsche Reichstag 1871–1873*, pp. 15–21 and passim; Bismarck, *Reflections and Reminiscences*, 2:135–95; Thomas Nipperdey, *Die Organisation der deutschen Parteien vor 1918*, pp. 102–5, 119, 161–65, and passim; Walter Tormin, *Geschichte der deutschen Parteien seit 1848*, pp. 79–83, 282–85; Rudolf Morsey, *Die oberste Reichsverwaltung unter Bismarck 1867–1890*; Harris, "Eduard Lasker," pp. 26–28, 68–69, 94–99, 205, and passim; Gordon R. Mork, "The Making of a German Nationalist," pp. 23–32; James F. Harris, "Eduard Lasker and Compromise Liberalism," pp. 342–60; Zucker, "Ludwig Bamberger," pp. 215–21 and passim; Gordon R. Mork, "Bismarck and the 'Capitulation' of German Liberalism," *Journal of Modern History*, 43 (1971):59–75; Wilhelm Otto Vollrath, *Der parlamentarische Kampf um das preussische Dreiklassenwahlrecht*, pp. 33, 45–54; Gagel, *Wahlrechtsfrage*, pp. 73–94; Gordon R. Mork, "The Prussian Railway Scandal of 1873," pp. 35–48; Ruth Lange, "Three Critical Years of the National Liberal Party of Germany, 1877, 1878, 1879," pp. 59–113 and passim (a survey based upon some of the published material available). A fully satisfactory study of Lasker remains to be done. I have sampled but not systematically used the University of Wisconsin microfilm of the Lasker *Nachlass* at Brandeis University.

15. Gagel, *Wahlrechtsfrage*, pp. 176–77; Tormin, *Geschichte der deutschen Parteien*, tables following p. 281; Schierbaum, *Die politischen Wahlen*, pp. 203–17. For further information and bibliography on German left-liberalism after 1871, see chapter 11, below.

16. For the beginnings of the Center party see the convenient sketch by Tormin, *Geschichte der deutschen Parteien*, pp. 60–65; Karl Buchheim, *Ultramontanismus und Demokratie*, pp. 215–33 (useful notwithstanding its argument that "ultramontanism was a form of democracy…in the epoch of the national state");

the following additional works by Buchheim: *Leidensgeschichte des zivilen Geistes oder die Demokratie in Deutschland*, p. 91 and passim, and "Die Frage nach der katholischen Partei," pp. 63–77; Kaiser, *Die politischen Strömungen*, pp. 18–277 passim; Emil Ritter, *Der Weg des politischen Katholizismus in Deutschland*, pp. 11–72, esp. pp. 71–72; Windell, *The Catholics and German Unity*, esp. pp. 6, 70–83, 118, 125–30, 134–47, 153n, 179–229, 246–52, 276–95, and Appendix; and Rudolf Lill, "Die deutschen Katholiken und Bismarcks Reichsgründung," pp. 345–65.

17. Emiliana P. Noether, "Vatican Council I," pp. 218–33; Lillian Parker Wallace, *The Papacy and European Diplomacy, 1869–1878*, pp. 3–14, 52–186 passim; Franciscus Hanus, *Die preussische Vatikangesandtschaft 1747–1920*, pp. 306–10; Georg Franz-Willing, *Die bayerische Vatikangesandtschaft 1803–1934*, pp. 56–80; the letters from Augusta to William I in Adelheid Constabel, ed., *Die Vorgeschichte des Kulturkampfes*, pp. 18–68 and passim (an important collection of documents from D.D.R. archives in Merseburg); the excellent two-part article by Heinrich Bornkamm, "Die Staatsidee im Kulturkampf," pp. 41–72, 273–306; Rudolf Morsey, "Bismarck und der Kulturkampf," pp. 232–70; Georg Franz, *Kulturkampf*, pp. 277 and 185–276 passim; Windell, *The Catholics and German Unity*, pp. 123–24, 246–52. For the chancellor's own account, which emphasizes his concern about the Polish minority in Prussia, see Bismarck, *Reflections and Reminiscences*, 2:135–54, 184–87.

18. Huber, *Verfassungsgeschichte*, 4:672–767; Constabel, ed., *Die Vorgeschichte des Kulturkampfes*, pp. 104–13, 124, 131–33, and passim; Stoltenberg, *Der deutsche Reichstag*, pp. 32–36 and passim; Knaplund, ed., *Letters from the Berlin Embassy*, 2:71; Buchheim, *Ultramontanismus und Demokratie*, pp. 234–54; Hanus, *Die preussische Vatikangesandtschaft*, pp. 310–29; Wallace, *The Papacy and European Diplomacy*, pp. 187–260; Kaiser, *Die politischen Strömungen*, pp. 278–360; Elvira L. Heybeg, "The German Liberal Parties in the Kulturkampf, 1871–1876,"

19. Nipperdey, *Die Organisation der deutschen Parteien vor 1918*, pp. 265–87; Buchheim, *Ultramontanismus und Demokratie*, pp. 271–90 passim; Ernst Deuerlein, "Ludwig Windthorst," pp. 277–97; Koppel S. Pinson, *Modern Germany*, p. 190 (for the hate-love quotation); Hans Dietzel, *Die preussischen Wahlrechtsreformbestrebungen von der Oktroyierung des Dreiklassenwahlrechts bis zum Beginn des Weltkrieges*, pp. 15–31; Gagel, *Wahlrechtsfrage*, pp. 74–75; Windell, *The Catholics and German Unity*, p. 50; Tormin, *Geschichte der deutschen Parteien*, p. 282ff.; Kaiser, *Die politischen Strömungen*, pp. 258–63, 360–93.

20. Bismarck, *Reflections and Reminiscences*, 2:196–204; Ivo Nikolai Lambi, *Free Trade and Protection in Germany 1868–1879*, pp. 99–240 passim; also Lambi's article, "The Protectionist Interests of the German Iron and Steel Industry, 1873–1879," pp. 59–70; Böhme, *Deutschlands Weg zur Grossmacht*, pp. 309–20, 341–564 passim; Morsey, "Bismarck und der Kulturkampf," pp. 267–69; Huber, *Verfassungsgeschichte*, 4:767–831; Lillian Parker Wallace, *Leo XIII and the Rise of Socialism*, pp. 79–143 passim; Ritter, *Der Weg des politischen Katholizismus*, pp. 84–85 (Windthorst comment of May 1879, quoted above).

21. For this and other contemporary comments see Jeanette Keim, *Forty Years of German-American Political Relations*, pp. 30, 31n, 33n.

VIII A NEW LEFT

1. The quotations are from: the addendum Engels wrote in 1874 to the preface of the 2d ed. of his long 1850 essay on *The Peasant War in Germany*, republished

by Leonard Krieger, ed., *The German Revolutions*, pp. 13, 15; and Engels to Marx, Aug. 15, 1870, quoted by Hans-Josef Steinberg, "Sozialismus, Internationalismus und Reichsgründung," p. 334.

2. For an introduction, one can still profitably read William Harbutt Dawson, *German Socialism and Ferdinand Lassalle*, for example, on Rodbertus, pp. 61–90. This has not seemed an appropriate, much less a requisite, place for a lengthy discussion of Marx or of Marxism. I have tried to suggest in a few concise sentences the essential character of Marxism as it affected rank and file German Social Democrats. In going beyond this, it seems sensible to regard as effectively "Marxist" what Marx published rather than what he chose not to publish, though I am aware of various "discoveries" of the "real" Marx in unpublished notebooks and drafts, such as those of 1844 and 1857–58. For selections from the latter see, for example, David McLellan, ed., *The Grundrisse: Karl Marx* (New York, 1971). For selected bibliographical references regarding Marx and Marxism, see above, chapter 3, n. 16. For the origins and development of socialism in Germany before 1863 see: Franz Mehring, *Geschichte der deutschen Sozialdemokratie*, vols. 1 and 2; Richard Lipinski, *Die Sozialdemokratie von ihren Anfängen bis zur Gegenwart*, 1:13–135; Hedwig Wachenheim, *Die deutsche Arbeiterbewegung 1844 bis 1914*, pp. 1–63; G. D. H. Cole, *A History of Socialist Thought*, 1:esp. pp. 219–60, 2:esp. pp. 12–31. The eclecticism of German Social Democracy is rightly emphasized by Susanne Miller, *Das Problem der Freiheit im Sozialismus*, pp. 23–176.

3. Hans Rosenberg, *Die Weltwirtschaftskrisis von 1857–1859*, pp. 174–83; Hans Rosenberg, *Grosse Depression und Bismarckzeit*, pp. 38–57 and passim; Gerhard Bry, *Wages in Germany, 1871–1945*, pp. 4, 14–79, 361–62; Ashok V. Desai, *Real Wages in Germany, 1871–1913*, p. 125 and passim; Wolfram Fischer, *Der Staat und die Anfänge der Industrialisierung in Baden 1800–1850*, 1:343–51; Jürgen Kuczynski, *Die Geschichte der Lage der Arbeiter unter dem Kapitalismus*, 2:127–211, 3:251–416, 18:101–64, esp. 2:129, 122, 180, 3:300, 302, 18:105; A. Sartorius von Waltershausen, *Deutsche Wirtschaftsgeschichte 1815–1914*, pp. 237–327, 501; Karl Erich Born, "Der soziale und wirtschaftliche Strukturwandel Deutschlands am Ende des 19. Jahrhunderts," pp. 361–76; Robert E. Dickinson, *The West European City*, pp. 238–45; and J. H. Clapham, *The Economic Development of France and Germany, 1815–1914*, pp. 278–322. Useful statistical compilations are available in Walter G. Hoffmann, Franz Grumbach, and Helmut Hesse, *Das Wachstum der deutschen Wirtschaft seit der Mitte des 19. Jahrhunderts*.

4. The quotations from Marx and Engels are from Max Eastman, ed., *Capital, the Communist Manifesto, and Other Writings by Karl Marx*, p. 359 (see also pp. 345–46, 357–67); Krieger, ed., *German Revolutions*, pp. 8, 9. On the leading roles played by artisans and other middle-class democrats in the organization of the workers of the 1860's see: Theodore S. Hamerow, *The Social Foundations of German Unification, 1858–1871*, 1:163–80; Frolinde Balser, *Sozial-Demokratie 1848/49–1863*, 1:350–51, 409–13, 484–96; Rolf Engelsing, "Zur politischen Bildung der deutschen Unterschichten 1789–1863," pp. 337–69; Gustav Meyer, "Die Trennung der proletarischen von der bürgerlichen Demokratie in Deutschland (1863–1870)," pp. 8–67 (an enduring monograph); Karl-Heinz Leidigkeit, *Wilhelm Liebknecht und August Bebel in der deutschen Arbeiterbewegung 1862–1869*, pp. 11–22, 70–84, and passim; Rolf Weber, *Kleinbürgerliche Demokraten in der deutschen Einheitsbewegung 1863–1866*. The studies by Leidigkeit and Weber are representative of much research in East Germany since World War II on the history of democracy, socialism, and labor in the 1860's. For other works see the articles, documents, and bibliographical references in the *Zeitschrift für Geschichtswis-*

senschaft (the main East German historical periodical) and in the *Beiträge zur Geschichte der deutschen Arbeiterbewegung* (a periodical published since 1959 by the Institute for Marxism-Leninism of the Central Committee of the Sozialistische Einheitspartei Deutschlands).

5. For an informed argument that Lassalle sought unsuccessfully to superimpose his authoritarian will upon the democratically inclined associations of workers, see Shlomo Na'aman, *Demokratische und soziale Impulse in der Frühgeschichte der deutschen Arbeiterbewegung der Jahre 1862/63*, pp. 76–93. See also: Dawson, *German Socialism and Ferdinand Lassalle*, pp. 114–218; Hermann Oncken, *Lassalle: Eine politische Biographie*, 3d. ed. (Stuttgart, 1920); David Footman, *Ferdinand Lassalle, Romantic Revolutionary*; Mehring, *Geschichte der deutschen Sozialdemokratie*, 3:1–164 passim; Miller, *Das Problem der Freiheit im Sozialismus*, pp. 39 and 23–176 passim; Thomas Nipperdey, *Die Organisation der deutschen Parteien vor 1918*, pp. 294–301; Johannes Hohlfeld and Klaus Hohlfeld, eds., *Dokumente der deutschen Politik und Geschichte von 1848 bis zur Gegenwart*, 1:115–24, 127–29; Hamerow, *Social Foundations of German Unification*, 1:115, 227–50; Paul Löbe, *Der Weg war lang: Lebenserinnerungen*, pp. 46–59; Roger Morgan, *The German Social Democrats and the First International, 1864–1872*, pp. 34–62; Edmund Silberner and Werner Blumenberg, eds., *Moses Hess*, pp. 225–478.

6. Max Hochdorf, *August Bebel*, pp. 7–95 passim; August Bebel, *Aus meinem Leben*, 1:1–22, 51–53, 72; Leidigkeit, *Liebknecht und Bebel*, pp. 56–69; and, for other sources (by and about Bebel), see Ernst Schraepler, *August-Bebel Bibliographie*.

7. Leidigkeit, *Liebknecht und Bebel*, pp. 32–84, 92–119; Bebel, *Aus meinem Leben*, 1:129–31, 169; Hochdorf, *August Bebel*, pp. 62–72; Mayer, "Die Trennung,"; Morgan, *German Social Democrats*, pp. 62–117. Liebknecht's relationships to 1866 with Marx and Engels, including his occasional appeals to the latter for funds, are documented in Georg Eckert, ed., *Wilhelm Liebknecht*, pp. 15–78.

8. Liebknecht to Engels, Dec. 11, 1867, and Jan. 20, 1868, in Eckert, ed., *Wilhelm Liebknecht*, pp. 82–101; Friedrich Engels, Preface to the 2d ed. (1870) of *The Peasant War in Germany*, in Krieger, ed., *German Revolutions*, p. 6 ("there is only one serious enemy of the Revolution in Germany at the present time—the Prussian government"); Hohlfeld and Hohlfeld, eds., *Dokumente*, 1:253–54 (the Eisenach program of August 1869); Mehring, *Geschichte der deutschen Sozialdemokratie*, 3:349–69; Mayer, "Die Trennung der proletarischen"; Sinclair W. Armstrong, "The Internationalism of the Early Social Democrats of Germany," p. 246; Leidigkeit, *Liebknecht und Bebel*, pp. 85–203; Morgan, *German Social Democrats*, pp. 117–99 (goes beyond Leidigkeit in research, giving more credit to Becker and Bebel and less to Liebknecht for the radicalization of the Verband); Arnold Heinz Schuetz, "Johann Jacoby—A Prussian Democrat," pp. 234–79; and on local manifestations of the rivalry between Lassalleans and Eisenachers, see Hugo Eckert, *Liberal-oder Sozialdemokratie*, pp. 156–83 and passim, and the section referring to this schism in Wolf-Arno Kropat, *Frankfurt zwischen Provinzialismus und Nationalismus*, pp. 89–91, 203–8. The minutes of the founding congress have been made available in a photo-reprint of the 1869 original: W. Liebknecht, A. Bebel, et al., eds., *Protokoll über die Verhandlungen des allgemeinen deutschen sozial-demokratischen Arbeiterkongresses zu Eisenach am 7., 8., und 9. August 1869*.

9. For basic documentation and court testimony on the attitudes of the leading socialists during the war of 1870/–71, see Wilhelm Liebknecht, ed., *Der Hochverraths-Prozess wider Karl Liebknecht, Bebel, Hepner vor dem Schwurgericht zu Leipzig*

vom 11. bis 26. März 1872, esp. pp. 393–638. For the above paragraph see also: Steinberg, "Sozialismus, Internationalismus und Reichsgründung," pp. 319–44; Sinclair W. Armstrong, "The Social Democrats and the Unification of Germany, 1863–71," pp. 500–507, and 485–509 passim; Gustav Mayer, *Friedrich Engels*, pp. 210–11; Hochdorf, *August Bebel*, pp. 105, 124; Morgan, *German Social Democrats*, pp. 199–215; Eckert, *Liberal-oder Sozialdemokratie*, pp. 184–186; Reinhard Höhn, *Sozialismus und Heer*, 1:309–38 (a third volume is projected); Eckert, ed., *Wilhelm Liebknecht*, pp. 105–25; Werner Conze and Dieter Groh, *Die Arbeiterbewegung in der nationalen Bewegung*, pp. 86–113. The question of partisan attitudes toward the annexation of Alsace-Lorraine also agitated nonsocialist democrats. In the Reichstag elections of 1871 in Frankfurt am Main, for instance, Leopold Sonnemann, a democrat, but no socialist who opposed the annexations, convincingly defeated four conservative and liberal opponents who supported them. Cf. Kropat, *Frankfurt zwischen Provinzialismus und Nationalismus*, pp. 179–80, 208.

10. Armstrong, "Social Democrats and Unification," pp. 507–9; Morgan, *German Social Democrats*, pp. 215–38; Wachenheim, *Die deutsche Arbeiterbewegung*, pp. 129–82; Mehring, *Geschichte der deutschen Sozialdemokratie*, 4:85–93; Nipperdey, *Die Organisation der deutschen Parteien*, pp. 304–6; Eckert, ed., *Wilhelm Liebknecht*, pp. 125–92, 229; Bebel, *Aus meinem Leben*, 2:330–34; Werner Blumenberg, ed., *August Bebels Briefwechsel mit Friedrich Engels*, pp. 26–39, 406–20.

11. Werner Pöls, *Sozialistenfrage und Revolutionsfurcht in ihrem Zusammenhang mit den angeblichen Staatsstreichplänen Bismarcks*, pp. 25–47; Wolfgang Pack, *Das parlamentarische Ringen um das Sozialistengesetz Bismarcks 1878–1890*, pp. 29–114, 243–63; Eckert, *Liberal-oder Sozialdemokratie*, pp. 186–233; Wachenheim, *Die deutsche Arbeiterbewegung*, pp. 182–208; Karl Kautsky, *Erinnerungen und Erörterungen*, p. 354; Adalbert Wahl, *Deutsche Geschichte von der reichsgründung bis zum Ausbruch des Weltkrieges (1871 bis 1914)*, 1:279, 521–39; Karl Schlottenloher, *Flugblatt und Zeitung*, p. 418; Rolf Engelsing, *Massenpublikum und Journalistentum im 19. Jahrhundert in Nordwestdeutschland*, pp. 78–99, 230–49; Hohlfeld and Hohlfeld, eds., *Dokumente*, 1:367–74 (for excerpts from debates, the draft, and the law).

12. Pack, *Das parlamentarische Ringen*, pp. 259–63 (text of the 1878 laws), 115–235 (enforcement and renewals to 1890); Vernon L. Lidtke, *The Outlawed Party*, pp. 78–345 passim (text of 1878 law in English translation, pp. 339–45); Dieter Fricke, "Eine wichtige Quelle zur Geschichte der deutschen Arbeiterbewegung," pp. 94–103; Mehring, *Geschichte der deutschen Sozialdemokratie*, 4:153–324; Lipinski, *Die Sozialdemokratie*, 2:40–141; Schlottenloher, *Flugblatt und Zeitung*, p. 418; Kurt Koszyk, *Anfänge und frühe Entwicklung der sozialdemokratische Presse im Ruhrgebiet (1875–1908)*, pp. 14, 30–33, 35; Hochdorf, *August Bebel*, pp. 162–202; Bebel, *Aus meinem Leben*, vol. 3. For a record of the 1878–90 court actions against Social Democrats and their punishments see Peter Rassow and Karl Erich Born, eds., *Akten zur staatlichen Sozialpolitik in Deutschland 1890–1914*, pp. 64–71. See also Reinhard Höhn, ed., *Die vaterlandslosen Gesellen*, vol. 1.

13. For a study that is useful, notwithstanding its Nazi interpretations, see Otto Quandt, *Die Anfänge der Bismarckschen Sozialgesetzgebung und die Haltung der Parteien (Das Unfallversicherungsgesetz 1881–1884)*. See also: Walter Vogel, *Bismarcks Arbeiterversicherung*; Werner Frauendienst, "Sozialpolitik Bismarcks—und Heute," pp. 730–32 (text of Bismarck's letter of March 13, 1879).

14. Nipperdey, *Die Organisation der deutschen Parteien*, pp. 306–17; Lidtke, *Outlawed Party*, pp. 78–97. On Eduard Bernstein's uncle, Aaron Bernstein, see Adolf Kober, "Jews in the Revolution of 1848 in Germany," p. 153; Peter Gay, *The Dilemma of Democratic Socialism*, chap. 1–2; Kautsky, *Erinnerungen und Erörterungen*, pp. 433–36; Helmut Hirsch, ed., *Eduard Bernsteins Briefwechsel mit*

Friedrich Engels, pp. 15, 19, 25, 31, 39, 250 for Engels to Bernstein, Feb. 2, March 12, April 14, and Aug. 17, 1881, and Bernstein to Engels, Oct. 14, 1881, and March 5, 1884; Ernst Engelberg, *Revolutionäre Politik und rote Feldpost 1878–1890*, pp. 172–291 and passim (which combines valuable historical data with denunciations of the current politics of the West German SPD); Höhn, ed., *Die vaterlandslosen Gesellen*, pp. 28, 42, 43, 247, and passim, for police reports on the smuggling of the *Sozialdemokrat* into Germany.

15. The tensions between the Social Democratic Reichstag caucus and the Marxist theorists who rallied around the *Sozialdemokrat* and *Die neue Zeit* are reflected, sometimes with considerable passion, in the following collections of correspondence: Benedikt Kautsky, ed., *Friedrich Engels' Briefwechsel mit Karl Kautsky*, pp. 70, 80, 82, and 70–250 passim; Hirsch, ed., *Bernsteins Briefwechsel mit Engels*, pp. 64–75, 208–26, 271–77, 316–30, 433–36, and passim. On the founding of *Die neue Zeit* and its editor, see also Kautsky, *Erinnerungen and Erörterungen*. The more general tendencies noted above are discussed in detail by Lidtke, *Outlawed Party*; Hans-Josef Steinberg, *Sozialismus und deutsche Sozialdemokratie*, pp. 13–75 and passim.

16. For Hasenclever's election campaign of 1884 see Karl A. Hellfaier, "Die sozialdemokratische Bewegung in Halle/Saale (1865–1890)," pp. 104–6. Several socialist election leaflets of 1884 in Berlin may be found in the Nachlass Goldschmidt, German Foreign Ministry Archives filmed at Whaddon Hall, National Archives Microcopy T-291, Roll 3, frames 00535–00544. For the paragraphs above, see also: Engelberg, *Revolutionäre Politik*, pp. 35–135 and passim; Miller, *Das Problem der Freiheit im Sozialismus*, pp. 92–122, 179–98; Lidtke, *Outlawed Party*, pp. 97–290 passim; Heinrich Gemkow, ed., "Briefe August Bebels aus den Jahren 1886–1887," pp. 135–53; Gustav Seeber, *Die deutsche Sozialdemokratie und die Entwicklung ihrer revolutionären Parlamentstaktik von 1867 bis 1893*, pp. 32–50; Eckert, ed., *Wilhelm Liebknecht*, pp. 267–368; Blumenberg, ed., *Bebels Briefwechsel mit Engels*, pp. 102–9, 136–42, 178–84, 191–201, 272–75, 293, 361–63, and passim.

17. Lidtke, *Outlawed Party*, pp. 97–290 passim; Dieter Fricke, *Die deutsche Arbeiterbewegung 1869–1890* (a paperback handbook by an East German historian, containing much information on the party and unions during the years of repression); Höhn, ed., *Die vaterlandslosen Gesellen*, pp. 14–16, 24, 54–65, 96, 120, 146, 196, 244–45, 264, and passim; Walter Tormin, *Geschichte der deutschen Parteien seit 1848*, pp. 282ff. (electoral statistics); Engelsing, *Massenpublikum und Journalistentum*, pp. 99–102, 250; Hermann Grossmann, *Die kommunale Bedeutung des Strassenbahnwesens beleuchtet am Werdegange der Dresdener Strassenbahnen*, Table IV and passim. Studies are needed of the technological, social, and political aspects of the development of electric street railways in Germany from the 1870's to 1914. Sources that might be examined include: the *Zeitschrift für das gesammte Local-& Strassenbahnwesen*; *Brockhaus' Konversations-Lexikon*, 14th ed., 17 vols. (Leipzig, 1908), 2:789–91; Erich Giese, *Schnellstrassenbahnen*; F. Van der Gragt, *Europe's Greatest Tramway Network*. For evidence of German socialist disputations in the 1880's concerning "die elektrotechnische Revolution" see Hirsch ed., *Bernsteins Briefwechsel mit Engels*, pp. 186, 189–93, 196–97.

18. Lidtke, *Outlawed Party*, pp. 291–319; Pack, *Das parlamentarische Ringen*, pp. 204–36; Pöls, *Sozialistenfrage und Revolutionsfurcht*, pp. 83–99; Wilhelm Mommsen, *Bismarcks Sturz und die Parteien*, pp. 24–154; Otto von Bismarck, *Erinnerung und Gedanke*, vol. 3 of his memoirs, pp. 48–110, 163–70; Egmont Zechlin, *Staatsstreichpläne Bismarcks und Wilhelms II. 1890–1894*, pp. 3–84, 178–84; Rudolf Vier-

haus, ed., *Das Tagebuch der Baronin Spitzemberg geb. Freiin v. Varnbüler*, pp. 266, 311; Norman Rich, *Friedrich von Holstein*, 1:255–84; Engels to Bebel, Feb. 17, 1890, in Blumenberg, ed., *Bebels Briefwechsel mit Engels*, p. 380, see also pp. 377–84.

19. For a concise statement of the Marxist distinction between political democracy as a means and as an end, see Engels to Bernstein, March 24, 1884, in Hirsch, ed., *Bernsteins Briefwechsel mit Engels*, pp. 253–54. The problem of harmonizing pledges to achieve democracy with endorsement of the dictatorship of the proletariat led to contradictions in contemporary socialist writings, and they in turn have given rise to contradictions in the works of historians. Note, for example, the conflicting generalizations to be found in the generally excellent study by Lidtke, *Outlawed Party*, on p. 326 ("if the German Social Democrats were not scornful of political democracy by 1890, at least they were very little concerned about it") and on p. 317 ("in political theory and practice, [Social Democracy] was in historical reality a party of radical democratic liberalism").

IX OBSTACLES TO DEMOCRACY

1. For the wedding details, see Robert K. Massie, *Nicholas and Alexandra*, p. 33. On Ernst Ludwig cf. *Festschrift zum fünfundzwanzigjährigen Regierungsjubiläum Seiner Königlichen Hoheit, des Grossherzogs Ernst Ludwig von Hessen und bei Rhein*, pp. 9–110. In 1901 the marriage which caused the festivities ended in divorce.

2. The history of the reign of William I and his successor may be followed in two standard accounts: Adalbert Wahl, *Deutsche Geschichte von der Reichsgründung bis zum Ausbruch des Weltkrieges (1871 bis 1914)*, offers a detailed survey from a conservative-nationalist viewpoint; for a liberal interpretation see Johannes Ziekursch, *Politische Geschichte des neuen deutschen Kaiserreiches*. On the ill-fated Frederick see, among many other publications: Andreas Dorpalen, "Emperor Frederick III and the German Liberal Movement," pp. 1–31; Frederic B. M. Hollyday, *Bismarck's Rival*, pp. 31–42, 64, 66, 124–34, 149, 179, and 217–36 passim; Michael Freund, *Das Drama der 99 Tage*, esp. pp. 351–93. Research scholars interested in imperial Germany should consult Thomas E. Skidmore, "Survey of Unpublished Sources on the Central Government and Politics of the German Empire, 1871–1918," pp. 848–59. For additional data on many matters treated in this chapter, see Ernst Rudolf Huber, *Deutsche Verfassungsgeschichte seit 1789*, vol. 4.

3. Michael Stürmer, "Staatsstreichgedanken im Bismarckreich," pp. 566–615, is very useful for its treatment of the events of 1878, as is the same author's subsequent "Bismarck in Perspective," esp. pp. 291–97, 304–17, a translation of Sturmer's "Bismarck—Mythos und Historie." Huber, *Verfassungsgeschichte*, 4:214–28, strongly argues that Bismarck talked of a *Staatsstreich* in 1890 to arrange an alliance with the Center. On major aspects of Bismarck's chancellorship, including this question, see: Otto von Bismarck, *Erinnerung und Gedanke*, vol. 3 of his memoirs, pp. 48, 110, 163–70; Norman Rich, *Friedrich von Holstein*, 1:273–84; Wolfgang Pack, *Das parlamentarische Ringen um das Sozialistengesetz Bismarcks 1878–1890*, pp. 204–36; Erich Eyck, *Bismarck*, 3:543–99; John C. G. Röhl, "The Disintegration of the *Kartell* and the Politics of Bismarck's Fall From Power, 1887–90," pp. 60–89; Wilhelm Mommsen, *Bismarcks Sturz und die Parteien*, pp. 24–199; Karl Friedrich Nowak, *Kaiser and Chancellor*, pp. 155–206; Egmont Zechlin, *Staatsstreichpläne Bismarcks und Wilhelms II, 1890–1894*, pp. 3–84, 178–84; John C. G. Röhl, "Staatsstreichplan oder Staatsstreichbereitschaft? Bismarcks Politik in der Entlassungskrise," pp. 610–24.

4. The following are suggestive on the personality and political philosophy of the kaiser: Michael Balfour, *The Kaiser and His Times*, pp. 138–66 and passim, which reemphasizes themes treated earlier by E. F. Benson, *The Kaiser and English Relations*; Joachim von Kürenberg (pseud. J. von Reichel), *The Kaiser*, pp. 24, 73–74, 82, 90, 154 (an impressionistic but perceptive portrait); Erich Eyck, *Das persönliche Regiment Wilhelms II*, p. 148 and passim. Unconvincing attempts to rehabilitate the reputation of the kaiser are offered by J. Daniel Chamier, *Fabulous Monster*, and Hans Helfritz, *Wilhelm II als Kaiser und König*, esp. pp. 11–72. For the paragraphs above see also: William II, *Ereignisse und Gestalten aus den Jahren 1878–1918*; Robert von Zedlitz-Trützschler, *Twelve Years at the Imperial Court*, esp. pp. 56–84, 115–72; Johannes Haller, ed., *Philip Eulenburg*, 1:31, 116, 165, 206–7, 214, 265, 293, 2:61, 63; Erhard von Wedel, *Zwischen Kaiser und Kanzler*, pp. 212–18; Bernhard von Bülow, *Memoirs of Prince von Bülow*, 1:5, 255, 605–9, 632, 2:160–62, 3:332, and passim; Rich, *Friedrich von Holstein*, 2:499 and passim; Rudolf Vierhaus, ed., *Das Tagebuch der Baronin Spitzemberg geb. Freiin v. Varnbüler*, pp. 297–98, 353–54, and passim; Josef Kliersfeld, *Die Haltung Kaiser Wilhelms II. zur Arbeiterbewegung und zur Sozialdemokratie*; Zechlin, *Staatsstreich pläne*, pp. 87–152, 184–225; Max Buchner, *Kaiser Wilhelm II*, p. 167. For the emperor's public remarks in 1891 (and German press comment on them) see German Foreign Ministry Archives, 1867–1920, Whaddon Hall, National Archives Microcopy T-149, Reel 188.

5. J. Alden Nichols, *Germany after Bismarck*, pp. 29–364; John C. G. Röhl, *Germany without Bismarck*, pp. 56–117; Rich, *Friedrich von Holstein*, 1:375–430 and 287–430 passim; Zechlin, *Staatsstreichpläne*, pp. 87–152, 184–225; Eyck, *Das persönliche Regiment*, pp. 47–61, 81; Charlotte Sempell, "The Constitutional and Political Problems of the Second Chancellor, Leo von Caprivi," pp. 234–54; Helmuth Rogge, ed., *Holstein und Hohenlohe*, pp. 404–13; Karl Erich Born, *Staat und Sozialpolitik seit Bismarcks Sturz*, pp. 84–118; Peter Rassow and Karl Erich Born, eds., *Akten zur staatlichen Sozialpolitik in Deutschland 1890–1914*, pp. 1–24, 30–56; Thomas Elliott Skidmore, "The Chancellorship of Caprivi," pp. 92–393 (draws upon some unpublished material but adds no significant new information).

6. Röhl, *Germany without Bismarck*, pp. 118–279; Gunther Blieffert, "Die Innenpolitik des Reichskanzlers Fürst Chlodwig zu Hohenlohe-Schillingsfürst 1894–1900," esp. pp. 73, 117, 137, 250; Chlodwig zu Hohenlohe-Schillingsfürst, *Denkwürdigkeiten der Reichskanzlerzeit*, esp. pp. 20–24, 45–54, 59–67, 92–112, 296–99, 320–64, 385–86, 440–41, 451–53; Chlodwig of Hohenlohe-Schillings-fürst, *Memoirs*, 2:465–66, 470, and passim; Rich, *Friedrich von Holstein*, 2:433–610; Heinz Josef Varain, *Freie Gewerkschaften, Sozialdemokratie und Staat*, pp. 19–21; Jonathan Steinberg, *Yesterday's Deterrent*; Eckart Kehr, *Der Primat der Innenpolitik*, pp. 111–48, and, more important, Kehr's *Schlachtflottenbau und Parteipolitik 1894–1901*, pp. 34–167 and passim; Rassow and Born, eds., *Akten zur staatlichen Sozialpolitik*, pp. 56–128; Born, *Staat und Sozialpolitik seit Bismarcks Sturz*, pp. 118–66. For Bebel's comment on Hohenlohe, see Werner Blumenberg, ed., *August Bebels Briefwechsel mit Friedrich Engels*, p. 789.

7. Besides the six larger states—Prussia, Bavaria, Saxony, Württemberg, Baden, and Hesse—and the imperial territory of Alsace-Lorraine, the German Empire included the republican city-states of Bremen, Hamburg, and Lübeck and the princely states of Anhalt, Braunschweig, Lippe, Mecklenburg-Schwerin, Mecklenburg-Strelitz, Oldenburg, Reuss (Older Line), Reuss (Younger Line), Saxe-Altenburg, Saxe-Coburg-Gotha, Saxe-Meiningen, Saxe-Weimar, Schaum-

burg-Lippe, Schwarzburg-Rudolstadt, Schwarzburg-Sondershausen, and Waldeck. The text of the constitution, as revised in 1870–71, appears in Bureau des Reichstags, ed., *Reichstags-Handbuch, 13*, pp. 7–78. Administrative relationships between the central and the state governments are treated by Herbert Jacob, *German Administration since Bismarck*, pp. 22–66. An extended analysis of the structure of the imperial government is provided by Huber, *Verfassungsgeschichte*, 3:766–1074.

8. For the key constitutional articles concerning the positions and powers of kaiser and chancellor, see Bureau des Reichstags, ed., *Reichstags-Handbuch*, pp. 17–20, 41, 43, 79–80. See also: Huber, *Verfassungsgeschichte*, 3:809–46, 930–44, 988, 1006, 1012, 1015; Gordon A. Craig, *The Politics of the Prussian Army, 1640–1945*, pp. 217–30; Gerhard Ritter, *Staatskunst und Kriegshandwerk*, vol. 2; and Martin Kitchen, *The German Officer Corps, 1890–1914*. More generally, see Elisabeth Fehrenbach, *Wandlungen des deutschen Kaisergedankens 1871–1918*, pp. 52–88 and passim.

9. Julius Hatschek, *Das Parlamentsrecht des Deutschen Reiches*; Ernst Deuerlein, ed., *Der Reichstag*, pp. 13–73, 125–43; Willy Kremer, *Der soziale Aufbau der Parteien des deutschen Reichstages von 1871–1918*, pp. 79–80; Thomas Nipperdey, *Die Organisation der deutschen Parteien vor 1918*; Wolfgang Conrad Haussman, *Die Durchsetzung des parlamentarischen Systems im deutschen Kaiserreich*, p. 56; Otto von Bismarck, *Bismarck, the Man and the Statesman, Being the Reflections and Reminiscences of Otto, Prince von Bismarck*, 1:63–64 and passim; Walter Tormin, *Geschichte der deutschen Parteien seit 1848*, pp. 71–126 passim; James J. Sheehan, "Political Leadership in the German Reichstag, 1871–1918," pp. 511–28; Huber, *Verfassungsgeschichte*, 3:874.

10. Bureau des Reichstags, ed., *Reichstags-Handbuch*, pp. 13–17, 47; Huber, *Verfassungsgeschichte*, 3:848–60, 880, 1064–74; James Harvey Robinson, *The German Bundesrath: A Study in Comparative Constitutional Law*, vol. 3, no. 1 in the *Political Economy and Public Law Series*, University of Pennsylvania (Philadelphia, 1891), pp. 5, 24, and passim. Bismarck, *Reflections and Reminiscences*, 1:320–22, 325, 391–412, and his *Erinnerung und Gedanke*, p. 15; George G. Windell, "The Bismarckian Empire as a Federal State, 1866–1880," pp. 299–311. The statement of 1884 is quoted from a memorandum sent by Vice-Chancellor Helfferich to the minister-presidents of the federal states on April 23, 1917 (German Foreign Ministry Archives, Whaddon Hall, National Archives Microcopy T149, Reel 331).

11. On state and local government in Prussia after 1871 see Hue de Grais, *Handbuch der Verfassung und Verwaltung in Preussen und dem Deutschen Reiche*, esp. pp. 36–89; Heinrich Heffter, *Die deutsche Selbstverwaltung im 19. Jahrhundert*, pp. 6, 329, 335, 546–56, 588–99; Hellmut von Gerlach, *Von Rechts nach Links*, p. 91; Fritz Hartung, *Deutsche Verfassungsgeschichte vom 15. Jahrhundert bis zur Gegenwart*, pp. 297–303. See also: John C. G. Röhl, "Higher Civil Servants in Germany, 1890–1900," pp. 101–21.

12. Ivo Nikolai Lambi, *Free Trade and Protection in Germany, 1868–1879*, pp. 150–90, 207–25, and passim; Nipperdey, *Die Organisation der deutschen Parteien*, pp. 102–5, 119, and 86–175 passim; James Fremont Harris, "Eduard Lasker, 1829–1884"; Uriel Tal, "Liberal Protestantism and the Jews in the Second Reich, 1870–1914," p. 24; Bismarck, *Reflections and Reminiscences*, 2:196–204; Lenore O'Boyle, "Liberal Political Leadership in Germany, 1867–1884," pp. 341, 345; Joachim H. Knoll, *Führungsauslese in Liberalismus und Demokratie*, pp. 170–83; Theodor Eschenburg, *Das Kaiserreich am Scheideweg*, pp. 112, 115; Kremer, *Der soziale Aufbau der Parteien*, pp. 13–23; Karl Erich Born, "Der soziale und wirt-

schaftliche Strukturwandel Deutschlands am Ende des 19. Jahrhunderts," pp. 361–76, esp. pp. 372–73; Julius Heyderhoff and Paul Wentzcke, eds., *Deutscher Liberalismus im Zeitalter Bismarcks*, 2:363–456 passim.

13. Wilhelm Otto Vollrath, *Der parlamentarische Kampf um das preussische Dreiklassenwahlrecht*, pp. 33, 45–54, 75; Hans Dietzel, *Die preussischen Wahlrechtsreformbestrebungen von der Oktroyierung des Dreiklassenwahlrechts bis zum Beginn des Weltkrieges*, pp. 11–14, 46–47 (corrects several points in the Vollrath study); Walter Gagel, *Die Wahlrechtsfrage in der Geschichte der deutschen liberalen Parteien 1848–1918*, pp. 74, 103–5, 126–27; Mommsen, *Bismarcks Sturz und die Parteien*, pp. 98–99.

14. Kremer, *Der soziale Aufbau der Parteien*, pp. 13–23; Erich Brandenburg, *Fünfzig Jahre Nationalliberale Partei 1867–1914*, pp. 11–23; Gagel, *Wahlrechtsfrage*, pp. 100–103, 116. There are convenient tables of statistics on all the Reichstag elections in Tormin, *Geschichte der deutschen Parteien*, pp. 282–85. See also Helmuth Croon, *Die gesellschaftlichen Auswirkungen des Gemeindewahlrechts in den Gemeinden und Kreisen des Rheinlandes und Westfalens im 19. Jahrhundert*, pp. 32–37, 59, and passim; Nipperdey, *Die Organisation der deutschen Parteien*, pp. 100–101, 149–50, and 86–175 passim; Eschenburg, *Das Kaiserreich am Scheideweg*, pp. 60–61; Haller, ed., *Philip Eulenburg*, 1:113–14; Karola Bassermann, *Ernst Bassermann*.

15. Eschenburg, *Das Kaiserreich am Scheideweg*, pp. 3–26, 60–61; Bassermann, *Ernst Bassermann*, pp. 145–46, 153, and passim; Ernst Müller-Meiningen, *Parlamentarismus*, pp. 176–77; Bogdan Hutten-Czapski, *Sechzig Jahre Politik und Gesellschaft*, 2:6–7, 9–12; and the revealing documentary collection, Klaus-Peter Reiss, ed., *Von Bassermann zu Stresemann*, pp. 11–31, 89–191.

16. Nichols, *Germany after Bismarck*, pp. 70, 188, 216, 217, 237, 250–53, 256, 294, 309; Georg von Hertling, *Erinnerungen aus meinem Leben* (which carry only to 1902); Klaus Epstein, *Matthias Erzberger and the Dilemma of German Democracy*, pp. 39–44; E. Wetterle, *Behind the Scenes in the Reichstag*, pp. 62–67; Haussmann, *Die Durchsetzung des parlamentarischen Systems*, p. 35; Bülow, *Memoirs*, 1:611–12; Karl Bachem, *Vorgeschichte, Geschichte und Politik der deutschen Zentrumspartei*, 9:502 and passim; and Rudolf Morsey, *Die deutsche Zentrumspartei 1917–1923*, pp. 33–52.

17. Insolde Rieger, *Die Wilhelminischen Presse im Überblick 1888–1918*, pp. 114–18; John K. Zeender, "The German Center Party during World War I," pp. 442–47, 452n; Morsey, *Die deutsche Zentrumspartei*, p. 43; Hohenlohe-Schillingsfürst, *Memoirs*, 2:474; Bachem, *Zentrumspartei*, 9:504–9; and *Arbeiter-Jugend* (Berlin), March 9, 1918, for statistics on the *Verband der katholischen Jünglingsvereinigungen Deutschlands*.

18. These generalizations are based upon literature cited in the foregoing and following notes and upon research in the Carl Bachem Nachlass and Bachem Familienarchiv in the Stadtarchiv, Cologne (hereinafter cited as Bachem Nachlass). Carl Bachem closely collaborated with his brother, Franz X. Bachem, publisher of the *Kölnische Volkszeitung*, whose leading editor, Julius Bachem, was a cousin. I have used Carl Bachem's general letter files, 1905–14, and other files most relevant to this volume for the period 1890–1914. The quotation above is from a lengthy memorandum sent by Center party leaders to Cardinal Rampolla, Feb. 7, 1900. With preliminary drafts and other related materials, it is in Folder 37, Bachem Nachlass. Excerpts from Julius Bachem's article of March 1, 1906, "Wir müssen aus dem Turm heraus," are reprinted in Wilhelm Mommsen, ed., *Deutsche Parteiprogramme*, pp. 240–44. For a concise and accurate discussion of

the controversy between the Cologne and Berlin orientations within the party, see Huber, *Verfassungsgeschichte*, 4:49–63.

19. Röhl, *Germany without Bismarck*, p. 216. For other material in the above paragraphs see: Lillian Parker Wallace, *Leo XIII and the Rise of Socialism*, pp. 79–143; Mommsen, *Bismarcks Sturz und die Parteien*, pp. 44–139 passim; Nichols, *Germany after Bismarck*, p. 71 and passim; Dan P. Silverman, "Political Catholicism and Social Democracy in Alsace-Lorraine, 1871–1914," pp. 52–53 and passim; Gagel, *Wahlrechtsfrage*, p. 126; Eyck, *Das persönliche Regiment*, pp. 100, 108, 150, and passim; Hartung, *Deutsche Verfassungsgeschichte*, p. 292; Buchner, *Kaiser Wilhelm II*; and the essay by Klaus Müller in Konrad Repgen and Stephan Skalweit, eds., *Spiegel der Geschichte*, pp. 828–57. Eckart Kehr exaggerated the Center's desire to influence policy into an ambition for *Hegemonie* and *Herrschaft* during the Hohenlohe chancellorship: *Schlachtflottenbau und Parteipolitik*, pp. 128–67, 365–79.

20. Karl Heidemann, *Bismarcks Sozialpolitik und die Zentrumspartei 1881–1884*, pp. 15–16, 117, and passim; Michael P. Fogarty, *Christian Democracy in Western Europe, 1820–1953*, pp. 427–28; Karl Buchheim, *Ultramontanismus und Demokratie*, pp. 447–536 passim; Emil Ritter, *Die katholisch-soziale Bewegung Deutschlands im 19. Jahrhundert und der Volksverein*, pp. 129–351 passim.

21. Josef Deutz, *Adam Stegerwald*, esp. pp. 29, 36–37, 40–41, 44, 52, 67–68, 73; Helmut J. Schorr, *Adam Stegerwald*, pp. 16–56; Ludwig Frey, *Die Stellung der christlichen Gewerkschaften Deutschlands zu den politischen Parteien*, pp. 7–9, 11, 26, 62, 67, 107, 110 (a useful but not exhaustive dissertation); Max Jürgen Koch, *Die Bergarbeiterbewegung im Ruhrgebiet zur Zeit Wilhelms II (1889–1914)*, pp. 25–26, 47, 60–62, 123–29, 132; Zeender, "German Center Party," pp. 443, 445, 449n, 458, and passim. The director of the central office of the Volksverein estimated in 1904 that about thirty thousand members of the Christian Trade Unions were Protestants; August Pieper to Franz Brandts, Feb. 23, 1904, Folder 215, Bachem Nachlass.

22. The memorandum, earlier drafts, and correspondence concerning it are in Folder 215, Bachem Nachlass. On the Christian Trade Unions see also: Folder 980, Bachem Nachlass; Kremer, *Der soziale Aufbau der Parteien*, pp. 27–38; Frey, *Die Stellung der christlichen Gewerkschaften*, pp. 107, 110; Bachem, *Zentrumspartei*, 9:509; Morsey, *Die deutsche Zentrumspartei*, p. 50 (for table on occupations of Center Reichstag deputies, 1903–18).

23. *Germania* (Berlin), March 27, 1904 (clipping in Folder 215, Bachem Nachlass); the following folders in the Bachem Nachlass: 290 (clippings from the *Kölnische Volkszeitung* of May 2, 1910, and other dates criticizing reform proposals of the government and the National Liberal party; also Carl Bachem's *Pro notitia* dated April 22, 1910, and Bachem to Porsch, April 22, Bachem to Wallraf, April 25 and 26, and Wallraf to Bachem, April 30 plus unsent draft, Bachem to Wallraf, April 23); 325 (brochure of 47 pages distributed in 1910–11 in thousands of copies in anticipation of the next elections: *Das Zentrum und die Wahlrechts-Reform in Preussen*; also in this folder the election leaflet, *Nimm alle Kraft zusammen!*, published by the Bachem firm and distributed by the general secretariat of the Rhenish Center party, Cologne, April 1913). See also, for the paragraph above, Vollrath, *Der parlamentarische Kampf um das preussische Dreiklassenwahlrecht*, pp. 33, 48–54; Dietzel, *Die preussischen Wahlrechtsreformbestrebungen*, pp. 15–31, 38–39; Emil Ritter, *Der Weg des politischen Katholizismus*, pp. 11–148 passim and 245; Ernst Deuerlein, "Verlauf und Ergebnis des 'Zentrumsstreites' (1906–1909)," pp. 103–26; Haussmann, *Die Durchsetzung des parlamentarischen Systems*, pp. 35–37; Croon, *Die gesellschaftlichen Auswirkungen des Gemeindewahlrechtes*, pp. 27–28 and passim.

24. See the suggestive article by John K. Zeender, "German Catholics and the Concept of an Interconfessional Party, 1900–1922," pp. 424–28; Schorr, *Adam Stegerwald*, pp. 51–55; Theodor Eschenburg, "Carl Sonnenschein," pp. 333–61.

25. On the origin and development of both parties to about 1876 see: Otto-Ernst Schüddekopf, *Die deutsche Innenpolitik im letzten Jahrhundert und der konservative Gedanke*, pp. 5–67; Kremer, *Der soziale Aufbau der Parteien*, pp. 4–11; Hans Booms, *Die deutschkonservative Partei*, pp. 6–7; Fredrick Aandahl, "The Rise of German Free Conservatism," pp. 1–155 (for the origins of the party and its development to 1871); Nipperdey, *Die Organisation der deutschen Parteien*, pp. 18–20 and 241–64 passim; Tormin, *Geschichte der deutschen Parteien*, pp. 282–85.

26. Booms, *Die deutschkonservative Partei*, pp. 6–8, 34–58, 62; Schüddekopf, *Die deutsche Innenpolitik*, p. 124; Alexander Gerschenkron, *Bread and Democracy in Germany*, pp. 22–23, 86, 88; Gerlach, *Von Rechts nach Links*, pp. 34, 161; Kremer, *Der soziale Aufbau der Parteien*, pp. 4–7; Gagel, *Wahlrechtsfrage*, pp. 116, 176–77; Lysbeth Walker Muncy, *The Junker in the Prussian Administration under William II, 1888–1914*, pp. 223, 227–29; Ernst Kohn-Bramstedt, *Aristocracy and the Middle-Classes in Germany*, pp. 228–340; Oscar Stillich, *Die politischen Parteien in Deutschland*, 1:1–29, 66–67, 126–60; Andreas Dorpalen, "The German Conservatives and the Parliamentarization of Imperial Germany," pp. 184–99; Born, "Der soziale und wirtschaftliche Strukturwandel Deutschlands," p. 369 (for the Heydebrand comment); Kurt Schreinert, ed., *Theodor Fontane Briefe an Friedlaender*, pp. 255–56; Eyck, *Das persönliche Regiment*, pp. 76–77; Nikolaus von Preradovich, *Die Führungsschichten in Österreich und Preussen (1804–1918) mit einem Ausblick bis zum Jahre 1945*, pp. 78–84, 106–7, 160–68; Aandahl, "German Free Conservatism," p. 185 and passim; Abraham Ascher, "Baron von Stumm, Advocate of a Feudal Capitalism," pp. 271–85; and Hans Rosenberg, *Probleme der deutschen Sozialgeschichte*, pp. 7–80 and passim.

27. Aandahl, "German Free Conservatism," pp. 42–43n, 67–70, 284–333, 345, and passim; Ascher, "Baron von Stumm," pp. 271–85; Müller-Meiningen, *Parlamentarismus*, pp. 176, 178; Kuno von Westarp, *Konservative Politik im letzten Jahrzehnt des Kaiserreiches*, 1:348–58 and passim; Annelise Thimme, *Hans Delbrück als Kritiker der Wilhelminischen Epoche*, p. 64n; Rieger, *Die Wilhelminische Presse*, pp. 111–14.

28. Hans Rosenberg, *Grosse Depression und Bismarckzeit*, pp. 88–117; P. G. J. Pulzer, *The Rise of Political Anti-Semitism in Germany and Austria*, pp. 88–101, 226–35, and passim; Wanda Kampmann, "Adolf Stoecker und die Berliner Bewegung," pp. 558–79; Bismarck, *Erinnerung und Gedanke*, pp. 19–20; Nichols, *Germany after Bismarck*, pp. 218, 238, 250; George L. Mosse, *The Crisis of German Ideology*, pp. 126–222 passim; Fritz Stern, *The Politics of Cultural Despair*; Fritz Stern, "Money, Morals, and the Pillars of Bismarck's Society," pp. 49–65; Johannes Hohlfeld and Klaus Hohlfeld, eds., *Dokumente der deutschen Politik und Geschichte von 1848 bis zur Gegenwart*, 2:143–46, 149–53 (for quote of Tivoli program); Kremer, *Der soziale Aufbau der Parteien*, p. 59; Paul W. Massing, *Rehearsal for Destruction*, pp. 21–59, 66, 104, 123, 246–47; Alfred Kruck, *Geschichte des Alldeutschen Verbandes 1890–1939*, pp. 45–46; Tormin, *Geschichte der deutschen Parteien*, p. 99; and Ernest Hamburger, *Juden im öffentlichen Leben Deutschlands*. On political anti-Semitism see Richard S. Levy, "Anti-Semitic Political Parties in the German Empire," pp. 55–128.

29. Andreas Dorpalen, *Heinrich von Treitschke*, pp. 234, 251, 294–95, and passim; Hannah Arendt, *The Origins of Totalitarianism*, p. 222 and passim; Mildred S. Wertheimer, *The Pan-German League, 1890–1914*; Lothar Werner, *Der*

Alldeutsche Verband 1890–1918; Kruck, *Geschichte des Alldeutschen Verbandes;* Booms, *Die Deutschkonservative Partei,* pp. 120–29.

30. Sarah Rebecca Tirrell, *German Agrarian Politics after Bismarck's Fall,* esp. pp. 158–206 (a carefully executed study); Wilhelm Mattes, *Die bayerischen Bauernräte,* p. 39; Elard von Oldenburg-Januschau, *Erinnerungen,* pp. 32–61; Hohlfeld and Hohlfeld, eds., *Dokumente,* 2:35–36 (for the February 1893 founding program of the Bund der Landwirte); and the masterful study of Hans-Jürgen Puhle, *Agrarische Interessenpolitik und preussischer Konservatismus im Wilhelminischen Reich (1893–1914),* pp. 168–72, 213–73, *and passim.*

31. Helmut Böhme, *Deutschlands Weg zur Grossmacht,* pp. 504 and 359–604 passim; Gerhard Schulz, "Über die Entstehung und Formen von Interessengruppen in Deutschland seit Beginn der Industrialisierung," pp. 124–54; Thomas Nipperdey, "Interessenverbände und Parteien in Deutschland vor dem Ersten Weltkrieg," pp. 262–80; Hartmut Kaelble, *Industrielle Interessenpolitik in der Wilhelminischen Gesellschaft,* pp. 7–21, 137–46, 164–74, 189–96, and passim; Gerhard Erdmann, *Die deutschen Arbeitgeberverbände im sozialgeschichtlichen Wandel der Zeit,* pp. 52–84 (which is largely based, for the period before 1914, upon the two following informative apologias by administrators of their respective organizations: H. A. Bueck, *Der Centralverband Deutscher Industrieller 1876–1901,* 1:145–54, 193, 3:684–88, and passim; Fritz Tänzler, *Die deutschen Arbeitgeberverbände 1904–1929,* pp. 11–12, 16–18, and passim.) See also: Lambi, *Free Trade,* pp. 90–149, 207–11, and passim; Aandahl, "German Free Conservatism," pp. 42–71 and passim; Rassow and Born, eds., *Akten zur staatlichen Sozialpolitik,* pp. 130–34 (on the "12,000 Mark Affäre"); Donald Warren, Jr., *The Red Kingdom of Saxony,* p. 9 (the quotation from Bassermann to Stresemann on Bueck, July 9, 1908) and passim.

32. George Dunlap Crothers, *The German Elections of 1907,* pp. 162 and 163; Kaelble, *Industrielle Interessenpolitik,* pp. 7–21, 114-23, 136–46, 189–200, 215–24; Hans Jaeger, *Unternehmer in der deutschen Politik (1890–1918);* Annelise Thimme, *Gustav Stresemann,* pp. 15–20; Warren, *Red Kingdom of Saxony,* pp. 38–90 passim (for Stresemann's activity as organizer and director of the Verband Sächsischer Industrieller—the affiliate in Saxony of the Bund der Industriellen); Nipperdey, "Interessenverbände und Parteien," p. 271.

33. Tormin, *Geschichte der deutschen Parteien,* p. 108; Nipperdey, *Die Organisation der deutschen Parteien,* p. 139; Jacob Toury, *Die politischen Orientierungen der Juden in Deutschland,* pp. 230n, 233; Kaelble, *Industrielle Interessenpolitik,* pp. 181–83, 219–22; Fritz Fischer, *Krieg der Illusionen,* pp. 56–58 (which draws upon a Hamburg dissertation, typescript, 1968 that I have not consulted: Dirk Stegmann, "Parteien und Verbände 1897–1918: Studien zur Sammlungspolitik im Wilhelminischen Deutschland"); Stern, "Money, Morals, and the Pillars of Bismarck's Society," pp. 49–72; Lamar Cecil, *Albert Ballin,* pp. 98–142 and passim; and Lamar Cecil, "The Creation of Nobles in Prussia, 1871–1918," pp. 757–95.

34. Both the socioeconomic and the political history of the bureaucracy in imperial Germany need study. An excellent starting point is the perceptive essay of 1911 by Otto Hintze on "Der Beamtenstand," now available in Hintze, *Soziologie und Geschichte,* pp. 66–125. In various writings from the 1890's through World War I, Max Weber criticized the Junker spirit of the Prussian bureaucracy and saw it becoming the model for other state bureaucracies in Germany. One might also profitably consult (I have not) the *Monatsschrift für Deutsche Beamte,* started in 1877 by the Preussische Beamtenverein (founded in 1875). See also the text and bibliography in Jacob, *German Administration since Bismarck;* John Gillis, "Aristocracy and Bureaucracy in Nineteenth-Century Prussia," pp. 105–29. On

the clandestine sympathies of a few civil servants with Social Democracy see: Philipp Scheidemann, *Memorien eines Sozialdemokraten*, 1:93–94, 170–71; Bebel to Engels, Oct. 29, 1891, in Werner Blumenberg, ed., *August Bebels Briefwechsel mit Friedrich Engels*, p. 468.

35. The basic work is by Kurt Koszyk, *Deutsche Presse im 19. Jahrhundert*, pp. 130–308 (rich in information and bibliography). See further: Klaus Werecke, *Der Wille zur Weltgeltung*, pp. 11–25; Arthur Spurgeon Drake, "The Struggle for Freedom of the Press in the German Empire, 1871–1874"; E. Malcolm Carroll, *Germany and the Great Powers, 1866–1914*, p. 18 and passim; Rolf Engelsing, *Massenpublikum und Journalistentum im 19. Jahrhundert in Nordwestdeutschland*, pp. 63–289 passim; Irene Fischer-Frauendienst, *Bismarcks Pressepolitik*, pp. 21–22 and passim; Eberhard Naujoks, "Bismarck und die Organisation der Regierungspresse," pp. 46–80; Rieger, *Die Wilhelminische Presse*, pp. 78–122 and passim; articles on "Zeitungswesen" and "Pressgesetzgebung" in *Brockhaus' Konversations-Lexikon*, 14th ed., 17 vols. (Leipzig, 1908), 5:71–78, 13:379–81; Herman Ullstein, *The Rise and Fall of the House of Ullstein*, pp. 69–100; Hans Erman, *August Scherl*; Gotthart Schwarz, *Theodor Wolff und das "Berliner Tageblatt"* pp. 1–72 passim.

36. See the following works by Karl Kupisch: "Bürgerliche Frömmigkeit im Wilhelminischen Zeitalter," pp. 123–41; *Zwischen Idealismus und Massendemokratie*, pp. 85–142; and *Quellen zur Geschichte des deutschen Protestantismus (1871–1945)*, pp. 9–28, 45–140 (quotations above are from pp. 74–75, 85–88), from which selected documents have been translated by E. Bramsted, "The Position of the Catholic Church in Germany, 1871–1933" pp. 314–34. See also: Kürenberg, *The Kaiser*, pp. 143, 145; Tal, "Liberal Protestantism and the Jews," pp. 23–41; Andrew Landale Drummond, *German Protestantism since Luther*, pp. 221–29; Wolfgang Marienfeld, *Wissenschaft und Schlachtflottenbau in Deutschland 1897–1906*, pp. 49–52, 94–95, 110; Hartmut Lehmann, "Friedrich von Bodelschwingh und das Sedanfest," pp. 542–73; J. Rathje, *Die Welt des freien Protestantismus, dargestellt an Leben und Werk von Martin Rade*; Karl-Wilhelm Dahm, *Pfarrer und Politik*, pp. 50–58 and passim; *Brockhaus' Konversations-Lexikon*, 14th ed., 6:27–28, 67–69, 17:808–9. Also on the organization of the Protestant churches, see Huber, *Verfassungsgeschichte*, 4:842–75 (accurate and of basic importance).

37. *Brockhaus' Konversations-Lexikon*, 14th ed., 5:27–28, 67–69, 17: insert pp. 4–5 between 808 and 809; Kürenberg, *The Kaiser*, p. 184; Buchner, *Kaiser Wilhelm II*, esp. pp. 26, 53–94, 109–18, 126, 131, 171–200 (a work that is as strongly nationalist as it is Catholic); Ritter, *Der Weg des politischen Katholizismus*; *Katholische Monatsbriefe*, No. 26 (January 1918); Dahm, *Pfarrer und Politik*, pp. 51–52; and other works cited on the Catholic Center party in notes 16–24, above.

38. *Brockhaus' Konversations-Lexikon*, 14th ed., 5:69–70; Hans-Heinrich Plickat, *Die Schule als Instrument des sozialen Aufstiegs*; R. H. Samuel and R. Hinton Thomas, *Education and Society in Modern Germany* (comprehensive, but thin before 1914); Edward H. Reisner, *Nationalism and Education since 1789*, pp. 176–215; William Setchel Learned, *The Oberlehrer*, pp. 67–123; I. L. Kandel, *The Training of Elementary School Teachers in Germany*, pp. 19–131; Matthew Arnold, *Higher Schools and Universities in Germany*, pp. 82, 96, 152, and passim; Eduard Sack, *Die preussische Schule im Dienste gegen die Freiheit*, pp. 11–22, 172, 180–95, and passim; Fritz Blättner, *Das Gymnasium*, pp. 173–247; Walter Consuelo Langsam, "Nationalism and History in the Prussian Elementary Schools under William II," pp. 241–60; Georg G. Iggers, *The German Conception of History*, pp.

3–123; Horst Schallenberger, *Untersuchungen zum Geschichtsbild der Wilhelminischen Ära und der Weimarer Zeit*, pp. 53–162; Karl Bungardt, *Die Odyssee der Lehrerschaft*, pp. 71–99 (disappointingly thin); Mosse, *Crisis of German Ideology*, pp. 149–203 passim; Karl Heinrich Höfele, "Selbstverständnis und Zeitkritik des deutschen Bürgertums vor dem ersten Weltkrieg," pp. 40–56; Reinhard Höhn, *Die Armee als Erziehungsschule der Nation*, pp. 303–11; Fritz K. Ringer, "Higher Education in Germany in the Nineteenth Century," pp. 123–38; W. Lexis, *A General View of the History and Organisation of Public Education in the German Empire*; Ernst Christian Helmreich, *Religious Education in German Schools*, pp. 53–100; Friedrich Paulsen, *German Education*, pp. 197–261; Huber, *Verfassungsgeschichte*, 4:942 (and, more generally, pp. 876–970 passim).
39. George M. Schwarz, "Political Attitudes in the German Universities during the Reign of William II," pp. 249–346 and passim; Abraham Ascher, "Professors as Propagandists," pp. 282–302; Friedrich Paulsen, *The German Universities and University Study*, pp. 76–110, 125–59, 227–62, 352– 61, and passim; Dieter Fricke, "Zur Militarisierung des deutschen Geisteslebens im Wilhelminischen Kaiserreich," pp. 1069–1107; Klaus Schwabe, "Zur politischen Haltung der deutschen Professoren im Ersten Weltkrieg," p. 601; James J. Sheehan, *The Career of Lujo Brentano*, pp. 89, 178–87, and passim; Friedrich Meinecke, *Strassburg, Freiburg, Berlin 1901–1919*; Bülow, *Memoirs*, 1:159; Utz-Friedebert Taube, *Ludwig Quidde*, pp. 1–67 and passim; Marienfeld, *Wissenschaft und Schlachtflottenbau*, pp. 7, 34–40, 56–63, 110–15, and passim; Gustav Schmidt, *Deutscher Historismus und der Übergang zur parlamentarischen Demokratie*; Dieter Lindenlaub, *Richtungskämpfe im Verein für Sozialpolitik* (excellent in research and interpretation); Friedrich Schmidt-Ott, *Erlebtes und Erstrebtes 1860–1950*, pp. 16–138 (a thin account of service in the Prussian Ministry of Culture, 1888–1914, by an official who became *Kultusminister* in 1917); Iggers, *German Conception of History*, pp. 124–228; and the valuable study by Fritz K. Ringer, *The Decline of the German Mandarins*, pp. 30–61, 81–180, and passim.
40. The impact of the natural sciences on political attitudes in imperial Germany needs scholarly investigation. Several of the works mentioned in the foregoing note are suggestive as are the following: H. Stuart Hughes, *Consciousness and Society*; Gerhard Masur, *Prophets of Yesterday*; Friedrich Naumann, *Demokratie und Kaisertum*, p. 81 and passim (Darwinist political vocabulary); Hans Delbrück, *Government and the Will of the People*, pp. 60–63; Robert Michels, *Political Parties*; Hedwig Wachenheim, *Die deutsche Arbeiterbewegung 1844 bis 1914*, pp. 498–99; Ernst Haeckel, *Die Welträthsel*, Volks-Ausgabe, bringing the total number of copies in print up to 107,000, pp. 131–32; Daniel Gasman, *The Scientific Origins of National Socialism*, pp. 14, 39–43, 90–92, 157–59, and passim (which overemphasizes the proto-Nazi features of Monism); Niles Robert Holt, "The Social and Political Ideas of the German Monist Movement, 1871–1914," pp. 101–88 and passim (which overemphasizes the differences between Monism and Nazism); Mosse, *Crisis of German Ideology*, pp. 99–103 (on Woltmann); Fritz Bolle, "Darwinismus und Zeitgeist," pp. 143–78. The statements about the physician-parliamentarians rest upon my analysis of biographical data presented by Max Schwarz, ed., *MdR*, pp. 43–112 (1848) and pp. 251–506 (1867–1918). In the latter period, 52 physician-deputies can be identified out of a total of 2,769 (1.9 percent); but one joined no party, while 4 from Alsace-Lorraine and 4 Poles did not join a German party. Of the remaining 43, 14 of the 17 left-liberals and socialists were elected before 1882, while 9 of the 15 National Liberals were first elected after 1882. The median year of birth of the left-liberals and socialists was 1820, while that of the National Liberals was 1830. In other words, the

physician-deputies born and elected later in the century were, on the whole, more conservative than those born and elected earlier.

41. Höhn, *Die Armee als Erziehungsschule der Nation*, pp. 101–502 passim; Karl Demeter, *The German Officer-Corps in Society and State, 1650–1945*, pp. 28, 34, 40, 43–44, 171, 224–25; Steinberg, *Yesterday's Deterrent*, p. 40; Craig, *Prussian Army*, pp. 217–54, 362n; Gustav Mayer, *Friedrich Engels*, pp. 258–61; Gerhard Ritter, "The Military and Politics in Germany," p. 265; Ritter, *Staatskuns und Kriegshandwerk*, 2:115–31; and Kitchen, *German Officer Corps*.

42. In a number of essays, 1902–14, Otto Hintze pointed to the fundamental importance of social psychology in shaping constitutional forms. He repeatedly emphasized that Germany's internal divisions and her position in international affairs made parliamentary government impractical for the German Empire. See Otto Hintze, *Staat und Verfassung*, pp. 319–20 and passim. More recently Ralf Dahrendorf has identified aversion to domestic conflict as a major obstacle to the achievement of liberal democracy in Germany, while only vaguely hinting that the strength of the German aversion to conflict arose from the very strength and pervasiveness of the conflict itself: *Society and Democracy in Germany*, pp. 202–3, 129–203 passim. For suggestive general insights and bibliographical references on the relationship between anxiety and politics, see Franz Neumann, *The Democratic and the Authoritarian State*, pp. 270–300. Manifestations of anxiety and alienation are apparent in some of the individuals treated by Hans Kohn, *The Mind of Germany*. They are more explicitly explored by Stern, *Politics of Cultural Despair*; see also his essay, "Money, Morals, and the Pillars of Bismarck's Society," pp. 70–72. For some striking illustrations of the concern felt by the kaiser, the chancellor, and leading military authorities see Fischer, *Krieg der Illusionen*, pp. 175–77, 270–71, and passim. Though Fischer emphasizes the offensive aims of German policy, many of his quotations vividly reveal an acute sense of insecurity in high places.

43. Heinrich Mann, *Der Untertan*, pp. 65–67, 122, 124, and passim.

X GROWTH OF SOCIAL DEMOCRACY

1. Edward H. Reisner, *Nationalism and Education since 1789*, p. 194.
2. A Sartorius von Waltershausen, *Deutsche Wirtschaftsgeschichte 1815–1914*, pp. 399–400, 503, 599, and 378–632 passim; Jürgen Kuczynski, *Die Geschichte der Lage der Arbeiter unter dem Kapitalismus*, 3: 123, 4:63; Lamar Cecil, *Albert Ballin*; Wolfgang Köllmann, "The Population of Germany in the Age of Industrialism"; Wolfgang Köllmann, "The Process of Urbanization in Germany at the Height of the Industrialization Period," pp. 69–73; see also: Gerhard Masur, *Imperial Berlin*.
3. Peter N. Stearns, "Adaptation to Industrialization," suggests the heterogeneity of working-class attitudes.
4. Karl Erich Born, *Staat und Sozialpolitik seit Bismarcks Sturz*, pp. 7–105, 129–31; Josef Kliersfeld, *Die Haltung Kaiser Wilhelms II. zur Arbeiterbewegung und zur Sozialdemokratie*, pp. 24, 48–55, and passim.
5. Born, *Staat und Sozialpolitik*, pp. 190, 192 (quotations), and 105–77 passim; Peter Rassow and Karl Erich Born, eds., *Akten zur staatlichen Sozialpolitik in Deutschland 1890–1914*, pp. 48–128.
6. Helmut Seidl, *Streikkämpfe der mittel-und ostdeutschen Braunkohlenbergarbeiter von 1890 bis 1914*, p. 25; Ashok V. Desai, *Real Wages in Germany, 1871–1913*, pp. 112, 117, 125, 171; Kuczynski, *Geschichte der Lage der Arbeiter*, pt. 1, 3:322–23, 4:330; Georg Kotowski, *Friedrich Ebert*, 1: 74–75n.

7. Desai, *Real Wages*, p. 25; Masur, *Imperial Berlin*; Hsi-Huey Liang, "Lower-Class Immigrants in Wilhelmine Berlin," pp. 94–111.
8. Born, *Staat und Sozialpolitik*, pp. 177–251; Rassow and Born, eds., *Akten zur staatlichen Sozialpolitik*, pp. 272–343 and passim; Ernst Rudolf Huber, *Deutsche Verfassungsgeschichte seit 1789*, 3:1208–56; Kuczynski, *Geschichte der Lage der Arbeiter*, 4:111–12, 164–89; Hedwig Wachenheim, *Die deutsche Arbeiterbewegung 1844 bis 1914*, pp. 300–307, 386–97.
9. Gustav Hartmann, *Fünfzig Jahre Deutsche Gewerkvereine (Hirsch-Duncker) (1868–1918)*, pp. 6–8, 26–27; W. A. McConagha, *Development of the Labor Movement in Great Britain, France, and Germany*, pp. 150–52 and passim.
10. Heinz Josef Varain, *Freie Gewerkschaften, Sozialdemokratie und Staat*, pp. 10–40; Gerhard Bry, *Wages in Germany, 1871–1945*, pp. 30–32; Gerhard A. Ritter, *Die Arbeiterbewegung im Wilhelminischen Reich*, pp. 124–27; Gerhard A. Ritter, "Die politische Arbeiterbewegung Deutschlands 1863–1914," Appendix IV; Dieter Fricke, *Zur Organisation und Tätigkeit der deutschen Arbeiterbewegung (1890–1914)*, pp. 208–62; Kuczynski, *Geschichte der Lage der Arbeiter*, 18:183; Jacqueline Strain, "Feminism and Political Radicalism in the German Social Democratic Movement, 1890–1914," pp. 106–13, 267; Wachenheim, *Arbeiterbewegung*, pp. 385–86 and passim.
11. Hans-Alexander Apolant, *Die wirtschaftsfriedliche nationale Arbeiterbewegung (Gelbe Gewerkschaften) in Deutschland*, pp. 5–41, 136–48, and passim; Ritter, "Politische Arbeiterbewegung," Appendix IV.
12. Ritter, "Politische Arbeiterbewegung," Appendix IV; Ritter, *Arbeiterbewegung im Wilhelminischen Reich*, pp. 101–27, 150–75; Wachenheim, *Arbeiterbewegung*, pp. 277–321, 382–85, and passim; Seidl, *Streikkämpfe*, pp. 42–50 and passim; Wilhelm Keil, *Erlebnisse eines Sozialdemokraten*, 1:42–43 (Legien quote). Varain, *Freie Gewerkschaften, Sozialdemokratie und Staat*, pp. 10, 38–39, 185–86.
13. Werner Blumenberg, ed., *August Bebels Briefwechsel mit Friedrich Engels*, pp. 392–402, 403, 409–11, 508, 513, 530, 552, 760, 766, 771–72, 777, and passim; Ritter, *Arbeiterbewegung im Wilhelminischen Reich*, pp. 46–62, 228–29; Erich Matthias and Eberhard Pikart, eds., *Die Reichstagsfraktion der deutschen Sozialdemokratie 1898 bis 1918*, Part I, pp. lxvii–cxxii; Philipp Scheidemann, *Memoiren eines Sozialdemokraten*, 1:114–21, 173 (on Bebel and Singer); Ernest Hamburger, *Juden im öffentlichen Leben Deutschlands*, pp. 419–26; Hans-Josef Steinberg, *Sozialismus und deutsche Sozialdemokratie*, pp. 32–33, 34, 111–25; Wachenheim, *Arbeiterbewegung*, pp. 142, 144, 181, 293, 353, and passim; George Eckert, ed., *Wilhelm Liebknecht*, pp. 394–99 and passim.
14. On the invention of the telephone and the above data on its rapid adoption in Germany, see: Silvanus P. Thompson, *Philipp Reis*; Alvin F. Harlow, *Old Wires and New Waves*, pp. 344–48, 364, 366; Richard Hennig, *Die älteste Entwickelung der Telegraphie und Telephonie* (Leipzig, 1908), pp. 184–85, 163–87; C. Erfurth, *Haustelegraphie, Telephonie und Blitzableiter in Theorie und Praxis*, pp. 109–61; A. R. Bennett, *The Telephone Systems of the Continent of Europe*, pp. 17–19, 29, 51, 178, 182, 217, 430, 436, and passim (especially informative); J. E. Kingsbury, *The Telephone and Telephone Exchanges*, pp. 530–31. For evidence of its use by the SPD in the early 1890's, see Bebel to Engels, Sept. 29, 1891, in Blumenberg, ed., *Bebels Briefwechsel mit Engels*, p. 435; Ritter, *Arbeiterbewegung im Wilhelminischen Reich*, p. 52 (reports two telephones in SPD central office in the early 1890's); W. Liebknecht to Engels, Nov. 15, 1894, in Eckert, ed., *Wilhelm Liebknecht*, pp. 393–94; Kurt Koszyk, *Deutsche Presse im 19. Jahrhundert*, p. 214; Posadowsky's recommendation is quoted by Chlodwig zu Hohenlohe-Schillingsfürst, *Denkwürdigkeiten der Reichskanzlerzeit*, p. 543.

15. Koszyk, *Deutsche Presse*, pp. 184–209; Strain, "Feminism and Poltical Radicalism," p. 267; Fricke, *Organisation und Tätigkeit der deutschen Arbeiterbewegung*, pp. 133, 143, 146, 149, 150, 160; Engels to Bernstein, Feb. 27–March 1, 1883, in Helmut Hirsch, ed., *Eduard Bernsteins Briefwechsel mit Friedrich Engels*, 1:197; Rolf Engelsing, *Massenpublikum und Journalistentum im 19. Jahrhundert in Nordwestdeutschland*, pp. 102–6, 250–67; Isolde Rieger, *Die Wilhelminische Presse im Überblick 1888–1918*, pp. 103–11; Hamburger, *Juden im öffentlichen Leben*, pp. 419–26, and Jacob Toury, *Die politischen Orientierungen der Juden in Deutschland*, p. 195 (on Singer); Matthias and Pikart, eds., *Reichstagsfraktion der deutschen Sozialdemokratie*, 1:6, 7, 17, 23, 25–26, 52–53, 63, 148 (for criticisms of press organs, 1898–1901, and of *Vorwärts* in 1905); Keil, *Erlebnisse*, 1:43–44, suggests the impact even a simple union publication made upon a young artisan ("the first newspaper that I regularly read"); Keil became a socialist newspaper editor, and his memoirs tell a good bit about the state of socialist journalism in the period 1890–1914 (1:92–95, 130–41, 152–62, 192–200, and passim); see also Scheidemann, *Memoiren*, 1:9, 50–98.

16. Scheidemann, *Memoiren*, 1:61–72 and passim; Keil, *Erlebnisse*, 1:151–76 and passim; Kotowski, *Friedrich Ebert*, 1:53–54.

17. Rassow and Born, eds., *Akten zur staatlichen Sozialpolitik*, pp. 63–107; Kotowski, *Friedrich Ebert*, 1:42, 58, 69n; Bebel to Engels, Sept. 29, 1892, in Blumenberg, ed., *Bebels Briefwechsel mit Engels*, p. 595; Paul Löbe, *Der Weg war lang*, pp. 46–51; Hajo Holborn, "Prussia and the Weimar Republic," p. 339 (Haase-Braun); Richard Lipinski, *Die Sozialdemokratie von Ihren Anfängen bis zur Gegenwart*, 2:142 (citing *Vorwärts*); Haenisch to Franz, Feb. 24, May 25, and June 28, 1909, Konrad Haenisch Letters to Rudolf Franz, 1907–15, Hoover Institution; emphasis in the quotation is that of Haenisch.

18. Strain, "Feminism and Political Radicalism," pp. 13–24, 32–42, 52, 61, 65, 71–105, and passim; Bebel to Engels, Sept. 29, 1891, in Blumenberg, ed., *Bebels Briefwechsel mit Engels*, pp. 435–36; Kotowski, *Friedrich Ebert*, 1:53.

19. Strain, "Feminism and Political Radicalism," pp. 25–31, 46–48, 72, 78–82, 131–38, 152–238; Wachenheim, *Arbeiterbewegung*, pp. 286, 288 (on Ihrer); J. P. Nettl, *Rosa Luxemburg*, 1:136, 194 and passim; Amy Hackett, "Feminism and Liberalism in Wilhelmine Germany," pp. 10–11 (Braun).

20. Strain, "Feminism and Political Radicalism," pp. 66, 153, 230–67.

21. Karl Korn, *Die Arbeiterjugendbewegung*, pp. 15–16, 32–256 passim; Viktor Engelhardt, *An der Wende des Zeitalters*, pp. 41–42, 47–49; Walter Sieger, *Das erste Jahrzehnt der deutschen Arbeiterjugendbewegung, 1904–1914*; Walter Sieger, *Die junge Front*; Babette Dross, *Willi Münzenburg*, pp. 19–59; David Childs, *Germany since 1918*, p. 65; Max Peters, *Friedrich Ebert, erster Präsident der deutschen Republik; sein Werden und Wirken*, pp. 61–69; Karl W. Meyer, *Karl Liebknecht, Man without a Country*, pp. 36–41, 89; Fricke, *Organisation und Tätigkeit der deutschen Arbeiterbewegung*, p. 90; Koszyk, *Deutsche Presse*, p. 209; Heinrich Muth, "Jugendpflege und Politik," pp. 597–619; Harold Eugene Kist, "Wilhelm Sollmann," pp. 24–46 (Sollmann was chairman of the youth committee in Cologne).

22. Keil, *Erlebnisse*, 1:68–69, 80, 104; Steinberg, *Sozialismus und deutsche Sozialdemokratie*, pp. 12–142; Karl-Wilhelm Dahm, *Pfarrer und Politik*, p. 135.

23. Edmund Silberner, *Sozialisten zur Judenfrage*, pp. 107–80, 198–230; Bebel to Engels, June 24, 1892, in Blumenberg, ed., *Bebels Briefwechsel mit Engels*, pp. 549–50; Donald L. Niewyk, *Socialist, Anti-Semite, and Jew*, pp. 14–28; Donald L. Niewyk, "German Social Democracy and the Problem of Anti-Semitism, 1906–1914"; Hamburger, *Juden im öffentlichen Leben*, pp. 147, 250–54, 404–7, 411, 412;

Toury, *Die politischen Orientierungen der Juden*, pp. 229–30. The SPD Reichstag deputies elected in January 1912 who identified themselves as Jews were Oskar Cohn (lawyer), Georg Davidsohn (editor), Ludwig Frank (lawyer), Hugo Haase (lawyer), and Emanuel Waron (editor). Those of Jewish family background were Eduard Bernstein (writer), Georg Grundwasser (editor), Josef Herzfeld (lawyer), Gustav Hoch (editor and local labor secretary), Otto Landsberg (lawyer), Max Queeck (editor), Arthur Stadthagen (lawyer and writer), and Georg Weill (writer). Eight members of this group did not comment on their religion for the *Reichstag-Handbuch*. The other five listed themselves as having no religion or no religious affiliation. Carl Förster (merchant) identified himself simply as a "dissident" which in Germany meant that he belonged to no church. Upon his death in November 1912, his seat was taken by Max Cohen-Reuss (writer) who identified himself as a "dissident," but was of Jewish descent. In preparing these ratings, I have slightly modified and supplemented the identifications provided by Toury, *Die politischen Orientierungen der Juden*, and Hamburger, *Juden im öffentlichen Leben*, (which differ slightly and fail to mention Förster) by using Max Schwarz, ed., *MdR*, and Germany, Bureau des Reichstags, *Reichstags Handbuch*. Among the SPD writers and editors of Jewish family background before 1914 were Josef Block, Adolf Braun, Kurt Eisner, Curt Geyer, Alexander Helphand ("Parvus"), Rudolf Hilferding, Rosa Luxemburg, Karl Radek, and Friedrich Stampfer.

24. Bebel to Engels, Oct. 12, 1886, Oct. 24, 1891, and Aug. 20, 1892, in Blumenberg, ed., *Bebels Briefwechsel mit Engels*, pp. 294, 468, 577; Ritter, *Arbeiterbewegung im Wilhelminischen Reich*, p. 77n, reporting and criticizing the 1905 estimate by R. Blank.

25. Reinhard Jansen, *Georg von Vollmar*, pp. 56–63 and passim; Scheidemann, *Memoiren*, 1:63–72; Bebel to Engels, July 10 and Aug. 4, 1894, July 17, 1895, in Blumenberg, ed., *Bebels Briefwechsel mit Engels*, pp. 769–70, 772, 803; Eduard David, *Sozialismus und Landwirtschaft*; Ritter, *Arbeiterbewegung im Wilhelminischen Reich*, pp. 43n, 67–78, 134–48; Matthias and Pikart, eds., *Reichstagsfraktion der deutschen Sozialdemokratie*, 1:xvi–xvii; Oron J. Hale, *The Great Illusion, 1900–1914*, pp. 43–45.

26. For the same statistics and other data on the growth of the SPD see: Fricke, *Organisation und Tätigkeit*, pp. 50, 65–69; Walter Tormin, *Geschichte der deutschen Parteien seit 1848*, Appendix; Adolf Neumann-Hofer, *Die Entwicklung der Sozialdemokratie bei den Wahlen zum deutschen Reichstag 1871–1903*, pp. 8–24, 30–51; Ritter, *Arbeiterbewegung im Wilhelminischen Reich*, pp. 67–78; Gerhard A. Ritter, "Kontinuität und Umformung des deutschen Parteiensystems 1918–1920," p. 377. On the figures for Saxony province, see Thomas Klein, "Reichstagswahlen und-Abgeordnete der Provinz Sachsen und Anhalt, 1867–1918. Ein Überblick," pp. 70, 97–100, 103–4.

27. Matthias and Pikart, eds., *Reichstagsfraktion der deutschen Sozialdemokratie*, 1:lxxxv; Paul Hirsch, *Der Weg der Sozialdemokratie zur Macht in Preussen*, pp. 20–28; Huber, *Verfassungsgeschichte*, 4:122; Ritter, *Arbeiterbewegung im Wilhelminischen Reich*, pp. 177–82, 216, 232–34; Ritter, "Politische Arbeiterbewegung," Appendix III; Hans Drüner, *Im Schatten des Weltkrieges*, p. 35; Paul Hirsch and Hugo Lindemann, *Das kommunale Wahlrecht*; James J. Sheehan, "Literalism and the City in Nineteenth-Century Germany," p. 132; Fricke, *Organisation und Tätigkeit der deutschen Arbeiterbewegung*, p. 122, credits the SPD with only 25 seats in Saxony, 13 in Baden.

XI MARXIST THEORY AND REVISIONIST PRACTICE

1. James Joll, *The Second International, 1889–1914*, p. 76.
2. G. D. H. Cole, *A History of Socialist Thought*, 3:253–54.
3. Joll, *The Second International*, p. 58.
4. Karl W. Meyer, *Karl Liebknecht, Man Without a Country*, pp. 21–49, 138; Karl Liebknecht, *Ausgewählte Reden, Briefe und Aufsätze*, p. 166; Karl Liebknecht, *Ausgewählte Reden und Schriften*, pp. v–xxvi, 32, 46–48, 61–78, 127–30, 308–18; Martha Globig, ed., "Ein unbekannter Brief August Bebels an Karl Liebknecht vom 10. November 1908," pp. 253–56.
5. Fred Oelssner, *Rosa Luxemburg*, pp. 9–54 ("critical" from a Stalinist viewpoint); Paul Frölich, *Rosa Luxemburg*, pp. 15–57 (sympathetic and valuable, based upon Luxemburg papers in the author's possession); J. P. Nettl, *Rosa Luxemburg*, abridged ed., pp. 10–12, 31–32, 41–46, 68–71, 254–59, 365–68; Cole, *Socialist Thought*, 3:67, 92, 500; Bebel to V. Adler, Nov. 24, 1899, in Rosa Luxemburg et al., "Einige Briefe Rosa Luxemburgs und andere Dokumente," p. 30.
6. Frölich, *Rosa Luxemburg*, pp. 71–75, 106–14; Oelssner, *Rosa Luxemburg*, pp. 34–35; Institut für Marxismus-Leninismus beim ZK der SED, *Rosa Luxemburg, Gesammelte Werke*, 1:pt. 2, 337–38, 554–55, 619–22; Liebknecht, *Ausgewählte Reden, Briefe und Aufsätze*, pp. 84–86; Leo Stern, ed., *Die Auswirkungen der ersten russischen Revolution von 1905–1907 auf Deutschland*, pp. xxiv–xxviii, 25–26, 71–75, and passim; Max Jürgen Koch, *Die Bergarbeiterbewegung im Ruhrgebiet zur Zeit Wilhelms II (1889–1914)*, pp. 85–101, 143; Richard W. Reichard, "The German Working Class and the Russian Revolution of 1905," pp. 136–53; Carl Schorske, *German Social Democracy, 1905–1917*, pp. 37, 39–40, 43; Charles Easton Rothwell, "Rosa Luxemburg and the German Social Democratic Party," esp. pp. 558–622 for a penetrating analysis of the content and significance of Luxemburg's major theoretical work, *Akumulation des Kapitals* (1912). For a post-1945 Soviet view of the German left-extremists see Henry J. Tobias and John L. Snell, "A Soviet Interpretation of the SPD, 1895–1933," pp. 61–66.
7. Cole, *Socialist Thought*, 3:40 (for Kautsky resolution of 1900); M. J. Bonn, *Wandering Scholar* (London, 1949), p. 210; Boris Goldenberg, *Beiträge zur Soziologie der deutschen Vorkriegssozialdemokratie*, p. 16; Kautsky to V. Adler, Nov. 15, 1901, June 9, 1902, Oct. 18, 1904, June 26 and Oct. 8, 1913, and Feb. 13, 1914, in Friedrich Adler, ed., *Victor Adler*, pp. 377, 405, 433, 573–74, 582–83, 592; Schorske, *German Social Democracy*, p. 112.
8. Reinhard Jansen, *Georg von Vollmar*, esp. pp. 11–50, 52, 83, 101 (an ably executed survey based upon some unpublished materials, but not definitive); Walter Gagel, *Die Wahlrechtsfrage in der Geschichte der deutschen liberalen Parteien 1848–1918*, p. 156; Schorske, *German Social Democracy*, p. 7; Cole, *Socialist Thought*, 3:273.
9. Peter Gay, *The Dilemma of Democratic Socialism*, pp. 66–67; Erika Rikli, *Der Revisionismus*, esp. pp. 31–32, 102–13 (a highly respectable analysis that is more flattering to revisionist theory than is Gay); for a good summary of Bernstein's *période radicale*, as well as for an extensive analysis of his metamorphosis during the London years, see the intellectual biography by Pierre Angel, *Eduard Bernstein et l'évolution du socialisme allemand*, pp. 66–89, 99–260. Another mirror of the same development, extending, however, only as far as 1895 and providing more insight on the Swiss than on the early years of Bernstein's English exile, can be found in Helmut Hirsch, ed., *Eduard Bernsteins Briefwechsel mit Friedrich Engels*, esp. Eduard Bernstein to Engels, Feb. 6, 1881 (pp. 16–18), Sept. 9, 1881 (pp. 33–38), Oct. 14, 1881 (pp. 38–44), and Oct. 15, 1885 (pp. 327–30). Eduard

Bernstein, *Entwicklungsgang eines Sozialisten*, pp. 1–37, is useful, but thin, while James W. Hulse, *Revolutionists in London*, pp. 138–66 examines a variety of influences which may have affected Bernstein's development during his London sojourn including his studies of the English revolution of the seventeenth century.

10. *Voraussetzungen des Sozialismus und die Aufgaben der Sozialdemokratie*, English ed.: Eduard Bernstein, *Evolutionary Socialism*.

11. Bernstein to Bebel, Oct. 20, 1898, in Adler, ed., *Victor Adler*, p. 261, see also pp. 254–65, 272–78, for Bebel to Bernstein, Oct. 16, 22, 1898, Bebel to V. Adler, Oct. 26, 1898, and Kautsky to Bernstein, Oct. 23, 1898. Note also Luxemburg to Bebel, Oct. 31, 1898, in Luxemburg et al., "Einige Briefe Rosa Luxemburgs," pp. 14–15.

12. Aaron Noland, *The Founding of the French Socialist Party (1893–1905)*, pp. 144–46, 157; Joll, *The Second International*, pp. 85–105; Cole, *Socialist Thought*, 3:37–42.

13. Kautsky to V. Adler, May 31 and Sept. 9, 1901, and Oct. 18, 1904, in Adler, ed., *Victor Adler*, pp. 352, 367, 433; Bebel to Kautsky, Sept. 4, 1901, as cited in Luxemburg et al., "Einige Briefe Rosa Luxemburgs," p. 26.

14. Schorske, *German Social Democracy*, pp. 188–95.

15. Cole, *Socialist Thought*, 3:313; Heinz Josef Varain, *Freie Gewerkschaften, Sozialdemokratie und Staat*, pp. 38–39; Hedwig Wachenheim, *Die deutsche Arbeiterbewegung 1844 bis 1914*, pp. 398–400.

16. Siegfried Nestriepke, *Die Gewerkschaftsbewegung*, 1:192–95; Paul Umbreit, *25 Jahre deutscher Gewerkschaftsbewegung 1890–1915*, pp. 155–62, 164, 172–84; Paul Ufermann, ed., *Alwin Brandes*, pp. 19–22; Theodor Cassau, *Die Gewerkschaftsbewegung*, pp. 1–2, 15–20; Fritz Opel, *Der deutsche Metallarbeiter-Verband während des ersten Weltkrieges und der Revolution*, p. 26; Heinz Langerhans, "Richtungsgewerkschaft und gewerkschaftliche Autonomie 1890–1914," pp. 24–28, 34; Varain, *Freie Gewerkschaften, Sozialdemokratie und Staat*, pp. 10–13, 20, 23–24, 27–29, 33–36, 57–60; Schorske, *German Social Democracy*, pp. 12–13; Koch, *Die Bergarbeiterbewegung im Ruhrgebiet*, pp. 25–26, 47; Stern, ed., *Die Auswirkungen der ersten russischen Revolution*, pp. xx–xxiii, 272; Carl Severing, *Mein Lebensweg*, 1:191; Kautsky to V. Adler, Oct. 15, 1892, in Adler, ed., *Victor Adler*, p. 109; Franz Josef Furtwängler, *Männer die ich sah und kannte*, p. 96; Curt Geyer, *Macht und Masse von Bismarck zu Hitler*, p. 39; Harry J. Marks, "The Sources of Reformism in the Social Democratic Party of Germany, 1890–1914," p. 336; Helmut Drüner, *Im Schatten des Weltkrieges*, pp. 30, 474n.

17. Germany, Reichstag, *Das Werk des Untersuchungsausschusses der deutschen verfassungsgebenden Nationalversammlung und des deutschen Reichstages 1919–1926*, 5:50–51; Langerhans, "Richtungsgewerkschaft," pp. 36–38 and passim; *Rundschreiben an die Vorstände und Mitglieder aller der freien Vereinigung deutscher Gewerkschaften angeschlossenen Vereine*, Sept. 15, 1915, Feb. 1, 1916, and July 1, 1916.

18. The Mannheim resolution is republished in the *Sozialistische Monatshefte*, Aug. 6, 1918, p. 755. See also: Schorske, *German Social Democracy*, pp. 49–53, 278; Wachenheim, *Arbeiterbewegung*, pp. 414–22, 438, 443; Adolf Braun, *Gewerkschaften und Sozialdemokratie*, esp. p. 5; Cassau, *Die Gewerkschaftsbewegung*, pp. 284–94; Gay, *The Dilemma of Democratic Socialism*, pp. 119–30.

19. Koch, *Die Bergarbeiterbewegung im Ruhrgebiet*, pp. 57–59; Varain, *Freie Gewerkschaften, Sozialdemokratie und Staat*, pp. 33, 45, 64; Gustav Noske, *Erlebtes aus Aufstieg und Niedergang einer Demokratie*, p. 27; Schorske, *German Social Democracy*, pp. 13–16; Langerhans, "Richtungsgewerkschaft," p. 204; Wachenheim, *Arbeiterbewegung*, pp. 522–23; John L. Snell, "German Socialists in the Last Imperial Reichstag, 1912–1918," pp. 198, 203.

20. Liebknecht, *Ausgewählte Reden, Briefe und Aufsätze*, pp. 142, 150, 167, 267; Konrad Haenisch to Rudolf Franz, Feb. 2, 1910, Haenisch-Franz Manuscripts, Hoover Institution; Kautsky to V. Adler, June 20, 1907. Adler, June 21, 1907, in Adler, ed., *Victor Adler*, pp. 479–80, 482–83; K. Frohme, *Monarchie oder Republic? Kulturgeschichtliche Streifzüge* (a socialist attack against monarchy in general and the rule of William II in particular); Wolfgang Neumann, "Die Innenpolitik des Fürsten Bülow von 1900–1906," p. 133; Joll, *The Second International*, p. 103; Schorske, *German Social Democracy*, pp. 184–85; Dieter Grosser, *Vom monarchischen Konstitutionalismus zur parlamentarischen Demokratie*, pp. 52–55.

21. Schorske, *German Social Democracy*, pp. 59–63; George Dunlap Crothers, *The German Elections of 1907*, pp. 211–29; Brigitte Haberland, "Die Innenpolitik des Reiches unter der Kanzlerschaft Bethmann Hollwegs 1909–1914," pp. 11–12, loaned to me by courtesy of Otto Becker; Richard Hostetter, "The S.P.D. and the General Strike as an Anti-war Weapon, 1905–1914," pp. 30–31; Sinclair W. Armstrong, "The Internationalism of the Early Social Democrats of Germany," p. 258; William H. Maehl, "The Triumph of Nationalism in the German Socialist Party on the Eve of the First World War," p. 33 and passim.

22. Carlton J. H. Hayes, "The History of German Socialism Reconsidered," pp. 86, 88; Edwyn Bevan, *German Social Democracy during the War*, pp. 264–65; Noske, *Erlebtes*, pp. 28–30, 35–36, 39, 42; Bertram D. Wolfe, *Three Who Made a Revolution*, pp. 572–73; Evelyn Anderson, *Hammer or Anvil*, p. 20 (an excellent though highly unflattering survey); Arthur Rosenberg, *The Birth of the German Republic, 1871–1918*, p. 69; William George Vettes, "The German Social Democrats and the Eastern Question, 1849–1900," pp. 86–100; Geyer, *Macht und Masse*, pp. 43–47.

23. Friedrich Meinecke, *The German Catastrophe*, pp. 16–19 and passim.

24. Schorske, *German Social Democracy*, pp. 209–13; Kautsky to V. Adler, June 26, Oct. 8, 1913, in Adler, ed., *Victor Adler*, pp. 573–74, 585; Eric Dombrowski, *German Leaders of Yesterday and Today*, p. 210.

25. Philipp Scheidemann, *Der Zusammenbruch*, p. 1; Bernhard von Bülow, *Memoirs of Prince von Bülow*, 1:234; Max Peters, *Friedrich Ebert, erster Präsident der deutschen Republik*, p. 73; Ben Hecht, *A Child of the Century*, p. 267.

26. Georg Kotowski, *Friedrich Ebert, Eine politische Biographie*, 1:34–217 and passim; Peters, *Friedrich Ebert*, pp. 11–76; Emil Felden, *Eines Menschen Weg* (a generally authentic and enthusiastic novel); Karl Radek, *Portraits and Pamphlets*, p. 53; Schorske, *German Social Democracy*, pp. 212–13, 285n.

27. Konrad Haenisch to Rudolf Franz, Jan. 15, 1911, April 2, 1912, Haenisch-Franz Manuscripts, Hoover Institution.

28. For an interesting single example of the mechanics, see Konrad Haenisch to Rudolf Franz, April 2, 1912, Haenisch-Franz Manuscripts, Hoover Institution.

29. Kautsky to V. Adler, June 26, 1913, in Adler, ed., *Victor Adler*, pp. 573–74; Kurt Mandelbaum, *Die Erörterungen innerhalb der deutschen Sozialdemokratie über das Problem des Imperialismus (1895–1914)*, pp. 57–58, a useful but not exhaustive Ph.D. dissertation.

30. Quoted in Koppel S. Pinson, *Modern Germany*, p. 202.

31. Kautsky to V. Adler, Sept. 26, 1909, in Adler, ed., *Victor Adler*, p. 501.

32. William H. Dawson, *The German Empire, 1867–1914, and the Unity Movement*, 2:372; Ernst Troeltsch, *Deutsche Zukunft*, p. 41; Friedrich Naumann, *Demokratie und Kaisertum*, p. 61; Hugo Preuss, *Das deutsche Volk und die Politik*, p. 70.

33. Max Weber, *Essays in Sociology*, p. 71.

34. August Bebel, *Aus meinem Leben*, 3:222.
35. Bebel to V. Adler, April 10, 1911, in Adler, ed., *Victor Adler*, p. 531; Schorske, *German Social Democracy*, pp. 216–220; Heinrich Ströbel, *The German Revolution and After*, pp. 10–11; Sozialdemokratische Partei Deutschlands, Vorstand, *Protokolle der Sitzungen des Parteiausschusses*, January 1915, for a regional and personal list of representatives in the *Parteiausschuss* (this source is available at The Hoover Institution); Snell, "German Socialists in the Last Imperial Reichstag," pp. 196–205 and passim; Weber, *Essays in Sociology*, p. 112; Anon., "Three German Socialists on the War," *Outlook*, 62 (Jan. 26, 1916): 182–84; Philipp Scheidemann, *The Making of New Germany*, 1:226, 316.

XII BOURGEOIS DEMOCRATS IN WILHELMIAN GERMANY

1. Wilson H. Coates and Hayden V. White, *An Intellectual History of Western Europe*, 2:17–241.
2. Eugene N. Anderson, *The Social and Political Conflict in Prussia, 1858–1864*, pp. 423–26; Julius Heyderhoff and Paul Wentzcke, eds., *Deutscher Liberalismus im Zeitalter Bismarcks*, 2:230–357, 365–66 (Gustav Freytag quote); Gustav Seeber, *Zwischen Bebel und Bismarck*, pp. 8–10, 24–29, 127–205; Ludwig Elm, *Zwischen Fortschritt und Reaktion*, pp. 2–8, 14–15, 27, 210–22 (both equally valuable and painstakingly documented works of East German historians). For two reliable West German survey treatments of left-liberal factions, consult Ernst Rudolf Huber, *Deutsche Verfassungsgeschichte seit 1789*, 4:75–86; and Thomas Nipperdey, *Die Organisation der deutschen Parteien vor 1918*, pp. 192–240. There exists no study of the Deutsche Volkspartei after 1871. The data on the composition of the Württemberg Landtag for the period were extracted from Max Miller and Paul Sauer, *Die württembergische Geschichte von der Reichsgründung bis heute*, pp. 44, 56, 70, 82, 92, 104–6, 116. For the 1910 fusion and its immediate results, note Jürgen Bertram, *Die Wahlen zum Deutschen Reichstag vom Jahre 1912*, pp. 64, 207–8, 213–15, 243–45, and S. T. Robson, "Left Wing Liberalism in Germany, 1900–19," pp. 96–97. John Dillard Hunley, "Society and Politics in the Düsseldorf Area, 1867–1878," pp. 396–99, details a clear instance of the Progressives losing their constituency to Center and SPD in a Catholic district during a period of rapid industrialization. In Silesia this process seems to have been repeated after the turn of the century.
3. Rudolf Vierhaus, ed., *Das Tagebuch der Baronin Spitzemberg geb. Freiin von Varnbüler*, pp. 192–202; Wilhelm Mommsen, ed., *Deutsche Parteiprogramme*, pp. 173–76; Walter Gagel, *Die Wahlrechtsfrage in der Geschichte der deutschen liberalen Parteien 1848–1918*, pp. 105–12, 119, 143–62; Hans Dietzel, *Die preussischen Wahlrechtsreformbestrebungen von der Oktroyierung des Dreiklassenwahlrechts bis zum Beginn des Weltkrieges*, pp. 32–37; Wilhelm Otto Vollrath, *Der parlamentarische Kampf um das preussische Dreiklassenwahlrecht*, pp. 30–54; Nipperdey, *Die Organisation der deutschen Parteien*, pp. 232–40; Donald J. Ziegler, *Prelude to Democracy*, pp. 26–43; Beverley Anne Heckert, "From Bassermann to Bebel," pp. 44–47, 188–94.
4. K. J. Rohfleisch, "Eugen Richter, Opponent to Bismarck," pp. 242–43.
5. W. A. McConagha, *Development of the Labor Movement in Great Britain, France, and Germany*, pp. 150–52 (a useful survey for the neophyte). Equally summary, but more solid, is Helga Grebing, *Geschichte der deutschen Arbeiterbewegung*, pp. 125–38; Gustav Hartmann, *Fünfzig Jahre deutsche Gewerkvereine (Hirsch-Duncker) (1868–1918)*, pp. 6, 8, 26–27; Josef Deutz, *Adam Stegerwald*, p. 14; *Die Hilfe: Wochenschrift für Politik, Literatur und Kultur*, Nov. 30, 1916, Sept. 12,

19, 1918; Lujo Brentano, *Mein Leben im Kampf um die soziale Entwicklung Deutschlands*, pp. 72–84, 230, 280; James J. Sheehan, *The Career of Lujo Brentano*, pp. 39n, 67–94, 101, 173, and passim; Franz Boese, *Geschichte des Vereins für Sozialpolitik 1872–1932*, pp. 2, 32, 60, 108, 113, 256; Dieter Lindenlaub, *Richtungskämpfe im Verein für Sozialpolitik: Wissenschaft und Sozialpolitik im Kaiserreich vornehmlich vom Beginn des 'neuen Kurses' bis zum Ausbruch des Ersten Weltkrieges (1890–1914)*, 1:20–21, 238–71, 2:393–443; Martin Wenck, *Friedrich Naumann*, pp. 36–56, 73.

6. E. Wetterlé, *Behind the Scenes in the Reichstag*, p. 51; Friedrich Naumann, *Demokratie und Kaisertum*, pp. 181–230; Hellmut von Gerlach, *Von Rechts nach Links*, pp. 151–230; Brentano, *Mein Leben*, pp. 230–76; Sheehan, *Lujo Brentano*, pp. 143–54; Wenck, *Friedrich Naumann*, pp. 81–99, 124–25; William O. Shanahan, "Liberalism and Foreign Affairs," pp. 188–89; Elisabeth Fehrenbach, *Wandlungen des deutschen Kaisergedankens, 1871–1918*, pp. 200–216; Joachim H. Knoll, *Führungsauslese in Liberalismus und Demokratie*, pp. 126–42; for the brief course of the National Social Society, see the useful monograph by Ralph Walz, "Friedrich Naumann's National Social Society, 1896–1903."

7. Klemens von Klemperer, *Germany's New Conservatism*, p. 41; Naumann, *Demokratie und Kaisertum*, esp. pp. 34–62, 67–69, 72, 132, 187; Alfred Milatz, ed., *Friedrich-Naumann-Bibliographie*, lists 2,100 items from Naumann's pen and 380 pieces about him. Friedrich Meinecke, *The German Catastrophe*, pp. 18–19; Theodor Heuss, *Friedrich Naumann*, esp. pp. 121–22, 171–72; Ernst Jäckh, *Der goldene Pflug*, pp. 104–5; Paul Rohrbach, *Um des Teufels Handschrift*, pp. 7–181 passim; Theodor Heuss, *Vorspiel des Lebens*, pp. 191–201; Hans Bott and Hermann Leins, eds., *Begegnungen mit Theodor Heuss*, pp. 29, 36, 42, 101; Wenck, *Friedrich Naumann*, pp. 124–25; J. P. Mayer, *Max Weber and German Politics*; Ilse E. Nelson, "The Practical Aspects of Max Weber's Political Philosophy: Max Weber's Attitude toward the Political Problems of Germany, 1885–1920" (Ph.D. diss., University of Chicago, 1950), pp. 8, 13, 69, 114, and passim. (Nelson overemphasizes the thesis that Weber was essentially "not a democratic thinker.")

8. Gertrud Bäumer, *Im Licht der Erinnerung*, pp. 119–64 passim; Bott and Leins, eds., *Begegnungen mit Theodor Heuss*, pp. 29, 447; Theodor Heuss, *Robert Bosch*, p. 313 and passim; Richard W. Sterling, *Ethics in a World of Power*, p. ix and passim (a sensitive account, in which sympathy is tempered by proper critical scholarship); Alfred Milatz, "Friedrich Naumann (1860–1919)," pp. 42–55; Heinz Josef Varain, *Freie Gewerkschaften, Sozialdemokratie und Staat*, p. 30.

9. *Brockhaus' Konversations-Lexikon*, 14th ed., 17 vols. (Leipzig, 1908), 7:105, 115–17; Friedrich C. Sell, *Die Tragödie des deutschen Liberalismus*, pp. 310–11; Anneliese Thimme, *Hans Delbrück als Kritiker der wilhelminischen Epoche*, p. 152n; Walz, "Friedrich Naumann's National Social Society," pp. 72–76; Jacqueline Strain, "Feminism and Political Radicalism in the German Social Democratic Movement, 1890–1914," pp. 10n, 124; Huber, *Verfassungsgeschichte*, 4:922–24; Arthur Mitzman, *The Iron Cage*, pp. 44–45.

10. Bäumer, *Im Licht der Erinnerungen*, pp. 119–64; Else Ulich-Beil, *Ich ging meinen Weg*, pp. 19, 30, 99–103, 109–14; Amy Hackett, "The German Women's Movement and Suffrage, 1890–1914," pp. 354–86; Arianna Giachi, "Helene Lange (1848–1930)," pp. 30–41; Ortwin Fink, "Gertrud Bäumer (1873–1954)," pp. 83–96; Strain, "Feminism and Political Radicalism," pp. 11, 17, 114–17, 126–29, 145–47, 201–8, 223–26; Amy Hackett, "Feminism and Liberalism in Wilhelmine Germany," pp. 13–19.

11. Jacob Toury, *Die politischen Orientierungen der Juden in Deutschland*, pp. 123–318; Ernest Hamburger, *Juden im öffentlichen Leben Deutschlands*, pp. 150–254,

302–11, 404–7; Werner Angress, "Prussia's Army and the Jewish Reserve Officer Controversy"; Paul W. Massing, *Rehearsal for Destruction*, p. 125 and passim; P. G. J. Pulzer, *The Rise of Political Anti-Semitism in Germany and Austria*, pp. 9–15, 260, 346–47; Marjorie Lamberti, "The Attempt to Form a Jewish Bloc," pp. 73–93; Lamar Cecil, *Albert Ballin*, pp. 98–112; Herman Ullstein, *The Rise and Fall of the House of Ullstein*, p. 80; Klaus Gerteis, *Leopold Sonnemann*, pp. 96–103.

12. Erich Eyck, *Das persönliche Regiment Wilhelms II*, pp. 171–72; Joachim von Kürenberg (pseud. J. von Reichel), *The Kaiser*, p. 127; Hans Wehberg, *Die Führer der deutschen Friedensbewegung (1890 bis 1923)*, pp. 7–10, 19–23, 26–31, 53–63; Hans Wehberg, ed., *Ludwig Quidde*, pp. 28–29; Utz-Friedebert Taube, *Ludwig Quidde*, pp. 4–68, 72–83, 93–97, 101–12, 125–63; Irwin Abrams, "Berta von Suttner and the Nobel Peace Prize," pp. 286–307; Gerlach, *Von Rechts nach Links*, p. 183; Roger P. Chickering, "Pacifism in Germany, 1900–1914," pp. 3–28, 63–90, 97–113, 128–31, 143–80, now partly published as "A Voice of Moderation in Imperial Germany," pp. 147–64; Herbert Burger, *Politik und politische Ethik bei F. W. Foerster*, pp. 69–73; Norman Angell, *Europe's Optical Illusion*, pp. 118–19; Robson, "Left Wing Liberalism in Germany," p. 38; Eckart Kehr, *Schlachtflottenbau und Parteipolitik 1894–1901*, pp. 298–304.

13. E. Malcolm Carroll, *Germany and the Great Powers, 1866–1914*; Sell, *Die Tragödie des deutschen Liberalismus*, pp. 275–98 passim; William H. Dawson, *The German Empire, 1867–1914, and the Unity Movement*, 2:373; Paul Hirsch, *Der Weg Weg des Sozialdemokratie zur Macht in Preussen*, p. 47.

14. Gerlach, *Von Rechts nach Links*, p. 150 and passim; Wetterlé, *Behind the Scenes in the Reichstag*, pp. 49–50; *Frankfurter Zeitung*, June 12, 1917, for a suggestive sketch of Payer by Conrad Haussmann. See also: Friedrich Payer, *Von Bethmann Hollweg bis Ebert*; Conrad Haussmann, *Schlaglichter*.

15. Kurt Koszyk, *Deutsche Presse im 19. Jahrhundert*, pp. 153–59; Germany, Kriegspresseamt, *Handbuch deutscher Zeitungen 1917*, pp. 10–11; Ullstein, *House of Ullstein*, pp. 100, 118–25. See also: Theodor Wolff, *Through Two Decades*; Wolff's *Vollendete Tatsachen 1914–1917*; and Gotthart Schwarz, *Theodor Wolff und das "Berliner Tageblatt,"* pp. 3–72 and passim.

16. Helmut Drüner, *Im Schatten des Weltkrieges*, pp. 25–53; Anon., *Geschichte der Frankfurter Zeitung, 1856 bis 1906*, (Frankfurt-am-Main, 1906) pp. 7–9, 906; Gerteis, *Leopold Sonnemann*; Hamburger, *Juden im öffentlichen Leben*, pp. 311–21.

17. Lyford P. Edwards, *The Natural History of Revolution*, p. 38.

18. Crane Brinton, *The Anatomy of Revolution*, p. 53. See also Eric Hoffer, *The True Believer*, pp. 129–31 and passim.

19. Eugen Schiffer, *Sturm über Deutschland*, p. 9.

20. Sell, *Die Tragödie des deutschen Liberalismus*, pp. 322–28.

21. Heinrich Heffter, *Die deutsche Selbstverwaltung im 19. Jahrhundert*, pp. 763–64; Friedrich Meinecke, *Weltbürgertum und Nationalstaat*, pp. 492–95; Carl Schmitt, *Hugo Preuss*, pp. 13–15; Fehrenbach, *Wandlungen des deutschen Kaisergedankens*, p. 198; Fritz K. Ringer, *The Decline of the German Mandarins*, pp. 128–80; Gerhard Anschütz, "Lebenserinnerungen" (carbon typescript in the possession of Hans A. Schmitt), pp. 182–88; Georg G. Iggers, *The German Conception of History*, pp. 124–288; Gustav Schmidt, *Deutscher Historismus und der Übergang zur parlamentarischen Demokratie*; Waldemar Besson, "Friedrich Meinecke und die Weimarer Republik," pp. 113–29; Robert A. Pois, *Friedrich Meinecke and German Politics in the Twentieth Century*, pp. 7–8, 16.

22. Marianne Weber, *Max Weber*, pp. 142–43, 446, 453, and passim. There exist now five full-scale studies of Weber's thought and person to which these summary remarks cannot do justice, but on which they have drawn: Wolfgang

Mommsen, *Max Weber und die deutsche Politik 1890–1920*, pp. 165–68, 191–206; Reinhard Bendix, *Max Weber*, pp. 15–38; Eduard Baumgarten, *Max Weber, Werk und Person*, pp. 80–81, 307–11, 316–17, 331–33; Mitzman, *The Iron Cage*, pp. 148–63, 170–75, 423–68; Ilse Dronberger, *The Political Thought of Max Weber*; on Weber's limitations as a political leader, see Gerhard Schulz, "Geschichtliche Theorie und politisches Denken bei Max Weber," pp. 325–50.

23. Quoted from Wilhelm Raabe, *Horacker*, pp. 155–56, and Georg Lukács, "Wilhelm Raabe," in Hermann Helmers, ed., *Raabe in neuer Sicht* (Stuttgart, 1968), p. 52.

24. Jürgen Kuczynski, *Gestalten und Werke*, pp. 194–203; Ernst Kohn-Bramstedt, *Aristocracy and the Middle-Classes in Germany*; J. Dresch, *Le roman social en Allemagne (1850–1900)*, pp. 194–96, 234–50.

25. Kurt Schreinert, ed., *Theodor Fontane, Briefe an Georg Friedländer*, pp. 70, 140, 146–47, 161–62, 170, 309; Erich Behrend, *Theodor Fontane's Roman 'Der Stechlin'*; Maximilian von Hagen, "Theodor Fontane's politische Wandlung," pp. 106–12; Kenneth Attwood, *Fontane und das Preussentum*, pp. 287–89.

26. Quoted from Michael Hamburger, *Contraries, Studies in German Literature*, p. 235.

27. Walter H. Sokel, *The Writer in Extremis, Expressionism in Twentieth Century German Literature*, pp. 95, 102. See also Walter A. Kaufmann, *Nietzsche* (a first-rate interpretation based on intensive study); Theobald Ziegler, *Die geistigen und sozialen Strömungen Deutschlands im 19. und 20. Jahrhundert*, pp. 519–33; Friedrich Glum, *Philosophen im Spiegel und Zerrspiegel*, p. 136 and passim; Erich Heller, *The Disinherited Mind*; Karl Löwith, *Von Hegel zu Nietzsche*, pp. 392–98; Georg Lukács, *Von Nietzsche bis Hitler oder der Irrationalismus in der deutschen Politik*, pp. 37–39 and passim.

28. On publication figures, see Koszyk, *Deutsche Presse*, p. 299, and for a solid as well as lively introduction, Harry Pross, *Literatur und Politik, Geschichte und Programme der politisch-literarischen Zeitschriften im deutschen Sprachgebiet seit 1870*, pp. 54–57, 61–66. The two standard monographs are Eugen Roth, *Simplicissimus*, and Harry F. Young, *Maximilian Harden, Censor Germaniae*. A representative example of a serious and comprehensive attack on the kaiser by a regular *Simplicissimus* contributor is Ludwig Thoma's review article of 1907 "Die Reden Kaiser Wilhelms II," *Gesammelte Werke*, 1:554–74.

29. As does the analysis of Karl Pfannkuch, "Zeitgeist um die Jahrhundertwende," pp. 119–20.

30. Cf. Alfred Vagts, *Deutsch-Amerikanische Rückwanderung*, p. 55.

31. Harry Slochower, *Richard Dehmel, der Mensch und der Denker*, pp. 110–25; Leroy R. Shaw, *Gerhard Hauptmann, Witness of Deceit*, pp. 25–67.

32. André Bernuls, *Heinrich Mann*, pp. 94–106; David Roberts, *Artistic Consciousness and Political Conscience*, pp. 108–16, 125–35.

33. H. Ihering, *Heinrich Mann, sein Leben und sein Werk*, p. 64; Slochower, *Richard Dehmel*, pp. 128–29.

34. Quoted from Fritz Martini, *Deutsche Literaturgeschichte von den Anfängen bis zur Gegenwart*, p. 440.

XIII PUBLIC POLICY AND THE DEMOCRATIC IMPULSE

1. Johannes Haller, *Philipp Eulenburg*, 1:262; Peter Rassow and Karl Erich Born, eds., *Akten zur staatlichen Sozialpolitik in Deutschland 1890–1914*, pp. 138–43; Norman Rich, *Friedrich von Holstein*, 2:501; Ivo Nikolai Lambi, "The Agrarian-

Industrial Front in Bismarckian Politics, 1873–1879," p. 396; Peter-Christian Witt, *Die Finanzpolitik des Deutschen Reiches von 1903 bis 1913*, pp. 69–74; Lamar Cecil, *Albert Ballin*, p. 114; Bernhard von Bülow, *Memoirs of Prince von Bülow*, 1:510, 2:243; Wolfgang Neumann, "Die Innenpolitik des Fürsten Bülow von 1900–1906," pp. ii, 165–70, 189, kindly lent by the library of Univ. of Kiel; Germany, Bureau des Reichstags, *Reichstags Handbuch, 13*, pp. 137–40.

2. See above, chapter 9, pp. 7–9; Leo Stern, ed., *Die Auswirkungen der ersten russischen Revolution von 1905–1907 auf Deutschland*, pp. iv, 156–68, 204–85; Robert C. Williams, "Russians in Germany," pp. 121–49; Karl Erich Born, *Staat und Sozialpolitik seit Bismarcks Sturz*, pp. 196–99; Konrad H. Jarausch, *The Enigmatic Chancellor*, pp. 47–48; Volker R. Berghahn, "Zu den Zielen des deutschen Flottenbaus unter Wilhelm II," pp. 52–57; Josef Kliersfeld, *Die Haltung Kaiser Wilhelms II. zur Arbeiterbewegung und zur Sozialdemokratie*, p. 58.

3. Beverly Anne Heckart, "From Bassermann to Bebel," pp. 13–31, 48–74; Hans Dietzel, *Die preussischen Wahlrechtsreformbestrebungen von der Oktroyierung des Dreiklassenwahlrechts bis zum Beginn des Weltkrieges*, pp. 40–43; Erich Eyck, *Das persönliche Regiment Wilhelms II*, p. 461; Bülow, *Memoirs*, 2:581.

4. On the constitutional structure and position of the German colonies, see Ernst Rudolf Huber, *Deutsche Verfassungsgeschichte seit 1789*, 4:604–34; on the political controversies over colonialism in 1906–7 consult Stadtarchiv Köln, Bachem Nachlass, Folders 500–501; Bülow, *Memoirs*, 2:305; Hans-Georg Hartmann, "Die Innenpolitik des Fürsten Bülow 1906–1909," pp. 8–10; George D. Crothers, *The German Elections of 1907*, pp. 81, 119–53, 170, 194–210; Klaus Epstein, *Matthias Erzberger and the Dilemma of German Democracy*, pp. 52–60; Bruce B. Frye, "Matthias Erzberger and German Politics, 1914–1921," pp. 1–18; Hans-Jürgen Puhle, *Agrarische Interessenpolitik und preussischer Konservativismus im Wilhelminischen Reich (1893–1914)*, pp. 149–50; Hans-Alexander Apolant, *Die wirtschaftsfriedliche nationale Arbeiterbewegung (Gelbe Gewerkschaften) in Deutschland*, p. 83; for National Liberal election pamphlets, see *German Foreign Office Archives, 1870–1920*, Microfilm T 291, Roll 3, Frames 54–55, 76.

5. Rudolf Vierhaus, ed., *Das Tagebuch der Baronin Spitzemberg, geb. Freiin Von Varnbüler*, pp. 472–506; Harry F. Young, *Maximilian Harden, Censor Germaniae*, pp. 82–113, 120–25; Rich, *Friedrich von Holstein*, 2:757–97; Hartmann, "Die Innenpolitik des Fürsten Bülow," pp. 34–45; Bülow, *Memoirs*, 2:272, 321–23, 344–50; Joachim von Kürenberg (pseud. J. von Reichel), *The Kaiser*, pp. 123, 136, 174–76; Haller, *Philipp Eulenburg*, 2:5, 188–224.

6. Rassow and Born, eds., *Akten zur staatlichen Sozialpolitik*, pp. 272–343; Adalbert Wahl, *Deutsche Geschichte von der Reichsgründung bis zum Ausbruch des Weltkrieges (1871 bis 1914)*, 4:10–13; James J. Sheehan, *The Career of Lujo Brentano*, pp. 168–70; Richard Lipinski, *Die Sozialdemokratie von ihren Anfängen bis zur Gegenwart*, 1:7.

7. Cf. Friedrich Naumann to Conrad Haussmann, Sept. 22, 1908, Württembergisches Hauptstaatsarchiv Stuttgart: *Nachlass Haussmann; Stenographische Berichte über die Verhandlungen des preussischen Hauses der Abgeordneten*, 21. Legislaturperiode, II, Session 1908/09, I (Oct. 20, 1908), pp. 1–6; Dietzel, *Die preussischen Wahlrechtsreformbestrebungen*, pp. 49, 53, 58, 61; Eyck, *Das persönliche Regiment*, pp. 461–68.

8. Born, *Staat und Sozialpolitik*, pp. 233–36; Wahl, *Deutsche Geschichte*, 4:19–27.

9. Jonathan Steinberg, *Yesterday's Deterrent*, pp. 17–29 and passim; on the general ineptness of German foreign policy, see also the same author's brilliant case study, "Germany and the Russo-Japanese War," pp. 1965–86; Fritz Fischer, *Krieg der Illusionen*, pp. 413–58 passim; on the ultimately offensive design of

German naval expansion consult Berghahn, "Zu den Zielen des deutschen Flottenbaus," pp. 63–65; Joe Stroud, "Sir Eyre Crowe and the Shaping of British Policy toward Germany, 1905–1914"; Samuel R. Williamson Jr., *The Politics of Grand Strategy*, pp. 5–29 passim, postulates the Entente Cordiale's lack of aggressive intent toward Germany, as does, though less emphatically, Christopher Andrew, *Théophile Delcassé and the Making of the Entente Cordiale*, pp. 213–15, 265–67, 269–70. For the demoralizing impact of the Anglo-French rapprochement on the German Foreign Office, see Vierhaus, ed., *Das Tagebuch der Baronin Spitzemberg*, p. 439; A. J. P. Taylor, *The Struggle for Mastery in Europe, 1848–1918*, pp. xxviii–xxx; Eyck, *Das persönliche Regiment*, p. 504.

10. Bülow, *Memoirs*, 2:396; E. Malcolm Carroll, *Germany and the Great Powers, 1866–1914*, pp. 337–46, 456, 485–572.

11. Wilhelm Schüssler, *Die Daily-Telegraph Affaire*, pp. 1–38; Hartmann, "Die Innenpolitik des Fürsten Bülow," pp. 121–59; Norman Rich and M. H. Fisher, eds., *The Holstein Papers*, 1:203–7; Bülow, *Memoirs*, 2:389–436; Eyck, *Das persönliche Regiment*, p. 493.

12. Ernst Deuerlein, *Der Bundesratsauschuss für die Auswärtigen Angelegenheiten 1870–1918*, pp. 94, 142, 148–60; *Verhandlungen des Reichstags*, XII. Legislaturperiode, 1. Session (Nov. 10–11, Dec. 2–3, 1908), pp. 5374–5439 and 5903–76 contain the principal debates on the *Daily Telegraph* Affair. See also, Bülow, *Memoirs*, 2:402–9; Elard von Oldenburg-Januschau, *Erinnerungen*, pp. 97–98; Vierhaus, ed., *Das Tagebuch der Baronin Spitzemberg*, pp. 489–516; Schüssler, *Die Daily-Telegraph Affaire*, pp. 42–43.

13. See debates cited in note 12; Theodor Eschenburg, *Das Kaiserreich am Scheideweg*, pp. 131–75; Anneliese Thimme, *Hans Delbrück als Kritiker der Wilhelminischen Epoche*, pp. 18, 20–21.

14. A view shared by some more open-minded National Liberals, cf., Heckart, "From Bassermann to Bebel," pp. 119–20.

15. In the debates cited in note 12, compare the positions taken by Progressive speakers such as Haussmann, Schrader, and Wiemer. See also, Wolfgang Conrad Haussmann, *Die Durchsetzung des parlamentarischen Systems im Deutschen Kaiserreich*, p. 38; Eyck, *Das persönliche Regiment*, p. 500; Hartmann, "Die Innenpolitik des Fürsten Bülow," pp. 121–59; Klaus Simon, *Die Württembergischen Demokraten*, pp. 135–38; Marianne Weber, *Max Weber*, pp. 446–53; Eduard Baumgarten, *Max Weber, Werk und Person*, pp. 487–89.

16. Bülow, *Memoirs*; Dieter Grosser, *Vom monarchischen Konstitutionalismus zur parlamentarischen Demokratie*, pp. 51–52; Erich Matthias und Eberhard Pikart, eds., *Die Reichstagsfraktion der deutschen Sozialdemokratie 1898 bis 1918*, pp. 198–203.

17. Rich and Fisher, eds., *Holstein Papers*, 4:592–93; Vierhaus, ed., *Das Tagebuch der Baronin Spitzemberg*, pp. 406–7.

18. Since Eyck's *Das persönliche Regiment*, this has been the majority verdict, and the damaging effects on foreign policy emerge with particular clarity from the subsequent Rich, *Friedrich von Holstein*, 2:847 and passim. Ernst Rudolf Huber remains the major challenger of the Eyck thesis. For a recent summation, see his "Das persönliche Regiment Wilhelms II," pp. 282–310. For another interesting attempt at a dispassionate assessment of the substance and excesses of the Wilhelmian regime, note Otto Graf zu Stolberg-Wernigerode, *Die unentschiedene Generation*, pp. 111–25.

19. *Stenographische Berichte über die Verhandlungen des preussischen Hauses der Abgeordneten*, 21. Legislaturperiode, II. Session 1908/09, 1 (Jan. 25–26, 1909), pp. 1184–1292; 2–3 (Feb. 5–March 27, 1909); Eyck, *Das persönliche Regiment*, p. 469;

Dietzel, *Die preussischen Wahlrechtsreformbestrebungen*, p. 65; Weber, *Max Weber*, p. 445; Karl Liebknecht, *Ausgewählte Reden, Briefe und Aufsätze*, p. 142.

20. Rich and Fisher, eds., *Holstein Papers*, 4:615–17; Bülow, *Memoirs*, 2:304–14, 497–579 passim; Heckart, "From Bassermann to Bebel," pp. 121–30; Hartmann, "Die Innenpolitik des Fürsten Bülow," pp. 160–236; Eyck, *Das persönliche Regiment*, pp. 525–41; Huber, *Verfassungsgeschichte*, 4: 315–17.

21. Huber, *Verfassungsgeschichte*, 4:318.

22. Arthur Rosenberg, *The Birth of the German Republic, 1871*–1918, p. 55.

23. Bernhard Guttmann and Rudolf Kirchner, *Bethmann-Tirpitz-Ludendorff*, p. 7.

24. Jarausch, *Enigmatic Chancellor*, pp. 41–49, 51–58, 63–68. Illustrative of Bethmann's "reforming conservatism" is his long memorandum to Bülow on electoral reform, dated March 22, 1907, Deutsches Zentral Archiv, Potsdam, *Reichskanzlei*, Fasc. 1070, esp. p. 4, a photocopy of which was kindly provided Professor Snell by Professor Jarausch. On the Lübeck Bundesrat delegate's judgment, see Brigitte Haberland, "Die Innenpolitik des Reiches unter der Kanzlerschaft Bethmann Hollwegs 1909–1914," Appendix I. See also: James W. Gerard, *My First Eighty-Three Years in America*, pp. 200–201, and Cecil, *Albert Ballin*, p. 122.

25. Haberland, "Die Innenpolitik des Reiches," pp. 19, 22, 125; Hans-Günter Zmarzlik, *Bethmann Hollweg als Reichskanzler*, pp. 30–37, 42, 72, 76–77, 83, 138–39; Theobald von Bethmann-Hollwegg, *Betrachtungen zum Weltkriege*, 1:15, 18–20; Paul Herre, *Kronprinz Wilhelm*, pp. 1–85 passim; William H. Dawson, *The German Empire, 1867–1914, and the Unity Movement*, 2:348.

26. Bogdan Hutten-Czapski, *Sechzig Jahre Politik und Gesellschaft*, 2: 8–25; Zmarzlik, *Bethmann Hollweg*, pp. 42–83 passim; Haberland, "Die Innenpolitik des Reiches," pp. 42–99, 119–63; Matthias and Pikart, eds., *Die Reichstagsfraktion der deutschen Sozialdemokratie*, 1:cxxvn; Carl Schorske, *German Social Democracy, 1905–1917*, pp. 264–67; Rassow and Born, eds., *Akten zur staatlichen Sozialpolitik*, pp. 412–38; Huber, *Verfassungsgeschichte*, 4:1243, 1247–49.

27. Johannes Hohlfeld and Klaus Hohlfeld, eds., *Dokumente der deutschen Politik und Geschichte von 1848 bis zur Gegenwart*, 2:224–25; Stadtarchiv Köln, Bachem Nachlass, Folders 215, 290, 325; Paul Hirsch, *Der Weg der Sozialdemokratie zur Macht in Preussen*, p. 30; Bethmann-Hollweg, *Betrachtungen zum Weltkriege*, 1:97; Jarausch, *Enigmatic Chancellor*, pp. 73–79; Born, *Staat und Sozialpolitik*, pp. 236–38; Kuno von Westarp, *Konservative Politik im letzten Jahrzehnt des Kaiserreiches*, 1:107–18; Hutten-Czapski, *Sechzig Jahre Politik und Gesellschaft*, 2:9–12; Dietzel, *Die preussischen Wahlrechtsreformbestrebungen*, pp. 61–73; Haberland, "Die Innenpolitik des Reiches," pp. 23–41; Donald Warren, Jr., *The Red Kingdom of Saxony*, p. 79; Fischer, *Krieg der Illusionen*, p. 51; Thomas Nipperdey, *Die Organisation der deutschen Parteien*, pp. 97–98; Klaus-Peter Reiss, ed., *Von Bassermann zu Stresemann*, pp. 22–23; Grosser, *Vom monarchischen Konstitutionalismus*, pp. 69–75; Heckart, "From Bassermann to Bebel," pp. 251–57.

28. Schorske, *German Social Democracy*, pp. 171–85; Liebknecht, *Ausgewählte Reden, Briefe und Aufsätze*, pp. 161–67, 267; Fred Oelssner, *Rosa Luxemburg, Eine kritische biographische Skizze*, p. 78; Peter Franz Stubmann, *Ballin*, p. 231.

29. Fischer, *Krieg der Illusionen*, pp. 117–19, 140–44; Klaus Wernecke, *Der Wille zur Weltgeltung*, pp. 40–143 passim (incl. the quote from the *Hamburger Nachrichten*).

30. Fischer, *Krieg der Illusionen*, pp. 37–61, 147, 155, 333–37; Stradtarchiv Köln, Bachem Nachlass, Folders 317 and 318; Jürgen Bertram, *Die Wahlen zum deutschen Reichstag vom Jahre 1912*, pp. 200–238 passim; Heckart, "From Bassermann to

Bebel," pp. 305–19; Philipp Scheidemann, *Memoiren eines Sozialdemokraten*, 1:107–13; Schorske, *German Social Democracy*, pp. 226–33.

31. Fischer, *Krieg der Illusionen*, pp. 150–54, 159–64, 384–412; Egmont Zechlin and Hans Joachim Bieter, *Die deutsche Politik und die Juden im ersten Weltkrieg*, pp. 45–49; Richard S. Levy, "Anti-Semitic Political Parties in the German Empire," pp. 353–63.

32. Warren, *Red Kingdom of Saxony*, pp. 25–40; Henry Ashby Turner, Jr., *Stresemann and the Politics of the Weimar Republic*, p. 8; Fischer, *Krieg der Illusionen*, p. 154; Reiss, ed., *Von Bassermann zu Stresemann*, pp. 24–29, 89–104; Heckart, "From Bassermann to Bebel," pp. 307, 317–18, 339–74.

33. Epstein, *Matthias Erzberger*, pp. 3–95; Klaus Epstein, "Erzberger's Position in the Zentrumsstreit before World War I," pp. 1–16; Scheidemann, *Memoiren*, 1:203–18; Heckart, "From Bassermann to Bebel," pp. 319–38; Matthias and Pikart, eds., *Die Reichstagsfraktion der deutschen Sozialdemokratie*, 1:cxxxv–cxliii; Fischer, *Krieg der Illusionen*, pp. 155–57, 167.

34. Schorske, *German Social Democracy*, pp. 235–41; Hans Delbrück, *Government and the Will of the People*, p. 103. See also Haussmann, *Die Durchsetzung des parlamentarischen Systems*, p. 17, and the retrospective comments in Stresemann to Traub, Jan. 7, 1917, and Stresemann to Bassermann, April 9, 1917, in U.S. National Archives, Stresemann Nachlass, Microfilm 3077 (Frames 135528-30) and 3061 (Frames 125738-39).

35. Schorske, *German Social Democracy*, pp. 268, 274–75, 278; Ludwig Bergsträsser, *Die preussische Wahlrechtsfrage und die Entstehung der Osterbotschaft 1917*, pp. 13–14; Oelssner, *Rosa Luxemburg*, pp. 82–83. See also the useful communist study, Kurt Stenkwitz, *Gegen Bajonette und Dividende*, pp. 224–52 and passim.

36. Bülow, *Memoirs*, 2:336; Neumann, "Die Innenpolitik des Fürsten Bülow," p. 104 and passim; Theodor Schieder, *Das deutsche Kaiserreich von 1871 als Nationalstaat*, pp. 19, 26, 95–124; Werner Blumenberg, ed., *August Bebel's Briefwechsel mit Friedrich Engels*, p. 405; Oswald Hauser, "Polen und Dänen im Deutschen Reich," pp. 291–309; Hans-Ulrich Wehler, *Sozialdemokratie und Nationalstaat*, pp. 187–90; Alfred E. Senn, *The Emergence of Modern Lithuania*, pp. 2–3, 13–15, 22.

37. Hans Peter Hanssen, *Diary of a Dying Empire*, pp. xvii–xxxvii, 40; Bülow, *Memoirs*, 2:336; Hauser, "Polen und Dänen im deutschen Reich," pp. 309–18; Wehler, *Sozialdemokratie und Nationalstaat*, pp. 76–92; for a contemporary history of the question from the Danish viewpoint, see M. Mackeprang, *Nord-Schleswig von 1864–1911*. The work of Oswald Hauser on Schleswig-Holstein has treated both the ethnic questions (*Preussische Staatsräson und nationaler Gedanke*, esp. pp. 13–25 and 62–160 passim) and the preference among Schleswig-Holsteiners for incorporation into Germany as a separate *Land* (*Staatliche Einheit und regionale Vielfalt in Preussen*, pp. 7, 106) which did not obtain satisfaction until 1945.

38. For Alsace-Lorraine's constitutional position in the empire, see Huber, *Verfassungsgeschichte*, 4:437–79. The most recent history of the region under German governance has just been completed by Dan P. Silvermann, *Reluctant Union*, esp. pp. 36–64, 91–132. On the German failure to transform the population into loyal Germans, note the testimony of Chlodwig zu Hohenlohe-Schillingsfürst, imperial governor from 1885 to 1894, in his *Denkwürdigkeiten der Reichskanzlerzeit*, p. 430, and Helmuth Rogge, eds., *Holstein und Hohenlohe*, pp. 272–73.

39. Silvermann, *Reluctant Union*, pp. 145–50; Jean-Marie Mayeur, *Autonomie et politique en Alsace*, pp. 73–127 passim.

40. Delbrück, *Government and the Will of the People*, p. 1; Jarausch, *Enigmatic Chancellor*, pp. 100–103; Silvermann, *Reluctant Union*, pp. 190–98; Kurt Stenkwitz, *"Immer feste druff!" Zabernaffäre 1913*; Hans-Ulrich Wehler, "Der Fall Zabern," pp. 27–46. See also Richard W. Mackey, "The Zabern Affair, 1913–1914," esp. pp. 47–67, 111–86, and for the last quote, Ernst Toller, *I was a German*, p. 67.

41. Jarausch, *Enigmatic Chancellor*, pp. 71–72; Gunther Blieffert, "Die Innenpolitik des Reichskanzlers Fürst Chlodwig zu Hohenlohe-Schillingsfürst 1894–1900," pp. 185–215; Ernst zu Reventlow, *Von Potsdam nach Doorn*, pp. 121, 341; Karl Alexander von Müller, *Aus Gärten der Vergangenheit*, pp. 133, 141–42, 213; Robert H. Lowie, *Toward Understanding Germany*, pp. 48–49; Hohenlohe, *Denkwürdigkeiten der Reichskanzlerzeit*, pp. 368–69, 390–96, 407–8, 426–28, 462–64, 474; Vierhaus, ed., *Tagebuch der Baronin Spitzemberg*, pp. 358–467 passim; Elisabeth Fehrenbach, *Wandlungen des deutschen Kaisergedankens, 1871–1918*, pp. 143–57.

42. Joachim H. Knoll, *Führungsauslese in Liberalismus und Demokratie*, pp. 70–72; Huber, *Verfassungsgeschichte*, 4:385–401; Willy Albrecht, *Landtag und Regierung in Bayern am Vorabend der Revolution von 1918*, pp. 35, 43, 46–47.

43. Albert Eugen Adam, *Ein Jahrhundert württembergische Verfassung*, pp. 188–208 passim; Wilhelm Keil, *Erlebnisse eines Sozialdemokraten*, 1: 144–47, 179; Walter Grube, *Der Stuttgarter Landtag 1457–1957*, pp. 544–55; Georg H. Kleine, *Der württembergische Ministerpräsident Freiherr Hermann von Mittnacht (1825–1909)*, pp. 46–53, 60–82.

44. Huber, *Verfassungsgeschichte*, 4:415–18, 420–21.

45. Albrecht, *Landtag und Regierung in Bayern*, pp. 39–42; Johannes Schulte, *Geschichte der Hamburger Arbeiterschaft 1890–1919*, pp. 69–78; Ulrich Seemann, "Die Kämpfe der Hamburger Arbeiter gegen die Verschlechterung ihres Wahlrechts in den Jahren 1905/06," pp. 63–100; Richard A. Comfort, *Revolutionary Hamburg*, pp. 16–18.

46. Huber, *Verfassungsgeschichte*, 4:400–411; Warren, *Red Kingdom of Saxony*, pp. 18–23, 41–49, 52–58; Friedrich Kracke, *Friedrich August III, Sachsens volkstümlichster König*, pp. 86–87, 104–5.

47. Manfred Hamann, *Das staatliche Werden Mecklenburgs*, pp. 50–51. The head of Mecklenburg's last prerevolutionary government, Adolf Langfeld, provides a detailed "inside" account of the abortive struggle for reform in *Mein Leben*, pp. 252–80. For an interesting sketch of Mecklenburg society under its anachronistic political order, see Joachim von Dissow, *Adel im Übergang*, pp. 69–70.

48. Haller, *Philipp Eulenburg*, 1:288.

49. Quote by Richard Sexau, "Die 'wilhelminische' Epoche," p. 276.

50. Hohlfeld and Hohlfeld, eds., *Dokumente der deutschen Politik*, 2: 268–69.

51. Reventlow, *Von Potsdam nach Doorn*, pp. 436–44; Wernecke, *Der Wille zur Weltgeltung*, pp. 14–15, 30.

52. Bülow, *Memoirs*, 2:462; Kürenberg, *The Kaiser*, p. 352; Robert von Zedlitz-Trützschler, *Twelve Years at the Imperial German Court*, p. 52 and passim.

53. Cf. Irène Petit, "Kautsky et les discussions autour du problème de l'impérialisme dans le parti social-démocrate allemand de 1907 à 1914," p. 337 (see also the interesting articles by Annie Kriegel, P. Angel, and Dieter Groh in the same issue); Jacob Toury, *Die politischen Orientierungen der Juden in Deutschland*, p. 232; Hellmut von Gerlach, *Von Rechts nach Links*, p. 240; Wahl, *Deutsche Geschichte*, 4:237; Rupert Emerson, *State and Sovereignty in Modern Germany*, p. 75 and passim.

54. See also, Count Johann Bernstorff to Foreign Office, Feb. 5, May 1, 1913; Bethmann Hollweg to Bernstorff, May 3, 1913, German Foreign Ministry Archives 1867–1920, Microfilm T-149, Reel 189.

55. Quoted by Donald J. Ziegler, *Prelude to Democracy*, p. 100.

56. Carroll, *Germany and the Great Powers*, p. 727.

57. Sidney B. Fay, *The Origins of the World War*, 2:203–4; Jarausch, *Enigmatic Chancellor*, pp. 155–59.

58. Gerhard Ritter, *Der Schlieffenplan*, pp. 53, 57–58, 68–69, 71, 81, 95, 145–60 (the draft of December 1905), 178–80 (Moltke's comments of 1911), 181–90 (Schlieffen's memorandum of 1912). Although offering far greater detail, Ritter's definitive monograph does not challenge the excellent brief survey by Gordon A. Craig, *The Politics of the Prussian Army, 1640–1945*, pp. 277–95.

59. Reiss, ed., *Von Bassermann zu Stresemann*, p. 109; Fischer, *Krieg der Illusionen*, pp. 166–67, 290–92, 342–43; Carroll, *Germany and the Great Powers*, p. 815.

60. J. W. Wheeler-Bennett, *Three Episodes in the Life of Kaiser Wilhelm II*, p. 24.

61. In 1961 the historical controversy over the origins and causes of World War I was reopened by Fritz Fischer's *Griff nach der Weltmacht*, 3d ed. Several major responses to Fischer, and his own reactions to such critics, have been brought together in Ernst Wilhelm, Graf Lynar ed., *Deutsche Kriegsziele 1914–1918*. The articles of Klaus Epstein, Immanuel Geiss, Wolfgang J. Mommsen, Jonathan Steinberg, and Norman Stone in the *Journal of Contemporary History*, I (July 1966), constitute another useful and stimulating introduction to the debate, as do such additional recent contributions as Fischer's own *Krieg der Illusionen*, esp. pp. 272–74, 359–60, 366–67, 542–64, 583–84, 636–59, 671, and 684; Jarausch, *Enigmatic Chancellor*, pp. 148–84; and Fritz Stern's significant essay in Leonard Krieger and Fritz Stern, eds., *The Responsibility of Power*, pp. 252–87.

BIBLIOGRAPHY

I MANUSCRIPT SOURCES

Anschütz, Gerhard. "Lebenserinnerungen" (carbon typescript in the possession of Hans A. Schmitt).
Deutsches Zentral Archiv, Potsdam, Reichskanzlei Fasc. 1070.
German Foreign Ministry Archives, 1867–1920, Whaddon Hall, National Archives Microcopy T-149, Reels 31, 188–189, 331.
Konrad Haenisch Letters to Rudolf Franz, 1907–1915, Manuscripts, The Hoover Institution, Stanford University.
Stadtarchiv Köln, Bachem Nachlass, Folders 215, 290, 325, 317, 318, 500–501.
Württembergisches Hauptstaatsarchiv Stuttgart, Hachlass Haussman.
United States National Archives, *Stresemann Nachlass*, Microfilm, 3061 and 3077.

II PRINTED SOURCES, MEMOIRS, CONTEMPORARY COMMENTARIES

Adler, Friedrich, ed. *Victor Adler: Briefwechsel mit August Bebel und Karl Kautsky*. Vienna, 1954.
Bassermann, Karola. *Ernst Bassermann: Das Lebensbild eines Parlamentariers aus Deutschlands glücklicher Zeit*. Mannheim, n.d. [1919].
Bäumer, Gertrud. *Im Licht der Erinnerung*. Tübingen, 1953.
Bebel, August. *Aus meinem Leben*. 3 vols. Stuttgart, 1914.
Becker, Johann Philipp and Christian Esselen. *Geschichte der Süddeutschen Mai-Revolution des Jahres 1849*. Geneva, 1849.
[Berlin]. *Rundschreiben an die Vorstände und Mitglieder aller der freien Vereinigung deutscher Gewerkschaften angeschlossenen Vereine*. Sept. 15, 1915, Feb. 1, July 1, 1916.
Bernhard, Duke of Saxe-Weimar-Eisenach. *Travels through North America during the Years 1825 and 1826*. 2 vols. Philadelphia, 1828.
Bernstein, Eduard. *Entwicklungsgang eines Sozialisten*. Leipzig, 1930.

————. *Evolutionary Socialism*. Translated by Edith C. Harvey. New York, 1909.

Bethmann-Hollweg, Theobald von. *Betrachtungen zum Weltkriege*. 2 vols. Berlin, 1919–21.

Bismarck, Otto von. *Bismarck, the Man and the Statesman, Being the Reflections and Reminiscences of Otto, Prince von Bismarck.* Translated by A. J. Butler. 2 vols. New York, 1898.

————. *Errinerung und Gedanke*, vol. 3 of his memoirs. Stuttgart, 1919.

Blumenberg, Werner, ed. *August Bebels Briefwechsel mit Friedrich Engels*. Quellen und Untersuchungen zur Geschichte der deutschen und österreichischen Arbeiterbewegung, vol. 6. The Hague, 1965.

Braun, Adolf. *Gewerkschaften und Sozialdemokratie*. Berlin, 1914.

Brentano, Lujo. *Mein Leben im Kampf um die soziale Entwicklung Deutschlands*. Jena, 1931.

Büchner, Ludwig. *Kraft und Stoff, oder Grundzüge der natürlichen Weltordnung, nebst einer darauf gebauten Moral oder Sittenlehre*. Leipzig, 1904.

Bülow, Bernhard von. *Memoirs of Prince von Bülow*. 4 vols. Boston, 1931– 32.

Bureau des Reichstags, ed. *Reichstags-Handbuch, 13. Legislaturperiode*. Berlin, 1912.

Constabel, Adelheid, ed. *Die Vorgeschichte des Kulturkampfes: Quellenveröffentlichung aus dem Deutschen Zentralarchiv*. Berlin, 1956.

Delbrück, Hans. *Government and the Will of the People: Academic Lectures*. Translated by Roy S. MacElwee. New York, 1923.

Eastman, Max, ed. *Capital, the Communist Manifesto, and Other Writings by Karl Marx*. New York, 1932.

Eckert, Georg, ed. *Wilhelm Liebknecht: Briefwechsel mit Karl Marx und Friedrich Engels*. Quellen und Untersuchungen zur Geschichte der deutschen und österreichischen Arbeiterbewegung, vol. 5. The Hague, 1963.

Engels, Friedrich. *Germany: Revolution and Counter Revolution*. Chicago, 1967.

Feibleman, James K. Edited by Huntington Cairns. *The Two-Story World: Selected Writings of James K. Feibleman*. New York, 1966.

Festschrift zum fünfundzwanzigjährigen Regierungsjubiläum Seiner Königlichen Hoheit, des Grossherzogs Ernst Ludwig von Hessen und bei Rhein. Leipzig, 1917.

Foerster, Friedrich Wilhelm. *Erlebte Weltgeschichte 1869–1953: Memoiren.* Nuremberg, 1953.

Freund, Max, ed. *Gustav Dresel's Houston Journal: Adventures in North America and Texas, 1837–1841.* Austin, 1954.

Fricke, Dieter. *Zur Organisation und Tatigkeit der deutschen Arbeiterbewegung (1890–1914): Dokumente und Materialien.* Leipzig, 1962.

Furtwängler, Franz Josef. *Männer die ich sah und kannte.* Hamburg, 1951.

Gemkow, Heinrich, ed. "Briefe August Bebels aus den Jahren 1886/1887," *Beiträge zur Geschichte der deutschen Arbeiterbewegung* 2 (1960).

Gerard, James W. *My First Eighty-Three Years in America: The Memoirs of James W. Gerard.* Garden City, 1951.

Gerlach, Hellmut von. *Von Rechts nach Links.* Zürich, 1937.

Germany, War Press Office. *Handbuch deutscher Zeitungen 1917.* Berlin, 1917.

Germany, Reichstag. *Das Werk des Untersuchungsausschusses der deutschen verfassungsgebenden Nationalversammlung und des deutschen Reichstags 1919–1926.* 4th ser., *Die Ursachen des deutschen Zusammenbruches im Jahre 1918.* 12 vols. Berlin, 1925–29.

Globig, Martha, ed. "Ein unbekannter Brief August Bebels an Karl Liebknecht vom 10. November 1908," *Beiträge zur Geschichte der deutschen Arbeiterbewegung* 3 (1961).

Grais, Hue de. *Handbuch der Verfassung und Verwaltung in Preussen und dem Deutschen Reiche.* Berlin, 1881, and many subsequent editions.

Griesinger, Theodor. *Freiheit und Sclaverei unter dem Sternenbanner oder Land und Leute in Amerika.* 2 vols. Stuttgart, 1862.

Gugelmeier, Erwin. *Das schwarze Jahr (1917–1918); Erlebtes aus dem letzten Kriegsjahr.* Freiburg-im-Breisgau, 1926.

Hanssen, Hans Peter. *Diary of a Dying Empire.* Bloomington, Ind., 1955.

Haussmann, Conrad. *Schlaglichter: Reichstagsbriefe und Aufzeichnungen.* Frankfurt am Main, 1924.

Hecht, Ben. *A Child of the Century.* Signet ed. New York, 1955.

Hertling, Georg von. *Erinnerungen aus meinem Leben.* 2 vols. Kempten, 1919–20.

Heuss, Theodor. *Vorspiel des Lebens: Jugenderinnerungen.* Tübingen, 1953.

Heyderhoff, Julius, and Paul Wentzcke, eds. *Deutscher Liberalismus im Zeitalter Bismarcks: Eine politische Briefsammlung.* 2 vols. Deutsche Geschichtsquellen des 19. und 20. Jahrhunderts, vols. 18, 24. 1925–26. Reprint. Osnabrück, 1967.

Hirsch, Helmut, ed. *Eduard Bernsteins Briefwechsel mit Friedrich Engels*. Quellen und Untersuchungen zur Geschichte der deutschen und österreichischen Arbeiterbewegung, N. F. vol. 1. Assen, 1970.

Höhn, Reinhard, ed. *Die vaterlandslosen Gesellen: Der Sozialismus im Lichte der Geheimberichte der preussischen Polizei 1878–1914*. Vol. I, *1878–1890*. Cologne, 1964.

Hohenlohe-Schillingsfürst, Chlodwig zu. Edited by Karl Alexander von Müller. *Denkwürdigkeiten der Reichskanzlerzeit*. Quellen zur deutschen Geschichte des 19. Jahrhunderts und 20. Jahrhunderts, vol. 28. 1931. Reprint. Osnabrück, 1967.

Hohenlohe-Schillingsfürst, Chlodwig of. *Memoirs*. Translated by George W. Chrystal. 2 vols. London, 1906.

Hohlfeld, Johannes, and Klaus Hohlfeld, eds. *Dokumente der deutschen Politik und Geschichte von 1848 bis zur Gegenwart*. 8 vols. Berlin, 1951–55.

Huber, Ernst Rudolf, ed. *Dokumente zur deutschen Verfassungsgeschichte*. 3 vols. Stuttgart, 1961–66.

Hutten-Czapski, Bogdan. *Sechzig Jahre Politik und Gesellschaft*. 2 vols. Berlin, 1936.

Institute für Marxismus-Leninismus beim ZK der SED. *Rosa Luxemburg, Gesammelte Werke*. Vol. I, *1893–1905*. E. Berlin, 1972.

Jäckh, Ernst. *Der goldene Pflug: Lebensernte eines Weltbürgers*. Stuttgart, 1954.

Kautsky, Benedikt, ed. *Friedrich Engels Briefwechsel mit Karl Kautsky*. Vienna, 1955.

Kautsky, Karl. Edited by Benedikt Kautsky. *Erinnerungen und Erörterungen*. The Hague, 1960.

Keil, Wilhelm. *Erlebnisse eines Sozialdemokraten*. 2 vols. Stuttgart, 1947–48.

Kessel, Eberhard, ed. *Die Briefe von Carl Schurz an Gottfried Kinkel*. Heidelberg, 1965.

Knaplund, Paul, ed. *Letters from the Berlin Embassy, 1871–1874, 1880– 1885*. Vol. 2. Annual Report of the American Historical Association for the Year 1942, vol. 2. Washington, 1944.

Kretzschmar, Hellmut, and Horst Schlechte, eds. *Französische und sächsische Gesandtschaftsberichte aus Dresden und Paris 1848– 1849*. Berlin, 1956.

Kupisch, Karl, ed. *Quellen zur Geschichte des deutschen Protestantismus (1871–1945)*. Gottingen, 1960.

Langfeld, Adolf. *Mein Leben*. Schwerin, 1930.

Liebknecht, Karl. *Ausgewählte Reden, Briefe und Aufsätze*. Berlin, 1952.

————. *Ausgewählte Reden und Schriften.* Vol. I, Edited and introduced by Helmut Böhme. Frankfurt, 1969.

Liebknecht, Wilhelm, ed. *Der Hochverraths-Prozess wider Liebknecht, Bebel, Hepner vor dem Schwurgericht zu Leipzig vom 11. bis 26. März 1872.* Berlin, 1894.

Liebknecht, W., A. Bebel, et al. *Protokoll über die Verhandlungen des allgemeinen deutschen sozial-demokratischen Arbeiterkongresses zu Eisenach am 7., 8., und 9. August 1869.* E. Berlin, 1969.

Lobe, Paul. *Der Weg war lang: Lebenserinnerungen.* 2d ed. Berlin, 1954.

Luxemburg, Rosa, et al. "Einige Briefe Rosa Luxemburgs und andere Dokumente." *Bulletin of the International Institute for Social History* no. 1 (1952).

Matthias, Erich, and Eberhard Pikart, eds. *Die Reichstagsfraktion der deutschen Sozialdemokratie 1898 bis 1918.* Quellen zur Geschichte des Parlamentarismus und der politischen Parteien, ser. 1: Von der konstitutionellen Monarchie zur parlamentarischen Republik, vol. 3/I. Düsseldorf, 1966.

Mayer, J. P., ed. *Alexis de Tocqueville: Werke und Briefe.* Vols. 1–2, *Über die Demokratie in Amerika.* 2 vols. Stuttgart, 1959–62.

Meinecke, Friedrich. *Strassburg, Freiburg, Berlin 1901–1919: Erinnerungen.* Stuttgart, 1949.

Metternich, Richard, ed. *Memoirs of Prince Metternich.* Translated by Gerald W. Smith. 5 vols. New York, 1880–82.

Moleschott, Jacob. *Für meine Freunde: Lebens-Erinnerungen.* Giessen, 1894.

Müller, Karl Alexander von. *Aus Gärten der Vergangenheit: Erinnerungen 1882–1914.* Stuttgart, 1951.

Müller-Meiningen, Ernst. *Parlamentarismus: Betrachtungen, Lehren und Erinnerungen aus deutschen Parlamenten.* Berlin, 1926.

Naumann, Friedrich. *Demokratie und Kaisertum.* 4th ed. Berlin, 1905.

Noske, Gustav. *Erlebtes aus Aufstieg und Niedergang einer Demokratie.* Offenbach-Main, 1947.

Oldenburg-Januschau, Elard von. *Erinnerungen.* Leipzig, 1936.

Oncken, Hermann, ed. *Die Rheinpolitik Kaiser Napoleons III von 1863 bis 1870 und der Ursprung des Krieges von 1870/71.* Deutsche Geschichtsquellen des 19. Jahrhunderts. Vol. 19–21. Stuttgart, 1926.

Paine, Thomas. *Geschichte der Revolution von Nord-Amerika vom Abt Raynal. Nebst Anmerkungen über diese Geschichte von Thomas Paine.* Translated by F. H. Wernitz. Berlin, 1786.

Payer, Friedrich. *Von Bethmann-Hollweg bis Ebert: Erinnerungen und Bilder.* Frankfurt am Main, 1923.

Radek, Karl. *Portraits and Pamphlets*. London, 1935.

Rapp, Adolf, ed. *Briefwechsel zwischen Strauss und Vischer*. 2 vols. Stuttgart, 1952–53.

Raschdau, L., ed. *Die politischen Berichte des Fürsten Bismarck aus Petersburg und Paris (1859–1862)*. 2 vols. Berlin, 1920

Rassow, Peter, and Karl Erich Born, eds. *Akten zur staatlichen Sozialpolitik in Deutschland 1890–1914*. Wiesbaden, 1959.

Raumer, Friedrich von. *Die Vereinigten Staaten von Nordamerika*. 2 vols. Leipzig, 1845.

Reiss, Klaus-Peter, ed. *Von Bassermann zu Stresemann: Die Sitzungen des national liberalen Zentralovorstandes 1912–1917*. Quellen zur Geschichte des Parlamentarismus und der politischen Parteien, I. Series: Von der Konstitutionellen Monarchie zur parlamentarischen Republik, Vol. 5. Düsseldorf, 1967.

Reventlow, Ernst zu. *Von Potsdam nach Doorn*. 12th ed. Berlin, 1940.

Rich, Norman, and M. H. Fischer, eds. *The Holstein Papers*. 4 vols. Cambridge, 1955–63.

Rogge, Helmuth, ed. *Holstein und Hohenlohe. Neue Beiträge zu Friedrich von Holsteins Tätigkeit als Mitarbeiter Bismarcks und als Ratgeber Hohenlohes. Nach Briefen und Aufzeichnungen aus dem Nachlass des Fürsten Chlodwig zu Hohenlohe-Schillingsfürst 1874–1894*. Stuttgart, 1957.

Rohrbach, Paul. *Um des Teufels Handschrift: Zwei Menschenalter erlebter Weltgeschichte*. Hamburg, 1953.

Sack, Eduard. Edited by Karl-Heinz Günther. *Die preussische Schule im Dienste gegen die Freiheit: Schulpolitische Kampfschriften*. Berlin, 1961.

Scheidemann, Philipp. *The Making of New Germany*. Translated by J. E. Michell. 2 vols. New York, 1929.

———. *Memorien eines Sozialdemokraten*. 2 vols. Dresden, 1928.

———. *Der Zusammenbruch*. Berlin, 1921.

Schiffer, Eugen. *Sturm über Deutschland*. Berlin, 1932.

Schmidt, Friedrich. *Versuch über den politischen Zustand der Vereinigten Staaten von Nord-Amerika*. 2 vols. Stuttgart, 1822.

Schmidt-Ott, Friedrich. *Erlebtes und Estrebtes 1860–1950*. Wiesbaden, 1952.

Schwarz, Robert, ed. *Aus Justus Liebigs und Friedrich Wöhlers Briefwechsel in den Jahren 1829–1873*. Weinheim/Bergstr., 1958.

Schreinert, Kurt, ed. *Theodor Fontane, Briefe an Georg Friedländer*. Heidelberg, 1954.

Severing, Carl. *Mein Lebensweg*. 2 vols. Cologne, 1950.

Silberner, Edmund, and Werner Blumenberg, eds. *Moses Hess: Briefwechsel*. The Hague, 1959.

Stenographische Berichte über die Verhandlungen des preussischen Hauses der Abgeordneten, 21. Legislaturperiode, II. Session 1908/09, I.

Tocqueville, Alexis de. Edited by John Lukacs. *"The European Revolution" and Correspondence with Gobineau*. Garden City, N.Y., 1959.

Toller, Ernst. *I Was a German*. New York, 1934.

Ulich-Beil, Else. *Ich ging meinen Weg: Lebenserinnerungen*. Berlin, 1961.

Ullstein, Herman. *The Rise and Fall of the House of Ullstein*. New York, 1944.

Umbreit, Paul. *25 Jahre deutscher Gewerkschaftsbewegung 1890–1915*. Berlin, 1915.

Venedey, Jakob. *Die deutschen Republikaner unter der französischen Republik*. Leipzig, 1870.

Vierhaus, Rudolf, ed. *Das Tagebuch der Baronin Spitzemberg geb. Freiin von Varnbüler. Aufzeichnungen aus der Hofgesellschaft des Hohenzollernreiches*. Deutsche Geschichtsquellen des 19. und 20. Jahrhunderts, vol. 43. Göttingen, 1960.

Weber, Marianne. *Max Weber: Ein Lebensbild*. Heidelberg, 1950.

Weber, Max. *Essays in Sociology*. Translated by H. H. Gerth and C. Wright Mills. New York, 1946.

Wedel, Erhard von. *Zwischen Kaiser und Kanzler: Aufzeichnungen des Generaladjutanten Grafen Carl von Wedel aus den Jahren 1890–1894*. Leipzig, 1943.

Wentzcke, Paul, and Wolfgang Klötzer, eds. *Deutscher Liberalismus im Vormärz: Heinrich von Gagern, Briefe und Reden 1815–1848*. Göttingen, 1959.

Westarp, Kuno von. *Konservative Politik im letzten Jahrzehnt des Kaiserreiches*. 2 vols. Berlin, 1935.

Wetterlé, E. *Behind the Scenes in the Reichstag: Sixteen Years of Parliamentary Life in Germany*. Translated by George Frederic Lees. New York, 1918.

Wigard, Franz, ed. *Stenographischer Bericht über die Verhandlungen der deutschen constituirenden Nationalversammlung zu Frankfurt am Main*. 9 vols. Frankfurt, 1848–49.

William II. *Ereignisse und Gestalten aus den Jahren 1878–1918*. Leipzig, 1922.

Winshaw. "On the Present State of Electro-Telegraphic Communication in England, Prussia, and America." *Journal of the Franklin Institute* 49 (1850).

Wislizenus, G. A. *Aus Amerika*. 2 vols. Leipzig, 1854.
Wolff, Theodor. *Through Two Decades*. Translated by E. W. Dickes. London, 1936
————. *Vollendete Tatsachen 1914–1917*. Berlin, 1918.
Zedlitz-Trützschler, Robert von. *Twelve Years at the Imperial Court*. London, 1924.

III SECONDARY WORKS

Ackerknecht, Erwin H. *Rudolf Virchow: Doctor, Statesman, Anthropologist*. Madison, Wis., 1953.
Adam, Albert Eugen. *Ein Jahrhundert württembergische Verfassung*. Stuttgart, 1919.
Adams, Henry M. *Prussian-American Relations, 1775–1871*. Cleveland, 1960.
Albrecht, Willy. *Landtag und Regierung in Bayern am Vorabend der Revolution von 1918. Studien zur gesellschaftlichen und staatlichen Entwicklung Deutschlands 1912–1918*. Beiträge zu einer historischen Strukturanalyse Bayerns im Industriezeitalter, vol. 2. Berlin, 1968.
Amelung, Eberhard. *Die demokratischen Bewegungen des Jahres 1848 im Urteil der protestantischen Theologie*. Marburg/Lahn, [1955].
Anderson, Eugene N. *The Social and Political Conflict in Prussia, 1858–1864*. Lincoln, Neb., 1954.
Anderson, Evelyn. *Hammer or Anvil: The Story of the German Working Class Movement*. London, 1945.
Andrew, Christopher. *Théophile Delcassé and the Making of the Entente Cordiale*. New York, 1968.
Angel, Pierre. *Eduard Bernstein et l'évolution du socialisme allemand*. Paris, 1961.
Angell, Norman. *Europe's Optical Illusion*. London, 1909.
Angermann, Erich. *Robert von Mohl 1799–1875: Leben und Werk eines altliberalen Staatsgelehrten*. Neuwied, 1962.
Apolant, Hans-Alexander. *Die wirtschaftsfriedliche nationale Arbeiterbewegung (Gelbe Gewerkschaften) in Deutschland: Ihr Werden, ihr Wesen und ihr Wollen*. Altenburg, 1926.
Arendt, Hannah. *The Origins of Totalitarianism*. New York, 1951.
Aris, Reinhold. *History of Political Thought in Germany from 1789 to 1815*. London, 1936.
Armytage, W. H. G. *The Rise of the Technocrats: A Social History*. London, 1965.

Arnold, Matthew. *Higher Schools and Universities in Germany*. 2d ed. London, 1882.

Attwood, Kenneth. *Fontane und das Preussentum*. Berlin, 1970.

Bachem, Karl. *Vorgeschichte, Geschichte und Politik der deutschen Zentrumspartei*. 9 vols. Cologne, 1927–32.

Baginsky, Paul Ben, ed. *German Works Relating to America, 1493–1800*. New York, 1942.

Balfour, Michael. *The Kaiser and His Times*. Boston, 1964.

Balser, Frolinde. *Sozial-Demokratie 1848/49–1863: Die erste deutsche Arbeiterorganisation*. 2 vols. Stuttgart, 1962.

Baumgarten, Eduard. *Max Weber, Werk und Person*. Tübingen, 1964.

Becker, Otto. Edited by Alexander Scharff. *Bismarcks Ringen um Deutschlands Gestaltung*. Heidelberg, 1958.

Behrend, Erich. *Theodor Fontane's Roman 'Der Stechlin'*. Marburg, 1929.

Bendix, Reinhard. *Max Weber: An Intellectual Portrait*. New York, 1960.

Bennett, A. R. *The Telephone Systems of the Continent of Europe*. London, 1895.

Benson, E. F. *The Kaiser and English Relations*. London, 1936.

Bergsträsser, Ludwig. *Die Entwicklung des Parlamentarismus in Deutschland*. Schloss Laupheim, 1954.

――――. *Geschichte der politischen Parteien in Deutschland*. 8th and 9th eds. in one. Munich, 1955.

――――. *Die preussische Wahlrechtsfrage und die Entstehung der Osterbotschaft 1917*. Tübingen, 1929.

――――. *Die Verfassung des deutschen Reiches vom Jahre 1849*. Kleine Texte für Vorlesungen und Übungen, no. 114. Bonn, 1913.

Berlin, Isaiah. *Karl Marx: His Life and Environment*. Rev. ed. New York, 1959.

Bernuls, André. *Heinrich Mann*. Sprache und Literatur, vol. 62. Stuttgart, 1970.

Bertram, Jürgen. *Die Wahlen zum deutschen Reichstag vom Jahre 1912. Parteien und Verbände in der Innenpolitik des wilhelminischen Reiches*. Beiträge zur Geschichte des Parlamentarismus und der politischen Parteien, vol. 28. Düsseldorf, 1964.

Bevan, Edwyn. *German Social Democracy during the War*. London, 1918.

Binkley, Robert C. *Realism and Nationalism, 1852–1871*. New York, 1935.

Biro, Sidney Seymour. *The German Policy of Revolutionary France:*

A Study in French Diplomacy during the War of the First Coalition, 1792–1797. 2 vols. Cambridge, Mass., 1957.

Black, C. E. *The Dynamics of Modernization: A Study in Comparative History*. New York, 1966.

Blättner, Fritz. *Das Gymnasium: Aufgaben der höheren Schule in Geschichte und Gegenwart*. Heidelberg, 1960.

Bleiber, Helmut. *Zwischen Reform und Revolution: Lage und Kämpfe der schlesischen Bauern und Landarbeiter im Vormärz 1840–1847*. Berlin, 1966.

Blum, Hans. *Die deutsche Revolution 1848–1849 mit 256 authentischen Faksimilebeilagen*. Jena, 1905.

Boberach, Heinz. *Wahlrechtsfragen im Vormärz: Die Wahlrechtsanschauung im Rheinland 1815–1849 und die Entstehung des Dreiklassenwahlrechts*. Düsseldorf, 1959.

Böckenförde, Ernst-Wolfgang. *Die deutsche verfassungsgeschichtliche Forschung im 19. Jahrhundert*. Berlin, 1961.

Böhme, Helmut. *Deutschlands Weg zur Grossmacht: Studien zum Verhältnis von Wirtschaft und Staat während der Reichsgründungszeit 1848–1881*. Cologne, 1966.

Boese, Franz. *Geschichte des Vereins für Sozialpolitik 1872–1932*. Berlin, 1939.

Booms, Hans, *Die deutschkonservative Partei: Preussischer Charakter, Reichsauffassung, Nationalbegriff*. Beiträge zur Geschichte des Parlamentarismus und der politischen Parteien, vol. 3. Düsseldorf, 1954.

Born, Karl Erich, ed. *Bismarck-Bibliographie: Quellen und Literatur zur Geschichte Bismarcks und seiner Zeit*. Cologne, 1966.

————. *Staat und Sozialpolitik seit Bismarcks Sturz: Ein Beitrag zur Geschichte der innenpolitischen Entwicklung des Deutschen Reiches 1890–1914*. Historische Forschungen, vol. 1. Wiesbaden, 1957.

Bossenbrook, William J. *The German Mind*. Detroit, 1961.

Bott, Hans, and Hermann Leins, eds. *Begegnungen mit Theodor Heuss*. Tübingen, 1954.

Bowle, John. *Politics and Opinion in the Nineteenth Century: An Historical Introduction*. London, 1954.

Bramsted, Ernest Kohn. *Aristocracy and the Middle-Classes in Germany: Social Types in German Literature, 1830–1900*. London, 1937.

Brandenburg, Erich. *Fünfzig Jahre Nationalliberale Partei 1867–1917*. Berlin, 1917.

————. *Die Reichsgründung*. 2 vols. Leipzig, 1916.

Brandt, Hartwig. *Landständische Repräsentation im deutschen Vor-*

märz: Politisches Denken im Einflussfeld des monarchischen Prinzips. Neuwied, 1968.

Brinton, Crane. *The Anatomy of Revolution*. Rev. ed. New York, 1952.

Bruford, W. H. *Germany in the Eighteenth Century: The Social Background of the Literary Revival*. Rev. ed. Cambridge, 1952.

Bry, Gerhard. *Wages in Germany, 1871–1945*. Princeton, 1960.

Buchheim, Karl. *Leidensgeschichte des zivilen Geistes oder die Demokratie in Deutschland*. Munich, 1951.

──────. *Ultramontanismus und Demokratie: Der Weg der deutschen Katholiken im 19. Jahrhundert*. Munich, 1963.

Büchner, Anton. *Die Familie Büchner: George Büchners Vorfahren, Eltern und Geschwister*. Darmstadt, 1963.

Buchner, Max. *Kaiser Wilhelm II: Seine Weltanschauung und die deutschen Katholiken*. Liepzig, 1929.

Buchner, Rudolf. *Die deutsch-französische Tragödie 1848–1864: Politische Beziehungen und psychologisches Verhältnis*. Würzburg, 1965.

Bueck, H. A. *Der Centralverband Deutscher Industrieller 1876–1901*. 3 vols. Berlin, n.d.

Bungardt, Karl. *Die Odyssee der Lehrerschaft: Sozialgeschichte eines Standes*. 2d ed. Hanover, 1965.

Butler, E. M. *The Saint-Simonian Religion in Germany: A Study of the Young German Movement*. Cambridge, 1926.

Büttner, Ludwig. *Georg Büchner, Revolutionär und Pessimist: Ein Beitrag zur Geistesgeschichte des XIX. Jahrhunderts*. Nuremberg, 1948.

Burger, Herbert. *Politik und politische Ethik bei F. W. Foerster*. Schriften zur Rechtslehre und Politik, vol. 60. Bonn, 1969.

Cameron, Rondo, et al. *Banking in the Early Stages of Industrialization: A Study in Comparative Economic History*. New York, 1967.

Carr, W. *Schleswig-Holstein, 1815–48: A Study in National Conflict*. Manchester, 1963.

Carroll, E. Malcolm. *Germany and the Great Powers, 1866–1914: A Study in Public Opinion and Foreign Policy*. New York, 1938.

Carsten, F. L. *Princes and Parliaments in Germany from the Fifteenth to the Eighteenth Century*. Oxford, 1959.

Case, Lynn M. *French Opinion on War and Diplomacy during the Second Empire*. Philadelphia, 1954.

Cassau, Theodor. *Die Gewerkschaftsbewegung: Ihre Soziologie und ihr Kampf*. Halberstadt, 1925.

Cecil, Lamar. *Albert Ballin: Business and Politics in Imperial Germany, 1888–1918*. Princeton, 1967.

Chamier, J. Daniel. *Fabulous Monster*. London, 1934.

Childs, David. *Germany since 1918*. New York, 1971.

Clapham, J. H. *The Economic Development of France and Germany, 1815–1914*. 4th ed. Cambridge, 1961.

Clark, Chester Wells. *Franz Joseph and Bismarck: The Diplomacy of Austria before the War of 1866*. Cambridge, Mass., 1934.

Clark, Thomas D., ed. *Travels in the Old South: A Bibliography*. 3 vols. Norman, Okla., 1956–59.

Coates, Wilson H., and Hayden V. White. *An Intellectual History of Western Europe*, Vol. 2, *The Ordeal of Liberal Humanism*. New York, 1970.

Cole, G. D. H. *A History of Socialist Thought*. London, 1953–56. Vol. 1, *Socialist Thought: The Forerunners, 1789–1850*, 1953. Vol. 2, *Socialist Thought: Marxism and Anarchism, 1850–1890*, 1954. Vol. 3, *The Second International, 1889–1914*, 1956.

Comfort, Richard A. *Revolutionary Hamburg: Labor Politics in the Early Weimar Republic*. Stanford, 1966.

Commager, Henry Steele, ed. *America in Perspective: The United States Through Foreign Eyes*. New York, 1947.

Connelly, Owen. *Napoleon's Satellite Kingdoms*. New York, 1965.

Conze, Werner, and Dieter Groh. *Die Arbeiterbewegung in der nationalen Bewegung: Die deutsche Sozialdemokratie vor, während und nach der Reichsgründung*. Stuttgart, 1966.

Conze, Werner, et al. *Staat und Gesellschaft im deutschen Vormärz 1815–1848*. Stuttgart, 1962.

Craig, Gordon A. *The Battle of Königgratz: Prussia's Victory over Austria, 1866*. Philadelphia, 1964.

————. *The Politics of the Prussian Army*, 1640–1945. Oxford, 1955.

————. *War, Politics, and Diplomacy*. New York, 1966.

Croon, Helmuth. *Die gesellschaftlichen Auswirkungen des Gemeindewahlrechts in den Gemeinden und Kreisen des Rheinlandes und Westfalens im 19. Jahrhundert*. Cologne, 1960.

Crothers, George Dunlap. *The German Elections of 1907*. New York, 1941.

Dahm, Karl-Wilhelm. *Pfarrer und Politik: Soziale Position und politische Mentalität des deutschen evangelischen Pfarrerstandes zwischen 1918 und 1933*. Dortmunder Schriften zur Sozialforschung, vol. 29. Cologne, 1965.

Dahrendorf, Ralf. *Society and Democracy in Germany*. Anchor Books ed. of a study published in German in 1964. Garden City, N.Y., 1969.

David, Eduard. *Sozialismus und Landwirtschaft*. Leipzig, 1922.

Dawson, Jerry F. *Friedrich Schleiermacher: The Evolution of a Nationalist*. Austin, Tex., 1966.

Dawson, William H. *The German Empire, 1867–1914, and the Unity Movement*. 2 vols. London, 1919.

────. *German Socialism and Ferdinand Lassalle: A Biographical History of German Socialistic Movements during This Century*. Rev. ed. New York, 1899.

Demeter, Karl. *The German Officer-Corps in Society and State, 1650–1945*. London, 1965.

Demiaskovich, Michael. *The National Mind: English, French, German*. New York, 1938.

Desai, Ashok V. *Real Wages in Germany, 1871–1913*. Oxford, 1968.

Deuerlein, Ernst. *Der Bundesratsauschuss für die Auswärtigen Angelegenheiten 1870–1918*. Regensburg, 1955.

────. ed. *Der Reichstag: Aufsätze, Protokolle und Darstellungen zur Geschichte der parlamentarischen Vertretung des deutschen Volkes 1871–1933*. Frankfurt, 1963.

Deutsch, Harold C. *The Genesis of Napoleonic Imperialism*. Cambridge, Mass., 1938.

Deutz, Josef. *Adam Stegerwald: Gewerkschaftler, Politiker, Minister 1874–1945*. Cologne, 1952.

Dickinson, Robert E. *Germany: A General and Regional Geography*. New York, 1953.

────. *The West European City: A Geographical Interpretation*. London, 1951.

Diesel, Eugen. *Germany and the Germans*. Translated by W. D. Robson-Scott. New York, 1931.

Dietzel, Hans. *Die preussischen Wahlrechtsreformbestrebungen von der Oktroyierung des Dreiklassenwahlrechts bis zum Beginn des Weltkrieges*. Emsdetten, 1934.

Dissow, Joachim von. *Adel im Übergang: Ein kritischer Standesgenosse berichtet aus Residenzen und Gutshäusern*. Stuttgart, 1961.

Dobert, Eitel Wolf. *Deutsche Demokraten in Amerika: Die Achtundvierziger und ihre Schriften*. Göttingen, 1958.

Doeberl, Michael. *Bayern und die Deutsche Frage in der Epoche des Frankfurter Parlaments*. Munich, 1922.

────.*Entwicklungsgeschichte Bayerns*. 3 vols. Munich, 1931.

Döhner, Otto, Jr. *Georg Büchner's Naturauffassung*. Marburg, 1967.

Doll, Eugene Edgar. *American History as Interpreted by German Historians from 1770 to 1815*. Transactions of the American Philosophical Society, N. S., vol. 38. Philadelphia, 1948.

Dombrowski, Eric. *German Leaders of Yesterday and Today*. New York, 1920.

Dorpalen, Andreas. *Heinrich von Treitschke*. New Haven, 1957.

Dresch, J. *Le roman social en Allemagne (1850–1900)*. Paris, 1913.

Dreisbach-Olsen, Jutta. *Ludwig Büchner: Zur soziologischen Analyse naturwissenschaftlich-materialistischen Denkens im 19. Jahrhundert*. Marburg/Lahn, 1969.

Dreyfus, F. G. *Sociétés et mentalités à Mayence dans la seconde moitié du XVIIIe siècle*. Paris, 1968.

Dronberger, Ilse. *The Political Thought of Max Weber*. New York, 1971.

Dross, Babette. *Willi Münzenberg: Eine politische Biographie*. Schriftenreihe der Vierteljahrshefte für Zeitgeschichte, vol. 14/15. Stuttgart, 1967.

Droz, Jacques. *L'Allemagne et la révolution française*. Paris, 1949.

————. *Le Libéralisme rhenan, 1815-1848: Contribution à l'histoire du libéralisme allemand*. Paris, 1940.

————. *Le Romantisme allemand et l'état: Résistance et collaboration dans l'Allemagne napoléonienne*. Paris, 1966.

————. and Ernest Tonnelat, *Les Révolutions allemandes de 1848*. Paris, 1957.

Drummond, Andrew Landale. *German Protestantism since Luther*. London, 1951.

Drüner, Helmut. *Im Schatten des Weltkrieges: Zehn Jahre Frankfurter Geschichte von 1914–1924*. Frankfurt am Main, 1934.

Dunk, Hermann von der. *Der deutsche Vormärz und Belgien 1830/48*. Wiesbaden, 1966.

Dunning, William Archibald. *A History of Political Theories: From Rousseau to Spencer*. New York, 1970.

Easum, Chester V. *Prince Henry of Prussia: Brother of Frederick the Great*. Madison, Wis., 1942.

Eckert, Hugo. *Liberal-oder Sozialdemokratie: Frühgeschichte der Nürnberger Arbeiterbewegung*. Stuttgart, 1968.

Edwards, Lyford P. *The Natural History of Revolution*. Chicago, 1927.

Ehmke, Horst. *Karl von Rotteck, der "politische Professor"*. Karlsruhne, 1964.

Eichholtz, Dietrich. *Junker und Bourgeoisie vor 1848 in der preussischen Eisenbahngeschichte*. Berlin, 1962.

Eisfeld, Gerhard. *Die Entstehung der liberalen Parteien in Deutschland 1858–1870: Studie zu den Organisationen und Programmen der Liberalen und Demokraten*. Hanover, 1969.

Elbogen, Ismar, and Eleonore Sterling. *Die Geschichte der Juden in Deutschland: Eine Einführung*. Frankfurt am Main, 1966.

Ellwein, Thomas. *Das Erbe der Monarchie in der deutschen Staatskrise: Zur Geschichte des Verfassungsstaates in Deutschland*. Munich, 1954.

Elm, Ludwig. *Zwischen Fortschritt und Reaktion. Geschichte der Parteien der liberalen Bourgeoisie in Deutschland 1893–1918*. Berlin, 1968.

Emerson, Rupert. *State and Sovereignty in Modern Germany*. New Haven, 1928.

Engelberg, Ernst. *Revolutionäre Politik und rote Feldpost 1878–1890*. Berlin, 1959.

Engelhardt, Viktor. *An der Wende des Zeitalters: Individualistische oder sozialistische Kultur*. Berlin, 1925.

Engelsing, Rolf. *Massenpublikum und Journalistentum im 19. Jahrhundert in Nordwestdeutschland*. Berlin, 1966.

Epstein, Klaus. *The Genesis of German Conservatism*. Princeton, 1966.

————. *Matthias Erzberger and the Dilemma of German Democracy*. Princeton, 1959.

Erdmann, Gerhard. *Die deutschen Arbeitgeberverbände im sozialgeschichtlichen Wandel der Zeit*. Neuwied, 1966.

Erfurth, C. *Haustelegraphie, Telephonie und Blitzableiter in Theorie und Praxis*. Berlin, 1885.

Erman, Hans. *August Scherl: Dämonie und Erfolg in Wilhelminischer Zeit*. Berlin, 1954.

Eschenburg, Theodor. *Das Kaiserreich am Scheideweg: Bassermann, Bülow und der Block*. Introduction by Gustav Stresemann. Berlin 1929.

Eyck, Erich. *Auf Deutschlands politischem Forum: Deutsche Parlamentarier und Studien zur neuesten deutschen Geschichte*. Erlenbach-Zürich, 1963.

————. *Bismarck: Leben und Werk*. 3 vols. Zurich, 1941–44.

————. *Das persönliche Regiment Wilhelms II: Politische Geschichte des deutschen Kaiserreiches von 1890 bis 1914*. Erlenbach-Zürich, 1948.

Eyck, Frank. *The Frankfurt Parliament, 1848–1849*. New York, 1968.

Faber, Karl-Georg. *Die national-politische Publizistik Deutschlands von 1866 bis 1871: Eine kritische Bibliographie*. 2 vols. Düsseldorf, 1963.

————. *Die Rheinlande zwischen Restauration und Revolution: Prob-*

leme der rheinischen Geschichte von 1814 bis 1848 im Spiegel der zeitgenössischen Publizistik. Wiesbaden, 1966.

Fay, Sidney B. *The Origins of the World War*. 2 vols. 2d rev. ed. New York, 1932.

Federici, Federico, ed. *Der deutsche Liberalismus: Die Entwicklung einer politischen Idee von Immanuel Kant bis Thomas Mann*. Zurich, 1946.

Fehrenbach, Elisabeth. *Wandlungen des deutschen Kaisergedankens 1871–1918*. Studien zur Geschichte des neunzehnten Jahrhunderts, vol. 1. Munich, 1969.

Felden, Emil. *Eines Menschen Weg: Ein Fritz-Ebert-Roman*. Bremen, 1927.

Fischer, Fritz. *Griff nach der Weltmacht: Die Kriegszielpolitik des kaiserlichen Deutschland 1914/18*. 3d ed. Düsseldorf, 1964.

———. *Krieg der Illusionen: Die deutsche Politik von 1911 bis 1914*. Düsseldorf, 1969.

Fischer, Wolfram. *Der Staat und die Anfänge der Industrialisierung in Baden 1800–1850*. Vol. 1, *Die Staatliche Gewerbepolitik*. Berlin, 1962.

Fischer-Frauendienst, Irene. *Bismarcks Pressepolitik*. Münster, 1963.

Fisher, Herbert A. L. *The Republican Tradition in Europe*. London, 1911.

———. *Studies in Napoleonic Statesmanship: Germany*. Oxford, 1903.

Fletcher, Willard Allen. *The Mission of Vincent Benedetti to Berlin, 1864–1870*. The Hague, 1965.

Flitner, Andreas. *Die politische Erziehung in Deutschland: Geschichte und Probleme 1750–1880*. Tübingen, 1957.

Fogarty, Michael P. *Christian Democracy in Western Europe, 1820–1953*. London, 1957.

Footman, David. *Ferdinand Lassalle, Romantic Revolutionary*. New Haven, 1947.

Ford, Guy Stanton. *Stein and the Era of Reform in Prussia, 1807–1815*. Princeton, 1922.

Fraenkel, Ernst, ed. *Amerika im Spiegel des deutschen politischen Denkens*. Cologne, 1959.

Fraenkel, Josef, ed. *The Jews of Austria: Essays on Their Life, History and Destruction*. London, 1967.

Franz, Eckart G. *Das Amerikabild der deutschen Revolution von 1848/49: Zum Problem der Übertragung gewachsener Verfassungs-*

formen. Beihefte zum *Jahrbuch für Amerikastudien*, vol. 2. Heidelberg, 1958.

Franz, Georg. *Kulturkampf: Staat und katholische Kirche in Mitteleuropa von der Säkularisation bis zum Abschluss des preussischen Kulturkampfes*. Munich, n.d. [1954].

Franz-Willing, Georg. *Die bayerische Vatikangesandtschaft 1803–1934*. Munich, 1965.

Freund, Michael. *Das Drama der 99 Tage: Krankheit und Tod Friedrichs III*. Cologne, 1966.

Frey, Ludwig. *Die Stellung der christlichen Gewerkschaften Deutschlands zu den politischen Parteien*. Würzburg, 1931.

Fricke, Dieter. *Die deutsche Arbeiterbewegung 1869–1890: Ihre Organisation und Tätigkeit*. Leipzig, 1964.

Friedrich, Carl J. *The Impact of American Constitutionalism Abroad*. Boston, 1967.

Frölich, Paul. *Rosa Luxemburg: Gedanke und Tat*. Hamburg, 1949.

Frohme, K. *Monarchie oder Republik? Kulturgeschichtliche Streifzüge*. Hamburg, 1904.

Gagel, Walter. *Die Wahlrechtsfrage in der Geschichte der deutschen liberalen Parteien 1848–1918*. Düsseldorf, 1958.

Gall, Lothar. *Der Liberalismus als regierende Partei: Das Grossherzogtum Baden zwischen Restauration und Reichsgründung*. Wiesbaden, 1968.

Gallin, Mary Alice. *German Resistance to Hitler; Ethical and Religious Factors*. Washington, D.C. 1962.

Gasman, Daniel. *The Scientific Origins of National Socialism: Social Darwinism in Ernst Haeckel and the German Monist League*. New York, 1971.

Gay, Peter. *The Dilemma of Democratic Socialism: Eduard Bernstein's Challenge to Marx*. New York, 1952.

Gerhard, Dietrich. *Alte und neue Welt in vergleichender Geschichtsbetrachtung*. Göttingen, 1962.

Gerlach, Hellmut von. *Die Geschichte des preussischen Wahlrechts*. Berlin, 1908.

Gerschenkron, Alexander. *Bread and Democracy in Germany*. Berkeley, 1943.

Gerteis, Klaus. *Leopold Sonnemann: Ein Beitrag zur Geschichte des demokratischen Nationalstaatsgedankens in Deutschland*. Studien zur Frankfurter Geschichte, vol. 3. Frankfurt am Main, 1970.

Geuss, Herbert. *Bismarck und Napoleon III: Ein Beitrag zur Geschichte der preussisch-französischen Beziehungen 1851–1871*. Cologne, 1959.

Geyer, Curt. *Macht und Masse von Bismarck zu Hitler*. Hanover, 1948.

Giesberg, Robert I. *The Treaty of Frankfort: A Study in Diplomatic History, September 1870–September 1873*. Philadelphia, 1966.

Giese, Erich. *Schnellstrassenbahnen: Eine Untersuchung . . . unter besonderer Berücksichtigung der Verhältnisse in Gross Berlin*. Berlin, 1917.

Gillespie, Charles Coulston, ed. *Dictionary of Scientific Biography*. 4 vols. New York, 1970–72.

Glum, Friedrich. *Philosophen im Spiegel und Zerrspiegel: Deutschlands Weg in den Nationalismus und Nationalsozialismus*. Munich, 1954.

Goldenberg, Boris. *Beiträge zur Soziologie der deutschen Vorkriegssozialdemokratie*. Berlin, n.d.

Gooch, G. P. *Frederick the Great: The Ruler, the Writer, the Man*. London, 1947.

————. *Studies in German History*. London, 1948.

Grab, Walter. *Demokratische Strömungen in Hamburg und Schleswig-Holstein zur Zeit der ersten französischen Republik*. Hamburg, 1966.

Grauer, Karl-Johannes. *Wilhelm I. König von Württemberg. Ein Bild seines Lebens und seiner Zeit*. Stuttgart, 1960.

Grebing, Helga. *Geschichte der deutschen Arbeiterbewegung. Ein Überblick*. Munich, 1966.

Groote, Wolfgang v. and Ursula v. Gersdorff, eds. *Entscheidung 1866: Der Krieg zwischen Österreich und Preussen*. Stuttgart, 1966.

Grosser, Dieter. *Vom monarchischen Konstitutionalismus zur parlamentarischen Demokratie. Die Verfassungspolitik der deutschen Parteien im letzten Jahrzehnt des Kaiserreiches*. The Hague, 1970.

Grossmann, Hermann. *Die kommunale Bedeutung des Strassenbahnwesens beleuchtet am Werdegange der Dresdener Strassenbahnen*. Dresden, 1903.

Grube, Walter. *Der Stuttgarter Landtag 1457–1957: Von den Landständen zum demokratischen Parlament*. Stuttgart, 1957.

Gutkind, E. A. *Urban Development in Central Europe*. Glencoe, Ill., 1964.

Guttmann, Bernhard, and Rudolf Kirchner. *Bethmann-Tirpitz-Ludendorff: Regierung und Nebenregierung*. Frankfurt am Main, 1919.

Haeckel, Ernst. *Das Welträthsel: Gemeinverständliche Studien über monistische Philosophie*. Stuttgart, n.d. [1903].

Bibliography [457]

Hale, Oron J. *The Great Illusion, 1900-1914*. New York, 1971.
Haller, Johannes. *Philip Eulenburg: The Kaiser's Friend*. Translated
by Ethel Colburn Mayne. 2 vols. New York, 1930.
Hallowell, John H. *The Decline of Liberalism as an Ideology, with
Particular Reference to German Politico-Legal Thought*. Berkeley,
1945.
Hamann, Manfred. *Das staatliche Werden Mecklenburgs*. Mittel-
deutsche Forschungen, vol. 24. Cologne, 1962.
Hamburger, Ernest. *Juden im öffentlichen Leben Deutschlands:
Regierungsmitglieder, Beamte und Parlamentarier in der monarch-
ischen Zeit 1848-1918*. Tübingen, 1968.
Hamburger, Michael. *Contraries, Studies in German Literature*.
New York, 1970.
Hamerow, Theodore S. *Restoration, Revolution, Reaction: Eco-
nomics and Politics in Germany, 1815-1871*. Princeton, 1958.
_____. *The Social Foundations of German Unification, 1858-1871*.
Vol. 1. Princeton, 1969.
Hammen, Oscar J. *The Red '48ers: Karl Marx and Friedrich Engels*.
New York, 1969.
Handlin, Oscar, ed. *This Was America*. Cambridge, Mass., 1949.
Hanus, Franciscus. *Die preussische Vatikangesandtschaft 1747-
1920*. Munich, 1954.
Harlow, Alvin F. *Old Wires and New Waves: The History of the
Telegraph, Telephone, and Wireless*. New York, 1936.
Hartmann, Gustav. *Fünfzig Jahre Deutsche Gewerkvereine (Hirsch-
Duncker) (1868-1918)*. Jena, 1918.
Hartung, Fritz. *Deutsche Verfassungsgeschichte vom 15. Jahrhundert
bis zur Gegenwart*. 6th ed. Stuttgart, 1954.
Hasek, C. W. *The Introduction of Adam Smith's Doctrines in Ger-
man*. Studies in History, Economics, and Public Law...of Co-
lumbia University, vol. 67. New York, 1925.
Hatschek, Julius. *Das Parlamentsrecht des Deutschen Reiches*. Ber-
lin, 1915.
Hauser, Oswald. *Preussische Staatsräson und nationaler Gedanke*.
Quellen und Forschungen zur Geschichte Schleswig-Holsteins,
vol. 42. Neumünster, 1960.
_____. *Staatliche Einheit und regionale Vielfalt in Preussen. Der
Aufbau der Verwaltung in Schleswig-Holstein nach 1867*. Neu-
münster, 1967.
Haussman, Wolfgang Conrad. *Die Durchsetzung des parlamentari-
schen Systems im deutschen Kaiserreich*. Heidelberg, 1927.
Hawgood, John A. *Political and Economic Relations between the*

United States of America and the German Provisional Central Government at Frankfurt-am-Main in 1848–1849. Heidelberg, 1928.

———. The Tragedy of German-America: The Germans in the United States of America during the Nineteenth Century–and After. New York, 1940.

Heffter, Heinrich. Die deutsche Selbstverwaltung im 19. Jahrhundert: Geschichte der Ideen und Institutionen. Stuttgart, 1950.

Heidemann, Karl. Bismarcks Sozialpolitik und die Zentrumspartei 1881–1884. Herford, 1930.

Helfritz, Hans. Wilhelm II als Kaiser und König: Eine historische Studie. [Zurich], 1954.

Heller, Erich. The Disinherited Mind: Essays in Modern German Literature and Thought. Rev. ed. New York, 1951.

Helmreich, Ernst Christian. Religious Education in German Schools: An Historical Appraisal. Cambridge, Mass., 1959.

Henderson, W. O. The State and the Industrial Revolution in Prussia, 1740–1870. Liverpool, 1958.

———. The Zollverein. Cambridge, 1939.

Hennig, Richard. Die älteste Entwicklung der Telegraphie und Telephonie. Leipzig, 1908.

Herre, Paul. Kronprinz Wilhelm: Seine Rolle in der deutschen Politik. Munich, 1954.

Hertz, Frederick. The Development of the German Public Mind: A Social History of German Political Sentiments, Aspirations, and Ideas. New York, 1957.

Hess, Adalbert. Das Parlament das Bismarck widerstrebte: Zur Politik und sozialen Zusammensetzung des preussischen Abgeordnetenhauses der Konfliktszeit (1862–1866). Politische Forschungen, vol. 6. Cologne, 1964.

———. Die Landtags-und Reichstagswahlen im Grossherzogtum Hessen 1865–1871. Oberursel/Taunus, n.d. [1958].

Heuss, Theodor. Friedrich Naumann: Der Mann, das Werk, die Zeit. Stuttgart, 1937.

———. Robert Bosch: Leben und Leistung. Stuttgart, 1946.

Hintze, Otto. Soziologie und Geschichte: Gesammelte Abhandlungen zur Soziologie, Politik und Theorie der Geschichte. 2d ed. Göttingen, 1964.

———. Staat und Verfassung: Gesammelte Abhandlungen zur allgemeinen Verfassungsgeschichte. 2d ed. Göttingen, 1962.

Hirsch, Paul. Der Weg der Sozialdemokratie zur Macht in Preussen. Berlin, 1929.

———, and Hugo Lindemann. Das kommunale Wahlrecht. Sozialdemokratische Gemeindepolitik: Kommunalpolitische Abhandlungen, vol. 1. Berlin, 1905.

Hochdorf, Max. *August Bebel: Geschichte einer politischen Vernunft.* Berlin, 1932.

Hock, Wolfgang. *Liberales Denken im Zeitalter der Paulskirche: Droysen und die Frankfurter Mitte.* Münster, 1957.

Höhn, Reinhard. *Die Armee als Erziehungsschule der Nation: Das Ende einer Idee.* Bad Harzburg, 1963.

————. *Sozialismus und Heer.* 2 vols. Bad Homburg, 1959.

————. *Verfassungskampf und Heereseid: Der Kampf des Bürgertums um das Heer (1815–1850).* Leipzig, 1938.

Hoffer, Eric. *The True Believer: Thoughts on the Nature of Mass Movements.* New York, 1951.

Hoffman, Walther G., Franz Grumbach, and Helmut Hesse. *Das Wachstum der deutschen Wirtschaft seit der Mitte des 19. Jahrhunderts.* Berlin, 1965.

Holborn, Hajo. *A History of Modern Germany: The Reformation.* New York, 1959.

————. *A History of Modern Germany: 1648–1840.* New York, 1964.

Hollyday, Frederic B. M. *Bismarck's Rival: A Political Biography of General and Admiral Albrecht von Stosch.* Durham, N.C., 1960.

Holtman, Robert B. *Napoleonic Propaganda.* Baton Rouge, 1950.

Howard, Michael. *The Franco-Prussian War: The German Invasion of France, 1870–1871.* New York, 1962.

Huber, Ernst Rudolf. *Deutsche Verfassungsgeschichte seit 1789.* 4 vols. Stuttgart, 1957–69.

Hughes, H. Stuart. *Consciousness and Society: The Reorientation of European Social Thought, 1890–1930.* New York, 1958.

Hulse, James W. *Revolutionists in London; A Study of Five Unorthodox Socialists.* Oxford, 1970.

Iggers, Georg G. *The German Conception of History: The National Tradition of Historical Thought from Herder to the Present.* Middletown, Conn., 1968.

Ihering, H. *Heinrich Mann, sein Leben und sein Werk.* Berlin, 1951.

Jacob, Herbert. *German Administration since Bismarck: Central Authority versus Local Autonomy.* New Haven, 1963.

Jaeger, Hans. *Unternehmer in der deutschen Politik (1890–1918).* Bonn, 1967.

Jansen, Reinhard. *Georg von Vollmar: Eine politische Biographie.* Düsseldorf, 1958.

Jantke, Carl, and Dietrich Hilger, eds. *Die Eigentumslosen: Der deutsche Pauperismus und die Emanzipationskrise in Darstellungen und Deutungen der Zeitgenössischen Literatur*. Freiburg, 1965.

Jarausch, Konrad H. *The Enigmatic Chancellor: Bethmann-Hollweg and the Hubris of Imperial Germany*. New Haven, 1973.

Joll, James. *The Second International, 1889–1914*. New York, 1956.

Kaeber, Ernst. *Berlin 1848: Zur Hundertjahrfeier...* Berlin, 1948.

Kaelble, Hartmut. *Industrielle Interessenpolitik in der Wilhelminischen Gesellschaft: Centralverband Deutscher Industrieller 1895–1914*. Berlin, 1967.

Kaiser, Renate. *Die politischen Strömungen in den Kreisen Bonn und Rheinbach 1848–1878*. Bonn, 1963.

Kandel, I. L. *The Training of Elementary School Teachers in Germany*. New York, 1910.

Kann, Robert A. *The Multinational Empire: Nationalism and National Reform in the Habsburg Monarchy, 1848–1918*. 2 vols. New York, 1950.

Kaufmann, Walter A. *Nietzsche: Philosopher, Psychologist, Anti-Christ*. Princeton, 1950.

Kautz, Klara. *Das deutsche Frankreichbild in der ersten Hälfte des 19. Jahrhunderts nach Reisebeschreibungen, Tagebüchern und Briefen*. Cologne, 1957.

Kehr, Eckart. *Der Primat der Innenpolitik: Gesammelte Aufsätze zur preussisch-deutschen Sozialgeschichte im 19. und 20. Jahrhundert*. Berlin, 1965.

———. *Schlachtflottenbau und Parteipolitik 1894–1901*. Historische Studien, vol. 197. Berlin, 1930.

Keim, Jeanette. *Forty Years of German-American Political Relations*. Philadelphia, 1919.

Kingsbury, J. E. *The Telephone and Telephone Exchanges: Their Invention and Development*. London, 1965.

Kissinger, Henry A. *A World Restored*. Universal Library. New York, 1964.

Kitchen, Martin. *The German Officer Corps, 1890–1914*. Oxford, 1968.

Klein, Ernst. *Von der Reform zur Restoration: Finanzpolitik und Reformgesetzgebung des preussischen Staatskanzlers Karl August von Hardenberg*. Berlin, 1965.

Kleine, Georg H. *Der württembergische Ministerpräsident Freiherr Hermann von Mittnacht (1825–1909)*. Veröffentlichungen der Kommission für geschichtliche Landeskunde in Baden-Württemberg, Series B: Forschungen, vol. 50. Stuttgart, 1969.

Klemperer, Klemens von. *Germany's New Conservatism: Its History and Dilemma in the Twentieth Century*. Princeton, 1957.

Kliersfeld, Josef. *Die Haltung Kaiser Wilhelms II. zur Arbeiterbewegung und zur Sozialdemokratie*. Kallmünz, 1933.

Knoll, Joachim H. *Führungsauslese in Liberalismus und Demokratie: Zur politischen Geistesgeschichte der letzten hundert Jahre*. Stuttgart, 1957.

Koch, Max Jürgen. *Die Bergarbeiterbewegung im Ruhrgebiet zur Zeit Wilhelms II (1889–1914)*. Düsseldorf, 1954.

Kohn, Hans. *The Mind of Germany: The Education of a Nation*. New York, 1960.

———. *Prelude to Nation-States: The French and German Experience, 1789–1815*. Princeton, 1967.

Kohn-Bramstedt, Ernst. *Aristocracy and the Middle-Classes in Germany: Social Types in German Literature, 1830–1900*. London, 1937.

Köllmann, Wolfgang. *Friedrich Harkort*. Vol. 1, *1793–1838*. Düsseldorf, 1964.

Korn, Karl. *Die Arbeiterjugendbewegung: Einführung in ihre Geschichte*. Berlin, 1922.

Koselleck, Reinhart. *Preussen zwischen Reform und Revolution: Allgemeines Landrecht, Verwaltung und soziale Bewegung von 1791 bis 1848*. Stuttgart, 1967.

Koszyk, Kurt. *Anfänge und frühe Entwicklung der sozialdemokratische Presse im Ruhrgebiet (1875–1908)*. Dortmund, 1953.

———. *Deutsche Presse im 19. Jahrhundert*. Berlin, 1966.

Kotowski, Georg. *Friedrich Ebert: Eine politische Biographie*. Vol. 1, *Der Aufstieg eines deutschen Arbeiterführers 1871 bis 1917*. Wiesbaden, 1963.

Kötzschke, Rudolf, and Hellmut Kretzschmar. *Sächsische Geschichte*. 1925. Reprint. Frankfurt am Main, 1965.

Kracke, Friedrich. *Friedrich August III, Sachsens volkstümlichster König. Ein Bild seines Lebens und seiner Zeit*. Schriftenreihe für sächsische Geschichte und Kultur, vol. 3. Munich, 1964.

Kraehe, Enno E. *Metternich's German Policy*. Vol. 1, *The Contest with Napoleon, 1799–1814*. Princeton, 1963.

Krause, Hans. *Die demokratische Partei von 1848 und die soziale Frage: Ein Beitrag zur Geschichte der ersten deutschen Revolution*. Frankfurt, 1923.

Kremer, Willy. *Der soziale Aufbau der Parteien des deutschen Reichstages von 1871–1918*. Emsdetten, 1934.

Krieger, Leonard. *The German Idea of Freedom: History of a Political Tradition*. Boston, 1957.

————, ed. *The German Revolutions*. Chicago, 1967.

————, and Fritz Stern, eds. *The Responsibility of Power: Historical Essays in Honor of Hajo Holborn*. New York, 1967.

Kropat, Wolf-Arno. *Frankfurt zwischen Provinzialismus und Nationalismus. Die Eingliederung der "Freien Stadt" in den Preussischen Staat (1866–1871)*. Studien zur Frankfurter Geschichte, vol. 4. Frankfurt am Main, 1971.

Kruck, Alfred. *Geschichte des Alldeutschen Verbandes 1890–1939*. Wiesbaden, 1954.

Kuczynski, Jürgen. *Die Geschichte der Lage der Arbeiter unter dem Kapitalismus*. 37 vols. Berlin, 1961–67.

————. *Gestalten und Werke. Soziologische Studien zur deutschen Literatur*. Berlin, 1969.

Kuhn, Annettte. *Die Kirche im Ringen mit dem Sozialismus 1803–1848: Eine historische Studie*. Munich, 1965.

Kupisch, Karl. *Die deutschen Landeskirchen im 19. und 20. Jahrhundert*. Göttingen, 1966.

————. *Zwischen Idealismus und Massendemokratie: Eine Geschichte der evangelischen Kirche in Deutschland von 1815–1945*. Berlin, 1955.

Kürenberg, Joachim von (pseud. J. von Reichel). *The Kaiser: A Life of Wilhelm II, Last Emperor of Germany*. Translated by H. T. Russell and Herta Hagen. London, 1954.

Lambi, Ivo Nikolai. *Free Trade and Protection in Germany, 1868–1879*. Wiesbaden, 1963.

Lamer, Reinhard J. *Der englische Parlamentarismus in der deutschen politischen Theorie im Zeitalter Bismarcks (1857–1890)*. Lübeck, 1963.

Langer, William L. *Political and Social Upheaval, 1832–1852*. New York, 1969.

Learned, William Setchel. *The Oberlehrer: A Study of the Social and Professional Evolution of the German Schoolmaster*. Cambridge, Mass., 1914.

Lefèbvre, Georges. *The French Revolution from 1793 to 1799*. Translated by John Hall Stewart and James Friguglietti. London, 1964.

Legge, J. G. *Rhyme and Revolution in Germany: A Study in German History, Life, Literature and Character, 1813–1850*. New York, 1919.

Leidigkeit, Karl-Heinz. *Wilhelm Liebknecht und August Bebel in der deutschen Arbeiterbewegung 1862–1869*. Berlin, 1957.

Lexis, W. *A General View of the History and Organisation of Public*

Education in the German Empire. Translated by G. J. Tamson. Berlin, 1904.

Lichtheim, George. *The Origins of Socialism.* New York, 1969.

Lidtke, Vernon L. *The Outlawed Party: Social Democracy in Germany, 1878–1890.* Princeton, 1966.

Liebel, Helen P. *Enlightened Bureaucracy versus Enlightened Despotism in Baden, 1750–1792.* Transactions of the American Philosophical Society, N.S., vol. 55. Philadelphia, 1965.

Lindenberger, Herbert. *Georg Büchner.* Carbondale, Ill., 1964.

Lindenlaub, Dieter. *Richtungskämpfe im Verein für Sozialpolitik: Wissenschaft und Sozialpolitik im Kaiserreich vornehmlich vom Beginn des "neuen Kurses" bis zum Ausbruch des Ersten Weltkrieges (1890–1914).* 2 vols. Wiesbaden, 1967.

Lipinski, Richard. *Die Sozialdemokratie von ihren Anfängen bis zur Gegenwart.* 2 vols. Berlin, 1927–28.

Losch, Philipp. *Geschichte des Kurfürstentums Hessen, 1803 bis 1866.* Marburg, 1922.

Lowie, Robert H. *Toward Understanding Germany,* Chicago, 1954.

Löwith, Karl. *From Hegel to Nietzsche: The Revolution in Nineteenth-Century Thought.* Translated by David E. Green. Garden City, N.Y., 1967.

Lukács, Georg. *Von Nietzsche bis Hitler oder der Irrationalismus in der deutschen Politik.* Hamburg, 1966.

Mackeprang, M. *Nord-Schleswig von 1864–1911.* Jena, 1912.

McConagha, W. A. *Development of the Labor Movement in Great Britain, France and Germany.* Chapel Hill, 1942.

Mandelbaum, Kurt. *Die Erörterungen innerhalb der deutschen Sozialdemokratie über das Problem des Imperialismus (1895–1914).* Frankfurt, 1926.

Mann, Golo. *Deutsche Geschichte des neunzehnten und zwanzigsten Jahrhunderts.* Frankfurt, 1958.

Mann, Heinrich. *Der Untertan.* Leipzig, 1918.

Marcks, Erich. *Kaiser Wilhelm I.* Leipzig, 1897.

Marienfeld, Wolfgang. *Wissenschaft und Schlachtflottenbau in Deutschland 1897–1906.* Supplement 2 of the *Marine Rundschau.* Berlin, 1957.

Martini, Fritz. *Deutsche Literaturgeschichte von den Anfängen bis zur Gegenwart.* 4th ed. Stuttgart, 1952.

Massie, Robert K. *Nicholas and Alexandra.* New York, 1971.

Massing, Paul W. *Rehearsal for Destruction: A Study of Political Anti-Semitism in Imperial Germany.* New York, 1949.

Masur, Gerhard. *Imperial Berlin.* New York, 1970.

————. *Prophets of Yesterday: Studies in European Culture, 1890–1914.* New York, 1961.

Mattes, Wilhelm. *Die bayerischen Bauernräte: Eine soziologische und historische Untersuchung über bäuerliche Politik*. Stuttgart, 1921.

Mayer, Arno J. *Dynamics of Counterrevolution in Europe, 1870– 1956: An Analytic Framework*. New York, 1971.

Mayer, Gustav. *Friedrich Engels: A Biography*. New York, 1936.

Mayer, J. P. *Max Weber and German Politics: A Study in Political Sociology*. London, 1944.

Mayeur, Jean-Marie. *Autonomie et politique en Alsace. La Constitution de 1911*. Paris, 1970.

Mehring, Franz. *Geschichte der deutschen Sozialdemokratie*. 12th ed. 4 books in 2 vols. Berlin, 1922.

Meinecke, Friedrich. *The German Catastrophe: Reflections and Recollections*. Translated by Sidney B. Fay. Cambridge, Mass., 1950.

————. *Weltbürgertum und Nationalstaat: Studien zur Genesis des deutschen Nationalstaates*. Munich, 1908. English translation of 7th ed. (1928), *Cosmopolitanism and the National State*. Translated by Robert B. Kimber. Princeton, 1970.

Mesmer-Strupp, Beatrix. *Arnold Ruges Plan einer Alliance intellectuelle zwischen Deutschen und Franzosen*. Bern, 1963.

Meyer, Arnold Oskar. *Bismarck: Der Mensch und der Staatsmann*. Stuttgart, 1949.

————. *Bismarcks Kampf mit Österreich am Bundestag zu Frankfurt (1851 bis 1859)*. Berlin, 1927.

Meyer, Gustav. *Friedrich Engels: A Biography*. New York, 1936.

Meyer, Karl W. *Karl Liebknecht, Man without a Country*. Introduction by C. V. Easum. Washington, 1957.

Michels, Robert. *Political Parties: A Sociological Study of the Oligarchical Tendencies of Modern Democracy*. Translated by Eden Paul and Cedar Paul. New York, 1915.

Mieck, Ilja. *Preussische Gewerbepolitik in Berlin 1806–1844: Staatshilfe und Privatinitiative zwischen Merkantilismus und Liberalismus*. Berlin, 1965.

Milatz, Alfred, ed. *Friedrich-Naumann-Bibliographie*. Düsseldorf, 1957.

Miller, Max and Paul Sauer. *Die württembergische Geschichte von der Reichsgründung bis heute*. Stuttgart, 1971.

Miller, Susanne. *Das Problem der Freiheit im Sozialismus: Freiheit, Staat und Revolution in der Programmatik der Sozialdemokratie von Lassalle bis zum Revisionismusstreit*. Frankfurt am Main, 1964.

Millman, Richard. *British Foreign Policy and the Coming of the Franco-Prussian War*. Oxford, 1965.

Misteli, Herman. *Carl Vogt: Seine Entwicklung vom angehenden naturwissenschaftlichen Materialisten zum idealen Politiker der Paulskirche (1817–1849)*. Zurich, 1938.

Mitzman, Arthur. *The Iron Cage: An Historical Interpretation of Max Weber*. New York, 1970.

Mommsen, Wilhelm. *Bismarcks Sturz und die Parteien*. Stuttgart, 1924.

————, ed. *Deutsche Parteiprogramme*. Munich, 1960.

————. *Grösse und Versagen des deutschen Bürgertums: Ein Beitrag zur politischen Bewegung des 19. Jahrhunderts, insbesondere zur Revolution 1848/49*. 2d ed. Munich, 1964.

Mommsen, Wolfgang. *Max Weber und die deutsche Politik 1890–1920*. Tübingen, 1959.

Morgan, Roger. *The German Social Democrats and the First International, 1864–1872*. Cambridge, 1965.

Morsey, Rudolf. *Die deutsche Zentrumspartei 1917–1923*. Beiträge zur Geschichte des Parlamentarismus und der politischen Parteien, vol. 32. Düsseldorf, 1966.

————. *Die oberste Reichsverwaltung unter Bismarck 1867–1890*. Münster, 1957.

Mosse, George L. *The Crisis of German Ideology: Intellectual Origins of the Third Reich*. New York, 1964.

Mosse, W. E. *The European Powers and the German Question, 1848–71, with Special Reference to England and Russia*. Cambridge, 1958.

Müller, Gunther. *König Max II. und die soziale Frage*. Politische Studien, Supplement 1. Munich, 1964.

Muncy, Lysbeth Walker. *The Junker in the Prussian Administration under William II, 1888–1914*. Providence, R.I., 1944.

Na'aman, Shlomo. *Demokratische und soziale Impulse in der Frühgeschichte der deutschen Arbeiterbewegung der Jahre 1862/63*. Wiesbaden, 1969.

Naher, Walter. *Arnold Ruge als Politiker und politischer Schriftsteller: Ein Beitrag zur deutschen Geschichte des 19. Jahrhunderts*. Heidelberg, 1933.

Nauwerck, Karl. *Statistisches Wörterbuch über die Vereinigten Staaten*. Leipzig, 1853.

Neitzke, Paul. *Die deutschen politischen Flüchtlinge in der Schweiz 1848–49*. Charlottenburg, 1926.

Nestriepke, Siegfried. *Die Gewerkschaftsbewegung*. 3 vols. Stuttgart, 1922–23.

Nettl, J. P. *Rosa Luxemburg*, 2 vols. London, 1966. Also an abridged ed., Oxford, 1969.

Neumann, Franz. Edited by Herbert Marcuse. *The Democratic and the Authoritarian State: Essays in Political and Legal Theory.* Glencoe, Ill., 1957.

Neumann, Sigmund. *Die Stufen des preussischen Konservatismus: Ein Beitrag zum Staats-und-Gesellschaftsbild Deutschlands im 19. Jahrhundert.* Berlin, 1930.

Neumann-Hofer, Adolf. *Die Entwicklung der Sozialdemokratie bei den Wahlen zum deutschen Reichstag 1871–1903.* Berlin, 1903.

Nichols, J. Alden. *Germany after Bismarck: The Caprivi Era, 1890–1894.* Cambridge, Mass., 1958.

Niewyk, Donald L. *Socialist, Anti-Semite, and Jew: German Social Democracy Confronts the Problem of Anti-Semitism, 1918–1933.* Baton Rouge, 1971.

Nipperdey, Thomas. *Die Organisation der deutschen Parteien vor 1918.* Beiträge zur Geschichte des Parlamentarismus und der politische Parteien, vol. 18. Düsseldorf, 1961.

Noland, Aaron. *The Founding of the French Socialist Party (1893–1905).* Cambridge, Mass., 1956.

Nowak, Karl Friedrich. *Kaiser and Chancellor: The Opening Years of the Reign of Kaiser William II.* Translated by E. W. Dickes. New York, 1930.

Noyes, P. H. *Organization and Revolution: Working-Class Associations in the German Revolutions of 1848–1849.* Princeton, 1966.

Oelssner, Fred. *Rosa Luxemburg: Eine kritische biographische Skizze.* 2d ed. Berlin, 1952.

Olden, Rudolf. *The History of Liberty in Germany.* London, 1946.

Oncken, Hermann. *Lassalle: Eine politische Biographie.* 3d ed. Stuttgart, 1920.

Opel, Fritz. *Der deutsche Metallarbeiter-Verband während des ersten Weltkrieges und der Revolution.* Hanover, 1957.

Pack, Wolfgang. *Das parlamentarische Ringen um das Sozialistengesetz Bismarcks 1878–1890.* Düsseldorf, 1961.

Pagel, Karl. *Mecklenburg, Biographie eines deutschen Landes.* Göttingen, 1969.

Palmer, R. R. *The Age of the Democratic Revolution.* 2 vols. Princeton, 1959–64.

Paret, Peter. *Yorck and the Era of Prussian Reform, 1807–1815.* Princeton, 1966.

Paulsen, Friedrich. *German Education: Past and Present.* Translated by T. Lorenz. New York, 1912.

———. *The German Universities and University Study.* Translated by Frank Thilly and William Y. Elwang. New York, 1906.

Perkins, Dexter. *Hands Off: A History of the Monroe Doctrine*. Boston, 1941.

Perry, Thomas Sergeant, ed. *The Life and Letters of Francis Lieber*. Boston, 1882.

Peters, Max. *Friedrich Ebert, erster Präsident der deutschen Republik; sein Werden und Wirken*. 2d ed. Berlin, 1954.

Pflanze, Otto. *Bismarck and the Development of Germany: The Period of Unification, 1815–1871*. Princeton, 1963.

Pinson, Koppel S. *Modern Germany: Its History and Civilization*. New York, 1954.

Plickat, Hans-Heinrich. *Die Schule als Instrument des sozialen Aufstiegs*. Weinheim/Bergstrasse, 1959.

Pochmann, Henry A. *German Culture in America: Philosophical and Literary Influences, 1600–1900*. Madison, Wisc., 1957.

Pois, Robert A. *Friedrich Meinecke and German Politics in the Twentieth Century*. Berkeley, 1972.

Pöls, Werner. *Sozialistenfrage und Revolutionsfurcht in ihrem Zusammenhang mit den angeblichen Staatsstreichplänen Bismarcks*. Historische Studien, vol. 277. Lübeck, 1960.

Pothoff, Heinrich. *Die deutsche Politik Beusts von seiner Berufung zum österreichischen Aussenminister Oktober 1866 bis zum Ausbruch des deutsch-französischen Krieges 1870/71*. Bonner Historische Forschungen, vol. 31. Bonn, 1968.

Pottinger, E. Ann. *Napoleon III and the German Crisis, 1865–1866*. Cambridge, Mass., 1966.

Preradovich, Nikolaus von. *Die Führungsschichten in Österreich und Preussen (1804–1918) mit einem Ausblick bis zum Jahre 1945*. Wiesbaden, 1955.

Preuss, Hugo. *Das deutsche Volk und die Politik*. Jena, 1915.

Pross, Harry. *Literatur und Politik, Geschichte und Programme der politisch-literarischen Zeitschriften im deutschen Sprachgebiet seit 1870*. Olten, 1963.

Puhle, Hans-Jürgen. *Agrarische Interessenpolitik und preussischer Konservatismus im Wilhelminischen Reich (1893–1914): Ein Beitrag zur Analyse des Nationalismus in Deutschland am Beispiel des Bundes der Landwirte und der Deutsch Konservativen Partei*. Hanover, 1966.

Pulzer, P. G. J. *The Rise of Political Anti-Semitism in Germany and Austria*. New York, 1964.

Puppke, Ludwig. *Sozialpolitik und soziale Anschauungen frühindustrieller Unternehmer in Rheinland-Westfalen*. Cologne, 1966.

Quandt, Otto. *Die Anfänge der Bismarckschen Sozialgesetzgebung und die Haltung der Parteien (Das Unfallversicherungsgesetz 1881–1884)*. Berlin, 1938.

Raabe, Wilhelm. *Horacker*. Berlin, 1931.

Raack, R. C. *The Fall of Stein*. Cambridge, Mass., 1965.

Ramm, Agatha. *Germany, 1789–1919: A Political History*. London, 1967.

Rang, Adalbert. *Der politische Pestalozzi*. Frankfurt am Main, 1967.

Rapp, Adolf. *Der Kampf um die Demokratie in Deutschland seit der grossen französischen Revolution*. Berlin, 1923.

————. *Die Württemberger und die nationale Frage 1863–1871*. Stuttgart, 1910.

Rath, R. John. *The Viennese Revolution of 1848*. Austin, Tex., 1957.

Rathje, J. *Die Welt des freien Protestantismus, dargestellt an Leben und Werk von Martin Rade*. Stuttgart, 1952.

Real, Willy. *Der Deutsche Reformverein: Grossdeutsche Stimmen und Kräfte zwischen Villafranca und Königgrätz*. Historische Studien, vol. 395. Lübeck, 1966.

Reddaway, W. F. *Frederick the Great and the Rise of Prussia*. New York, 1904.

Rein, Gustav Adolf. *Die Revolution in der Politik Bismarcks*. Göttingen, 1957.

Reiners, Ludwig. *Bismarck*. 2 vols. Munich, 1956–57.

Reisner, Edward H. *Nationalism and Education since 1789: A Social and Political History of Modern Education*. New York, 1922.

Repgen, Konrad. *Märzbewegung und Maiwahlen des Revolutionsjahres 1848 im Rheinland*. Bonn, 1955.

————, and Stephan Skalweit, eds. *Spiegel der Geschichte: Festgabe für Max Braubach zum 10. April 1964*. Münster, 1964.

Rich, Norman. *Friedrich von Holstein: Politics and Diplomacy in the Era of Bismarck and William II*. 2 vols. Cambridge, 1965.

Richter, Werner. *Bismarck*. Translated by Brian Battershaw. London, 1964.

Rieger, Isolde. *Die Wilhelminische Presse im Überblick 1888–1918*. Munich, 1957

Rikli, Erika. *Der Revisionismus: Ein Revisions-Versuch der deutschen Marxistischen Theorie (1890–1914)*. Zürich, 1936.

Ringer, Fritz K. *The Decline of the German Mandarins: The German Academic Community, 1890–1933*. Cambridge, Mass., 1969.

Ritter, Emil. *Die katholisch-soziale Bewegung Deutschlands im 19. Jahrhundert und der Volksverein*. Cologne, 1954.

————. *Der Weg des politischen Katholizismus in Deutschland*. Breslau, 1934.

Ritter, Gerhard. *Das deutsche Problem: Grundfragen deutschen Staatslebens gestern und heute*. Munich, 1962.

————. *Friedrich der Grosse: Ein historisches Profil*. 3d ed. Heidelberg, 1954.

————. *Lebendige Vergangenheit: Beiträge zur historisch-politischen Selbstbesinnung*. Munich, 1958.

————. *Der Schlieffenplan: Kritik eines Mythos*. Munich, 1956.

————. *Staatskunst und Kriegshandwerk: Das Problem des "Militarismus" in Deutschland*. 4 vols. Munich, 1954–68.

Ritter, Gerhard A. *Die Arbeiterbewegung im Wilhelminischen Reich: Die Sozialdemokratische Partei und die Freien Gewerkschaften 1890–1900*. Berlin-Dahlem, 1959.

Roberts, David. *Artistic Consciousness and Political Conscience: The Novels of Heinrich Mann, 1900–1938*. Australisch-Neuseeländische Studien zur deutschen Sprache und Literatur, vol. 2. Berne, 1971.

Robertson, Charles Grant. *Bismarck*. New York, 1919.

Robertson, Priscilla. *Revolutions of 1848: A Social History*. Princeton, 1952.

Robinson, James Harvey. *The German Bundesrath: A Study in Comparative Constitutional Law*. University of Pennsylvania Political Economy and Public Law Series, vol. 3, no. 1. Philadelphia, 1891.

Robson-Scott, W. B. *German Travellers in England, 1400–1800*. Oxford, 1953.

Röhl, J. C. G. *Germany without Bismarck: The Crisis of Government in the Second Reich, 1890–1900*. Berkeley, 1967.

Rohr, Donald G. *The Origins of Social Liberalism in Germany*. Chicago, 1963.

Röhrbein, Waldemar. *Hamburg und der hannoversche Verfassungskonflikt 1837–1840*. Quellen und Darstellungen zur Geschichte Niedersachsens, vol. 67. Hildesheim, 1965.

Rosenberg, Arthur. *The Birth of the German Republic, 1871–1918*. Translated by Ian F. D. Morrow. New York, 1931.

Rosenberg, Hans. *Bureaucracy, Aristocracy, and Autocracy: The Prussian Experience, 1660–1815*. Cambridge, Mass., 1958.

————. *Grosse Depression und Bismarckzeit: Wirtschaftsablauf, Gesellschaft und Politik in Mitteleuropa*. Berlin, 1967.

————, ed. *Die nationalpolitische Publizistik Deutschlands vom Eintritt der neuen Ära in Preussen bis zum Ausbruch des deutschen Krieges: Eine kritische Bibliographie*. 2 vols. Munich, 1935.

————. *Probleme der deutschen Sozialgeschichte*. Frankfurt, 1969.

————. *Rudolf Haym und die Anfänge des klassischen Liberalismus*. Munich, 1933.

————. *Die Weltwirtschaftskrisis von 1857–1859*. Vierteljahrschrift für Sozial-und Wirtschaftsgeschichte, Supplement 30. Stuttgart, 1934.

Rössler, Hellmuth. *Österreichs Kampf um Deutschlands Befreiung: Die deutsche Politik der nationalen Führer Österreichs 1805–1815*. 2 vols. Hamburg, 1940.

Roth, Eugen. *Simplicissimus: Ein Rückblick auf die satirische Zeitschrift*. Hanover, 1954.

Ruggiero, Guido de. *The History of European Liberalism*. Translated by R. G. Collingwood. Oxford, 1927.

Samuel, R. H. and R. Hinton Thomas. *Education and Society in Modern Germany*. London, 1949.

Schallenberger, Horst. *Untersuchungen zum Geschichtsbild der Wilhelminischen Ära und der Weimarer Zeit: Eine vergleichende Schulbuchanalyse deutscher Schulgeschichtsbücher aus der Zeit von 1888 bis 1933*. Ratingen bei Düsseldorf, 1964.

Schieder, Theodor. *Das deutsche Kaiserreich von 1871 als National-staat*. Wissenschaftliche Abhandlungen der Arbeitsgemeinschaft für Forschung des Landes Nordrhein-Westfalen, vol. 20. Cologne, 1961.

————. *Die kleindeutsche Partei in Bayern in den Kämpfen um die nationale Einheit 1863–1871*. Munich, 1936.

————. *Staat und Gesellschaft im Wandel unserer Zeit: Studien zur Geschichte des 19. und 20. Jahrhunderts*. Munich, 1958.

Schieder, Wolfgang. *Anfänge der deutschen Arbeiterbewegung: Die Auslandsvereine im Jahrzehnt nach der Julirevolution von 1830*. Stuttgart, 1963.

Schierbaum, Hansjürgen. *Die politischen Wahlen in den Eifel-und Moselkreisen des Regierungsbezirks Trier 1849–1867*. Düsseldorf, 1960.

Schilfert, Gerhard. *Sieg und Niederlage des demokratischen Wahlrechts in der deutschen Revolution 1848/49*. Berlin, 1952.

Schlick, Werner. *Das Georg Büchner-Schrifttum bis 1965; Eine internationale Bibliographie*. Hildesheim, 1968.

Schlieper, Inge. *Wurzeln der Demokratie in der deutschen Geschichte*. Bonn, 1967.

Schlottenloher, Karl. *Flugblatt und Zeitung: Ein Wegweiser durch das gedruckte Tagesschrifttum*. Berlin, 1922.

Schmidt, Gustav. *Deutscher Historismus und der Übergang zur parlamentarischen Demokratie: Untersuchungen zu den politischen*

Gedanken von Meinecke, Troeltsch, Max Weber. Historische Studien, vol. 389. Lübeck, 1964.

Schmidt, Heinrich. *Die deutschen Flüchtlinge in der Schweiz 1833–1836.* Zurich, 1899.

Schmitt, Carl. *Hugo Preuss: Sein Staatsbegriff und seine Stellung in der deutschen Staatslehre.* Tübingen, 1930.

————. *Staatsgefüge und Zusammenbruch des zweiten Reiches: Der Sieg des Bürgers über den Soldaten.* Hamburg, 1934.

Schnabel, Franz. *Deutsche Geschichte im neunzehnten Jahrhundert.* 4th ed. 4 vols. Freiburg im Breisgau, 1948.

Schneider, Hans. *Der preussische Staatsrat 1817–1918.* Munich, 1952.

Schorr, Helmut J. *Adam Stegerwald: Gewerkschaftler und Politiker der ersten deutschen Republik.* Recklinghausen, 1966.

Schorske, Carl. *German Social Democracy, 1905–1917: The Great Schism.* Cambridge, Mass., 1955.

Schraepler, Ernst. *August-Bebel Bibliographie.* Düsseldorf, 1962.

Schramm, Percy Ernst. *Neun Generationen: Dreihundert Jahre deutscher "Kulturgeschichte" im Lichte der Schicksale einer Hamburger Bürgerfamilie (1648–1948).* 2 vols. Göttingen, 1964.

Schroeder, Paul W. *Metternich's Diplomacy at Its Zenith, 1820–1823.* Austin, Tex., 1962.

Schüddekopf, Otto Ernst. *Die deutsche Innenpolitik im letzten Jahrhundert und der konservative Gedanke.* Braunschweig, 1951.

Schult, Johannes. *Geschichte der Hamburger Arbeiterschaft 1890–1919.* Hanover, 1967.

Schüssler, Wilhelm. *Die Daily-Telegraph Affaire: Fürst Bülow, Kaiser Wilhelm und die Krise des zweiten Reiches 1908.* Göttingen, 1952.

Schwab, Rudolf. *Der deutsche Nationalverein, seine Entstehung und sein Wirken.* Frauenfeld, 1902.

Schwarz, Gotthart. *Theodor Wolff und das "Berliner Tageblatt": Eine liberale Stimme in der deutschen Politik 1906–1933.* Tübinger Studien zur Geschichte und Politik, vol. 25. Tübingen, 1968.

Schwarz, Max, ed. *MdR: Biographisches Handbuch der Reichstage.* Hanover, 1965.

Seeber, Gustav. *Die deutsche Sozialdemokratie und die Entwicklung ihrer revolutionären Parlamentstaktik von 1867 bis 1893.* Berlin, 1966.

————. *Zwischen Bebel und Bismarck: Zur Geschichte des Linksliberalismus in Deutschland 1871–1893.* Berlin, 1965.

Seidl, Helmut. *Streikkämpfe der mittel-und ostdeutschen Braunkohlenbergarbeiter von 1890 bis 1914.* Freiberger Forschungshefte. Leipzig, 1964.

Seier, Hellmut. *Die Staatsidee Heinrich von Sybels in den Wand-lungun der Reichsgründungszeit 1862/71*. Historische Studien, vol. 383. Lübeck, 1961.

Sell, Friedrich C. *Die Tragödie des deutschen Liberalismus*. Stutt-gart, 1953.

Senn, Alfred E. *The Emergence of Modern Lithuania*. New York, 1959.

Shanahan, William O. *German Protestants Face the Social Question*. Notre Dame, 1954.

————. *Prussian Military Reforms, 1786–1813*. New York, 1945.

Shaw, Leroy R. *Gerhard Hauptmann, Witness of Deceit*. University of California Publications in Modern Philology, vol. 50. Berke-ley, 1958.

Sheehan, James J. *The Career of Lujo Brentano: A Study of Liberalism and Social Reform in Imperial Germany*. Chicago, 1966.

Sieburg, Heinz-Otto. *Deutschland und Frankreich in der Geschichts-schreibung des neunzehnten Jahrhunderts*. Wiesbaden, 1954.

Sieger, Walter. *Das erste Jahrzehnt der deutschen Arbeiterjugend-bewegung, 1904–1914*. Schriftenreihe des Instituts für Deutsche Geschichte an der Karl-Marx-Universität, Leipzig, vol. 4. Ber-lin, 1958.

————. *Die junge Front; Die revolutionäre Arbeiterjugend im Kampf gegen den Ersten Weltkrieg*. Berlin, 1958.

Silberner, Edmund. *Moses Hess: Geschichte seines Lebens*. Leiden, 1966.

————. *Sozialisten zur Judenfrage: Ein Beitrag zur Geschichte des Sozialismus vom Anfang des 19. Jahrhunderts bis 1914*. Berlin, 1962.

Silverman, Dan P. *Reluctant Union, Alsace-Lorraine and Imperial Germany, 1871–1918*. University Park, Pa., 1972.

Simon, Klaus. *Die Württembergischen Demokraten: Ihre Stellung und Arbeit im Partein- und Verfassungssystem in Württemberg und im Deutschen Reich 1890–1920*. Veröffentlichungen der Kom-mission für Geschichtliche Landeskunde in Baden-Württem-berg, Ser. B, vol. 52. Stuttgart, 1969.

Simon, Walter M. *The Failure of the Prussian Reform Movement*. Ithaca, 1955.

Slochower, Harry. *Richard Dehmel, der Mensch und der Denker*. Dresden, 1928.

Smith, G. Barnett. *William I and the German Empire: A Biographical and Historical Sketch*. Chicago, 1888.

Snell, John L. *Wartime Origins of the East-West Dilemma over Germany*. New Orleans, 1959.

Sokel, Walter H. *The Writer in Extremis, Expressionism in Twentieth Century German Literature*. Stanford, 1959.

Sontag, Raymond James. *Germany and England: Background of Conflict, 1848–1898*. New York, 1938.

Srbik, Heinrich von. *Deutsche Einheit: Idee und Wirklichkeit vom Heiligen Reich bis Königgrätz*. 3d ed. 4 vols. Munich, 1940–42.

———. *Metternich: Der Staatsmann und der Mensch*. 3 vols. Munich, 1925–54.

Stadelmann, Rudolf. *Soziale und politische Geschichte der Revolution von 1848*. Munich, 1948.

Steefel, Lawrence D. *Bismarck, the Hohenzollern Candidacy, and the Origins of the Franco-German War of 1870*. Cambridge, Mass., 1962.

Steinberg, Hans-Josef. *Sozialismus und deutsche Sozialdemokratie: Zur Ideologie der Partei vor dem I. Weltkrieg*. Schriftenreihe des Forschungsinstituts der Friedrich Ebert-Stiftung: Historisch-politische Schriften. Hanover, 1967.

Steinberg, Jonathan. *Yesterday's Deterrent: Tirpitz and the Birth of the German Battle Fleet*. New York, 1965.

Stenkwitz, Kurt. *Gegen Bajonette und Dividende: Die politische Krise in Deutschland am Vorabend des ersten Weltkrieges*. Berlin, 1960.

———. *"Immer feste druff!" Zabernaffäre 1913*. Berlin, 1962.

Sterling, Richard W. *Ethics in a World of Power: The Political Ideas of Friedrich Meinecke*. Princeton, 1958.

Stern, Fritz. *The Politics of Cultural Despair*. Berkeley, 1961.

Stern, Leo, ed. *Die Auswirkungen der ersten russischen Revolution von 1905–1907 auf Deutschland*. Berlin, 1955.

Stillich, Oscar. *Die politischen Parteien in Deutschland*. 2 vols. Leipzig, 1908.

Stolberg-Wernigerode, Otto Graf zu. *Die unentschiedene Generation. Deutschlands konservative Führungsschichten am Vorabend des Ersten Weltkrieges*. Munich, 1968.

Stoltenberg, Gerhard. *Der deutsche Reichstag 1871–1873*. Düsseldorf, 1955.

Ströbel, Heinrich. *The German Revolution and After*. Translated by H. J. Stenning. London, 1923.

Stubmann, Peter Franz. *Ballin: Leben und Werk eines deutschen Reeders*. Berlin, 1926.

Tänzler, Fritz. *Die deutschen Arbeitgeberverbände 1904–1929: Ein Beitrag zur Geschichte der deutschen Arbeitgeberbewegung*. Berlin, 1929.

Taube, Utz-Friedebert. *Ludwig Quidde: Ein Beitrag zur Geschichte des demokratischen Gedankens in Deutschland*. Kallmünz, 1963.

Taylor, A. J. P. *Bismarck: The Man and the Statesman*. London, 1955.

――――. *The Struggle for Mastery in Europe, 1848–1918*. Oxford, 1954.

Thimme, Annelise. *Gustav Stresemann: Eine politische Biographie zur Geschichte der Weimarer Republic*. Hanover, 1957.

――――. *Hans Delbrück als Kritiker der Wilhelminischen Epoche*. Düsseldorf, 1955.

Thomas, R. Hinton. *Liberalism, Nationalism and the German Intellectuals (1822–1847): An Analysis of the Academic and Scientific Conferences of the Period*. Cambridge, 1951.

Thompson, Silvanus P. *Philipp Reis: Inventor of the Telephone*. London, 1883.

Tilly, Richard. *Financial Institutions and Industrialization in the Rhineland, 1815–1870*. Madison, Wis., 1966.

Tirrell, Sarah Rebecca. *German Agrarian Politics after Bismarck's Fall: The Formation of the Farmer's League*. New York, 1951.

Tormin, Walter. *Geschichte der deutschen Parteien seit 1848*. Stuttgart, 1966.

Toury, Jacob. *Die politischen Orientierungen der Juden in Deutschland: Von Jena bis Weimar*. Tübingen, 1966.

Treitschke, Heinrich von. *Deutsche Geschichte im neunzehnten Jahrhundert*. 5 vols. Leipzig, 1879–94.

Troeltsch, Ernst. *Deutsche Zukunft*. Berlin, 1916.

Tschirch, Otto. *Geschichte der öffentlichen Meinung in Preussen vom Baseler Frieden bis zum Zusammenbruch des Staates (1795–1806)*. 2 vols. Weimar, 1933–34.

Turner, Henry Ashby, Jr. *Stresemann and the Politics of the Weimar Republic*. Princeton, 1963.

Ufermann, Paul, ed. *Alwin Brandes: Leben und Wirken eines deutschen Gewerkschaftsführers*. Berlin, 1949.

Ullman, Richard K., and Stephen King-Hall. *German Parliaments: A Study of the Development of Representative Institutions in Germany*. New York, 1954.

Ullner, Rudolf. *Die Idee des Föderalismus im Jahrzehnt der deutschen Einigungskriege dargestellt unter besonderer Berücksichtigung des Modells der amerikanischen Verfassung für das deutsche politische Denken*. Historische Studien, vol. 393. Lübeck, 1965.

Vagts, Alfred. *Deutsch-Amerikanische Rückwanderung*. Heidelberg, 1960.

Valentin, Veit. *1848: Chapters of German History*. Translated by Ethel Talbot Scheffauer. London, 1940.

————. *Geschichte der deutschen Revolution von 1848–49*. 2 vols. Berlin, 1930–31.

Valjavec, Fritz. *Die Entstehung der politischen Strömungen in Deutschland 1770–1815*. Munich, 1951.

Van der Gragt, F. *Europe's Greatest Tramway Network: Tramways in the Rhein-Ruhr Area of Germany*. Leiden, 1968.

Varain, Heinz Josef. *Freie Gewerkschaften, Sozialdemokratie und Staat: Die Politik der Generalkommission unter der Führung Carl Legiens (1890–1920)*. Düsseldorf, 1956.

Viëtor, Karl. *Georg Büchner: Politik, Dichtung, Wissenschaft*. Bern, 1949.

Vitense, Otto. *Geschichte von Mecklenburg*. Gotha, 1920.

Vogel, Walter. *Bismarcks Arbeiterversicherung: Ihre Entstehung im Kräftespiel der Zeit*. Braunschweig, 1951.

Vollrath, Wilhelm Otto. *Der parlamentarische Kampf um das preussische Dreiklassenwahlrecht*. Jena, 1931.

Vossler, Otto. *Die amerikanischen Revolutionsideal in ihrem Verhältnis zu den europäischen untersucht an Thomas Jefferson*. Historische Zeitschrift, Supplement 18. Munich, 1929.

Wachenheim, Hedwig. *Die deutsche Arbeiterbewegung 1844 bis 1914*. Cologne, 1967.

Wahl, Adalbert, *Deutsche Geschichte von der Reichsgründung bis zum Ausbruch des Weltkrieges (1871 bis 1914)*. 4 vols. Stuttgart, 1926–36.

Walker, Mack. *Germany and the Emigration, 1816–1885*. Cambridge, Mass., 1964.

Wallace, Lillian Parker. *Leo XIII and the Rise of Socialism*. Durham, N.C., 1966.

————. *The Papacy and European Diplomacy, 1869–1878*. Chapel Hill, N.C., 1948.

Waltershausen, A. Sartorius von. *Deutsche Wirtschaftsgeschichte 1815–1914*. 2d rev. ed. Jena, 1923.

Warren, Donald, Jr. *The Red Kingdom of Saxony: Lobbying Grounds for Gustav Stresemann, 1901–1919*. The Hague, 1964.

Webb, Walter Prescott. *The Great Frontier*. Boston, 1952.

Weber, Paul C. *America in Imaginative German Literature in the First Half of the Nineteenth Century*. New York, 1926.

Weber, Rolf. *Kleinbürgerliche Demokraten in der deutschen Einheitsbewegung 1863–1866*. Berlin, 1962.

————. *Die Revolution in Sachsen 1848/49. Entwicklung und Analyse ihre Triebkräfte*. Berlin, 1970.

Wehberg, Hans. *Die Führer der deutschen Friedensbewegung (1890 bis 1923)*. Leipzig, 1923.

————, ed. *Ludwig Quidde: Ein deutscher Demokrat und Vorkämpfer der Völkerverständigung*. Offenbach-am-Main, 1948.

Wehler, Hans-Ulrich. *Sozialdemokratie und Nationalstaat: Die deutsche Sozialdemokratie und die Nationalitätenfrage in Deutschland von Karl Marx bis zum Ausbruch des ersten Weltkrieges*. Würzburg, 1962.

Wenck, Martin. *Friedrich Naumann: Ein Lebensbild*. Berlin, 1920.

Wentzcke, Paul. *Geschichte der deutschen Burschenschaft . . . bis zu den Karlsbader Beschlüssen*. 1919. Reprint. Heidelberg, 1965.

Wernecke, Klaus. *Der Wille zur Weltgeltung: Aussenpolitik und Öffenlichkeit im Kaiserreich am Vorabend des Ersten Weltkrieges*. Düsseldorf, 1970.

Werner, Lothar. *Der Alldeutsche Verband 1890–1918*. Berlin, 1935.

Wertheimer, Mildred S. *The Pan-German League, 1890–1914*. New York, 1924.

Westra, Pier. *Georg Büchner dans ses rapports avec ses contemporains*. Paris, 1946.

Wheeler-Bennett, J. W. *Three Episodes in the Life of Kaiser Wilhelm II*. The Leslie Stephens Lecture. Oxford, 1955.

Wiegler, Paul. *Wilhelm der Erste: Sein Leben und seine Zeit*. Hellerau bei Dresden, 1927.

Wilhelm, Graf Lynar, Ernst, ed. *Deutsch Kriegsziele 1914–1918: Eine Diskussion*. Frankfurt am Main, 1964.

Wilhelm, Theodor. *Die englische Verfassung und der vormärzliche deutsche Liberalismus: Eine Darstellung und Kritik des Verfassungsbildes der liberalen Führer*. Stuttgart, 1928.

Williamson, Samuel R., Jr. *The Politics of Grand Strategy: Britain and France Prepare for War, 1904–1914*. Cambridge, Mass., 1969.

Windell, George G. *The Catholics and German Unity, 1866–1871*. Minneapolis, 1954.

Winkler, Heinrich August. *Preussischer Liberalismus und deutscher Nationalstaat: Studien zur Geschichte der deutschen Fortschrittspartei 1861–1866*. Tübingen, 1964.

Witt, Peter-Christian. *Die Finanzpolitik des Deutschen Reiches von 1903 bis 1913. Eine Studie zur Innenpolitik des Wilhelminischen Deutschland*. Historische Studien, vol. 415. Lübeck, 1970.

Wittke, Carl. *Against the Current: The Life of Karl Heinzen (1809–80)*. Chicago, 1945.

————. *Refugees of Revolution: The German Forty-Eighters in America*. Philadelphia, 1952.

Wolfe, Bertram D. *Three Who Made a Revolution: A Biographical History*. New York, 1948.

Young, Harry F. *Maximilian Harden, Censor Germaniae*. The Hague, 1958.

Zechlin, Egmont. *Staatsstreichpläne Bismarcks und Wilhelms II, 1890–1894*. Stuttgart, 1929.

———, and Hans Joachim Bieter. *Die deutsche Politik und die Juden im ersten Weltkrieg*. Göttingen, 1969.

Zehntner, Hans. *Das Staats Lexikon von Rotteck und Welcker: Eine Studie zur Geschichte des deutschen Frühliberalismus*. Jena, 1929.

Ziegler, Donald J. *Prelude to Democracy: A Study of Proportional Representation and the Heritage of Weimar Germany, 1871–1920*. Lincoln, Neb., 1958.

Ziegler, Theobald. *Die geistigen und sozialen Strömungen Deutschlands im 19. und 20. Jahrhundert*. 7th ed. Berlin, 1921.

Ziekursch, Johannes. *Politische Geschichte des neuen deutschen Kaiserreiches*. 3 vols. Frankfurt am Main, 1925–30.

Zmarzlik, Hans-Günter. *Bethmann Hollweg als Reichskanzler: Studien zu Möglichkeiten und Grenzen seiner innerpolitischen Machstellung*. Düsseldorf, 1957.

Zunkel, Friedrich. *Der rheinisch-westfälische Unternehmer 1834–1879: Ein Beitrag zur Geschichte des deutschen Bürgertums im 19. Jahrhundert*. Cologne, 1962.

IV ARTICLES

Abrams, Irwin. "Berta von Suttner and the Nobel Peace Prize," *Journal of Central European Affairs* 22 (1962).

Adam, R. "Johann Jacoby's politischer Werdegang 1805–1840," *Historische Zeitschrift* 143 (1931).

Anon. "Three German Socialists on the War." *Outlook* 62 (Jan. 26, 1916).

Armstrong, Sinclair W. "The Internationalism of the Early Social Democrats of Germany." *American Historical Review* 48 (1942).

———. "The Social Democrats and the Unification of Germany, 1863–71." *Journal of Modern History* 12 (1940).

Ascher, Abraham. "Baron von Stumm, Advocate of a Feudal Capitalism." *Journal of Central European Affairs* 22 (1962).

———. "Professors as Propagandists: The Politics of the *Kathedersozialisten*." *Journal of Central European Affairs* 23 (1963).

Beaton, K. B. "Der konservative Roman in Deutschland nach der Revolution von 1848." *Zeitschrift für Religions-und Geistesgeschichte* 19 (1967).

Becker, Josef. "Zum Problem der Bismarckschen Politik in der Spanischen Thronfrage 1870." *Historische Zeitschrift* 212 (1971).

Berdahl, Robert H. "New Thoughts on German Nationalism," *American Historical Review* 77 (1972).

Berghahn, Volker R. "Zu den Zielen des deutschen Flottenbaus unter Wilhelm II." *Historische Zeitschrift* 210 (1970).

Besson, Waldemar. "Friedrich Meinecke und die Weimarer Republik." *Vierteljahrshefte für Zeitgeschichte* 8 (1959).

Bigler, Robert M. "The Rise of Political Protestantism in Nineteenth Century Germany: The Awakening of Political Consciousness and the Beginnings of Political Activity in the Protestant Clergy of Pre-March Prussia." *Church History* 34 (1965).

Blasius, Dirk. "Lorenz von Stein und Preussen." *Historische Zeitschrift* 212 (1971).

Blumenberg, Werner. "Zur Geschichte des Bundes der Kommunisten: Die Aussagen des Peter Gerhardt Röser." *International Review of Social History* 9 (1964).

Bolle, Fritz. "Darwinismus und Zeitgeist." *Zeitschrift für Religions-und Geistesgeschichte* 14 (1962).

Born, Karl Erich. "Der soziale und wirtschaftliche Strukturwandel Deutschlands am Ende des 19. Jahrhunderts." *Vierteljahrsschrift für Sozial-und Wirtschaftsgeschichte* 50 (1963).

Bornkamm, Heinrich. "Die Staatsidee im Kulturkampf." *Historische Zeitschrift* 170 (1950).

Bramsted, E. "The Position of the Catholic Church in Germany, 1871–1933: Part I." *Journal of Religious History* 2 (1962–63).

Brandenburg, Erich. "Zum älteren deutschen Parteiwesen." *Historische Zeitschrift* 119 (1919).

Buchheim, Karl. "Die Frage nach der katholischen Partei." *Zeitschrift für Politik*, N.F. 10 (1963).

Bussmann, Walter. "Zur Geschichte des deutschen Liberalismus im 19. Jahrhundert." *Historische Zeitschrift* 186 (1958).

Cameron, Rondo E. "Founding the Bank of Darmstadt." *Explorations in Entrepreneurial History* 8 (1955–56).

Cecil, Lamar. "The Creation of Nobles in Prussia, 1871–1918." *American Historical Review* 75 (1970).

Chickering, Roger P. "A Voice of Moderation in Imperial Germany: The 'Verband für Internationale Verständigung,' 1911–1914." *Journal of Contemporary History* 8 (1973).

Coupe, W. A. "The German Cartoon and the Revolution of 1848." *Comparative Studies in Society and History* 9 (1967).

Craig, Gordon A. "Engagement and Neutrality in Germany:

The Case of Georg Forster, 1754–94." *Journal of Modern History* 41 (1969).

————. "Wilhelm von Humboldt as Diplomat." In *Studies in International History*, edited by K. Bourne and D. C. Watt, London, 1967.

De Kay, Drake. "Encyclopedia Americana, First Edition." *Journal of Library History* 3 (1968).

Deuerlein, Ernst. "Ludwig Windthorst." *Stimmen der Zeit* 169 (1961–62).

————. "Verlauf und Ergebnis des 'Zentrumsstreites' (1906–1909)." *Stimmen der Zeit* 156 (1955).

Dorpalen, Andreas. "Emperor Frederick III and the German Liberal Movement." *American Historical Review* 54 (1948).

————. "The German Conservatives and the Parliamentarization of Imperial Germany." *Journal of Central European Affairs* 11 (1951).

————. "The German Struggle against Napoleon: The East German View." *Journal of Modern History* 41 (1969).

————. "Die Revolution von 1848 in der Geschichtsschreibung der DDR." *Historische Zeitschrift* 210 (1970).

Douglass, Elisha P. "German Intellectuals and the American Revolution." *William and Mary Quarterly* 17 (1960).

Droz, Jacques. "Religious Aspects of the Revolutions of 1848 in Europe." In *French Society and Culture since the Old Regime*, edited by Evelyn M. Acomb and Marvin L. Brown, New York, 1967.

Duroselle, Jean-Baptiste. "Die europäischen Staaten und die Gründung des Deutschen Reiches." In *Reichsgründung 1870/71: Tatsachen, Kontroverse, Interpretationen*, edited by Theodor Schieder and Ernst Deuerlein, Stuttgart, 1970.

Eckert, Georg. "Aus der Korrespondenz des Kommunistenbundes (Fraktion Willich-Schapper)." *Archiv für Sozialgeschichte* 5 (1965).

Engelsing, Rolf. "Zur politischen Bildung der deutschen Unterschichten 1789–1863." *Historische Zeitschrift* 206 (1968).

Epstein, Klaus. "Erzberger's Position in the *Zentrumsstreit* before World War I." *Catholic Historical Review* 44 (1958).

Eschenburg, Theodor. "Carl Sonnenschein." *Vierteljahrshefte für Zeitgeschichte* 11 (1963).

Eyck, F. Gunther. "English and French Influences on German Liberalism before 1848." *Journal of the History of Ideas* 18 (1957).

————. "Mazzini's Young Europe." *Journal of Central European Affairs* 17 (1958).

Fehrenbach, Elisabeth. "Die Reichsgründung in der deutschen Geschichtsschreibung." In *Reichsgründung 1870/71: Tatsachen, Kontroverse, Interpretationen*, edited by Theodor Schieder and Ernst Deuerlein, Stuttgart, 1970.

Fink, Ortwin. "Gertrud Bäumer (1873–1954)." In *Deutsche Demokratie von Bebel bis Heuss: Geschichte in Lebensbildern*, edited by Friedrich Andrae and Sybille Schönfeldt, 2d ed. Frankfurt am Main, 1968.

Fischer, Fritz. "Der deutsche Protestantismus und die Politik im 19. Jahrhundert." *Historische Zeitschrift* 171 (1951).

Fischer, Wolfram. "Government Activity and Industrialization in Germany (1815–70)." In *Economics of Take-Off into Sustained Growth*, edited by W. W. Rostow, New York, 1963.

――――. "Soziale Unterschichten im Zeitalter der Frühhindustrialisierung." *International Review of Social History* 8 (1963).

Frauendienst, Werner. "Sozialpolitik Bismarcks—und Heute." *Deutsche Rundschau* 82 (1956).

Fricke, Dieter. "Zur Militarisierung des deutschen Geisteslebens im Wilhelminischen Kaiserreich. Der Fall Leon Arons." *Zeitschrift für Geschichtswissenschaft* 8 (1960).

――――. "Eine wichtige Quelle zur Geschichte der deutschen Arbeiterbewegung." *Beiträge zur Geschichte der deutschen Arbeiterbewegung* 3 (1961).

Gerhard, Dietrich. "The Frontier in Comparative View." *Comparative Studies in Society and History* 1 (1958–59).

Giachi, Arianna. "Helene Lange (1848–1930)." In *Deutsche Demokratie von Bebel bis Heuss: Geschichte in Lebensbildern*, edited by Friedrich Andrae and Sybille Schönfeldt, 2d ed. Frankfurt am Main, 1968.

Gillis, John. "Aristocracy and Bureaucracy in Nineteenth-Century Prussia." *Past and Present* No. 41 (1968).

Gollwitzer, H. "Der Cäsarismus Napoleons III. im Widerhall der öffentlichen Meinung Deutschlands." *Historische Zeitschrift* 173 (1952).

Hackett, Amy. "The German Women's Movement and Suffrage, 1890–1914." In *Modern European Social History*, edited by Robert Bezucha, Lexington, Mass., 1972.

Hagen, Maximilian von. "Theodor Fontanes politische Wandlung." *Die Welt als Geschichte* 17 (1975).

Hale, Douglas D., Jr. "Friedrich Adolph Wislizenus: From Student Rebel to Southwestern Explorer." *Missouri Historical Review* 62 (1968).

_____. "Gustav Bunsen: A German Rebel in the Texas Revolution." *East Texas Historical Journal* 6 (1968).

_____. "The Making of a Liberal Leader: Heinrich von Gagern, 1799–1848." *The Historian* 32 (1969).

Hamerow, Theodor S. "1848," In *The Responsibility of Power: Historical Essays in Honor of Hajo Holborn*, edited by Leonard Krieger and Fritz Stern, Garden City, N.Y., 1967.

_____. "The Elections to the Frankfurt Parliament." *Journal of Modern History* 33 (1961).

_____. "History and the German Revolution of 1848." *American Historical Review* 60 (1954).

Hammen, Oscar J. "Economic and Social Factors in the Prussian Rhineland in 1848." *American Historical Review* 54 (1949).

_____. "The Failure of an Attempted Franco-German Liberal Rapprochement, 1830–1840." *American Historical Review* 52 (1946).

_____. "The Specter of Communism in the 1840's." *Journal of the History of Ideas* 14 (1953).

_____. "The Young Marx Reconsidered." *Journal of the History of Ideas* 31 (1970).

Harris, James F. "Eduard Lasker and Compromise Liberalism." *Journal of Modern History* 42 (1970).

Hartung, Fritz. "Der aufgeklärte Absolutismus." *Historische Zeitschrift* 180 (1955).

Hauser, Oswald. "Polen und Dänen im Deutschen Reich." In *Reichsgründung 1870/71: Tatsachen, Kontroverse, Interpretationen*, edited by Theodor Schieder and Ernst Deuerlein, Stuttgart, 1970.

Hayes, Carlton J. H. "The History of German Socialism Reconsidered." *American Historical Review* 23 (1917).

Hellfaier, Karl-Alexander. "Die politische Funktion der Burschenschaft von ihren Anfängen 1814 bis zum Revolutionsjahr 1848 an der Universität Halle-Wittenberg." *Jahrbuch für die Geschichte Mittel-und Ostdeutschlands* 12 (1963).

_____. "Die sozialdemokratische Bewegung in Halle/Saale 1865–1890)." *Archiv für Sozialgeschichte* 1 (1961).

Hennig, Hansjoachim. "Preussische Sozialpolitik im Vormärz? Ein Beitrag zu den arbeiterfreundlichen Bestrebungen in Unternehmen der preussischen Seehandlung unter Christian von Rother." *Vierteljahrschrift für Sozial-und Wirtschaftsgeschichte* 52 (1965).

Hirsch, Felix. "Eduard von Simson: Das Problem der deutschjüdischen Symbiose im Schatten Goethes und Bismarcks." *Geschichte in Wissenschaft und Unterricht* 16 (1965).

Höfele, Karl Heinrich. "Königgratz und die Deutschen von 1866." *Geschichte in Wissenschaft und Unterricht* 17 (1966).

―――. "Selbstverständnis und Zeitkritik des deutschen Bürgertums vor dem ersten Weltkrieg." *Zeitschrift für Religions-und Geistesgeschichte* 8 (1956).

Hoffman, Walther G. "The Take-Off in Germany." In *The Economics of Take-Off into Sustained Growth*, edited by W. W. Rostow, New York, 1963.

Holborn, Hajo. "Prussia and the Weimar Republic." *Social Research* 23 (1956).

Hostetter, Richard. "The S.P.D. and the General Strike as an Anti-War Weapon, 1905–1914." *The Historian* 13 (1950).

Huber, Ernst Rudolf. "Das persönliche Regiment Wilhelms II." In *Moderne deutsche Verfassungsgeschichte (1815–1918)*, edited by Ernst-Wolfgang Böckenförde, Neue wissenschaftliche Bibliothek, vol. 51. Cologne, 1972.

Hübner, Hans. "Die ostpreussischen Landarbeiter im Kampf gegen junkerliche Ausbeutung und Willkür (1848–1914)." *Zeitschrift für Geschichtswissenschaft* 11 (1963).

Iggers, Georg G. "Heinrich Heine and the Saint-Simonians: A Reëxamination." *Comparative Literature* 10 (1958).

Kampmann, Wanda. "Adolf Stoecker und die Berliner Bewegung: Ein Beitrag zur Geschichte des Antisemitismus." *Geschichte in Wissenschaft und Unterricht* 13 (1962).

Kantzenbach, Friedrich Wilhelm. "Zur geistig-religiösen Situation der christlichen Konfessionen zwischen 1850 und 1860." *Zeitschrift für Religions-und Geistegeschichte* 18 (1966).

Kessel, Eberhard. "Carl Schurz and Gottfried Kinkel." In *Europa und Übersee: Festschrift für Egmont Zechlin*, edited by Otto Brunner and Dietrich Gerhard, Hamburg, 1961.

Klein, Thomas. "Reichstagswahlen und-Abgeordnete der Provinz Sachsen und Anhalt, 1867–1918. Ein Überblick." In *Festschrift für Friedrich Zahn*, vol. I: *Zur Geschichte und Volkskunde Mitteldeutschlands*, edited by Walter Schlesinger, Mitteldeutsche Forschungen, vol. 50/I. Cologne, 1968.

Kober, Adolf. "Jews in the Revolution of 1848 in Germany." *Jewish Social Studies* 10 (1948).

Köllman, Wolfgang. "The Population of Germany in the Age of Industrialism." In *Population Movements in Modern European History*, edited by Herbert Moller, New York, 1964.

_____. "The Process of Urbanization in Germany at the Height of the Industrialization Period." *Journal of Contemporary History* 4 (1969).

Kolb, Eberhard. "Bismarck und das Aufkommen der Annexionsforderung 1870." *Historische Zeitschrift* 209 (1969).

Koszyk, Kurt. "Carl D'Ester als Gemeinderat und Parlamentarier (1846–1849)." *Archiv für Sozialgeschichte* 1 (1961).

Kraehe, Enno E. "Austria and the Problem of Reform in the German Confederation, 1851–1863." *American Historical Review* 61 (1951).

_____."Raison d'état et idéologie dans la politique allemande de Metternich (1809–1820)." *Revue d'histoire moderne et contemporaine* 13 (1966).

Kren, George M. "Gustav Freytag and the Assimilation of the German Middle Class." *American Journal of Economics and Sociology* 22 (1963).

Kupisch, Karl. "Bürgerliche Frömmigkeit im Wilhelminischen Zeitater." *Zeitschrift für Religions-und Geistesgeschichte* 14 (1962).

_____. "Der Deutsche zwischen 1850 und 1865." *Zeitschrift für Religions-und Geistesgeschichte* 18 (1966).

Lamberti, Marjorie. "The Attempt to Form a Jewish Bloc: Jewish Notables and Politics in Wilhelmian Germany." *Central European History* 3 (1970).

Lambi, Ivo Nikolai. "The Agrarian-Industrial Front in Bismarckian Politics, 1873–1879." *Journal of Central European Affairs* 20 (1961).

_____. "The Protectionist Interests of the German Iron and Steel Industry, 1873–1879." *Journal of Economic History* 22 (1962).

Langer, William L. "The Pattern of Urban Revolution in 1848." In *French Society and Culture since the Old Regime*, edited by Evelyn M. Acomb and Marvin L. Brown, New York, 1966.

Langerhans, Heinz. "Richtungsgewerkschaft und gewerkschaftliche Autonomie 1890–1914." *International Review of Social History* 2 (1957).

Langsam, Walter Consuelo. "Nationalism and History in the Prussian Elementary Schools under William II." In *Nationalism and Internationalism: Essays Inscribed to Carlton J. H. Hayes*, edited by Edward Mead Earle, New York, 1950.

Lehmann, Hartmut. "Friedrich von Bodelschwingh und das Sedanfest: Ein Beitrag zum nationalen Denken der politisch-aktiven Richtung im deutschen Pietismus des 19. Jahrhunderts." *Historische Zeitschrift* 202 (1966).

Lenk, Leonhard. "Revolutionär-kommunistische Umtriebe im Königreich Bayern: Ein Beitrag zur Entwicklung von Staat und Gesellschaft 1848–1864." *Zeitschrift für bayerische Landesgeschichte* 28 (1965).

Liang, Hsi-Huey. "Lower-Class Immigrants in Wilhelmine Berlin." *Central European History* 3 (1970).

Liebel, Helen P. "The Bourgeoisie in Southwestern Germany, 1500–1789; A Rising Class?" *International Review of Social History* 10 (1965).

Lill, Rudolf. "Die deutschen Katholiken und Bismarcks Reichsgründung." In Schieder und Deuerlein (eds.), *Reichsgründung, 1870/71*, pp. 345–65.

Lukács, Georg. "Wilhelm Raabe." In *Raabe in neuer Sicht*, edited by Herman Helmers, Stuttgart, 1968.

Lutz, Rolland R. "The German Revolutionary Student Movement." *Central European History* 4 (1971).

McClelland, Charles E. "History in the Service of Politics: A Reassessment of G. G. Gervinus." *Central European History* 4 (1971).

Maehl, William H. "The Triumph of Nationalism in the German Socialist Party on the Eve of the First World War." *Journal of Modern History* 24 (1952).

Marks, Harry J. "The Sources of Reformism in the Social Democratic Party of Germany, 1890–1914." *Journal of Modern History* 11 (1939).

Mattheisen, Donald T. "Voters and Parliaments in the German Revolution of 1848: An Analysis of the Prussian Constituent Assembly." *Central European History* 5 (1972).

Mayer, Gustav. "Die Trennung der proletarischen von der bürgerlichen Demokratie in Deutschland (1863–1870)." *Archiv für die Geschichte des Sozialismus und der Arbeiterbewegung* 2 (1912).

Meinecke, Friedrich. "Zur Geschichte des älteren deutschen Parteiwesens." *Historische Zeitschrift* 117 (1917).

―――. "The Year 1848 in German History: Reflections on a Centenary." *Review of Politics* 10 (1948).

Mieck, Ilja. "Das Berliner Fabriken-Gericht (1815–1875): Ein Beitrag zur Geschichte der Arbeitsgerichtsbehörden." *Jahrbuch für die Geschichte Mittel-und Ostdeutschlands* 7 (1958).

Milatz, Alfred. "Friedrich Naumann (1860–1919)." In *Deutsche Demokratie von Bebel bis Heuss: Geschichte in Lebensbildern*, edited by Friedrich Andrae and Sybille Schönfeldt, 2d ed. Frankfurt am Main, 1968.

Mommsen, Wilhelm. "Julius Fröbel, Wirrnis und Weitsicht." *Historische Zeitschrift* 181 (1956).

Mork, Gordon R. "Bismarck and the 'Capitulation' of German Liberalism." *Journal of Modern History* 43 (1971).

————. "The Making of a German Nationalist: Eduard A. Lasker's Early Years, 1829–1847." *Societas* 1 (1971).

————. "The Prussian Railway Scandal of 1873: Economics and Politics in the German Empire." *European Studies Review* 1 (1971).

Morsey, Rudolf. "Bismarck und der Kulturkampf: Ein Forschungs-und Literaturbericht 1945–1957. Unter Verwendung neuen Materials." *Archiv für Kulturgeschichte* 39 (1957).

Muth, Heinrich. "Jugendpflege und Politik: Zur Jugend-und Innenpolitik des Kaiserreichs." *Geschichte in Wissenschaft und Unterricht* 12 (1961).

Na'aman, Schlomo. "Zur Geschichte des Bundes der Kommunisten in Deutschland in der zweiten Phase seines Bestehens." *Archiv für Sozialgeschichte* 5 (1965).

Naujoks, Eberhard. "Bismarck und die Organisation der Regierungspresse." *Historische Zeitschrift* 205 (1967).

Neu, Heinrich. "Bismarcks Versuch einer Eiflussnahme auf die 'Kölnische Zeitung': Ein Beitrag zur Geschichte der rheinischen Presse in der Zeit der Reaktion." *Rheinische Vierteljahrsblätter* 30 (1965).

Nipperdey, Thomas. "Interessenverbände und Parteien in Deutschland vor dem Ersten Weltkrieg." *Politische Vierteljahrsschrift* 2 (1961).

————. "Die Organisation der bürgerlichen Parteien in Deutschland vor 1918." *Historische Zeitschrift* 185 (1958).

Noether, Emiliana P. "Vatican Council I: Its Political and Religious Setting." *Journal of Modern History* 40 (1968).

Obermann, Karl. "Zur Geschichte der deutschen Arbeiterbewegung nach der Revolution von 1848/49 zu Beginn der fünfziger Jahre." *Beiträge zur Geschichte der deutschen Arbeiterbewegung* 3 (1961).

O'Boyle, Lenore. "The Democratic Left in Germany, 1848." *Journal of Modern History* 33 (1961).

————. "The German Nationalverein." *Journal of Central European Affairs* 16 (1957).

————. "The Image of the Journalist in France, Germany, and England, 1815–1848." *Comparative Studies in Society and History* 10 (1968).

———. "Klassische Bildung und soziale Struktur in Deutschland zwischen 1800 und 1848." *Historische Zeitschrift* 207 (1968).

———. "Liberal Political Leadership in Germany, 1867–1884." *Journal of Modern History* 28 (1956).

———. "The Problem of an Excess of Educated Men in Western Europe, 1800–1850." *Journal of Modern History* 42 (1970).

Petit, Irène. "Kautsky et les discussions autour du problème de l'impéralisme dans le parti social-démocrate allemand de 1907 à 1914." *Revue d'Allemagne* 1 (1969).

Pfannkuch, Karl. "Zeitgeist um die Jahrhundertwende; Methodisches-Philosophisches-Literarisches." *Zeitschrift für Religions-und Zeitgeschichte* 14 (1962).

Pflanze, Otto. "Juridicial and Political Responsibility in Nineteenth-Century Germany." In *The Responsibility of Power: Historical Essays in Honor of Hajo Holborn*, edited by Leonard Krieger and Fritz Stern, Garden City, N.Y., 1967.

Raumer, Kurt von. "Das Hambacher Fest." In *Staat und Volkstum: Neue Studien zur bairischen und deutschen Geschichte und Volkskunde: Festgabe für Karl Alexander von Müller*, edited by Eugen Franz et al., Diessen nr. Munich, 1933.

Redlich, Fritz. "The Leaders of the German Steam-Engine Industry during the First Hundred Years." *Journal of Economic History* 4 (1944).

Reichard, Richard W. "The German Working Class and the Russian Revolution of 1905." *Journal of Central European Affairs* 13 (1953).

Richter, Gregor. "Der Staat und die Presse in Württemberg bis zur Mitte des 19. Jahrhunderts." *Zeitschrift für Württembergische Landesgeschichte* 25 (1966).

Riedel, Manfred. "Vom Biedermeier zum Maschinenzeitalter: Zur Kulturgeschichte der ersten Eisenbahnen in Deutschland." *Archiv für Kulturgeschichte* 43 (1961).

Ringer, Fritz K. "Higher Education in Germany in the Nineteenth Century." *Journal of Contemporary History* 2 (1967).

Ritter, Gerhard. "The Military and Politics in Germany." *Journal of Central European Affairs* 17 (1957).

Ritter, Gerhard A. "Kontinuität und Umformung des deutschen Parteiensystems 1918–1920." In *Entstehung und Wandel der modernen Gesellschaft: Festschrift für Hans Rosenberg zum 65. Geburtstag*, edited by G. A. Ritter, Berlin, 1970.

———. "Die politische Arbeiterbewegung Deutschlands 1863–

1914." In *Aus Politik und Zeitgeschichte: Beilage zur Wochenzeitung Das Parlament*, May 22, 1963.

Röhl, John C. G. "The Disintegration of the *Kartell* and the Politics of Bismarck's Fall from Power, 1887–90." *Historical Journal* 9 (1966).

———. "Higher Civil Servants in Germany, 1890–1900." *Journal of Contemporary History* 2 (1967).

———. "Staatsstreichplan oder Staatsstreichbereitschaft? Bismarcks Politik in der Entlassungskrise." *Historische Zeitschrift* 203 (1966).

Rohlfes, Joachim. "Staat, Nation und evangelische Kirche im Zeitalter der deutschen Einigung (1848–1871)." *Geschichte in Wissenschaft und Unterricht* 9 (1958).

Rose, Carol. "The Issue of Parliamentary Suffrage at the Frankfurt National Assembly." *Central European History* 5 (1972).

Rosenberg, Hans, ed. "Honoratiorenpolitiker und 'grossdeutsche' Sammlungsbestrebungen im Reichsgründungsjahrzehnt." *Jahrbuch für die Geschichte Mittel-und Ostdeutschlands* 19 (1970).

Schieder, Theodor. "Die Theorie der Partei im älteren deutschen Liberalismus." In *Festschrift zum 70. Geburtstag von Ludwig Bergsträsser: Aus Geschichte und Politik*, edited by Alfred Herrmann, Düsseldorf, 1954.

Schlawe, Fritz. "Die junghegelische Publizistik." *Die Welts als Geschichte* 20 (1960).

Schmidt, Siegfried. "Zur Frühgeschichte der bürgerlichen Parteien in Deutschland." *Zeitschrift für Geschichtswissenschaft* 13 (1965).

Schmidt, Walter. "Der Bund der Kommunisten und die Versuche einer Zentralisierung der deutschen Arbeitervereine im April und Mai 1848." *Zeitschrift für Geschichtswissenschaft* 9 (1961).

Schmitt, Hans A. "Count Beust and Germany, 1866–1870: Reconquest, Realignment, or Resignation?" *Central European History* 1 (1968).

Schoeps, Hans-Joachim, ed. "Metternichs Kampf gegen die Revolution: Weltanschaaung in Briefen." *Historische Zeitschrift* 205 (1967).

Schraepler, Ernst. "Der Bund der Gerechten: Seine Tätigkeit in London, 1840–1847." *Archiv für Sozialgeschichte* 2 (1962).

Schroeder, Paul W. "Metternich Studies since 1925." *Journal of Modern History* 33 (1961).

Schulz, Gerhard. "Geschichtliche Theorie und politisches

Denken bei Max Weber." *Vierteljahrshefte für Zeitgeschichte* 12 (1964).

————. "Über die Entstehung und Formen von Interessengruppen in Deutschland seit Beginn der Industrialisierung." *Politische Vierteljahrsschrift* 2 (1961).

Schwabe, Klaus. "Zur politischen Haltung der deutschen Professoren im Ersten Weltkrieg." *Historische Zeitschrift* 193 (1961).

Schwann, Stanislaw. "Die Neue Oder-Zeitung und Karl Marx als ihr Korrespondent." *International Review of Social History* 4 (1959).

Seemann, Ulrich. "Die Kämpfe der Hamburger Arbeiter gegen die Verschlechterung ihres Wahlrechts in den Jahren 1905/06." *Wissenschaftliche Zeitung der Universität Rostock* 10 (1961).

Sempell, Charlotte. "The Constitutional and Political Problems of the Second Chancellor, Leo von Caprivi." *Journal of Modern History* 25 (1953).

Sexau, Richard. "Die 'wilhelminische' Epoche." *Neues Abendland* 11 (1956).

Shanahan, William O. "Liberalism and Foreign Affairs: Naumann and the Prewar German View." *Review of Politics* 21 (1959).

Sheehan, James J. "Literalism and the City in Nineteenth-Century Germany." *Past and Present*, no. 51 (1971).

————. "Political Leadership in the German Reichstag, 1871–1918." *American Historical Review* 74 (1968).

Siemers, Bruno. "Die Vereinigten Staaten und die deutsche Einheitsbewegung." In *Geschichtliche Kräfte und Entscheidungen: Festschrift zum Fünfunsechzigsten Geburtstag von Otto Becker*, edited by Martin Göhring and Alexander Scharff, Wiesbaden, 1954.

Silverman, Dan P. "Political Catholicism and Social Democracy in Alsace-Lorraine, 1871–1914." *Catholic Historical Review* 52 (1966).

Skidmore, Thomas E. "Survey of Unpublished Sources on the Central Government and Politics of the German Empire, 1871–1918." *American Historical Review* 65 (1960).

Snell, John L. "German Socialists in the Last Imperial Reichstag, 1912–1918." *Bulletin of the International Institute for Social History*, no. 3 (1952).

Stadler, Peter. "Wirtschaftskrise und Revolution bei Marx und Engels: Zur Entwicklung ihres Denkens in den 1850er Jahren." *Historische Zeitschrift* 199 (1964).

Stearns, Peter N. "Adaptation to Industrialization: German Workers as a Test Case." *Central European History* 3 (1970).

Steinberg, Hans-Josef. "Sozialismus, Internationalismus und Reichsgründung." In *Reichsgründung 1870/71: Tatsachen, Kontroverse, Interpretationen*, edited by Theodor Schieder and Ernst Deuerlein, Stuttgart, 1970.

Stern, Fritz. "Money, Morals, and the Pillars of Bismarck's Society." *Central European History* 3 (1970).

Sterne, Margaret. "The End of the Free City of Frankfurt." *Journal of Modern History* 30 (1958).

Struck, Wolf-Heino. "Das Streben nach bürgerlicher Freiheit und nationaler Einheit in der Sicht des Herzogtums Nassau." *Nassauische Annalen* 77 (1966).

Stürmer, Michael. "Bismarck-Mythos und Historie." *Beilage zur Wochenzeitung Das Parlament*, Jan. 16, 1971.

_____. "Bismarck in Perspective." *Central European History* 4 (1971).

_____. "Staatsstreichgedanken im Bismarckreich." *Historische Zeitschrift* 209 (1969).

Tal, Uriel. "Liberal Protestantism and the Jews in the Second Reich, 1870–1914." *Jewish Social Studies* 26 (1964).

Thoma, Ludwig. "Die Reden Kaiser Wilhelms II. Ein Beitrag zur Geschichte unserer Zeit." In *Gesammelte Werke*, vol. II, Munich, 1927.

Tilly, Richard. "Germany (1815–1870)." In *Banking in the Early Stages of Industrialization: A Study in Comparative Economic History*, edited by Rondo Cameron et al., New York, 1967.

_____. "The Political Economy of Public Finance and the Industrialization of Prussia, 1815–1866." *Journal of Economic History* 26 (1966).

Tobias, Henry J., and John L. Snell. "A Soviet Interpretation of the SPD, 1895–1933." *Journal of Central European Affairs* 13 (1953).

Treue, Wilhelm. "Dagobert Oppenheim: Zeitungsherausgeber, Bankier und Unternehmer in der Zeit des Liberalismus und Neumerkantilismus." *Tradition* 9 (1964).

Trübner, Georg. "Johann Phillipp Becker und die Revolution 1848." *International Review of Social History* 10 (1965).

Vettes, William George. "The German Social Democrats and the Eastern Question, 1849–1900." *American Slavic and Eastern European Review* 17 (1958).

Vossler, Otto. "Humboldts Idee der Universität." *Historische Zeitschrift* 178 (1954).

Wagner, Jonathan F. "Georg Gottfried Gervinus: The Tribulations of a Liberal Federalist." *Central European History* 4 (1971).

Weber, Frank G. "Palmerston and German Liberalism, 1848." *Journal of Modern History* 35 (1963).

Weber, Rolf. "Die Beziehungen zwischen sozialer Struktur und politischer Ideologie des Kleinbürgertums in der Revolution von 1848/49." *Zeitschrift für Geschichtswissenschaft* 13 (1965).

Wehler, Hans-Ulrich. "Der Fall Zabern: Rückblick auf eine Verfassungskrise des wilhelminischen Kaiserreichs." *Die Welt als Geschichte* 23 (1963).

Weiss, John. "Dialectical Idealism and the Work of Lorenz von Stein." *International Review of Social History* 8 (1963).

――――. "Karl Marlo, Guild Socialism, and the Revolutions of 1848." *International Review of Social History* 5 (1960).

Wentzcke, Paul. "Bayerische Stimmen aus der Paulskirche (Juni-Juli 1848): Nachlese und Vorschau aus oberfränkischen Privatarchiven." *Archivalische Zeitschrift* 50–51 (1955).

Williams, Robert C. "Russians in Germany: 1900–1914." *Journal of Contemporary History* 1 (1966).

Windell, George G. "The Bismarckian Empire as a Federal State, 1866–1880: A Chronicle of Failure." *Central European History* 2 (1969).

Wittich, Dieter. "Zur Geschichte und Deutung des Materialismus von Karl Vogt, Jakob Moleschott und Ludwig Büchner." *Wissenschaftliche Zeitschrift der Humboldt Universität zu Berlin* 12 (1963).

Zeender, John K. "German Catholics and the Concept of an Interconfessional Party, 1900–1922." *Journal of Central European Affairs* 23 (1964).

――――. "The German Center Party during World War I. An Internal Study." *Catholic Historical Review* 42 (1957).

Ziebura, Gilbert. "Anfänge des deutschen Parlamentarismus: Geschäftsverfahren und Entscheidungsprozess in der ersten deutschen Nationalversammlung 1848/49." In *Faktoren der politischen Entscheidung: Festgabe für Ernst Fraenkel zum 65. Geburtstag*, edited by Gerhard A. Ritter and Gilbert Ziebura, Berlin 1963.

Zorn, Wolfgang. "Wirtschafts-und sozialgeschichtliche Zusammenhänge der deutschen Reichsgründungszeit (1850–1879)." *Historische Zeitschrift* 197 (1963).

V. UNPUBLISHED DISSERTATIONS, THESES, AND PAPERS

Aandahl, Frederick. "The Rise of German Free Conservatism." Ph.D. dissertation, Princeton University, 1955.

Angress, Werner. "Prussia's Army and the Jewish Reserve Officer Controversy." Paper presented at the 1971 meeting of the American Historical Association.

Blieffert, Gunther. "Die Innenpolitik des Reichskanzlers Fürst Chlodwig zu Hohenlohe-Schillingsfürst 1894–1900." Ph.D. dissertation, Univ. of Kiel, 1949.

Chickering, Roger P. "Pacifism in Germany, 1900–1914: A Study of Nationalism and Wilhelmine Society." Ph.D. dissertation, Stanford University, 1968.

Christofferson, Thomas Rodney. "The Revolution of 1848 in Marseille." Ph.D. dissertation, Tulane University, 1968.

Drake, Arthur Spurgeon. "The Struggle for Freedom of the Press in the German Empire, 1871–1874." Master's thesis, University of North Carolina, 1968.

Frye, Bruce B. "Matthias Erzberger and German Politics, 1914–1921." Ph.D. dissertation, Stanford University, 1953.

Haberland, Brigitte. "Die Innenpolitik des Reiches unter der Kanzlerschaft Bethmann Hollwegs 1909–1914." Ph.D. dissertation, Univ. of Kiel, 1950.

Hackett, Amy. "Feminism and Liberalism in Wilhelmine Germany." Paper presented at the 1971 meeting of the American Historical Association.

Hale, Douglas D., Jr. "The Press and Fatherland Society in 1832: Common Ancestor to German Progressivism." Manuscript made available by the author.

Harris, James Fremont. "Eduard Lasker, 1829–1884: An Analysis of the Political Ideas of a Left-Wing Liberal." Ph.D. dissertation, University of Wisconsin, 1968.

Hartmann, Hans-Georg. "Die Innenpolitik des Fürsten Bülow 1906– 1909." Ph.D. dissertation, Univ. of Kiel, 1950.

Heckart, Beverley Anne. "From Bassermann to Bebel: The Relationship between Liberals and Social Democrats in Germany, 1905–1914." Ph.D. dissertation, Washington University of St. Louis, 1968.

Heybeg, Elvira L. "The German Liberal Parties in the Kulturkampf, 1871–1876." Master's thesis, University of North Carolina, 1970.

Holden, Catherine Magill. "A Decade of Dissent in Germany: An Historical Study of the Society of Protestant Friends, and the German-Catholic Church, 1840–1848." Ph.D. dissertation, Yale University, 1954.

Holt, Niles Robert. "The Social and Political Ideas of the German Monist Movement, 1871–1941." Ph.D. dissertation, Yale University, 1967.

Hunley, John Dillard. "Society and Politics in the Düsseldorf Area, 1867– 1878." Ph.D. dissertation, University of Virginia, 1973.

Kist, Harold Eugene. "Wilhelm Sollmann: The Emergence of a Social Democratic Leader." Ph.D. dissertation, University of Pennsylvania, 1969.

Lange, Ruth. "Three Critical Years of the National Liberal Party of Germany, 1877, 1878, 1879." Ph.D. dissertation, New York University, 1968.

Lees, Andrew. "Revolution and Reflection: The German Intellectuals, 1849–1859." Revised draft of a Ph.D. dissertation, Harvard University, 1968.

Levy, Richard S. "Anti-Semitic Political Parties in the German Empire." Ph.D. dissertation, Yale University, 1969.

McClelland, Charles Edgar. "The German Historians and England: A Study of Nineteenth Century Views." Ph.D. dissertation, Yale University, 1967.

Mackey, Richard W. "The Zabern Affair, 1913–1914." Ph.D. dissertation, University of California, Los Angeles, 1967.

Nelson, Ilse E. "The Practical Aspects of Max Weber's Political Philosophy: Max Weber's Attitude toward the Political Problems of Germany, 1885–1920." Ph.D. dissertation, University of Chicago, 1950.

Neumann, Wolfgang. "Die Innenpolitik des Fürsten Bülow von 1900– 1906." Ph.D. dissertation, Univ. of Kiel, 1949.

Niewyk, Donald L. "German Social Democracy and the Problem of Anti-Semitism, 1906–1914." Master's thesis, Tulane University, 1964.

Rohfleisch, K. J. "Eugen Richter, Opponent to Bismarck." Ph.D. dissertation, University of California, Berkeley, 1946.

Robson, S. T. "Left Wing Liberalism in Germany, 1900–19." Ph.D. dissertation, St. Antony's, Oxford University, 1966.

Rothwell, Charles Easton. "Rosa Luxemburg and the German Social Democratic Party." Ph.D. dissertation, Stanford University, 1939.

Schuetz, Arnold Heinz. "Johann Jacoby—A Prussian Democrat:

The Years 1847–1877." Ph.D. dissertation, University of Wisconsin, 1971.

Schwarz, George M. "Political Attitudes in the German Universities during the Reign of William II." Ph.D. dissertation, Oxford University, 1961.

Skidmore, Thomas Elliott. "The Chancellorship of Caprivi: A Constitutional Study." Ph.D. dissertation, Harvard University, 1960.

Strain, Jacqueline. "Feminism and Political Radicalism in the German Social Democratic Movement, 1890–1914." Ph.D. dissertation, University of California, Berkeley, 1964.

Stroud, Joe. "Sir Eyre Crowe and the Shaping of British Policy toward Germany, 1905–1914." Master's thesis, Tulane University, 1959.

Walz, Ralph. "Friedrich Naumann's National Social Society, 1896–1903." Ph.D. dissertation, New York University, 1971.

Zucker, Stanley. "Ludwig Bamberger and the Crisis of German Liberalism." Ph.D. dissertation, University of Wisconsin, 1968.

INDEX

Schoder, Adolf, 115, 132
Schönlein, Johann Lukas, 32
Schopenhauer, Arthur, 137, 140
Schulze-Delitzsch, Hermann, 156, 159, 188
Schurz, Carl, 124
Schweitzer, Albert, 314
Schweitzer, Johann Baptist von, 190, 192
Sealsfield, Charles. *See* Postl, Karl Anton
Sigel, Franz, 90, 122, 124
Simon, Ludwig, 97, 117, 118, 124
Simson, Eduard, 119, 128, 158, 164
Singer, Paul, 258–59, 298
Social Democratic party of Germany (SPD), 208, 212, 232, 236, 256–303, 307, 309–11, 314, 320–21, 335, 339–41, 349, 351, 353, 355–58, 359–62, 364–66, 368, 378, 382
Social Democratic Workers' party, 193
Socialist Workers' party of Germany, 194–99, 202–8
Society of Protestant Friends, 67–68, 136
Sonnemann, Leopold, 151, 307, 320, 324
Spahn, Peter, 223, 365
Spielhagen, Friedrich, 327
Stahl, Friderich Julius, 137
Stegerwald, Adam, 226, 228
Stein, Baron Karl vom, 15–17, 336
Stein, Lorenz von, 138
Stoecker, Adolf, 231–32
Strauss, David Friedrich, 50, 60, 126
Stresemann, Gustav, 235, 364–65
Struve, Gustav von, 66–67, 71, 88, 89, 92, 93–94, 104–5, 121, 123–24
Stumm, Carl Ferdinand von, 230
Stüve, Carl Bertram, 85
Suttner, Bertha von, 321–22
Sybel, Heinrich von, 137, 141, 158

T

Tellkampf, Johann Ludwig, 56
Tirpitz, Admiral Alfred von, 339–40
Trimborn, Karl, 223
Troeltsch, Ernst, 301, 322
Twesten, Karl, 153, 156, 168

U

Uhland, Ludwig, 96
Uhlich, Leberecht, 68–69, 136
Ullstein, Leopold, 319, 323–24
Union of Industrialists, 234, 235
Unruh, Hans Viktor von, 156

V

Venedey, Jakob, 97–98, 117, 118, 124, 147
Virchow, Rudolph, 32, 83, 153, 156, 169
Vogt, Karl, 98, 117, 118, 121, 124
Vollmar, Georg von, 198, 199, 276, 288–89, 291
Vorparlament, 92–94

W

Wagner, Adolf, 242, 243
Wagner, Richard, 120
Waldeck, Benedikt, 109, 153, 156
Wangenheim, Baron Conrad von, 233
Weber, Helene, 315–16
Weber, Marianne, 315
Weber, Max, 236, 243, 244, 301, 311, 314, 322, 325–27, 332–33, 348–49, 350
Wedekind, Benjamin Franklin, 331
Weitling, Wilhelm, 59–60, 61, 110
Weizsäcker, Karl von, 372
Welcker, Karl Theodor, 36, 54–55, 58, 65, 70, 89, 96, 116, 137, 146
Wiener, Otto, 348
Wigard, Franz, 69–70, 71, 98, 117, 118
William I, king of Prussia and German emperor, 151–57, 161, 164, 167–68, 172–73, 196, 210, 305, 308
William II, German emperor and king of Prussia, 204–5, 209, 211–15, 225, 238–39, 248, 249, 250–51, 264, 321, 328, 330, 337, 339, 343, 351, 353–54, 357, 359, 369, 371–72, 377, 381–82; *Daily Telegraph* incident, 344–50; celebration of his silver jubilee in the United States, 378–79
Windthorst, Ludwig, 180, 182, 211, 222
Wirth, Johann Georg August, 38–39
Wislizenus, Friedrich Adolph, 32
Wislizenus, Gustav Adolf, 68–69, 136, 140